Readings in the

Theory of Knowledge

THE CENTURY PHILOSOPHY SERIES
Sterling P. Lamprecht, Editor

Readings in the

Theory of Knowledge

JOHN V. CANFIELD
Cornell University

FRANKLIN H. DONNELL, JR.
University of Kansas

APPLETON-CENTURY-CROFTS
EDUCATIONAL DIVISION
New York MEREDITH CORPORATION

Preface

Theory of knowledge, or epistemology, is concerned with what it is to know and other questions pertinent to this: what it is to believe, be certain, perceive, remember, justify or have grounds for what one claims to know; what it is to be true or to be probably true; what concepts, properties, and propositions are. These are questions about what we ought to understand by statements such as "He knows" or "This is probably true." We might say that such questions concern the concepts or notions of knowing, believing, perceiving, truth, probability, and so forth, and that they should be roughly distinguished from such factual questions about learning, retention, or discrimination as may interest the psychologist. "What is it to remember?" in contrast to "How much reinforcement is needed to remember this?" is a question which is distinctively philosophical and part of epistemology. There is little that might be done in psychological laboratories or interviews to determine an answer to "What is memory?" though there is obviously much that could be done to find out when people remember and when they do not.

In addition to such conceptual investigations, theory of knowledge is concerned with whether we may claim to know the truth of any members of large classes of statements. With regard to our claims to knowledge about science or religion or philosophy, about what we see, about the past, or about the thoughts and feelings of others, philosophers have sometimes presented fascinating and provocative considerations which seem to undermine our precritical assurance that we can find out such things. Discussion of these considerations and their importance for our beliefs is obviously a matter of first importance for philosophy, and a topic generally worthy of serious intellectual concern.

Issues raised in epistemology have bearing throughout philosophy, and a discussion of them may easily drift into ethics, aesthetics, metaphysics, or philosophy of religion. In compiling this volume we have sought to avoid topics that might properly be investigated within other branches of philosophy and to restrict our subject matter to a few expressly epistemological issues. Even many of the questions posed above—clearly epistemological—had to be excluded for the anthology to be of reasonable size. Those issues which have been emphasized, however, have all received considerable discussion in the course of the history of philosophy; they are: the nature of knowing, rationalism and empiricism, truth, induction, and perception. While the selections on these issues cannot be said to reveal all the points of view that the history of philosophy may disclose, they broach many considerations which have been suggestive and important. The readings, moreover, have been selected for their clarity and their accessibility to close philosophic study and discussion. The serious philosophy student should find them both demanding and fruitful.

We wish to thank Professors J. C. M. Brentano, K. Fischer, and R. Chisholm for use of the previously unpublished translation of Franz Brentano's *Wahrheit und Evidenz,* and Professor D. Gustafson both for advice about the selections and many helpful comments.

J. V. C.
F. H. D., Jr.

Contents

PART ONE

Knowledge

Introduction

knowledge, like being, is analogous

Clearly there is some difference in meaning between "He knows that juniper is evergreen" and "He believes (thinks, is of the opinion) that juniper is evergreen." All the discussions in this section take some stand as to what this difference is. Each, that is, presents a view of what must be true of the situation in which a person knows. In the selection from Plato's *Theaetetus,* the first extended study of epistemological questions in philosophical literature, various answers to the question "What is knowing?" are broached and examined, together with other issues concerning belief or judgment. As in many of the Platonic dialogues, no final answer to the initial question is reached. An answer is to be found, however, in the pages of the *Republic,* Plato's great dialogue about the ordering of society. A quite different account is presented at length in Aristotle's *Posterior Analytics.*

A main impetus to discussion of the nature of knowing has come from philosophical scepticism, i.e. from claims that we are really unable to know anything about the truth of large categories of statements (for example, statements about the past or what is seen) that we ordinarily suppose we can know. Justification for these claims sometimes rests on a specification of what knowing really is: the passages from the *Republic* and *Posterior Analytics* show how accounts of knowing justify claims about the limitation of knowledge. Another such example is found in the writings of René Descartes. In the celebrated opening pages of the *Meditations* he demands an exclusion from the category of knowledge of all that is not immune from doubt or demonstrable from what is so immune. This demand is the basis of a sceptical outlook, often called Methodological Scepticism, which is critical of our ordinary corpus of beliefs for failing to meet these standards, yet is critical of them for the purpose of discovering some certainty that can be a starting point for the proper construction of knowledge. Descartes' contentions are criticized by the late influential Oxford don H. A. Prichard, who also presents an account of the nature of knowing. His account, which may be contrasted with that of Bertrand Russell, is itself criticized in the paper by Professor Norman Malcolm of Cornell.

The descriptions of knowing given by Descartes, Prichard, and Russell obviously lie in philosophic traditions that stem from the epistemological writings of Plato and Aristotle. A different approach to the problem may be found in the selection from Bernard Bosanquet's *Essentials of Logic.* This selection is one of three drawn from epistemological idealism (see Blanshard in the chapter on truth, Campbell in the chapter on perception). Certain historical antecedents of these points of view may be seen in the selections from Berkeley and Kant. Idealism as a doctrine about what exists (ontological idealism) is the view that nothing can exist that is not in some sense mental in nature. This doctrine was expressly advanced by Berkeley, and is also held by Bosanquet, though his interpretation of it differs widely from Berkeley's. As an epistemological doctrine, however, idealism dwells on the importance of mind to the character of objects perceived, maintaining that it is only through belief or judgment about what is perceived that objects of perception gain such characteristics as they may have. Reasons for this contention may be found in the selection from Bosanquet, as well as in that from Kant.

It is largely because of the creativity that Bosanquet ascribes to knowing that his account of it differs from those of Plato and Aristotle. To them knowing was being appraised of the character of things whose nature was antecedent to and unaffected by their being known. That knowing something is not *ipso facto* crucial to its being what it is may indeed seem only common sense. Nevertheless Bosanquet maintains that knowing an object or knowing that something is the case is really the bringing of order to experience through the imposition of a conceptual structure. Even the belief that one is seeing a table, it might be said, cannot be separated from the application to present experience of categories of space and time, unity and plurality, as well as such notions as "support," "furniture," and "convenience," all of which can be assumed to be the contributions of thought or intelligence to this situation. Thus judging that something is the case will be, in a sense, the creation of this very circumstance through a focusing of intelligence. This doctrine of the creativity of knowing obviously requires its own picture of what it is for a judgment to be true. Blanshard's essay on the coherence theory of truth gives an account of truth consonant with the notion that knowing is a producing of what is known.

ONE

Object of Knowledge

PLATO (427- 347 B.C.)

I

From *Theaetetus**

SOCRATES. Well then, Theaetetus, here is a point for you to consider. The answer you gave was that knowledge is perception, wasn't it?

THEAETETUS. Yes.

SOCR. Now suppose you were asked: 'When a man sees white or
black things or hears high or low tones, what does he see or hear with?'
I suppose you would say: 'With eyes and ears'.

THEAET. Yes, I should.

SOCR. To use words and phrases in an easy-going way without
scrutinising them too curiously is not, in general, a mark of ill-breeding;
on the contrary there is something low-bred in being too precise. But
sometimes there is no help for it, and this is a case in which I must take
exception to the form of your answer. Consider: is it more correct to
say that we see and hear *with* our eyes and ears or *through* them?

THEAET. I should say we always perceive through them, rather than
with them.

SOCR. Yes; it would surely be strange that there should be a number of senses ensconced inside us, like the warriors in the Trojan horse,
and all these things should not converge and meet in some single nature
—a mind, or whatever it is to be called—*with* which we perceive all the
objects of perception *through* the senses as instruments.

THEAET. Yes, I think that is a better description.

SOCR. My object in being so precise is to know whether there is
some part of ourselves, the same in all cases, with which we apprehend

* From "Theaetetus," in *Plato's Theory of Knowledge* by F. M. Cornford (London,
Routledge & Kegan Paul Ltd., 1935). Reprinted by permission of the publishers.

black or white through the eyes, and objects of other kinds through the other senses. Can you, if the question is put to you, refer all such acts of apprehension to your body? Perhaps, however, it would be better you should speak for yourself in reply to questions, instead of my taking the words out of your mouth. Tell me: all these instruments through which you perceive what is warm or hard or light or sweet are parts of the body, aren't they?—not of anything else.

THEAET.   Of nothing else.

SOCR.   Now will you also agree that the objects you perceive through one faculty cannot be perceived through another—objects of hearing, for instance, through sight, or objects of sight through hearing?

THEAET.   Of course I will.

SOCR.   Then, if you have some thought about both objects at once, you cannot be having a perception including both at once through either the one or the other organ.

THEAET.   No.

SOCR.   Now take sound and colour. Have you not, to begin with, this thought which includes both at once—that they both *exist?*

THEAET.   I have.

SOCR.   And, further, that each of the two is *different* from the other and the *same* as itself?

THEAET.   Naturally.

SOCR.   And again, that both together are *two,* and each of them is *one?*

THEAET.   Yes.

SOCR.   And also you can ask yourself whether they are *unlike* each other or *alike?*

THEAET.   No doubt.

SOCR.   Then through what organ do you think all this about them both? What is common to them both cannot be apprehended either through hearing or through sight. Besides, here is further evidence for my point. Suppose it were possible to inquire whether sound and colour were both brackish or not, no doubt you could tell me what faculty you would use—obviously not sight or hearing, but some other.

THEAET.   Of course: the faculty that works through the tongue.

SOCR.   Very good. But now, through what organ does that faculty work, which tells you what is common not only to these objects but to all things—what you mean by the words 'exists' and 'does not exist' and the other terms applied to them in the questions I put a moment ago? What sort of organs can you mention, corresponding to all these terms, through which the perceiving part of us perceives each one of them?

THEAET.   You mean existence and non-existence, likeness and un-likeness, sameness and difference, and also unity and numbers in general as applied to them; and clearly your question covers 'even' and 'odd' and all that kind of notions. You are asking, through what part of the body our mind perceives these?

Socr. You follow me most admirably, Theaetetus; that is exactly my question.

Theaet. Really, Socrates, I could not say, except that I think there is no special organ at all for these things, as there is for the others. It is clear to me that the mind in itself is its own instrument for contemplating the common terms that apply to everything.

Socr. In fact, Theaetetus, you are handsome, not ugly as Theodorus said you were; for in a discussion handsome is that handsome does. And you have treated me more than handsomely in saving me the trouble of a very long argument, if it is clear to you that the mind contemplates some things through its own instrumentality, others through the bodily faculties. That was indeed what I thought myself; but I wanted you to agree.

Theaet. Well, it is clear to me.

Socr. Under which head, then, do you place existence? For that is, above all, a thing that belongs to everything.

Theaet. I should put it among the things that the mind apprehends by itself.

Socr. And also likeness and unlikeness and sameness and difference?

Theaet. Yes.

Socr. And how about 'honourable' and 'dishonourable' and 'good' and 'bad'?

Theaet. Those again seem to me, above all, to be things whose being is considered, one in comparison with another, by the mind, when it reflects within itself upon the past and the present with an eye to the future.

Socr. Wait a moment. The hardness of something hard and the softness of something soft will be perceived by the mind through touch, will they not?

Theaet. Yes.

Socr. But their existence and the fact that they both exist, and their contrariety to one another and again the existence of this contrariety are things which the mind itself undertakes to judge for us, when it reflects upon them and compares one with another.

Theaet. Certainly.

Socr. Is it not true, then, that whereas all the impressions which penetrate to the mind through the body are things which men and animals alike are naturally constituted to perceive from the moment of birth, reflections about them with respect to their existence and usefulness only come, if they come at all, with difficulty through a long and troublesome process of education?

Theaet. Assuredly.

SOCR. Is it possible, then, to reach truth when one cannot reach existence?

THEAET. It is impossible.

SOCR. But if a man cannot reach the truth of a thing, can he possibly know that thing?

THEAET. No, Socrates, how could he?

SOCR. If that is so, knowledge does not reside in the impressions, but in our reflection upon them. It is there, seemingly, and not in the impressions, that it is possible to grasp existence and truth.

THEAET. Evidently.

SOCR. Then are you going to give the same name to two things which differ so widely?

THEAET. Surely that would not be right.

SOCR. Well then, what name do you give to the first one—to seeing, hearing, smelling, feeling cold and feeling warm?

THEAET. Perceiving. What other name is there for it?

SOCR. Taking it all together, then, you call this perception?

THEAET. Necessarily.

SOCR. A thing which, we agree, has no part in apprehending truth, since it has none in apprehending existence.

THEAET. No, it has none.

SOCR. Nor, consequently, in knowledge either.

THEAET. No.

SOCR. Then, Theaetetus, perception and knowledge cannot possibly be the same thing.

THEAET. Evidently not, Socrates. Indeed, it is now perfectly plain that knowledge is something different from perception.

SOCR. But when we began our talk it was certainly not our object to find out what knowledge is not, but what it is. Still, we have advanced so far as to see that we must not look for it in sense-perception at all, but in what goes on when the mind is occupied with things by itself, whatever name you give to that.

THEAET. Well, Socrates, the name for that, I imagine, is 'making judgments'.

SOCR. You are right, my friend. Now begin all over again. Blot out all we have been saying, and see if you can get a clearer view from the position you have now reached. Tell us once more what knowledge is.

THEAET. I cannot say it is judgment as a whole, because there is false judgment; but perhaps true judgment is knowledge. You may take that as my answer. If, as we go further, it turns out to be less convincing than it seems now, I will try to find another.

SOCR. Good, Theaetetus; this promptness is much better than hanging back as you did at first. If we go on like this, either we shall find what we are after, or we shall be less inclined to imagine we know something of which we know nothing whatever; and that surely is a reward not to be despised. And now, what is this you say: that there are two sorts of judgment, one true, the other false, and you define knowledge as judgment that is true?

THEAET.   Yes; that is the view I have come to now.

SOCR.   Then, had we better go back to a point that came up about judgment?

THEAET.   What point do you mean?

SOCR.   A question that worries me now, as often before, and has much perplexed me in my own mind and also in talking to others. I cannot explain the nature of this experience we have, or how it can arise in our minds.

THEAET.   What experience?

SOCR.   Making a false judgment. At this moment I am still in doubt and wondering whether to let that question alone or to follow it further, not as we did a while ago, but in a new way.

THEAET.   Why not, Socrates, if it seems to be in the least necessary? Only just now, when you and Theodorus were speaking of leisure, you said very rightly that there is no pressing hurry in a discussion of this sort.

SOCR.   A good reminder; for this may be the right moment to go back upon our track. It is better to carry through a small task well than make a bad job of a big one.

THEAET.   Certainly it is.

SOCR.   How shall we set about it, then? What is it that we do mean? Do we assert that there is in every case a false judgment, and that one of us thinks what is false, another what is true, such being the nature of things?

THEAET.   Certainly we do.

SOCR.   And, in each and all cases, it is possible for us either to know a thing or not to know it? I leave out of account for the moment becoming acquainted with things and forgetting, considered as falling between the two. Our argument is not concerned with them just now.

THEAET.   Well then, Socrates, there is no third alternative left in any case, besides knowing and not knowing.

SOCR.   And it follows at once that when one is thinking he must be thinking either of something he knows or of something he does not know?

THEAET.   Necessarily.

SOCR.   And further, if you know a thing, you cannot also not know it; and if you do not know it, you cannot also know it?

THEAET.   Of course.

SOCR.   Then is the man who thinks what is false supposing that things he knows are not those things but other things he knows, so that, while he knows both, he fails to recognise either?

THEAET.   No, that is impossible, Socrates.

SOCR.   Well then, is he supposing that things he does *not* know are other things he does not know? Is this possible—that a man who knows neither Theaetetus nor Socrates should take it into his head that Socrates is Theaetetus or Theaetetus Socrates?

THEAET.   No. How could he?

SOCR.   But surely a man does not imagine that things he does know are things he does not know, or that things he does not know are things he knows?

THEAET.   No, that would be a miracle.

SOCR.   What other way is there, then, of judging falsely? There is, presumably, no possibility of judging outside these alternatives, granted that everything is either known by us or not known; and inside them there seems to be no room for a false judgment.

THEAET.   Quite true.

SOCR.   Perhaps, then, we had better approach what we are looking for by way of another alternative. Instead of 'knowing or not knowing', let us take 'being or not being'.

THEAET.   How do you mean?

SOCR.   May it not simply be that one who thinks *what is not* about anything cannot but be thinking what is false, whatever his state of mind may be in other respects?

THEAET.   There is some likelihood in that, Socrates.

SOCR.   Then what shall we say, Theaetetus, if we are asked: 'But is what you describe possible for anyone? Can any man think what is not, either about something that is or absolutely?' I suppose we must answer to that: 'Yes, when he believes something and what he believes is not true.' Or what are we to say?

THEAET.   We must say that.

SOCR.   Then is the same sort of thing possible in any other case?

THEAET.   What sort of thing?

SOCR.   That a man should see something, and yet what he sees should be nothing.

THEAET.   No. How could that be?

SOCR.   Yet surely if what he sees is something, it must be a thing that is. Or do you suppose that 'something' can be reckoned among things that have no being at all?

THEAET.   No, I don't.

SOCR.   Then, if he sees something, he sees a thing that is.

THEAET.   Evidently.

SOCR.   And if he hears a thing, he hears something and hears a thing that is.

THEAET.   Yes.

SOCR. And if he touches a thing, he touches something, and if something, then a thing that is.

THEAET. That also is true.

SOCR. And if he thinks, he thinks something, doesn't he?

THEAET. Necessarily.

SOCR. And when he thinks something, he thinks a thing that is?

THEAET. I agree.

SOCR. So to think what is not is to think nothing.

THEAET. Clearly.

SOCR. But surely to think nothing is the same as not to think at all.

THEAET. That seems plain.

SOCR. If so, it is impossible to think what is not, either about anything that is, or absolutely.

THEAET. Evidently.

SOCR. Then thinking falsely must be something different from thinking what is not.

THEAET. So it seems.

SOCR. False judgment, then, is no more possible for us on these lines than on those we were following just now.

THEAET. No, it certainly is not.

SOCR. We do recognise the existence of false judgment as a sort of misjudgment, that occurs when a person interchanges in his mind two things, both of which are, and asserts that the one is the other. In this way he is always thinking of something which is, but of one thing in place of another, and since he misses the mark he may fairly be said to be judging falsely.

THEAET. I believe you have got it quite right now. When a person thinks 'ugly' in place of 'beautiful' or 'beautiful' in place of 'ugly', he is really and truly thinking what is false.

SOCR. I can see that you are no longer in awe of me, Theaetetus, but beginning to despise me.

THEAET. Why, precisely?

SOCR. I believe you think I shall miss the opening you give me by speaking of 'truly thinking what is false', and not ask you whether a thing can be slowly quick or heavily light or whether any contrary can desert its own nature and behave like its opposite. However, I will justify your boldness by letting that pass. So you like this notion that false judgment is mistaking.

THEAET. I do.

SOCR. According to you, then, it is possible for the mind to take one thing for another, and not for itself.

THEAET. Yes, it is.

SOCR. And when the mind does that, must it not be thinking either of both things or of one of the two?

THEAET. Certainly it must, either at the same time or one after the other.

SOCR. Excellent. And do you accept my description of the process of thinking?

THEAET. How do you describe it?

SOCR. As a discourse that the mind carries on with itself about any subject it is considering. You must take this explanation as coming from an ignoramus; but I have a notion that, when the mind is thinking, it is simply talking to itself, asking questions and answering them, and saying Yes or No. When it reaches a decision—which may come slowly or in a sudden rush—when doubt is over and the two voices affirm the same thing, then we call that its 'judgment'. So I should describe thinking as discourse, and judgment as a statement pronounced, not aloud to someone else, but silently to oneself.

THEAET. I agree.

SOCR. It seems, then, that when a person thinks of one thing as another, he is affirming to himself that the one is the other.

THEAET. Of course.

SOCR. Now search your memory and see if you have ever said to yourself 'Certainly, what is beautiful is ugly', or 'what is unjust is just'. To put it generally, consider if you have ever set about convincing yourself that any one thing is certainly another thing, or whether, on the contrary, you have never, even in a dream, gone so far as to say to yourself that odd numbers must be even, or anything of that sort.

THEAET. That is true.

SOCR. Do you suppose anyone else, mad or sane, ever goes so far as to talk himself over, in his own mind, into stating seriously that an ox must be a horse or that two must be one?

THEAET. Certainly not.

SOCR. So, if making a statement to oneself is the same as judging, then, so long as a man is making a statement or judgment about both things at once and his mind has hold of both, he cannot say or judge that one of them is the other. You, in your turn, must not cavil at my language; I mean it in the sense that no one thinks: 'the ugly is beautiful' or anything of that kind.

THEAET. I will not cavil, Socrates. I agree with you.

SOCR. So long, then, as a person is thinking of both, he cannot think of the one as the other.

THEAET. So it appears.

SOCR. On the other hand, if he is thinking of one only and not of the other at all, he will never think that the one is the other.

THEAET. True; for then he would have to have before his mind the thing he was not thinking of.

SOCR. It follows, then, that 'mistaking' is impossible, whether he thinks of both things or of one only. So there will be no sense in defining false judgment as 'misjudgment'. It does not appear that false judgment exists in us in this form any more than in those we dismissed earlier.

THEAET.   So it seems.

SOCR.   And yet, Theaetetus, if we cannot show that false judgment does exist, we shall be driven into admitting all sorts of absurdities.

THEAET.   For instance?

SOCR.   I will not mention them until I have tried to look at the question from every quarter. So long as we cannot see our way, I should feel some shame at our being forced into such admissions. But if we find the way out, then, as soon as we are clear, it will be time to speak of others as caught in the ludicrous position we shall have ourselves escaped; though, if we are completely baffled, then, I suppose, we must be humble and let the argument do with us what it will, like a sailor trampling over sea-sick passengers. So let me tell you where I still see an avenue open for us to follow.

THEAET.   Do tell me.

SOCR.   I shall say we were wrong to agree that a man cannot think that things he knows are things he does not know and so be deceived. In a way it is possible.

THEAET.   Do you mean something that crossed my mind at the moment when we said that was impossible? It occurred to me that sometimes I, who am acquainted with Socrates, imagine that a stranger whom I see at a distance is the Socrates whom I know. In a case like that a mistake of the kind you describe does occur.

SOCR.   And we were shy of saying that, because it would have made us out as both knowing and not knowing what we know?

THEAET.   Exactly.

SOCR.   We must, in fact, put the case in a different way. Perhaps the barrier will yield somewhere, though it may defy our efforts. Anyhow, we are in such straits that we must turn every argument over and put it to the test. Now, is there anything in this? Is it possible to become acquainted with something one did not know before?

THEAET.   Surely.

SOCR.   And the process can be repeated with one thing after another?

THEAET.   Of course.

SOCR.   Imagine, then, for the sake of argument, that our minds contain a block of wax, which in this or that individual may be larger or smaller, and composed of wax that is comparatively pure or muddy, and harder in some, softer in others, and sometimes of just the right consistency.

THEAET.   Very well.

SOCR.   Let us call it the gift of the Muses' mother, Memory, and say that whenever we wish to remember something we see or hear or conceive in our own minds, we hold this wax under the perceptions or ideas and imprint them on it as we might stamp the impression of a seal-ring. Whatever is so imprinted we remember and know so long as the image remains; whatever is rubbed out or has not succeeded in leaving an impression we have forgotten and do not know.

THEAET. So be it.

SOCR. Now take a man who knows things in this way, and is attending to something that he sees or hears. Is there not here a possibility of his making a false judgment?

THEAET. How?

SOCR. By thinking that things he knows are other things he knows, or sometimes things he does not know. We were wrong when we agreed earlier that this was impossible.

THEAET. What do you think about it now? . . .

SOCR. There remain, then, the following cases in which, if anywhere, false judgment can occur.

THEAET. What are they? Perhaps they may help me to understand better. At present I cannot follow.

SOCR. Take things you know: you can suppose them to be other things which you both know and perceive; or to be things you do not know, but do perceive; or you can confuse two things which you both know and perceive.

THEAET. Now I am more in the dark than ever.

SOCR. Let me start again, then, and put it in this way. I know Theodorus and have a memory in my mind of what he is like, and the same with Theaetetus. At certain moments I see or touch or hear or otherwise perceive them; at other times, though I have no perception of you and Theodorus, I nevertheless remember you both and have you before my mind. Isn't that so?

THEAET. Certainly.

SOCR. That, then, is the first point I want to make clear—that it is possible either to perceive or not to perceive something one is acquainted with.

THEAET. True.

SOCR. And it is also possible, when one is not acquainted with a thing, sometimes not to perceive it either, sometimes merely to perceive it and nothing more.

THEAET. That is possible too.

SOCR. Then see if you can follow me better now. If Socrates knows Theodorus and Theaetetus, but sees neither and has no sort of present perception of them, he can never think in his own mind that Theaetetus is Theodorus. Is that good sense?

THEAET.   Yes, that is true.

SOCR.   Well, that was the first of the cases I mentioned.

THEAET.   Yes.

SOCR.   And the second was this: if I know one of you but not the other and perceive neither, once more I could never think that the one I know is the other whom I do not know.

THEAET.   True.

SOCR.   And thirdly, if I neither know nor perceive either of you, I cannot think that one unknown person is another unknown person. And now take it as if I had gone over the whole list of cases again, in which I shall never judge falsely about you and Theodorus, whether I know both or neither or only one of you. And the same applies to perceiving, if you follow me.

THEAET.   I follow now.

SOCR.   It remains, then, that false judgment should occur in a case like this: when I, who know you and Theodorus and possess imprints of you both like seal-impressions in the waxen block, see you both at a distance indistinctly and am in a hurry to assign the proper imprint of each to the proper visual perception, like fitting a foot into its *own footmark to effect* a recognition; and then make the mistake of interchanging them, like a man who thrusts his feet into the wrong shoes, and apply the perception of each to the imprint of the other. Or my mistake might be illustrated by the sort of thing that happens in a mirror when the visual current transposes right to left. In that case mistaking or false judgment does result.

THEAET.   I think it does, Socrates. That is an admirable description of what happens to judgment.

SOCR.   Then there is also the case where I know both and perceive only one, and do not get the knowledge I have of that one to correspond with my perception. That is the expression I used before, which you did not understand.

THEAET.   No, I did not.

SOCR.   Well, that is what I was saying: if you know one of two people and also perceive him and if you get the knowledge you have to correspond with the perception of him, you will never think he is another person whom you both know and perceive, if your knowledge of him likewise is got to correspond with the perception. That was so, wasn't it?

THEAET.   Yes.

SOCR.   But there was left over the case I have been describing now, in which we say false judgment does occur: the possibility that you may know both and see or otherwise perceive both, but not get the two imprints to correspond each with its proper perception. Like a bad archer, you may shoot to one side and miss the mark—which is indeed another phrase we use for error.

THEAET. With good reason.

SOCR. Also, when a perception is present which belongs to one of the imprints, but none which belongs to the other, and the mind fits to the present perception the imprint belonging to the absent one, in all such cases it is in error. To sum up: in the case of objects one does not know and has never perceived, there is, it seems, no possibility of error or false judgment, if our present account is sound; but it is precisely in the field of objects both known and perceived that judgment turns and twists about and proves false or true—true when it brings impressions straight to their proper imprints; false when it misdirects them cross-wise to the wrong imprint.

THEAET. Surely that is a satisfactory account, isn't it, Socrates?

SOCR. You will think still better of it when you hear the rest. To judge truly is a fine thing and there is something discreditable in error.

THEAET. Of course.

SOCR. Well, they say the differences arise in this way. When a man has in his mind a good thick slab of wax, smooth and kneaded to the right consistency, and the impressions that come through the senses are stamped on these tables of the 'heart'—Homer's word hints at the mind's likeness to wax—then the imprints are clear and deep enough to last a long time. Such people are quick to learn and also have good memories, and besides they do not interchange the imprints of their perceptions but think truly. These imprints being distinct and well-spaced are quickly assigned to their several stamps—the 'real things' as they are called—and such men are said to be clever. Do you agree?

THEAET. Most emphatically.

SOCR. When a person has what the poet's wisdom commends as a 'shaggy heart', or when the block is muddy or made of impure wax, or over soft or hard, the people with soft wax are quick to learn, but forgetful, those with hard wax the reverse. Where it is shaggy or rough, a gritty kind of stuff containing a lot of earth or dirt, the impressions obtained are indistinct; so are they too when the stuff is hard, for they have no depth. Impressions in soft wax also are indistinct, because they melt together and soon become blurred. And if, besides this, they overlap through being crowded together into some wretched little narrow mind, they are still more indistinct. All these types, then, are likely to judge falsely. When they see or hear or think of something, they cannot quickly assign things to their several imprints. Because they are so slow and sort things into the wrong places, they constantly see and hear and think amiss, and we say they are mistaken about things and stupid.

THEAET. Your description could not be better, Socrates.

SOCR. We are to conclude, then, that false judgments do exist in us?

THEAET. Most certainly.

SOCR. And true ones also, I suppose?

THEAET. True ones also.

SOCR. At last, then, we believe we have reached a satisfactory agreement that both these kinds of judgments certainly exist?

THEAET. Most emphatically.

SOCR. It really does seem to be true, Theaetetus, that a garrulous person is a strange and disagreeable creature.

THEAET. Why, what makes you say that?

SOCR. Disgust at my own stupidity. I am indeed garrulous: what else can you call a man who goes on bandying arguments to and fro because he is such a dolt that he cannot make up his mind and is loath to surrender any one of them?

THEAET. But why are you disgusted with yourself?

SOCR. I am not merely disgusted but anxious about the answer I shall make if someone asks: 'So, Socrates, you have made a discovery: that false judgment resides, not in our perceptions among themselves nor yet in our thoughts, but in the fitting together of perception and thought?' I suppose I shall say, Yes, and plume myself on this brilliant discovery of ours.

THEAET. I don't see anything to be ashamed of in what you have just pointed out, Socrates.

SOCR. 'On the other hand,' he will continue, 'you also say that we can never imagine that a man whom we merely think of and do not see is a horse which again we do not see or touch but merely think of without perceiving it in any way?' I suppose I shall say, Yes, to that.

THEAET. And rightly.

SOCR. 'On that showing,' he will say, 'a man could never imagine that 11, which he merely thinks of, is 12, which again he merely thinks of.' Come, you must find the answer now.

THEAET. Well, I shall answer that, if he saw or handled eleven things, he might suppose they were twelve; but he will never make that judgment about the 11 and the 12 he has in his thoughts.

SOCR. Well now, does a man ever consider in his own mind 5 and 7—I don't mean five men and seven men or anything of that sort, but just 5 and 7 themselves, which we describe as records in that waxen block of ours, among which there can be no false judgment—does anyone ever take these into consideration and ask himself in his inward conversation how much they amount to; and does one man believe and state that they make 11, another that they make 12, or does everybody agree they make 12?

THEAET. Far from it; many people say 11; and if larger numbers are involved, the more room there is for mistakes; for you are speaking generally of any numbers, I suppose.

SOCR.   Yes, that is right. Now consider what happens in this case. Is it not thinking that the 12 itself that is stamped on the waxen block is 11?

THEAET.   It seems so.

SOCR.   Then haven't we come round again to our first argument? For when this happens to someone, he is thinking that one thing he knows is another thing he knows; and that, we said, was impossible. That was the very ground on which we were led to make out that there could be no such thing as false judgment: it was in order to avoid the conclusion that the same man must at the same time know and not know the same thing.

THEAET.   Quite true.

SOCR.   If so, we must account for false judgment in some other way than as the misfitting of thought to perception. If it were that, we should never make mistakes among our thoughts themselves. As the case stands now, either there is no such thing as false judgment, or it is possible not to know what one does know. Which alternative do you choose?

THEAET.   I see no possible choice, Socrates.

SOCR.   But the argument is not going to allow both alternatives. However, we must stick at nothing: suppose we try being quite shameless.

THEAET.   In what way?

SOCR.   By making up our minds to describe what knowing is like.

THEAET.   How is that shameless?

SOCR.   You seem to be unaware that our whole conversation from the outset has been an inquiry after the nature of knowledge on the supposition that we did not know what it was.

THEAET.   No, I am quite aware of that.

SOCR.   Then, doesn't it strike you as shameless to explain what knowing is like, when we don't know what knowledge is? The truth is, Theaetetus, that for some time past there has been a vicious taint in our discussion. Times out of number we have said: 'we know', 'we do not know', 'we have knowledge', 'we have no knowledge', as if we could understand each other while we still know nothing about knowledge. At this very moment, if you please, we have once more used the words 'know nothing' and 'understand', as if we had a right to use them while we are still destitute of knowledge.

THEAET.   Well, but how are you going to carry on a discussion, Socrates, if you keep clear of those words?

SOCR.   I cannot, being the man I am, though I might if I were an expert in debate. If such a person were here now, he would profess to keep clear of them and rebuke us severely for my use of language. As we are such bunglers, then, shall I be so bold as to describe what knowing is like? I think it might help us.

THEAET. Do so, then, by all means. And if you cannot avoid those words, you shall not be blamed.

SOCR. Well, you have heard what 'knowing' is commonly said to be?

THEAET. Possibly; but I don't remember at the moment.

SOCR. They say it is 'having knowledge'.

THEAET. True.

SOCR. Let us make a slight amendment and say: 'possessing knowledge'.

THEAET. What difference would you say that makes?

SOCR. None, perhaps; but let me tell you my idea and you shall help me test it.

THEAET. I will if I can.

SOCR. 'Having' seems to me different from 'possessing'. If a man has bought a coat and owns it, but is not wearing it, we should say he possesses it without having it about him.

THEAET. True.

SOCR. Now consider whether knowledge is a thing you can possess in that way without having it about you, like a man who has caught some wild birds—pigeons or what not—and keeps them in an aviary he has made for them at home. In a sense, of course, we might say he 'has' them all the time inasmuch as he possesses them, mightn't we?

THEAET. Yes.

SOCR. But in another sense he 'has' none of them, though he has got control of them, now that he has made them captive in an enclosure of his own; he can take and have hold of them whenever he likes by catching any bird he chooses, and let them go again; and it is open to him to do that as often as he pleases.

THEAET. That is so.

SOCR. Once more then, just as a while ago we imagined a sort of waxen block in our minds, so now let us suppose that every mind contains a kind of aviary stocked with birds of every sort, some in flocks apart from the rest, some in small groups, and some solitary, flying in any direction among them all.

THEAET. Be it so. What follows?

SOCR. When we are babies we must suppose this receptacle empty, and take the birds to stand for pieces of knowledge. Whenever a person acquires any piece of knowledge and shuts it up in his enclosure, we must say he has learnt or discovered the thing of which this is the knowledge, and that is what 'knowing' means.

THEAET. Be it so.

SOCR. Now think of him hunting once more for any piece of knowledge that he wants, catching and holding it, and letting it go again. In what terms are we to describe that—the same that we used of the original process of acquisition, or different ones? An illustration may help you to see what I mean. There is a science you call 'arithmetic'.

THEAET.   Yes.

SOCR.   Conceive that, then, as a chase after pieces of knowledge about all the numbers, odd or even.

THEAET.   I will.

SOCR.   That, I take it, is the science in virtue of which a man has in his control pieces of knowledge about numbers and can hand them over to someone else.

THEAET.   Yes.

SOCR.   And when he hands them over, we call it 'teaching', and when the other takes them from him, that is 'learning', and when he has them in the sense of possessing them in that aviary of his, that is 'knowing'.

THEAET.   Certainly.

SOCR.   Now observe what follows. The finished arithmetician knows all numbers, doesn't he? There is no number the knowledge of which is not in his mind.

THEAET.   Naturally.

SOCR.   And such a person may sometimes count either the numbers themselves in his own head or some set of external things that have a number.

THEAET.   Of course.

SOCR.   And by counting we shall mean simply trying to find out what some particular number amounts to?

THEAET.   Yes.

SOCR.   It appears, then, that the man who, as we admitted, knows every number, is trying to find out what he knows as if he had no knowledge of it. No doubt you sometimes hear puzzles of that sort debated.

THEAET.   Indeed I do.

SOCR.   Well, our illustration from hunting pigeons and getting possession of them will enable us to explain that the hunting occurs in two ways: first, before you possess your pigeon in order to have possession of it; secondly, after getting possession of it, in order to catch and hold in your hand what you have already possessed for some time. In the same way, if you have long possessed pieces of knowledge about things you have learnt and know, it is still possible to get to know the same things again, by the process of recovering the knowledge of some particular thing and getting hold of it. It is knowledge you have possessed for some time, but you had not got it handy in your mind.

THEAET.   True.

SOCR.   That, then, was the drift of my question, what terms should be used to describe the arithmetician who sets about counting or the literate person who sets about reading; because it seemed as if, in such a case, the man was setting about learning again from himself what he already knew.

THEAET. That sounds odd, Socrates.

SOCR. Well, but can we say he is going to read or count something he does *not* know, when we have already granted that he knows all the letters or all the numbers?

THEAET. No, that is absurd too.

SOCR. Shall we say, then, that we care nothing about words, if it amuses anyone to turn and twist the expressions 'knowing' and 'learning'? Having drawn a distinction between possessing knowledge and having it about one, we agree that it is impossible not to possess what one does possess, and so we avoid the result that a man should not know what he does know; but we say that it is possible for him to get hold of a false judgment about it. For he may not have about him the knowledge of that thing, but a different piece of knowledge instead, if it so happens that, in hunting for some particular piece of knowledge, among those that are fluttering about, he misses it and catches hold of a different one. In that case, you see, he mistakes 11 for 12, because he has caught hold of the knowledge of 11 that is inside him, instead of his knowledge of 12, as he might catch a dove in place of a pigeon.

THEAET. That seems reasonable.

SOCR. Whereas, when he catches the piece of knowledge he is trying to catch, he is not mistaken but thinks what is true. In this way both true and false judgments can exist, and the obstacles that were troubling us are removed. You will agree to this, perhaps? Or will you not?

THEAET. I will.

SOCR. Yes; for now we are rid of the contradiction about people not knowing what they do know. That no longer implies our not possessing what we do possess, whether we are mistaken about something or not. But it strikes me that a still stranger consequence is coming in sight.

THEAET. What is that?

SOCR. That the interchange of pieces of knowledge should ever result in a judgment that is false.

THEAET. How do you mean?

SOCR. In the first place, that a man should have knowledge of something and at the same time fail to recognise that very thing, not for want of knowing it but by reason of his own knowledge; and next that he should judge that thing to be something else and *vice versa*— isn't that very unreasonable: that when a piece of knowledge presents itself, the mind should fail to recognise anything and know nothing? On this showing, the presence of ignorance might just as well make us know something, or the presence of blindness make us see—if knowledge can ever make us fail to know.

THEAT. Perhaps, Socrates, we were wrong in making the birds stand for pieces of knowledge only, and we ought to have imagined pieces of ignorance flying about with them in the mind. Then, in chasing them, our man would lay hold sometimes of a piece of knowledge, sometimes of a piece of ignorance; and the ignorance would make him judge falsely, the knowledge truly, about the same thing.

SOCR. It is not easy to disapprove of anything you say, Theaetetus; but think again about your suggestion. Suppose it is as you say; then the man who lays hold of the piece of ignorance will judge falsely. Is that right?

THEAET. Yes.

SOCR. But of course he will not think he is judging falsely.

THEAET. Of course not.

SOCR. No; he will think he is judging truly; and his attitude of mind will be the same as if he knew the thing he is mistaken about.

THEAET. Naturally.

SOCR. So he will imagine that, as a result of his chase, he has got hold of a piece of knowledge, not a piece of ignorance.

THEAET. Clearly.

SOCR. Then we have gone a long way round only to find ourselves confronted once more with our original difficulty. Our destructive critic will laugh at us. 'You wonderful people,' he will say, 'are we to understand that a man knows both a piece of knowledge and a piece of ignorance, and then supposes that one of these things he knows is the other which he also knows? Or does he know neither, and then judge that one of these unknown things is the other? Or does he know only one, and identify this known thing with the unknown one, or the unknown one with the known? Or are you going to tell me that there are yet further pieces of knowledge *about* your pieces of knowledge and ignorance, and that their owner keeps these shut up in yet another of your ridiculous aviaries or waxen blocks, knowing them so long as he possesses them, although he may not have them at hand in his mind? On that showing you will find yourselves perpetually driven round in a circle and never getting any further.' What are we to reply to that, Theaetetus?

THEAET. Really, Socrates, I don't know what we are to say.

SOCR. Maybe, my young friend, we have deserved this rebuke, and the argument shows that we were wrong to leave knowledge on one side and look first for an explanation of false judgment. That cannot be understood until we have a satisfactory account of the nature of knowledge.

THEAET. As things now stand, Socrates, one cannot avoid that conclusion.

Socr.   To start all over again, then: what is one to say that knowledge is? For surely we are not going to give up yet.

Theaet.   Not unless you do so.

Socr.   Then tell me: what definition can we give with the least risk of contradicting ourselves?

Theaet.   The one we tried before, Socrates. I have nothing else to suggest.

Socr.   What was that?

Theaet.   That true belief is knowledge. Surely there can at least be no mistake in believing what is true and the consequences are always satisfactory.

Socr.   Try, and you will see, Theaetetus, as the man said when he was asked if the river was too deep to ford. So here, if we go forward on our search, we may stumble upon something that will reveal the thing we are looking for. We shall make nothing out, if we stay where we are.

Theaet.   True; let us go forward and see.

Socr.   Well, we need not go far to see this much: you will find a whole profession to prove that true belief is not knowledge.

Theaet.   How so? What profession?

Socr.   The profession of those paragons of intellect known as orators and lawyers. There you have men who use their skill to produce conviction, not by instruction, but by making people believe whatever they want them to believe. You can hardly imagine teachers so clever as to be able, in the short time allowed by the clock, to instruct their hearers thoroughly in the true facts of a case of robbery or other violence which those hearers had not witnessed.

Theaet.   No, I cannot imagine that; but they can convince them.

Socr.   And by convincing you mean making them believe something.

Theaet.   Of course.

Socr.   And when a jury is rightly convinced of facts which can be known only by an eye-witness, then, judging by hearsay and accepting a true belief, they are judging without knowledge, although, if they find the right verdict, their conviction is correct?

Theaet.   Certainly.

Socr.   But if true belief and knowledge were the same thing, the best of jurymen could never have a correct belief without knowledge. It now appears that they must be different things.

Theaet.   Yes, Socrates, I have heard someone make the distinction. I had forgotten, but now it comes back to me. He said that true belief with the addition of an account (*logos*) was knowledge, while belief without an account was outside its range. Where no account could be given of a thing, it was not 'knowable'—that was the word he used—where it could, it was knowable.

SOCR. A good suggestion. But tell me how he distinguished these knowable things from the unknowable. It may turn out that what you were told tallies with something I have heard said.

THEAET. I am not sure if I can recall that; but I think I should recognise it if I heard it stated.

SOCR. If you have had a dream, let me tell you mine in return. I seem to have heard some people say that what might be called the first elements of which we and all other things consist are such that no account can be given of them. Each of them just by itself can only be named; we cannot attribute to it anything further or say that it exists or does not exist; for we should at once be attaching to it existence or non-existence, whereas we ought to add nothing if we are to express just it alone. We ought not even to add 'just' or 'it' or 'each' or 'alone' or 'this', or any other of a host of such terms. These terms, running loose about the place, are attached to everything, and they are distinct from the things to which they are applied. If it were possible for an element to be ex-pressed in any formula exclusively belonging to it, no other terms ought to enter into that expression; but in fact there is no formula in which any element can be expressed: it can only be named, for a name is all there is that belongs to it. But when we come to things composed of these ele-ments, then, just as these things are complex, so the names are combined to make a description (*logos*), a description being precisely a combina-tion of names. Accordingly, elements are inexplicable and unknowable, but they can be perceived; while complexes ('syllables') are knowable and explicable, and you can have a true notion of them. So when a man gets hold of the true notion of something without an account, his mind does think truly of it, but he does not know it; for if one cannot give and receive an account of a thing, one has no knowledge of that thing. But when he has also got hold of an account, all this becomes possible to him and he is fully equipped with knowledge.

Does that version represent the dream as you heard it, or not?

THEAET. Perfectly.

SOCR. So this dream finds favour and you hold that a true notion with the addition of an account is knowledge?

THEAET. Precisely.

SOCR. Can it be, Theaetetus, that, all in a moment, we have found out to-day what so many wise men have grown old in seeking and have not found?

THEAET. I, at any rate, am satisfied with our present statement, Socrates.

SOCR. Yes, the statement just in itself may well be satisfactory; for how can there ever be knowledge without an account and right belief? But there is one point in the theory as stated that does not find favour with me.

THEAET.   What is that?

SOCR.   What might be considered its most ingenious feature: it says that the elements are unknowable, but whatever is complex ('syllables') can be known.

THEAET.   Is not that right?

SOCR.   We must find out. We hold as a sort of hostage for the theory the illustration in terms of which it was stated.

THEAET.   Namely?

SOCR.   Letters—the elements of writing—and syllables. That and nothing else was the prototype the author of this theory had in mind, don't you think?

THEAET.   Yes, it was.

SOCR.   Let us take up that illustration, then, and put it to the question, or rather put the question to ourselves: did we learn our letters on that principle or not? To begin with: is it true that an account can be given of syllables, but not of letters?

THEAET.   It may be so.

SOCR.   I agree, decidedly. Suppose you are asked about the first syllable of 'Socrates': 'Explain, Theaetetus; what is SO?' How will you answer?

THEAET.   S and O.

SOCR.   And you have there an account of the syllable?

THEAET.   Yes.

SOCR.   Go on, then; give me a similar account of S.

THEAET.   But how can one state the elements of an element? The fact is, of course, Socrates, that S is one of the consonants, nothing but a noise, like a hissing of the tongue; while B not only has no articulate sound but is not even a noise, and the same is true of most of the letters. So they may well be said to be inexplicable, when the clearest of them, the seven vowels themselves, have only a sound, and no sort of account can be given of them.

SOCR.   So far, then, we have reached a right conclusion about knowledge.

THEAET.   Apparently.

SOCR.   But now, have we been right in declaring that the letter cannot be known, though the syllable can?

THEAET.   That seems all right.

SOCR.   Take the syllable then: do we mean by that both the two letters or (if there are more than two) all the letters? Or do we mean a single entity that comes into existence from the moment when they are put together?

THEAET.   I should say we mean all the letters.

SOCR.   Then take the case of the two letters S and O. The two together are the first syllable of my name. Anyone who knows that syllable knows both the letters, doesn't he?

THEAET. Naturally.

SOCR. So he knows the S and the O.

THEAET. Yes.

SOCR. But has he, then, no knowledge of *each* letter, so that he knows both without knowing either?

THEAET. That is a monstrous absurdity, Socrates.

SOCR. And yet, if it is necessary to know each of two things before one can know both, he simply must know the letters first, if he is ever to know the syllable; and so our fine theory will vanish and leave us in the lurch.

THEAET. With a startling suddenness.

SOCR. Yes, because we are not keeping a good watch upon it. Perhaps we ought to have assumed that the syllable was not the letters but a single entity that arises out of them with a unitary character of its own and different from the letters.

THEAET. By all means. Indeed, it may well be so rather than the other way.

SOCR. Let us consider that. We ought not to abandon an imposing theory in this poor-spirited manner.

THEAET. Certainly not.

SOCR. Suppose, then, it is as we say now: the syllable arises as a single entity from any set of letters which can be combined; and that holds of every complex, not only in the case of letters.

THEAET. By all means.

SOCR. In that case, it must have no parts.

THEAET. Why?

SOCR. Because, if a thing has parts, the whole thing must be the same as all the parts.

SOCR. Or do you say that a whole likewise is a single entity that arises out of the parts and is different from the aggregate of the parts?

THEAET. Yes, I do.

SOCR. Then do you regard the sum (τὸ πᾶν) as the same thing as the whole, or are they different?

THEAET. I am not at all clear; but you tell me to answer boldly, so I will take the risk of saying they are different.

SOCR. Your boldness, Theaetetus, is right; whether your answer is so, we shall have to consider.

THEAET. Yes, certainly.

SOCR. Well, then, the whole will be different from the sum, according to our present view.

THEAET. Yes.

SOCR. Well but now, is there any difference between the sum and all the things it includes? For instance, when we say, 'one, two, three, four, five, six', or 'twice three' or 'three times two' or 'four and two' or 'three and two and one', are we in all these cases expressing the same thing or different things?

THEAET.   The same.

SOCR.   Just six, and nothing else?

THEAET.   Yes.

SOCR.   In fact, in each form of expression we have expressed all the six.

THEAET.   Yes.

SOCR.   But when we express them all, is there no sum that we express?

THEAET.   There must be.

SOCR.   And is that sum anything else than 'six'?

THEAET.   No.

SOCR.   Then, at any rate in the case of things that consist of a number, the words 'sum' and 'all the things' denote the same thing.

THEAET.   So it seems.

SOCR.   Let us put our argument, then, in this way. The number of (square feet in) an acre, and the acre are the same thing, aren't they?

THEAET.   Yes.

SOCR.   And so too with the number of (feet in) a mile?

THEAET.   Yes.

SOCR.   And again with the number of (soldiers in) an army and the army, and so on, in all cases. The total number is the same as the total thing in each case.

THEAET.   Yes.

SOCR.   But the number of (units in) any collection of things cannot be anything but *parts* of that collection?

THEAET.   No.

SOCR.   Now, anything that has parts consists of parts.

THEAET.   Evidently.

SOCR.   But all the parts, we have agreed, are the same as the sum, if the total number is to be the same as the total thing.

THEAET.   Yes.

SOCR.   The whole, then, does not consist of parts; for if it were all the parts it would be a sum.

THEAET.   Apparently not.

SOCR.   But can a part be a part of anything but its whole?

THEAET.   Yes; of the sum.

SOCR.   You make a gallant fight of it, Theaetetus. But does not 'the sum' mean precisely something from which nothing is missing?

THEAET.   Necessarily.

SOCR.   And is not a whole exactly the same thing—that from which nothing whatever is missing? Whereas, when something is removed, the thing becomes neither a whole nor a sum: it changes at the same moment from being both to being neither.

THEAET. I think now that there is no difference between a sum and a whole.

SOCR. Well, we were saying—were we not?—that when a thing has parts, the whole or sum will be the same thing as all the parts?

THEAET. Certainly.

SOCR. To go back, then, to the point I was trying to make just now; if the syllable is not the same thing as the letters, does it not follow that it cannot have the letters as parts of itself; otherwise, being the same thing as the letters, it would be neither more nor less knowable than they are?

THEAET. Yes.

SOCR. And it was to avoid that consequence that we supposed the syllable to be different from the letters.

THEAET. Yes.

SOCR. Well, if the letters are not parts of the syllable, can you name any things, other than its letters, that are parts of a syllable?

THEAET. Certainly not, Socrates. If I admitted that it had any parts, it would surely be absurd to set aside the letters and look for parts of any other kind.

SOCR. Then, on the present showing, a syllable will be a thing that is absolutely one and cannot be divided into parts of any sort?

THEAET. Apparently.

SOCR. Do you remember then, my dear Theaetetus, our accepting a short while ago a statement that we thought satisfactory: that no account could be given of the primary things of which other things are composed, because each of them, taken just by itself, was incomposite; and that it was not correct to attribute even 'existence' to it, or to call it 'this', on the ground that these words expressed different things that were extraneous to it; and this was the ground for making the primary thing inexplicable and unknowable?

THEAET. I remember.

SOCR. Then is not exactly this, and nothing else, the ground of its being simple in nature and indivisible into parts? I can see no other.

THEAET. Evidently there is no other.

SOCR. Then has not the syllable now turned out to be a thing of the same sort, if it has no parts and is a unitary thing?

THEAET. Certainly.

SOCR. To conclude, then: if, on the one hand, the syllable is the same thing as a number of letters and is a whole with the letters as its parts, then the letters must be neither more nor less knowable and explicable than syllables, since we made out that all the parts are the same thing as the whole.

THEAET.   True.

SOCR.   But if, on the other hand, the syllable is a unity without parts, syllable and letter likewise are equally incapable of explanation and unknowable. The same reason will make them so.

THEAET.   I see no way out of that.

SOCR.   If so, we must not accept this statement: that the syllable can be known and explained, the letter cannot.

THEAET.   No, not if we hold by our argument.

SOCR.   And again, would not your own experience in learning your letters rather incline you to accept the opposite view?

THEAET.   What view do you mean?

SOCR.   This: that all the time you were learning you were doing nothing else but trying to distinguish by sight or hearing each letter by itself, so as not to be confused by any arrangement of them in spoken or written words.

THEAET.   That is quite true.

SOCR.   And in the music school the height of accomplishment lay precisely in being able to follow each several note and tell which string it belonged to; and notes, as everyone would agree, are the elements of music.

THEAET.   Precisely.

SOCR.   Then, if we are to argue from our own experience of elements and complexes to other cases, we shall conclude that elements in general yield knowledge that is much clearer than knowledge of the complex and more effective for a complete grasp of anything we seek to know. If anyone tells us that the complex is by its nature knowable, while the element is unknowable, we shall suppose that, whether he intends it or not, he is playing with us.

THEAET.   Certainly.

SOCR.   Indeed we might, I think, find other arguments to prove that point. But we must not allow them to distract our attention from the question before us, namely, what can really be meant by saying that an account added to true belief yields knowledge in its most perfect form.

THEAET.   Yes, we must see what that means.

SOCR.   Well then, what is this term 'account' intended to convey to us? I think it must mean one of three things.

THEAET.   What are they?

SOCR.   The first will be giving overt expression to one's thought by means of vocal sound with names and verbs, casting an image of one's notion on the stream that flows through the lips, like a reflection in a mirror or in water. Do you agree that expression of that sort is an 'account'?

THEAET. I do. We certainly call that expressing ourselves in speech (λέγειν).

SOCR. On the other hand, that is a thing that anyone can do more or less readily. If a man is not born deaf or dumb, he can signify what he thinks on any subject. So in this sense anyone whatever who has a correct notion evidently will have it 'with an account', and there will be no place left anywhere for a correct notion apart from knowledge.

THEAET. True.

SOCR. Then we must not be too ready to charge the author of the definition of knowledge now before us with talking nonsense. Perhaps that is not what he meant. He may have meant: being able to reply to the question, what any given thing is, by enumerating its elements.

THEAET. For example, Socrates?

SOCR. For example, Hesiod says about a wagon, 'In a wagon are a hundred pieces of wood.' I could not name them all; no more, I imagine, could you. If we were asked what a wagon is, we should be content if we could mention wheels, axle, body, rails, yoke.

THEAET. Certainly.

SOCR. But I dare say he would think us just as ridiculous as if we replied to the question about your own name by telling the syllables. We might think and express ourselves correctly, but we should be absurd if we fancied ourselves to be grammarians and able to give such an account of the name Theaetetus as a grammarian would offer. He would say it is impossible to give a scientific account of anything, short of adding to your true notion a complete catalogue of the elements, as, I think, was said earlier.

THEAET. Yes, it was.

SOCR. In the same way, he would say, we may have a correct notion of the wagon, but the man who can give a complete statement of its nature by going through those hundred parts has thereby added an account to his correct notion and, in place of mere belief, has arrived at a technical knowledge of the wagon's nature, by going through all the elements in the whole.

THEAET. Don't you approve, Socrates?

SOCR. Tell me if you approve, my friend, and whether you accept the view that the complete enumeration of elements is an account of any given thing, whereas description in terms of syllables or of any larger unit still leaves it unaccounted for. Then we can look into the matter further.

THEAET. Well, I do accept that.

SOCR. Do you think, then, that anyone has knowledge of whatever it may be, when he thinks that one and the same thing is a part sometimes of one thing, sometimes of a different thing; or again when he believes now one and now another thing to be part of one and the same thing?

THEAET. Certainly not.

SOCR. Have you forgotten, then, that when you first began learning to read and write, that was what you and your schoolfellows did?

THEAET. Do you mean, when we thought that now one letter and now another was part of the same syllable, and when we put the same letter sometimes into the proper syllable, sometimes into another?

SOCR. That is what I mean.

THEAET. Then I have certainly not forgotten; and I do not think that one has reached knowledge so long as one is in that condition.

SOCR. Well then, if at that stage you are writing 'Theaetetus' and you think you ought to write T and H and E and do so, and again when you are trying to write 'Theodorus', you think you ought to write T and E and do so, can we say that you know the first syllable of your two names?

THEAET. No; we have just agreed that one has not knowledge so long as one is in that condition.

SOCR. And there is no reason why a person should not be in the same condition with respect to the second, third, and fourth syllables as well?

THEAET. None whatever.

SOCR. Can we, then, say that whenever in writing 'Theaetetus' he puts down all the letters in order, then he is in possession of the complete catalogue of elements together with correct belief?

THEAET. Obviously.

SOCR. Being still, as we agree, without knowledge, though his beliefs are correct?

THEAET. Yes.

SOCR. Although he possesses the 'account' in addition to right belief. For when he wrote he was in possession of the catalogue of the elements, which we agreed was the 'account'.

THEAET. True.

SOCR. So, my friend, there is such a thing as right belief together with an account, which is not yet entitled to be called knowledge.

THEAET. I am afraid so.

SOCR. Then, apparently, our idea that we had found the perfectly true definition of knowledge was no better than a golden dream. Or shall we not condemn the theory yet? Perhaps the meaning to be given to 'account' is not this, but the remaining one of the three, one of which we said must be intended by anyone who defines knowledge as correct belief together with an account.

THEAET. A good reminder; there is still one meaning left. The first was what might be called the image of thought in spoken sound; and the one we have just discussed was going all through the elements to arrive at the whole. What is the third?

SOCR. The meaning most people would give: being able to name some mark by which the thing one is asked about differs from everything else.

THEAET.   Could you give me an example of such an account of a thing?

SOCR.   Take the sun as an example. I dare say you will be satisfied with the account of it as the brightest of the heavenly bodies that go round the earth.

THEAET.   Certainly.

SOCR.   Let me explain the point of this example. It is to illustrate what we were just saying: that if you get hold of the difference distinguishing any given thing from all others, then, so some people say, you will have an 'account' of it; whereas, so long as you fix upon something common to other things, your account will embrace all the things that share it.

THEAET.   I understand. I agree that what you describe may fairly be called an 'account'.

SOCR.   And if, besides a right notion about a thing, whatever it may be, you also grasp its difference from all other things, you will have arrived at knowledge of what, till then, you had only a notion of.

THEAET.   We do say that, certainly.

SOCR.   Really, Theaetetus, now I come to look at this statement at close quarters, it is like a scene-painting: I cannot make it out at all, though, so long as I kept at a distance, there seemed to be some sense in it.

THEAET.   What do you mean? Why so?

SOCR.   I will explain, if I can. Suppose I have a correct notion about you; if I add to that the account of you, then, we are to understand, I know you. Otherwise I have only a notion.

THEAET.   Yes.

SOCR.   And 'account' means putting your differentness into words.

THEAET.   Yes.

SOCR.   So, at the time when I had only a notion, my mind did not grasp any of the points in which you differ from others?

THEAET.   Apparently not.

SOCR.   Then I must have had before my mind one of those common things which belong to another person as much as to you.

THEAET.   That follows.

SOCR.   But look here! If that was so, how could I possibly be having a notion of you rather than of anyone else? Suppose I was thinking: Theaetetus is one who is a man and has a nose and eyes and a mouth and so forth, enumerating every part of the body. Will thinking in that way result in my thinking of Theaetetus rather than of Theodorus or, as they say, of the man in the street?

THEAET.   How should it?

SOCR. Well, now suppose I think not merely of a man with a nose and eyes, but of one with a snub nose and prominent eyes, once more shall I be having a notion of you any more than of myself or anyone else of that description?

THEAET. No.

SOCR. In fact, there will be no notion of Theaetetus in my mind, I suppose, until this particular snubness has stamped and registered within me a record distinct from all the other cases of snubness that I have seen; and so with every other part of you. Then, if I meet you to-morrow, that trait will revive my memory and give me a correct notion about you.

THEAET. Quite true.

SOCR. If that is so, the correct notion of anything must itself include the differentness of that thing.

THEAET. Evidently.

SOCR. Then what meaning is left for getting hold of an 'account' in addition to the correct notion? If, on the one hand, it means adding the notion of how a thing differs from other things, such an injunction is simply absurd.

THEAET. How so?

SOCR. When we have a correct notion of the way in which certain things differ from other things, it tells us to add a correct notion of the way in which they differ from other things. On this showing, the most vicious of circles would be nothing to this injunction. It might better deserve to be called the sort of direction a blind man might give: to tell us to get hold of something we already have, in order to get to know something we are already thinking of, suggests a taste of the most absolute darkness.

THEAET. Whereas, if ——? The supposition you made just now implied that you would state some alternative; what was it?

SOCR. If the direction to add an 'account' means that we are to get to *know* the differentness, as opposed to merely having a notion of it, this most admirable of all definitions of knowledge will be a pretty business; because 'getting to know' means acquiring knowledge, doesn't it?

THEAET. Yes.

SOCR. So, apparently, to the question, What is knowledge? our definition will reply: 'Correct belief together with knowledge of a differentness'; for, according to it, 'adding an account' will come to that.

THEAET. So it seems.

SOCR. Yes; and when we are inquiring after the nature of knowledge, nothing could be sillier than to say that it is correct belief together with a *knowledge* of differentness or of anything whatever.

So, Theaetetus, neither perception, nor true belief, nor the addition of an 'account' to true belief can be knowledge.

THEAET. Apparently not.

SOCR.   Are we in labour, then, with any further child, my friend, or have we brought to birth all we have to say about knowledge?

THEAET.   Indeed we have; and for my part I have already, thanks to you, given utterance to more than I had in me.

SOCR.   All of which our midwife's skill pronounces to be mere wind-eggs and not worth the rearing?

THEAET.   Undoubtedly.

SOCR.   Then supposing you should ever henceforth try to conceive afresh, Theaetetus, if you succeed, your embryo thoughts will be the better as a consequence of to-day's scrutiny; and if you remain barren, you will be gentler and more agreeable to your companions, having the good sense not to fancy you know what you do not know. For that, and no more, is all that my art can effect; nor have I any of that knowledge possessed by all the great and admirable men of our own day or of the past. But this midwife's art is a gift from heaven; my mother had it for women, and I for young men of a generous spirit and for all in whom beauty dwells.

Now I must go to the portico of the King Archon to meet the indictment which Meletus has drawn up against me. But tomorrow morning, Theodorus, let us meet here again.

II

From *The Republic**

I said: *Until philosophers are kings, or the kings and princes of this world have the spirit and power of philosophy, and political greatness and wisdom meet in one, and those commoner natures who pursue either to the exclusion of the other are compelled to stand aside, cities will never have rest from their evils,—no, nor the human race, as I believe,—and then only will this our State have a possibility of life and behold the light of day.*

Such was the thought, my dear Glaucon, which I would fain have uttered if it had not seemed too extravagant; for to be convinced that in no other State can there be happiness private or public is indeed a hard thing.

Socrates, what do you mean? I would have you consider that the word which you have uttered is one at which numerous persons, and very respectable persons too, in a figure pulling off their coats all in a moment, and seizing any weapon that comes to hand, will run at you might and main, before you know where you are, intending to do heaven knows

* From "The Republic," translated by Benjamin Jowett.

what; and if you don't prepare an answer, and put yourself in motion, you will be 'pared by their fine wits,' and no mistake.

You got me into the scrape, I said.

And I was quite right; however, I will do all I can to get you out of it; but I can only give you good-will and good advice, and, perhaps, I may be able to fit answers to your questions better than another—that is all. And now, having such an auxiliary, you must do your best to show the unbelievers that you are right.

I ought to try, I said, since you offer me such invaluable assistance. And I think that, if there is to be a chance of our escaping, we must explain to them whom we mean when we say that philosophers are to rule in the State; then we shall be able to defend ourselves: There will be discovered to be some natures who ought to study philosophy and to be leaders in the State; and others who are not born to be philosophers, and are meant to be followers rather than leaders.

Then now for a definition, he said.

Follow me, I said, and I hope that I may in some way or other be able to give you a satisfactory explanation.

Proceed.

I dare say that you remember, and therefore I need not remind you, that a lover, if he is worthy of the name, ought to show his love, not to some one part of that which he loves, but to the whole.

I really do not understand, and therefore beg of you to assist my memory.

Another person, I said, might fairly reply as you do; but a man of pleasure like yourself ought to know that all who are in the flower of youth do somehow or other raise a pang or emotion in a lover's breast, and are thought by him to be worthy of his affectionate regards. Is not this a way which you have with the fair: one has a snub nose, and you praise his charming face; the hook-nose of another has, you say, a royal look; while he who is neither snub nor hooked has the grace of regularity: the dark visage is manly, the fair are children of the gods; and as to the sweet 'honey pale,' as they are called, what is the very name but the invention of a lover who talks in diminutives, and is not adverse to paleness if appearing on the cheek of youth? In a word, there is no excuse which you will not make, and nothing which you will not say, in order not to lose a single flower that blooms in the spring-time of youth.

If you make me an authority in matters of love, for the sake of the argument, I assent.

And what do you say of lovers of wine? Do you not see them doing the same? They are glad of any pretext of drinking any wine.

Very good.

And the same is true of ambitious men; if they cannot command an army, they are willing to command a file; and if they cannot be honoured by really great and important persons, they are glad to be honoured by lesser and meaner people,—but honour of some kind they must have.

Exactly.

Once more let me ask: Does he who desires any class of goods, desire the whole class or a part only?

The whole.

And may we not say of the philosopher that he is a lover, not of a part of wisdom only, but of the whole?

Yes, of the whole.

And he who dislikes learning, especially in youth, when he has no power of judging what is good and what is not, such an one we maintain not to be a philosopher or a lover of knowledge, just as he who refuses his food is not hungry, and may be said to have a bad appetite and not a good one?

Very true, he said.

Whereas he who has a taste for every sort of knowledge and who is curious to learn and is never satisfied, may be justly termed a philosopher? Am I not right?

Glaucon said: If curiosity makes a philosopher, you will find many a strange being will have a title to the name. All the lovers of sights have a delight in learning, and must therefore be included. Musical amateurs, too, are a folk strangely out of place among philosophers, for they are the last persons in the world who would come to anything like a philosophical discussion, if they could help, while they run about at the Dionysiac festivals as if they had let out their ears to hear every chorus; whether the performance is in town or country—that makes no difference—they are there. Now are we to maintain that all these and any who have similar tastes, as well as the professors of quite minor arts, are philosophers?

Certainly not, I replied; they are only an imitation.

He said: Who then are the true philosophers?

Those, I said, who are lovers of the vision of truth.

That is also good, he said; but I should like to know what you mean?

To another, I replied, I might have a difficulty in explaining; but I am sure that you will admit a proposition which I am about to make.

What is the proposition?

That since beauty is the opposite of ugliness, they are two?

Certainly.

And inasmuch as they are two, each of them is one?

True again.

And of just and unjust, good and evil, and of every other class, the same remark holds: taken singly, each of them is one; but from the various combinations of them with actions and things and with one another, they are seen in all sorts of lights and appear many?

Very true.

And this is the distinction which I draw between the sight-loving, art-loving, practical class and those of whom I am speaking, and who are alone worthy of the name of philosophers.

How do you distinguish them? he said.

The lovers of sounds and sights, I replied, are, as I conceive, fond of fine tones and colours and forms and all the artificial products that are made out of them, but their mind is incapable of seeing or loving absolute beauty.

True, he replied.

Few are they who are able to attain to the sight of this.

Very true.

And he who, having a sense of beautiful things has no sense of absolute beauty, or who, if another lead him to a knowledge of that beauty is unable to follow—of such an one I ask, Is he awake or in a dream only? Reflect: is not the dreamer, sleeping or waking, one who likens dissimilar things, who puts the copy in the place of the real object?

I should certainly say that such an one was dreaming.

But take the case of the other, who recognises the existence of absolute beauty and is able to distinguish the idea from the objects which participate in the idea, neither putting the objects in the place of the idea nor the idea in the place of the objects—is he a dreamer, or is he awake?

He is wide awake.

And may we not say that the mind of the one who knows has knowledge, and that the mind of the other, who opines only, has opinion.

Certainly.

But suppose that the latter should quarrel with us and dispute our statement, can we administer any soothing cordial or advice to him, without revealing to him that there is sad disorder in his wits?

We must certainly offer him some good advice, he replied.

Come, then, and let us think of something to say to him. Shall we begin by assuring him that he is welcome to any knowledge which he may have, and that we are rejoiced at his having it? But we should like to ask him a question: Does he who has knowledge know something or nothing? (You must answer for him.)

I answer that he knows something.

Something that is or is not?

Something that is; for how can that which is not ever be known?

And are we assured, after looking at the matter from many points of view, that absolute being is or may be absolutely known, but that the utterly non-existent is utterly unknown?

Nothing can be more certain.

Good. But if there be anything which is of such a nature as to be and not to be, that will have a place intermediate between pure being and the absolute negation of being?

Yes, between them.

And, as knowledge corresponded to being and ignorance or necessity to not-being, for that intermediate between being and not-being there has to be discovered a corresponding intermediate between ignorance and knowledge, if there be such?

Certainly.

Do we admit the existence of opinion?

Undoubtedly.

As being the same with knowledge, or another faculty?

Another faculty.

Then opinion and knowledge have to do with different kinds of matter corresponding to this difference of faculties?

Yes.

And knowledge is relative to being and knows being. But before I proceed further I will make a division.

What division?

I will begin by placing faculties in a class by themselves: they are powers in us, and in all other things, by which we do as we do. Sight and hearing, for example, I should call faculties. Have I clearly explained the class which I mean?

Yes, I quite understand.

Then let me tell you my view about them. I do not see them, and therefore the distinctions of figure, colour, and the like, which enable me to discern the differences of some things, do not apply to them. In speaking of a faculty I think only of its sphere and its result; and that which has the same sphere and the same result I call the same faculty, but that which has another sphere and another result I call different. Would that be your way of speaking?

Yes.

And will you be so very good as to answer one more question? Would you say that knowledge is a faculty, or in what class would you place it?

Certainly knowledge is a faculty, and the mightiest of all faculties.

And is opinion also a faculty?

Certainly, he said; for opinion is that with which we are able to form an opinion.

And yet you were acknowledging a little while ago that knowledge is not the same as opinion?

Why, yes, he said: how can any reasonable being ever identify that which is infallible with that which errs?

An excellent answer, proving, I said, that we are quite conscious of a distinction between them.

Yes.

Then knowledge and opinion having distinct powers have also distinct spheres or subject-matters?

That is certain.

Being is the sphere or subject-matter of knowledge, and knowledge is to know the nature of being?

Yes.

And opinion is to have an opinion?

Yes.

And do we know what we opine? or is the subject-matter of opinion the same as the subject-matter of knowledge?

Nay, he replied, that has been already disproven; if difference in faculty implies difference in the sphere or subject-matter, and if, as we were saying, opinion and knowledge are distinct faculties, then the sphere of knowledge and of opinion cannot be the same.

Then if being is the subject-matter of knowledge, something else must be the subject-matter of opinion?

Yes, something else.

Well then, is not-being the subject-matter of opinion? or, rather, how can there be an opinion at all about not-being? Reflect: when a man has an opinion, has he not an opinion about something? Can he have an opinion which is an opinion about nothing?

Impossible.

He who has an opinion has an opinion about some one thing?

Yes.

And not-being is not one thing but, properly speaking, nothing?

True.

Of not-being, ignorance was assumed to be the necessary corelative; of being, knowledge?

True, he said.

Then opinion is not concerned either with being or with not-being?

Not with either.

And can therefore neither be ignorance nor knowledge?

That seems to be true.

But is opinion to be sought without and beyond either of them, in a greater clearness than knowledge, or in a greater darkness than ignorance?

In neither.

Then I suppose that opinion appears to you to be darker than knowledge, but lighter than ignorance?

Both; and in no small degree.

And also to be within and between them?

Yes.

Then you would infer that opinion is intermediate?

No question.

But were we not saying before, that if anything appeared to be of a sort which is and is not at the same time, that sort of thing would appear also to lie in the interval between pure being and absolute not-being; and that the corresponding faculty is neither knowledge nor ignorance, but will be found in the interval between them?

True.

And in that interval there has now been discovered something which we call opinion?

There has.

Then what remains to be discovered is the object which partakes equally of the nature of being and not-being, and cannot rightly be termed either, pure and simple; this unknown term, when discovered, we may truly call the subject of opinion, and assign each to their proper faculty,—the extremes to the faculties of the extremes and the mean to the faculty of the mean.

True.

This being premised, I would ask the gentleman who is of opinion that there is no absolute or unchangeable idea of beauty—in whose opinion the beautiful is the manifold—he, I say, your lover of beautiful sights, who cannot bear to be told that the beautiful is one, and the just is one, or that anything is one—to him I would appeal, saying, Will you be so very kind, sir, as to tell us whether, of all these beautiful things, there is one which will not be found ugly; or of the just, which will not be found unjust; or of the holy, which will not also be unholy?

No, he replied; the beautiful will in some point of view be found ugly; and the same is true of the rest.

And may not the many which are doubles be also halves?—doubles, that is, of one thing, and halves of another?

Quite true.

And things great and small, heavy and light, as they are termed, will not be denoted by these any more than by the opposite names?

True; both these and the opposite names will always attach to all of them.

And can any one of those many things which are called by particular names be said to be this rather than not to be this?

He replied: They are like the punning riddles which are asked at feasts or the children's puzzle about the eunuch aiming at the bat, with what he hit him, as they say in the puzzle, and upon what the bat was sitting. The individual objects of which I am speaking are also a riddle, and have a double sense: nor can you fix them in your mind, either as being or not-being, or both, or neither.

Then what will you do with them? I said. Can they have a better place than between being and not-being? For they are clearly not in greater darkness or negation than not-being, or more full of light and existence than being.

That is quite true, he said.

Thus we seem to have discovered that the many ideas which the multitude entertain about the beautiful and about all other things are tossing about in some region which is half-way between pure being and pure not-being?

We have.

Yes; and we had before agreed that anything of this kind which we might find was to be described as matter of opinion, and not as matter of knowledge; being the intermediate flux which is caught and detained by the intermediate faculty.

Quite true.

Then those who see the many beautiful, and who yet neither see absolute beauty, nor can follow any guide who points the way thither; who see the many just, and not absolute justice, and the like,—such persons may be said to have opinion but not knowledge?

That is certain.

But those who see the absolute and eternal and immutable may be said to know, and not to have opinion only?

Neither can that be denied.

The one love and embrace the subjects of knowledge, the other those of opinion? The latter are the same, as I dare say you will remember, who listened to sweet sounds and gazed upon fair colours, but would not tolerate the existence of absolute beauty.

Yes, I remember.

Shall we then be guilty of any impropriety in calling them lovers of opinion rather than lovers of wisdom, and will they be very angry with us for thus describing them?

I shall tell them not to be angry; no man should be angry at what is true.

But those who love the truth in each thing are to be called lovers of wisdom and not lovers of opinion.

Assuredly. . . .

I must remind you of what I have mentioned in the course of this discussion, and at many other times.

What?

The old story, that there is a many beautiful and a many good, and so of other things which we describe and define; to all of them 'many' is applied.

True, he said.

And there is an absolute beauty and an absolute good, and of other things to which the term 'many' is applied there is an absolute; for they may be brought under a single idea, which is called the essence of each.

Very true.

The many, as we say, are seen but not known, and the ideas are known but not seen.

Exactly.

And what is the organ with which we see the visible things?

The sight, he said.

And with the hearing, I said, we hear, and with the other senses perceive the other objects of sense?

True.

But have you remarked that sight is by far the most costly and complex piece of workmanship which the artificer of the senses ever contrived?

No, I never have, he said.

Then reflect: has the ear or voice need of any third or additional nature in order that the one may be able to hear and the other to be heard?

Nothing of the sort.

No, indeed, I replied; and the same is true of most, if not all, the other senses—you would not say that any of them requires such an addition?

Certainly not.

But you see that without the addition of some other nature there is no seeing or being seen?

How do you mean?

Sight being, as I conceive, in the eyes, and he who has eyes wanting to see; colour being also present in them, still unless there be a third nature specially adapted to the purpose, the owner of the eyes will see nothing and the colours will be invisible.

Of what nature are you speaking?

Of that which you term light, I replied.

True, he said.

Noble, then, is the bond which links together sight and visibility, and great beyond other bonds by no small difference of nature; for light is their bond, and light is no ignoble thing?

Nay, he said, the reverse of ignoble.

And which, I said, of the gods in heaven would you say was the lord of this element? Whose is that light which makes the eye to see perfectly and the visible to appear?

You mean the sun, as you and all mankind say.

May not the relation of sight to this deity be described as follows?

How?

Neither sight nor the eye in which sight resides is the sun?

No.

Yet of all the organs of sense the eye is the most like the sun?

By far the most like.

And the power which the eye possesses is a sort of effluence which is dispensed from the sun?

Exactly.

Then the sun is not sight, but the author of sight who is recognised by sight.

True, he said.

And this is he whom I call the child of the good, whom the good begat in his own likeness, to be in the visible world, in relation to sight and the things of sight, what the good is in the intellectual world in relation to mind and the things of mind.

Will you be a little more explicit? he said.

Why, you know, I said, that the eyes, when a person directs them towards objects on which the light of day is no longer shining, but the moon and stars only, see dimly, and are nearly blind; they seem to have no clearness of vision in them?

Very true.

But when they are directed towards objects on which the sun shines, they see clearly and there is sight in them?

Certainly.

And the soul is like the eye: when resting upon that on which truth and being shine, the soul perceives and understands and is radiant with intelligence; but when turned towards the twilight of becoming and perishing, then she has opinion only, and goes blinking about, and is first of one opinion and then of another, and seems to have no intelligence?

Just so.

Now, that which imparts truth to the known and the power of knowing to the knower is what I would have you term the idea of good, and this you will deem to be the cause of science, and of truth in so far as the latter becomes the subject of knowledge; beautiful too, as are both truth and knowledge, you will be right in esteeming this other nature as more beautiful than either; and, as in the previous instance, light and sight may be truly said to be like the sun, and yet not to be the sun, so in this other sphere, science and truth may be deemed to be like the good, but not the good; the good has a place of honour yet higher.

What a wonder of beauty that must be, he said, which is the author of science and truth, and yet surpasses them in beauty; for you surely cannot mean to say that pleasure is the good?

God forbid, I replied; but may I ask you to consider the image in another point of view?

In what point of view?

You would say, would you not, that the sun is not only the author of visibility in all visible things, but of generation and nourishment and growth, though he himself is not generation?

Certainly.

In like manner the good may be said to be not only the author of knowledge to all things known, but of their being and essence, and yet the good is not essence, but far exceeds essence in dignity and power.

Glaucon said, with a ludicrous earnestness: By the light of heaven, how amazing!

Yes, I said, and the exaggeration may be set down to you; for you made me utter my fancies.

And pray continue to utter them; at any rate let us hear if there is anything more to be said about the similitude of the sun.

Yes, I said, there is a great deal more.

Then omit nothing, however slight.

I will do my best, I said; but I should think that a great deal will have to be omitted.

You have to imagine, then, that there are two ruling powers, and that one of them is set over the intellectual world, the other over the visible. I do not say heaven, lest you should fancy that I am playing upon the name (οὐρανός, ὁρατός). May I suppose that you have this distinction of the visible and intelligible fixed in your mind?

I have.

Now take a line which has been cut into two unequal parts, and divide each of them again in the same proportion, and suppose the two main divisions to answer, one to the visible and the other to the intelligible, and then compare the subdivisions in respect of their clearness and want of clearness, and you will find that the first section in the sphere of the visible consists of images. And by images I mean, in the first place, shadows, and in the second place, reflections in water and in solid, smooth and polished bodies and the like: Do you understand?

Yes, I understand.

Imagine, now, the other section, of which this is only the resemblance, to include the animals which we see, and everything that grows or is made.

Very good.

Would you not admit that both the sections of this division have different degrees of truth, and that the copy is to the original as the sphere of opinion is to the sphere of knowledge?

Most undoubtedly.

Next proceed to consider the manner in which the sphere of the intellectual is to be divided.

In what manner?

Thus:—There are two subdivisions, in the lower of which the soul uses the figures given by the former division as images; the enquiry can only be hypothetical, and instead of going upwards to a principle descends to the other end; in the higher of the two, the soul passes out of hypotheses, and goes up to a principle which is above hypotheses, making no use of images as in the former case, but proceeding only in and through the ideas themselves.

I do not quite understand your meaning, he said.

Then I will try again; you will understand me better when I have made some preliminary remarks. You are aware that students of geometry, arithmetic, and the kindred sciences assume the odd and the even and the figures and three kinds of angles and like in their several branches of science; these are their hypotheses, which they and every body are supposed to know, and therefore they do not deign to give any account of them either to themselves or others; but they begin with them, and go on until they arrive at last, and in a consistent manner, at their conclusion?

Yes, he said, I know.

And do you not know also that although they make use of the visible forms and reason about them, they are thinking not of these, but of the ideals which they resemble; not of the figures which they draw, but of the absolute square and the absolute diameter, and so on—the forms which they draw or make, and which have shadows and reflections in water of their own, are converted by them into images, but they are really seeking to behold the things themselves, which can only be seen with the eye of the mind?

That is true.

And of this kind I spoke as the intelligible, although in the search after it the soul is compelled to use hypotheses; not ascending to a first principle, because she is unable to rise above the region of hypothesis, but employing the objects of which the shadows below are resemblances in their turn as images, they having in relation to the shadows and reflections of them a greater distinctness, and therefore a higher value.

I understand, he said, that you are speaking of the province of geometry and the sister arts.

And when I speak of the other division of the intelligible, you will understand me to speak of that other sort of knowledge which reason herself attains by the power of dialectic, using the hypotheses not as first principles, but only as hypotheses—that is to say, as steps and points of departure into a world which is above hypotheses, in order that she may soar beyond them to the first principle of the whole; and clinging to this and then to that which depends on this, by successive steps she descends again without the aid of any sensible object, from ideas, through ideas, and in ideas she ends.

I understand you, he replied; not perfectly, for you seem to me to be describing a task which is really tremendous; but, at any rate, I understand you to say that knowledge and being, which the science of dialectic contemplates, are clearer than the notions of the arts, as they are termed, which proceed from hypotheses only: these are also contemplated by the understanding, and not only by the senses: yet, because they start from hypotheses and do not ascend to a principle, those who contemplate them appear to you not to exercise the higher reason upon them, although when a first principle is added to them they are cognizable by the higher reason. And the habit which is concerned with geometry and the cognate sciences I suppose that you would term understanding and not reason, as being intermediate between opinion and reason.

You have quite conceived my meaning, I said; and now corresponding to these four divisions, let there be four faculties in the soul—reason answering to the highest, understanding to the second, faith (or conviction) to the third, and perception of shadows to the last—and let there be a scale of them, and let us suppose that the several faculties have clearness in the same degree that their objects have truth.

I understand, he replied, and give my assent, and accept your arrangement.

TWO

Knowledge and Necessity

ARISTOTLE (384-322 B.C.)

From *Posterior Analytics**

FROM BOOK I

1. All instruction given or received by way of argument proceeds from pre-existent knowledge. This becomes evident upon a survey of all the species of such instruction. The mathematical sciences and all other speculative disciplines are acquired in this way, and so are the two forms of dialectical reasoning, syllogistic and inductive; for each of these latter makes use of old knowledge to impart new, the syllogism assuming an audience that accepts its premises, induction exhibiting the universal as implicit in the clearly known particular. Again, the persuasion exerted by rhetorical arguments is in principle the same, since they use either example, a kind of induction, or enthymeme, a form of syllogism.

The pre-existent knowledge required is of two kinds. In some cases admission of the fact must be assumed, in others comprehension of the meaning of the term used, and sometimes both assumptions are essential. Thus we assume that every predicate can be either truly affirmed or truly denied of any subject, and that 'triangle' means so and so; as regards 'unit' we have to make the double assumption of the meaning of the word and the existence of the thing. The reason is that these several objects are not equally obvious to us. Recognition of a truth may in some cases contain as factors both previous knowledge and also knowledge acquired simultaneously with that recognition—knowledge, this latter, of the particulars actually falling under the universal and therein already virtually known. For example, the student knew beforehand that the angles of every triangle are equal to two right angles; but it was only at the actual moment at which he was being led on to recognize this as true in the instance before him that he came to know 'this figure inscribed in the semicircle' to be a triangle. For some things (viz. the singulars finally reached which are not predicable of anything else as subject) are only learnt in this way, i.e. there is here no recognition through a middle of a minor term as subject to a major. Before he was led on to recognition or before

---

* From the *Oxford Translation of Aristotle,* by permission of the Clarendon Press.

he actually drew a conclusion, we should perhaps say that in a manner he knew, in a manner not.

If he did not in an unqualified sense of the term *know* the existence of this triangle, how could he *know* without qualification that its angles were equal to two right angles? No: clearly he *knows* not without qualification but only in the sense that he *knows* universally. If this distinction is not drawn, we are faced with the dilemma in the *Meno*: [1] either a man will learn nothing or what he already knows; for we cannot accept the solution which some people offer. A man is asked, 'Do you, or do you not, know that every pair is even?' He says he does know it. The questioner then produces a particular pair of the existence, and so *a fortiori* of the evenness, of which he was unaware. The solution which some people offer is to assert that they do not know that every pair is even, but only that everything which they know to be a pair is even: yet what they know to be even is that of which they have demonstrated evenness, i.e. what they made the subject of their premiss, viz. not merely every triangle or number which they know to be such, but any and every number of triangle without reservation. For no premiss is ever couched in the form 'every number which you know to be such', or 'every rectilinear figure which you know to be such': the predicate is always construed as applicable to any and every instance of the thing. On the other hand, I imagine there is nothing to prevent a man in one sense knowing what he is learning, in another not knowing it. The strange thing would be, not if in some sense he knew what he was learning, but if he were to know it in that precise sense and manner in which he was learning it.

2. We suppose ourselves to possess unqualified scientific knowledge of a thing, as opposed to knowing it in the accidental way in which the sophist knows, when we think that we know the cause on which the fact depends, as the cause of that fact and of no other, and, further, that the fact could not be other than it is. Now that scientific knowing is something of this sort is evident—witness both those who falsely claim it and those who actually possess it, since the former merely imagine themselves to be, while the latter are also actually, in the condition described. Consequently the proper object of unqualified scientific knowledge is something which cannot be other than it is.

There may be another manner of knowing as well—that will be discussed later. What I now assert is that at all events we do know by demonstration. By demonstration I mean a syllogism productive of scientific knowledge, a syllogism, that is, the grasp of which is *eo ipso* such knowledge. Assuming then that my thesis as to the nature of scientific knowing is correct, the premisses of demonstrated knowledge must be true, primary, immediate, better known than and prior to the conclusion,

1 Plato, *Meno*, 80 E.

which is further related to them as effect to cause. Unless these conditions are satisfied, the basic truths will not be 'appropriate' to the conclusion. Syllogism there may indeed be without these conditions, but such syllogism, not being productive of scientific knowledge, will not be demonstration. The premisses must be true: for that which is non-existent cannot be known—we cannot know, e.g., that the diagonal of a square is commensurate with its side. The premisses must be primary and indemonstrable; otherwise they will require demonstration in order to be known, since to have knowledge, if it be not accidental knowledge, of things which are demonstrable, means precisely to have a demonstration of them. The premisses must be the causes of the conclusion, better known than it, and prior to it; its causes, since we possess scientific knowledge of a thing only when we know its cause; prior, in order to be causes; antecedently known, this antecedent knowledge being not our mere understanding of the meaning, but knowledge of the fact as well. Now 'prior' and 'better known' are ambiguous terms, for there is a difference between what is prior and better known in the order of being and what is prior and better known to man. I mean that objects nearer to sense are prior and better known to man; objects without qualification prior and better known are those further from sense. Now the most universal causes are furthest from sense and particular causes are nearest to sense, and they are thus exactly opposed to one another. In saying that the premisses of demonstrated knowledge must be primary, I mean that they must be the 'appropriate' basic truths, for I identify primary premiss and basic truth. A 'basic truth' in a demonstration is an immediate proposition. An immediate proposition is one which has no other proposition prior to it. A proposition is either part of an enunciation, i.e. it predicates a single attribute of a single subject. If a proposition is dialectical, it assumes either part indifferently; if it is demonstrative, it lays down one part to the definite exclusion of the other because that part is true. The term 'enunciation' denotes either part of a contradiction indifferently. A contradiction is an opposition which of its own nature excludes a middle. The part of a contradiction which conjoins a predicate with a subject is an affirmation; the part disjoining them is a negation. I call an immediate basic truth of syllogism a 'thesis' when, though it is not susceptible of proof by the teacher, yet ignorance of it does not constitute a total bar to progress on the part of the pupil: one which the pupil must know if he is to learn anything whatever is an axiom. I call it an axiom because there are such truths and we give them the name of axioms *par excellence*. If a thesis assumes one part or the other of an enunciation, i.e. asserts either the existence or the non-existence of a subject, it is a hypothesis; if it does not so assert, it is a definition. Definition *is* a 'thesis' or a 'laying something down,' since the arithmetician lays it down that to be a unit is to be quantitatively indivisible;

but it is not a hypothesis, for to define what a unit is is not the same as to affirm its existence.

Now since the required ground of our knowledge—i.e. of our conviction—of a fact is the possession of such a syllogism as we call demonstration, and the ground of the syllogism is the facts constituting its premisses—some if not all of them—beforehand, but know them better than the conclusion: for the cause of an attribute's inherence in a subject always itself inheres in the subject more firmly than that attribute; e.g. the cause of our loving anything is dearer to us than the object of our love. So since the primary premisses are the cause of our knowledge—i.e. of our conviction—it follows that we know them better—that is, are more convinced of them—than their consequences, precisely because our knowledge of the latter is the effect of our knowledge of the premisses. Now a man cannot believe in anything more than in the things he knows, unless he has either actual knowledge of it or something better than actual knowledge. But we are faced with this paradox if a student whose belief rests on a demonstration has not prior knowledge; a man must believe in some, if not in all, of the basic truths more than in the conclusion. Moreover, if a man sets out to acquire the scientific knowledge that comes through demonstration, he must not only have a better knowledge of the basic truths and a firmer conviction of them than of the connexion which is being demonstrated: more than this, nothing must be more certain or better known to him than these basic truths in their character as contradicting the fundamental premisses which lead to the opposed and erroneous conclusion. For indeed the conviction of pure science must be unshakable.

3. Some hold that, owing to the necessity of knowing the primary premisses, there is no scientific knowledge. Others think there is, but that all truths are demonstrable. Neither doctrine is either true or a necessary deduction from the premisses. The first school, assuming that there is no way of knowing other than by demonstration, maintain that an infinite regress is involved, on the ground that if behind the prior stands no primary, we could not know the posterior through the prior (wherein they are right, for one cannot traverse an infinite series): if on the other hand—they say—the series terminates and there are primary premisses, yet these are unknowable because incapable of demonstration, which according to them is the only form of knowledge. And since thus one cannot know the primary premisses, knowledge of the conclusions which follow from them is not pure scientific knowledge nor properly knowing at all, but rests on the mere supposition that the premisses are true. The other party agree with them as regards knowing, holding that it is only possible by demonstration, but they see no difficulty in holding

that all truths are demonstrated, on the ground that demonstration may be circular and reciprocal.

Our own doctrine is that not all knowledge is demonstrative: on the contrary, knowledge of the immediate premisses is independent of demonstration. (The necessity of this is obvious; for since we must know the prior premisses from which the demonstration is drawn, and since the regress must end in immediate truths, those truths must be indemonstrable.) Such, then, is our doctrine, and in addition we maintain that besides scientific knowledge there is its originative source which enables us to recognize the definitions.

Now demonstration must be based on premisses prior to and better known than the conclusion; and the same things cannot simultaneously be both prior and posterior to one another: so circular demonstration is clearly not possible in the unqualified sense of 'demonstration,' but only possible if 'demonstration' be extended to include that other method of argument which rests on a distinction between truths prior to us and truths without qualification prior, i.e. the method by which induction produces knowledge. But if we accept this extension of its meaning, our definition of unqualified knowledge will prove faulty; for there seem to be two kinds of it. Perhaps, however, the second form of demonstration, that which proceeds from truths better known to us, is not demonstration in the unqualified sense of the term.

The advocates of circular demonstration are not only faced with the difficulty we have just stated: in addition their theory reduces to the mere statement that if a thing exists, then it does exist—an easy way of proving anything. That this is so can be clearly shown by taking three terms, for to constitute the circle it makes no difference whether many terms or few or even only two are taken. Thus by direct proof, if A is, B must be; if B is, C must be; therefore if A is, C must be. Since then—by the circular proof—if A is, B must be, and if B is, A must be, A may be substituted for C above. Then 'if B is, A must be' = 'if B is, C must be', which above gave the conclusion 'if A is, C must be': but C and A have been identified. Consequently the upholders of circular demonstration are in the position of saying that if A is, A must be—a simple way of proving anything. Moreover, even such circular demonstration is impossible except in the case of attributes that imply one another, viz. 'peculiar' properties.

Now, it has been shown that the positing of one thing—be it one term or one premiss—never involves a necessary consequent: [2] two premisses constitute the first and smallest foundation for drawing a conclusion at all and therefore a fortiori for the demonstrative syllogism of science. If, then, A is implied in B and C, and B and C are reciprocally

[2] *An. Pr.* i, ch. 25.

implied in one another and in *A,* it is possible, as has been shown in my writings on the syllogism, [3] to prove all the assumptions on which the original conclusion rested, by circular demonstration in the first figure. But it has also been shown that in the other figures either no conclusion is possible, or at least none which proves both the original premises. [4] Propositions the terms of which are not convertible cannot be circularly demonstrated at all, and since convertible terms occur rarely in actual demonstrations, it is clearly frivolous and impossible to say that demonstration is reciprocal and that therefore everything can be demonstrated.

4. Since the object of pure scientific knowledge cannot be other than it is, the truth obtained by demonstrative knowledge will be necessary. And since demonstrative knowledge is only present when we have a demonstration, it follows that demonstration is an inference from necessary premises. So we must consider what are the premises of demonstration—i.e. what is their character: and as a preliminary, let us define what we mean by an attribute 'true in every instance of its subject,' an 'essential' attribute, and a 'commensurate and universal' attribute. I call 'true in every instance' which is truly predicable of all instances—not of one to the exclusion of others—and at all times, not at this or that time only; e.g. if animal is truly predicable of every instance of man, then if it be true to say 'this is a man,' 'this is an animal' is also true, and if the one be true now the other is true now. A corresponding account holds if point is in every instance predicable as contained in line. There is evidence for this in the fact that the objection we raise against a proposition put to us as true in every instance is either an instance in which, or an occasion on which, it is not true. Essential attributes are (1) such as belong to their subject as elements in its essential nature (e.g. line thus belongs to triangle, point to line; for the very being or 'substance' of triangle and line is composed of these elements, which are contained in the formulae defining triangle and line): (2) such that, while they belong to certain subjects, the subjects to which they belong are contained in the attribute's own defining formula. Thus straight and curved belong to line, odd and even, prime and compound, square and oblong, to number; and also the formula defining any one of these attributes contains its subject—e.g. line or number as the case may be.

Extending this classification to all other attributes, I distinguish those that answer the above description as belonging essentially to their respective subjects; whereas attributes related in neither of these two ways to their subjects I call accidents or 'coincidents'; e.g. musical or white is a 'coincident' of animal.

3 *Ibid.* ii, ch. 5.
4 *Ibid.* ii, cc. 5 and 6.

Further (a) that is essential which is not predicated of a subject other than itself; e.g. 'the walking (thing)' walks and is white in virtue of being something else besides; whereas substance, in the sense of whatever signifies a 'this somewhat,' is not what it is in virtue of being something else besides. Things, then, not predicated of a subject I call essential; things predicated of a subject I call accidental or 'coincidental.'

In another sense again (b) a thing consequentially connected with anything is essential; one not so connected is 'coincidental.' An example of the latter is 'While he was walking it lightened': the lightning was not due to his walking; it was, we should say, a coincidence. If, on the other hand, there is a consequential connexion, the predication is essential; e.g. if a beast dies when its throat is being cut, then its death is also essentially connected with the cutting, because the cutting was the cause of death, not death a 'coincident' of the cutting.

So far then as concerns the sphere of connexions scientifically known in the unqualified sense of that term, all attributes which (within that sphere) are essential either in the sense that their subjects are contained in them, or in the sense that they are contained in their subjects, are necessary as well as consequentially connected with their subjects. For it is impossible for them not to inhere in their subjects—either simply or in the qualified sense that one or other of a pair of opposites must inhere in the subject; e.g. in line must be either straightness or curvature, in number either oddness or evenness. For within a single identical genus the contrary of a given attribute is either its privative or its contradictory; e.g. within number what is not odd is even, inasmuch as within this sphere even is a necessary consequent of not-odd. So, since any given predicate must be either affirmed or denied of any subject, essential attributes must inhere in their subjects of necessity.

Thus, then, we have established the distinction between the attribute which is 'true in every instance' and the 'essential' attribute.

I term 'commensurately universal' an attribute which belongs to every instance of its subject, and to every instance essentially and as such; from which it clearly follows that all commensurate universals inhere *necessarily* in their subjects. The essential attribute, and the attribute that belongs to its subject as such, are identical. E.g. point and straight belong to line essentially, for they belong to line as such; and triangle as such has two right angles, for it is *essentially* equal to two right angles.

An attribute belongs commensurately and universally to a subject when it can be shown to belong to any random instance of that subject and when the subject is the first thing to which it can be shown to belong. Thus, e.g., (1) the equality of its angles to two right angles is not a commensurately universal attribute of figure. For though it is possible to show that a figure has its angles equal to two right angles, this attribute cannot be demonstrated of any figure selected at haphazard, nor in demonstrating does one take a figure at random—a square is a figure but its angles are not equal to two right angles. On the other hand, any isosceles triangle has its angles equal to two right angles, yet isosceles triangle is not the primary subject of this attribute but triangle is prior. So whatever can be shown to have its angles equal to two right angles, or to possess any other attribute, in any random instance of itself and primarily—that is the first subject to which the predicate in question belongs commensurately and universally, and the demonstration, in the essential sense, of any predicate is the proof of it as belonging to this first subject commensurately and universally: while the proof of it as belonging to the other subjects to which it attaches is demonstration only in a secondary and unessential sense. Nor again (2) is equality to two right angles a commensurately universal attribute of isosceles; it is of wider application.

6. Demonstrative knowledge must rest on necessary basic truths; for the object of scientific knowledge cannot be other than it is. Now attributes attaching essentially to their subjects attach necessarily to them: for essential attributes are either elements in the essential nature of their subjects, or contain their subjects as elements in their own essential nature. (The pairs of opposites which the latter class includes are necessary because one member or the other necessarily inheres.) It follows from this that premisses of the demonstrative syllogism must be connexions essential in the sense explained: for all attributes must inhere essentially or else be accidental, and accidental attributes are not necessary to their subjects.

We must either state the case thus, or else premise that the conclusion of demonstration is necessary and that a demonstrated conclusion cannot be other than it is, and then infer that the conclusion must be developed from necessary premisses. For though you may reason from true premisses without demonstrating, yet if your premisses are necessary you will assuredly demonstrate—in such necessity you have at once a distinctive character of demonstration. That demonstration proceeds from necessary premisses is also indicated by the fact that the objection we raise against a professed demonstration is that a premiss of it is not a necessary truth—whether we think it altogether devoid of necessity, or at any rate so far as our opponent's previous argument goes. This shows how naïve it is to suppose one's basic truths rightly chosen if one starts with a proposition which is (1) popularly accepted and (2) true, such as the sophists' assumption that to know is the same as to possess knowledge. For (1) popular acceptance or rejection is no criterion of a basic truth, which can only be the primary law of the genus constituting the subject matter of the demonstration; and (2) not *all* truth is 'appropriate.'

A further proof that the conclusion must be the development of necessary premises is as follows. Where demonstration is possible, one who can give no account which includes the cause has no scientific knowledge. If, then, we suppose a syllogism in which, though A necessarily inheres in C, yet B, the middle term of the demonstration, is not necessarily connected with A and C, then the man who argues thus has no reasoned knowledge of the conclusion, since this conclusion does not owe its necessity to the middle term; for though the conclusion is necessary, the mediating link is a contingent fact. Or again, if a man is without knowledge now, though he still retains the steps of the argument, though there is no change in himself or in the fact and no lapse of memory on his part; then neither had he knowledge previously. But the mediating link, not being necessary, may have perished in the interval; and if so, though there be no change in him nor in fact, and though he will still retain the steps of the argument, yet he has not knowledge, and therefore had not knowledge before. Even if the link has not actually perished but is liable to perish, this situation is possible and might occur. But such a condition cannot be knowledge.

When the conclusion is necessary, the middle through which it was proved may yet quite easily be non-necessary. You can in fact infer the necessary even from a non-necessary premiss, just as you can infer the true from the not true. On the other hand, when the middle is necessary the conclusion must be necessary; just as true premises always give a true conclusion. Thus, if A is necessarily predicated of B and B of C, then A is necessarily predicated of C. But when the conclusion is non-necessary the middle cannot be necessary either. Thus let A be predicated non-necessarily of C but necessarily of B, and let B be a necessary predicate of C; then A too will be a necessary predicate of C, which by hypothesis it is not.

To sum up, then: demonstrative knowledge must be knowledge of a necessary nexus, and therefore must clearly be obtained through a necessary middle term; otherwise its possessor will know neither the cause nor the fact that his conclusion is a necessary connexion. Either he will mistake the non-necessary for the necessary and believe the necessity of the conclusion without knowing it, or else he will not even believe it—in which case he will be equally ignorant, whether he actually infers the mere fact through middle terms or the reasoned fact and from immediate premises.

Of accidents that are not essential according to our definition of essential there is no demonstrative knowledge; for since an accident, in the sense in which I here speak of it, may also not inhere, it is impossible to prove its inherence as a necessary conclusion. A difficulty, however, might be raised as to why in dialectic, if the conclusion is not a necessary connexion, such and such determinate premisses should be proposed in order to deal with such and such determinate problems. Would not the result be the same if one asked any questions whatever and then merely stated one's conclusion? The solution is that determinate questions have to be put, not because the replies to them affirm facts which necessitate facts affirmed by the conclusion, but because these answers are propositions which if the answerer affirm, he must affirm the conclusion—and affirm it with truth if they are true.

Since it is just those attributes within every genus which are essential and possessed by their respective subjects as such that are necessary, it is clear that both the conclusions and the premisses of demonstrations which produce scientific knowledge are essential. For accidents are not necessary: and, further, since accidents are not necessary one does not necessarily have reasoned knowledge of a conclusion drawn from them (this is so even if the accidental premisses are invariable but not essential, as in proofs through signs; for though the conclusion be actually essential, one will not know it as essential nor know its reason); but to have reasoned knowledge of a conclusion is to know it through its cause. We may conclude that the middle must be consequentially connected with the minor, and the major with the middle. . . .

8. It is also clear that if the premisses from which the syllogism proceeds are commensurately universal, the conclusion of such demonstration—demonstration, i.e., in the unqualified sense—must also be eternal. Therefore no attribute can be demonstrated nor known by strictly scientific knowledge to inhere in perishable things. The proof can only be accidental, because the attribute's connexion with its perishable subject is not commensurately universal but temporary and special. If such a demonstration is made, one premiss must be perishable and not commensurately universal (perishable because only if it is perishable will the conclusion be perishable; not commensurately universal, because the predicate will be predicable of some instances of the subject and not of others); so that the conclusion can only be that a fact is true at the moment—not commensurately and universally. The same is true of definitions, since a definition is either a primary premiss or a conclusion of a demonstration, or else only differs from a demonstration in the order of its terms. Demonstration and science of merely frequent occurrences—e.g. of eclipse as happening to the moon—are, as such, clearly eternal: whereas so far as they are not eternal they are not fully commensurate. Other subjects too have properties attaching to them in the same way as eclipse attaches to the moon.

10. I call the basic truths of every genus those elements in it the existence of which cannot be proved. As regards both these primary truths

and the attributes dependent on them the meaning of the name is assumed. The fact of their existence as regards the primary truths must be assumed; but it has to be proved of the remainder, the attributes. Thus we assume the meaning alike of unity, straight, and triangular; but while as regards unity and magnitude we assume also the fact of their existence, in the case of the remainder proof is required.

Of the basic truths used in the demonstrative sciences some are peculiar to each science, and some are common, but common only in the sense of analogous, being of use only in so far as they fall within the genus constituting the province of the science in question.

Peculiar truths are, e.g., the definitions of line and straight; common truths are such as 'take equals from equals and equals remain.' Only so much of these common truths is required as falls within the genus in question: for a truth of this kind will have the same force even if not used generally but applied by the geometer only to magnitudes, or by the arithmetician only to numbers. Also peculiar to a science are the subjects the existence as well as the meaning of which it assumes, and the essential attributes of which it investigates, e.g. in arithmetic units, in geometry points and lines. Both the existence and the meaning of the subjects are assumed by these sciences; but of their essential attributes only the meaning is assumed. For example arithmetic assumes the meaning of odd and even, square and cube, geometry that of incommensurable, or of deflection or verging of lines, whereas the existence of these attributes is demonstrated by means of the axioms and from previous conclusions as premises. Astronomy too proceeds in the same way. For indeed every demonstrative science has three elements: (1) that which it posits, the subject genus whose essential attributes it examines; (2) the so-called axioms, which are primary premises of its demonstration; (3) the attributes, the meaning of which it assumes. Yet some sciences may very well pass over some of these elements; e.g. we might not expressly posit the existence of the genus if its existence were obvious (for instance, the existence of hot and cold is more evident than that of number); or we might omit to assume expressly the meaning of the attributes if it were well understood. In the same way the meaning of axioms, such as 'Take equals from equals and equals remain,' is well known and so not expressly assumed. Nevertheless in the nature of the case the essential elements of demonstration are three: the subject, the attributes, and the basic premises.

That which expresses necessary self-grounded fact, and which we must necessarily believe, is distinct both from the hypotheses of a science and from illegitimate postulate—I say 'must believe,' because all syllogism, and therefore *a fortiori* demonstration, is addressed not to the spoken word, but to the discourse within the soul, and though we can always raise objections to the spoken word, to the inward discourse we cannot always object. That which is capable of proof but assumed by the teacher without proof is, if the pupil believes and accepts it, hypothesis, though only in a limited sense hypothesis—that is, relatively to the pupil; if the pupil has no opinion or a contrary opinion on the matter, the same assumption is an illegitimate postulate. Therein lies the distinction between hypothesis and illegitimate postulate: the latter is the contrary of the pupil's opinion, demonstrable, but assumed and used without demonstration.

The definitions—viz. those which are not expressed as statements that anything is or is not—are not hypotheses: but it is in the premises of a science that its hypotheses are contained. Definitions require only to be understood, and this is not hypothesis—unless it be contended that the pupil's hearing is also an hypothesis required by the teacher. Hypotheses, on the contrary, postulate facts on the being of which depends the being of the fact inferred. Nor are the geometer's hypotheses false, as some have held, urging that one must not employ falsehood and that the geometer is uttering falsehood in stating that the line which he draws is a foot long or straight, when it is actually neither. The truth is that the geometer does not draw any conclusion from the being of the particular line of which he speaks, but from what his diagrams symbolize. A further distinction is that all hypotheses and illegitimate postulates are either universal or particular, whereas a definition is neither.

31. Scientific knowledge is not possible through the act of perception. Even if perception as a faculty is of 'the such' and not merely of a 'this somewhat,' yet one must at any rate actually perceive a 'this somewhat,' and at a definite present place and time: but that which is commensurately universal and true in all cases one cannot perceive, since it is not 'this' and it is not 'now'; if it were, it would not be commensurately universal—the term we apply to what is always and everywhere. Seeing, therefore, that demonstrations are commensurately universal and universals imperceptible, we clearly cannot obtain scientific knowledge by the act of perception: nay, it is obvious that even if it were possible to perceive that a triangle has its angles equal to two right angles, we should still be looking for a demonstration—we should not (as some say) possess knowledge of it; for perception must be of a particular, whereas scientific knowledge involves the recognition of the commensurate universal. So if we were on the moon, and saw the earth shutting out the sun's light, we should not know the cause of the eclipse: we should perceive the present fact of the eclipse, but not the reasoned fact at all, since the act of perception is not of the commensurate universal. I do not, of course, deny that by watching the frequent recurrence of this event we might, after tracking the commensurate universal, possess a

demonstration, for the commensurate universal is elicited from the several groups of singulars.

The commensurate universal is precious because it makes clear the cause; so that in the case of facts like these which have a cause other than themselves universal knowledge is more precious than sense-perceptions and than intuition. (As regards primary truths there is of course a different account to be given.) Hence it is clear that knowledge of things demonstrable cannot be acquired by perception, unless the term perception is applied to the possession of scientific knowledge through demonstration. Nevertheless certain points do arise with regard to connexions to be proved which are referred for their explanation to a failure in sense-perception: there are cases when an act of vision would terminate our inquiry, not because in seeing we should be knowing, but because we should have elicited the universal from seeing; if, for example, we saw the pores in the glass and the light passing through, the reason of the kindling would be clear to us because we should at the same time see it in each instance and intuit that it must be so in all instances.

33. Scientific knowledge and its object differ from opinion and the object of opinion in that scientific knowledge is commensurately universal and proceeds by necessary connexions, and that which is necessary cannot be otherwise. So though there are things which are true and real and yet can be otherwise, *scientific knowledge* clearly does not concern them: if it did, things which can be otherwise would be incapable of being otherwise. Nor are they any concern of *rational intuition*—by rational intuition I mean an originative source of scientific knowledge—nor of indemonstrable knowledge, which is the grasping of the immediate premiss. Since then rational intuition, science, and opinion, and what is revealed by these terms, are the only things that can be 'true,' it follows that it is *opinion* that is concerned with that which may be true or false, and can be otherwise: opinion in fact is the grasp of a premiss which is immediate but not necessary. This view also fits the observed facts, for opinion is unstable, and so is the kind of being we have described as its object. Besides, when a man thinks a truth incapable of being otherwise he always thinks that he knows it, never that he opines it. He thinks that he opines when he thinks that a connexion, though actually so, may quite easily be otherwise; for he believes that such is the proper object of opinion, while the necessary is the object of knowledge.

In what sense, then, can the same thing be the object of both opinion and knowledge? And if any one chooses to maintain that all that he knows he can also opine, why should not opinion be knowledge? For he that knows and he that opines will follow the same train of thought through the same middle terms until the immediate premisses are reached; because it is possible to opine not only the fact but also the reasoned fact, and the reason is the middle term; so that, since the former knows, he that opines also has knowledge.

The truth perhaps is that if a man grasp truths that cannot be other than they are, in the way in which he grasps the definitions through which demonstrations take place, he will have not opinion but knowledge: if on the other hand he apprehends these attributes as inhering in their subjects, but not in virtue of the subjects' substance and essential nature, he possesses opinion and not genuine knowledge; and his opinion, if obtained through immediate premises, will be both of the fact and of the reasoned fact; if not so obtained, of the fact alone. The object of opinion and knowledge is not quite identical; it is only in a sense identical, just as the object of true and false opinion is in a sense identical. The sense in which some maintain that true and false opinion can have the same object leads them to embrace many strange doctrines, particularly the doctrine that what a man opines falsely he does not opine at all. There are really many senses of 'identical,' and in one sense the object of true and false opinion can be the same, in another it cannot. Thus, to have a true opinion that the diagonal is commensurate with the side would be absurd: but because the diagonal with which they are both concerned is the same, the two opinions have objects so far the same: on the other hand, as regards their essential definable nature these objects differ. The identity of the objects of knowledge and opinion is similar. Knowledge is the apprehension of, e.g. the attribute 'animal' as incapable of being otherwise, opinion the apprehension of 'animal' as capable of being otherwise—e.g. the apprehension that animal is an element in the essential nature of man is knowledge; the apprehension of animal as predicable of man but not as an element in man's essential nature is opinion: man is the subject in both judgments, but the mode of inherence differs.

This also shows that one cannot opine and know the same thing simultaneously; for then one would apprehend the same thing as both capable and incapable of being otherwise—an impossibility. Knowledge and opinion of the same thing can coexist in two different people in the sense we have explained, but not simultaneously in the same person. That would involve a man's simultaneously apprehending, e.g., (1) that man is essentially animal—i.e. cannot be other than animal—and (2) that man is not essentially animal, that is, we may assume, may be other than animal.

Further consideration of modes of thinking and their distribution under the heads of discursive thought, intuition, science, art, practical wisdom, and metaphysical thinking, belongs rather partly to natural science, partly to moral philosophy.

FROM BOOK II

1. The kinds of question we ask are as many as the kinds of things which we know. They are in fact four:—(1) whether the connexion of an attribute with a thing is a fact, (2) what is the reason of the connexion, (3) whether a thing exists, (4) what is the nature of the thing. Thus, when our question concerns a complex of thing and attribute and we ask whether the thing is thus or otherwise qualified—whether, e.g., the sun suffers eclipse or not—then we are asking as to the fact of a connexion. That our inquiry ceases with the discovery that the sun does suffer eclipse is an indication of this; and if we know from the start that the sun suffers eclipse, we do not inquire whether it does so or not. On the other hand, when we know the fact we ask the reason; as, for example, when we know that the sun is being eclipsed and that an earthquake is in progress, it is the reason of eclipse or earthquake into which we inquire.

Where a complex is concerned, then, those are the two questions we ask; but for some objects of inquiry we have a different kind of question to ask, such as whether there is or is not a centaur or a God. (By 'is or is not' I mean 'is or is not, without further qualification'; as opposed to 'is or is not (e.g.) white.') On the other hand, when we have ascertained the thing's existence, we inquire as to its nature, asking, for instance, 'what, then, is God?' or 'what is man?'.

2. These, then, are the four kinds of question we ask, and it is in the answers to these questions that our knowledge consists.

Now when we ask whether a connexion is a fact, or whether a thing without qualification *is*, we are really asking whether the connexion or the thing has a 'middle'; and when we have ascertained either that the connexion is a fact or that the thing *is*—i.e. ascertained either the partial or the unqualified being of the thing—and are proceeding to ask the reason of the connexion or the nature of the thing, then we are asking what the 'middle' is.

(By distinguishing the fact of the connexion and the existence of the thing as respectively the partial and the unqualified being of the thing, I mean that if we ask 'does the moon suffer eclipse?', or 'does the moon wax?', the question concerns a part of the thing's being; for what we are asking in such questions is whether a thing is this or that, i.e. has or has not this or that attribute: whereas, if we ask whether the moon or night exists, the question concerns the unqualified being of a thing.)

We conclude that in all our inquiries we are asking either whether there is a 'middle' or what the 'middle' is: for the 'middle' here is precisely the cause, and it is the cause that we seek in all our inquiries. Thus, 'Does the moon suffer eclipse?' means 'Is there or is there not a cause producing eclipse of the moon?', and when we have learnt that there is, our next question is, 'What, then, is this cause?'; for the cause through which a thing *is*—not *is this or that,* i.e. has this or that attribute, but without qualification *is*—and the cause through which it is—not *is* without qualification, but *is this or that* as having some essential attribute or some accident—are both alike the 'middle.' By that which *is* without qualification I mean the subject, e.g. moon or earth or sun or triangle; by that which a subject *is* (in the partial sense) I mean a property, e.g. eclipse, equality or inequality, interposition or non-interposition. For in all these examples it is clear that the nature of the thing and the reason of the fact are identical: the question 'What is eclipse?' and its answer 'The privation of the moon's light by the interposition of the earth' are identical with the question 'What is the reason of eclipse?' or 'Why does the moon suffer eclipse?' and the reply 'Because of the failure of light through the earth's shutting it out.' Again, for 'What is a concord? A commensurate numerical ratio of a high and a low note,' we may substitute 'What reason makes a high and a low note concordant? Their relation according to a commensurate numerical ratio.' 'Are the high and the low note concordant?' is equivalent to 'Is their ratio commensurate?'; and when we find that it is commensurate, we ask 'What, then, is their ratio?'.

Cases in which the 'middle' is sensible show that the object of our inquiry is always the 'middle': we inquire, because we have not perceived it, whether there is or is not a 'middle' causing e.g. an eclipse. On the other hand, if we were on the moon we should not be inquiring either as to the fact or the reason, but both fact and reason would be obvious simultaneously. For the act of perception would have enabled us to know the universal too; since, the present fact of an eclipse being evident, perception would then at the same time give us the present fact of the earth's screening the sun's light, and from this would arise the universal.

Thus, as we maintain, to know a thing's nature is to know the reason why it is; and this is equally true of things in so far as they are said without qualification to *be* as opposed to being possessed of some attribute, and in so far as they are said to be possessed of some attribute such as equal to two right angles, or greater or less.

11. We think we have scientific knowledge when we know the cause,

and there are four causes: (1) the definable form, (2) an antecedent which necessitates a consequent, (3) the efficient cause, (4) the final cause. Hence each of these can be the middle term of a proof, for (a) though the inference from antecedent to necessary consequent does not hold if only one premiss is assumed—two is the minimum—still when there are two it holds on condition that they have a single common middle term. So it is from the assumption of this single middle term that the conclusion follows necessarily. The following example will also show this. Why is the angle in a semicircle a right angle?—or from what assumption does it follow that it is a right angle? Thus, let A be right angle, B the half of two right angles, C the angle in a semicircle. Then B is the cause in virtue of which A, right angle, is attributable to C, the angle in a semicircle, since $B = A$ and the other, viz. $C, = B$, for C is half of two right angles. Therefore it *is* the assumption of B, the half of two right angles, from which it follows that A is attributable to C, i.e. that the angle in a semicircle is a right angle. Moreover, B is identical with (b) the defining form of A, since it is what A's definition signifies. Moreover, the formal cause has already been shown to be the middle. (c) 'Why did the Athenians become involved in the Persian war?' means 'What cause originated the waging of war against the Athenians?' and the answer is, 'Because they raided Sardis with the Eretrians,' since this originated the war. Let A be war, B unprovoked raiding, C the Athenians. Then B, unprovoked raiding, is true of C, the Athenians, and A is true of B, since men make war on the unjust aggressor. So A, having war waged upon them, is true of B, the initial aggressors, and B is true of C, the Athenians, who were the aggressors. Hence here too the cause —in this case the efficient cause—is the middle term. (d) This is no less true where the cause is the final cause. E.g. why does one take a walk after supper? For the sake of one's health. Why does a house exist? For the preservation of one's goods. The end in view is in the one case health, in the other preservation. To ask the reason why one must walk after supper is precisely to ask to what end one must do it. Let C be walking after supper, B the non-regurgitation of food, A health. Then let walking after supper possess the property of preventing food from rising to the orifice of the stomach, and let this condition be healthy; since it seems that B, the non-regurgitation of food, is attributable to C, taking a walk, and that A, health, is attributable to B. What, then, is the cause through which A, the final cause, inheres in C? It is B, the non-regurgitation of food; but B is a kind of definition of A, for A will be explained by it. Why is B the cause of A's belonging to C? Because to be in a condition such as B is to be in health. The definitions must be transposed, and then the detail will become clearer. Incidentally, here the order of coming to be is the reverse of what it is in proof through the efficient cause: in the efficient order the middle term must come to be first, whereas in the teleological order the minor, C, must first take place, and the end in view comes last in time.

The same thing may exist for an end and be necessitated as well. For example, light shines through a lantern (1) because that which consists of relatively small particles necessarily passes through pores larger than those particles—assuming that light does issue by penetration —and (2) for an end, namely to save us from stumbling. If, then, a thing can exist through two causes, can it come to be through two causes—as for instance if thunder be a hiss and a roar necessarily produced by the quenching of fire, and also designed, as the Pythagoreans say, for a threat to terrify those that lie in Tartarus? Indeed, there are very many such cases, mostly among the processes and products of the natural world; for nature, in different senses of the term 'nature,' produces now for an end, now by necessity.

Necessity too is of two kinds. It may work in accordance with a thing's natural tendency, or by constraint and in opposition to it; as, for instance, by necessity a stone is borne both upwards and downwards, but not by the same necessity.

Of the products of man's intelligence some are never due to chance or necessity but always to an end, as for example a house or a statue; others, such as health or safety, may result from chance as well.

It is mostly in cases where the issue is indeterminate (though only where the production does not originate in chance, and the end is consequently good), that a result is due to an end, and this is true alike in nature or in art. By chance, on the other hand, nothing comes to be for an end.

19. As regards syllogism and demonstration, the definition of, and the conditions required to produce each of them, are now clear, and with that also the definition of, and the conditions required to produce, demonstrative knowledge, since it is the same as demonstration. As to the basic premisses, how they become known and what is the developed state of knowledge of them is made clear by raising some preliminary problems.

We have already said that scientific knowledge through demonstration is impossible unless a man knows the primary immediate premisses. But there are questions which might be raised in respect of the apprehension of these immediate premisses: one might not only ask whether it is of the same kind as the apprehension of the conclusions, but also whether there is or is not scientific knowledge of both; or scientific knowledge of the latter, and of the former a different kind of knowledge; and, further, whether the developed states of knowledge are not innate but come to be in us, or are innate but at first unnoticed. Now it is strange if we possess them from birth: for it means that we possess apprehensions more accurate than demonstration and fail to notice them. If on the other hand we acquire them and do not previously possess them, how could we apprehend and learn without a basis of pre-existent knowledge? For that is impossible, as we used to find in the case of demonstration. So it emerges that neither can we possess them from birth, nor can they come to be in us if we are without knowledge of them to the extent of having no such developed state at all. Therefore we must possess a capacity of some sort, but not such as to rank higher in accuracy than these developed states. And this at least is an obvious characteristic of all animals, for they possess a congenital discriminative capacity which is called sense-perception. But though sense-perception is innate in all animals, in some the sense-impression comes to persist, in others it does not. So animals in which this persistence does not come to be have either no knowledge at all outside the act of perceiving, or no knowledge of objects of which no impression persists; animals in which it does come into being have perception and can continue to retain the sense-impression in the soul: and when such persistence is frequently repeated a further distinction at once arises between those which out of the persistence of such sense-impressions develop a power of systematizing them and those which do not. So out of sense-perception comes to be what we call memory, and out of frequently repeated memories of the same thing develops experience; for a number of memories constitute a single experience. From experience again—i.e. from the universal now stabilized in its entirety within the soul, the one besides the many which is a single identity within them all—originate the skill of the craftsman and the knowledge of the man of science, skill in the sphere of coming to be and science in the sphere of being.

We conclude that these states of knowledge are neither innate in a determinate form, nor developed from other higher states of knowledge, but from sense-perception. It is like a rout in battle stopped by first one man making a stand and then another, until the original formation has been restored. The soul is so constituted as to be capable of this process.

Let us now restate the account given already, though with insufficient clearness. When one of a number of logically indiscriminable particulars has made a stand, the earliest universal is present in the soul: for though the act of sense-perception is of the particular, its content is universal—is man, for example, not the man Callias. A fresh stand is made among these rudimentary universals, and the process does not cease until the indivisible concepts, the true universals, are established: e.g. such and such a species of animal is a step towards the genus animal, which by the same process is a step towards a further generalization.

Thus it is clear that we must get to know the primary premisses by induction; for the method by which even sense-perception implants the universal is inductive. Now of the thinking states by which we grasp truth, some are unfailingly true, others admit of error—opinion, for instance, and calculation, whereas scientific knowing and intuition are always true: further, no other kind of thought except intuition is more accurate than scientific knowledge, whereas primary premisses are more knowable than demonstrations, and all scientific knowledge is discursive. From these considerations it follows that there will be no scientific knowledge of the primary premisses, and since except intuition nothing can be truer than scientific knowledge, it will be intuition that apprehends the primary premisses—a result which also follows from the fact that demonstration cannot be the originative source of demonstration, nor, consequently, scientific knowledge of scientific knowledge. If, therefore, it is the only other kind of true thinking except scientific knowing, intuition will be the originative source of scientific knowledge. And the originative source of science grasps the original basic premiss, while science as a whole is similarly related as originative source to the whole body of fact.

THREE

Geometry As a Model for Knowledge

RENE DESCARTES (1596-1650)

I

From *Rules for the Direction of the Mind**

RULE I

The end of study should be to direct the mind towards the enunciation of sound and correct judgments on all matters that come before it.

Whenever men notice some similarity between two things, they are wont to ascribe to each, even in those respects in which the two differ, what they have found to be true of the other. Thus they erroneously compare the sciences, which entirely consist in the cognitive exercise of the mind, with the arts, which depend upon an exercise and disposition of the body. They see that not all the arts can be acquired by the same man, but that he who restricts himself to one, most readily becomes the best executant, since it is not so easy for the same hand to adapt itself both to agricultural operations and to harp-playing, or to the performance of several such tasks as to one alone. Hence they have held the same to be true of the sciences also, and distinguishing them from one another according to their subject matter, they have imagined that they ought to be studied separately, each in isolation from all the rest. But this is certainly wrong. For since the sciences taken all together are identical with human wisdom, which always remains one and the same, however applied to different subjects, and suffers no more differentiation proceeding from them than the light of the sun experiences from the variety of the things which it illumines, there is no need for minds to be confined at all within limits; for neither does the knowing of one truth have an effect like that of the acquisition of one art and prevent us from finding out another, it rather aids us to do so. Certainly it appears to me strange

* From "Rules for the Direction of the Mind," in *The Philosophical Works of Descartes,* translated by Haldane and Ross (Cambridge University Press, 1931). Reprinted by permission of the publishers.

Knowledge is univocal for Descartes n'est ce pas?

that so many people should investigate human customs with such care, the virtues of plants, the motions of the stars, the transmutations of metals, and the objects of similar sciences, while at the same time practically none bethink themselves about good understanding or universal Wisdom, though nevertheless all other studies are to be esteemed not so much for their own value as because they contribute something to this. Consequently we are justified in bringing forward this as the first rule of all, since there is nothing more prone to turn us aside from the correct way of seeking out truth than this directing of our inquiries, not towards their general end, but towards certain special investigations. I do not here refer to perverse and censurable pursuits like empty glory or base gain; obviously counterfeit reasonings and quibbles suited to vulgar understanding open up a much more direct route to such a goal than does a sound apprehension of the truth. But I have in view even honourable and laudable pursuits, because these mislead us in a more subtle fashion. For example take our investigations of those sciences conducive to the conveniences of life or which yield that pleasure which is found in the contemplation of truth, practically the only joy in life that is complete and untroubled with any pain. There we may indeed expect to receive the legitimate fruits of scientific inquiry; but if, in the course of our study, we think of them, they frequently cause us to omit many facts which are necessary to the understanding of other matters, because they seem to be either of slight value or of little interest. Hence we must believe that all the sciences are so inter-connected, that it is much easier to study them all together than to isolate one from all the others. If, therefore, anyone wishes to search out the truth of things in serious earnest, he ought not to select one special science; for all the sciences are conjoined with each other and interdependent: he ought rather to think how to increase the natural light of reason, not for the purpose of resolving this or that difficulty of scholastic type, but in order that his understanding may light his will to its proper choice in all the contingencies of life. In a short time he will see with amazement that he has made much more progress than those who are eager about particular ends, and that he has not only obtained all that they desire, but even higher results than fall within his expectation.

RULE II

That is: we should study only that which is certain.

Only those objects should engage our attention to the sure and indubitable knowledge of which our mental powers seem to be adequate.

Science in its entirety is true and evident cognition. He is no more learned who has doubts on many matters than the man who has never thought of them; nay he appears to be less learned if he has formed wrong opinions on any particulars. Hence it were better not to study at all than to occupy one's self with objects of such difficulty, that, owing to our inability to distinguish true from false, we are forced to regard the doubtful as certain; for in those matters any hope of augmenting our knowledge is exceeded by the risk of diminishing it. Thus in accordance with the above maxim we reject all such merely probable knowledge and make it a rule to trust only what is completely known and incapable of being doubted. No doubt men of education may persuade themselves that there is but little of such certain knowledge, because, forsooth, a common failing of human nature has made them deem it too easy and open to everyone, and so led them to neglect to think upon such truths; but I nevertheless announce that there are more of these than they think —truths which suffice to give a rigorous demonstration of innumerable propositions, the discussion of which they have hitherto been unable to free from the element of probability. Further, because they have believed that it was unbecoming for a man of education to confess ignorance on any point, they have so accustomed themselves to trick out their fabricated explanations, that they have ended by gradually imposing on themselves and thus have issued them to the public as genuine.

But if we adhere closely to this rule we shall find left but few objects of legitimate study. For there is scarce any question occurring in the sciences about which talented men have not disagreed. But whenever two men come to opposite decisions about the same matter one of them at least must certainly be in the wrong, and apparently there is not even one of them who knows; for if the reasoning of the second was sound and clear he would be able so to lay it before the other as finally to succeed in convincing *his* understanding also. Hence apparently we cannot attain to a perfect knowledge in any such case of probable opinion, for it would be rashness to hope for more than others have attained to. Consequently if we reckon correctly, of the sciences already discovered, Arithmetic and

couldn't he be half wrong?

Geometry alone are left, to which the observance of this rule reduces us.

Yet we do not therefore condemn that method of philosophizing which others have already discovered and those weapons of the school-men, probable syllogisms, which are so well suited for polemics. They indeed give practice to the wits of youths and, producing emulation among them, act as a stimulus; and it is much better for their minds to be moulded by opinions of this sort, uncertain though they appear, as being objects of controversy among the learned, than to be left entirely to their own devices. For thus through lack of guidance they might stray into some abyss; but as long as they follow in their masters' footsteps, though they may diverge at times from the truth, they will yet certainly find a path which is at least in this respect safer, that it has been approved of by more prudent people. We ourselves rejoice that we in earlier years experienced this scholastic training; but now, being released from that oath of allegiance which bound us to our old masters, and since, as becomes our riper years, we are no longer subject to the ferule, if we wish in earnest to establish for ourselves those rules which shall aid us in scaling the heights of human knowledge, we must admit assuredly among the primary members of our catalogue that maxim which forbids us to abuse our leisure as many do, who neglect all easy quests and take up their time only with difficult matters; for they, though certainly making all sorts of subtle conjectures and elaborating most plausible arguments with great ingenuity, frequently find too late that after all their labours they have only increased the multitude of their doubts, without acquiring any knowledge whatsoever.

But now let us proceed to explain more carefully our reasons for saying, as we did a little while ago, that of all the sciences known as yet, Arithmetic and Geometry alone are free from any taint of falsity or uncertainty. We must note then that there are two ways by which we arrive at the knowledge of facts, viz. by experience and by deduction. We must further observe that while our inferences from experience are frequently fallacious, deduction, or the pure illation of one thing from another, though it may be passed over, if it is not seen through, cannot be erroneous when performed by an understanding that is in the least degree rational. And it seems to me that the operation is profited but little by those constraining bonds by means of which the Dialecticians claim to control human reason, though I do not deny that that discipline may be serviceable for other purposes. My reason for saying so is that none of the mistakes which men can make (men, I say, not beasts) are due to faulty inference; they are caused merely by the fact that we found upon a basis of poorly comprehended experiences, or that propositions are posited which are hasty and groundless.

This furnishes us with an evident explanation of the great superiority in certitude of Arithmetic and Geometry to other sciences. The former alone deal with an object so pure and uncomplicated, that they need make no assumptions at all which experience renders uncertain, but wholly consist in the rational deduction of consequences. They are on that account much the easiest and clearest of all, and possess an object such as we require, for in them it is scarce humanly possible for anyone to err except by inadvertence. And yet we should not be surprised to find that plenty of people of their own accord prefer to apply their intelligence to other studies, or to Philosophy. The reason for this is that every person permits himself the liberty of making guesses in the matter of an obscure subject with more confidence than in one which is clear, and that it is much easier to have some vague notion about any subject, no matter what, than to arrive at the real truth about a single question however simple that may be.

But one conclusion now emerges out of these considerations, viz. not, indeed, that Arithmetic and Geometry are the sole sciences to be studied, but only that in our search for the direct road towards truth we should busy ourselves with no object about which we cannot attain a certitude equal to that of the demonstrations of Arithmetic and Geometry.

RULE III

In the subjects we propose to investigate, our inquiries should be directed, not to what others have thought, nor to what we ourselves conjecture, but to what we can clearly and perspicuously behold and with certainty deduce; for knowledge is not won in any other way.

To study the writings of the ancients is right, because it is a great boon for us to be able to make use of the labours of so many men; and we should do so, both in order to discover what they have correctly made out in previous ages, and also that we may inform ourselves as to what in the various sciences is still left for investigation. But yet there is a great danger lest in a too absorbed study of these works we should become infected with their errors, guard against them as we may. For it is the way of writers, whenever they have allowed themselves rashly and credulously to take up a position in any controverted matter, to try with the subtlest of arguments to compel us to go along with them. But when, on the contrary, they have happily come upon something certain and evident, in displaying it they never fail to surround it with ambiguities, fearing, it would seem, lest the simplicity of their explanation should make us respect their discovery less, or because they grudge us an open vision of the truth.

Further, supposing now that all were wholly open and candid, and never thrust upon us doubtful opinions as true, but expounded every matter in good faith, yet since scarce anything has been asserted by any one man the contrary of which has not been alleged by another, we should be eternally uncertain which of the two to believe. It would be no use to total up the testimonies in favour of each, meaning to follow that opinion which was supported by the greater number of authors; for if it is a question of difficulty that is in dispute, it is more likely that the truth would have been discovered by few than by many. But even though all these men agreed among themselves, what they teach us would not suffice for us. For we shall not, e.g. all turn out to be mathematicians though we know by heart all the proofs that others have elaborated, unless we have an intellectual talent that fits us to resolve difficulties of any kind. Neither, though we have mastered all the arguments of Plato and Aristotle, if yet we have not the capacity for passing a solid judgment on these matters, shall we become Philosophers; we should have acquired the knowledge not of a science, but of history.

I lay down the rule also, that we must wholly refrain from ever mixing up conjectures with our pronouncements on the truth of things. This warning is of no little importance. There is no stronger reason for our finding nothing in the current Philosophy which is so evident and certain as not to be capable of being controverted, than the fact that the learned, not content with the recognition of what is clear and certain, in the first instance hazard the assertion of obscure and ill-comprehended theories, at which they have arrived merely by probable conjecture. Then afterwards they gradually attach complete credence to them, and mingling them promiscuously with what is true and evident, they finish by being unable to deduce any conclusion which does not appear to depend upon some proposition of the doubtful sort, and hence is not uncertain.

But lest we in turn should slip into the same error, we shall here take note of all those mental operations by which we are able, wholly without fear of illusion, to arrive at the knowledge of things. Now I admit only two, viz. intuition and deduction.

By *intuition* I understand, not the fluctuating testimony of the senses, nor the misleading judgment that proceeds from the blundering constructions of imagination, but the conception which an unclouded and attentive mind gives us so readily and distinctly that we are wholly freed from doubt about that which we understand. Or, what comes to the same thing, *intuition* is the undoubting conception of an unclouded and attentive mind, and springs from the light of reason alone; it is more certain that deduction itself, in that it is simpler, though deduction, as we have noted above, cannot by us be erroneously conducted. Thus each individual can mentally have intuition of the fact that he exists, and that he thinks; that the triangle is bounded by three lines only, the sphere by a single superficies, and so on. Facts of such a kind are far more numerous than many people think, disdaining as they do to direct their attention upon such simple matters.

But in case anyone may be put out by this new use of the term intuition and of other terms which in the following pages I am similarly compelled to dissever from their current meaning, I here make the general announcement that I pay no attention to the way in which particular terms have of late been employed in the schools, because it would have been difficult to employ the same terminology while my theory was wholly different. All that I take note of is the meaning of the Latin of each word, when, in cases where an appropriate term is lacking, I wish to transfer to the vocabulary that expresses my own meaning those that I deem most suitable.

This evidence and certitude, however, which belongs to intuition, is required not only in the enunciation of propositions, but also in discursive reasoning of whatever sort. For example consider this consequence: 2 and 2 amount to the same as 3 and 1. Now we need to see intuitively not only that 2 and 2 make 4, and that likewise 3 and 1 make 4, but further that the third of the above statements is a necessary conclusion from these two.

Hence now we are in a position to raise the question as to why we have, besides intuition, given this supplementary method of knowing, viz. knowing by *deduction*, by which we understand all necessary inference from other facts that are known with certainty. This, however, we could not avoid, because many things are known with certainty, though not be themselves evident, but only deduced from true and known principles by the continuous and uninterrupted action of a mind that has a clear vision of each step in the process. It is in a similar way that we know that the last link in a long chain is connected with the first, even though we do not take in by means of one and the same act of vision all the intermediate links on which that connection depends, but only remember that we have taken them successively under review and that each single one is united to its neighbour, from the first even to the last. Hence we distinguish this mental intuition from deduction by the fact that into the conception of the latter there enters a certain movement or succession, into that of the former there does not. Further deduction does not require an immediately presented evidence such as intuition possesses; its certitude is rather conferred upon it in some way by memory. The upshot of the matter is that it is possible to say that those propositions indeed which are immediately deduced from first principles are known now by intuition, now by deduction, i.e. in a way that differs according to our point of view. But the first principles themselves are given by intuition alone, while, on the contrary, the remote conclusions are furnished only by deduction.

These two methods are the most certain routes to knowledge, and the mind should admit no others. All the rest should be rejected as suspect of error and dangerous. But this does not prevent us from believing matters that have been divinely revealed as being more certain than our surest knowledge, since belief in these things, as all faith in obscure matters, is an action not of our intelligence, but of our will. They should be heeded also since, if they have any basis in our understanding, they can and ought to be, more than all things else, discovered by one or other of the ways above-mentioned, as we hope perhaps to show at greater length on some future opportunity.

seems like a narrow mind to me.

II

From *Meditations**

MEDITATION I

Of the things which may be brought within the sphere of the doubtful.

It is now some years since I detected how many were the false beliefs that I had from my earliest youth admitted as true, and how doubtful was everything I had since constructed on this basis; and from that time I was convinced that I must once for all seriously undertake to rid myself of all the opinions which I had formerly accepted, and commence to build anew from the foundation, if I wanted to establish any firm and permanent structure in the sciences. But as this enterprise appeared to be a very great one, I waited until I had attained an age so mature that I could not hope that at any later date I should be better fitted to execute my design. This reason caused me to delay so long that I should feel that I was doing wrong were I to occupy in deliberation the time that yet remains to me for action. To-day, then, since very opportunely for the plan I have in view I have delivered my mind from every care (and am happily agitated by no passions) and since I have procured for myself an assured leisure in a peaceable retirement, I shall at last seriously and freely address myself to the general upheaval of all my former opinions.

* From "Meditations on the First Philosophy in which the Existence of God and the Distinction between Mind and Body are Demonstrated," in *The Philosophical Works of Descartes,* translated by Haldane and Ross (Cambridge University Press, 1931). Reprinted by permission of the publishers.

Now for this object it is not necessary that I should show that all of these are false—I shall perhaps never arrive at this end. But inasmuch as reason already persuades me that I ought no less carefully to withhold my assent from matters which are not entirely certain and indubitable than from those which appear to me manifestly to be false, if I am able to find in each one some reason to doubt, this will suffice to justify my rejecting the whole. And for that end it will not be requisite that I should examine each in particular, which would be an endless undertaking; for owing to the fact that the destruction of the foundations of necessity brings with it the downfall of the rest of the edifice, I shall only in the first place attack those principles upon which all my former opinions rested.

All that up to the present time I have accepted as most true and certain I have learned either from the senses or through the senses; but it is sometimes proved to me that these senses are deceptive, and it is wiser not to trust entirely to any thing by which we have once been deceived.

Senses are occasions of deception.

But it may be that although the senses sometimes deceive us concerning things which are hardly perceptible, or very far away, there are yet many others to be met with as to which we cannot reasonably have any doubt, although we recognise them by their means. For example, there is the fact that I am here, seated by the fire, attired in a dressing gown, having this paper in my hands and other similar matters. And how could I deny that these hands and this body are mine, were it not perhaps that I compare myself to certain persons, devoid of sense, whose cerebella are so troubled and clouded by the violent vapours of black bile, that they constantly assure us that they think they are kings when they are really quite poor, or that they are clothed in purple when they are really without covering, or who imagine that they have an earthenware head or are nothing but pumpkins or are made of glass. But they are mad, and I should not be any the less insane were I to follow examples so extravagant.

At the same time I must remember that I am a man, and that consequently I am in the habit of sleeping, and in my dreams representing to myself the same things or sometimes even less probable things, than do those who are insane in their waking moments. How often has it happened to me that in the night I dreamt that I found myself in this particular place, that I was dressed and seated near the fire, whilst in reality I was lying undressed in bed! At this moment it does indeed seem to me that it is with eyes awake that I am looking at this paper; that this head which I move is not asleep, that it is deliberately and of set purpose that I extend my hand and perceive it; what happens in sleep does not appear so clear nor so distinct as does all this. But in thinking over this I remind myself that on many occasions I have in sleep been deceived by similar illusions, and in dwelling carefully on this reflection I see so manifestly that there are no certain indications by which we may clearly distinguish wakefulness from sleep that I am lost in astonishment. And my astonishment is such that it is almost capable of persuading me that I now dream.

Now let us assume that we are asleep and that all these particulars, e.g. that we open our eyes, shake our head, extend our hands, and so on, are but false delusions; and let us reflect that possibly neither our hands nor our whole body are such as they appear to us to be. At the same time we must at least confess that the things which are represented to us in sleep are like painted representations which can only have been formed as the counterparts of something real and true, and that in this way those general things at least, i.e. eyes, a head, hands and a whole body, are not imaginary things, but things really existent. For, as a matter of fact, painters, even when they study with the greatest skill to represent sirens and satyrs by forms the most strange and extraordinary, cannot give them natures which are entirely new, but merely make a certain medley of the members of different animals; or if their imagination is extravagant enough to invent something so novel that nothing similar has ever before been seen, and that then their work represents a thing purely fictitious and absolutely false, it is certain all the same that the colours of which this is composed are necessarily real. And for the same reason, although these general things, to wit, [a body], eyes, a head, and such like, may be imaginary, we are bound at the same time to confess that there are at least some other objects yet more simple and more universal, which are real and true; and of these just in the same way as with certain real colours, all these images of things which dwell in our thoughts, whether true and real or false and fantastic, are formed.

To such a class of things pertains corporeal nature in general, and its extension, the figure of extended things, their quantity or magnitude and number, as also the place in which they are, the time which measures their duration, and so on.

That is possibly why our reasoning is not unjust when we conclude from this that Physics, Astronomy, Medicine and all other sciences which have as their end the consideration of composite things, are very dubious and uncertain; but that Arithmetic, Geometry and other sciences of that kind which only treat of things that are very simple and very general, without taking great trouble to ascertain whether they are actually existent or not, contain some measure of certainty and an element of the indubitable. For whether I am awake or asleep, two or three together always form five, and the square can never have more than four sides, and it does not seem possible that truths so clear and apparent can be suspected of any falsity [or uncertainty].

Nevertheless I have long had fixed in my mind the belief that an all-powerful God existed by whom I have been created such as I am. But how do I know that He has not brought it to pass that there is no earth, no heaven, no extended body, no magnitude, no place, and that nevertheless [I possess the perceptions of all these things and that] they seem to me to exist just exactly as I now see them? And, besides, as I sometimes imagine that others deceive themselves in the things which they think they know best, how do I know that I am not deceived every time that I add two and three, or count the sides of a square, or judge of things yet simpler, if anything simpler can be imagined? But possibly God has not desired that I should be thus deceived, for He is said to be supremely good. If, however, it is contrary to His goodness to have made me such that I constantly deceive myself, it would also appear to be contrary to His goodness to permit me to be sometimes deceived, and nevertheless I cannot doubt that He does permit this.

There may indeed be those who would prefer to deny the existence of a God so powerful, rather than believe that all other things are uncertain. But let us not oppose them for the present, and grant that all that is here said of a God is a fable; nevertheless in whatever way they suppose that I have arrived at the state of being that I have reached—whether they attribute it to fate or to accident, or make out that it is by a continual succession of antecedents, or by some other method—since to err and deceive oneself is a defect, it is clear that the greater will be the probability of my being so imperfect as to deceive myself ever, as is the Author to whom they assign my origin the less powerful. To these reasons I have certainly nothing to reply, but at the end I feel constrained to confess that there is nothing in all that I formerly believed to be true, of which I cannot in some measure doubt, and that not merely through want of thought or through levity, but for reasons which are very powerful and maturely considered; so that henceforth I ought not the less carefully to refrain from giving credence to these opinions than to that which is manifestly false, if I desire to arrive at any certainty [in the sciences].

But it is not sufficient to have made these remarks, we must also be careful to keep them in mind. For these ancient and commonly held opinions still revert frequently to my mind, long and familiar custom having given them the right to occupy my mind against my inclination and rendered them almost masters of my belief; nor will I ever lose the habit of deferring to them or of placing my confidence in them, so long as I consider them as they really are, i.e. opinions in some measure doubtful, as I have just shown, and at the same time highly probable, so that there is much more reason to believe in than to deny them. That is why I consider that I shall be not acting amiss, if, taking of set purpose a contrary belief, I allow myself to be deceived, and for a certain time pretend that all these opinions are entirely false and imaginary, until at last, having thus balanced my former prejudices with my latter [so that they cannot divert my opinions more to one side than to the other], my judgment will no longer be dominated by bad usage or turned away from the right knowledge of the truth. For I am assured that there can be neither peril nor error in this course, and that I cannot at present yield too much to distrust, since I am not considering the question of action, but only of knowledge.

I shall then suppose, not that God who is supremely good and the fountain of truth, but some evil genius not less powerful than deceitful, has employed his whole energies in deceiving me; I shall consider that the heavens, the earth, colours, figures, sound, and all other external things are nought but the illusions and dreams of which this genius has availed himself in order to lay traps for my credulity; I shall consider myself as having no hands, no eyes, no flesh, no blood, nor any senses, yet falsely believing myself to possess all these things; I shall remain obstinately attached to this idea, and if by this means it is not in my power to arrive at the knowledge of any truth, I may at least do what is in my power (i.e. suspend my judgment), and with firm purpose avoid giving credence to any false thing, or being imposed upon by this arch deceiver, however powerful and deceptive he may be. But this task is a laborious one, and insensibly a certain lassitude leads me into the course of my ordinary life. And just as a captive who in sleep enjoys an imaginary liberty, when he begins to suspect that his liberty is but a dream, fears to awaken, and conspires with these agreeable illusions that the deception may be prolonged, so insensibly of my own accord I fall back into my former opinions, and I dread awakening from this slumber, lest the laborious wakefulness which would follow the tranquillity of this repose should have to be spent not in daylight, but in the excessive darkness of the difficulties which have just been discussed.

MEDITATION II

Of the Nature of the Human Mind; and that it is more easily known than the Body.

The Meditation of yesterday filled my mind with so many doubts that it is no longer in my power to forget them. And yet I do not see in what manner I can resolve them; and, just as if I had all of a sudden fallen into very deep water, I am so disconcerted that I can neither make certain of setting my feet on the bottom, nor can I swim and so support myself on the surface. I shall nevertheless make an effort and follow anew the same path as that on which I yesterday entered, i.e. I shall proceed by setting aside all that in which the least doubt could be supposed to exist, just as if I had discovered that it was absolutely false; and I shall ever follow in this road until I have met with something which is certain, or at least, if I can do nothing else, until I have learned for certain that there is nothing in the world that is certain. Archimedes, in order that he might draw the terrestrial globe out of its place, and transport it elsewhere, demanded only that one point should be fixed and immovable; in the same way I shall have the right to conceive high hopes if I am happy enough to discover one thing only which is certain and indubitable.

I suppose, then, that all the things that I see are false; I persuade myself that nothing has ever existed of all that my fallacious memory represents to me. I consider that I possess no senses; I imagine that body, figure, extension, movement and place are but the fictions of my mind. What, then, can be esteemed as true? Perhaps nothing at all, unless that there is nothing in the world that is certain.

But how can I know there is not something different from those things that I have just considered, of which one cannot have the slightest doubt? Is there not some God, or some other being by whatever name we call it, who puts these reflections into my mind? That is not necessary, for is it not possible that I am capable of producing them myself? I myself, am I not at least something? But I have already denied that I had senses and body. Yet I hesitate, for what follows from that? Am I so dependent on body and senses that I cannot exist without these? But I was persuaded that there was nothing in all the world, that there was no heaven, no earth, that there were no minds, nor any bodies: was I not then likewise persuaded that I did not exist? Not at all; of a surety I myself did exist since I persuaded myself of something [or merely because I thought of something]. But there is some deceiver or other, very powerful and very cunning, who ever employs his ingenuity in deceiving me. Then without doubt I exist also if he deceives me, and let him deceive me as much as he will, he can never cause me to be nothing so long as I think that I am something. So that after having reflected well and carefully examined all things, we must come to the definite conclusion that this proposition: I am, I exist, is necessarily true each time that I pronounce it, or that I mentally conceive it.

But I do not yet know clearly enough what I am, I who am certain that I am; and hence I must be careful to see that I do not imprudently take some other object in place of myself, and thus that I do not go astray in respect of this knowledge that I hold to be the most certain and most evident of all that I have formerly learned. That is why I shall now consider anew what I believed myself to be before I embarked upon these last reflections; and of my former opinions I shall withdraw all that might even in a small degree be invalidated by the reasons which I have just brought forward, in order that there may be nothing at all left beyond what is absolutely certain and indubitable.

What then did I formerly believe myself to be? Undoubtedly I be-

sounds like Sartre

lieved myself to be a man. But what is a man? Shall I say a reasonable animal? Certainly not; for then I should have to inquire what an animal is, and what is reasonable; and thus from a single question I should insensibly fall into an infinitude of others more difficult; and I should not wish to waste the little time and leisure remaining to me in trying to unravel subtleties like these. But I shall rather stop here to consider the thoughts which of themselves spring up in my mind, and which were not inspired by anything beyond my own nature alone when I applied myself to the consideration of my being. In the first place, then, I considered myself as having a face, hands, arms, and all that system of members composed of bones and flesh as seen in a corpse which I designated by the name of body. In addition to this I considered that I was nourished, that I walked, that I felt, and that I thought, and I referred all these actions to the soul: but I did not stop to consider what the soul was, or if I did stop, I imagined that it was something extremely rare and subtle like a wind, a flame, or an ether, which was spread throughout my grosser parts. As to body I had no manner of doubt about its nature, but thought I had a very clear knowledge of it; and if I had desired to explain it according to the notions that I had then formed of it, I should have described it thus: By the body I understand all that which can be defined by a certain figure: something which can be confined in a certain place, and which can fill a given space in such a way that every other body will be excluded from it; which can be perceived either by touch, or by sight, or by hearing, or by taste, or by smell: which can be moved in many ways not, in truth, by itself, but by something which is foreign to it, by which it is touched (and from which it receives impressions): for to have the power of self-movement, as also of feeling or of thinking, I did not consider to appertain to the nature of body: on the contrary, I was rather astonished to find that faculties similar to them existed in some bodies.

But what am I, now that I suppose that there is a certain genius which is extremely powerful, and, if I may say so, malicious, who employs all his powers in deceiving me? Can I affirm that I possess the least of all those things which I have just said pertain to the nature of body? I pause to consider, I resolve all these things in my mind, and find none of which I can say that it pertains to me. It would be tedious to stop to enumerate them. Let us pass to the attributes of soul and see if there is any one which is in me? What of nutrition or walking [the first mentioned]? But if it is so that I have no body it is also true that I can neither walk nor take nourishment. Another attribute is sensation. But one cannot feel without body, and besides I have thought I perceived many things during sleep that I recognised in my waking moments as not having been experienced at all. What of thinking? I find here that thought is an attribute that belongs to me; it alone cannot be separated from me. I am, I exist, that is certain. But how often? Just when I think; for it

might possibly be the case if I ceased entirely to think, that I should likewise cease altogether to exist. I do not now admit anything which is not
necessarily true: to speak accurately I am not more than a thing which
thinks, that is to say a mind or a soul, or an understanding, or a reason,
which are terms whose significance was formerly unknown to me. I am,
however, a real thing and really exist; but what thing? I have answered:
a thing which thinks.

And what more? I shall exercise my imagination [in order to see if I
am not something more]. I am not a collection of members which we call
the human body: I am not a subtle air distributed through these members, I am not a wind, a fire, a vapour, a breath, nor anything at all which
I can imagine or conceive; because I have assumed that all these were
nothing. Without changing that supposition I find that I only leave myself certain of the fact that I am somewhat. But perhaps it is true that
these same things which I supposed were non-existent because they are
unknown to me, are really not different from the self which I know. I am
not sure about this, I shall not dispute about it now; I can only give judgment on things that are known to me. I know that I exist, and I inquire
what I am, I whom I know to exist. But it is very certain that the knowledge of my existence taken in its precise significance does not depend on
things whose existence is not yet known to me; consequently it does not
depend on those which I can feign in imagination. And indeed the very
term *feign* in imagination proves to me my error, for I really do this if I
image myself a something, since to imagine is nothing else than to contemplate the figure or image of a corporeal thing. But I already know for
certain that I am, and that it may be that all these images, and, speaking
generally, all things that relate to the nature of body are nothing but
dreams (and chimeras). For this reason I see clearly that I have as little
reason to say, 'I shall stimulate my imagination in order to know more
distinctly what I am,' than if I were to say, 'I am now awake, and I perceive somewhat that is real and true: but because I do not yet perceive it
distinctly enough, I shall go to sleep of express purpose, so that my
dreams may represent the perception with greatest truth and evidence.'
And, thus, I know for certain that nothing of all that I can understand by
means of my imagination belongs to this knowledge which I have of myself, and that it is necessary to recall the mind from this mode of thought
with the utmost diligence in order that it may be able to know its own
nature with perfect distinctness.

But what then am I? A thing which thinks. What is a thing which
thinks? It is a thing which doubts, understands, [conceives], affirms,
denies, wills, refuses, which also imagines and feels.

Certainly it is no small matter if all these things pertain to my
nature. But why should they not so pertain? Am I not that being who
now doubts nearly everything, who nevertheless understands certain

things, who affirms that one only is true, who denies all the others, who desires to know more, is averse from being deceived, who imagines many things, sometimes indeed despite his will, and who perceives many likewise, as by the intervention of the bodily organs? Is there nothing in all this which is as true as it is certain that I exist, even though I should always sleep and though he who has given me being employed all his ingenuity in deceiving me? Is there likewise any one of these attributes which can be distinguished from my thought, or which might be said to be separated from myself? For it is so evident of itself that it is I who doubts, who understands, and who desires, that there is no reason here to add anything to explain it. And I have certainly the power of imagining likewise; for although it may happen (as I formerly supposed) that none of the things which I imagine are true, nevertheless this power of imagining does not cease to be really in use, and it forms part of my thought. Finally, I am the same who feels, that is to say, who perceives certain things, as by the organs of sense, since in truth I see light, I hear noise, I feel heat. But it will be said that these phenomena are false and that I am dreaming. Let it be so; still it is at least quite certain that it seems to me that I see light, that I hear noise and that I feel heat. That cannot be false; properly speaking it is what is in me called feeling; and used in this precise sense that is no other thing than thinking.

From this time I begin to know what I am with a little more clearness and distinction than before; but nevertheless it still seems to me, and I cannot prevent myself from thinking, that corporeal things, whose images are framed by thought, which are tested by the senses, are much more distinctly known than that obscure part of me which does not come under the imagination. Although really it is very strange to say that I know and understand more distinctly these things whose existence seems to me dubious, which are unknown to me, and which do not belong to me than others of the truth of which I am convinced, which are known to me and which pertain to my real nature, in a word, than myself. But I see clearly how the case stands: my mind loves to wander, and cannot yet suffer itself to be retained within the just limits of truth. Very good, let us once more give it the freest rein, so that, when afterwards we seize the proper occasion for pulling up, it may the more easily be regulated and controlled.

Let us begin by considering the commonest matters, those which we believe to be the most distinctly comprehended, to wit, the bodies which we touch and see; not indeed bodies in general, for these general ideas are usually a little more confused, but let us consider one body in particular. Let us take for example, this piece of wax: it has been taken quite freshly from the hive, and it has not yet lost the sweetness of the honey which it contains; it still retains somewhat of the odour of the flowers from which it has been culled; its colour, its figure, its size are apparent;

it is hard, cold, easily handled, and if you strike it with the finger, it will emit a sound. Finally all the things which are requisite to cause us distinctly to recognise a body, are met with in it. But notice that while I speak and approach the fire what remained of the taste is exhaled, the smell evaporates, the colour alters, the figure is destroyed, the size increases, it becomes liquid, it heats, scarcely can one handle it, and when one strikes it, no sound is emitted. Does the same wax remain after this change? We must confess that it remains; none would judge otherwise. What then did I know so distinctly in this piece of wax? It could certainly be nothing of all that the senses brought to my notice, since all these things which fall under taste, smell, sight, touch, and hearing, are found to be changed, and yet the same wax remains.

Perhaps it was what I now think, viz. that this wax was not that sweetness of honey, nor that agreeable scent of flowers, nor that particular whiteness, nor that figure, nor that sound, but simply a body which a little before appeared to me as perceptible under these forms, and which is now perceptible under others. But what, precisely, is it that I imagine when I form such conceptions? Let us attentively consider this, and, abstracting from all that does not belong to the wax, let us see what remains. Certainly nothing remains excepting a certain extended thing which is flexible and movable. But what is the meaning of flexible and movable? Is it not that I imagine that this piece of wax being round is capable of becoming square and of passing from a square to a triangular figure? No, certainly it is not that, since I imagine it admits of an infinitude of similar changes, and I nevertheless do not know how to compass the infinitude by my imagination, and consequently this conception which I have of the wax is not brought about by the faculty of imagination. What now is this extension? Is it not also unknown? For it becomes greater when the wax is melted, greater when it is boiled, and greater still when the heat increases; and I should not conceive [clearly] according to truth what wax is, if I did not think that even this piece that we are considering is capable of receiving more variations in extension than I have ever imagined. We must then grant that I could not even understand through the imagination what this piece of wax is, and that it is my mind alone which perceives it. I say this piece of wax in particular, for as to wax in general it is yet clearer. But what is this piece of wax which cannot be understood excepting by the [understanding or] mind? It is certainly the same that I see, touch, imagine, and finally it is the same which I have always believed it to be from the beginning. But what must particularly be observed is that its perception is neither an act of vision, nor of touch, nor of imagination, and has never been such although it may have appeared formerly to be so, but only an intuition of the mind, which may be imperfect and confused as it was formerly, or clear and distinct as it is at present, according as my attention is more or less directed to the elements which are found in it, and of which it is composed.

Yet in the meantime I am greatly astonished when I consider [the great feebleness of mind] and its proneness to fall [insensibly] into error; for although without giving expression to my thoughts I consider all this in my own mind, words often impede me and I am almost deceived by the terms of ordinary language. For we say that we see the same wax, if it is present, and not that we simply judge that it is the same from its having the same colour and figure. From this I should conclude that I knew the wax by means of vision and not simply by the intuition of the mind; unless by chance I remember that, when looking from a window and saying I see men who pass in the street, I really do not see them, but infer that what I see is men, just as I say that I see wax. And yet what do I see from the window but hats and coats which may cover automatic machines? Yet I judge these to be men. And similarly solely by the faculty of judgment which rests in my mind, I comprehend that which I believed I saw with my eyes.

A man who makes it his aim to raise his knowledge above the common should be ashamed to derive the occasion for doubting from the forms of speech invented by the vulgar; I prefer to pass on and consider whether I had a more evident and perfect conception of what the wax was when I first perceived it, and when I believed I knew it by means of the external senses or at least by the common sense as it is called, that is to say by the imaginative faculty, or whether my present conception is clearer now that I have most carefully examined what it is, and in what way it can be known. It would certainly be absurd to doubt as to this. For what was there in this first perception which was distinct? What was there which might not as well have been perceived by any of the animals? But when I distinguish the wax from its external forms, and when, just as if I had taken from it its vestments, I consider it quite naked, it is certain that although some error may still be found in my judgment, I can nevertheless not perceive it thus without a human mind.

But finally what shall I say of this mind, that is, of myself, for up to this point I do not admit in myself anything but mind? What then, I who seem to perceive this piece of wax distinctly, do I not know myself, not only with much more truth and certainty, but also with much more distinctness and clearness? For if I judge that the wax is or exists from the fact that I see it, it certainly follows much more clearly that I am or that I exist myself from the fact that I see it. For it may be that what I see is not really wax, it may also be that I do not possess eyes with which to see anything; but it cannot be that when I see, or (for I no longer take account of the distinction) when I think I see, that I myself who think am nought. So if I judge that the wax exists from the fact that I touch it, the same thing will follow, to wit, that I am; and if I judge that my imagination, or some other cause, whatever it is, persuades me that the wax exists, I shall still conclude the same. And what I have here remarked of wax may be applied to all other things which are external to me [and which are met with outside of me]. And further, if the [notion or] perception of wax has seemed to me clearer and more distinct, not only after the sight or the touch, but also after many other causes have rendered it quite manifest to me, with how much more [evidence] and distinctness must it be said that I now know myself, since all the reasons which contribute to the knowledge of wax, or any other body whatever, are yet better proofs of the nature of my mind! And there are so many other things in the mind itself which may contribute to the elucidation of its nature, that those which depend on body such as these just mentioned, hardly merit being taken into account.

But finally here I am, having insensibly reverted to the point I desired, for, since it is now manifest to me that even bodies are not properly speaking known by the senses or by the faculty of imagination, but by the understanding only, and since they are not known from the fact that they are seen or touched, but only because they are understood, I see clearly that there is nothing which is easier for me to know than my mind. But because it is difficult to rid oneself so promptly of an opinion to which one was accustomed for so long, it will be well that I should halt a little at this point, so that by the length of my meditation I may more deeply imprint on my memory this new knowledge.

if I perceive, I know I exist.
The perception can be wrong or right

MEDITATION III

I shall now close my eyes, I shall stop my ears, I shall call away all my senses, I shall efface even from my thoughts all the images of corporeal things, or at least (for that is hardly possible) I shall esteem them as vain and false; and thus holding converse only with myself and considering my own nature, I shall try little by little to reach a better knowledge of and a more familiar acquaintanceship with myself. I am a thing that thinks, that is to say, that doubts, affirms, denies, that knows a few things, that is ignorant of many [that loves, that hates], that wills, that desires, that also imagines and perceives; for as I remarked before, although the things which I perceive and imagine are perhaps nothing at all apart from me and in themselves, I am nevertheless assured that these modes of thought that I call perceptions and imaginations, inasmuch only as they are modes of thought, certainly reside [and are met with] in me.

And in the little that I have just said, I think I have summed up all that I really know, or at least all that hitherto I was aware that I knew. In order to try to extend my knowledge further, I shall now look around more carefully and see whether I cannot still discover in myself some other things which I have not hitherto perceived. I am certain that I am a thing which thinks; but do I not then likewise know what is requisite to render me certain of a truth? Certainly in this first knowledge there is nothing that assures me of its truth, excepting the clear and distinct perception of that which I state, which would not indeed suffice to assure me that what I say is true, if it could ever happen that a thing which I conceived so clearly and distinctly could be false; and accordingly it seems to me that already I can establish as a general rule that all things which I perceive very clearly and very distinctly are true.

At the same time I have before received and admitted many things to be very certain and manifest, which yet I afterwards recognised as being dubious. What then were these things? They were the earth, sky, stars and all other objects which I apprehended by means of the senses. But what did I clearly [and distinctly] perceive in them? Nothing more than that the ideas or thoughts of these things were presented to my mind. And not even now do I deny that these ideas are met with in me. But there was yet another thing which I affirmed, and which, owing to the habit which I had formed of believing it, I thought I perceived very clearly, although in truth I did not perceive it at all, to wit, that there were objects outside of me from which these ideas proceeded, and to which they were entirely similar. And it was in this that I erred, or, if perchance my judgment was correct, this was not due to any knowledge arising from my perception.

But when I took anything very simple and easy in the sphere of arithmetic or geometry into consideration, e.g. that two and three together made five, and other things of the sort, were not these present to my mind so clearly as to enable me to affirm that they were true? Certainly if I judged that since such matters could be doubted, this would not have been so for any other reason than that it came into my mind that perhaps a God might have endowed me with such a nature that I may have been deceived even concerning things which seemed to me most manifest. But every time that this preconceived opinion of the sovereign power of a God presents itself to my thought, I am constrained to confess that it is easy to Him, if He wishes it, to cause me to err, even in matters in which I believe myself to have the best evidence. And, on the other hand, always when I direct my attention to things which I believe myself to perceive very clearly, I am so persuaded of their truth that I let myself break out into words such as these: Let who will deceive me, He can never cause me to be nothing while I think that I am, or some day cause it to be true to say that I have never been, it being true now to say that I am, or that two and three make more or less than five, or any such thing in which I see a manifest contradiction. And, certainly I have no reason to believe that there is a God who is a deceiver, and as I have not yet satisfied myself that there is a God at all, the reason for doubt which depends on this opinion alone is very slight, and so to speak metaphysical. But in order to be able altogether to remove it, I must inquire whether there is a God as soon as the occasion presents itself; and if I find that there is a God, I must also inquire whether He may be a deceiver; for without a knowledge of these two truths I do not see that I can ever be certain of anything. . . .

III

From *Replies**

REASONS WHICH ESTABLISH THE EXISTENCE OF GOD, AND THE DISTINCTION BETWEEN THE MIND AND BODY OF MAN, DISPOSED IN GEOMETRICAL ORDER.

DEFINITIONS

I. By the term *thought* (*cogitatio, pensée*), I comprehend all that is in us, so that we are immediately conscious of it. Thus, all the operations of the will, intellect, imagination, and senses, are thoughts. But I have used the word *immediately* expressly to exclude whatever follows or depends upon our thoughts; for example, voluntary motion has, in truth, thought for its source (principle), but yet it is not itself thought. [Thus, walking is not a thought, but the perception or knowledge we have of our walking is.]

II. By the word *idea* I understand that form of any thought, by the immediate perception of which I am conscious of that same thought; so that I can express nothing in words, when I understand what I say, without making it certain, by this alone, that I possess the idea of the thing that is signified by these words. And thus I give the appellation idea not to the images alone that are depicted in the phantasy; on the contrary, I

---

* From "Reply to the Second Objections," in *The Philosophical Works of Descartes,* translated by John Veitch (Cambridge University Press, 1931). Reprinted by permission of the publishers.

do not here apply this name to them, in so far as they are in the corporeal phantasy, that is to say, in so far as they are depicted in certain parts of the brain, but only in so far as they inform the mind itself, when turned towards that part of the brain.

III. By the *objective reality of an idea* I understand the entity or being of the thing represented by the idea, in so far as this entity is in the idea; and, in the same manner, it may be called either an objective perfection, or objective artifice, etc. (*artificium objectivum*). For all that we conceive to be in the objects of the ideas is objectively [or by representation] in the ideas themselves.

IV. The same things are said to be *formally* in the objects of the ideas when they are in them such as we conceive them; and they are said to be in the objects *eminently* when they are not indeed such as we conceive them, but are so great that they can supply this defect by their excellence.

V. Everything in which there immediately resides, as in a subject, or by which there exists any object we perceive, that is, any property, or quality, or attribute of which we have in us a real idea, is called *substance*. For we have no other idea of substance, accurately taken, except that it is a thing in which exists formally or eminently this property or quality which we perceive, or which is objectively in some one of our ideas, since we are taught by the natural light that nothing can have no real attribute.

VI. The substance in which thought immediately resides is here called *mind (mens, esprit)*. I here speak, however, of *mens* rather than of *anima,* for the latter is equivocal, being frequently applied to denote a corporeal object.

VII. The substance which is the immediate subject of local extension, and of the accidents that presuppose this extension, as figure, situation, local motion, etc., is called *body*. But whether the substance which is called mind be the same with that which is called body, or whether they are two diverse substances, is a question to be hereafter considered.

VIII. The substance which we understand to be supremely perfect, and in which we conceive nothing that involves any defect, or limitation of perfection, is called *God.*

IX. When we say that some attribute is contained in the nature or concept of a thing, this is the same as if we said that the attribute is true of the thing, or that it may be affirmed of the thing itself.

X. Two substances are said to be really distinct, when each of them may exist without the other.

Postulates

1st. I request that my readers consider how feeble are the reasons that have hitherto led them to repose faith in their senses, and how uncertain are all the judgments which they afterwards founded on them; and that they will revolve this consideration in their mind so long and so frequently, that, in fine, they may acquire the habit of no longer trusting so confidently in their senses; for I hold that this is necessary to render one capable of apprehending metaphysical truths.

2d. That they consider their own mind, and all those of its attributes of which they shall find they cannot doubt, though they may have supposed that all they ever received by the senses was entirely false, and that they do not leave off considering it until they have acquired the habit of conceiving it distinctly, and of believing that it is more easy to know than any corporeal object.

3d. That they diligently examine such propositions as are self-evident, which they will find within themselves, as the following:—That the same thing cannot at once be and not be; that nothing cannot be the efficient cause of anything, and the like;—and thus exercise that clearness of understanding that has been given them by nature, but which the perceptions of the senses are wont greatly to disturb and obscure—exercise it, I say, pure and delivered from the objects of sense; for in this way the truth of the following axioms will appear very evident to them.

4th. That they examine the ideas of those natures which contain in them an assemblage of several attributes, such as the nature of the triangle, that of the square, or of some other figure; as also the nature of mind, the nature of body, and above all that of God, or of a being supremely perfect. And I request them to observe that it may with truth be affirmed that all these things are in objects, which we clearly conceive to be contained in them: for example, because that, in the nature of the rectilineal triangle, this property is found contained—viz., that its three angles are equal to two right angles, and that in the nature of body or of an extended thing, divisibility is comprised (for we do not conceive any extended thing so small that we cannot divide it, at least in thought)—it is true that the three angles of a rectilineal triangle are equal to two right angles, and that all body is divisible.

5th. That they dwell much and long on the contemplation of the supremely perfect Being, and, among other things, consider that in the ideas of all other natures, possible existence is indeed contained, but that in the idea of God is contained not only possible but absolutely necessary existence. For, from this alone, and without any reasoning, they will discover that God exists: and it will be no less evident in itself than that two is an equal and three an unequal number, with other truths of this sort. For there are certain truths that are thus manifest to some without proof, which are not comprehended by others without a process of reasoning.

6th. That carefully considering all the examples of clear and distinct perception, and all of obscure and confused, of which I spoke in my Meditations, they accustom themselves to distinguish things that are clearly known from those that are obscure, for this is better learnt by example than by rules; and I think that I have there opened up, or at least in some degree touched upon, all examples of this kind.

7th. That readers adverting to the circumstance that they never discovered any falsity in things which they clearly conceived, and that, on the contrary, they never found, unless by chance, any truth in things which they conceived but obscurely, consider it to be wholly irrational, if, on account only of certain prejudices of the senses, or hypotheses which contain what is unknown, they call in doubt what is clearly and distinctly conceived by the pure understanding; for they will thus readily admit the following axioms to be true and indubitable, though I confess that several of them might have been much better unfolded, and ought rather to have been proposed as theorems than as axioms, if I had desired to be more exact.

AXIOMS OR COMMON NOTIONS

I. Nothing exists of which it cannot be inquired what is the cause of its existing; for this can even be asked respecting God; not that there is need of any cause in order to his existence, but because the very immensity of his nature is the cause or reason why there is no need of any cause of his existence.

II. The present time is not dependent on that which immediately preceded it; for this reason, there is not need of a less cause for conserving a thing than for at first producing it.

III. Any thing or any perfection of a thing actually existent cannot have *nothing*, or a thing non-existent, for the cause of its existence.

IV. All the reality or perfection which is in a thing is found formally or eminently in its first and total cause.

V. Whence it follows likewise, that the objective reality of our ideas requires a cause in which this same reality is contained, not simply objectively, but formally or eminently. And it is to be observed that this axiom must of necessity be admitted, as upon it alone depends the knowledge of all things, whether sensible or insensible. For whence do we know, for example, that the sky exists? Is it because we see it? But this vision does not affect the mind unless in so far as it is an idea, and an idea inhering in the mind itself, and not an image depicted on the phantasy; and, by reason of this idea, we cannot judge that the sky exists unless we suppose that every idea must have a cause of its objective reality which is really existent; and this cause we judge to be the sky itself, and so in the other instances.

VI. There are diverse degrees of reality, that is, of entity [or perfection]: for substance has more reality than accident or mode, and infinite substance than finite; it is for this reason also that there is more objective reality in the idea of substance than in that of accident, and in the idea of infinite than in the idea of finite substance.

VII. The will of a thinking being is carried voluntarily and freely, for that is of the essence of will, but nevertheless infallibly, to the good that is clearly known to it; and, therefore, if it discover any perfections which it does not possess, it will instantly confer them on itself if they are in its power; [for it will perceive that to possess them is a greater good than to want them].

VIII. That which can accomplish the greater or more difficult, can also accomplish the less or the more easy.

IX. It is a greater and more difficult thing to create or conserve a substance than to create or conserve its attributes or properties; but this creation of a thing is not greater or more difficult than its conservation, as has been already said.

X. In the idea or concept of a thing existence is contained, because we are unable to conceive anything unless under the form of a thing which exists; but with this difference that, in the concept of a limited thing, possible or contingent existence is alone contained, and in the concept of a being sovereignly perfect, perfect and necessary existence is comprised.

Proposition I

The existence of God is known from the consideration of his nature alone.

Demonstration

To say that an attribute is contained in the nature or in the concept of a thing, is the same as to say that this attribute is true of this thing, and that it may be affirmed to be in it. (Definition IX.)

But necessary existence is contained in the nature or in the concept of God (by Axiom X).

Hence it may with truth be said that necessary existence is in God, or that God exists.

And this syllogism is the same as that of which I made use in my *producing something beyond our mind,*

if our own ideas are incapable of

reply to the sixth article of these objections; and its conclusion may be
known without proof by those who are free from all prejudice, as has
been said in Postulate V. But because it is not so easy to reach so great
perspicacity of mind, we shall essay to establish the same thing by other
modes.

PROPOSITION II

The existence of God is demonstrated, *a posteriori,* from this
alone, that his idea is in us.

DEMONSTRATION

The objective reality of each of our ideas requires a cause in
which this same reality is contained, not simply objectively, but formally
or eminently (by Axiom V).

But we have in us the idea of God (by Definitions II and VIII), and
of this idea the objective reality is not contained in us, either formally
or eminently (by Axiom VI), nor can it be contained in any other except
in God himself (by Definition VIII).

Therefore this idea of God which is in us demands God for its cause,
and consequently God exists (by Axiom III).

PROPOSITION III

The existence of God is also demonstrated from this, that we
ourselves, who possess the idea of him, exist.

DEMONSTRATION

If I possessed the power of conserving myself, I should likewise have the power of conferring, *a fortiori,* on myself, all the perfections that are awanting to me (by Axioms VIII and IX), for these perfections are only attributes of substance whereas I myself am a substance.

But I have not the power of conferring on myself these perfections,
for otherwise I should already possess them (by Axiom VII).

Hence, I have not the power of self-conservation.

Further, I cannot exist without being conserved, so long as I exist,
either by myself, supposing I possess the power, or by another who has
this power (by Axioms I and II).

But I exist, and yet I have not the power of self-conservation, as I
have recently proved. Hence I am conserved by another.

Further, that by which I am conserved has in itself formally or
eminently all that is in me (by Axiom IV).

But I have in me the perception of many perfections that are awanting to me, and that also of the idea of God (by Definitions II and VIII). Hence the perception of these same perfections is in him by whom I am conserved.

Finally, that same being by whom I am conserved cannot have the perception of any perfections that are awanting to him, that is to say, which he has not in himself formally or eminently (by Axiom VII); for having the power of conserving me, as has been recently said, he should have, *a fortiori*, the power of conferring these perfections on himself, if they were awanting to him (by Axioms VIII and IX).

But he has the perception of all the perfections which I discover to be wanting to me, and which I conceive can be in God alone, as I recently proved:

Hence he has all these in himself, formally or eminently, and thus he is God.

COROLLARY

God has created the sky and the earth and all that is therein contained; and besides this he can make all the things which we clearly conceive in the manner in which we conceive them.

proof of the world

DEMONSTRATION

All these things clearly follow from the preceding proposition. For in it we have proved the existence of God, from its being necessary that some one should exist in whom are contained formally or eminently all the perfections of which there is in us any idea.

But we have in us the idea of a power so great, that by the being alone in whom it resides, the sky and the earth, etc., must have been created, and also that by the same being all the other things which we conceive as possible can be produced.

Hence, in proving the existence of God, we have also proved with it all these things.

PROPOSITION IV

The mind and body are really distinct.

Platonic?

DEMONSTRATION

All that we clearly conceive can be made by God in the manner in which we conceive it (by foregoing Corollary).

But we clearly conceive mind, that is, a substance which thinks, without body, that is to say, without an extended substance (by Postulate II); and, on the other hand, we as clearly conceive body without mind (as every one admits).

Hence, at least, by the omnipotence of God, the mind can exist without the body, and the body without the mind.

Now, substances which can exist independently of each other, are really distinct (by Definition X).

But the mind and the body are substances (by Definitions V, VI, and VII), which can exist independently of each other, as I have recently proved:

Hence the mind and the body are really distinct.

And it must be observed that I have here made use of the omnipotence of God in order to found my proof on it, not that there is need of any extraordinary power in order to separate the mind from the body, but for this reason, that, as I have treated of God only in the foregoing propositions, I could not draw my proof from any other source than from him: and it matters very little by what power two things are separated in order to discover that they are really distinct.

FOUR

Knowledge Is in the Form of Judgments

BERNARD BOSANQUET (1848-1923)

From *The Essentials of Logic**

FROM LECTURE I

Schopenhauer called his great work, *The World as Will and Idea*. Leaving out Will for the moment, let us consider the world "as Idea."

" 'The world is my idea'; this is a truth which holds good for everything that lives and knows, though man alone can bring it into reflective and abstract consciousness. If he really does this, he has attained to philosophical wisdom. It then becomes clear and certain to him that what he knows is not a sun and an earth, but only an eye that sees a sun, a hand that feels an earth; that the world which surrounds him is there only as an idea, *i.e.* only in relation to something else, the consciousness which is himself. If any truth can be asserted *a priori*, it is this; for it is the expression of the most general form of all possible and thinkable experience: a form which is more general than time, space, or causality, for they all pre-suppose it.

*   *   *   *   *   *

"No truth, therefore, is more certain, more independent of all others, and less in need of proof than this, that all that exists for knowledge, and, therefore, this whole world, is only object in relation to subject, perception of a perceiver, in a word, idea. This is obviously true of the past and the future, as well as of the present, of what is farthest off, as of what is near; for it is true of time and space themselves, in which alone these distinctions arise. All that in any way belongs or can belong to the world is inevitably thus conditioned through the subject and exists only for the subject. The world is idea."

The world, then, for each of us, exists in the medium of our mind. It is a sort of building of which the materials are our ideas and perceptions.

*From *The Essentials of Logic* by Bernard Bosanquet (New York, The Macmillan Company, c1895).

So much for "idea." What do we mean by "world"? A succession of images passing before us, or rather making up our consciousness, like a dream, is not a world. The term is very expressive; it is a favourite word in Shakespeare. When the courtier says—

"Hereafter, in a better world than this,
I shall desire more love and knowledge of you,"

he does not mean, as I used to think, "in heaven"; he means in a better condition of social affairs. In "mad world, mad kings, mad composition," the term means more especially the set of political and family connections within which extraordinary reversals of behaviour have just taken place. Often we use the expression, with a qualifying epithet, to indicate some particular sphere of connected action, "the ecclesiastical world," "the political world," and so forth. Always there seems to be implied the notion of a set of things or persons bound together by some common quality which enables them to act upon each other, and to constitute what is technically termed a "whole." *The* "world" *par excellence,* then, ought to mean the one connected set of things and persons which we all recognise and refer to as the same, and as including ourselves along with all who use the word in the same sense.

Then the "world as idea" means no less than this, that the system of things and persons which surrounds all of us, and which each of us speaks of and refers to as the same for every one, exists for each of us as something built up in his own mind—the mind attached to his own body—and out of the material of his own mind.

Let us illustrate this building up by thinking of the world, our surroundings, as an animal must be aware of it. The lowest beginnings of sight, for example, give no colour and no shape. An animal in this stage can, probably, only just take warning if a dark object comes between him and the light. Therefore he cannot have the ordered visual image of space definitely stretching away all round him, which is the primary basis of our idea of a world. He can move, no doubt, but there is nothing to make us suppose that he records and co-ordinates the results of his movements into anything like that permanent order of objects which must be constructed in some way by a human being even though born blind. Succession, we might say, is much more powerful with animals than co-existence; but we should have to guard ourselves against supposing that this was what we mean by succession, that is, a process definitely recognised as in time, with a connection of some reasonable kind between its phases. For the most part with animals out of sight is out of mind; if so, the present is not interpreted, enlarged, and arranged with reference to what is not present in time or space by them as it is by us. And therefore the consciousness of a single system of things, permanent, and distinct from the momentary presentations of the senses, cannot, in all probability, grow up for them. If so, they have no real world, but only a dream world,[1] *i.e.* a world not contrasted with the stream of presentation, nor taken as the common theatre of all actions and events. This difference between the world of an animal and that of a human being is a rough measure of what man does by mental or intellectual construction in making his world.

We have now got the idea of a "world," as a system of things and persons connected together, taken to be the same for oneself at different times and for different minds at the same time, yet existing, for oneself, in the medium of one's individual consciousness.

We see at once that we cannot stop here. We have really got a contradiction. If the parts of our world are connected with each other, they are not merely dependent upon us, that is, upon the changes of our consciousness. And we all take them to be independent of us, in the sense that we do not suppose the presence or absence of our perception to make any difference to the world except by the continuance or cessation of our perception of it or of its parts. This is the state of mind in which we practically live, philosophers and all. I do not really take notice of any difference in mode of existence between the wall in front of me, which I see, and the wall behind me, which I do not see. While you are in this lecture-hall, if you think of your rooms at home, you think of them as they look, that is, as they would look if you were there to see them. How else, indeed, could you think of them? This is practically necessary, and therefore, for practical purposes, true.

But if you take it as a theory, omitting the hypothetical factor, "if I was there to see," you go wrong. You then treat your world as being, outside your consciousness, the same that it is inside your consciousness, without allowing for the withdrawal of your consciousness. You are then on the way to think that the world, *as you see, hear, and feel it,* is outside your mind, and that the sight, hearing, feeling, and the ideas born of them, are inside your mind as a sort of faint and imperfect *copy* of the world which you then call "external," in the sense of outside the mind.

i. The first position was that of common sense. The second is that of common-sense theory. Common sense is quite justified. It says, "Things affect each other, but the mere presence and absence of our perception does not affect them." For practical purposes we must treat them as being, when unapprehended by our minds, just the same as when

[1] The character of the sensory powers, which are strongest in many animals, contributes to this conclusion. Mr. F. H. Bradley is sure that his dog's system of logic, if he had one, would run, "What exists smells; what does not smell is nothing." The sense of smell can scarcely give rise to the idea of a world of objects. It has hardly any capacity of structural discernment.

apprehended by our minds. This is the first idea or rather postulate—for it is not a theoretical idea—of objectivity. Objective = "independent of our consciousness for practical purposes."

ii. In describing the second position as that of common-sense theory I do not refer to the doctrine of any regular school of philosophers. There was a Scotch school of philosophy—the school of Reid in the eighteenth century—commonly called the common-sense school. I will say below how I think this school was related to the position which I am now describing. But my present purpose is to hit off the simple theory of reality which common-sense people make for themselves when they reflect. Now this theory, in which we all live except when we make a special effort, accepts the distinction between things and the mind. For example, it defines truth as the conformity of ideas to objects. That means something of this kind: the ideas are inside our heads, and the objects are outside our heads. If we are to have knowledge, the objects have to be represented inside our heads, and they get in through the senses. And then you have two similar forms of the world, one outside our heads, which is real, and another like it but less perfect and without solidity or causal power, inside our heads, which is ideal or mental. This is what I call the common-sense theory of the Objective. Like common sense, it assumes that there is a world which the withdrawal of our individual consciousness does not affect, but which persists and acts all the same. Unlike common sense, it lays down an assertion as to the nature of this world, viz. that it is, apart from our consciousness, the same as it is for our consciousness. The world in consciousness, it assumes, is subjective, the world out of consciousness is objective, and the former is an imperfect copy of the latter in a feebler material.

The schools of common-sense philosophy, such as are represented by Locke and Reid, are not quite so simple-minded as the reflection of ordinary common sense, because every systematic thinker sees at once that the question stares him in the face, "If the world outside the mind is copied by the world inside the mind, how can we ever know whether the copy conforms to the original?" We are by the hypothesis inside the mind; whatever has passed through the senses is inside the mind. We cannot as at present advised get at anything outside the senses or outside the mind. In face of this question, the common-sense philosophies have two courses open. They may start from the idea of things outside the mind, but admit that in passing through the senses the things are in some partial respects transformed—as for instance, that they acquire colour, sound, and smell in passing through the senses—this is what Locke says. Or again, still starting from the idea of things outside the mind, they may simply assert that perception is of such a nature that it gives us things as they really are. The former was the view of Locke, the latter that of Reid. This latter view obviously might pass into the most extreme idealism, and its interpretation, if it does not so pass, is exceedingly difficult.

But whatever may have been the view of the historical "common-sense school," the common-sense theory which we all make for ourselves involves a separation between the mind and reality. The objective world is the world as independent of mind, and independent of mind means existing and acting outside mind, exactly, or almost exactly, as it seems to exist and act before the mind.

Now this is an absolute *cul-de-sac*. If the objective is that which is outside perception, the objective is out of our reach, and the world of our perception can never be objective. This is the pass to which we are brought by taking common sense as the guide of theory and not as its material.

iii. There is no way out but by retracing our steps, and avoiding a false turn which we took in passing from common sense to common-sense theory. It was quite true that the world is unaffected by the withdrawal of my individual perception and consciousness (except in so far as I acted *qua* bodily thing in the world); but it does not follow from this that *if* it becomes the object of a consciousness in me, it can be so otherwise than as presented within that consciousness. We must distinguish between the idea that the objective is outside consciousness and therefore not in consciousness, and the idea that the objective can be in the individual consciousness, but identified with something beyond the individual consciousness. It may be that consciousness is capable of containing a world, not as a copy of a ready-made original, but as something which it makes for itself by a necessary process, and which refers beyond this finite and momentary consciousness.

According to these ideas, the objective is, shortly stated, whatever we are obliged to think. This, though it is *in* our thought, is not considered merely *as* our thought, or as a train of images or whole of presentation in our minds. That is an artificial point of view, the point of view of psychology, and we must carefully avoid starting from it. But knowledge refers beyond its mental self, and has no limitation in time or in kind except its own necessity. Thus, I am forced to think, by a certain context of ideas and perceptions, that there is now a fire burning in my study at home. This judgment is not barred by the fact that my mind, as a function attached to my body, is here three miles away. The thought is objective for me, so long as I am obliged to think it. My presence in or absence from the room where the fire is burning has no effect on the question, except as it furnishes me with evidence one way or the other. Not only absence in space is no obstacle, but succession in time is no obstacle. My thought, which *is* here and now, refers confidently to what has happened in long intervals of time, if the necessity of consistency obliges it to do so. Thus if I go back to my room and find the fire out and the room very cold, I infer without hesitation to certain acts and events which are needed to explain this state of things. And interpretations or explanations of this kind make up my world, which is for me in my thought, but is presented as more than my thought, and cannot be a world at all unless it is more than in my thought. It is in as far as my thought constructs and presents a world which is more than my momentary psychical state, that my thought, and the world as presented to me in it, is objective. The world is not a set of my ideas, but it is a set of objects and relations of which I frame an idea, and the existence of which has no meaning for me except as presented in the idea which I frame. We are not to think of (i) Ideas, and (ii) Things which they represent; the ideas, taken as parts of a world, *are* the things.

We begin to see, then, how the nature of knowledge meets the puzzle which I stated above. How, I asked, can a connected "world," whose parts act on one another quite independently of my perception, be in my individual mind? I answer that it does not follow, because the world *is for me* only in my presentation, that my presentation is the only thing which goes on in the world. "What I am obliged to think" may represent a real development depending on laws and a system which is not confined to my individual course of consciousness. The "objective" in this sense is for Logic an assumption, or rather a fact to be analysed. We do not attempt to prove its existence, except in the sense of calling attention to its nature in detail. It will be seen that "outside the mind" ceases, on this view of objectivity, to have meaning as regards anything that can be related to us. "Outside" is a relation of bodies to one another; but everything, about which we can so much as ask a question, is so far inside the mind, *i.e.* given in its continuum of presentation or idea.

I will recapitulate the three conceptions of the "objective."

(1) According to practical "common sense" the objective is independent of our consciousness in the sense that the presence or absence of our consciousness makes no difference to the operation of things upon each other.

(2) According to "common-sense theory" the objective is independent of our consciousness in the sense that the presence or absence of our consciousness makes no difference in the mode of being of things (viz. that the world in consciousness approaches objectivity by resembling or reproducing a similar and quite objective world outside consciousness).

(3) According to philosophical theory the objective is independent of our consciousness in the sense that it is what we are constrained to think in order to make our consciousness consistent with itself. "What

we are constrained to think" is not confined, in its *reference,* to our thought, or to thought at all.

Thus, for the purposes of Logic, we must turn our usual ideas upside down. We must try to imagine something of this kind. We have all seen a circular panorama. Each one of us, we must think, is shut up alone inside such a panorama, which is movable and flexible, and follows him wherever he goes. The things and persons depicted in it move and act upon one another; but all this is in the panorama, and not beyond. The individual cannot get outside this encircling scenery, and no one else can get inside it. Apart from it, prior to it, we have no self; it is indeed the stuff of which oneself is made. Is every one's panorama exactly the same? No, they are not exactly the same. They are formed round different centres, each person differing from all the others by individual qualities, and by his position towards the points and processes which determine his picture. For—and here is the remarkable point— every one of us has painted for himself the picture within which he is shut up, and he is perpetually painting and re-painting it, not by copy- ing from some original, but by arranging and completing confused im- ages and tints that are always appearing magically on his canvas. Now this magical panorama, from which the individual cannot escape, and the laws of which are the laws of his experience, is simply his own mind regarded as a content or a world. His own body and mind, regarded as things, are within the panorama, just as other people's bodies and minds are. The whole world, for each of us, *is* our course of consciousness, in so far as this is regarded as a system of objects which we are obliged to think. Not, in so far as it really *is* a system, for an onlooker, say for a psychologist. For no doubt every child's mind, and every animal's mind, *is* a working system of presentations, which a psychologist may study and analyse from without. Consciousness is consciousness of a world only in so far as it *presents* a system, a whole of objects, acting on one another, and therefore independent of the presence or absence of the consciousness which presents them. . . .

Thus, I repeat, the world for each of us is our course of conscious- ness, looked at in that way in which it presents a systematic, organised picture of inter-acting objects, not in that way in which it is a stream of ideas and feelings, taking place in our several heads. In the former point of view it is the world as our idea; in the latter point of view it is simply the consciousness attached to our body. We might soon puzzle ourselves with the contradictions which arise if we fail to distinguish these points of view. In one sense my mind is in my head, in the other sense my head is in my mind. In the one sense I am in space, in the other sense space is in me. Just so, however rough the metaphor, from one point of view the microscope is one among a host of things seen from the outside; from the other point of view all that we see is in the microscope, which is itself not seen at all.

It is in this latter sense that our mental equipment is looked at, when it is regarded as knowledge; and it is in this sense that it forms a panorama which absolutely shuts in every one of us into his own circle of ideas. (It is not implied, we should carefully observe, that his ideas or experience are in any way secondary to his self, or separable from it, or an adjective of it.) Then how does it happen that our separate worlds, the panoramas which we construct, do not contradict one another?

The answer is, that they *correspond*. It is this conception from which we must start in Logic. We must learn to regard our separate worlds of knowledge as something constructed by definite processes, and corresponding to each other in consequence of the common nature of these processes. We know that we begin apart. We begin in fact, though not conscious of our limits, with feelings and fancies and unorganised experiences which give us little or no common ground and power of co-operation with other people. But as the constructive process advances, the correspondence between our worlds is widened and deepened, and the greater proportion of what we are obliged to think is in harmony with what other people are obliged to think. Now of course this would not be so unless reality, the whole actual system in which we find our-selves, were self-consistent. But more than that, it would not be so unless the nature of intelligence were the same in every mind. It is this common nature of intelligence, together with its differentiated adaptations to reality, that we have to deal with in Logic.

Thus the separate worlds, in which we are all shut up, must be considered as corresponding so far as they are objective, that is, so far as they approach what we are ultimately obliged to think. I say "cor-responding," because that is the term which expresses the relation between systems which represent the same thing by the same rules, but with different starting-points. Drawings in perspective of the same build-ing from different points of view are such corresponding systems; the parts represented answer each to each, but the same part is near or large in one drawing, and distant and small in another; not, however, by chance, but as a definite consequence of the same laws. Our separate worlds may be compared to such drawings: the things in them are iden-tified by their relations and functions, so that we can understand each other, *i.e.* make identical references, though my drawing be taken from the east, and yours from the west. The things do not look quite the same in our different worlds; besides being taken from different standpoints, both drawings are imperfect and incorrect. But so long as we can make out the correspondence, we have a basis for co-operation and for discussion. Logic shows us the principles and processes by which, under the given influences, these drawings are constructed. . . .

FROM LECTURE II

Therefore we say, coming closer to our subject, that *"Knowledge is the medium in which our world, as an interrelated whole, exists for us."* This is more than saying that it exists in mind or presentation, because the mere course of consciousness need not amount to Knowledge. A world, that is, a system of things acting on one another, could not exist merely in the course of our ideas. But *Knowledge,* we said, is the mental construction of reality. It consists of what we are obliged to assert in thought, and because we are all obliged to think assertorily according to the same methods, the results of our thinking form corresponding systems—systems that correspond alike to each other and to reality. (I may be asked, does not this agreement of our knowledge depend on the agreement of the physical stimuli supplied to us by nature, as well as on the homogeneousness of our intelligences? The answer is, that these stimuli, or nature, have no priority in Knowledge. Their identity is merely a case or consequence of the identity of our experience as a whole. We are regarding nature as a system developed in experience, not as an unknown somewhat behind it. To suppose that solid or extended existence somehow comes before and accounts for everything else, is a form of the common-sense theory we have dismissed. Knowledge and Truth have their limitations as forms of Reality, but an appeal to solidity or extension will not furnish the required supplementation.)

All that we have been saying about Knowledge is summed up in the sentence, "Knowledge is a judgment, an affirmation." We need not trouble ourselves yet about negation. We all know what affirmative assertion is and it is near enough for the present to say that all knowledge is judgment in the sense of affirmative assertion.

I will explain how we sum up all we have said of knowledge by calling it a judgment.

Judgment or affirmation always implies three properties, though they are not always recognised.

It is (a) necessary, (b) universal, and (γ) constructive.

(a) Judgment is necessary. In saying this, we express all that we said about the objectivity of the world in knowledge. "Objective" meant, we concluded, what we are obliged to think. And judgment is necessary, because it expresses what we are obliged to think; obliged, that is, not as we are obliged to feel pain, as an unexplained and isolated fact, but obliged by a necessity operative within the movement of our consciousness, though not, of course, theoretically recognised as necessity in common thinking. Thus, in the simplest phases of Judgment, necessity does begin to approach the kind of necessity by which we feel pain or are visited by persistent irrational associations.

We can trace an explicit sense of necessity in any scientific matter, or in any doubtful and complex matters in which we are aware of our own reflections. We constantly hear and read such phrases as, "I am unable to resist the conclusion"; "I am forced to believe"; "I am driven to think"; "I have no alternative but to suppose." These are every-day phrases in controversy and in theoretical discussion. And what they all mean is just what was insisted on in the last lecture; the objective or real for us is what we are obliged to think. Given our perceptive state and our mental equipment, the judgment follows.

In trivial or simple judgments this necessity is harder to observe within consciousness, and approaches more and more to the mere constraint exercised upon us by physical reality. In a judgment of mere sensuous comparison, such as a "colour-match," the necessity is not that of an intellectual system, but almost that of a feeling which we cannot dispel. The chief intellectual labour is here negative, and consists in precautions to remove all disturbing influences, both mental and material, so as to let the perception operate freely on the mind. But yet here *is* necessity; we never for a moment think that we can modify the result; our aim is simply to distinguish from all others the particular strand of necessity by which we desire to be guided.

It is easy for an observer to detect intellectual necessity in judgment, even where the judging subject is wholly unreflective. If you contradict an obvious judgment made by an uneducated man, we will no doubt be quite unable to point out the intellectual necessity which constrains him to it, *i.e.* to argue in support of it; but he will be bewildered and probably indignant, which shows that, unknown to himself, his whole intellectual existence is really impeached by impeachment of a necessary conclusion from it. Many people cannot see the difference between impeaching their argument and impeaching their veracity; and this confusion arises, I presume, from a just feeling that their whole mind is on its trial in the one case as in the other, although they do not distinguish between the forms of its action which are concerned. We are told, indeed, in formal logic, that ordinary statements of fact do not claim necessity; but this merely arises from confining necessity to explicit necessity expressed in a special grammatical form.

But, it may be objected, we do not always feel that every trivial judgment emanates from and so implicates our whole mental constitution and equipment. If I say to a friend, "I saw you at Charing Cross yesterday," and he says, "No, you could not, for I was out of town," then, unless I was very certain indeed, I should admit having made a mistake, and think no more about the matter. That only means, (1) that the unity of the mind is not thoroughly complete—there are many more or less detached systems in the mind, and one of them may not be very deeply inwrought in the whole intellectual frame; and (2) the necessity of thought may itself modify the certainty of the fact, *e.g.* I know that a mistake of identity is quite a common thing, and this knowledge cooperates with my friend's denial.

But in any perceptive judgment, however unimportant its immediate content, if it is clear and persistent, a contradiction is a most serious thing. There is a well-known form of bewilderment connected with the judgment of direction; if you forget or do not know of a turn that you have taken, and come out, for example, on familiar ground from the North when you think you are coming on it from the South, so that objects have the reverse position of what you expected, then, supposing that you cannot explain the contradiction, the result is sometimes a very grave perplexity; some men are quite unhinged by it for the moment, and a psychologist in France [1] has given it a new name, "Vertigo of Direction." This again shows how your whole intellectual nature is staked upon the most trifling perception, and if you seem to be forced to a flat contradiction even in the simplest judgment you are almost "beside yourself."

(b) Judgment is universal. There are different senses of "universal" as of "necessary." We are now speaking only in the widest sense, in which universality is a property of all judgment whatever. If we assume that all our intellectual natures are the same, then to be universal is a mere consequence of being necessary. I not only feel that my judgment is inevitable for me, but I never think of doubting that, given the same materials, it is obligatory for every other intelligent being. If some one disagrees with a judgment of mine, I try to put the case before him as it is in my mind. And I am absolutely sure that if I could do so, he would be obliged to judge as I do. If it were not so, we should never think of arguing. We should simply say, "Perhaps his mind is differently constituted from mine," as, in fact, with reference to special sets of dominant ideas, and to special provinces of experience, we often do say. But these we regard as hindrances, imperfections, accidents. We do not doubt that the system of reason is active in him as in us.

And thus, as reason is essentially a system, the universality of judgment involves something more. We not only think that our judgment is

---

[1] M. Binet. See *Mind*, x. 156.

obligatory upon every one else, in as far as they have the same materials, but we think that it must be *consistent with* the judgments of all other persons, just as much as with our own. If it is inconsistent with any other judgment, we think that one of the two must be wrong; that is, we will not admit the possibility that the real world, as others construct it, is out of harmony with the real world as we construct it.

Thus, knowledge, being judgment, is necessary and universal, and in the widest sense this is true of all judgments.

(γ) These are two properties of the Judgment, but they do not tell us what it is. We shall of course examine its nature more fully in the later lectures. At present we need only think of it as affirmation. This may be simply described as "pronouncing the interpretation of our perceptions to form one system with the data of our perceptions." We may at once admit the distinction between *data* and interpretation to be only relative. Its relativity is the consequence of the constructed or so to speak artificial character of our real world. We can get at no data unqualified by judgment.

We may take as an example our perception of things in space. How much of what we see is given in present sense-perception? This is a question to which there is no definite answer. We do not know what the presentations of vision were like before we had learnt to see as a fully conscious human being sees. We have no right to assume, that after we have learned to see in this way the actual sense-presentation remains the same as it was in a different stage of our visual education. We can give no precise meaning in the way of a time-limit to the *presentness* of perception. But we know this much, that it takes a long time and many kinds of experience to learn to see as an educated human being sees, and that this acquired capacity is never at a stand-still, but is always being extended or diminished according to the vitality, growth, or atrophy of our apperceptive masses. There is always a certain element of amplification or interpretation, which by experience or attentive introspection we can eliminate from the data apparently forced upon us by reality, although these data themselves are modified through and through both by habitual interpretation, and by the very defining attention which aims at eliminating all amplification from them.

But yet the whole of sense-perception has a peculiar quality in being *present*. Artificial though it is, it yet, relatively speaking, contains an irreducible datum. It is distinguishable from everything which is not present. It is pervaded by something which we cannot reduce to intellectual relation, though if we withdrew from it all that is relation, the apparent datum would be gone.

Now Knowledge is the affirmation or judgment which identifies the constructive interpretation of our present perception with the reality which present perception forces upon us. This is clear enough to begin with, but will have to be modified below to suit the more circuitous or mediate types of Judgment.

I take two examples, one from sight and one from sound.

Here is a table. In common language we should all say, "We see that is a table." The expression is quite correct, because human seeing is a judgment. But yet, if you were asked to reduce your perception to terms of sight pure and simple—I mean of visual sensation—why, unless you were an analytic psychologist or a very skilful artist, you would not be able to do it. To speak of one point only, you would have to eliminate the attribute of depth and distance. That is all, so far as mere vision is concerned, your theory and your interpretation. The problem for an artist is to get back, at his high plane of perceptive power, to what in theory would be the lower plane. He has to re-translate his perception of a thing in space into a flat coloured surface. The difference between his flat picture and a real object in space is a rough measure of the difference made by interpretation or implication in the datum of sense-perception when we say, judging by sight only, "That is a table." All the experiences of touch and motion, from which we have learned to perceive the solidity of the object, are, theoretically speaking, put into the judgment by us. They are not given by the eye alone, although we cannot now separate them from that which is given by the eye alone. For the artist's flat picture, which I used as an illustration, is not a stage in our visual education. Our visual education has proceeded *pari passu* with our education by touch and motion; and we saw objects in space as solids, long before we reflected that for the eye alone a coloured surface would naturally appear as flat.[2]

But this impossibility of getting at an original datum only shows how entirely we are right in saying that our world is constructed by judgment. For the process of interpretative amplification passes quite continuously from the unconscious to the conscious; and every definitely expressed judgment, though perfectly homogeneous with the processes which have qualified its datum, and though it may fall wholly within the maximum of what in ordinary parlance we should call a simple given perception, contains an identification of some ideal element, enlargement, or interpretation, with that relatively given element which reveals itself through a peculiar quality of presentness pervading the "given" perception.

In the example "That is a table," the unity of judgment is so well shown that the identification becomes almost unreal. In fact, we never judge except to satisfy an interest, and so simple a judgment used as an

[2] The view that depth is a visual datum in the same sense as breadth seems to me in flagrant contradiction with experience. But for our present purpose the question is only one of degree, as no one maintains that either depth or breadth are seen without education as an adult sees them.

example, apart from any context which could explain the need for it, has an air of unreality. You may hear a child make such a judgment constantly in the sheer pleasure of recognition. An adult would never make it explicitly unless in some particular context; but it is made, as I shall maintain below, by the mere glance of his eye which takes in the table as a real object in a real world of space. Its appearance to the eye is in this case the datum, while the interpretation consists in construing this appearance as a solid individual existence in space.

We will look at an example in which the discrimination of elements is easier. Take the affirmation, "That is a cab," assuming it to be made from merely hearing a sound. In this we can much more nearly separate the datum or minimum of sense from our enlargement or interpretation of it, and we know that our interpretation is liable to be wrong; that is to say, the reality into which we ought to construe the sound may be some other kind of vehicle, and not a cab. Now compare this with the affirmation, "That (which I see) is a cab." This judgment of sight-perception, though its terms are more inextricably interwoven, has just the same elements in it as the judgment of sound-perception, "That (which I hear) is a cab." In the sound-perception the structure is quite plain. A particular complex quality in the sound suggests as its objective explanation, what is perfectly distinguishable from it in thought, the movement of a cab on a particular kind of pavement. The quality of the sound, its roughness, loudness, increase and decrease, all form points of connection with the sound of a cab as we know it, and with the speed, weight, etc. of such a vehicle. But it is quite easy to consider the sound in itself apart from its interpretation, and we sometimes feel the interpretation to be more immediate, and sometimes more inferential. We sometimes say, "I hear a cab," just as we say, "I see one," but in case of sound we more often perhaps say, "That sounds like—" such and such a thing, which indicates a doubt, and the beginning of conscious inference.

Thus we see how continuous is the mental construction of reality. From our unreflective education in seeing, hearing, and touching, to the explicit judgment of the trained observer, which in its turn passes readily into inference, there is no definite break. Once the idea of reality, or of a world, is applied in practice (I do not say reflectively grasped), there is no further difficulty in principle throughout the whole process of its construction.

We may then sum up so far: our knowledge, or our world in knowledge, exists for us as a judgment, that is, as an affirmation in which our present perception is amplified by an ideal interpretation which is identified with it. This interpretation or enlargement claims necessity or universality, and is therefore objective as our world, *i.e.* is what we are *obliged* to think, and what we are *all* obliged to think. The whole system in process of construction, viz. our present perception as extended by interpretation, is what we mean by reality, only with a reservation in favour of forms of experience which are not intellectual at all. Every judgment then affirms something to be real, and therefore affirms reality to be defined, in part, by that something. Knowledge exists in the form of affirmations about reality. And our world as existing for us in the medium of knowledge consists, for us, of a standing affirmation about reality.

This standing affirmation about reality may be described in other words as "the continuous affirmative judgment of the waking consciousness." In the common logic-books you will find judgment treated only as the "proposition," that is, as an assertion made in language. That is a very convenient way of treating the judgment, and is not false, if you remember that the proposition, that is, the assertory sentence, is rather a translation of the judgment than the judgment itself. But the judgment expressed in a proposition is always some one definite assertion, with a limited subject and predicate. We shall speak of the judgment in this sense—the usual sense—later. But to-day I want to describe the judgment in a more extended sense, that is, as co-extensive with the waking human consciousness, so far as aware of a world.

If judgment consists in the extension of our perceptions by an interpretation considered as equally real with their content, it clearly is not confined to the particular facts and truths which from time to time we utter in language. And more than this, everything that we do definitely utter, implies a great deal which is not definitely uttered. If I say, "I have to catch the train at Sloane Square to go down to Essex Hall," I only mention the reality of one train, one square, and one building. But my assertion shades off into innumerable facts, the equal reality of which as elements in my world is necessary to make this judgment intelligible and true. It implies the real existence of the underground railway, which implies that of London, and therefore that of the surface of our globe in a certain definite order, and of the civilised world. It implies the reality of this building and of the meetings which we hold in it, of the University Extension system, and of my own life and habits as enabling me to take part in the work of that system. Only a part of this is in the focus of my attention as I judge; but the whole is a continuous context, the parts of which are inseparable; and although I do not affirm the whole of it in so many words, when I say that I am coming down here by train this evening, yet if any part of it was not affirmed the rest would, so to speak, fall to pieces, i.e. would lose relations in the absence of which its meaning would be destroyed. Other detached parts of one's life and knowledge may seem to be separable from the content of such a judgment; but on looking closely we see that this is not the case. So long as we are awake, our whole world is conceived as real, and forms for us a single immense affirmation, which hangs from present perception, and shares its constraining power. My present perception is the illuminated spot, and shades off gradually into the rest which forms the background, receiving from this background its organised systematic individuality, while impressing upon it a relation to its own sensuous presentness. We have only to reflect, in order to illustrate this connection, on the way in which the idea of London forms a determining background for the present perception of this room, while on the other hand it is perceived by us as real in our presentation of this room.

And indeed the simplest example of what I am pointing out is the arrangement of objects and places in space. The visual picture which each of us forms of this room is certainly an affirmative judgment. It is a judgment because it consists of ideas affirmed as true of reality. As we look round, all the distances of the objects and the walls from each other, and their shapes and position, seem to be imprinted on our minds without an effort. But really they are conclusions from long education in the art of seeing and from the experience of the other senses. They are an enlargement or interpretation of sense-perception, taken as real, *i.e.* as forming a system which is one with the content of sense-perception, and touches us through sense-perception, and therefore they exist for us in the form of Judgment. And, as I described before, our whole world, both of things in space and of our own history and circumstances, is also affirmed as the background implied in this picture. That is to say, it is all connected together, it is all taken as equally real, and it is all vouched for by its connection with what is given to us in perception. What do we mean by saying that the Antipodes are real, and implied in my perception of this room? We mean that they are an element, necessary to educated thought, in the same system with which I am in contact at this moment by sight, touch, and hearing, the system of reality. And though I may not have explicitly thought of them since entering the room till now, yet, if they were no part of my affirmed system of ideas, my perception of anything in space would be quite different from what it is.

This sense of necessary connection is confined, I think, to our *waking* consciousness. Of course there are degrees between waking and dreaming; but I should be inclined to set up the presence or absence of judgment as a very fair test of those degrees. We say that a man is *awake* in as far as he is aware (i.) of a reality which is not his mere course of consciousness, and (ii.) of the same reality of which other people are aware; *i.e.* in as far as he identifies his present perception with a reality, and that the real reality. It is said that surprise, *i.e.* the sense of conflict between expectation and the reality, is absent in dreams, and in a very remarkable passage Æschylus identifies the life of the savage in his (imaginary) primitive state with a dream-life, considered as a life of sensuous presentation, in which the interpretative judgment of perception was absent. With extraordinary profoundness, in portraying this all but animal existence, he strikes out all those relations to the objective world by which man forms for himself a system that goes beyond the present, so as to leave the stream of presentation without any background of organised reality.[3]

It may be asked, "Why should not a man form for himself a system which interprets his own perception, but is discrepant from the system of every one else? Should we in that case count him as awake?" Yes, he would be awake, but he would be mad. Suppose, being a common man, he interprets all his perceptions into a system which makes him out to be King of England; in such a case he cannot be set down as dreaming, because he is alleging a connection which goes beyond his present perception, and has, ostensibly, been propounded as an interpretation of it into a systematic order of things. He has in short *a* world, but he has broken away from *the* world, and therefore we pronounce him mad. A completely new vision of life may cause a man to be thought mad.

The whole world, then, of our waking consciousness may be treated as a single connected predicate affirmed as an enlargement of present perception. All that we take to be real is by the mere fact of being so taken, brought within an affirmative judgment.

---

[3] I quote from Mrs. Browning's Translation of the *Prometheus Bound,* which seems close enough for the present purpose.

> "And let me tell you, not as taunting men,
> But teaching you the intention of my gifts,
> How first, *beholding, they beheld in vain,*
> *And hearing, heard not,* but, *like shapes in dreams,*
> Mixed all things wildly down the tedious time,
> Nor knew to build a house against the sun
> With wicketed sides, nor any woodwork knew,
> But lived, like silly ants, beneath the ground,
> In hollow caves unsunned. There came to them
> No steadfast sign of winter, nor of spring
> Flower-perfumed, nor of summer full of fruit,
> But blindly and lawlessly they did all things,
> Until I taught them how the stars do rise
> And set in mystery, and devised for them
> Number, the inducer of philosophies,
> The synthesis of letters, and besides,
> The artificer of all things, Memory,
> That sweet muse-mother."—Pr., v. 445, ft.

The expression "seeing saw not, and hearing heard not" appears to suggest the contrast of presentation and objective perception.

FIVE

Knowledge, Error, and Probable Opinion

BERTRAND RUSSELL (1872-   )

From *The Problems of Philosophy**

The question as to what we mean by truth and falsehood, which we considered in the preceeding chapter, is of much less interest than the question as to how we can know what is true and what is false. This question will occupy us in the present chapter. There can be no doubt that *some* of our beliefs are erroneous; thus we are led to inquire what certainty we can ever have that such and such a belief is not erroneous. In other words, can we ever *know* anything at all, or do we merely sometimes by good luck believe what is true? Before we can attack this question, we must, however, first decide what we mean by 'knowing,' and this question is not so easy as might be supposed.

At first sight we might imagine that knowledge could be defined as 'true belief.' When what we believe is true, it might be supposed that we had achieved a knowledge of what we believe. But this would not accord with the way in which the word is commonly used. To take a very trivial instance: If a man believes that the late Prime Minister's name began with a B, he believes what is true, since the late Prime Minister was Sir Henry Campbell Bannerman. But if he believes that Mr. Balfour was the late Prime Minister, he will still believe that the late Prime Minister's last name began with a B, yet this belief, though true, would not be thought to constitute knowledge. If a newspaper, by an intelligent anticipation, announces the result of a battle before any telegram giving the result has been received, it may by good fortune announce what afterwards turns out to be the right result, and it may produce belief in some of its less experienced readers. But in spite of the truth of their belief, they cannot be said to have knowledge. Thus it is clear that a true belief is not knowledge when it is deduced from a false belief.

In like manner, a true belief cannot be called knowledge when it is

* From *The Problems of Philosophy* by Bertrand Russell (London, Oxford University Press, c1912). Reprinted by permission of the publishers.

deduced by a fallacious process of reasoning, even if the premisses from which it is deduced are true. If I know that all Greeks are men and that Socrates was a man, and I infer that Socrates was a Greek, I cannot be said to *know* that Socrates was a Greek, because, although my premisses and my conclusion are true, the conclusion does not follow from the premisses.

But are we to say that nothing is knowledge except what is validly deduced from true premisses? Obviously we cannot say this. Such a definition is at once too wide and too narrow. In the first place, it is too wide, because it is not enough that our premisses should be *true,* they must also be *known.* The man who believes that Mr. Balfour was the late Prime Minister may proceed to draw valid deductions from the true premiss that the late Prime Minister's name began with a B, but he cannot be said to *know* the conclusions reached by these deductions. Thus we shall have to amend our definition by saying that knowledge is what is validly deduced from *known* premisses. This, however, is a circular definition: it assumes that we already know what is meant by 'known premisses.' It can, therefore, at best define one sort of knowledge, the sort we call derivative, as opposed to intuitive knowledge. We may say: '*Derivative* knowledge is what is validly deduced from premisses known intuitively.' In this statement there is no formal defect, but it leaves the definition of *intuitive* knowledge still to seek.

Leaving on one side, for the moment, the question of intuitive knowledge, let us consider the above suggested definition of derivative knowledge. The chief objection to it is that it unduly limits knowledge. It constantly happens that people entertain a true belief, which has grown up in them because of some piece of intuitive knowledge from which it is capable of being validly inferred, but from which it has not, as a matter of fact, been inferred by any logical process.

Take, for example, the beliefs produced by reading. If the newspapers announce the death of the King, we are fairly well justified in believing that the King is dead, since this is the sort of announcement which would not be made if it were false. And we are quite amply justified in believing that the newspaper asserts that the King is dead. But here the intuitive knowledge upon which our belief is based is knowledge of the existence of sense-data derived from looking at the print which gives the news. This knowledge scarcely rises into consciousness, except in a person who cannot read easily. A child may be aware of the shapes of the letters, and pass gradually and painfully to a realization of their meaning. But anybody accustomed to reading passes at once to what the letters mean, and is not aware, except on reflection, that he has derived this knowledge from the sense-data called seeing the printed letters. Thus although a valid inference from the letters to their meaning is possible, and *could* be performed by the reader, it is not in fact performed, since he does not in fact perform any operation which can be called logical inference. Yet it would be absurd to say that the reader does not *know* that the newspaper announces the King's death.

We must, therefore, admit as derivative knowledge whatever is the result of intuitive knowledge even if by mere association, provided there *is* a valid logical connexion, and the person in question could become aware of this connexion by reflection. There are in fact many ways, besides logical inference, by which we pass from one belief to another: the passage from the print to its meaning illustrates these ways. These ways may be called 'psychological inference.' We shall, then, admit such psychological inference as a means of obtaining derivative knowledge, provided there is a discoverable logical inference which runs parallel to the psychological inference. This renders our definition of derivative knowledge less precise than we could wish, since the word 'discoverable' is vague: it does not tell us how much reflection may be needed in order to make the discovery. But in fact 'knowledge' is not a precise conception: it merges into 'probable opinion,' as we shall see more fully in the course of the present chapter. A very precise definition, therefore, should not be sought, since any such definition must be more or less misleading.

The chief difficulty in regard to knowledge, however, does not arise over derivative knowledge, but over intuitive knowledge. So long as we are dealing with derivative knowledge, we have the test of intuitive knowledge to fall back upon. But in regard to intuitive beliefs, it is by no means easy to discover any criterion by which to distinguish some as true and others as erroneous. In this question it is scarcely possible to reach any very precise result: all our knowledge of truths is infected with *some* degree of doubt, and a theory which ignored this fact would be plainly wrong. Something may be done, however, to mitigate the difficulties of the question.

Our theory of truth, to begin with, supplies the possibility of distinguishing certain truths as self-evident in a sense which ensures infallibility. When a belief is true, we said, there is a corresponding fact, in which the several objects of the belief form a single complex. The belief is said to constitute *knowledge* of this fact, provided it fulfils those further somewhat vague conditions which we have been considering in the present chapter. But in regard to any fact, besides the knowledge constituted by belief, we may also have the kind of knowledge constituted by *perception* (taking this word in its widest possible sense). For example, if you know the hour of the sunset, you can at that hour know the fact that the sun is setting: this is knowledge of the fact by way of knowledge of *truths;* but you can also, if the weather is fine, look to the west and actually see the setting sun: you then know the same fact by the way of knowledge of *things.*

Thus in regard to any complex fact, there are, theoretically, two ways in which it may be known: (1) by means of a judgment, in which its several parts are judged to be related as they are in fact related: (2) by means of *acquaintance* with the complex fact itself, which may (in a large sense) be called perception, though it is by no means confined to objects of the senses. Now it will be observed that the second way of knowing a complex fact, the way of acquaintance, is only possible when there really is such a fact, while the first way, like all judgement, is liable to error. The second way gives us the complex whole, and is therefore only possible when its parts do actually have that relation which makes them combine to form such a complex. The first way, on the contrary, gives us the parts and the relation severally, and demands only the reality of the parts and the relation: the relation may not relate those parts in that way, and yet the judgement may occur.

It will be remembered that at the end of Chapter XI we suggested that there might be two kinds of self-evidence, one giving an absolute guarantee of truth, the other only a partial guarantee. These two kinds can now be distinguished.

We may say that a truth is self-evident in the first and most absolute sense, when we have acquaintance with the fact which corresponds to the truth. When Othello believes that Desdemona loves Cassio, the corresponding fact, if his belief were true, would be 'Desdemona's love for Cassio.' This would be a fact with which no one could have acquaintance except Desdemona; hence in the sense of self-evidence that we are considering, the truth that Desdemona loves Cassio (if it were a truth) could only be self-evident to Desdemona. All mental facts, and all facts concerning sense-data, have this same privacy: there is only one person to whom they can be self-evident in our present sense, since there is only one person who can be acquainted with the mental things or the sense-data concerned. Thus no fact about any particular existing thing can be self-evident to more than one person. On the other hand, facts about universals do not have this privacy. Many minds may be acquainted with the same universals; hence a relation between universals may be known by acquaintance to many different people. In all cases where we know by acquaintance a complex fact consisting of certain terms in a certain relation, we say that the truth that these terms are so related has the first or absolute kind of self-evidence, and in these cases the judgement that the terms are so related *must* be true. Thus this sort of self-evidence is an absolute guarantee of truth.

But although this sort of self-evidence is an absolute guarantee of truth, it does not enable us to be *absolutely* certain, in the case of any given judgement, that the judgement in question is true. Suppose we first perceive the sun shining, which is a complex fact, and thence proceed to make the judgement 'the sun is shining.' In passing from the per-

ception to the judgement, it is necessary to analyse the given complex
fact: we have to separate out 'the sun' and 'shining' as constituents of
the fact. In this process it is possible to commit an error; hence even
where a *fact* has the first or absolute kind of self-evidence, a judgement
believed to correspond to the fact is not absolutely infallible, because
it may not really correspond to the fact. But if it does correspond (in
the sense explained in the preceding chapter), then it *must* be true.

The second sort of self-evidence will be that which belongs to judgements in the first instance, and is not derived from direct perception of a
fact as a single complex whole. This second kind of self-evidence will
have degrees, from the very highest degree down to a bare inclination in
favour of the belief. Take, for example, the case of a horse trotting
away from us along a hard road. At first our certainty that we hear the
hoofs is complete; gradually, if we listen intently, there comes a moment
when we think perhaps it was imagination or the blind upstairs or our
own heartbeats; at last we become doubtful whether there was any
noise at all; then we *think* we no longer hear anything, and at last we
know we no longer hear anything. In this process, there is a continual
gradation of self-evidence from the highest degree to the least, not in
the sense-data themselves, but in the judgements based on them.

Or again: Suppose we are comparing two shades of colour, one blue
and one green. We can be quite sure they are different shades of colour;
but if the green colour is gradually altered to be more and more like
the blue, becoming first a blue-green, then a greeny-blue, then blue,
there will come a moment when we are doubtful whether we can see
any difference, and then a moment when we know that we cannot see
any difference. The same thing happens in tuning a musical instrument,
or in any other case where there is a continuous gradation. Thus self-
evidence of this sort is a matter of degree; and it seems plain that the
higher degrees are more to be trusted than the lower degrees.

In derivative knowledge our ultimate premisses must have some
degree of self-evidence, and so must their connexion with the conclusions deduced from them. Take for example a piece of reasoning in
geometry. It is not enough that the axioms from which we start should
be self-evident: it is necessary also that, at each step in the reasoning,
the connexion of premiss and conclusion should be self-evident. In
difficult reasoning, this connexion has often only a very small degree of
self-evidence; hence errors of reasoning are not improbable where the
difficulty is great.

From what has been said it is evident that, both as regards intuitive
knowledge and as regards derivative knowledge, if we assume that intuitive knowledge is trustworthy in proportion to the degree of its self-
evidence, there will be a gradation in trustworthiness, from the existence
of noteworthy sense-data and the simpler truths of logic and arithmetic,

which may be taken as quite certain, down to judgements which seem only just more probable than their opposites. What we firmly believe, if it is true, is called *knowledge*, provided it is either intuitive or inferred (logically or psychologically) from intuitive knowledge from which it follows logically. What we firmly believe, if it is not true, is called error. What we firmly believe, if it is neither knowledge nor error, and also what we believe hesitatingly, because it is, or is derived from, something which has not the highest degree of self-evidence, may be called probable opinion. Thus the greater part of what would commonly pass as knowledge is more or less probable opinion.

In regard to probable opinion, we can derive great assistance from *coherence*, which we rejected as the *definition* of truth, but may often use as a *criterion*. A body of individually probable opinions, if they are mutually coherent, become more probable than any one of them would be individually. It is in this way that many scientific hypotheses acquire their probability. They fit into a coherent system of probable opinions, and thus become more probable than they would be in isolation. The same thing applies to general philosophical hypotheses. Often in a single case such hypotheses may seem highly doubtful, while yet, when we consider the order and coherence which they introduce into a mass of probable opinion, they become pretty nearly certain. This applies, in particular, to such matters as the distinction between dreams and waking life. If our dreams, night after night, were as coherent one with another as our days, we should hardly know whether to believe the dreams or the waking life. As it is, the test of coherence condemns the dreams and confirms the waking life. But this test, though it increases probability where it is successful, never gives absolute certainty, unless there is certainty already at some point in the coherent system. Thus the mere organization of probable opinion will never, by itself, transform it into indubitable knowledge.

SIX

Descartes

H. A. PRICHARD (1871-1947)

From *Knowledge and Perception**

At the beginning of Meditation II Descartes considers that as the result of the process reached in Meditation I, he has reached the stage of believing all his previous beliefs about the world false, or, rather, uncertain.

He then asks: 'Though I am thus believing the existence of everything in the world uncertain, do I not at least know that of something else, viz. some being who caused my belief in physical things?'

To this he answers, rather artificially, 'No, because I myself may have caused this belief'.

And then he finds in his own existence a limit to what he can doubt. 'In being persuaded that there was nothing in the world, was I not also persuaded that *I* did not exist. Far from it; I without doubt existed, since I was thus persuaded. The proposition "I am, I exist", is necessarily true every time I state or conceive it.' And here, though he does not say so, he is implying that along with being certain of his own existence, he is also certain that in this state of certainty no being *can* be deceiving him. For he is stating his certainty that his thought that he exists is necessarily true, and to say this is to imply that this thought cannot have been due to a deceiver.

Descartes continues thus:

Though assured *that* I am, I am not sufficiently assured of *what* I am. Before I began to doubt I thought I was a being possessed of a body and that I walked and thought and that these actions belonged to the soul. But though I thought I knew what a body was I did not stay to consider what a soul was, or, if I did, I imagined it was a rare and subtle wind or ether spread through my body.

But now I *cannot* say that I possess the attributes of a body (extension, tangibility, visibility, &c.)—since I think that there are no bodies. And I cannot say that I walk; for walking implies a body. But thinking, i.e. really being conscious, is another matter. This does belong to me, for if I cease to think I cease to be.

* From H. A. Prichard, *Knowledge and Perception;* by permission of the Clarendon Press, Oxford.

And, a little later, he explains that a thinking being is a thing which doubts, understands, affirms, denies, wills, imagines, and perceives; and he urges that imagining and perceiving are still real, even though nothing which I imagine is true and no reality corresponds to my perceiving.

The net result, then, is that Descartes represents the process of trying to doubt as ending in a state in which he is certain of his own existence as a thinking being, and uncertain of the existence of everything else whatever.

To consider this view fully would be to anticipate much that is better considered later.

But certain comments are appropriate at once.

1. Even on Descartes's own showing, the process he describes does not succeed in conforming to his own plan for it. Since it is Descartes's object to scrutinize the truth of all his existing convictions, it must be part of his plan in carrying out the scrutiny not to make use of either these convictions or any others like them, which equally need scrutiny, i.e. we must not accept as true at any stage any thought which we can doubt.

But in what he represents as the execution of his plan he neither does nor can avoid using such a conviction at every stage. And the reason is simple. A doubt requires a positive ground or basis: or, more fully, it is only possible to doubt one thing, if we are *convinced of* or, more accurately, *think without question* something else. Thus if I come to doubt whether the noise I heard was due to a car, as I at first thought without doubting, it is only because I am thinking without question that such a noise can be caused by something other than a car, say, an aeroplane.

And Descartes, each time he introduces a new doubt, has, in order to do so, to introduce a new thought or conviction. Thus to represent himself as doubting whether any of his thoughts based on perception were true, he has to represent himself as thinking without question that certain of these past thoughts were false. Again, to take one more instance, to represent himself as doubting whether he is awake, he has to represent himself as thinking without doubt that dreaming is not distinguished from waking by any difference of character. But he has no business to use such a thought or conviction, and he need only have reflected, to have doubted the truth of the thought and therefore to have removed the thought, and therefore also the doubt to which it gave rise. The whole process which he says he has conducted is self-destructive in the sense that when faithfully carried out, though one step creates a doubt, the next step can be used to destroy the doubt, and the net result is nothing. On the other hand, if he had tried to carry out his plan in the way his plan requires, i.e. abstaining from taking for granted any conviction the truth of which he had not scrutinized, he could not even have got started, because *ex hypothesi* he has no such conviction to start from. The fact is that, Descartes's plan being what it was, either he cannot start at all or if he does he can be forced to retrace any step he takes.

2. Of Descartes's reasons for doubting the truth of various thoughts, obviously the most important is the thought that God or some demon might have made our intelligence defective. But if Descartes really had this thought in the process of doubting, as he said he did, it is difficult to see why he did not at once stop the process at that point. For once we have that thought we shall think that any thought we subsequently attain, whether it be about our own existence or anything else, may be defective and so not possibly knowledge.

3. Descartes fails to notice that on his own principles he ought to have doubted even his own existence. He says in effect 'I cannot doubt my existence, since my persuasion that there is no world implies the existence of myself who am thus persuaded'. But it could be retorted that he can only make this statement because he is *persuaded* that he had this persuasion and also that such a persuasion implies the existence of a being who is persuaded; and that just as he had doubted the truth of his persuasion that there was no world, because some being might be deceiving him, so he ought for the same reason to have doubted these new persuasions, and therefore that of his own existence.

Descartes might have replied: 'I was not *persuaded* that I was persuaded; I *knew* that I was.' But to this it might be replied: 'Well, you spoke of your *persuasion* that there is no world and not of your *knowledge* that there is no world; and if you call the state you are thinking of here one of persuasion, you should equally speak of your *persuasion* that you were persuaded.'

The fact is that when Descartes comes to consider what we call an act of self-consciousness, i.e. the consciousness of our own state, it simply does not occur to him even to ask whether the truth of this consciousness is doubtful. He just takes it for granted that it is not; yet as he avowedly doubts the competence of our intelligence, he ought as much to have doubted the truth of this consciousness as the truth of any other state of himself.

Descartes considers that by the process he has described in the first two Meditations he has become certain of and so knows his own existence, though doubtful of the existence of everything else.

He then in effect asks himself: 'As I have attained this one certainty, is it not now open to me to attain others and so come to have other knowledge?' His reader naturally expects him to answer 'no'; for he has expressly said that he has found the existence of everything else doubtful, and that seems to finish the matter. Indeed, the plan on which he proceeds in the first two Meditations really requires him to stop—as having finished the task he has set himself.

Descartes, however, inconsistently, thinks otherwise. His idea (a fallacious idea) is that by analysing the process by which he has become certain of his own existence, he can discover the general nature of the process of becoming certain of something, and that once we know its general nature, we can use this knowledge to attain other certainties, and indeed all such certainties as we are capable of attaining.

Descartes at once proceeds to carry out this analysis. In fact, however, he gives a different account from that implied in the second Meditation, and we should first consider the latter.

The key to the earlier account is to be found in Descartes's saying in effect: 'The mere fact that I was persuaded of something, whether truly or falsely, e.g. that there was no such thing as a world, involves my existence.' This statement implies that if he had been asked, when writing the second Meditation, what rendered him certain of his own existence, he would have had to say that it was his *certainty* that he had had a certain persuasion, together with the certainty that any persuasion involves the existence of a self which is persuaded, distinct from the persuasion. And we could say that according to this account we become certain of some fact in nature by consideration of certain other facts in nature.

The account of the Third Meditation is, however, different. Unfortunately it is obscure. What he says is:

In this first knowledge, doubtless, there is nothing which makes me certain of its truth except the clear and distinct perception of what I say, which would not indeed suffice to make me certain that that which I say is true, if it could ever happen that a thing which I conceived thus clearly and distinctly should prove false; and accordingly it seems to me that already I can establish as a general rule that all the things which we conceive very clearly and very distinctly are true.

Here, if we put in what is necessary to complete the sense, what Descartes appears to be saying is this:

In this knowledge that I exist, what renders me certain that the thought that I exist is true, is my *certainty* that this thought is an act of perceiving clearly and distinctly that I exist; but this certainty would not be sufficient to do this, unless I was also certain, that any state of perceiving clearly and distinctly is necessarily true.

And he should have added not—as he does—'hence it now *seems* to me that any such state must be true', but 'hence I now know that I have already been certain, and so already know that any such state must be true'. Also, he should have added that this knowledge that I exist requires an additional certainty, viz. that where a thought is necessarily true, the fact must correspond.

This account is obviously different in two ways. For (1) it introduces a new note—that of perceiving something clearly and distinctly, and (2) according to this account we become certain of a fact in nature only indirectly, by considering a certain state of our own mind. We first come to perceive clearly and distinctly that we exist, presumably by perceiving clearly and distinctly that some persuasion of ours implies our existence —this perceiving not being the being certain; then by reflecting on this state we become certain that it is one of clear and distinct perception, and so necessarily true, and thence become certain that we exist.

Further (2), it should be noticed, if 'perceiving clearly' had to be introduced into the *earlier* account, it could be done only by assuming that Descartes considered that what he calls perceiving clearly is the same thing as the 'being certain' of this earlier account.

One implication of the new account is obvious. This is that there is at least one certainty which we must have before we can be certain even of our own existence, viz. the certainty that any state which is one of clear perceiving is necessarily true—so that in this respect, too, the second account is inconsistent with the first.

The differences between the two accounts can be put generally thus: Suppose I am to become certain that an *A* is *B*, e.g. that a three-sided figure has also three angles. According to the first account, I must first, by considering the nature of an *A* and of *B*-ness, become certain that something in the nature of an *A* and of *B*-ness necessitates that an *A* is *B*— this being certain being what Descartes calls perceiving clearly and distinctly. According to the second account, I must first, by considering the nature of an *A* and *B*-ness, come to perceive clearly that an *A* is *B*, this perceiving clearly *not* being the same as being certain; then secondly, by considering the nature of my state of mind become certain that it is one of perceiving clearly; and then thirdly, become certain that this fact necessitates that *A* is *B*. The difference is fundamental, because while according to the first account we attain knowledge by consideration of the facts, according to the second we do so by a consideration of the state of mind which we reach by considering the facts. Thus, suppose we had tried to discover the product of 7 and 9 and were doubtful about our conclusion, according to the first account the proper procedure would be to do the sum again, while according to the second account we should consider once more the state of mind we had previously reached in doing the sum.

Strangely enough Descartes does not notice that the two accounts are different. What we find is the two accounts left side by side undistinguished. For later on he often treats perceiving clearly as if it were the same as being certain, thereby reverting to the first account.

Descartes, having formulated this second account, then finds himself harassed by two reasons for doubting whether a state of clear perceiving *is* necessarily true. And he naturally goes on to consider whether they are good reasons, since as according to this account all our other certainties are based on the certainty that such a state is necessarily true, then if such a state is not necessarily true, in being certain of something we do not *know*, since no state in which we may be mistaken can possibly be one of knowledge.

And it may be noticed that on his other version of the process of becoming certain, he would equally have to consider these reasons. For on this version, perceiving clearly is the same thing as being certain, and therefore on this version also, if perceiving clearly is a state in which we are liable to error, in being certain of something we are not knowing.

Moreover the reasons are important for *us* to consider, because we, too, when we reflect begin to doubt whether we know even when we are certain, and if we do not, knowledge seems unattainable—since no better state seems possible than that of being certain.

Descartes's general contention in favour of this doubt is that we often have perceived things very clearly and yet afterwards been convinced that we have or at least may have been mistaken. In favour of this contention Descartes puts forward two types of case.

1. He says he has received the existence of the various objects of the senses, i.e. the earth, the sky, the stars, &c., as very certain and manifest; i.e. he has very clearly and distinctly perceived their existence, and yet afterwards has found their existence doubtful.

This particular source of doubt, he thinks, however, can be easily disposed of. What, he asks, did I distinctly perceive about these objects? Simply that ideas of them were present to my mind, and this, he says, I do not even now think doubtful. But besides distinctly perceiving this, I did something else; I thought I perceived clearly that realities independent of me existed from which these ideas proceeded, and it was in having this thought that I was or at least may have been mistaken.

This reply enables Descartes to save the view that where our state *is* one of clear perceiving it is necessarily true.

He fails, however, to notice that in taking this step he has only gone from Scylla to Charybdis. For he has only saved his view (that a state of clear perceiving is necessarily true) at the cost of admitting that we may always be mistaken in being certain that a state in which we are is one of clear perceiving; and if this be so, since the certainty of anything else will imply such a certainty, then in being certain of anything we shall not be knowing it.

2. The second type of case is one which Descartes thinks much more difficult to dispose of. It is that of our state of mind when considering some easy proposition in arithmetic or geometry. If we read what Des-

cartes says here in the third Meditation with the passage from Meditation V, we can say that what Descartes is saying to himself is this:

While I am actually following the argument put forward in support of any simple proposition such as 'The angles of a triangle are equal to two right angles', it does most clearly appear to me that the angles are equal to two right angles. In this case, unlike the preceding type of case, there is no doubt about it. Here I do perceive clearly. So much is this so that, when in this condition, I find it impossible to believe otherwise; i.e. I am certain. Indeed if at such a time I ask myself whether even an omnipotent deity can have been deceiving me here by giving me a nature which makes me mistaken in my present state, though certain, I answer 'No. Even such a thing could not do this.' Yet afterwards I can doubt whether even when in this state I was not mistaken. For once I cease to follow the proof, then even though I remember I did follow it, I can think that in my past state an omnipotent deity may have been deceiving me.

Consequently, even in those cases where unquestionably my state is one of perceiving something clearly and distinctly, I may be mistaken, i.e. the state is not necessarily true, so that in being certain as I was that such a state, as being one of clear perceiving, is necessarily true I may have been mistaken, and consequently in being certain I am not knowing.

The conclusion which Descartes draws is that in order to know something it is necessary not only to have and to know that we have a clear and distinct perception of it; we must also come to know, and know by having some proof, that in such a state God cannot be deceiving us; and that therefore in order to know anything else whatever we must first come to know that there is a deity who does not deceive us when we are in such a state.

Naturally, therefore, his next step is to inquire whether there is a God and whether, if there is, he can be a deceiver.

Here we may notice two things by the way.

1. The existence of God is the third thing Descartes has come in the course of his thought to say we must know first, i.e. as a condition of knowing anything else, the other two being, of course, our existence, and the truth of a clear and distinct perception. Yet plainly Descartes can at best have only one thing as what we must know first.

2. Though Descartes says the ground of doubt is slight, it is not really so. The ground is serious. When, however, he adds that it is metaphysical, though he is saying what is important (viz. that it arises only when we come to consider whether we have the capacity to know, and not from doubts raised in ordinary life), to say this does not make the difficulty any less serious.

We are now in a position to consider the tenability of this view of

Descartes. There is no need to wait until we are acquainted with the proof of God's existence which Descartes goes on to offer, because whatever the proof the general nature of the view will be the same.

The first thing to be noticed is that Descartes could, and indeed should, have stated the reason for doubt more generally, in a way which is independent of a theological setting. He could have said that we can only have come to perceive something clearly by using such a capacity of thought as we have, i.e. our intelligence—this being necessarily so however we have acquired this capacity, i.e. whether it be due to God or not; and that consequently the doubt arises whether this capacity is equal to the task of attaining a state in which we cannot be mistaken. Therefore, he could have said, before we know anything else we must come to know that our capacity of thought is such that the use of it will give us knowledge; or, to put it otherwise, before we can know that in any particular state we cannot be mistaken and so must know some particular thing, we must first come to know that the use of our intelligence is capable of giving us knowledge. This indeed is the more general form in which the doubt presents itself to us, and in fact it was the form in which Locke presented it to himself.

The next thing to be observed is that Descartes's idea of how the doubt has to be allayed, if at all, is obviously mistaken; and we can see that it is mistaken without even considering the actual way in which Descartes considers that he allays it, viz. by discovering what he considers a *proof* that there exists a deity who is no deceiver. For as Descartes is representing the matter, such a proof could only consist in perceiving clearly and distinctly that certain things which he perceives clearly involve a necessity that such a God exists; and as precisely what he is doubtful of is whether even when he perceives something clearly and distinctly he is not mistaken, he will become doubtful, when he reflects on his having this proof, whether here, too, he is not mistaken. In exactly the same way, if we were to come to perceive clearly that our capacity of thought is competent to yield knowledge, the mere reflection that this perception is the result of our capacity would produce the very doubt about the truth of this state, which we are trying to dissipate generally. In other words, any process by which we seek to dissipate the doubt by proving it to be mistaken will itself be exposed to the very doubt which we are anxious to dissipate.

Descartes, therefore, it is obvious, is setting himself an impossible task; and we can discover it to be impossible without considering his attempt to execute it. Admitting as he does the existence of the general doubt, he would have done better to admit that it was irremovable, and that therefore even when we are certain we do not know. But if he had, he would also have had to allow that our certainty of anything could only be momentary, since on becoming certain of something we should have only to reflect on our certainty to become certain that it is not knowledge, and so to become uncertain of the thing.

Yet, as it is easy to see, there must be something wrong about Descartes's doctrine, for as we see if we reflect, we can only be uncertain of one thing because we are certain of something else, and therefore to maintain, as the sceptic does, that we are uncertain of everything is impossible.

Still what we really want to discover is what precisely is wrong with Descartes's position and what is the proper way to deal with Descartes's doubt. And to do this is not easy.

To succeed, there are two things which we absolutely must do first.

1. We must first recognize the fundamental nature of the difference between knowing and believing.

2. We must recognize that whenever we know something we either do, or at least can, by reflecting, directly know that we are knowing it, and that whenever we believe something, we similarly either do or can directly know that we are believing it and not knowing it.

As regards (1), that there is such a fundamental difference is not something which everyone will readily admit, and some will go on to the end denying it. Nevertheless, I am confident that at least the more you consider the matter the more difficult you will find it to deny the existence of the difference.

For the sake of brevity and clearness I propose to try to state dogmatically the nature of the difference, and in doing so, I shall for the most part only be trying to state Cook Wilson's view.[1] In saying that I am going to speak dogmatically I mean two things. I mean first that I am not going to offer reasons for what I am going to assert. These for the most part would from the nature of the case have to take the form of trying to meet objections; and this I propose to try to do later. I mean secondly that the statements are meant to express what I know to be *knowledge* on my part and not *opinion,* and so what is beyond controversy.

But if 'controversial' stands for any doctrine which has been disputed, then my statements will express a doctrine which is controversial, and controversial in the highest degree. Thus any of you who have had the benefit of knowing or hearing Professor J. A. Smith or Professor Joachim will realize that they would deny the truth of every statement I am going to make. But, of course, it does not follow from the mere fact that a statement is controversial in this sense that it does not express knowledge on the part of the individual who states it, and that therefore, since everything is controversial in this sense, it is useless for you to try to attain knowledge about anything.

1. Knowing is absolutely different from what is called indifferently

---

[1] Cook Wilson, *Statement and Inference,* Part I, chap. 11; Part II, chaps. 1, 2, 3.

believing or being convinced or being persuaded or having an opinion or thinking, in the sense in which we oppose thinking to knowing, as when we say 'I think so but am not sure'. Knowing is not something which differs from being convinced by a difference of degree of something such as a feeling of confidence, as being more convinced differs from being less convinced, or as a fast movement differs from a slow movement. Knowing and believing differ in kind as do desiring and feeling, or as do a red colour and a blue colour. Their difference in kind is not that of species and genus, like that of a red colour and a colour. To know is not to have a belief of a special kind, differing from beliefs of other kinds; and no improvement in a belief and no increase in the feeling of conviction which it implies will convert it into knowledge. Nor is their difference that of being two species of a common genus. It is not that there is a general kind of activity, for which the name would have to be thinking, which admits of two kinds, the better of which is knowing and the worse believing, nor is knowing something called thinking at its best, thinking not at its best being believing. Their relatedness consists rather in the facts (a) that believing presupposes knowing, though, of course, knowing something other than what we believe, and (b) that believing is a stage we some-times reach in the endeavour to attain knowledge.

To convince ourselves of the difference between knowing and be-lieving we need only notice that on the one hand we should only say that we know something when we are certain of it, and conversely, and that in the end we have to allow that the meaning of the terms is iden-tical; whereas, on the other hand, when we believe something we are uncertain of it.

Further there are certain things about knowing and believing which it is essential to recognize, i.e. know, when we are considering Descartes.

(a) Though obviously knowledge is not false, and though obviously, when we know, we are not mistaken, knowledge is not *true*. It is neither true nor false, just as a colour is neither heavy nor light. On the other hand, beliefs are either true or false.

(b) Though some beliefs are true and others are false, there is no special kind of belief distinguished from others by some special char-acteristic such as that of being a condition of perceiving something clearly and distinctly, which, as being the kind it is, is necessarily true. Or, to put this otherwise, there is no such thing as a kind of opinion called true opinion—as Plato often implies that there is. In fact there is no sort of condition of mind of which it can truly be said that it is necessarily true; what seems nearest to this is the condition of knowing, which is neces-sarily not false, but yet is not true. And it may be noticed here that it is a tribute to Plato's philosophical insight, that though he considered there was a kind of opinion called true opinion, a kind which if it existed would be necessarily true, in the *Theaetetus*, where he tries to answer the question 'What is knowledge?', he will have nothing to do with the view that it is true opinion.

2. Consider the second condition, which I said must be satisfied before we can get the matter straight. We must recognize that when we know something we either do, or by reflecting can, know that our condition is one of knowing that thing, while when we believe something, we either do or can know that our condition is one of believing and not of knowing: so that we cannot mistake belief for knowledge or vice versa.

Consider instances: When knowing, for example, that the noise we are hearing is loud, we do or can know that we are knowing this and so cannot be mistaken, and when believing that the noise is due to a car we know or can know that we are believing and not knowing this. The knowledge, however, is in both cases direct; we do not know, for example, that our state is one of knowing that the noise we hear is loud indirectly, i.e. by knowing that it has some character, other than that of knowing, which we know any state must have if it is to be one of knowing—such as that of being an act of clear and distinct perceiving; we know directly that it is of the sort which knowing is; and so, too, with our knowledge that our state is one of believing.

Further, it should be noticed that in knowing that some state in which we are is one of knowing or of believing, as the case may be, we are necessarily knowing the sort of thing which knowing is and the sort of thing which believing is, even though it is impossible for us or anyone else to define either, i.e. to state its nature in terms of the nature of something else. This is obvious, because even in knowing in a given case that my condition is one of believing and not of knowing, I must be knowing the sort of thing that knowing is, since otherwise I should not know that my condition is not one of knowing, just as in knowing that some line is not straight, I must—as Plato saw—be knowing what straightness is.

Now with these two considerations in mind return to Descartes's doubt whether he was not mistaken in some past state in which he was following the proof that the angles of a triangle are equal to two right angles; and consider what we can say about it. The first thing to do is obviously to answer the question 'Was the condition of mind on which Descartes was reflecting one of knowing, or was it one of believing, or (as we say) of being convinced, as when we say we are convinced it was X who killed Y?' And, obviously, only one answer is possible. Descartes here was *knowing*; it was not a case of being *convinced*. This is something that we *know*, and to know this all we have to do is to follow the argument ourselves and then ask ourselves 'Is this condition in which, as Descartes would say, we perceive clearly for certain reasons that the angles are equal to two right angles one of *knowing*, or is it only one of being convinced?' We can only answer 'Whatever may be our state on other occasions, here we are knowing this'. And this statement is an expression of our *knowing* that we are knowing this; for we do not *believe* that we are knowing this, we know that we are.

But if that is the proper answer about Descartes's state of mind, then, of course, we know that in it he could not have been liable to deception; and therefore for ourselves we have cut off the doubt at its source. We do not require a proof of God's existence, because we know that Descartes could not have been deceived. In the same way, if his doubt had been the wider doubt whether he was not deceived because his state might have resulted from the use of an imperfect intelligence, that also is cut off for us for the same reason. For obviously a condition of knowing cannot be the result of the use of imperfect faculties.

Further, if someone were to object that after all Descartes's condition may have been liable to error, because for all we know we can later on discover some fact which is incompatible with a triangle's having angles that are equal to two right angles, we can answer that we *know* that there can be no such fact, for in knowing that a triangle must have such angles we also know that nothing can exist which is incompatible with this fact.

Further we can add: Descartes himself is just on the verge of discovering the truth when he says that *at the time,* i.e. when following the argument, he finds it impossible to believe otherwise, and finds himself saying 'Here no one can be deceiving me', and that it is only afterwards he can think that he may have been wrong. Plainly, this is just on the verge of saying 'If I consider my state at the time, I *know* that it is one of knowing'. And plainly also he afterwards only comes in fact to doubt whether even in such a state he may not have been mistaken, because he has somehow in the interval come to misrepresent to himself the character of his past state. If he had not, he could no more have doubted the truth of his state then than, as he admits, he could doubt it at the time.

And an indication that there is misrepresentation is to be found in the fact that he has to give different accounts of his state while following the demonstration, according as he describes it as it presented itself to him at the time, and as he describes it as it presented itself to him afterwards. As it presented itself at the time, he describes it as one of perceiving clearly that the angles are equal to two right angles; as it presented itself afterwards, he describes it as one in which he only *thought* he perceived clearly; and although only one of these descriptions can be true he has to introduce the second, because otherwise he could not have represented himself as afterwards doubting the truth of that state.

On Descartes's own showing, therefore, he is thinking of the state differently at the time and afterwards.

We therefore can get Descartes out of the impasse, provided we allow, *as we can,* that the state to which he referred as one of perceiving clearly was in fact one of knowing, and one which he could have known at the time to be one of knowing. By doing this we stop the rot from starting. Descartes's trouble was that he let the rot begin, and once it is allowed to start, it cannot be prevented from going on indefinitely. . . .

The doctrine I have been either stating or implying to be true can, I think, be summarized thus:

1. We are certain of certain things, e.g. that we are wondering what is going to happen next, that we did wonder a short time ago what was going to happen next (an act of memory), that a three-sided figure is three-angled and again that the three-sidedness of a three-sided figure necessitates that the number of its angles is three, that there cannot be a test of truth.

2. To be certain of something is to know it.

3. To know something is one thing and to believe something is another.

4. When we know something, we either do or can directly know that we are knowing it, and when we believe something we know or can know that we are believing and not knowing it, and in view of the former fact, we *know* that in certain instances of its use our intelligence is not defective, so that Descartes's difficulties fall to the ground.

Now I think you will find that the objections which you may feel will reduce to two. And these are best considered separately.

The first is really only a repetition of an objection which Descartes felt to the truth of his idea that a state in which we perceive something clearly is necessarily true. It will be urged that it is preposterous to maintain that, when we are certain, we know, since obviously we and others have often been certain, and yet afterwards found that we were mistaken. Men, for example, were at one time certain that the sun goes round the earth, or that local spirits interfered with the course of nature; again two men are frequently certain of contrary things, e.g. that motion is absolute and that it is relative, that space might have a fourth dimension and that it could not, that space is infinite and that it is not. But in such cases only one can be *right*, and as both are in the same kind of state, even the one who is right cannot *know*.

In considering this objection, we should first notice that there is a state of mind which we may fail to distinguish from one of certainty, and so regard as one of certainty when it is not. This is what we may describe as an unquestioning frame of mind—or as one in which it did not occur to us to doubt something, or—as Cook Wilson described it—one of 'being under the impression that'. I, for example, might be, as we say, thinking without question that the thing in front of me is a table, or that to-day is Tuesday, or that so and so came to see me last week. Cook Wilson said of this state that it stimulates knowledge since, as is obvious, in this state there is no doubt or uncertainty. But it obviously is not the same as *being certain*. In such states we are, of course, constantly being mistaken, and unless we distinguish such states from being certain, we are apt to take instances of them as instances of our being certain and yet mistaken. And once we have noticed the distinction, we are forced to allow that we are certain of very much less than we should have said otherwise. Thus, we have to allow that we are not certain of the truth of any inductive generalization, e.g. that all men are mortal, or that sugar is sweet, for we are not *certain* that anything in the nature of a man requires that he shall at some time die; we are not even certain that the sun will rise to-morrow. And if you were asked in a law court, 'Are you certain of the truth of what you have just said?', you would probably answer, 'Well, if it comes to that there is precious little I am certain of'. It is no use to object, 'Well, if you are going to restrict what we know to what we are certain of, you are going to reduce what we know to very little'. For nothing is gained by trying to make out that we know when we do not, and the important thing is to be able to convince ourselves that there are at least some things that we know, whether the knowledge of them is important or not, especially as, if there were nothing which we knew, all our beliefs would be worthless, as having no basis in knowledge.

Next we should ask ourselves whether when we are prepared to say we know we are also prepared to say we are certain, or *vice versa*. Now, unquestionably, we should answer to the first question 'Yes'. For we should never think of ourselves as knowing something unless we thought of ourselves as certain. The converse, however, is not so obvious, viz. that where we should say we are certain, we should be prepared to say we know. But consider what is the alternative. If when we are certain, for example, that the square of three must be an odd number, we do not know, what *do* we do? The only possible answer is, 'In such a state we *think* we know'. But then consider what can be meant by a state of thinking we know this. The answer must be, 'Only thinking this', i.e. thinking that the square of three must be odd, as opposed to knowing that it must. But if we consider our state of mind, the retort is obvious—we do not *think* this, we *know* it. In fact, in the end it seems impossible to distinguish the meaning of knowing and being certain; any reluctance to admit this comes from a failure to distinguish being certain from what we may call thinking without question.

Now if we bear these considerations in mind, we shall come to allow that many asserted instances of mistaken certainties were not really instances of certainties. We should say, for example, 'Though many have thought without question that the sun went round the earth, and many also have been certain that they had certain perceptions, no one has ever been *certain* that it was the sun which went round the earth rather than that it was the earth which went round the sun.' And we should add, as Descartes in effect did, that anyone who said that he was *certain* that the

sun moved would, when the difference between being certain and thinking without question had been pointed out to him, end by saying that
what really he was certain of was that he had had certain perceptions. . . .

The second objection is one which it is specially important for us to
consider because Descartes himself felt it acutely and also gets very near
to answering it.

The certainties of which Descartes was thinking are all certainties
attained by the operation or activity of thinking, in the sense in which
we say that when we reason we *think*, a sense in which we speak of thinking as something opposed to perceiving and to being self-conscious and
to remembering. As an indication of this, we should all be prepared to
give a *reason* for the certainties of which Descartes was thinking, saying,
for example, 'We are certain that we exist, *since* our persuasion that there
is no world requires or necessitates the existence of ourselves as the subject of the persuasion, i.e. as that which is persuaded.' [Contrast an act
of memory—'I am certain that I heard a sound a short time ago'. If someone asked me 'Why?', I should answer, 'I have no reason for being certain
of this, I am simply certain of it'.]

Now the objection relates to our certainties reached by thinking—
and it may be put thus:

The object of knowledge, i.e. what is known, if there be knowledge,
is some part of an independent world of reality, i.e. some part of a reality
which exists independently of the knower and whose character is independent of that of the knower. Now the only way in which the nature of
anything in this independent world can come to be known is either by
observing it, i.e. perceiving it, or, should the thing be a state of ourselves,
by an act of reflection on our part which is analogous to perception. If we
perceive something to have a certain characteristic, that is knowing it to
have that characteristic, and that is all that need be said. And there is no
other way of knowing it.

Now the states of which Descartes is thinking are unquestionably
states of certainty. Moreover, in them there is something which renders
it inevitable or necessary that we are certain of that of which we are certain—something which, as we say, makes us certain. In being certain that
a three-sided figure is also three-angled, I am not simply certain of this,
there is something which necessitates that I am certain that it is three-
angled and not four-angled or five-angled, or in some instances three-
angled and in others, say, seven-angled.

But, though we know this to be so, yet if we ask, 'Must the things
about which we are certain correspond with our certainty by really having
the property which we are certain they have?', we have to answer 'No'. For
even though there is something which renders it necessary that we are

certain that the thing has that property and not another, our being certain that it has it does not require or necessitate that it *has it*. For its possession or non-possession of the property depends on its nature and not on the nature of any attitude of ours towards its possession or non-possession of it. And even though there is something which renders it inevitable that we are certain that it has it, this something does not render it inevitable that it has it. For this something can only be something in our own minds, and this cannot render anything in the real world necessary or inevitable.

In fact, as Descartes put it in effect with reference to another instance, and using the language of thinking and conceiving clearly where he might have substituted 'being certain': 'Though I conceive, i.e. conceive clearly and distinctly, that God exists, and though I cannot conceive God except as existing, i.e. though there is something which makes it necessary that I conceive God as existing and not as not existing, it does not follow that God exists: for my thought imposes no necessity on things.' That is, my thought that, e.g., God exists, even though there be something which renders it necessary that I should think this, does not render it necessary that God does exist. Consequently to be certain is *not* to know, for since a thing is not required to have a property by our being certain that it has it, even though something renders our certainty inevitable, our certainty may be mistaken, and so cannot (not 'may not') be knowledge. And even if afterwards we observed some of the triangles we had been certain about to have three angles, this would not show that our certainty about them was knowledge.

The objection is of course serious, since it implies that general knowledge, i.e. knowledge that all things of a certain kind have a certain property, is obtainable only by observation of all the particular things, and that therefore to attempt to gain it, in advance of observations, by thinking is futile. And its seriousness is increased so far as knowledge of things in the physical world is concerned, as soon as we discover, as sooner or later we must, that we do not observe, i.e. perceive, physical things at all.

This being the difficulty, what are we to do about it?

The objection, of course, allows that in the certainties to which it applies there is something which makes us certain, i.e. renders it necessary or inevitable that we are certain. Now this something is what we should call our reason for being certain. And, as consideration of instances will show, we mean by our reason for being certain that an *A* is *B*, another certainty, and a certainty of something of a special kind, viz. our certainty that a certain characteristic of an *A* requires or necessitates that an *A* is *B*. Thus if we were asked what is our reason for being certain that a three-sided figure is three-angled, we should answer, 'Our certainty that the possession by a three-sided figure of the characteristic of being three-sided requires that the figure also has the characteristic of being three-angled'. And if we were to become certain by what we call a process of argument that a picture A on a wall was higher than a picture B, and if we were then asked, 'What made us certain', we might give some such answer as, 'Our certainty that A's being higher than X and B's being lower than X necessitated that of A and B, A was the higher'. To say this, is only to give our reason for being certain, in the same way that we might give our reason for thinking so and so, in the sense of believing so and so.

The objection therefore allows what is in fact true, that there is no such thing as our being barely or merely certain that an A is B, i.e. certain without having a reason; i.e. really, that our certainty that an A is B involves or implies our certainty that an A's possessing a certain characteristic requires it to have the characteristic of B-ness.

But once we realize this the objection assumes quite a different complexion. In fact the most direct answer to the question becomes paradoxically simple. For the objection is expressed in the statement, 'Though I am certain, for example, that a three-sided figure is three-angled, and though there is something which makes me certain of this, viz., my certainty that the three-sidedness of a three-sided figure requires it to be three-angled as well, yet a three-sided figure need not be three-angled.' And to this it can now be replied that the statement is really only mere words, and not an expression of an activity of our minds, whether one of being certain or one of having an opinion. For it means: 'Though I am certain that a certain definite character possessed by a three-sided figure in nature requires such a figure to have three angles, there is no definite character of such a thing in nature which requires this.' And obviously we do not actually think there is no such character, when *ex hypothesi* we are certain that there is such a character.

We ought, however, to go rather more below the surface. First we should ask, 'Can the certainty which is the reason for our certainty that an A is B be said to be knowledge; i.e. do we know, for example, that our certainty that the three-sidedness of a three-sided figure requires it to have three angles is knowledge?' Here, if we face the issue, the answer can only be 'Yes'. It may be objected that this state cannot really even be one of certainty, and so not one of knowledge, since it itself is something for which we have no reason. But to this the answer is, as we shall see if we think it out, that there cannot be such a thing as a reason for a reason, or more fully our having a reason for having a reason, and that the certainty that one thing necessitates another is in one respect analogous to such a certainty as that now our condition is one of perplexity, viz. in being simple, in the sense that our certainty does not depend on a reason.

Secondly, we should consider what has now become of the objection that our certainty that an A is B cannot be knowledge because an A need not in the real world conform to our certainty by being B. The fact is that it has simply vanished. For now admittedly it is a condition of our being certain that an A is B, that we know a certain fact in nature, viz. that the possession by an A of a certain characteristic, a, necessitates its having the characteristic of being B, and knowing this we cannot even raise the question, 'Need an A in nature have the characteristic B?', because we know that a certain definite characteristic which it has requires it to have that characteristic.

The only possible ground on which this might be disputed would be the contention that what is called the necessitation of B-ness in an A by an A's having a characteristic, a, is *not* a fact in the real world. But this contention is merely the result of the childlike and almost childish idea—though the idea chiefly appears in grown-ups and especially in those whose interests are chiefly scientific—that only that is real which is sensible, observable, or perceptible.

It is now possible to see—at any rate if you grant that what I have been saying is true—how very nearly Descartes got to the truth in trying to meet his own objection. For, speaking of what he considers to be his inevitably conceiving that God exists, he says, not that God's existence is brought about by my thought, or that my thought imposes any necessity on things, i.e. renders it necessary that the things about which I think correspond to my thought, but on the contrary that the necessity of the existence of God (i.e. really the fact that certain facts in nature necessitate that a God exists) determines me to think in this way. Here Descartes seems just on the verge of stating the truth, and if he had substituted for 'the necessity' 'my thought of the necessity', or rather 'my knowledge of the necessity', he would have got it right, for he would then have been saying what in principle can be stated thus: what renders me certain that an A is B is my certainty or knowledge of that which in nature necessitates that an A is B; with the implication that just for that reason in being certain that an A is B, I cannot possibly be mistaken.

SEVEN

Knowledge and Belief*

NORMAN MALCOLM (1911-   )

"We must recognize that when we know something we either do, or by reflecting, can know that our condition is one of knowing that thing, while when we believe something, we either do or can know that our condition is one of believing and not of knowing: so that we cannot mistake belief for knowledge or vice versa." [1]

This remark is worthy of investigation. Can I discover *in myself* whether I know something or merely believe it?

Let us begin by studying the ordinary usage of "know" and "believe". Suppose, for example, that several of us intend to go for a walk and that you propose that we walk in Cascadilla gorge. I protest that I should like to walk beside a flowing stream and that at this season the gorge is probably dry. Consider the following cases:

(1) You say "I believe that it won't be dry although I have no particular reason for thinking so". If we went to the gorge and found a flowing stream we should not say that you *knew* that there would be water but that you thought so and were right.

(2) You say "I believe that it won't be dry because it rained only three days ago and usually water flows in the gorge for at least that long after a rain". If we found water we should be inclined to say that you knew that there would be water. It would be quite natural for you to say "I knew that it wouldn't be dry"; and we should tolerate your remark. This case differs from the previous one in that here you had a *reason*.

(3) You say "I know that it won't be dry" and give the same reason as in (2). If we found water we should have very little hesitation in saying that you knew. Not only had you a reason, but you *said* "I know" instead of "I believe". It may seem to us now that the latter should not make a difference—but it does.

(4) You say "I know that it won't be dry" and give a stronger reason,

---

*Norman Malcolm, "Knowledge and Belief," *Mind*, vol. LXI, NS, no. 242. Apr., 1952.

[1] H. A. Prichard, *Knowledge and Perception* (Oxford, 1950), p. 88. (See pp. 118-135 this volume) ed.

e.g. "I saw a lot of water flowing in the gorge when I passed it this morning". If we went and found water, there would be no hesitation at all in saying that you knew. If, for example, we later met someone who said "Weren't you surprised to see water in the gorge this morning?" you would reply "No, I *knew* that there would be water; I had been there earlier in the day". We should have no objection to this statement.

(5) Everything happens as in (4), except that upon going to the gorge we find it to be dry. We should not say that you knew, but that you *believed* that there would be water. And this is true even though you declared that you knew, and even though your evidence was the same as it was in case (4) in which you did know.

I wish to make some comments on the usage of "know", "knew", "believe", and "believed", as illustrated in the preceding cases:

(a) Whether we should say that you knew, depends in part on whether you had grounds for your assertion and on the strength of those grounds. There would certainly be less hesitation to say that you knew in case (4) than in case (3), and this can be due only to the difference in the strength of the grounds.

(b) Whether we should say that you knew, depends in part on how *confident* you were. In case (2), if you had said "It rained only three days ago and usually water flows in the gorge for at least that long after a rain; but, of course, I don't feel absolutely sure that there will be water", then we should *not* have said that you knew that there would be water. If you lack confidence that p is true then others do not say that you know that p is true, even though *they* know that p is true. Being confident is a necessary condition for knowing.

(c) Prichard says that if we reflect we cannot mistake belief for knowledge. In case (4) you knew that there would be water, and in case (5) you merely believed it. Was there any way that you could have discovered by reflexion, in case (5), that you did not know? It would have been useless to have reconsidered your grounds for saying that there would be water, because in case (4), where you *did* know, your grounds were identical. They could be at fault in (5) only if they were at fault in (4), and they were not at fault in (4). Cases (4) and (5) differ in only one respect—namely, that in one case you did subsequently find water and in the other you did not. Prichard says that we can determine by reflexion whether we know something or merely believe it. But where, in these cases, is the material that reflexion would strike upon? There is none.

There is only one way that Prichard could defend his position. He would have to say that in case (4) you did *not* know that there would be water. And it is obvious that he would have said this. But this is false. It is an enormously common usage of language to say, in commenting upon just such an incident as (4), "He knew that the gorge wouldn't be dry because he had seen water flowing there that morning". It is a usage that all of us are familiar with. We so employ "know" and "knew" every day of our lives. We do not think of our usage as being loose or incorrect—and it is not. As philosophers we may be surprised to observe that it *can* be that the knowledge that *p* is true should differ from the belief that *p* is true *only* in the respect that in one case *p* is true and in the other false. But that is the fact.

There is an argument that one is inclined to use as a proof that you did not know that there would be water. The argument is the following: It could have turned out that you found no water; if it had so turned out you would have been mistaken in saying that you would find water; therefore you could have been mistaken; but if you could have been mistaken then you did not know.

Now it certainly *could* have turned out that the forge was quite dry when you went there, even though you saw lots of water flowing through it only a few hours before. This does not show, however, that you did not know that there would be water. What it shows is that *although you knew you could have been mistaken*.[2] This would seem to be a contradictory result; but it is not. It seems so because our minds are fixed upon another usage of "know" and "knew"; one in which "It could have turned out that I was mistaken", implies "I did not know".

When is "know" used in this sense? I believe that Prichard uses it in this sense when he says that when we go through the proof of the proposition that the angles of a triangle are equal to two right angles we *know* that the proposition is true (p. 128). He says that if we put to ourselves the question: Is our condition one of knowing this, or is it only one of being convinced of it?, then "We can only answer 'Whatever may be our state on other occasions, here we are knowing this.' And this statement is an expression of our *knowing* that we are knowing; for we do not *believe* that we are knowing this, we know that we are" (p. 128). He goes on to say that if someone were to object that we may be making a mistake "because for all we know we can later on discover some fact which is incompatible with a triangle's having angles that are equal to two right angles, we can answer that we *know* that there can be no such fact, for in knowing that a triangle must have such angles we also know that nothing can exist which is incompatible with this fact" (p. 129).

It is easy to imagine a non-philosophical context in which it would have been natural for Prichard to have said "I know that the angles of a triangle are equal to two right angles". Suppose that a young man just

---

2 Some readers seem to have thought that I was denying here that "I knew that *p*" entails "that *p*." That was not my intention, and my words do not have that implication. If I had said *"although you knew you were mistaken,"* I should have denied the above entailment and, also, I should have misused "knew." The difference between the strong and weak senses of "know" (and "knew") is not that this entailment holds for the strong but not for the weak sense. It holds for both. If it is false that *p*, then one does not (and did not) know that *p*.

beginning the study of geometry was in doubt as to whether that proposition is true, and had even constructed an ingenious argument that appeared to prove it false. Suppose that Prichard was unable to find any error in the argument. He might have said to the young man: "There must be an error in it. I know that the angles of a triangle are equal to two right angles."

When Prichard says that "nothing can exist which is incompatible with" the truth of that proposition, is he prophesying that no one will ever have the ingenuity to construct a flawless-looking argument against it? I believe not. When Prichard says that "we" *know* (and implies that *he* knows) that the proposition is true and *know* that nothing can exist that is incompatible with its being true, he is not making any *prediction* as to what the future will bring in the way of arguments or measurements. On the contrary, he is asserting that *nothing* that the future might bring could ever count as evidence against the proposition. He is implying that he would not *call* anything "evidence" against it. He is using "know" in what I shall call its "strong" sense. "Know" is used in this sense when a person's statement "I know that *p* is true" implies that the person who makes the statement would look upon nothing whatever as evidence that *p* is false.

It must not be assumed that whenever "know" is used in connexion with mathematical propositions it is used in the strong sense. A great many people have *heard* of various theorems of geometry, *e.g.* the Pythagorean. These theorems are a part of "common knowledge". If a schoolboy doing his geometry assignment felt a doubt about the Pythagorean theorem, and said to an adult, "Are you *sure* that it is true?", the latter might reply "Yes, I know that it is". He might make this reply even though he could not give proof of it and even though he had never gone through a proof of it. If subsequently he was presented with a "demonstration" that the theorem is false, or if various persons reputed to have a knowledge of geometry soberly assured him that it is false, he might be filled with doubt or even be convinced that he was mistaken. When he said "Yes, I know that it is true", he did not pledge himself to hold to the theorem through thick and thin. He did not absolutely exclude the possibility that something could prove it to be false. I shall say that he used "know" in the "weak" sense.

Consider another example from mathematics of the difference between the strong and weak senses of "know". I have just now rapidly calculated that 92 times 16 is 1472. If I had done this in the commerce of daily life where a practical problem was at stake, and if someone had asked "Are you sure that $92 \times 16 = 1472$?", I might have answered "I *know* that it is; I have just now calculated it". But also I might have answered "I know that it is; but I will calculate it again to *make sure*". And here my language points to a distinction. I say that I *know* that 92×16

= 1472. Yet I am willing to *confirm* it—that is, there is something that I should *call* "making sure"; and, likewise, there is something that I should *call* "finding out that it is false". If I were to do this calculation again and obtain the result that $92 \times 16 = 1372$, and if I were to carefully check this latter calculation without finding any error, I should be disposed to say that I was previously mistaken when I declared that $92 \times 16 = 1472$. Thus when I say that I know that $92 \times 16 = 1472$, I allow for the possibility of a *refutation*; and so I am using "know" in its weak sense.

Now consider propositions like $2 + 2 = 4$ and $7 + 5 = 12$. It is hard to think of circumstances in which it would be natural for me to say that I know that $2 + 2 = 4$, because no one ever questions it. Let us try to suppose, however, that someone whose intelligence I respect argues that certain developments in arithmetic have shown that $2 + 2$ does not equal 4. He writes out a proof of this in which I can find no flaw. Suppose that his demeanour showed me that he was in earnest. Suppose that several persons of normal intelligence became persuaded that his proof was correct and that $2 + 2$ does not equal 4. What would be my reaction? I should say "I can't see what is wrong with your proof; but it *is* wrong, because I *know* that $2 + 2 = 4$. Here I should be using "know" in its strong sense. I should not admit that any argument or any future development in mathematics could show that it is false that $2 + 2 = 4$.

The propositions $2 + 2 = 4$ and $92 \times 16 = 1472$ do not have the same status. There *can* be a demonstration that $2 + 2 = 4$. But a demonstration would be for me (and for any average person) only a curious exercise, a sort of *game*. We have no serious interest in proving that proposition.[3] It does not *need* a proof. It stands without one, and would not fall if a proof went against it. The case is different with the proposition that $92 \times 16 = 1472$. We take an interest in the demonstration (calculation) because that proposition *depends* upon its demonstration. A calculation may lead me to reject it as false. But $2 + 2 = 4$ does *not* depend on its demonstration. It does not depend on anything! And in the calculation that proves that $92 \times 16 = 1472$, there are steps that do not depend on any calculation (*e.g.* $2 \times 6 = 12$; $5 + 2 = 7$; $5 + 9 = 14$).

There is a correspondence between this dualism in the logical status of mathematical propositions and the two senses of "know". When I use "know" in the weak sense I am prepared to let an investigation (demonstration, calculation) determine whether the something that I claim to know is true or false. When I use "know" in the strong sense I am not prepared to look upon anything as an *investigation*; I do not concede that anything whatsoever could prove me mistaken; I do not regard the

---

[3] Some logicians and philosophers have taken an interest in proving that $2 + 2 = 4$ (*e.g.* Leibnitz, *New Essays on the Understanding*, Bk. IV, ch. 7, sec. 10; Frege, *The Foundations of Arithmetic*, §6). They have wished to show that it can be deduced from certain premises, and to determine what premises and rules of inference are required in the deduction. Their interest has not been in the *outcome* of the deduction.

matter as open to any *question;* I do not admit that my proposition could turn out to be false, that any future investigation *could* refute it or cast doubt on it.[4]

We have been considering the strong sense of "know" in its application to mathematical propositions. Does it have application anywhere in the realm of *empirical* propositions—for example, to propositions that assert or imply that certain physical things exist? Descartes said that we have a "moral assurance" of the truth of some of the latter propositions but that we lack a "metaphysical certainty".[5] Locke said that the perception of the existence of physical things is not "so certain as our intuitive knowledge, or the deductions of our reason" although "it is an assurance that deserves the name of knowledge".[6] Some philosophers have held that when we make judgments of perception such as that there are peonies in the garden, cows in the field, or dishes in the cupboard, we are "taking for granted" that the peonies, cows, and dishes exist, but not knowing it in the "strict" sense. Others have held that all empirical propositions, including judgments of perception, are merely hypotheses.[7] The thought behind this exaggerated mode of expression is that any empirical proposition whatever *could* be refuted by future experience—that is, it *could* turn out to be false. Are these philosophers right?

Consider the following propositions:

(i) The sun is about ninety million miles from the earth.
(ii) There is a heart in my body.
(iii) Here is an ink-bottle.

In various circumstances I should be willing to assert of each of these propositions that I know it to be true. Yet they differ strikingly. This I see when, with each, I try to imagine the possibility that it is false.

(i) If in ordinary conversation someone said to me "The sun is about 20 million miles from the earth, isn't it?" I should reply "No; it is about 90 million miles from us". If he said "I think that you are confusing the sun with Polaris", I should reply, "I *know* that 90 million miles is roughly the sun's distance from the earth". I might invite him to verify the figure in an encyclopedia. A third person who overheard our conversation could quite correctly report that I knew the distance to the

---

[4] Compare these remarks about the strong sense of "know" with some of Locke's statements about "intuitive knowledge": ". . . in this the mind is at no pains of proving or examining. . . ." "This part of knowledge . . . leaves no room for hesitation, doubt, or examination. . . ."

"It is on this intuition that depends all the certainty and evidence of all our knowledge; which certainly every one finds to be so great, that he cannot imagine, and therefore not require a greater. . . ." Locke, *Essay*, Bk. IV, Ch. 2, §1.

[5] Descartes, *Discourse on the Method*, Part IV.

[6] Locke, *Essay*, Book IV, Ch. 11, §3.

[7] *E.g.* ". . . no proposition, other than a tautology, can possibly be anything more than a probable hypothesis." A. J. Ayer, *Language, Truth and Logic* (New York: Dover Publications, 1951) (2nd edn.), p. 38.

sun, whereas the other man did not. But this knowledge of mine is little better than hearsay. I have seen that figure mentioned in a few books. I know nothing about the observations and calculations that led astronomers to accept it. If tomorrow a group of eminent astronomers announced that a great error had been made and that the correct figure is 20 million miles, I should not insist that they were wrong. It would surprise me that such an enormous mistake could have been made. But I should no longer be willing to say that I *know* that 90 million is the correct figure. Although I should *now* claim that I know the distance to be about 90 million miles, it is easy for me to envisage the possibility that some future investigation will prove this to be false.

(ii) Suppose that after a routine medical examination the excited doctor reports to me that the X-ray photographs show that I have no heart. I should tell him to get a new machine. I should be inclined to say that the fact that I have a heart is one of the few things that I can count on as absolutely certain. I can feel it beat. I know it's there. Furthermore, how could my blood circulate if I didn't have one? Suppose that later on I suffer a chest injury and undergo a surgical operation. Afterwards the astonished surgeons solemnly declare that they searched my chest cavity and found no heart, and that they made incisions and looked about in other likely places but found it not. They are convinced that I am without a heart. They are unable to understand how circulation can occur or what accounts for the thumping in my chest. But they are in agreement and obviously sincere, and they have clear photographs of my interior spaces. What would be my attitude? Would it be to insist that they were all mistaken? I think not. I believe that I should eventually accept their testimony and the evidence of the photographs. I should consider to be false what I now regard as an absolute certainty.

(iii) Suppose that as I write this paper someone in the next room were to call out to me "I can't find an ink-bottle; is there one in the house"? I should reply "Here is an ink-bottle". If he said in doubtful tone "Are you sure? I looked there before", I should reply "Yes, I know there is; come and get it".

Now could it turn out to be false that there is an ink-bottle directly in front of me on this desk? Many philosophers have thought so. They would say that many things could happen of such a nature that if they did happen it would be proved that I am deceived. I agree that many extraordinary things could happen, in the sense that there is no logical absurdity in the supposition. It could happen that when I next reach for this ink-bottle my hand should seem to pass *through* it and I should not feel the contact of any object. It could happen that in the next moment the ink-bottle will suddenly vanish from sight; or that I should find myself under a tree in the garden with no ink-bottle about; or that one or more persons should enter this room and declare with apparent sincerity that they see no ink-bottle on this desk; or that a photograph taken now of the top of the desk should clearly show all of the objects on it except the ink-bottle. Having admitted that these things *could* happen,[8] am I compelled to admit that if they did happen then it would be proved that there is no ink-bottle here *now?* Not at all! I could say that when my hand seemed to pass through the ink-bottle I should *then* be suffering from hallucination; that if the ink-bottle suddenly vanished it would have miraculously ceased to exist; that the other persons were conspiring to drive me mad, or were themselves victims of remarkable concurrent hallucinations; that the camera possessed some strange flaw or that there was trickery in developing the negative. I admit that in the next moment I could find myself under a tree or in the bathtub. But this is not to admit that it could be revealed in the next moment that I am now dreaming. For what I admit is that I might be instantaneously transported to the garden, but not that in the next moment I might *wake up* in the garden. There is nothing that could happen to me in the next moment that I should call "waking up"; and therefore nothing that could happen to me in the next moment would be accepted by me now as proof that I now dream.

Not only do I not *have* to admit that those extraordinary occurrences would be evidence that there is no ink-bottle here; the fact is that I *do not* admit it. There is nothing whatever that could happen in the next moment or the next year that would by me be called *evidence* that there is not an ink-bottle here now. No future experience or investigation could prove to me that I am mistaken. Therefore, if I were to say "I know that there is an ink-bottle here", I should be using "know" in the strong sense.

It will appear to some that I have adopted an *unreasonable* attitude toward that statement. There is, however, nothing unreasonable about it. It seems so because one thinks that the statement that here is an ink-bottle *must* have the same status as the statements that the sun is 90 million miles away and that I have a heart and that there will be water in the gorge this afternoon. But this is a *prejudice*.

In saying that I should regard nothing as evidence that there is no ink-bottle here now, I am not *predicting* what I should do if various astonishing things happened. If other members of my family entered this room and, while looking at the top of this desk, declared with apparent

---

[8] My viewpoint is somewhat different here from what it is in "The Verification Argument" (in *Philosophical Analysis*, Max Black, ed., Prentice-Hall, 1950). There I am concerned with bringing out the different ways in which such a remark as "these things *could* happen" can be taken. I wish to show, furthermore, that from none of the senses in which the remark is *true* does it follow that it is *not certain* that the things in question will *not* happen. Finally, I hold there, that it is perfectly certain that they will not happen. Here, I am not disagreeing with any of those points, but I am adding the further point that my admission that, in some sense, the things *could happen*, does not require me to admit that *if* they were to happen, that would be evidence that there is no ink-bottle here now.

sincerity that they see no ink-bottle, I might fall into a swoon or become mad. I *might* even come to believe that there is not and has not been an ink-bottle here. I cannot foretell with certainty how I should react. But if it is *not* a prediction, what is the meaning of my assertion that I should regard nothing as evidence that there is no ink-bottle here?

That assertion describes my *present* attitude towards the statement that here is an ink-bottle. It does not prophesy what my attitude *would* be if various things happened. My present attitude toward that statement is radically different from my present attitude toward those other statements (*e.g.* that I have a heart).[9] I do *now* admit that certain future occurrences would disprove the latter. Whereas no imaginable future occurrence would be considered by me *now* as proving that there is not an ink-bottle here.

These remarks are not meant to be autobiographical. They are meant to throw light on the common concepts of evidence, proof, and disproof. Everyone of us upon innumerable occasions of daily life takes this same attitude towards various statements about physical things, *e.g.* that here is a torn page, that this dish is broken, that the thermometer reads 70, that no rug is on the floor. Furthermore, the concepts of proof, disproof, doubt, and conjecture, *require* us to take this attitude. In order for it to be possible that any statements about physical things should *turn out to be false* it is necessary that some statements about physical things *cannot* turn out to be false.

This will be made clear if we ask ourselves the question, When do we *say* that something turned out to be false?; When do we use those words? Someone asks you for a dollar. You say "There is one in this drawer". You open the drawer and look, but it is perfectly empty. Your statement turned out to be false. This can be said because you *discovered* an empty drawer. It could not be said if it were only probable that the drawer is empty or were still open to question. Would it make sense to say "I had better make sure that it is empty; perhaps there is a dollar in it after all?" Sometimes; but not always. Not if the drawer lies open before your eyes. That remark is the prelude to a search. What search can there be when the emptiness of the drawer confronts you? In certain circumstances there is nothing that you would call "making sure" that the drawer is empty; and likewise nothing that you would call "its turning out to be false" that the drawer is empty. You *made* sure that the drawer is empty. One statement about physical things *turned out to be false*

---

[9] The word "attitude" is not very satisfactory, but I cannot think of another noun that would do the trick. By "my attitude" I mean, here, *what I should say and think* if various things were to happen. By "my *present* attitude" I mean what I should say and think now, when I imagine those things as happening, in contrast with what I should say and think at some future time if those things actually did happen at that time. It is this distinction that shows that my description of "my present attitude" is not a *prophecy*.

only because you *made sure* of another statement about physical things. The two concepts cannot exist apart. Therefore it is impossible that *every* statement about physical things *could* turn out to be false.

In a certain important respect some *a priori* statements and some empirical statements possess the same logical character. The statements that $5 \times 5 = 25$ and that here is an ink-bottle, both lie beyond the reach of doubt. On both my judgment and reasoning *rests*. If you could somehow undermine my confidence in either, you would not teach me *caution*. You would fill my mind with chaos! I could not even make *conjectures* if you took away those fixed points of certainty; just as a man cannot *try* to climb whose body has no support. A conjecture implies an understanding of what certainty could be. If it is not a certainty that $5 \times 5 = 25$ and that here is an ink-bottle, then I do not understand what it is. You cannot make me doubt either of these statements or treat them as hypotheses. You cannot persuade me that future experience could refute them. With both of them it is perfectly unintelligible to me to speak of a "possibility" that they are false. This is to say that I know both of them to be true, in the strong sense of "know". And I am inclined to think that the strong sense of "know" is what various philosophers have had in mind when they have spoken of "perfect", "metaphysical", or "strict certainty".[10]

It will be thought that I have confused a statement about my "sensations", or my "sense-data", or about the way something *looks* or *appears* to me, with a statement about physical things. It will be thought that the things that I have said about the statement "Here is an ink-bottle" could be true only if that statement is interpreted to mean something like "There appears to me to be an ink-bottle here", *i.e.* interpreted so as not to assert or imply that any physical thing exists. I wish to make it clear that my statement "Here is an ink-bottle" is *not* to be interpreted in that way. It would be utterly fantastic for me in my present circumstances to say "There appears to me to be an ink-bottle here". The usage of the latter sentence would be natural only in two sorts of circumstances: either when I know or believe that there is *not* an ink-bottle before me or when I am in doubt as to whether there is an ink-bottle before me. But I do not know or believe that there is not an ink-bottle here; nor am I in *doubt* as to whether there is—indeed, I *cannot* be in doubt, *i.e.* a doubt is unintelligible to me.

If someone were to call me on the telephone and say that he urgently

---

[10] Descartes, for example, apparently took as his criterion for something's being "entirely certain" that he could not *imagine* in it the least ground of doubt: ". . . je pensai qu'il fallait . . . que je retasse comme absolument faux tout ce en quoi je pourrais imaginer le moindre doute, afin de voir s'il ne me resterait point après cela quelque chose en ma créance qui fut entièrement indubitable" (*Discourse,* Part IV). And Locke (as previously noted) said of "intuitive knowledge" that one *cannot imagine* a greater certainty, and that it "leaves no room for hesitation, doubt, or examination" (*Essay,* Bk. IV, ch. 2, §1).

needed an ink-bottle I should invite him to come here and get this one. If he said that it was extremely urgent that he should obtain one immediately and that he could not afford to waste time going to a place where there might not be one, I should tell him that it is an absolute certainty that there is one here, that nothing could be more certain, that it is something I absolutely guarantee. But if my statement "There is an ink-bottle here" were a statement about my "sensations" or "sense-data", or if it meant that there *appears* to me to be an ink-bottle here or that something here *looks* to me like an ink-bottle, and if that is all that I meant by it—then I should react quite differently to his urgent request. I should say that there is probably an ink-bottle here but that I could not *guarantee* it, and that if he needs one very desperately and at once then he had better look elsewhere. In short, I wish to make it clear that my statement "Here is an ink-bottle" is strictly about physical things and not about "sensations", "sense-data", or "appearances".[11]

Let us go back to Prichard's remark that we can determine by reflection whether we know something or merely believe it. Prichard would think that "knowledge in the weak sense" is mere belief and not knowledge. This is wrong. But if we let ourselves speak this way, we can then see some justification for Prichard's remark. For then he would be asserting, among other things, that we can determine by reflection whether we know something in the strong sense or in the weak sense. This is not literally true; however, there is this truth in it—that reflection can make us realize that we are *using* "I know it" in the strong (or weak) sense in a particular case. Prichard says that reflection can show us that "our condition is one of knowing" a certain thing, or instead that "our condition is one of believing and not of knowing" that thing. I do not understand what could be meant here by "our condition." The way I should put it is that reflection on *what we should think* if certain things were to happen may make us realize that we should (or should not) call those things "proof" or "evidence" that what we claim to know is not so. I have tried to show that the distinction between strong and weak knowledge does not run parallel to the distinction between *a priori* and empirical knowledge but cuts across it, i.e., these two kinds of knowledge may be distinguished *within a priori* knowledge and *within* empirical knowledge.

Reflection can make me realize that I am using "know" in the strong sense; but can reflection show me that I *know* something in the strong sense (or in the weak)? It is not easy to state the logical facts here. On the one hand, if I make an assertion of the form "I know that *p*" it does

11 The remainder of the essay is newly written. The original conclusion was wrongly stated. The reader is referred to the following exchange between Richard Taylor and myself, in respect to the original paper: Taylor, "A Note on Knowledge and Belief," *Analysis*, XIII, June 1953; Malcolm, "On Knowledge and Belief," *Analysis*, XIV, March 1954; Taylor, "Rejoinder to Mr. Malcolm," *ibid.*

not *follow* that *p,* whether or not I am using "know" in the strong sense. If I have said to someone outside my room "Of course, I know that Freddie is in here," and I am speaking in the strong sense, it does not *follow* that Freddie is where I claim he is. This logical fact would not be altered even if I *realized* that I was using "know" in the strong sense. My reflection on what I should say if . . . , cannot show me that I *know* something. From the fact that I should not call anything "evidence" that Freddie is not here, it does not follow that he *is* here; therefore, it does not follow that I *know* he is here.

On the other hand, in an actual case of my using "know" in the strong sense, I cannot envisage a possibility that what I say to be true should turn out to be not true. If I were speaking of *another person's* assertion about something, I *could* think both that he is using "know" in the strong sense and that nonetheless what he claims he knows to be so might turn out to be not so. But *in my own case* I cannot have this conjunction of thoughts, and this is a logical and not a psychological fact. When *I* say that I know something to be so, using "know" in the strong sense, it is unintelligible *to me* (although perhaps not to others) to suppose that anything could prove that it is not so and, therefore, that I do not know it.[12]

[12] This is the best summary I can give of what is wrong and right in Prichard's claim that one can determine by reflection whether one knows something or merely believes it. A good part of the ideas in this essay were provoked by conversations with Wittgenstein. A brief and rough account of those talks is to be found in my *Ludwig Wittgenstein: A Memoir* (New York, Oxford University Press, 1958), p. 87-92.

Further Reading

The following books and papers contain discussions of knowing and other topics pertinent to this chapter.

AARON, R. I., *The Nature of Knowing* (London, Williams & Norgate Ltd., 1930).

Aristotelian Society Symposia: Is there knowledge by acquaintance? Suppl. II (1919); Suppl. XXIII (1949).

AUSTIN, J. L., "Other Minds," *Proceedings of the Aristotelian Society,* Suppl. XX (1946), pp. 148-187. Reprinted in A. Flew ed. *Logic and Language* II (Oxford, Basil Blackwell, 1959).

AYER, A. J., *Language, Truth & Logic* (London, Victor Gollancz, 1936). (New York, Dover Publications, Inc.).

———— *The Problem of Knowledge* (London, Macmillan and Co., Ltd., 1956).

BECK, L. J., *The Method of Descartes: A study of the Regulae* (Oxford, Clarendon Press, 1952).

BERGSON, H., *An Introduction to Metaphysics,* T. E. Hulme, trans. (New York, Liberal Arts Press, Inc., 1949).

CASSIRER, E., *Das Erkenntnisproblem in der Philosophie und Wissenschaft der neueren Zeit* (Berlin, B. Cassirer, 1922-3). Three volumes.

———— *The Problem of Knowledge: Philosophy, Science and History Since Hegel,* W. H. Woglon and C. W. Hendel, trans. (New Haven, Yale University Press, 1950).

CORNFORD, F. M., *Plato's Theory of Knowledge* (London, Routledge & Kegan Paul Ltd, 1935). (New York, Liberal Arts Press, Inc.).

DEWEY, J., *The Quest for Certainty* (New York, Minton, Balch & Co., 1929).

EWING, A. C., *Idealism* (London, Methuen and Co., 1934).

HARTLAND-SWANN, J., *An Analysis of Knowing* (London, Allen & Unwin, 1958).

HUSSERL, E., *Cartesian Meditations: An Introduction to Phenomenology* (The Hague, Martinus Nijhoff, 1960).

LAIRD, J., *Knowledge, Belief and Opinion* (New York, Appleton-Century-Crofts, 1930).

LEWIS, C. I., *An Analysis of Knowledge and Valuation* (LaSalle, Ill., Open Court Publishing Co., 1946).

———— *Mind and the World Order* (New York, Charles Scribner's Sons, 1929).

MORRIS, C. R., *Idealistic Logic: a Study of its Aim, Method and Achievement* (London, Macmillan & Co., Ltd., 1933).

PIERCE, C. S., *Collected Papers: Pragmatism and Pragmaticism,* Vol. 5 (Harvard University Press, 1960).

ROYCE, J., *The World and the Individual,* second series (New York, Dover Publications).

RUSSELL, B., *Analysis of Mind* (New York, W. W. Norton & Company, Inc.).

RYLE, G., *The Concept of Mind* (London, Hutchinson's University Library, 1949).

SCHLICK, M., *Allgemeine Erkenntnislehre* (Berlin, Springer, 1925).

SMITH, N. K., *New Studies in the Philosophy of Descartes* (London, Macmillan & Co., 1952).

SPINOZA, B., *On the Improvement of the Understanding* (New York, Dover Publications, Inc., 1951).

———— *Ethics,* part II (New York, Dover Publications, Inc., 1951).

STACE, W. T., *The Theory of Knowledge and Existence* (Oxford University Press, 1932).

STOUT, G. F., *God and Nature* (Cambridge University Press, 1952).

TAYLOR, A. E., "Knowing and Believing," *Proceedings of the Aristotelian Society,* Vol. XXIX (1928-9), pp. 1-30.

WERKMEISTER, W. H., *The Basis and Structure of Knowledge* (New York, Harper & Row, Publishers, 1948).

WILSON, J. C., *Statement and Inference,* Vol. 1 (Oxford University Press, 1926).

WOOZLEY, A. D., *Theory of Knowledge* (London, Hutchinson's University Library, 1949).

PART TWO

Rationalism
and Empiricism

Introduction

In the introduction to the *Critique of Pure Reason,* Immanuel Kant (1724–1804) develops two important distinctions. First, judgments are divided into two kinds, analytic and synthetic. A judgment is analytic if the predicate of the judgment is contained in the subject. For example, in the sentence "All bachelors are unmarried," the notion of being unmarried is contained in—is part of the meaning of—the subject term "bachelor"; thus the sentence is analytic. We can know that such a sentence is true simply by analyzing the meaning of the subject term. This is not the case with synthetic judgments. For example, the synthetic judgment, "Sugar dissolves in water," is not true simply because of the meaning of "sugar."

Kant's second distinction is between *a priori* knowledge and *a posteriori,* or empirical, knowledge. Something is known *a priori* if it is known independently of experience. On the other hand, experience is necessary to *a posteriori* knowledge.

Since empirical tests and marks of evidence are entirely out of place in judging the truth of an analytic sentence, it follows that all analytic judgments are *a priori.* Conversely, all truths known *a posteriori* are synthetic. The interesting question is, are there truths which are both *a priori* and synthetic? That is, are there any *a priori* truths which are not analytic?

Among the candidates for the role of synthetic *a priori* truths are truths of mathematics, science, ethics, and statements of metaphysics. With respect to the second of these, Kant would maintain that such propositions as "Every event has a cause," are both non-analytic and known *a priori.* Experience, he would claim, can never prove or refute such propositions; yet, though they are clearly non-analytic, we know them to be true. An empiricist such as John Stuart Mill (1806–1873) would treat such sentences quite differently. He would grant that they are non-analytic, but deny that they are *a priori.* He might say, for example, that the above proposition is supported by experience and only probably true; past events have been discovered to have had causes, hence it is reasonable to expect—on inductive grounds—that future events will have causes. On the other hand, an empiricist might treat the sentence as not really a proposition at all, that is, as neither true nor false. He might claim, for example, that it is actually a disguised *imperative* or methodological *rule* of science: "Search for the causes of all events!"

When we turn to mathematical statements the situation is in one respect more complex. While most philosophers would agree that "All events have causes" is not analytic, they have been divided on the analyticity of mathematical statements. While some rationalists and empiricists agree that "7 + 5 = 12" is analytic, others, such as Kant and Mill, argue that the sentence is non-analytic. But Kant and Mill have quite different reasons for their views. Kant treats "7 + 5 = 12" as synthetic *a priori*, whereas Mill views the proposition as known through induction. According to Mill, we know that "7 + 5 = 12" is true in the same way, roughly, that we know "All ravens are black" is true; namely, by examining actual instances of adding seven things to five other things (adding five apples to a pile of seven apples, for instance) and ascertaining the results of these additions.

Mill holds that the truths of logic and of all branches of mathematics, including geometry, are inductive generalizations from experience. In the selection from Gottlob Frege (1848–1925) reprinted here, Mill's view of the inductive character of mathematics is trenchantly criticized. The selection from A. J. Ayer, a contemporary British philosopher, defends the above mentioned theory that statements of mathematics are analytic.

The opening selection in this chapter is from John Locke's *Essay Concerning Human Understanding* (1690). Locke's views relate directly to some of the problems mentioned above. Locke maintains that the source of all our ideas is experience, and that these ideas either are, or can be reduced to, simple impressions from our senses or from introspection. This view leads him, on the one hand, to criticize the doctrine of "innate ideas," and, on the other, to hold that such complex ideas as that of infinity can be reduced to simple ideas of sense or reflection.

EIGHT

An Empiricist Outlook

JOHN LOCKE (1632-1704)

From An Essay Concerning Human Understanding*

INTRODUCTION

1. Since it is the *understanding* that sets man above the rest of sensible beings, and gives him all the advantage and dominion which he has over them; it is certain a subject, even for its nobleness, worth our labour to inquire into. The understanding, like the eye, whilst it makes us see and perceive all other things, takes no notice of itself; and it requires art and pains to set it at a distance and make it its own object. But whatever be the difficulties that lie in the way of this inquiry; whatever it be that keeps us so much in the dark to ourselves; sure I am that all the light we can let in upon our minds, all the acquaintance we can make with our own understandings, will not only be very pleasant, but bring us great advantage, in directing our thoughts in the search of other things.

2. This, therefore, being my purpose—to inquire into the original, certainty, and extent of *human knowledge,* together with the grounds and degrees of *belief, opinion,* and *assent;*—I shall not at present meddle with the physical consideration of the mind; or trouble myself to examine wherein its essence consists; or by what motions of our spirits or alterations of our bodies we come to have any *sensation* by our organs, or any *ideas* in our understandings; and whether those ideas do in their formation, any or all of them, depend on matter or not. These are speculations which, however curious and entertaining, I shall decline, as lying out of my way in the design I am now upon. It shall suffice to my present purpose, to consider the discerning faculties of a man, as they are employed about the objects which they have to do with. And I shall imagine I have not wholly misemployed myself in the thoughts I shall have on this occasion, if, in this historical, plain method, I can give any account of the ways whereby our understandings come to attain those notions of things we have; and can set down any measures of the certainty of our

* From *An Essay Concerning Human Understanding* by John Locke (1690).

knowledge; or the grounds of those persuasions which are to be found amongst men, so various, different, and wholly contradictory; and yet asserted somewhere or other with such assurance and confidence, that he that shall take a view of the opinions of mankind, observe their opposition, and at the same time consider the fondness and devotion wherewith they are embraced, the resolution and eagerness wherewith they are maintained, may perhaps have reason to suspect, that either there is no such thing as truth at all, or that mankind hath no sufficient means to attain a certain knowledge of it.

3. It is therefore worth while to search out the bounds between opinion and knowledge; and examine by what measures, in things whereof we have no certain knowledge, we ought to regulate our assent and moderate our persuasion. In order whereunto I shall pursue this following method:—

First, I shall inquire into the original of those *ideas,* notions, or whatever else you please to call them, which a man observes, and is conscious to himself he has in his mind; and the ways whereby the understanding comes to be furnished with them.

Secondly, I shall endeavour to show what *knowledge* the understanding hath by those ideas; and the certainty, evidence, and extent of it.

Thirdly, I shall make some inquiry into the nature and grounds of *faith* or *opinion*: whereby I mean that assent which we give to any proposition as true, of whose truth yet we have no certain knowledge. And here we shall have occasion to examine the reasons and degrees of *assent.*

4. If by this inquiry into the nature of the understanding, I can discover the powers thereof; how far they reach; to what things they are in any degree proportionate; and where they fail us, I suppose it may be of use to prevail with the busy mind of man to be more cautious in meddling with things exceeding its comprehension; to stop when it is at the utmost extent of its tether; and to sit down in a quiet ignorance of those things which, upon examination, are found to be beyond the reach of our capacities. We should not then perhaps be so forward, out of an affectation of an universal knowledge, to raise questions, and perplex ourselves and others with disputes about things to which our understandings are not suited; and of which we cannot frame in our minds any clear or distinct perceptions, or whereof (as it has perhaps too often happened) we have not any notions at all. If we can find out how far the understanding can extend its view; how far it has faculties to attain certainty; and in what cases it can only judge and guess, we may learn to content ourselves with what is attainable by us in this state.

5. For though the comprehension of our understandings comes exceeding short of the vast extent of things, yet we shall have cause enough to magnify the bountiful Author of our being, for that propor-

tion and degree of knowledge he has bestowed on us, so far above all the rest of the inhabitants of this our mansion. Men have reason to be well satisfied with what God hath thought fit for them, since he hath given them (as St. Peter says) πάντα πρὸς ζωὴν καὶ εὐσέβειαν, whatsoever is necessary for the conveniences of life and information of virtue; and has put within the reach of their discovery, the comfortable provision for this life, and the way that leads to a better. How short soever their knowledge may come of an universal or perfect comprehension of whatsoever is, it yet secures their great concernments, that they have light enough to lead them to the knowledge of their Maker, and the sight of their own duties. Men may find matter sufficient to busy their heads, and employ their hands with variety, delight, and satisfaction, if they will not boldly quarrel with their own constitution, and throw away the blessings their hands are filled with, because they are not big enough to grasp everything. We shall not have much reason to complain of the narrowness of our minds, if we will but employ them about what may be of use to us; for of that they are very capable. And it will be an unpardonable, as well as childish peevishness, if we undervalue the advantages of our knowledge, and neglect to improve it to the ends for which it was given us, because there are some things that are set out of the reach of it. It will be no excuse to an idle and untoward servant, who would not attend his business by candle light, to plead that he had not broad sunshine. The Candle that is set up in us shines bright enough for all our purposes. The discoveries we can make with this ought to satisfy us; and we shall then use our understandings right, when we entertain all objects in that way and proportion that they are suited to our faculties, and upon those grounds they are capable of being proposed to us; and not peremptorily or intemperately require demonstration, and demand certainty, where probability only is to be had, and which is sufficient to govern all our concernments. If we will disbelieve everything, because we cannot certainly know all things, we shall do muchwhat as wisely as he who would not use his legs, but sit still and perish, because he had no wings to fly.

6. When we know our own strength, we shall the better know what to undertake with hopes of success; and when we have well surveyed the *powers* of our own minds, and made some estimate what we may expect from them, we shall not be inclined either to sit still, and not set our thoughts on work at all, in despair of knowing anything; nor on the other side, question everything, and disclaim all knowledge, because some things are not to be understood. It is of great use to the sailor to know the length of his line, though he cannot with it fathom all the depths of the ocean. It is well he knows that it is long enough to reach the bottom, at such places as are necessary to direct his voyage, and caution him against running upon shoals that may ruin him. Our business here is not to know all things, but those which concern our

conduct. If we can find out those measures, whereby a rational creature, put in that state in which man is in this world, may and ought to govern his opinions, and actions depending thereon, we need not to be troubled that some other things escape our knowledge.

7. This was that which gave the first rise to this *Essay* concerning the understanding. For I thought that the first step towards satisfying several inquiries the mind of man was very apt to run into, was, to take a survey of our own understandings, examine our own powers, and see to what things they were adapted. Till that was done I suspected we began at the wrong end, and in vain sought for satisfaction in a quiet and sure possession of truths that most concerned us, whilst we let loose our thoughts into the vast ocean of Being; as if all that boundless extent were the natural and undoubted possession of our understandings, wherein there was nothing exempt from its decisions, or that escaped its comprehension. Thus men, extending their inquiries beyond their capacities, and letting their thoughts wander into those depths where they can find no sure footing, it is no wonder that they raise questions and multiply disputes, which, never coming to any clear resolution, are proper only to continue and increase their doubts, and to confirm them at last in perfect scepticism. Whereas, were the capacities of our understandings well considered, the extent of our knowledge once discovered, and the horizon found which sets the bounds between the enlightened and dark parts of things; between what is and what is not comprehensible by us, men would perhaps with less scruple acquiesce in the avowed ignorance of the one, and employ their thoughts and discourse with more advantage and satisfaction in the other.

8. Thus much I thought necessary to say concerning the occasion of this Inquiry into human Understanding. But, before I proceed on to what I have thought on this subject, I must here in the entrance beg pardon of my reader for the frequent use of the word *idea,* which he will find in the following treatise. It being that term which, I think, serves best to stand for whatsoever is the *object* of the understanding when a man thinks, I have used it to express whatever is meant by *phantasm, notion, species,* or *whatever it is which the mind can be employed about in thinking;* and I could not avoid frequently using it.

I presume it will be easily granted me, that there are such *ideas* in men's minds: every one is conscious of them in himself; and men's words and actions will satisfy him that they are in others.

Our first inquiry then shall be,—how they come into the mind.

NO INNATE SPECULATIVE
PRINCIPLES *refutation of Descartes and Plato ??*

I, i,   1. It is an established opinion amongst some men, that there
are in the understanding certain *innate principles;* some primary notions,
κοιναὶ ἔννοιαι, characters, as it were stamped upon the mind of man;
which the soul receives in its very first being, and brings into the world
with it. It would be sufficient to convince unprejudiced readers of the
falseness of this supposition, if I should only show (as I hope I shall in
the following parts of this Discourse) how men, barely by the use of
their natural faculties, may attain to all the knowledge they have, without
the help of any innate impressions; and may arrive at certainty, without
any such original notions or principles. For I imagine any one will easily
grant that it would be impertinent to suppose the ideas of colours innate
in a creature to whom God hath given sight, and a power to receive
them by the eyes from external objects: and no less unreasonable would
it be to attribute several truths to the impressions of nature, and innate
characters, when we may observe in ourselves faculties fit to attain as
easy and certain knowledge of them as if they were originally imprinted
on the mind.

But because a man is not permitted without censure to follow his
own thoughts in the search of truth, when they lead him ever so little
out of the common road, I shall set down the reasons that made me
doubt of the truth of that opinion, as an excuse for my mistake, if I be
in one; which I leave to be considered by those who, with me, dispose
themselves to embrace truth wherever they find it.

2. There is nothing more commonly taken for granted than that
there are certain *principles,* both *speculative* and *practical,* (for they
speak of both), universally agreed upon by all mankind: which therefore,
they argue, must needs be the constant impressions which the souls of men
receive in their first beings, and which they bring into the world with
them, as necessarily and really as they do any of their inherent faculties.

3. This argument, drawn from universal consent, has this misfor-
tune in it, that if it were true in matter of fact, that there were certain
truths wherein all mankind agreed, it would not prove them innate, if
there can be any other way shown how men may come to that universal
agreement, in the things they do consent in, which I presume may be
done.

4. But, which is worse, this argument of universal consent, which
is made use of to prove innate principles, seems to me a demonstration
that there are none such: because there are none to which all mankind
give an universal assent. I shall begin with the speculative, and instance
in those magnified principles of demonstration, 'Whatsoever is, is,' and

'It is impossible for the same thing to be and not to be'; which, of all others, I think have the most allowed title to innate. These have so settled a reputation of maxims universally received, that it will no doubt be thought strange if any one should seem to question it. But yet I take liberty to say, that these propositions are so far from having an universal assent, that there are a great part of mankind to whom they are not so much as known.

5. For, first, it is evident, that all children and idiots have not the least apprehension or thought of them. And the want of that is enough to destroy that universal assent which must needs be the necessary concomitant of all innate truths: it seeming to me near a contradiction to say, that there are truths imprinted on the soul, which it perceives or understands not: imprinting, if it signify anything, being nothing else but the making certain truths to be perceived. For to imprint anything on the mind without the mind's perceiving it, seems to me hardly intelligible. If therefore children and idiots have souls, have minds, with those impressions upon them, *they* must unavoidably perceive them, and necessarily know and assent to these truths; which since they do not, it is evident that there are no such impressions. For if they are not notions naturally imprinted, how can they be innate? and if they are notions imprinted, how can they be unknown? To say a notion is imprinted on the mind, and yet at the same time to say, that the mind is ignorant of it, and never yet took notice of it, is to make this impression nothing. No proposition can be said to be in the mind which it never yet knew, which it was never yet conscious of. For if any one may, then, by the same reason, all propositions that are true, and the mind is capable ever of assenting to, may be said to be in the mind, and to be imprinted: since, if any one can be said to be in the mind, which it never yet knew, it must be only because it is capable of knowing it; and so the mind is of all truths it ever shall know. Nay, thus truths may be imprinted on the mind which it never did, nor ever shall know; for a man may live long, and die at last in ignorance of many truths which his mind was capable of knowing, and that with certainty. So that if the capacity of knowing be the natural impression contended for, all the truths a man ever comes to know will, by this account, be every one of them innate; and this great point will amount to no more, but only to a very improper way of speaking; which, whilst it pretends to assert the contrary, says nothing different from those who deny innate principles. For nobody, I think, ever denied that the mind was capable of knowing several truths. The capacity, they say, is innate; the knowledge acquired. But then to what end such contest for certain innate maxims? If truths can be imprinted on the understanding without being perceived, I can see no difference there can be between any truths the mind is *capable* of knowing in respect of their original: they must all be innate or all adventitious:

in vain shall a man go about to distinguish them. He therefore that talks of innate notions in the understanding, cannot (if he intend thereby any distinct sort of truths) mean such truths to be in the understanding as it never perceived, and is yet wholly ignorant of. For if these words 'to be in the understanding' have any propriety, they signify to be understood. So that to be in the understanding, and not to be understood; to be in the mind and never to be perceived, is all one as to say anything is and is not in the mind or understanding. If therefore these two propositions, 'Whatsoever is, is,' and 'It is impossible for the same thing to be and not to be,' are by nature imprinted, children cannot be ignorant of them: infants, and all that have souls, must necessarily have them in their understandings, know the truth of them, and assent to it.

6. To avoid this, it is usually answered, that all men know and assent to them, *when they come to the use of reason;* and this is enough to prove them innate. I answer:

7. Doubtful expressions, that have scarce any significance, go for clear reasons to those who, being prepossessed, take not the pains to examine even what they themselves say. For, to apply this answer with any tolerable sense to our present purpose, it must signify one of these two things: either that as soon as men come to the use of reason these supposed native inscriptions come to be known and observed by them; or else, that the use and exercise of men's reason, assists them in the discovery of these principles, and certainly makes them known to them.

8. If they mean, that by the use of reason men may discover these principles, and that this is sufficient to prove them innate; their way of arguing will stand thus, viz. that whatever truths reason can certainly discover to us, and make us firmly assent to, those are all naturally imprinted on the mind; since that universal assent, which is made the mark of them, amounts to no more but this,—that by the use of reason we are capable to come to a certain knowledge of and assent to them; and, by this means, there will be no difference between the maxims of the mathematicians, and theorems they deduce from them: all must be equally allowed innate; they being all discoveries made by the use of reason, and truths that a rational creature may certainly come to know, if he apply his thoughts rightly that way.

9. But how can these men think the use of reason necessary to discover principles that are supposed innate, when reason (if we may believe them) is nothing else but the faculty of deducing unknown truths from principles or propositions that are already known? That certainly can never be thought innate which we have need of reason to discover; unless as I have said, we will have all the certain truths that reason ever teaches us, to be innate. We may as well think the use of reason necessary to make our eyes discover visible objects, as that there should be need of reason, or the exercise thereof, to make the understanding see what is

originally engraven on it, and cannot be in the understanding before it be perceived by it. So that to make reason discover those truths thus imprinted, is to say, that the use of reason discovers to a man what he knew before: and if men have those innate impressed truths originally, and before the use of reason, and yet are always ignorant of them till they come to the use of reason, it is in effect to say, that men know and know them not at the same time.

10. It will here perhaps be said that mathematical demonstrations, and other truths that are not innate, are not assented to as soon as proposed, wherein they are distinguished from these maxims and other innate truths. I shall have occasion to speak of assent upon the first proposing, more particularly by and by. I shall here only, and that very readily, allow, that these maxims and mathematical demonstrations are in this different: that the one have need of reason, using of proofs, to make them out and to gain our assent; but the other, as soon as understood, are, without any the least reasoning, embraced and assented to. But I withal beg leave to observe, that it lays open the weakness of this subterfuge, which requires the use of reason for the discovery of these general truths: since it must be confessed that in their discovery there is no use made of reasoning at all. And I think those who give this answer will not be forward to affirm that the knowledge of this maxim, 'That it is impossible for the same thing to be and not to be,' is a deduction of our reason. For this would be to destroy that bounty of nature they seem so fond of, whilst they make the knowledge of those principles to depend on the labour of our thoughts. For all reasoning is search, and casting about, and requires pains and application. And how can it with any tolerable sense be supposed, that what was imprinted by nature, as the foundation and guide of our reason, should need the use of reason to discover it?

11. Those who will take the pains to reflect with a little attention on the operations of the understanding, will find that this ready assent of the mind to some truths, depends not, either on native inscription, or the use of reason, but on a faculty of the mind quite distinct from both of them, as we shall see hereafter. Reason, therefore, having nothing to do in procuring our assent to these maxims, if by saying, that 'men know and assent to them, when they come to the use of reason,' be meant, that the use of reason assists us in the knowledge of these maxims, it is utterly false; and were it true, would prove them not to be innate.

12. If by knowing and assenting to them 'when we come to the use of reason,' be meant, that this is the time when they come to be taken notice of by the mind; and that as soon as children come to the use of reason, they come also to know and assent to these maxims; this also is false and frivolous. First, it is false; because it is evident these maxims are not in the mind so early as the use of reason; and therefore the coming

to the use of reason is falsely assigned as the time of their discovery. How many instances of the use of reason may we observe in children, a long time before they have any knowledge of this maxim, 'That it is impossible for the same thing to be and not to be?' And a great part of illiterate people and savages pass many years, even of their rational age, without ever thinking on this and the like general propositions. I grant, men come not to the knowledge of these general and more abstract truths, which are thought innate, till they come to the use of reason; and I add, nor then neither. Which is so, because, till after they come to the use of reason, those general abstract ideas are not framed in the mind, about which those general maxims are, which are mistaken for innate principles, but are indeed discoveries made and verities introduced and brought into the mind by the same way, and discovered by the same steps, as several other propositions, which nobody was ever so extravagant as to suppose innate. This I hope to make plain in the sequel of this Discourse. I allow therefore, a necessity that men should come to the use of reason before they get the knowledge of those general truths; but deny that men's coming to the use of reason is the time of their discovery.

13. In the mean time it is observable, that this saying, that men know and assent to these maxims 'when they come to the use of reason,' amounts in reality of fact to no more but this,—that they are never known nor taken notice of before the use of reason, but may possibly be assented to some time after, during a man's life; but when is uncertain. And so may all other knowable truths, as well as these; which therefore have no advantage nor distinction from others by this note of being known when we come to the use of reason; nor are thereby proved to be innate, but quite the contrary.

14. But, secondly, were it true that the precise time of their being known and assented to were, when men come to the use of reason; neither would that prove them innate. This way of arguing is as frivolous as the supposition itself is false. For, by what kind of logic will it appear that any notion is originally by nature imprinted in the mind in its first constitution, because it comes first to be observed and assented to when a faculty of the mind, which has quite a distinct province, begins to exert itself? And therefore the coming to the use of speech, if it were supposed the time that these maxims are first assented to, (which it may be with as much truth as the time when men come to the use of reason,) would be as good a proof that they were innate, as to say they are innate because men assent to them when they come to the use of reason. I agree then with these men of innate principles, that there is no knowledge of these general and self-evident maxims in the mind, till it comes to the exercise of reason: but I deny that the coming to the use of reason is the precise time when they are first taken notice of; and if that were the precise time, I deny that it would prove them innate. All that can with

any truth be meant by this proposition, that men 'assent to them when they come to the use of reason,' is no more but this,—that the making of general abstract ideas, and the understanding of general names, being a concomitant of the rational faculty, and growing up with it, children commonly get not those general ideas, nor learn the names that stand for them, till, having for a good while exercised their reason about familiar and more particular ideas, they are, by their ordinary discourse and actions with others, acknowledged to be capable of rational conversation. If assenting to these maxims, when men come to the use of reason, can be true in any other sense, I desire it may be shown; or at least, how in this, or any other sense, it proves them innate.

15. The senses at first let in *particular* ideas, and furnish the yet empty cabinet, and the mind by degrees growing familiar with some of them, they are lodged in the memory, and names got to them. Afterwards, the mind proceeding further, abstracts them, and by degrees learns the use of general names. In this manner the mind comes to be furnished with ideas and language, the *materials* about which to exercise its discursive faculty. And the use of reason becomes daily more visible, as these materials that give it employment increase. But though the having of general ideas and the use of general words and reason usually grow together, yet I see not how this any way proves them innate. The knowledge of some truths, I confess, is very early in the mind; but in a way that shows them not to be innate. For, if we will observe, we shall find it still to be about ideas, not innate, but acquired; it being about those first which are imprinted by external things, with which infants have earliest to do, which make the most frequent impressions on their senses. In ideas thus got, the mind discovers that some agree and others differ, probably as soon as it has any use of memory; as soon as it is able to retain and perceive distinct ideas. But whether it be then or no, this is certain, it does so long before it has the use of words; or comes to that which we commonly call 'the use of reason.' For a child knows as certainly before it can speak the difference between the ideas of sweet and bitter (i.e. that sweet is not bitter), as it knows afterwards (when it comes to speak) that wormwood and sugarplums are not the same thing. . . .

OF IDEAS IN GENERAL, AND THEIR ORIGINAL

II, i,   1. Every man being conscious to himself that he thinks; and that which his mind is applied about whilst thinking being the *ideas* that are there, it is past doubt that men have in their minds several ideas,— such as are those expressed by the words *whiteness, hardness, sweetness, thinking, motion, man, elephant, army, drunkenness,* and others: it is in the first place then to be inquired, *How he comes by them?*

I know it is a received doctrine, that men have native ideas, and original characters, stamped upon their minds in their very first being. This opinion I have at large examined already; and, I suppose what I have said in the foregoing Book will be much more easily admitted, when I have shown whence the understanding may get all the ideas it has; and by what ways and degrees they may come into the mind;—for which I shall appeal to every one's own observation and experience.

2. Let us then suppose the mind to be, as we say, white paper, void of all characters, without any ideas:—How comes it to be furnished? Whence comes it by that vast store which the busy and boundless fancy of man has painted on it with an almost endless variety? Whence has it all the *materials* of reason and knowledge? To this I answer, in one word, from EXPERIENCE. In that all our knowledge is founded; and from that it ultimately derives itself. Our observation employed either, about external sensible objects, or about the internal operations of our minds perceived and reflected on by ourselves, is that which supplies our understandings with all the *materials* of thinking. These two are the fountains of knowledge, from whence all the ideas we have, or can naturally have, do spring.

3. First, our Senses, conversant about particular sensible objects, do convey into the mind several distinct perceptions of things, according to those various ways wherein those objects do affect them. And thus we come by those *ideas* we have of *yellow, white, heat, cold, soft, hard, bitter, sweet,* and all those which we call sensible qualities; which when I say the senses convey into the mind, I mean, they from external objects convey into the mind what produces there those perceptions. This great source of most of the ideas we have, depending wholly upon our senses, and derived by them to the understanding, I call SENSATION.

4. Secondly, the other fountain from which experience furnisheth the understanding with ideas is,—the perception of the operations of our own mind within us, as it is employed about the ideas it has got;—which operations, when the soul comes to reflect on and consider, do furnish the understanding with another set of ideas, which could not be had from things without. And such are *perception, thinking, doubting, believing, reasoning, knowing, willing,* and all the different actings of our own minds;—which we being conscious of, and observing in ourselves, do from these receive into our understandings as distinct ideas as we do from bodies affecting our senses. This source of ideas every man has wholly in himself; and though it be not sense, as having nothing to do with external objects, yet it is very like it, and might properly enough be called *internal sense.* But as I call the other Sensation, so I call this REFLECTION, the ideas it affords being such only as the mind gets by reflecting on its own operations within itself. By reflection then, in the following part of this discourse, I would be understood to mean, that notice which the mind takes of its own operations, and the manner

of them, by reason whereof there come to be ideas of these operations in the understanding. These two, I say, viz. external material things, as the objects of SENSATION, and the operations of our own minds within, as the objects of REFLECTION, are to me the only originals from whence all our ideas take their beginnings. The term *operations* here I use in a large sense, as comprehending not barely the actions of the mind about its ideas, but some sort of passions arising sometimes from them, such as is the satisfaction or uneasiness arising from any thought.

5. The understanding seems to me not to have the least glimmering of any ideas which it doth not receive from one of these two. *External objects* furnish the mind with the ideas of sensible qualities, which are all those different perceptions they produce in us; and *the mind* furnishes the understanding with ideas of its own operations.

These, when we have taken a full survey of them, and their several modes, [combinations, and relations,] we shall find to contain all our whole stock of ideas; and that we have nothing in our minds which did not come in one of these two ways. Let any one examine his own thoughts, and thoroughly search into his understanding; and then let him tell me, whether all the original ideas he has there, are any other than of the objects of his senses, or of the operations of his mind, considered as objects of his reflection. And how great a mass of knowledge soever he imagines to be lodged there, he will, upon taking a strict view, see that he has not any idea in his mind but what one of these two have imprinted; —though perhaps, with infinite variety compounded and enlarged by the understanding, as we shall see hereafter.

6. He that attentively considers the state of a child, at his first coming into the world, will have little reason to think him stored with plenty of ideas, that are to be the matter of his future knowledge. It is *by degrees* he comes to be furnished with them. And though the ideas of obvious and familiar qualities imprint themselves before the memory begins to keep a register of time or order, yet it is often so late before some unusual qualities come in the way, that there are few men that cannot recollect the beginning of their acquaintance with them. And if it were worth while, no doubt a child might be so ordered as to have but a very few, even of the ordinary ideas, till he were grown up to a man. But all that are born into the world, being surrounded with bodies that perpetually and diversely affect them, variety of ideas, whether care be taken of it or not, are imprinted on the minds of children. Light and colours are busy at hand everywhere, when the eye is but open; sounds and some tangible qualities fail not to solicit their proper senses, and force an entrance to the mind;—but yet, I think, it will be granted easily, that if a child were kept in a place where he never saw any other but black and white till he were a man, he would have no more ideas

of scarlet or green, than he that from his childhood never tasted an oyster, or a pine-apple, has of those particular relishes.

7. Men then come to be furnished with fewer or more simple ideas from without, according as the objects they converse with afford greater or less variety; and from the operations of their minds within, according as they more or less reflect on them. For, though he that contemplates the operations of his mind, cannot but have plain and clear ideas of them; yet, unless he turn his thoughts that way, and considers them *attentively,* he will no more have clear and distinct ideas of all the operations of his mind, and all that may be observed therein, than he will have all the particular ideas of any landscape, or of the parts and motions of a clock, who will not turn his eyes to it, and with attention heed all the parts of it. The picture, or clock may be so placed, that they may come in his way every day; but yet he will have but a confused idea of all the parts they are made up of, till he applies himself with attention, to consider them each in particular.

8. And hence we see the reason why it is pretty late before most children get ideas of the operations of their own minds; and some have not any very clear or perfect ideas of the greatest part of them all their lives. Because, though they pass there continually, yet, like floating visions, they make not deep impressions enough to leave in their mind clear, distinct, lasting ideas, till the understanding turns inward upon itself, reflects on its own operations, and makes them the objects of its own contemplation. . . .

24. The impressions then that are made on our senses by outward objects that are extrinsical to the mind; and its own operations about these impressions, reflected on by itself, as proper objects to be contemplated by it, are, I conceive, the original of all knowledge. Thus the first capacity of human intellect is,—that the mind is fitted to receive the impressions made on it; either through the senses by outward objects, or by its own operations when it reflects on them. This is the first step a man makes towards the discovery of anything, and the groundwork whereon to build all those notions which ever he shall have naturally in this world. All those sublime thoughts which tower above the clouds, and reach as high as heaven itself, take their rise and footing here: in all that great extent wherein the mind wanders, in those remote speculations it may seem to be elevated with, it stirs not one jot beyond those ideas which *sense* or *reflection* have offered for its contemplation.

25. In this part the understanding is merely passive; and whether or no it will have these beginnings, and as it were materials of knowledge, is not in its own power. For the objects of our senses do, many of them, obtrude their particular ideas upon our minds whether we will

or not; and the operations of our minds will not let us be without, at least, some obscure notions of them. No man can be wholly ignorant of what he does when he thinks. These simple ideas, when offered to the mind, the understanding can no more refuse to have, nor alter when they are imprinted, nor blot them out and make new ones itself, than a mirror can refuse, alter, or obliterate the images or ideas which the objects set before it do therein produce. As the bodies that surround us do diversely affect our organs, the mind is forced to receive the impressions; and cannot avoid the perception of those ideas that are annexed to them.

OF SIMPLE IDEAS

II, ii,   1. The better to understand the nature, manner, and extent of our knowledge, one thing is carefully to be observed concerning the ideas we have; and that is, that some of them are *simple* and some *complex*.

Though the qualities that affect our senses are, in the things themselves, so united and blended, that there is no separation, no distance between them; yet it is plain, the ideas they produce in the mind enter by the senses simple and unmixed. For, though the sight and touch often take in from the same object, at the same time, different ideas;— as a man sees at once motion and colour; the hand feels softness and warmth in the same piece of wax: yet the simple ideas thus united in the same subject, are as perfectly distinct as those that come in by different senses. The coldness and hardness which a man feels in a piece of ice being as distinct ideas in the mind as the smell and whiteness of a lily; or as the taste of sugar, and smell of a rose. And there is nothing can be plainer to a man than the clear and distinct perception he has of those simple ideas; which, being each in itself uncompounded, contains in it nothing but *one uniform appearance, or conception in the mind,* and is not distinguishable into different ideas.

2. These simple ideas, the materials of all our knowledge, are suggested and furnished to the mind only by those two ways above mentioned, viz. sensation and reflection. When the understanding is once stored with these simple ideas, it has the power to repeat, compare, and unite them, even to an almost infinite variety, and so can make at pleasure new complex ideas. But it is not in the power of the most exalted wit, or enlarged understanding, by any quickness or variety of thought, to *invent* or *frame* one new simple idea in the mind, not taken in by the ways before mentioned: nor can any force of the understanding *destroy* those that are there. The dominion of man, in this little world of his own understanding being muchwhat the same as it is in the great world of visible things; wherein his power, however managed by art and skill, reaches no farther than to compound and divide the materials that are

made to his hand; but can do nothing towards the making the least particle of new matter, or destroying one atom of what is already in being. The same inability will every one find in himself, who shall go about to fashion in his understanding one simple idea, not received in by his senses from external objects, or by reflection from the operations of his own mind about them. I would have any one try to fancy any taste which had never affected his palate; or frame the idea of a scent he had never smelt: and when he can do this, I will also conclude that a blind man hath ideas of colours, and a deaf man true distinct notions of sounds.

3. This is the reason why—though we cannot believe it impossible to God to make a creature with other organs, and more ways to convey into the understanding the notice of corporeal things than those five, as they are usually counted, which he has given to man—yet I think it is not possible for any *man* to imagine any other qualities in bodies, howsoever constituted, whereby they can be taken notice of, besides sounds, tastes, smells, visible and tangible qualities. And had mankind been made but with four senses, the qualities then which are the objects of the fifth sense had been as far from our notice, imagination, and conception, as now any belonging to a sixth, seventh, or eighth sense can possibly be;—which, whether yet some other creatures, in some other parts of this vast and stupendous universe, may not have, will be a great presumption to deny. He that will not set himself proudly at the top of all things, but will consider the immensity of this fabric, and the great variety that is to be found in this little and inconsiderable part of it which he has to do with, may be apt to think that, in other mansions of it, there may be other and different intelligent beings, of whose faculties he has as little knowledge or apprehension as a worm shut up in one drawer of a cabinet hath of the senses or understanding of a man; such variety and excellency being suitable to the wisdom and power of the Maker. I have here followed the common opinion of man's having but five senses; though, perhaps, there may be justly counted more;—but either supposition serves equally to my present purpose.

NINE

On the Supersensible Element in Knowledge

GOTTFRIED WILHELM LEIBNIZ (1646-1716)

From *Leibniz Selections**

(Letter to Queen Charlotte of Prussia, 1702)

We use the external senses as, to use the comparison of one of the ancients, a blind man does a stick, and they make us know their particular objects, which are colors, sounds, odors, flavors, and the qualities of touch. But they do not make us know what these sensible qualities are or in what they consist. For example, whether red is the revolving of certain small globules which it is claimed cause light; whether heat is the whirling of a very fine dust; whether sound is made in the air as circles in the water when a stone is thrown into it, as certain philosophers claim; this is what we do not see. And we could not even understand how this revolving, these whirlings and these circles, if they should be real, should cause exactly these perceptions which we have of red, of heat, of noise. Thus it may be said that *sensible qualities* are in fact *occult qualities,* and that there must be others *more manifest* which can render the former more explicable. And far from understanding only sensible things, it is exactly these which we understand the least. And although they are familiar to us we do not understand them the better for that; as a pilot understands no better than another person the nature of the magnetic needle which turns toward the north, although he has it always before his eyes in the compass, and although he does not admire it any the more for that reason.

I do not deny that many discoveries have been made concerning the nature of these occult qualities, as, for example, we know by what kind of refraction blue and yellow are formed, and that these two colors mixed form green; but for all this we cannot yet understand how

* The selection from LEIBNIZ SELECTIONS, pp. 355-364, edited by Philip P. Wiener (Copyright 1951 Charles Scribner's Sons) is used by the permission of Charles Scribner's Sons.

the perception which we have of these three colors results from these causes. Also we have not even nominal definitions of such qualities by which to explain the terms. The purpose of nominal definitions is to give sufficient marks by which the thing may be recognized; for example, assayers have marks by which they distinguish gold from every other metal, and even if a man had never seen gold these signs might be taught him so that he would infallibly recognize it if he should some day meet with it. But it is not the same with these sensible qualities; and marks to recognize blue, for example, could not be given if we had never seen it. So that blue is its own mark, and in order that a man may know what blue is it must necessarily be shown to him.

It is for this reason that we are accustomed to say that the *notions* of these qualities are *clear,* for they serve to recognize them; but that these same notions are not *distinct,* because we cannot distinguish or develop that which they include. It is an *I know not what* of which we are conscious, but for which we cannot account. Whereas we can make another understand what a thing is of which we have some description or nominal definition, even although we should not have the thing itself at hand to show him. However, we must do the senses the justice to say that, in addition to these occult qualities, they make us know other qualities which are more manifest and which furnish more distinct notions. And these are those which we ascribe to the *common sense,* because there is no external sense to which they are particularly attached and belong. And here definitions of the terms or words employed may be given. Such is the idea of *numbers,* which is found equally in sounds, colors, and touches. It is thus that we perceive also *figures,* which are common to colors and to touches, but which we do not notice in sounds. Although it is true that in order to conceive distinctly numbers and even figures, and to form sciences of them, we must come to something which the senses cannot furnish, and which the understanding adds to the senses.

As therefore our soul compares (for example) the numbers and figures which are in colors with the numbers and figures which are found by touch, there must be an *internal sense,* in which the perceptions of these different external senses are found united. This is what is called the *imagination,* which comprises at once the *notions of the particular senses,* which are *clear* but *confused,* and the *notions of the common sense,* which are clear and distinct. And these clear and distinct ideas which are subject to the imagination are the objects of the *mathematical sciences,* namely of arithmetic and geometry, which are *pure* mathematical sciences, and of the application of these sciences to nature, forming mixed mathematics. It is evident also that particular sensible qualities are susceptible of explanations and of reasonings only in so far as they involve what is common to the objects of several external senses, and belong to the internal sense. For those who try to explain sensible qualities distinctly always have recourse to the ideas of mathematics, and these ideas always involve *size* or multitude of parts. It is true that the mathematical sciences would not be demonstrative, and would consist in a simple induction or observation, which would never assure us of the perfect generality of the truths there found, if something higher and which intelligence alone can furnish did not come to the aid of the *imagination* and the *senses*.

There are, therefore, objects of still other nature, which are not included at all in what is observed in the objects of the senses in particular or in common, and which consequently are not objects of the imagination either. Thus besides the *sensible* and *imageable,* there is that which is purely *intelligible,* as being the *object of the understanding alone,* and such is the object of my thought when I think of myself.

This thought of the *Ego,* which informs me of sensible objects, and of my own action resulting therefrom, adds something to the objects of the senses. To think a color and to observe that one thinks it, are two very different thoughts, as different as the color is from the Ego which thinks it. And as I conceive that other beings may also have the right to say *I,* or that it could be said for them, it is through this that I conceive what is called *substance* in general, and it is also the consideration of the Ego itself which furnishes other *metaphysical* notions, such as cause, effect, actions, similarity, etc., and even those of *logic* and of *ethics.* Thus it can be said that there is nothing in the understanding which does not come from the senses, except the understanding itself, or that which understands.

There are then three grades of notions: the *sensible only,* which are the objects appropriate to each sense in particular; *the sensible and at the same time intelligible,* which pertain to the common sense; and the *intelligible only,* which belong to the understanding. The first and the second are both imageable, but the third are above the imagination. The second and third are intelligible and distinct; but the first are confused, although they are clear or recognizable.

Being itself and *truth* are not known wholly through the senses; for it would not be impossible for a creature to have long and orderly dreams, resembling our *life,* of such a sort that everything which it thought it perceived through the senses would be but mere *appearances.* There must therefore be something beyond the senses, which distinguishes the true from the apparent. But the truth of the demonstrative sciences is exempt from these doubts, and must even serve for judging of the truth of sensible things. For as able philosophers, ancient and modern, have already well remarked:—if all that I should think that I see should be but a dream, it would always be true that I who think while dreaming, would be something, and would actually think in many ways, for which there must always be some reason.

Thus what the ancient Platonists have observed is very true, and is very worthy of being considered, that the existence of intelligible things and particularly of the *Ego* which thinks and which is called spirit or soul, is incomparably more sure than the existence of sensible things; and that thus it would not be impossible, speaking with metaphysical rigor, that there should be at bottom only these intelligible substances, and that sensible things should be but appearances. While on the other hand our lack of attention makes us take sensible things for the only true things. It is well also to observe that if I should discover any demonstrative truth, mathematical or other, while dreaming (as might in fact be), it would be just as certain as if I had been awake. This shows us how intelligible truth is independent of the truth or of the existence outside of us of sensible and material things.

This conception of *being* and of *truth* is found therefore in the Ego and in the understanding, rather than in the external senses and in the perception of external objects.

There we find also what it is to affirm, to deny, to doubt, to will, to act. But above all we find there the *force of the consequences of* reasoning, which are a part of what is called the *natural light*. For example, from this premise, that *no wise man is wicked,* we may, by reversing the terms, draw this conclusion, that *no wicked man is wise.* Whereas from this sentence, that *every wise man is praiseworthy,* we cannot conclude by converting it, that *every one praiseworthy is wise* but only that *some praiseworthy ones are wise.* Although we may always convert particular affirmative propositions, for example, if *some wise man is rich* it must also be that *some rich men are wise,* this cannot be done in particular negatives. For example, we may say that *there are charitable persons who are not just,* which happens when charity is not sufficiently regulated; but we cannot infer from this that *there are just persons who are not charitable;* for in justice are included at the same time charity and the rule of reason.

It is also by this *natural light* that the *axioms* of mathematics are recognized; for example, that *if from two equal things the same quantity be taken away the things which remain are equal;* likewise that *if in a balance everything is equal on the one side and on the other, neither will incline,* a thing which we foresee without ever having experienced it. It is upon such foundations that we construct arithmetic, geometry, mechanics and the other demonstrative sciences; in which, in truth, the senses are very necessary, in order to have certain ideas of sensible things, and experiments are necessary to establish certain facts, and even useful to verify reasonings as by a kind of proof. But the force of the demonstrations depends upon intelligible notions and truths, which alone are capable of making us discern what is necessary, and which, in the conjectural sciences, are even capable of determining demonstratively the degree of probability upon certain given suppositions, in order that we may choose rationally among opposite appearances, the one which is greatest. Nevertheless this part of the art of reasoning has not yet been cultivated as much as it ought to be.

But to return to *necessary truths,* it is generally true that we know them only by this natural light, and not at all by the experiences of the senses. For the senses can very well make known, in some sort, what is, but they cannot make known what *ought to be* or could not be otherwise.

For example, although we may have experienced numberless times that every massive body tends toward the centre of the earth and is not sustained in the air, we are not sure that this is necessary as long as we do not understand the reason of it. Thus we could not be sure that the same thing would occur in air at a higher altitude, at a hundred or more leagues above us; and there are philosophers who imagine that the earth is a magnet, and as the ordinary magnet does not attract the needle when a little removed from it, they think that the attractive force of the earth does not extend very far either. I do not say that they are right, but I do say that one cannot go very certainly beyond the experiences one has had, when one is not aided by reason.

This is why the geometricians have always considered that what is only proved by *induction* or by examples, in geometry or in arithmetic, is never perfectly proved. For example, experience teaches us that odd numbers continuously added together produce the square numbers, that is to say, those which come from multiplying a number by itself. Thus 1 and 3 make 4, that is to say 2 times 2. And 1 and 3 and 5 make 9, that is to say 3 times 3. And 1 and 3 and 5 and 7 make 16, that is 4 times 4. And 1 and 3 and 5 and 7 and 9 make 25, that is 5 times 5. And so on.

1	1	1	1
3	3	3	3
–	5	5	5
4	–	7	7
	9	–	9
		16	–
			25
2	3	4	5
×	×	×	×
2	3	4	5
–	–	–	–
4	9	16	25

However, if one should experience it a hundred thousand times, continuing the calculation very far, he may reasonably think that this will always follow; but he does not therefore have absolute certainty of it, unless he learns the demonstrative reason which the mathematicians found out long ago. And it is on this foundation of the uncertainty of inductions, but carried a little too far, that an Englishman has lately wished to maintain that we can avoid death. For (said he) the inference is not good: my father, my grandfather, my great-grandfather are dead and all the others who have lived before us; therefore we shall also die. For their death has no influence on us. The trouble is that we resemble them a little too much in this respect that the causes of their death subsist also in us. For the resemblance would not suffice to draw sure consequences without the consideration of the same reasons.

In truth there are *experiments* which succeed numberless times and ordinarily, and yet it is found in some extraordinary cases that there are *instances* where the experiment does not succeed. For example, if we should have found a hundred thousand times that iron put all alone on the surface of water goes to the bottom, we are not sure that this must always happen. And without recurring to the miracle of the prophet Elisha, who made iron float, we know that an iron pot may be made so hollow that it floats, and that it can even carry besides a considerable weight, as do boats of copper or of tin. And even the abstract sciences like geometry furnish cases in which what ordinarily occurs occurs no longer. For example, we ordinarily find that two lines which continually approach each other finally meet, and many people will almost swear that this could never be otherwise. And nevertheless geometry furnishes us with extraordinary lines, which are for this reason called *asymptotes*, which prolonged *ad infinitum* continually approach each other, and nevertheless never meet.

This consideration shows also that there is a *light born within us*. For since the senses and inductions could never teach us truths which are thoroughly universal, nor that which is absolutely necessary, but only that which is, and that which is found in particular examples; and since we nevertheless know necessary and universal truths of the sciences, a privilege which we have above the brutes; it follows that we have derived these truths in part from what is within us. Thus we may lead a child to these by simple interrogations, after the manner of Socrates, without telling him anything, and without making him experiment at all upon the truth of what is asked him. And this could very easily be practiced in numbers and other similar matters.

I agree, nevertheless, that in the present state the external senses are necessary to us for thinking, and that, if we had none, we could not think. But that which is necessary for something does not for all that constitute its essence. Air is necessary for life, but our life is something else than air. The senses furnish us the matter for reasoning, and we never have thoughts so abstract that something from the senses is not mingled therewith; but reasoning requires something else in addition to what is from the senses.

TEN

How Are A Priori Synthetic Judgments Possible?

IMMANUEL KANT (1724-1804)

From *Critique of Pure Reason**

I. THE DISTINCTION BETWEEN PURE AND EMPIRICAL KNOWLEDGE

There can be no doubt that all our knowledge begins with experience. For how should our faculty of knowledge be awakened into action did not objects affecting our senses partly of themselves produce representations, partly arouse the activity of our understanding to compare these representations, and, by combining or separating them, work up the raw material of the sensible impressions into that knowledge of objects which is entitled experience? In the order of time, therefore, we have no knowledge antecedent to experience, and with experience all our knowledge begins.

But though all our knowledge begins with experience, it does not follow that it all arises out of experience. For it may well be that even our empirical knowledge is made up of what we receive through impressions and of what our own faculty.of knowledge (sensible impressions serving merely as the occasion) supplies from itself. If our faculty of knowledge makes any such addition, it may be that we are not in a position to distinguish it from the raw material, until with long practice of attention we have become skilled in separating it.

This, then, is a question which at least calls for closer examination, and does not allow of any off-hand answer:—whether there is any knowledge that is thus independent of experience and even of all impressions of the senses. Such knowledge is entitled *a priori,* and distinguished from the *empirical,* which has its sources *a posteriori,* that is, in experience.

The expression 'a priori' does not, however, indicate with sufficient

* From *Critique of Pure Reason* by Immanuel Kant, translated by Norman Kemp Smith (London, Macmillan & Co. Ltd., 1929), Introduction. Reprinted by permission of St. Martin's Press Inc., New York, The Macmillan Company of Canada Limited, and Macmillan & Co., Ltd., London.

precision the full meaning of our question. For it has been customary to
say, even of much knowledge that is derived from empirical sources, that
we have it or are capable of having it *a priori,* meaning thereby that we
do not derive it immediately from experience, but from a universal rule—
a rule which is itself, however, borrowed by us from experience. Thus we
would say of a man who undermined the foundations of his house, that
he might have known *a priori* that it would fall, that is, that he need not
have waited for the experience of its actual falling. But still he could not
know this completely *a priori.* For he had first to learn through experience that bodies are heavy, and therefore fall when their supports are
withdrawn.

In what follows, therefore, we shall understand by *a priori* knowledge, not knowledge independent of this or that experience, but
knowledge absolutely independent of all experience. Opposed to it is
empirical knowledge, which is knowledge possible only *a posteriori,* that
is, through experience. *A priori* modes of knowledge are entitled pure
when there is no admixture of anything empirical. Thus, for instance,
the proposition, 'every alteration has its cause', while an *a priori* proposition, is not a pure proposition, because alteration is a concept which
can be derived only from experience.

II. WE ARE IN POSSESSION OF CERTAIN MODES OF *A PRIORI* KNOWLEDGE, AND EVEN THE COMMON UNDERSTANDING IS NEVER WITHOUT THEM

What we here require is a criterion by which to distinguish
with certainty between pure and empirical knowledge. Experience teaches
us that a thing is so and so, but not that it cannot be otherwise. First, then,
if we have a proposition which in being thought is thought as *necessary,*
it is an *a priori* judgment; and if, besides, it is not derived from any
proposition except one which also has the validity of a necessary judgment,
it is an absolutely *a priori* judgment. Secondly, experience never confers on
its judgments true or strict, but only assumed and comparative *universality,* through induction. We can properly only say, therefore, that, so far as
we have hitherto observed, there is no exception to this or that rule. If,
then, a judgment is thought with strict universality, that is, in such manner that no exception is allowed as possible, it is not derived from experience, but is valid absolutely *a priori.* Empirical universality is only an
arbitrary extension of a validity holding in most cases to one which holds
in all, for instance, in the proposition, 'all bodies are heavy'. When, on

the other hand, strict universality is essential to a judgment, this indicates a special source of knowledge, namely, a faculty of *a priori* knowledge. Necessity and strict universality are thus sure criteria of *a priori* knowledge, and are inseparable from one another. But since in the employment of these criteria the contingency of judgments is sometimes more easily shown than their empirical limitation, or, as sometimes also happens, their unlimited universality can be more convincingly proved than their necessity, it is advisable to use the two criteria separately, each by itself being infallible.

Now it is easy to show that there actually are in human knowledge judgments which are necessary and in the strictest sense universal, and which are therefore pure *a priori* judgments. If an example from the sciences be desired, we have only to look to any of the propositions of mathematics; if we seek an example from the understanding in its quite ordinary employment, the proposition, 'every alteration must have a cause', will serve our purpose. In the latter case, indeed, the very concept of a cause so manifestly contains the concept of a necessity of connection with an effect and of the strict universality of the rule, that the concept would be altogether lost if we attempted to derive it, as Hume has done, from a repeated association of that which happens with that which precedes, and from a custom of connecting representations, a custom originating in this repeated association, and constituting therefore a merely subjective necessity. Even without appealing to such examples, it is possible to show that pure *a priori* principles are indispensable for the possibility of experience, and so to prove their existence *a priori*. For whence could experience derive its certainty, if all the rules, according to which it proceeds, were always themselves empirical, and therefore contingent? Such rules could hardly be regarded as first principles. At present, however, we may be content to have established the fact that our faculty of knowledge does have a pure employment, and to have shown what are the criteria of such an employment.

Such *a priori* origin is manifest in certain concepts, no less than in judgments. If we remove from our empirical concept of a body, one by one, every feature in it which is [merely] empirical, the colour, the hardness or softness, the weight, even the impenetrability, there still remains the space which the body (now entirely vanished) occupied, and this cannot be removed. Again, if we remove from our empirical concept of any object, corporeal or incorporeal, all properties which experience has taught us, we yet cannot take away that property through which the object is thought as substance or as inhering in a substance (although this concept of substance is more determinate than that of an object in general). Owing, therefore, to the necessity with which this concept of substance forces itself upon us, we have no option save to admit that it has its seat in our faculty of *a priori* knowledge.

III. PHILOSOPHY STANDS IN NEED OF A SCIENCE WHICH SHALL DETERMINE THE POSSIBILITY, THE PRINCIPLES, AND THE EXTENT OF ALL *A PRIORI* KNOWLEDGE

But what is still more extraordinary than all the preceding is this, that certain modes of knowledge leave the field of all possible experiences and have the appearance of extending the scope of our judgments beyond all limits of experience, and this by means of concepts to which no corresponding object can ever be given in experience.

It is precisely by means of the latter modes of knowledge, in a realm beyond the world of the senses, where experience can yield neither guidance nor correction, that our reason carries on those enquiries which owing to their importance we consider to be far more excellent, and in their purpose far more lofty, than all that the understanding can learn in the field of appearances. Indeed we prefer to run every risk of error rather than desist from such urgent enquiries, on the ground of their dubious character, or from disdain and indifference. These unavoidable problems set by pure reason itself are *God, freedom,* and *immortality.* The science which, with all its preparations, is in its final intention directed solely to their solution is metaphysics; and its procedure is at first dogmatic, that is, it confidently sets itself to this task without any previous examination of the capacity or incapacity of reason for so great an undertaking.

Now it does indeed seem natural that, as soon as we have left the ground of experience, we should, through careful enquiries, assure ourselves as to the foundations of any building that we propose to erect, not making use of any knowledge that we possess without first determining whence it has come, and not trusting to principles without knowing their origin. It is natural, that is to say, that the question should first be considered, how the understanding can arrive at all this knowledge *a priori,* and what extent, validity, and worth it may have. Nothing, indeed, could be more natural, if by the term 'natural' we signify what fittingly and reasonably ought to happen. But if we mean by 'natural' what ordinarily happens, then on the contrary nothing is more natural and more intelligible than the fact that this enquiry has been so long neglected. For one part of this knowledge, the mathematical, has long been of established reliability, and so gives rise to a favourable presumption as regards the other part, which may yet be of quite different nature. Besides, once we are outside the circle of experience, we can be sure of not being *contradicted* by experience. The charm of extending our knowledge is so great that nothing short of encountering a direct contradiction can suffice to arrest us in our course; and this can be avoided, if we are careful in our fabrications—which none the less will still remain fabrications. Mathematics gives us a shining example of how far, independently of experience, we can progress in *a priori* knowledge. It does, indeed, occupy itself with objects and with knowledge solely in so far as they allow of being exhibited in intuition. But this circumstance is easily overlooked, since this intuition can itself be given *a priori,* and is therefore hardly to be distinguished from a bare and pure concept. Misled by such a proof of the power of reason, the demand for the extension of knowledge recognises no limits. The light dove, cleaving the air in her free flight, and feeling its resistance, might imagine that its flight would be still easier in empty space. It was thus that Plato left the world of the senses, as setting too narrow limits to the understanding, and ventured out beyond it on the wings of the ideas, in the empty space of the pure understanding. He did not observe that with all his efforts he made no advance—meeting no resistance that might, as it were, serve as a support upon which he could take a stand, to which he could apply his powers, and so set his understanding in motion. It is, indeed, the common fate of human reason to complete its speculative structures as speedily as may be, and only afterwards to enquire whether the foundations are reliable. All sorts of excuses will then be appealed to, in order to reassure us of their solidity, or rather indeed to enable us to dispense altogether with so late and so dangerous an enquiry. But what keeps us, during the actual building, free from all apprehension and suspicion, and flatters us with a seeming thoroughness, is this other circumstance, namely, that a great, perhaps the greatest, part of the business of our reason consists in analysis of the concepts which we already have of objects. This analysis supplies us with a considerable body of knowledge, which, while nothing but explanation or elucidation of what has already been thought in our concepts, though in a confused manner, is yet prized as being, at least as regards its form, new insight. But so far as the matter or content is concerned, there has been no extension of our previously possessed concepts, but only an analysis of them. Since this procedure yields real knowledge *a priori,* which progresses in an assured and useful fashion, reason is so far misled as surreptitiously to introduce, without itself being aware of so doing, assertions of an entirely different order, in which it attaches to given concepts others completely foreign to them, and moreover attaches them *a priori.* And yet it is not known how reason can be in position to do this. Such a question is never so much as thought of. I shall therefore at once proceed to deal with the difference between these two kinds of knowledge.

IV. THE DISTINCTION BETWEEN ANALYTIC AND SYNTHETIC JUDGMENTS

In all judgments in which the relation of a subject to the predicate is thought (I take into consideration affirmative judgments only, the subsequent application to negative judgments being easily made), this relation is possible in two different ways. Either the predicate B belongs to subject A, as something which is (covertly) contained in this concept A; or B lies outside the concept A, although it does indeed stand in connection with it. In the one case I entitle the judgment analytic, in the other synthetic. Analytic judgments (affirmative) are therefore those in which the connection of the predicate with the subject is thought through identity; those in which this connection is thought without identity should be entitled synthetic. The former, as adding nothing through the predicate to the concept of the subject, but merely breaking it up into those constituent concepts that have all along been thought in it, although confusedly, can also be entitled explicative. The latter, on the other hand, add to the concept of the subject a predicate which has not been in any wise thought in it, and which no analysis could possibly extract from it; and they may therefore be entitled ampliative. If I say, for instance, 'All bodies are extended', this is an analytic judgment. For I do not require to go beyond the concept which I connect with 'body' in order to find extension as bound up with it. To meet with this predicate, I have merely to analyse the concept, that is, to become conscious to myself of the manifold which I always think in that concept. The judgment is therefore analytic. But when I say, 'All bodies are heavy', the predicate is something quite different from anything that I think in the mere concept of body in general; and the addition of such a predicate therefore yields a synthetic judgment.

Judgments of experience, as such, are one and all synthetic. For it would be absurd to found an analytic judgment on experience. Since, in framing the judgment, I must not go outside my concept, there is no need to appeal to the testimony of experience in its support. That a body is extended is a proposition that holds *a priori* and is not empirical. For, before appealing to experience, I have already in the concept of body all the conditions required for my judgment. I have only to extract from it, in accordance with the principle of contradiction, the required predicate, and in so doing can at the same time become conscious of the necessity of the judgment—and that is what experience could never have taught me. On the other hand, though I do not include in the concept of a body in general the predicate 'weight', none the less this concept indicates an object of experience through one of its parts, and I can add to that part other parts of this same experience, as in this way belonging together with the concept. From the start I can apprehend the concept of body analytically through the characters of extension, impenetrability, figure, etc., all of which are thought in the concept. Now, however, looking back on the experience from which I have derived this concept of body, and finding weight to be invariably connected with the above characters, I attach it as a predicate to the concept; and in doing so I attach it synthetically, and am therefore extending my knowledge. The possibility of the synthesis of the predicate 'weight' with the concept of 'body' thus rests upon experience. While the one concept is not contained in the other, they yet belong to one another, though only contingently, as parts of a whole, namely, of an experience which is itself a synthetic combination of intuitions.

But in *a priori* synthetic judgments this help is entirely lacking. [I do not here have the advantage of looking around in the field of experience.] Upon what, then, am I to rely, when I seek to go beyond the concept A, and to know that another concept B is connected with it? Through what is the synthesis made possible? Let us take the proposition, 'Everything which happens has its cause'. In the concept of 'something which happens', I do indeed think an existence which is preceded by a time, etc., and from this concept analytic judgments may be obtained. But the concept of a 'cause' lies entirely outside the other concept, and signifies something different from 'that which happens', and is not therefore in any way contained in this latter representation. How come I then to predicate of that which happens something quite different, and to apprehend that the concept of cause, though not contained in it, yet belongs, and indeed necessarily belongs, to it? What is here the unknown = X which gives support to the understanding when it believes that it can discover outside the concept A a predicate B foreign to this concept, which it yet at the same time considers to be connected with it? It cannot be experience, because the suggested principle has connected the second representation with the first, not only with greater universality, but also with the character of necessity, and therefore completely *a priori* and on the basis of mere concepts. Upon such synthetic, that is, ampliative principles, all our *a priori* speculative knowledge must ultimately rest; analytic judgments are very important, and indeed necessary, but only for obtaining that clearness in the concepts which is requisite for such a sure and wide synthesis as will lead to a genuinely new addition to all previous knowledge.

V. IN ALL THEORETICAL SCIENCES OF REASON SYNTHETIC *A PRIORI* JUDGMENTS ARE CONTAINED AS PRINCIPLES

1. *All mathematical judgments, without exception, are synthetic.* This fact, though incontestably certain and in its consequences very important, has hitherto escaped the notice of those who are engaged in the analysis of human reason, and is, indeed, directly opposed to all their conjectures. For as it was found that all mathematical inferences proceed in accordance with the principle of contradiction (which the nature of all apodeictic certainty requires), it was supposed that the fundamental propositions of the science can themselves be known to be true through that principle. This is an erroneous view. For though a synthetic proposition can indeed be discerned in accordance with the principle of contradiction, this can only be if another synthetic proposition is presupposed, and if it can then be apprehended as following from this other proposition; it can never be so discerned in and by itself.

First of all, it has to be noted that mathematical propositions, strictly so called, are always judgments a priori, not empirical; because they carry with them necessity, which cannot be derived from experience. If this be demurred to, I am willing to limit my statements to *pure* mathematics, the very concept of which implies that it does not contain empirical, but only pure *a priori* knowledge.

We might, indeed, at first suppose that the proposition $7 + 5 = 12$ is a merely analytic proposition, and follows by the principle of contradiction from the concept of a sum of 7 and 5. But if we look more closely we find that the concept of the sum of 7 and 5 contains nothing save the union of the two numbers into one, and in this no thought is being taken as to what that single number may be which combines both. The concept of 12 is by no means already thought in merely thinking this union of 7 and 5; and I may analyse my concept of such a possible sum as long as I please, still I shall never find the 12 in it. We have to go outside these concepts, and call in the aid of the intuition which corresponds to one of them, our five fingers, for instance, or, as Segner does in his *Arithmetic,* five points, adding to the concept of 7, unit by unit, the five given in intuition. For starting with the number 7, and for the concept of 5 calling in the aid of the fingers of my hand as intuition, I now add one by one to the number 7 the units which I previously took together to form the number 5, and with the aid of that figure [the hand] see the number 12 come into being. That 5 should be added to 7, I have indeed already thought in the concept of a sum $= 7 + 5$, but not that this sum is equivalent to the number 12. Arithmetical propositions are therefore always synthetic. This is still more evident if we take larger numbers. For it is then obvious that, however we might turn and twist our concepts, we could never, by the mere analysis of them, and without the aid of intuition, discover what [the number is that] is the sum.

Just as little is any fundamental proposition of pure geometry analytic. That the straight line between two points is the shortest, is a synthetic proposition. For my concept of *straight* contains nothing of quantity, but only of quality. The concept of the shortest is wholly an addition, and cannot be derived, through any process of analysis, from the concept of the straight line. Intuition, therefore, must here be called in; only by its aid is the synthesis possible. What here causes us commonly to believe that the predicate of such apodeictic judgments is already contained in our concept, and that the judgment is therefore analytic, is merely the ambiguous character of the terms used. We are required to join in thought a certain predicate to a given concept, and this necessity is inherent in the concepts themselves. But the question is not what we *ought* to join in thought to the given concept, but what we *actually* think in it, even if only obscurely; and it is then manifest that, while the predicate is indeed attached necessarily to the concept, it is so in virtue of an intuition which must be added to the concept, not as thought in the concept itself.

Some few fundamental propositions, presupposed by the geometrician, are indeed, really analytic, and rest on the principle of contradiction. But, as identical propositions, they serve only as links in the chain of method and not as principles; for instance, $a = a$; the whole is equal to itself; or $(a + b) > a$, that is, the whole is greater than its part. And even these propositions, though they are valid according to pure concepts, are only admitted in mathematics because they can be exhibited in intuition.

2. *Natural science (physics) contains* a priori *synthetic judgments as principles.* I need cite only two such judgments: that in all changes of the material world the quantity of matter remains unchanged; and that in all communication of motion, action and reaction must always be equal. Both propositions, it is evident, are not only necessary, and therefore in their origin *a priori,* but also synthetic. For in the concept of matter I do not think its permanence, but only its presence in the space which it occupies. I go outside and beyond the concept of matter, joining to it *a priori* in thought something which I have not thought *in* it. The proposition is not, therefore, analytic, but synthetic, and yet is thought *a priori;* and so likewise are the other propositions of the pure part of natural science.

3. *Metaphysics,* even if we look upon it as having hitherto failed in all its endeavours, is yet, owing to the nature of human reason, a quite indispensable science, and *ought to contain* a priori *synthetic knowledge.* For its business is not merely to analyse concepts which we make for our-

selves *a priori* of things, and thereby to clarify them analytically, but to extend our *a priori* knowledge. And for this purpose we must employ principles which add to the given concept something that was not contained in it, and through *a priori* synthetic judgments venture out so far that experience is quite unable to follow us, as, for instance, in the proposition, that the world must have a first beginning, and such like. Thus metaphysics consists, at least *in intention,* entirely of *a priori* synthetic propositions.

VI. THE GENERAL PROBLEM
OF PURE REASON

Much is already gained if we can bring a number of investigations under the formula of a single problem. For we not only lighten our own task, by defining it accurately, but make it easier for others, who would test our results, to judge whether or not we have succeeded in what we set out to do. Now the proper problem of pure reason is contained in the question: How are *a priori* synthetic judgments possible? . . .

//*

When Galileo caused balls, the weights of which he had himself previously determined, to roll down an inclined plane; when Torricelli made the air carry a weight which he had calculated beforehand to be equal to that of a definite volume of water; or in more recent times, when Stahl changed metals into oxides, and oxides back into metal, by withdrawing something and then restoring it,[a] a light broke upon all students of nature. They learned that reason has insight only into that which it produces after a plan of its own, and that it must not allow itself to be kept, as it were, in nature's leading-strings, but must itself show the way with principles of judgments based upon fixed laws, constraining nature to give answer to questions of reason's own determining. Accidental observations, made in obedience to no previously thought-out plan, can never be made to yield a necessary law, which alone reason is concerned to discover. Reason, holding in one hand its principles, according to which alone concordant appearances can be admitted as equivalent to laws, and in the other hand the experiment which it has devised in conformity

---

* From *Critique of Pure Reason,* Preface.

a I am not, in my choice of examples, tracing the exact course of the history of the experimental method; we have indeed no very precise knowledge of its first beginnings.

with these principles, must approach nature in order to be taught by it. It must not, however, do so in the character of a pupil who listens to everything that the teacher chooses to say, but of an appointed judge who compels the witnesses to answer questions which he has himself formulated. Even physics, therefore, owes the beneficent revolution in its point of view entirely to the happy thought, that while reason must seek in nature, not fictitiously ascribe to it, whatever as not being knowable through reason's own resources has to be learnt, if learnt at all, only from nature, it must adopt as its guide, in so seeking, that which it has itself put into nature. It is thus that the study of nature has entered on the secure path of a science, after having for so many centuries been nothing but a process of merely random groping.

Metaphysics is a completely isolated speculative science of reason, which soars far above the teachings of experience, and in which reason is indeed meant to be its own pupil. Metaphysics rests on concepts alone— not, like mathematics, on their application to intuition. But though it is older than all other sciences, and would survive even if all the rest were swallowed up in the abyss of an all-destroying barbarism, it has not yet had the good fortune to enter upon the secure path of a science. For in it reason is perpetually being brought to a stand, even when the laws into which it is seeking to have, as it professes, an *a priori* insight are those that are confirmed by our most common experiences. Ever and again we have to retrace our steps, as not leading us in the direction in which we desire to go. So far, too, are the students of metaphysics from exhibiting any kind of unanimity in their contentions, that metaphysics has rather to be regarded as a battle-ground quite peculiarly suited for those who desire to exercise themselves in mock combats, and in which no participant has ever yet succeeded in gaining even so much as an inch of territory, not at least in such manner as to secure him in its permanent possession. This shows, beyond all questioning, that the procedure of metaphysics has hitherto been a merely random groping, and, what is worst of all, a groping among mere concepts.

What, then, is the reason why, in this field, the sure road to science has not hitherto been found? Is it, perhaps, impossible of discovery? Why, in that case, should nature have visited our reason with the restless endeavour whereby it is ever searching for such a path, as if this were one of its most important concerns? Nay, more, how little cause have we to place trust in our reason, if, in one of the most important domains of which we would fain have knowledge, it does not merely fail us, but lures us on by deceitful promises, and in the end betrays us! Or if it be only that we have thus far failed to find the true path, are there any indications to justify the hope that by renewed efforts we may have better fortune than has fallen to our predecessors?

The examples of mathematics and natural science, which by a single and sudden revolution have become what they now are, seem to me sufficiently remarkable to suggest our considering what may have been the essential features in the changed point of view by which they have so greatly benefited. Their success should incline us, at least by way of experiment, to imitate their procedure, so far as the analogy which, as species of rational knowledge, they bear to metaphysics may permit. Hitherto it has been assumed that all our knowledge must conform to objects. But all attempts to extend our knowledge of objects by establishing something in regard to them *a priori,* by means of concepts, have, on this assumption, ended in failure. We must therefore make trial whether we may not have more success in the tasks of metaphysics, if we suppose that objects must conform to our knowledge. This would agree better with what is desired, namely, that it should be possible to have knowledge of objects *a priori,* determining something in regard to them prior to their being given. We should then be proceeding precisely on the lines of Corpernicus' primary hypothesis. Failing of satisfactory progress in explaining the movements of the heavenly bodies on the supposition that they all revolved round the spectator, he tried whether he might not have better success if he made the spectator to revolve and the stars to remain at rest. A similar experiment can be tried in metaphysics, as regards the *intuition* of objects. If intuition must conform to the constitution of the objects, I do not see how we could know anything of the latter *a priori;* but if the object (as object of the senses) must conform to the constitution of our faculty of intuition, I have no difficulty in conceiving such a possibility. Since I cannot rest in these intuitions if they are to become known, but must relate them as representations to something as their object, and determine this latter through them, either I must assume that the *concepts,* by means of which I obtain this determination, conform to the object, or else I assume that the objects, or what is the same thing, that the *experience* in which alone, as given objects, they can be known, conform to the concepts. In the former case, I am again in the same perplexity as to how I can know anything *a priori* in regard to the objects. In the latter case the outlook is more hopeful. For experience is itself a species of knowledge which involves understanding; and understanding has rules which I must presuppose as being in me prior to objects being given to me, and therefore as being *a priori.* They find expression in *a priori* concepts to which all objects of experience necessarily conform, and with which they must agree. As regards objects which are thought solely through reason, and indeed as necessary, but which can never—at least not in the manner in which reason thinks them—be given in experience, the attempts at thinking them (for they must admit of being thought) will furnish an excellent touchstone of what we are adopting as our new method of thought, namely, that we can know *a priori* of things only what we ourselves put into them.

*III**

THE PURE CONCEPTS OF THE
UNDERSTANDING, OR CATEGORIES

General logic, as has been repeatedly said, abstracts from all content of knowledge, and looks to some other source, whatever that may be, for the representations which it is to transform into concepts by process of analysis. Transcendental logic, on the other hand, has lying before it a manifold of *a priori* sensibility, presented by transcendental aesthetic, as material for the concepts of pure understanding. In the absence of this material those concepts would be without any content, therefore entirely empty. Space and time contain a manifold of pure *a priori* intuition, but at the same time are conditions of the receptivity of our mind—conditions under which alone it can receive representations of objects, and which therefore must also always affect the concept of these objects. But if this manifold is to be known, the spontaneity of our thought requires that it be gone through in a certain way, taken up, and connected. This act I name *synthesis*.

By *synthesis*, in its most general sense, I understand the act of putting different representations together, and of grasping what is manifold in them in one [act of] knowledge. Such a synthesis is *pure*, if the manifold is not empirical but is given *a priori*, as is the manifold in space and time. Before we can analyse our representations, the representations must themselves be given, and therefore as regards *content* no concepts can first arise by way of analysis. Synthesis of a manifold (be it given empirically or *a priori*) is what first gives rise to knowledge. This knowledge may, indeed, at first, be crude and confused, and therefore in need of analysis. Still the synthesis is that which gathers the elements for knowledge, and unites them to [form] a certain content. It is to synthesis, therefore, that we must first direct our attention, if we would determine the first origin of our knowledge.

Synthesis in general, as we shall hereafter see, is the mere result of the power of imagination, a blind but indispensable function of the soul, without which we should have no knowledge whatsoever, but of which we are scarcely ever conscious. To bring this synthesis *to concepts* is a function which belongs to the understanding, and it is through this function of the understanding that we first obtain knowledge properly so called.

* From *Critique of Pure Reason,* Transcendental Analytic.

Pure synthesis, *represented in its most general aspect,* gives us the pure concept of the understanding. By this pure synthesis I understand that which rests upon a basis of *a priori* synthetic unity. Thus our counting, as is easily seen in the case of larger numbers, is a synthesis according to concepts, because it is executed according to a common ground of unity, as, for instance, the decade. In terms of this concept, the unity of the synthesis of the manifold is rendered necessary.

By means of analysis different representations are brought under one concept—a procedure treated of in general logic. What transcendental logic, on the other hand, teaches, is how we bring to concepts, not representations, but the *pure synthesis* of representations. What must first be given—with a view to the *a priori* knowledge of all objects—is the *manifold* of pure intuition; the second factor involved is the *synthesis* of this manifold by means of the imagination. But even this does not yet yield knowledge. The concepts which give *unity* to this pure synthesis, and which consist solely in the representation of this necessary synthetic unity, furnish the third requisite for the knowledge of an object; and they rest on the understanding.

The same function which gives unity to the various representations *in a judgment* also gives unity to the mere synthesis of various representa-

TABLE OF CATEGORIES

I
Of Quantity
Unity
Plurality
Totality

II		III
Of Quality		*Of Relation*
Reality		Of Inherence and Subsistence
Negation		(*substantia et accidens*)
Limitation		Of Causality and Dependence
		(*cause and effect*)
		Of Community (reciprocity between agent and patient)

IV
Of Modality
Possibility—Impossibility
Existence—Non-existence
Necessity—Contingency

tions *in an intuition;* and this unity, in its most general expression, we entitle the pure concept of the understanding. The same understanding, through the same operations by which in concepts, by means of analytical unity, it produced the logical form of a judgment, also introduces a transcendental content into its representations, by means of the synthetic unity of the manifold in intuition in general. On this account we are entitled to call these representations pure concepts of the understanding, and to regard them as applying *a priori* to objects—a conclusion which general logic is not in a position to establish.

In this manner there arise precisely the same number of pure concepts of the understanding which apply *a priori* to objects of intuition in general, as there have been found to be logical functions in all possible judgments. For these functions specify the understanding completely, and yield an exhaustive inventory of its powers. These concepts we shall, with Aristotle, call *categories,* for our primary purpose is the same as his, although widely diverging from it in manner of execution.

This then is the list of all original pure concepts of synthesis that the understanding contains within itself *a priori.* . . .

THE RELATION OF THE UNDER-STANDING TO OBJECTS IN GENERAL, AND THE POSSIBILITY OF KNOWING THEM *A PRIORI*

What we have expounded separately and singly in the preceding section, we shall now present in systematic inter-connection. There are three subjective sources of knowledge upon which rests the possibility of experience in general and of knowledge of its objects—*sense, imagination,* and *apperception.* Each of these can be viewed as empirical, namely, in its application to given appearances. But all of them are likewise *a priori* elements or foundations, which make this empirical employment itself possible. *Sense* represents appearances empirically in *perception, imagination* in *association* (and reproduction), *apperception* in the *empirical consciousness* of the identity of the reproduced representations with the appearances whereby they were given, that is, in recognition.

But all perceptions are grounded *a priori* in pure intuition (in time, the form of their inner intuition as representations), association in pure synthesis of imagination, and empirical consciousness in pure apperception, that is, in the thoroughgoing identity of the self in all possible representations.

If, now, we desire to follow up the inner ground of this connection of the representations to the point upon which they have all to converge in order that they may therein for the first time acquire the unity of knowledge necessary for a possible experience, we must begin with pure apperception. Intuitions are nothing to us, and do not in the least concern us if they cannot be taken up into consciousness, in which they may participate either directly or indirectly. In this way alone is any knowledge possible. We are conscious *a priori* of the complete identity of the self in respect of all representations which can ever belong to our knowledge, as being a necessary condition of the possibility of all representations. For in me they can represent something only in so far as they belong with all others to one consciousness, and therefore must be at least capable of being so connected. This principle holds *a priori,* and may be called the transcendental principle of the *unity* of all that is manifold in our representations, and consequently also in intuition. Since this unity of the manifold in one subject is synthetic, pure apperception supplies a principle of the synthetic unity of the manifold in all possible intuition.[1]

This synthetic unity presupposes or includes a synthesis, and if the former is to be *a priori* necessary, the synthesis must also be *a priori.* The transcendental unity of apperception thus relates to the pure synthesis of imagination, as an *a priori* condition of the possibility of all combination of the manifold in one knowledge. But only the *productive* synthesis of the imagination can take place *a priori;* the reproductive rests upon empirical conditions. Thus the principle of the necessary unity of pure (productive) synthesis of imagination, prior to apperception, is the ground of the possibility of all knowledge, especially of experience.

We entitle the synthesis of the manifold in imagination transcendental, if without distinction of intuitions it is directed exclusively to the *a priori* combination of the manifold; and the unity of this synthesis is called transcendental, if it is represented as *a priori* necessary in relation to the original unity of apperception. Since this unity of apperception

---

[1] This proposition is of great importance and calls for careful consideration. All representations have a necessary relation to a *possible* empirical consciousness. For if they did not have this, and if it were altogether impossible to become conscious of them, this would practically amount to the admission of their non-existence. But all empirical consciousness has a necessary relation to a transcendental consciousness which precedes all special experience, namely, the consciousness of myself as original apperception. It is therefore absolutely necessary that in my knowledge all consciousness should belong to a single consciousness, that of myself. Here, then, is a synthetic unity of the manifold (of consciousness), which is known *a priori,* and so yields the ground for synthetic *a priori* propositions which concern pure thought, just as do space and time for the propositions which refer to the form of pure intuition. The synthetic proposition, that all the variety of *empirical consciousness* must be combined in one single self-consciousness, is the *absolutely* first and synthetic principle of our thought in general. But it must not be forgotten that the bare representation 'I' in relation to all other representations (the collective unity of which it makes possible) is transcendental consciousness. Whether this representation is clear (empirical consciousness) or obscure, or even whether it ever actually occurs, does not here concern us. But the possibility of the logical form of all knowledge is necessarily conditioned by relation to this apperception *as a faculty.*

underlies the possibility of all knowledge, the transcendental unity of
the synthesis of imagination is the pure form of all possible knowledge;
and by means of it all objects of possible experience must be represented
a priori.

The unity of apperception in relation to the synthesis of imagination
is the *understanding*; and this same unity, with reference to the *transcendental synthesis* of the imagination, the *pure understanding*. In the understanding there are then pure *a priori* modes of knowledge which contain
the necessary unity of the pure synthesis of imagination in respect of all
possible appearances. These are the *categories*, that is, the pure concepts
of understanding. The empirical faculty of knowledge in man must therefore contain an understanding which relates to all objects of the senses,
although only by means of intuition and of its synthesis through imagination. All appearances, as data for a possible experience, are subject to this
understanding. This relation of appearances to possible experience is indeed necessary, for otherwise they would yield no knowledge and would
not in any way concern us. We have, therefore, to recognise that pure
understanding, by means of the categories, is a formal and synthetic principle of all experiences, and that appearances have *a necessary relation to
the understanding*.

We will now, starting from below, namely, with the empirical, strive
to make clear the necessary connection in which understanding, by means
of the categories, stands to appearances. What is first given to us is appearance. When combined with consciousness, it is called perception.
(Save through its relation to a consciousness that is at least possible, appearance could never be for us an object of knowledge, and so would be
nothing to us; and since it has in itself no objective reality, but exists only
in being known, it would be nothing at all.) Now, since every appearance
contains a manifold, and since different perceptions therefore occur in the
mind separately and singly, a combination of them, such as they cannot
have in sense itself, is demanded. There must therefore exist in us an
active faculty for the synthesis of this manifold. To this faculty I give the
title, imagination. Its action, when immediately directed upon perceptions, I entitle apprehension.[2] Since imagination has to bring the manifold of intuition into the form of an image, it must previously have taken
the impressions up into its activity, that is, have apprehended them.

But it is clear that even this apprehension of the manifold would not
by itself produce an image and a connection of the impressions, were it
not that there exists a subjective ground which leads the mind to reinstate

[2] Psychologists have hitherto failed to realise that imagination is a necessary in-
gredient of perception itself. This is due partly to the fact that that faculty has been
limited to reproduction, partly to the belief that the senses not only supply impressions
but also combine them so as to generate images of objects. For that purpose something
more than the mere receptivity of impressions is undoubtedly required, namely, a function for the synthesis of them.

a preceding perception alongside the subsequent perception to which it has passed, and so to form whole series of perceptions. This is the reproductive faculty of imagination, which is merely empirical.

If, however, representations reproduced one another in any order, just as they happened to come together, this would not lead to any determinate connection of them, but only to accidental collocations; and so would not give rise to any knowledge. Their reproduction must, therefore, conform to a rule, in accordance with which a representation connects in the imagination with some one representation in preference to another. This subjective and *empirical* ground of reproduction according to rules is what is called the *association* of representations.

Now if this unity of association had not also an objective ground which makes it possible that appearances should be apprehended by the imagination otherwise than under the condition of a possible synthetic unity of this apprehension, it would be entirely accidental that appearances should fit into a connected whole of human knowledge. For even though we should have the power of associating perceptions, it would remain entirely undetermined and accidental whether they would themselves be associable; and should they not be associable, there might exist a multitude of perceptions, and indeed an entire sensibility, in which much empirical consciousness would arise in my mind, but in a state of separation, and without belonging to a consciousness of myself. This, however, is impossible. For it is only because I ascribe all perceptions to one consciousness (original apperception) that I can say of all perceptions that I am conscious of them. There must, therefore, be an objective ground (that is, one that can be comprehended *a priori,* antecedently to all empirical laws of the imagination) upon which rests the possibility, nay, the necessity, of a law that extends to all appearances—a ground, namely, which constrains us to regard all appearances as data of the senses that must be associable in themselves and subject to universal rules of a thoroughgoing connection in their reproduction. This objective ground of all association of appearances I entitle their *affinity.* It is nowhere to be found save in the principle of the unity of apperception, in respect of all knowledge which is to belong to me. According to this principle all appearances, without exception, must so enter the mind or be apprehended, that they conform to the unity of apperception. Without synthetic unity in their connection, this would be impossible; and such synthetic unity is itself, therefore, objectively necessary.

The objective unity of all empirical consciousness in one consciousness, that of original apperception, is thus the necessary condition of all possible perception; and (this being recognised we can prove that) the affinity of all appearances, near or remote, is a necessary consequence of a synthesis in imagination which is grounded *a priori* on rules.

Since the imagination is itself a faculty of *a priori* synthesis, we assign to it the title, productive imagination. In so far as it aims at nothing but necessary unity in the synthesis of what is manifold in appearance, it may be entitled the transcendental function of imagination. That the affinity of appearances, and with it their association, and through this, in turn, their reproduction according to laws, and so [as involving these various factors] experience itself, should only be possible by means of this transcendental function of imagination, is indeed strange, but is none the less an obvious consequence of the preceding argument. For without this transcendental function no concepts of objects would together make up a unitary experience.

The abiding and unchanging 'I' (pure apperception) forms the correlate of all our representations in so far as it is to be at all possible that we should become conscious of them. All consciousness as truly belongs to an all-comprehensive pure apperception, as all sensible intuition, as representation, does to a pure inner intuition, namely, to time. It is this apperception which must be added to pure imagination, in order to render its function intellectual. For since the synthesis of imagination connects the manifold only as it *appears* in intuition, as, for instance, in the shape of a triangle, it is, though exercised *a priori,* always in itself sensible. And while concepts, which belong to the understanding, are brought into play through relation of the manifold to the unity of apperception, it is only by means of the imagination that they can be brought into relation to sensible intuition.

A pure imagination, which conditions all *a priori* knowledge, is thus one of the fundamental faculties of the human soul. By its means we bring the manifold of intuition on the one side, into connection with the condition of the necessary unity of pure apperception on the other. The two extremes, namely sensibility and understanding, must stand in necessary connection with each other through the mediation of this transcendental function of imagination, because otherwise the former, though indeed yielding appearances, would supply no objects of empirical knowledge, and consequently no experience. Actual experience, which is constituted by apprehension, association (reproduction), and finally recognition of appearances, contains in recognition, the last and highest of these merely empirical elements of experience, certain concepts which render possible the formal unity of experience, and therewith all objective validity (truth) of empirical knowledge. These grounds of the recognition of the manifold, so far as they concern *solely the form of an experience in general,* are the *categories.* Upon them is based not only all formal unity in the (transcendental) synthesis of imagination, but also, thanks to that synthesis, all its empirical employment (in recognition, reproduction, association, apprehension) in connection with the appearances. For only by means of these fundamental concepts can appearances belong to knowledge or even to our consciousness, and so to ourselves.

Thus the order and regularity in the appearances, which we entitle *nature,* we ourselves introduce. We could never find them in appearances, had not we ourselves, or the nature of our mind, originally set them there. For this unity of nature has to be a necessary one, that is, has to be an *a priori* certain unity of the connection of appearances; and such synthetic unity could not be established *a priori* if there were not subjective grounds of such unity contained *a priori* in the original cognitive powers of our mind, and if these subjective conditions, inasmuch as they are the grounds of the possibility of knowing any object whatsoever in experience, were not at the same time objectively valid.

We have already defined the understanding in various different ways: as a spontaneity of knowledge (in distinction from the receptivity of sensibility), as a power of thought, as a faculty of concepts, or again of judgments. All these definitions, when they are adequately understood, are identical. We may now characterise it as the *faculty of rules.* This distinguishing mark is more fruitful, and approximates more closely to its essential nature. Sensibility gives us forms (of intuition), but understanding gives us rules. The latter is always occupied in investigating appearances, in order to detect some rule in them. Rules, so far as they are objective, and therefore necessarily depend upon the knowledge of the object, are called laws. Although we learn many laws through experience, they are only special determinations of still higher laws, and the highest of these, under which the others all stand, issue *a priori* from the understanding itself. They are not borrowed from experience; on the contrary, they have to confer upon appearances their conformity to law, and so to make experience possible. Thus the understanding is something more than a power of formulating rules through comparison of appearances; it is itself the lawgiver of nature. Save through it, nature, that is, synthetic unity of the manifold of appearances according to rules, would not exist at all (for appearances, as such, cannot exist outside us—they exist only in our sensibility); and this nature, as object of knowledge in an experience, with everything which it may contain, is only possible in the unity of apperception. The unity of apperception is thus the transcendental ground of the necessary conformity to law of all appearances in one experience. This same unity of apperception in respect to a manifold of representations (determining it out of a unity) acts as the rule, and the faculty of these rules is the understanding. All appearances, as possible experiences, thus lie *a priori* in the understanding, and receive from it their formal possibility, just as, in so far as they are mere intuitions, they lie in the sensibility, and are, as regards their form, only possible through it.

However exaggerated and absurd it may sound, to say that the understanding is itself the source of the laws of nature, and so of its formal unity, such an assertion is none the less correct, and is in keeping with the object to which it refers, namely, experience. Certainly, empirical laws, as such, can never derive their origin from pure understanding. That is as little possible as to understand completely the inexhaustible multiplicity of appearances merely by reference to the pure form of sensible intuition. But all empirical laws are only special determinations of the pure laws of understanding, under which, and according to the norm of which, they first become possible. Through them appearances take on an orderly character, just as these same appearances, despite the differences of their empirical form, must none the less always be in harmony with the pure form of sensibility.

Pure understanding is thus in the categories the law of the synthetic unity of all appearances, and thereby first and originally makes experience, as regards its form, possible. This is all that we were called upon to establish in the transcendental deduction of the categories, namely, to render comprehensible this relation of understanding to sensibility, and, by means of sensibility, to all objects of experience. The objective validity of the pure *a priori* concepts is thereby made intelligible, and their origin and truth determined.

SUMMARY REPRESENTATION OF THE CORRECTNESS OF THIS DEDUCTION OF THE PURE CONCEPTS OF UNDERSTANDING, AND OF ITS BEING THE ONLY DEDUCTION POSSIBLE

If the objects with which our knowledge has to deal were things in themselves, we could have no *a priori* concepts of them. For from what source could we obtain the concepts? If we derived them from the object (leaving aside the question how the object could become known to us), our concepts would be merely empirical, not *a priori*. And if we derived them from the self, that which is merely in us could not determine the character of an object distinct from our representations, that is, could not be a ground why a thing should exist characterised by that which we have in our thought, and why such a representation should not, rather, be altogether empty. But if, on the other hand, we have to deal only with appearances, it is not merely possible, but necessary, that certain *a priori* concepts should precede empirical knowledge of objects. For since a mere modification of our sensibility can never be met with outside us, the objects, as appearances, constitute an object which is merely in us. Now to assert in this manner, that all these appearances, and consequently all objects with which we can occupy ourselves, are one and all in me, that is, are determinations of my identical self, is only another way of saying that there must be a complete unity of them in one and the same apperception. But this unity of possible consciousness also constitutes the form of all knowledge of objects; through it the manifold is thought as belonging to a single object. Thus the mode in which the manifold of sensible representation (intuition) belongs to one consciousness precedes all knowledge of the object as the intellectual form of such knowledge, and itself constitutes a formal *a priori* knowledge of all objects, so far as they are thought (categories). The synthesis of the manifold through pure imagination, the unity of all representations in relation to original apperception, precede all empirical knowledge. Pure concepts of understanding are thus *a priori* possible, and, in relation to experience, are indeed necessary; and this for the reason that our knowledge has to deal solely with appearances, the possibility of which lies in ourselves, and the connection and unity of which (in the representation of an object) are to be met with only in ourselves. Such connection and unity must therefore precede all experience, and are required for the very possibility of it in its formal aspect. From this point of view, the only feasible one, our deduction of the categories has been developed.

. . . When, to take another example, I perceive the freezing of water, I apprehend two states, fluidity and solidity, and these as standing to one another in a relation of time. But in time, which I place at the basis of the appearance [in so far] as [it is] inner *intuition,* I necessarily represent to myself synthetic *unity* of the manifold, without which that relation of time could not be given in an intuition as being *determined* in respect of time-sequence. Now this synthetic unity, as a condition *a priori* under which I combine the manifold of an *intuition in general,* is— if I abstract from the constant form of *my* inner intuition, namely, time— the category of *cause,* by means of which, when I apply it to my sensibility, I determine *everything that happens* in accordance with the relation which it prescribes, and I do so *in time in general.* Thus my apprehension of such an event, and therefore the event itself, considered as a possible perception, is subject to the concept of the *relation* of *effects* and *causes,* and so in all other cases.

Categories are concepts which prescribe laws *a priori* to appearances, and therefore to nature, the sum of all appearances (*natura materialiter spectata*). The question therefore arises, how it can be conceivable that nature should have to proceed in accordance with categories which yet are not derived from it, and do not model themselves upon its pattern; that is, how they can determine *a priori* the combination of the manifold of nature, while yet they are not derived from it. The solution of this seeming enigma is as follows.

That the *laws* of appearances in nature must agree with the understanding and its *a priori* form, that is, with its faculty of *combining* the manifold in general, is no more surprising than that the appearances themselves must agree with the form of *a priori* sensible intuition. For just as appearances do not exist in themselves but only relatively to the subject in which, so far as it has senses, they inhere, so the laws do not exist in the appearances but only relatively to this same being, so far as it has understanding. Things in themselves would necessarily, apart from any understanding that knows them, conform to laws of their own. But appearances are only representations of things which are unknown as regards what they may be in themselves. As mere representations, they are subject to no law of connection save that which the connecting faculty prescribes. Now it is imagination that connects the manifold of sensible intuition; and imagination is dependent for the unity of its intellectual synthesis upon the understanding, and for the manifoldness of its apprehension upon sensibility. All possible perception is thus dependent upon synthesis of apprehension, and this empirical synthesis in turn upon transcendental synthesis, and therefore upon the categories. Consequently, all possible perceptions, and therefore everything that can come to empirical consciousness, that is, all appearances of nature, must, so far as their connection is concerned, be subject to the categories. Nature, considered merely as nature in general, is dependent upon these categories as the original ground of its necessary conformity to law (*natura formaliter spectata*). Pure understanding is not, however, in a position, through mere categories, to prescribe to appearances any *a priori* laws other than those which are involved in a *nature in general*, that is, in the conformity to law of all appearances in space and time. Special laws, as concerning those appearances which are empirically determined, cannot in their specific character be *derived* from the categories, although they are one and all subject to them. To obtain any knowledge whatsoever of these special laws, we must resort to experience; but it is the *a priori* laws that alone can instruct us in regard to experience in general, and as to what it is that can be known as an object of experience.

We cannot think an object save through categories; we cannot *know* an object so thought save through intuitions corresponding to these concepts. Now all our intuitions are sensible; and this knowledge, in so far as its object is given, is empirical. But empirical knowledge is experience. *Consequently, there can be no* a priori *knowledge, except of objects of possible experience.*[3]

But although this knowledge is limited to objects of experience, it is not therefore all derived from experience. The pure intuitions [of receptivity] and the pure concepts of understanding are elements in knowledge,

[3] Lest my readers should stumble at the alarming evil consequences which may over-hastily be inferred from this statement, I may remind them that *for thought* the categories are not limited by the conditions of our sensible intuition, but have an unlimited field. It is only the *knowledge* of that which we think, the determining of the object, that requires intuition. In the absence of intuition, the thought of the object may still have its true and useful consequences, as regards the subject's *employment of reason*. The use of reason is not always directed to the determination of the object, that is, to knowledge, but also to the determination of the subject and of its volition—a use which cannot therefore be here dealt with.

and both are found in us *a priori*. There are only two ways in which we can account for a *necessary* agreement of experience with the concepts of its objects: either experience makes these concepts possible or these concepts make experience possible. The former supposition does not hold in respect of the categories (nor of pure sensible intuition); for since they are *a priori* concepts, and therefore independent of experience, the ascription to them of an empirical origin would be a sort of *generatio aequivoca*. There remains, therefore, only the second supposition—a system, as it were, of the *epigenesis* of pure reason—namely, that the categories contain, on the side of the understanding, the grounds of the possibility of all experience in general. How they make experience possible, and what are the principles of the possibility of experience that they supply in their application to appearances, will be shown more fully in the following chapter on the transcendental employment of the faculty of judgment.

A middle course may be proposed between the two above mentioned, namely, that the categories are neither *self-thought* first principles *a priori* of our knowledge nor derived from experience, but subjective dispositions of thought, implanted in us from the first moment of our existence, and so ordered by our Creator that their employment is in complete harmony with the laws of nature in accordance with which experience proceeds— a kind of *preformation-system* of pure reason. Apart, however, from the objection that on such an hypothesis we can set no limit to the assumption of predetermined dispositions to future judgments, there is this decisive objection against the suggested middle course, that the *necessity* of the categories, which belongs to their very conception, would then have to be sacrificed. The concept of cause, for instance, which expresses the necessity of an event under a presupposed condition, would be false if it rested only on an arbitrary subjective necessity, implanted in us, of connecting certain empirical representations according to the rule of causal relation. I would not then be able to say that the effect is connected with the cause in the object, that is to say, necessarily, but only that I am so constituted that I cannot think this representation otherwise than as thus connected. This is exactly what the sceptic most desires. For if this be the situation, all our insight, resting on the supposed objective validity of our judgments, is nothing but sheer illusion; nor would there be wanting people who would refuse to admit this subjective necessity, a necessity which can only be felt. Certainly a man cannot dispute with anyone regarding that which depends merely on the mode in which he is himself organised.

IV

From *The Prolegomena to Any Future Metaphysic**

HOW IS THE SCIENCE OF NATURE POSSIBLE?

Nature is the existence of things, so far as it is determined according to universal laws. Should nature signify the existence of things in themselves, we could never cognise it either *a priori* or *a posteriori*. Not *a priori*, for how can we know what belongs to things in themselves, since this never can be done by the dissection of our concepts (in analytical judgments)? We do not want to know what is contained in our concept of a thing (for the [concept describes what] belongs to its logical being), but what is in the actuality of the thing superadded to our concept, and by what the thing itself is determined in its existence outside the concept. Our understanding, and the conditions on which alone it can connect the determinations of things in their existence, do not prescribe any rule to things themselves; these do not conform to our understanding, but it must conform itself to them; they must therefore be first given us in order to gather these determinations from them, wherefore they would not be cognised *a priori*.

A cognition of the nature of things in themselves *a posteriori* would be equally impossible. For, if experience is to teach us laws, to which the existence of things is subject, these laws, if they regard things in themselves, must belong to them of necessity even outside our experience. But experience teaches us what exists and how it exists, but never that it must necessarily exist so and not otherwise. Experience therefore can never teach us the nature of things in themselves. . . .

How Is Nature Itself Possible?

This question—the highest point that transcendental philosophy can ever reach, and to which, as its boundary and completion, it must proceed—properly contains two questions.

First: How is nature at all possible in the material sense, by intuition, considered as the totality of appearances; how are space, time, and

* From *The Prolegomena to Any Future Metaphysic,* translated by P. Carus (LaSalle, Ill., Open Court Publishing Co., 1902).

that which fills both—the object of sensation, in general possible? The answer is: By means of the constitution of our Sensibility, according to which it is specifically affected by objects, which are in themselves unknown to it, and totally distinct from those phenomena. This answer is given in the *Critique* itself in the transcendental Aesthetic, and in these *Prolegomena* by the solution of the first general problem.

SECONDLY: How is nature possible in the formal sense, as the totality of the rules, under which all phenomena must come, in order to be thought as connected in experience? The answer must be this: It is only possible by means of the constitution of our Understanding, according to which all the above representations of the sensibility are necessarily referred to a consciousness, and by which the peculiar way in which we think (viz., by rules), and hence experience also, are possible, but must be clearly distinguished from an insight into the objects in themselves. This answer is given in the *Critique* itself in the transcendental Logic, and in these *Prolegomena,* in the course of the solution of the second main problem.

But how this peculiar property of our sensibility itself is possible, or that of our understanding and of the apperception which is necessarily its basis and that of all thinking, cannot be further analysed or answered, because it is of them that we are in need for all our answers and for all our thinking about objects.

There are many laws of nature, which we can only know by means of experience; but conformity to law in the connexion of appearances, i.e., in nature in general, we cannot discover by any experience, because experience itself requires laws which are *a priori* at the basis of its possibility.

The possibility of experience in general is therefore at the same time the universal law of nature, and the principles of the experience are the very laws of nature. For we do not know nature but as the totality of appearances, i.e., of representations in us, and hence we can only derive the laws of its connexion from the principles of their connexion in us, that is, from the conditions of their necessary union in consciousness, which constitutes the possibility of experience.

Even the main proposition expounded throughout this section—that universal laws of nature can be distinctly cognised *a priori*—leads naturally to the proposition: that the highest legislation of nature must lie in ourselves, i.e., in our understanding, and that we must not seek the universal laws of nature in nature by means of experience, but conversely must seek nature, as to its universal conformity to law, in the conditions of the possibility of experience, which lie in our sensibility and in our understanding. For how were it otherwise possible to know *a priori* these laws, as they are not rules of analytical cognition, but truly synthetical extensions of it?

Such a necessary agreement of the principles of possible experience with the laws of the possibility of nature, can only proceed from one of two reasons: either these laws are drawn from nature by means of experience, or conversely nature is derived from the laws of the possibility of experience in general, and is quite the same as the mere universal conformity to law of the latter. The former is self-contradictory, for the universal laws of nature can and must be cognised *a priori* (that is, independent of all experience), and be the foundation of all empirical use of the understanding; the latter alternative therefore alone remains.[4]

But we must distinguish the empirical laws of nature, which always presuppose particular perceptions, from the pure or universal laws of nature, which, without being based on particular perceptions, contain merely the conditions of their necessary union in experience. In relation to the latter, nature and possible experience are quite the same, and as the conformity to law here depends upon the necessary connexion of appearances in experience (without which we cannot cognise any object whatever in the sensible world), consequently upon the original laws of understanding, it seems at first strange, but is not the less certain, to say:

The understanding does not derive its laws (a priori) from, but prescribes them to, nature.

We shall illustrate this seemingly bold proposition by an example, which will show, that laws, which we discover in objects of sensuous intuition (especially when these laws are cognised as necessary), are commonly held by us to be such as have been placed there by the understanding, in spite of their being similar in all points to the laws of nature, which we ascribe to experience.

If we consider the properties of the circle, by which this figure combines so many arbitrary determinations of space in itself, at once in a universal rule, we cannot avoid attributing a constitution (*eine Natur*) to this geometrical thing. Two right lines, for example, which intersect one another and the circle, howsoever they may be drawn, are always divided so that the rectangle constructed with the segments of the one is equal to that constructed with the segments of the other. The question now is: Does this law lie in the circle or in the understanding, that is, Does this figure, independently of the understanding, contain in itself the ground of the law, or does the understanding, having constructed according to its concepts (according to the quality of the radii) the figure itself, introduce into it this law of the chords cutting one another in geometrical proportion? When we follow the proofs of this law, we soon perceive,

---

4 Crusius alone thought of a compromise: that a Spirit, who can neither err nor deceive, implanted these laws in us originally. But since false principles often intrude themselves, as indeed the very system of this man shows in not a few examples, we are involved in difficulties as to the use of such a principle in the absence of sure criteria to distinguish the genuine origin from the spurious as we can never know certainly what the Spirit of truth or the father of lies may have instilled into us.

that it can only be derived from the condition on which the understanding founds the construction of this figure, and which is that of the equality of the radii. But, if we enlarge this concept, to pursue further the unity of various properties of geometrical figures under common laws, and consider the circle as a conic section, which of course is subject to the same fundamental conditions of construction as other conic sections, we shall find that all the chords which intersect within the ellipse, parabola, and hyperbola, always intersect so that the rectangles of their segments are not indeed equal, but always bear a constant ratio to one another. If we proceed still farther, to the fundamental laws of physical astronomy, we find a physical law of reciprocal attraction diffused over all material nature, the rule of which is: "that it decreases inversely as the square of the distance from each attracting point, i.e., as the spherical surfaces increase, over which this force spreads," which law seems to be necessarily inherent in the very nature of things, and hence is usually propounded as cognisable *a priori.* Simple as the sources of this law are, merely resting upon the relation of spherical surfaces of different radii, its consequences are so valuable with regard to the variety of their agreement and its regularity, that not only are all possible orbits of the celestial bodies conic sections, but such a relation of these orbits to each other results, that no other law of attraction, than that of the inverse square of the distance, can be imagined as fit for a cosmical system.

Here accordingly is a nature that rests upon laws which the understanding cognises *a priori,* and chiefly from the universal principles of the determination of space. Now I ask:

Do the laws of nature lie in space, and does the understanding learn them by merely endeavoring to find out the enormous wealth of meaning that lies in space; or do they inhere in the understanding and in the way in which it determines space according to the conditions of the synthetical unity in which its concepts are all centred?

Space is something so uniform and as to all particular properties so indeterminate, that we should certainly not seek a store of laws of nature in it. Whereas that which determines space to assume the form of a circle or the figures of a cone and a sphere, is the understanding, so far as it contains the ground of the unity of their constructions.

The mere universal form of intuition, called space, must therefore be the substratum of all intuitions determinable to particular objects, and in it of course the condition of the possibility and of the variety of these intuitions lies. But the unity of the objects is entirely determined by the understanding, and on conditions which lie in its own nature; and thus the understanding is the origin of the universal order of nature, in that it comprehends all appearances under its own laws, and thereby first constructs, *a priori,* experience (as to its form), by means of which whatever is to be cognised only by experience, is necessarily subjected to its laws. For we are not now concerned with the nature of things in themselves, which is independent of the conditions both of our sensibility and our understanding, but with nature, as an object of possible experience, and in this case the understanding, whilst it makes experience possible, thereby insists that the sensuous world is either not an object of experience at all, or must be nature [viz., an existence of things, determined according to universal laws].

ELEVEN

All Deductive Sciences Are Inductive

JOHN STUART MILL (1806-1878)

From A System of Logic*

OF THE FUNCTIONS AND LOGICAL VALUE OF THE SYLLOGISM

We have shown what is the real nature of the truths with which the Syllogism is conversant, in contradistinction to the more superficial manner in which their import is conceived in the common theory; and what are the fundamental axioms on which its probative force or conclusiveness depends. We have now to inquire, whether the syllogistic process, that of reasoning from generals to particulars, is, or is not, a process of inference; a progress from the known to the unknown: a means of coming to a knowledge of something which we did not know before.

Logicians have been remarkably unanimous in their mode of answering this question. It is universally allowed that a syllogism is vicious if there be any thing more in the conclusion than was assumed in the premises. But this is, in fact, to say, that nothing ever was, or can be, proved by syllogism, which was not known, or assumed to be known, before. Is ratiocination, then, not a process of inference? And is the syllogism, to which the word reasoning has so often been represented to be exclusively appropriate, not really entitled to be called reasoning at all? This seems an inevitable consequence of the doctrine, admitted by all writers on the subject, that a syllogism can prove no more than is involved in the premises. Yet the acknowledgement so explicitly made, has not prevented one set of writers from continuing to represent the syllogism as the correct analysis of what the mind actually performs in discovering and proving the larger half of the truths, whether of science or of daily life, which we believe; while those who have avoided this inconsistency, and followed out the general theorem respecting the logical value of the syllogism to its legitimate corollary, have been led to impute uselessness and frivolity to the syllogistic theory itself, on the ground of the *petitio principii*

---

* From *A System of Logic* by John Stuart Mill (1843).

which they allege to be inherent in every syllogism. As I believe both these opinions to be fundamentally erroneous, I must request the attention of the reader to certain considerations, without which any just appreciation of the true character of the syllogism, and the functions it performs in philosophy, appears to me impossible; but which seem to have been either overlooked, or insufficiently adverted to, both by the defenders of the syllogistic theory and by its assailants.

It must be granted that in every syllogism, considered as an argument to prove the conclusion, there is a *petitio principii*. When we say,

> All men are mortal,
> Socrates is a man,
> therefore
> Socrates is mortal;

it is unanswerably urged by the adversaries of the syllogistic theory, that the proposition, Socrates is mortal, is presupposed in the more general assumption, All men are mortal: that we can not be assured of the mortality of all men, unless we are already certain of the mortality of every individual man: that if it be still doubtful whether Socrates, or any other individual we choose to name, be mortal or not, the same degree of uncertainty must hang over the assertion, All men are mortal: that the general principle, instead of being given as evidence of the particular case, can not itself be taken for true without exception, until every shadow of doubt which could affect any case comprised with it, is dispelled by evidence *aliunde;* and then what remains for the syllogism to prove? That, in short, no reasoning from generals to particulars can, as such, prove any thing: since from a general principle we can not infer any particulars, but those which the principle itself assumes as known.

This doctrine appears to me irrefragable; and if logicians, though unable to dispute it, have usually exhibited a strong disposition to explain it away, this was not because they could discover any flaw in the argument itself, but because the contrary opinion seemed to rest on arguments equally indisputable. In the syllogism last referred to, for example, or in any of those which we previously constructed, is it not evident that the conclusion may, to the person to whom the syllogism is presented, be actually and *bona fide* a new truth? Is it not matter of daily experience that truths previously unthought of, facts which have not been, and can not be, directly observed, are arrived at by way of general reasoning? We believe that the Duke of Wellington is mortal. We do not know this by direct observation, so long as he is not yet dead. If we were asked how, this being the case, we know the duke to be mortal, we should probably answer, Because all men are so. Here, therefore, we arrive at the knowledge of a truth not (as yet) susceptible of observation, by a reasoning which admits of being exhibited in the following syllogism:

All men are mortal,
The Duke of Wellington is a man,
therefore
The Duke of Wellington is mortal.

And since a large portion of our knowledge is thus acquired, logicians have persisted in representing the syllogism as a process of inference or proof; though none of them has cleared up the difficulty which arises from the inconsistency between that assertion, and the principle, that if there be any thing in the conclusion which was not already asserted in the premises, the argument is vicious. For it is impossible to attach any serious scientific value to such a mere salvo, as the distinction drawn between being involved by *implication* in the premises, and being directly asserted in them. When Archbishop Whately says [1] that the object of reasoning is "merely to expand and unfold the assertions wrapped up, as it were, and implied in those with which we set out, and to bring a person to perceive and acknowledge the full force of that which he has admitted," he does not, I think, meet the real difficulty requiring to be explained, namely, how it happens that a science, like geometry, *can* be all "wrapped up" in a few definitions and axioms. Nor does this defense of the syllogism differ much from what its assailants urge against it as an accusation, when they charge it with being of no use except to those who seek to press the consequences of an admission into which a person has been entrapped without having considered and understood its full force. When you admitted the major premise, you asserted the conclusion; but, says Archbishop Whately, you asserted it by implication merely: this, however, can here only mean that you asserted it unconsciously; that you did not know you were asserting it; but, if so, the difficulty revives in this shape—Ought you not to have known? Were you warranted in asserting the general proposition without having satisfied yourself of the truth of every thing which it fairly includes? And if not, is not the syllogistic art *prima facie* what its assailants affirm it to be, a contrivance for catching you in a trap, and holding you fast in it? [2]

[1] *Logic*, p. 239 (9th ed.).

[2] It is hardly necessary to say, that I am not contending for any such absurdity as that we *actually* "ought to have known" and considered the case of every individual man, past, present, and future, before affirming that all men are mortal: although this interpretation has been, strangely enough, put upon the preceding observations. There is no difference between me and Archbishop Whately, or any other defender of the syllogism, on the practical part of the matter; I am only pointing out an inconsistency in the logical theory of it, as conceived by almost all writers. I do not say that a person who affirmed, before the Duke of Wellington was born, that all men are mortal, *knew* that the Duke of Wellington was mortal; but I do say that he *asserted* it; and I ask for an explanation of the apparent logical fallacy, of adducing in proof of the Duke of Wellington's mortality, a general statement which presupposes it. Finding no sufficient resolution of this difficulty in any of the writers on Logic, I have attempted to supply one.

From this difficulty there appears to be but one issue. The proposition that the Duke of Wellington is mortal, is evidently an inference; it is got at as a conclusion from something else; but do we, in reality, conclude it from the proposition, All men are mortal? I answer, no.

The error committed is, I conceive, that of overlooking the distinction between two parts of the process of philosophizing, the inferring part, and the registering part; and ascribing to the latter the functions of the former. The mistake is that of referring a person to his own notes for the origin of his knowledge. If a person is asked a question, and is at the moment unable to answer it, he may refresh his memory by turning to a memorandum which he carries about with him. But if he were asked, how the fact came to his knowledge, he would scarcely answer, because it was set down in his note-book: unless the book was written, like the Koran, with a quill from the wing of the angel Gabriel.

Assuming that the proposition, The Duke of Wellington is mortal, is immediately an inference from the proposition, All men are mortal; whence do we derive our knowledge of that general truth? Of course from observation. Now, all which man can observe are individual cases. From these all general truths must be drawn, and into these they may be again resolved; for a general truth is but an aggregate of particular truths; a comprehensive expression, by which an indefinite number of individual facts are affirmed or denied at once. But a general proposition is not merely a compendious form for recording and preserving in the memory a number of particular facts, all of which have been observed. Generalization is not a process of mere naming, it is also a process of inference. From instances which we have observed, we feel warranted in concluding, that what we found true in those instances, holds in all similar ones, past, present and future, however numerous they may be. We then, by that valuable contrivance of language which enables us to speak of many as if they were one, record all that we have observed, together with all that we infer from our observations, in one concise expression; and have thus only one proposition, instead of an endless number, to remember or to communicate. The results of many observations and inferences, and instructions for making innumerable inferences in unforeseen cases, are compressed into one short sentence.

When, therefore, we conclude from the death of John and Thomas, and every other person we ever heard of in whose case the experiment had been fairly tried, that the Duke of Wellington is mortal like the rest; we may, indeed, pass through the generalization, All men are mortal, as an intermediate stage; but it is not in the latter half of the process, the descent from all men to the Duke of Wellington, that the *inference* resides. The inference is finished when we have asserted that all men are mortal. What remains to be performed afterward is merely deciphering our own notes.

Archbishop Whately has contended that syllogizing, or reasoning from generals to particulars, is not, agreeably to the vulgar idea, a peculiar *mode* of reasoning, but the philosophical analysis of *the* mode in which all men reason, and must do so if they reason at all. With the deference due to so high an authority, I can not help thinking that the vulgar notion is, in this case, the more correct. If, from our experience of John, Thomas, etc., who once were living, but are now dead, we are entitled to conclude that all human beings are mortal, we might surely without any logical inconsequence have concluded at once from those instances, that the Duke of Wellington is mortal. The mortality of John, Thomas, and others is, after all, the whole evidence we have for the mortality of the Duke of Wellington. Not one iota is added to the proof by interpolating a general proposition. Since the individual cases are all the evidence we can possess, evidence which no logical form into which we choose to throw it can make greater than it is; and since that evidence is either sufficient in itself, or, if insufficient for the one purpose, can not be sufficient for the other; I am unable to see why we should be forbidden to take the shortest cut from these sufficient premises to the conclusion, and constrained to travel the "high priori road," by the arbitrary fiat of logicians. I can not perceive why it should be impossible to journey from one place to another unless we "march up a hill, and then march down again." It may be the safest road, and there may be a resting-place at the top of the hill, affording a commanding view of the surrounding country; but for the mere purpose of arriving at our journey's end, our taking that road is perfectly optional; it is a question of time, trouble, and danger.

Not only *may* we reason from particulars to particulars without passing through generals, but we perpetually do so reason. All our earliest inferences are of this nature. From the first dawn of intelligence we draw inferences, but years elapse before we learn the use of general language. The child, who, having burned his fingers, avoids to thrust them again into the fire, has reasoned or inferred, though he has never thought of the general maxim, Fire burns. He knows from memory that he has been burned, and on this evidence believes, when he sees a candle, that if he puts his finger into the flame of it, he will be burned again. He believes this in every case which happens to arise; but without looking, in each instance, beyond the present case. He is not generalizing; he is inferring a particular from particulars. In the same way, also, brutes reason. There is no ground for attributing to any of the lower animals the use of signs, of such a nature as to render general propositions possible. But those animals profit by experience, and avoid what they have found to cause them pain, in the same manner, though not always with the same skill, as a human creature. Not only the burned child, but the burned dog, dreads the fire. . . .

From the considerations now adduced, the following conclusions seem to be established. All inference is from particulars to particulars: General propositions are merely registers of such inferences already made, and short formulæ for making more: The major premise of a syllogism, consequently, is a formula of this description: and the conclusion is not an inference drawn *from* the formula, but an inference drawn *according* to the formula: the real logical antecedent, or premise, being the particular facts from which the general proposition was collected by induction. Those facts, and the individual instances which supplied them, may have been forgotten: but a record remains, not indeed descriptive of the facts themselves, but showing how those cases may be distinguished, respecting which, the facts, when known, were considered to warrant a given inference. According to the indications of this record we draw our conclusion: which is, to all intents and purposes, a conclusion from the forgotten facts. For this it is essential that we should read the record correctly: and the rules of the syllogism are a set of precautions to insure our doing so.

There are weighty scientific reasons for giving to every science as much of the character of a Deductive Science as possible; for endeavoring to construct the science from the fewest and the simplest possible inductions, and to make these, by any combinations however complicated, suffice for proving even such truths, relating to complex cases, as could be proved, if we chose, by inductions from specific experience. Every branch of natural philosophy was originally experimental; each generalization rested on a special induction, and was derived from its own distinct set of observations and experiments. From being sciences of pure experiment, as the phrase is, or, to speak more correctly, sciences in which the reasonings mostly consist of no more than one step, and are expressed by single syllogisms, all these sciences have become to some extent, and some of them in nearly the whole of their extent, sciences of pure reasoning; whereby multitudes of truths, already known by induction from as many different sets of experiments, have come to be exhibited as deductions or corollaries from inductive propositions of a simpler and more universal character. Thus mechanics, hydrostatics, optics, acoustics, thermology, have successively been rendered mathematical; and astronomy was brought by Newton within the laws of general mechanics. Why it is that the substitution of this circuitous mode of proceeding for a process apparently much easier and more natural, is held, and justly, to be the greatest triumph of the investigation of nature, we are not, in this stage of our inquiry, prepared to examine. But it is necessary to remark, that although, by this progressive transformation, all sciences tend to become more and more Deductive, they are not, therefore, the less Inductive; every step in the Deduction is still an Induction. The opposition is not between the terms Deductive and Inductive, but between Deductive and Experimental. A science is experimental, in proportion as every new case, which presents any peculiar features, stands in need of a new set of observations and experiments—a fresh induction. It is deductive, in proportion as it can draw conclusions, respecting cases of a new kind, by processes which bring those cases under old induction; by ascertaining that cases which can not be observed to have the requisite marks, have, however, marks of those marks.

We can now, therefore, perceive what is the generic distinction between sciences which can be made Deductive, and those which must as yet remain Experimental. The difference consists in our having been able, or not yet able, to discover marks of marks. If by our various inductions we have been able to proceed no further than to such propositions as these, a a mark of b, or a and b marks of one another, c a mark of d, or c and d marks of one another, without anything to connect a or b with c or d; we have a science of detached and mutually independent generalizations, such as these, that acids redden vegetable blues, and that alkalies color them green; from neither of which propositions could we, directly or indirectly, infer the other: and a science, so far as it is composed of such propositions, is purely experimental. Chemistry, in the present state of our knowledge, has not yet thrown off this character. There are other sciences, however, of which the propositions are of this kind: a a mark of b, b a mark of c, c of d, d of e, etc. In these sciences we can mount the ladder from a to e by a process of ratiocination; we can conclude that a is a mark of e, and that every object which has the mark a has the property e, although, perhaps, we never were able to observe a and e together, and although even d, our only direct mark of e, may not be perceptible in those objects, but only inferable. Or, varying the first metaphor, we may be said to get from a to e underground: the marks b, c, d, which indicate the route, must all be possessed somewhere by the objects concerning which we are inquiring; but they are below the surface: a is the only mark that is visible, and by it we are able to trace in succession all the rest.

We can now understand how an experimental may transform itself into a deductive science by the mere progress of experiment. In an experimental science, the inductions, as we have said, lie detached, as, a a mark of b, c a mark of d, e a mark of f, and so on: now, a new set of instances, and a consequent new induction, may at any time bridge over the interval between two of these unconnected arches; b, for example, may be ascertained to be a mark of c, which enables us thenceforth to prove deductively that a is a mark of c. Or, as sometimes happens, some comprehensive induction may raise an arch high in the air, which bridges over hosts of them at once; b, d, f, and all the rest, turning out to be marks of some one thing, or of things between which a connection has already been traced. As when Newton discovered that the motions, whether regular or apparently anomalous, of all the bodies of the solar system (each of which motions had been inferred by a separate logical operation, from separate marks), were all marks of moving round a common centre, with a centripetal force varying directly as the mass, and inversely as the square of the distance from that centre. This is the greatest example which has yet occurred of the transformation, at one stroke, of a science which was still to a great degree merely experimental, into a deductive science.

Transformations of the same nature, but on a smaller scale, continually take place in the less advanced branches of physical knowledge, without enabling them to throw off the character of experimental sciences. Thus with regard to the two unconnected propositions before cited, namely, Acids redden vegetable blues, Alkalies make them green; it is remarked by Liebig, that all blue coloring matters which are reddened by acids (as well as, reciprocally, all red coloring matters which are rendered blue by alkalies) contain nitrogen: and it is quite possible that this circumstance may one day furnish a bond of connection between the two propositions in question, by showing that the antagonistic action of acids and alkalies in producing or destroying the color blue, is the result of some one, more general, law. Although this connecting of detached generalizations is so much gain, it tends but little to give a deductive character to any science as a whole; because the new courses of observation and experiment, which thus enable us to connect together a few general truths, usually make known to us a still greater number of unconnected new ones. Hence chemistry, though similar extensions and simplifications of its generalizations are continually taking place, is still in the main an experimental science; and is likely so to continue unless some comprehensive induction should be hereafter arrived at, which, like Newton's, shall connect a vast number of the smaller known inductions together, and change the whole method of the science at once. Chemistry has already one great generalization, which, though relating to one of the subordinate aspects of chemical phenomena, possesses within its limited sphere this comprehensive character; the principle of Dalton, called the atomic theory, or the doctrine of chemical equivalents: which by enabling us to a certain extent to foresee the proportions in which two substances will combine, before the experiment has been tried, constitutes undoubtedly a source of new chemical truths obtainable by deduction, as well as a connecting principle for all truths of the same description previously obtained by experiment.

The discoveries which change the method of a science from experimental to deductive, mostly consist in establishing, either by deduction or by direct experiment, that the varieties of a particular phenomenon uniformly accompany the varieties of some other phenomenon better known.

Thus the science of sound, which previously stood in the lowest rank of merely experimental science, became deductive when it was proved by experiment that every variety of sound was consequent on, and therefore a mark of, a distinct and definable variety of oscillatory motion among the particles of the transmitting medium. When this was ascertained, it followed that every relation of succession or co-existence which obtained between phenomena of the more known class, obtained also between the phenomena which correspond to them in the other class. Every sound, being a mark of a particular oscillatory motion, became a mark of every thing which, by the laws of dynamics, was known to be inferable from that motion; and everything which by those same laws was a mark of any oscillatory motion among the particles of an elastic medium, became a mark of the corresponding sound. And thus many truths, not before suspected, concerning sound, become deducible from the known laws of the propagation of motion through an elastic medium; while facts already empirically known respecting sound, become an indication of corresponding properties of vibrating bodies, previously undiscovered.

But the grand agent for transforming experimental into deductive sciences, is the science of number. The properties of number, alone among all known phenomena, are, in the most rigorous sense, properties of all things whatever. All things are not colored, or ponderable, or even extended; but all things are numberable. And if we consider this science in its whole extent, from common arithmetic up to the calculus of variations, the truths already ascertained seem all but infinite, and admit of indefinite extension.

These truths, though affirmable of all things whatever, of course apply to them only in respect of their quantity. But if it comes to be discovered that variations of quality in any class of phenomena, correspond regularly to variations of quantity either in those same or in some other phenomena; every formula of mathematics applicable to quantities which vary in that particular manner, becomes a mark of a corresponding general truth respecting the variations in quality which accompany them: and the science of quantity being (as far as any science can be) altogether deductive, the theory of that particular kind of qualities becomes, to this extent, deductive likewise.

The most striking instance in point which history affords (though not an example of an experimental science rendered deductive, but of an unparalleled extension given to the deductive process in a science which was deductive already), is the revolution in geometry which originated with Descartes, and was completed by Clairaut. These great mathematicians pointed out the importance of the fact, that to every variety of position in points, direction in lines, or form in curves or surfaces (all of which are Qualities), there corresponds a peculiar relation of quantity between either two or three rectilineal co-ordinates; insomuch that if the law were known according to which those co-ordinates vary relatively to one another, every other geometrical property of the line or surface in question, whether relating to quantity or quality, would be capable of being inferred. Hence it followed that every geometrical question could be solved, if the corresponding algebraical one could; and geometry received an accession (actual or potential) of new truths, corresponding to every property of numbers which the progress of the calculus had brought, or might in future bring, to light. In the same general manner, mechanics, astronomy, and in a less degree, every branch of natural philosophy commonly so called, have been made algebraical. The varieties of physical phenomena with which those sciences are conversant, have been found to answer to determinable varieties in the quantity of some circumstance or other; or at least to varieties of form or position, for which corresponding equations of quantity had already been, or were susceptible of being, discovered by geometers.

In these various transformations, the propositions of the science of number do but fulfill the function proper to all propositions forming a train of reasoning, viz., that of enabling us to arrive in an indirect method, by marks of marks, at such of the properties of objects as we can not directly ascertain (or not so conveniently) by experiment. We travel from a given visible or tangible fact, through the truths of numbers, to the facts sought. The given fact is a mark that a certain relation subsists between the quantities of some of the elements concerned; while the fact sought presupposes a certain relation between the quantities of some other elements: now, if these last quantities are dependent in some known manner upon the former, or *vice versa,* we can argue from the numerical relation between the one set of quantities, to determine that which subsists between the other set; the theorems of the calculus affording the intermediate links. And thus one of the two physical facts becomes a mark of the other, by being a mark of a mark of a mark of it.

OF DEMONSTRATION, AND NECESSARY TRUTHS

If, as laid down in the two preceding chapters, the foundation of all sciences, even deductive or demonstrative sciences, is Induction; if every step in the ratiocinations even of geometry is an act of induction; and if a train of reasoning is but bringing many inductions to bear upon the same subject of inquiry, and drawing a case within one induction by means of another; wherein lies the peculiar certainty always ascribed to the sciences which are entirely, or almost entirely, deductive? Why are they called the Exact Sciences? Why are mathematical certainty, and the evidence of demonstration, common phrases to express the very highest degree of assurance attainable by reason? Why are mathematics by almost all philosophers, and (by some) even those branches of natural philosophy which, through the medium of mathematics, have been converted into deductive sciences, considered to be independent of the evidence of experience and observation, and characterized as systems of Necessary Truth?

The answer I conceive to be, that this character of necessity, ascribed to the truths of mathematics, and (even with some reservations to be hereafter made) the peculiar certainty attributed to them, is an illusion; in order to sustain which, it is necessary to suppose that those truths relate to, and express the properties of, purely imaginary objects. It is acknowledged that the conclusions of geometry are deduced, partly at least, from the so-called Definitions, and that those definitions are assumed to be correct representations, as far as they go, of the objects with which geometry is conversant. Now we have pointed out that, from a definition as such, no proposition, unless it be one concerning the meaning of a word, can ever follow; and that what apparently follows from a definition, follows in reality from an implied assumption that there exists a real thing conformable thereto. This assumption, in the case of the definitions of geometry, is not strictly true: there exist no real things exactly conformable to the definitions. There exist no points without magnitude; no lines without breadth, nor perfectly straight; no circles with all their radii exactly equal, nor squares with all their angles perfectly right. It will perhaps be said that the assumption does not extend to the actual, but only to the possible, existence of such things. I answer that, according to any test we have of possibility, they are not even possible. Their existence, so far as we can form any judgment, would seem to be inconsistent with the physical constitution of our planet at least, if not of the universe. To get rid of this difficulty, and at the same time to save the credit of the supposed system of necessary truth, it is customary to say that the points, lines, circles, and squares which are the subject of geometry, exist in our conceptions merely, and are part of our minds; which minds, by working on their own materials, construct an *a priori* science, the evidence of which is purely mental, and has nothing whatever to do with outward experience. By howsoever high authorities this doctrine may have been sanctioned, it appears to me psychologically incorrect. The points, lines, circles, and squares which any one has in his mind, are (I apprehend) simply copies of the points, lines, circles, and squares which he has known in his experience. Our idea of a point, I apprehend to be simply our idea of the *minimum visibile,* the smallest portion of surface which we can see. A line, as defined by geometers, is wholly inconceivable. We can reason about a line as if it had no breadth; because we have a power, which is the foundation of all the control we can exercise over the operations of our minds; the power, when a perception is present to our senses, or a conception to our intellects, of *attending* to a part only of that perception or conception, instead of the whole. But we can not *conceive* a line without breadth; we can form no mental picture of such a line: all the lines which we have in our minds are lines possessing breadth. If any one doubts this, we may refer him to his own experience. I much question if any one who fancies that he can conceive what is called a mathematical line, thinks so from the evidence of his consciousness: I suspect it is rather because he supposes that unless such a conception were possible, mathematics could not exist as a science: a supposition which there will be no difficulty in showing to be entirely groundless.

Since, then, neither in nature, nor in the human mind, do there exist any objects exactly corresponding to the definitions of geometry, while yet that science can not be supposed to be conversant about nonentities; nothing remains but to consider geometry as conversant with such lines, angles, and figures, as really exist; and the definitions, as they are called, must be regarded as some of our first and most obvious generalizations concerning those natural objects. The correctness of those generalizations, *as* generalizations, is without a flaw: the equality of all the radii of a circle is true of all circles, so far as it is true of any one: but it is not exactly true of any circle; it is only nearly true; so nearly that no error of any importance in practice will be incurred by feigning it to be exactly true. When we have occasion to extend these inductions, or their consequences, to cases in which the error would be appreciable—to lines of perceptible breadth or thickness, parallels which deviate sensibly from equidistance, and the like—we correct our conclusions, by combining with them a fresh set of propositions relating to the aberration; just as we also take in propositions relating to the physical or chemical properties of the material, if those properties happen to introduce any modification into the result; which they easily may, even with respect to figure and magnitude, as in the case, for instance, of expansion by heat. So long, however, as there exists no practical necessity for attending to any of the properties of the object except its geometrical properties, or to any of the natural irregularities in those, it is convenient to neglect the consideration of the other properties and of the irregularities, and to reason as if these did not exist: accordingly, we formally announce in the definitions, that we intend to proceed on this plan. But it is an error to suppose, because we resolve to confine our attention to a certain number of the properties of an object, that we therefore conceive, or have an idea of, the object, denuded of its other properties. We are thinking, all the time, of precisely such objects as we have seen and touched, and with all the properties which naturally belong to them; but, for scientific convenience, we feign them to be divested of all properties, except those which are material to our purpose, and in regard to which we design to consider them.

The peculiar accuracy, supposed to be characteristic of the first principles of geometry, thus appears to be fictitious. The assertions on which the reasonings of the science are founded, do not, any more than in other sciences, exactly correspond with the fact; but we suppose that they do so, for the sake of tracing the consequences which follow from the supposition. The opinion of Dugald Stewart respecting the foundations of geometry, is, I conceive, substantially correct; that it is built on hypotheses; that it owes to this alone the peculiar certainty supposed to distinguish it; and that in any science whatever, by reasoning from a set of hypotheses, we may obtain a body of conclusions as certain as those of geometry, that is, as strictly in accordance with the hypotheses, and as irresistibly compelling assent, *on condition* that those hypotheses are true.[3]

When, therefore, it is affirmed that the conclusions of geometry are necessary truths, the necessity consists in reality only in this, that they correctly follow from the suppositions from which they are deduced. Those suppositions are so far from being necessary, that they are not even true; they purposely depart, more or less widely, from the truth. The only sense in which necessity can be ascribed to the conclusions of any scientific investigation, is that of legitimately following from some assumption, which, by the conditions of the inquiry, is not to be questioned. In this relation, of course, the derivative truths of every deductive science must stand to the inductions, or assumptions, on which the science is founded, and which, whether true or untrue, certain or doubtful in themselves, are always supposed certain for the purposes of the particular science. And therefore the conclusions of all deductive sciences were said by the ancients to be necessary propositions. We have observed already that to be predicated necessarily was characteristic of the predicable Proprium, and that a proprium was any property of a thing which could

3 It is justly remarked by Professor Bain (*Logic*, ii., 134) that the word Hypothesis is here used in a somewhat peculiar sense. An hypothesis, in science, usually means a supposition not proved to be true, but surmised to be so, because if true it would account for certain known facts; and the final result of the speculation may be to prove its truth. The hypotheses spoken of in the text are of a different character; they are known not to be literally true, while as much of them as is true is not hypothetical, but certain. The two cases, however, resemble in the circumstance that in both we reason, not from a truth, but from an assumption, and the truth therefore of the conclusions is conditional, not categorical. This suffices to justify, in point of logical propriety, Stewart's use of the term. It is of course needful to bear in mind that the hypothetical element in the definitions of geometry is the assumption that what is very nearly true is exactly so. This unreal exactitude might be called a fiction, as properly as an hypothesis; but that appellation, still more than the other, would fail to point out the close relation which exists between the fictitious point of line and the points and lines of which we have experience.

be deduced from its essence, that is, from the properties included in its definition. . . .

It remains to inquire, what is the ground of our belief in axioms—what is the evidence on which they rest? I answer, they are experimental truths; generalizations from observation. The proposition, Two straight lines can not inclose a space—or, in other words, Two straight lines which have once met, do not meet again, but continue to diverge—is an induction from the evidence of our senses.

This opinion runs counter to a scientific prejudice of long standing and great strength, and there is probably no proposition enunciated in this work for which a more unfavorable reception is to be expected. It is, however, no new opinion; and even if it were so, would be entitled to be judged, not by its novelty, but by the strength of the arguments by which it can be supported. I consider it very fortunate that so eminent a champion of the contrary opinion as Dr. Whewell has found occasion for a most elaborate treatment of the whole theory of axioms, in attempting to construct the philosophy of the mathematical and physical sciences on the basis of the doctrine against which I now contend. Whoever is anxious that a discussion should go to the bottom of the subject, must rejoice to see the opposite side of the question worthily represented. If what is said by Dr. Whewell, in support of an opinion which he has made the foundation of a systematic work, can be shown not to be conclusive, enough will have been done, without going elsewhere in quest of stronger arguments and a more powerful adversary.

It is not necessary to show that the truths which we call axioms are originally *suggested* by observation, and that we should never have known that two straight lines can not inclose a space if we had never seen a straight line: thus much being admitted by Dr. Whewell, and by all, in recent times, who have taken his view of the subject. But they contend, that it is not experience which *proves* the axiom; but that its truth is perceived *a priori*, by the constitution of the mind itself, from the first moment when the meaning of the proposition is apprehended; and without any necessity for verifying it by repeated trials, as is requisite in the case of truths really ascertained by observation.

They can not, however, but allow that the truth of the axiom, Two straight lines can not inclose a space, even if evident independently of experience, is also evident from experience. Whether the axiom needs confirmation or not, it receives confirmation in almost every instant of our lives; since we can not look at any two straight lines which intersect one another, without seeing that from that point they continue to diverge more and more. Experimental proof crowds in upon us in such endless profusion, and without one instance in which there can be even a suspicion of an exception to the rule, that we should soon have stronger ground for believing the axiom, even as an experimental truth, than we have for almost any of the general truths which we confessedly learn from the evidence of our senses. Independently of *a priori* evidence, we should certainly believe it with an intensity of conviction far greater than we accord to any ordinary physical truth: and this too at a time of life much earlier than that from which we date almost any part of our acquired knowledge, and much too early to admit of our retaining any recollection of the history of our intellectual operations at that period. Where then is the necessity for assuming that our recognition of these truths has a different origin from the rest of our knowledge, when its existence is perfectly accounted for by supposing its origin to be the same? when the causes which produce belief in all other instances, exist in this instance, and in a degree of strength as much superior to what exists in other cases, as the intensity of the belief itself is superior? The burden of proof lies on the advocates of the contrary opinion: it is for them to point out some fact, inconsistent with the supposition that this part of our knowledge of nature is derived from the same sources as every other part.[6]

This, for instance, they would be able to do, if they could prove chronologically that we had the conviction (at least practically) so early in infancy as to be anterior to those impressions on the senses, upon which, on the other theory, the conviction is founded. This, however, can not be proved: the point being too far back to be within the reach of memory, and too obscure for external observation. The advocates of the *a priori* theory are obliged to have recourse to other arguments. These are

[6] Some persons find themselves prevented from believing that the axiom, Two straight lines can not inclose a space, could ever become known to us through experience, by a difficulty which may be stated as follows: If the straight lines spoken of are those contemplated in the definition—lines absolutely without breadth and absolutely straight—that such are incapable of inclosing a space is not proved by experience, for lines such as these do not present themselves in our experience. If, on the other hand, the lines meant are such straight lines as we do meet with in experience, lines straight enough for practical purposes, but in reality slightly zigzag, and with some, however trifling, breadth; as applied to these lines the axiom is not true, for two of them may, and sometimes do, inclose a small portion of space. In neither case, therefore, does experience prove the axiom.

Those who employ this argument to show that geometrical axioms can not be proved by induction, show themselves unfamiliar with a common and perfectly valid mode of inductive proof; proof by approximation. Though experience furnishes us with no lines so unimpeachably straight that two of them are incapable of inclosing the smallest space, it presents us with gradations of lines possessing less and less either of breadth or of flexure, of which series the straight line of the definition is the ideal limit. And observation shows that just as much, and as nearly, as the straight lines of experience approximate to having no breadth or flexure, so much and so nearly does the space-inclosing power of any two of them approach to zero. The inference that if they had no breadth or flexure at all, they would inclose no space at all, is a correct inductive inference from these facts, conformable to one of the four Inductive Methods hereinafter characterized, the Method of Concomitant Variations; of which the mathematical Doctrine of Limits presents the extreme case.

reducible to two, which I shall endeavor to state as clearly and as forcibly as possible.

In the first place it is said, that if our assent to the proposition that two straight lines can not inclose a space, were derived from the senses, we could only be convinced of its truth by actual trial, that is, by seeing or feeling the straight lines; whereas, in fact, it is seen to be true by merely thinking of them. That a stone thrown into water goes to the bottom, may be perceived by our senses, but mere thinking of a stone thrown into the water would never have led us to that conclusion: not so, however, with the axioms relating to straight lines: if I could be made to conceive what a straight line is, without having seen one, I should at once recognize that two such lines can not inclose a space. Intuition is "imaginary looking"; [7] but experience must be real looking: if we see a property of straight lines to be true by merely fancying ourselves to be looking at them, the ground of our belief can not be the senses, or experience; it must be something mental.

To this argument it might be added in the case of this particular axiom (for the assertion would not be true of all axioms), that the evidence of it from actual ocular inspection is not only unnecessary, but unattainable. What says the axiom? That two straight lines *can not* inclose a space; that after having once intersected, if they are prolonged to infinity they do not meet, but continue to diverge from one another. How can this, in any single case, be proved by actual observation? We may follow the lines to any distance we please; but we can not follow them to infinity: for aught our senses can testify, they may, immediately beyond the farthest point to which we have traced them, begin to approach, and at last meet. Unless, therefore, we had some other proof of the impossibility than observation affords us, we should have no ground for believing the axiom at all.

To these arguments, which I trust I can not be accused of understating, a satisfactory answer will, I conceive, be found, if we advert to one of the characteristic properties of geometrical forms—their capacity of being painted in the imagination with a distinctness equal to reality: in other words, the exact resemblance of our ideas of form to the sensations which suggest them. This, in the first place, enables us to make (at least with a little practice) mental pictures of all possible combinations of lines and angles, which resemble the realities quite as well as any which we could make on paper; and in the next place, make those pictures just as fit subjects of geometrical experimentation as the realities themselves; inasmuch as pictures, if sufficiently accurate, exhibit of course all the properties which would be manifested by the realities at one given instant,

[7] Whewell's *History of Scientific Ideas*, i., 140.

and on simple inspection: and in geometry we are concerned only with such properties, and not with that which pictures could not exhibit, the mutual action of bodies one upon another. The foundation of geometry would therefore be laid in direct experience, even if the experiments (which in this case consist merely in attentive contemplation) were practiced solely upon what we call our ideas, that is, upon the diagrams in our minds, and not upon outward objects. For in all systems of experimentation we take some objects to serve as representatives of all which resemble them; and in the present case the conditions which qualify a real object to be the representative of its class, are completely fulfilled by an object existing only in our fancy. Without denying, therefore, the possibility of satisfying ourselves that two straight lines can not inclose a space, by merely thinking of straight lines without actually looking at them; I contend, that we do not believe this truth on the ground of the imaginary intuition simply, but because we know that the imaginary lines exactly resemble real ones, and that we may conclude from them to real ones with quite as much certainty as we could conclude from one real line to another. The conclusion, therefore, is still an induction from observation. And we should not be authorized to substitute observation of the image in our mind, for observation of the reality, if we had not learned by long-continued experience that the properties of the reality are faithfully represented in the image; just as we should be scientifically warranted in describing an animal which we have never seen, from a picture made of it with a daguerreotype; but not until we had learned by ample experience, that observation of such a picture is precisely equivalent to observation of the original.

These considerations also remove the objection arising from the impossibility of ocularly following the lines in their prolongation to infinity. For though, in order actually to see that two given lines never meet, it would be necessary to follow them to infinity; yet without doing so we may know that if they ever do meet, or if, after diverging from one another, they begin again to approach, this must take place not at an infinite, but at a finite distance. Supposing, therefore, such to be the case, we can transport ourselves thither in imagination, and can frame a mental image of the appearance which one or both of the lines must present at that point, which we may rely on as being precisely similar to the reality. Now, whether we fix our contemplation upon this imaginary picture, or call to mind the generalizations we have had occasion to make from former ocular observation, we learn by the evidence of experience, that a line which, after diverging from another straight line, begins to approach to it, produces the impression on our senses which we describe by the expression, "a bent line," not by the expression, "a straight line."

The preceding argument, which is, to my mind unanswerable, merges, however, in a still more comprehensive one, which is stated most clearly and conclusively by Professor Bain. The psychological reason why axioms, and indeed many propositions not ordinarily classed as such, may be learned from the idea only without referring to the fact, is that in the process of acquiring the idea we have learned the fact. The proposition is assented to as soon as the terms are understood, because in learning to understand the terms we have acquired the experience which proves the proposition to be true. "We required," says Mr. Bain, "concrete experience in the first instance, to attain to the notion of whole and part; but the notion, once arrived at, implies that the whole is greater. In fact, we could not have the notion without an experience tantamount to this conclusion. . . . When we have mastered the notion of straightness, we have also mastered that aspect of it expressed by the affirmation that two straight lines can not inclose a space. No intuitive or innate powers or perceptions are needed in such cases. . . . We can not have the full meaning of Straightness, without going through a comparison of straight objects among themselves, and with their opposites, bent or crooked objects. The result of this comparison is, *inter alia,* that straightness in two lines is seen to be incompatible with inclosing a space; the inclosure of space involves crookedness in at least one of the lines." And similarly, in the case of every first principle, "the same knowledge that makes it understood, suffices to verify it." The more this observation is considered the more (I am convinced) it will be felt to go to the very root of the controversy.

The first of the two arguments in support of the theory that axioms are *a priori* truths, having, I think, been sufficiently answered; I proceed to the second, which is usually the most relied on. Axioms (it is asserted) are conceived by us not only as true, but as universally and necessarily true. Now, experience can not possibly give to any proposition this character. I may have seen snow a hundred times, and may have seen that it was white, but this can not give me entire assurance even that all snow is white; much less that snow *must* be white. "However many instances we may have observed of the truth of a proposition, there is nothing to assure us that the next case shall not be an exception to the rule. If it be strictly true that every ruminant animal yet known has cloven hoofs, we still can not be sure that some creature will not hereafter be discovered which has the first of these attributes, without having the other. . . . Experience must always consist of a limited number of observations; and, however numerous these may be, they can show nothing with regard to the infinite number of cases in which the experiment has not been made." Besides, Axioms are not only universal, they are also necessary. Now "experience can not offer the smallest ground for the necessity of a proposition. She can observe and record what has happened; but she can not find, in any case, or in any accumulation of cases, any reason for what *must* happen. She may see objects side by side; but she can not see a reason why they must ever be side by side. She finds certain events to occur in succession; but the succession supplies, in its occurrence, no reason for its recurrence. She contemplates external objects; but she can not detect any internal bond, which indissolubly connects the future with the past, the possible with the real. To learn a proposition by experience, and to see it to be necessarily true, are two altogether different processes of thought." And Dr. Whewell adds, "If any one does not clearly comprehend this distinction of necessary and contingent truths, he will not be able to go along with us in our researches into the foundations of human knowledge; not, indeed, to pursue with success any speculation on the subject."

In the following passage, we are told what the distinction is, the non-recognition of which incurs this denunciation. "Necessary truths are those in which we not only learn that the proposition *is* true, but see that it *must be* true; in which the negation of the truth is not only false, but impossible; in which we can not, even by an effort of imagination, or in a supposition, conceive the reverse of that which is asserted. That there are such truths can not be doubted. We may take, for example, all relations of number. Three and Two added together make Five. We can not conceive it to be otherwise. We can not, by any freak of thought, imagine Three and Two to make Seven."

Although Dr. Whewell has naturally and properly employed a variety of phrases to bring his meaning more forcibly home, he would, I presume, allow that they are all equivalent; and that what he means by a necessary truth, would be sufficiently defined, a proposition the negation of which is not only false but inconceivable. I am unable to find in any of his expressions, turn them what way you will, a meaning beyond this, and I do not believe he would contend that they mean any thing more.

This, therefore, is the principle asserted: that propositions, the negation of which is inconceivable, or in other words, which we can not figure to ourselves as being false, must rest on evidence of a higher and more cogent description than any which experience can afford.

Now I can not but wonder that so much stress should be laid on the circumstance of inconceivableness, when there is such ample experience to show, that our capacity or incapacity of conceiving a thing has very little to do with the possibility of the thing in itself; but is in truth very much an affair of accident, and depends on the past history and habits of our own minds. There is no more generally acknowledged fact in human nature, than the extreme difficulty at first felt in conceiving any thing as possible, which is in contradiction to long established and familiar experience; or even to old familiar habits of thought. And this difficulty is a necessary result of the fundamental laws of the human mind. When we have often seen and thought of two things together, and have never in any one instance either seen or thought of them separately, there is by the primary law of association an increasing difficulty, which may in the end become insuperable, of conceiving the two things apart. This is most of all conspicuous in uneducated persons, who are in general utterly unable to separate any two ideas which have once become firmly associated in their minds; and if persons of cultivated intellect have any advantage on the point, it is only because, having seen and heard and read more, and being more accustomed to exercise their imagination, they have experienced their sensations and thoughts in more varied combinations, and have been prevented from forming many of these inseparable associations. But this advantage has necessarily its limits. The most practiced intellect is not exempt from the universal laws of our conceptive faculty. If daily habit presents to any one for a long period two facts in combination, and if he is not led during that period either by accident or by his voluntary mental operations to think of them apart, he will probably in time become incapable of doing so even by the strongest effort; and the supposition that the two facts can be separated in nature, will at last present itself to his mind with all the character of an inconceivable phenomenon. There are remarkable instances of this in the history of science: instances in which the most instructed men rejected as impossible, because inconceivable, things which their posterity, by earlier practice and longer perseverance in the attempt, found it quite easy to conceive, and which every body now knows to be true. There was a time when men of the most cultivated intellects, and the most emancipated from the dominion of early prejudice, could not credit the existence of antipodes; were unable to conceive, in opposition to old association, the force of gravity acting upward instead of downward. The Cartesians long rejected the Newtonian doctrine of the gravitation of all bodies toward one another, on the faith of a general proposition, the reverse of which seemed to them to be inconceivable—the proposition that a body can not act where it is not. All the cumbrous machinery of imaginary vortices, assumed without the smallest particle of evidence, appeared to these philosophers a more rational mode of explaining the heavenly motions, than one which involved what seemed to them so great an absurdity. And they no doubt found it as impossible to conceive that a body should act upon the earth from the distance of the sun or moon, as we find it to conceive an end to space or time, or two straight lines inclosing a space. Newton himself had not been able to realize the conception, or we should not have had his hypothesis of a subtle ether, the occult cause of gravitation; and his writings prove, that though he deemed the particular nature of the intermediate agency a matter of conjecture, the necessity of *some* such agency appeared to him indubitable.

If, then, it be so natural to the human mind, even in a high state of culture, to be incapable of conceiving, and on that ground to believe impossible, what is afterward not only found to be conceivable but proved to be true; what wonder if in cases where the association is still older, more confirmed, and more familiar, and in which nothing ever occurs to shake our conviction, or even suggest to us any conception at variance with the association, the acquired incapacity should continue, and be mistaken for a natural incapacity? It is true, our experience of the varieties in nature enables us, within certain limits, to conceive other varieties analogous to them. We can conceive the sun or moon falling; for though we never saw them fall, nor ever, perhaps, imagined them falling, we have seen so many other things fall, that we have innumerable familiar analogies to assist the conception; which, after all, we should probably have some difficulty in framing, were we not well accustomed to see the sun and moon move (or appear to move), so that we are only called upon to conceive a slight change in the direction of motion, a circumstance familiar to our experience. But when experience affords no model on which to shape the new conception, how is it possible for us to form it? How, for example, can we imagine an end to space or time? We never saw any object without something beyond it, nor experienced any feeling without something following it. When, therefore, we attempt to conceive the last point of space, we have the idea irresistibly raised of other points beyond it. When we try to imagine the last instant of time, we can not help conceiving another instant after it. Nor is there any necessity to assume, as is done by a modern school of metaphysicians, a peculiar fundamental law of the mind to account for the feeling of infinity inherent in our conceptions of space and time; that apparent infinity is sufficiently accounted for by simpler and universally acknowledged laws.

Now, in the case of a geometrical axiom, such, for example, as that two straight lines can not inclose a space—a truth which is testified to us by our very earliest impressions of the external world—how is it possible (whether those external impressions be or be not the ground of our belief) that the reverse of the proposition *could* be otherwise than inconceivable to us? What analogy have we, what similar order of facts in any other branch of our experience, to facilitate to us the conception of two straight lines inclosing a space? Nor is even this all. I have already called attention to the peculiar property of our impressions of form, that the ideas or mental images exactly resemble their prototypes, and adequately represent them for the purposes of scientific observation. From this, and from the intuitive character of the observation, which in this case reduces itself to simple inspection, we can not so much as call up in our imagination two straight lines, in order to attempt to conceive them inclosing a space, without by that very act repeating the scientific experiment which establishes the contrary. Will it really be contended that the inconceivableness of the thing, in such circumstances, proves any thing against the experimental origin of the conviction? Is it not clear that in whichever mode our belief in the proposition may have originated, the impossibility of our conceiving the negative of it must, on either hypothesis, be the same?

As, then, Dr. Whewell exhorts those who have any difficulty in recognizing the distinction held by him between necessary and contingent truths, to study geometry—a condition which I can assure him I have conscientiously fulfilled—I, in return, with equal confidence, exhort those who agree with him, to study the general laws of association; being convinced that nothing more is requisite than a moderate familiarity with those laws, to dispel the illusion which ascribes a peculiar necessity to our earliest inductions from experience, and measures the possibility of things in themselves, by the human capacity of conceiving them.

THE SAME SUBJECT CONTINUED

In the examination which formed the subject of the last chapter, into the nature of the evidence of those deductive sciences which are commonly represented to be systems of necessary truth, we have been led to the following conclusions. The results of those sciences are indeed necessary, in the sense of necessarily following from certain first principles, commonly called axioms and definitions; that is, of being certainly true if those axioms and definitions are so; for the word necessity, even in this acceptation of it, means no more than certainty. But their claim to the character of necessity in any sense beyond this, as implying an evidence independent of and superior to observation and experience, must depend on the previous establishment of such a claim in favor of the definitions and axioms themselves. With regard to axioms, we found that, considered as experimental truths, they rest on superabundant and obvious evidence. We inquired, whether, since this is the case, it be imperative to suppose any other evidence of those truths than experimental evidence, any other origin for our belief of them than an experimental origin. We decided, that the burden of proof lies with those who maintain the affirmative, and we examined, at considerable length, such arguments as they have produced. The examination having led to the rejection of those arguments, we have thought ourselves warranted in concluding that axioms are but a class, the most universal class, of inductions from experience; the simplest and easiest cases of generalization from the facts furnished to us by our senses or by our internal consciousness.

While the axioms of demonstrative sciences thus appeared to be experimental truths, the definitions, as they are incorrectly called, in those sciences, were found by us to be generalizations from experience which are not even, accurately speaking, truths; being propositions in which, while we assert of some kind of object, some property or properties which observation shows to belong to it, we at the same time deny that it possesses any other properties, though in truth other properties do in every individual instance accompany, and in almost all instances modify, the property thus exclusively predicated. The denial, therefore, is a mere fiction, or supposition, made for the purpose of excluding the consideration of those modifying circumstances, when their influence is of too trifling amount to be worth considering, or adjourning it, when important to a more convenient moment.

From these considerations it would appear that Deductive or Demonstrative Sciences are all, without exception, Inductive Sciences; that their evidence is that of experience; but that they are also, in virtue of the peculiar character of one indispensable portion of the general formulæ according to which their inductions are made, Hypothetical Sciences. Their conclusions are only true on certain suppositions, which are, or ought to be, approximations to the truth, but are seldom, if ever, exactly true; and to this hypothetical character is to be ascribed the peculiar certainty, which is supposed to be inherent in demonstration.

What we have now asserted, however, can not be received as universally true of Deductive or Demonstrative Sciences, until verified by being applied to the most remarkable of all those sciences, that of Numbers; the theory of the Calculus; Arithmetic and Algebra. It is harder to believe of the doctrines of this science than of any other, either that they are not truths a priori, but experimental truths, or that their peculiar certainty is owing to their being not absolute but only conditional truths. This, therefore, is a case which merits examination apart; and the more so, because on this subject we have a double set of doctrines to contend with; that of the a priori philosophers on one side; and on the other, a theory the most opposite to theirs, which was at one time generally received, and is still far from being altogether exploded, among metaphysicians.

This theory attempts to solve the difficulty apparently inherent in the case, by representing the propositions of the science of numbers as merely verbal, and its processes as simple transformations of language, substitutions of one expression for another. The proposition, Two and one is equal to three, according to these writers, is not a truth, is not the assertion of a really existing fact, but a definition of the word three; a statement that mankind have agreed to use the name three as a sign exactly equivalent to two and one; to call by the former name whatever is called by the other more clumsy phrase. According to this doctrine, the longest process in algebra is but a succession of changes in terminology, by which equivalent expressions are substituted one for another; a series of translations of the same fact, from one into another language; though how, after such a series of translations, the fact itself comes out changed (as when we demonstrate a new geometrical theorem by algebra), they have not explained; and it is a difficulty which is fatal to their theory.

It must be acknowledged that there are peculiarities in the processes of arithmetic and algebra which render the theory in question very plausible, and have not unnaturally made those sciences the stronghold of Nominalism. The doctrine that we can discover facts, detect the hidden processes of nature, by an artful manipulation of language, is so contrary to common sense, that a person must have made some advances in philosophy to believe it: men fly to so paradoxical a belief to avoid, as they think, some even greater difficulty, which the vulgar do not see. What has led many to believe that reasoning is a mere verbal process, is, that no other theory seemed reconcilable with the nature of the Science of Numbers. For we do not carry any ideas along with us when we use the symbols of arithmetic or of algebra. In a geometrical demonstration we have a mental diagram, if not one on paper; AB,AC, are present to our imagination as lines, intersecting other lines, forming an angle with one another, and the like; but not so *a* and *b*. These may represent lines or any other magnitudes, but those magnitudes are never thought of; nothing is realized in our imagination but *a* and *b*. The ideas which, on the particular occasion, they happen to represent, are banished from the mind during every intermediate part of the process, between the beginning, when the premises are translated from things into signs, and the end, when the conclusion is translated back from signs into things. Nothing, then, being in the reasoner's mind but the symbols, what can seem more inadmissible than to contend that the reasoning process has to do with any thing more? We seem to have come to one of Bacon's Prerogative Instances; an *experimentum crucis* on the nature of reasoning itself.

Nevertheless, it will appear on consideration, that this apparently so decisive instance is no instance at all; that there is in every step of an arithmetical or algebraical calculation a real induction, a real inference of facts from facts; and that what disguises the induction is simply its comprehensive nature, and the consequent extreme generality of the language. All numbers must be numbers of something: there are no such things as numbers in the abstract. *Ten* must mean ten bodies, or ten sounds, or ten beatings of the pulse. But though numbers must be numbers of something, they may be numbers of any thing. Propositions, therefore, concerning numbers, have the remarkable peculiarity that they are propositions concerning all things whatever; all objects, all existences of every kind, known to our experience. All things possess quantity; consist of parts which can be numbered; and in that character possess all the properties which are called properties of numbers. That half of four is two, must be true whatever the word four represents, whether four hours, four miles, or four pounds weight. We need only conceive a thing divided into four equal parts (and all things may be conceived as so divided), to be able to predicate of it every property of the number four, that is, every arithmetical proposition in which the number four stands on one side of the equation. Algebra extends the generalization still farther: every number represents that particular number of all things without distinction, but every algebraical symbol does more, it represents all numbers without distinction. As soon as we conceive a thing divided into equal parts, without knowing into what number of parts, we may call it a or x, and apply to it, without danger of error, every algebraical formula in the books. The proposition, $2(a + b) = 2a + 2b$, is a truth co-extensive with all nature. Since then algebraical truths are true of all things whatever, and not, like those of geometry, true of lines only or of angles only, it is no wonder that the symbols should not excite in our minds ideas of any things in particular. When we demonstrate the forty-seventh proposition of Euclid, it is not necessary that the words should raise in us an image of all right-angled triangles, but only of some one right-angled triangle: so in algebra we need not, under the symbol, a, picture to ourselves all things whatever, but only some one thing; why not, then, the letter itself? The mere written characters, a, b, x, y, z, serve as well for representatives of Things in general, as any more complex and apparently more concrete conception. That we are conscious of them, however, in their character of things, and not of mere signs, is evident from the fact that our whole process of reasoning is carried on by predicating of them the properties of things. In resolving an algebraic equation, by what rules do we proceed? By applying at each step to $a, b,$ and $x,$ the proposition that equals added to equals make equals; that equals taken from equals leave equals; and other propositions founded on these two. These are not properties of language, or of signs as such, but of magnitudes, which is as much as to say, of all things. The inferences, therefore, which are successively drawn, are inferences concerning things, not symbols; though as any Things whatever will serve the turn, there is no necessity for keeping the idea of the Thing at all distinct, and consequently the process of thought may, in this case, be allowed without danger to do what all processes of thought, when they have been performed often, will do if permitted, namely, to become entirely mechanical. Hence the general language of algebra comes to be used familiarly without exciting ideas, as all other general language is prone to do from mere habit, though in no other case than this can it be done with complete safety. But when we look back to see from whence the probative force of the process is derived, we find that at every single step, unless we suppose ourselves to be thinking and talking of the things, and not the mere symbols, the evidence fails.

There is another circumstance, which, still more than that which we have now mentioned, gives plausibility to the notion that the propositions of arithmetic and algebra are merely verbal. That is, that when considered as propositions respecting Things, they all have the appearance of being identical propositions. The assertion, Two and one is equal to three, considered as an assertion respecting objects, as for instance, "Two pebbles and one pebble are equal to three pebbles," does not affirm equality between two collections of pebbles, but absolute identity. It affirms that if we put one pebble to two pebbles, those very pebbles are three. The objects, therefore, being the very same, and the mere assertion that "objects are themselves" being insignificant, it seems but natural to consider the proposition, Two and one is equal to three, as asserting mere identity of signification between the two names.

This, however, though it looks so plausible, will not bear examination. The expression "two pebbles and one pebble," and the expression "three pebbles," stand indeed for the same aggregation of objects, but they by no means stand for the same physical fact. They are names of the same objects, but of those objects in two different states: though they *de*note the same things, their *con*notation is different. Three pebbles in two separate parcels, and three pebbles in one parcel, do not make the same impression on our senses; and the assertion that the very same pebbles may be an alteration of place and arrangement be made to produce either the one set of sensations or the other, though a very familiar proposition, is not an identical one. It is a truth known to us by early and constant experience: an inductive truth; and such truths are the foundation of the science of Number. The fundamental truths of that science all rest on the evidence of sense; they are proved by showing to our eyes and our fingers that any given number of objects—ten balls, for example—may by separation and re-arrangement exhibit to our senses all the different sets of numbers the sums of which is equal to ten. All the improved methods of teaching arithmetic to children proceed on a knowledge of this fact. All who wish to carry the child's *mind* along with them in learning arithmetic; all who wish to teach numbers, and not mere ciphers—now teach it through the evidence of the senses, in the manner we have described.

We may, if we please, call the proposition, "Three is two and one," a definition of the number three, and assert that arithmetic, as it has been asserted that geometry, is a science founded on definitions. But they are definitions in the geometrical sense, not the logical; asserting not the meaning of a term only, but along with it an observed matter of fact. The proposition, "A circle is a figure bounded by a line which has all its points equally distant from a point within it," is called the definition of a circle; but the proposition from which so many consequences follow, and which is really a first principle in geometry, is, that figures answering to this description exist. And thus we may call "Three is two and one" a definition of three; but the calculations which depend on that proposition do not follow from the definition itself, but from an arithmetical theorem presupposed in it, namely, that collections of objects exist, which while they impress the senses thus, $^{O\,O}_{\;O}$, may be separated into two parts, thus, O OO. This proposition being granted, we term all such parcels Threes, after which the enunciation of the above-mentioned physical fact will serve also for a definition of the word Three.

The Science of Number is thus no exception to the conclusion we previously arrived at, that the processes even of deductive sciences are altogether inductive, and that their first principles are generalizations from experience. It remains to be examined whether this science resembles geometry in the further circumstance, that some of its inductions are not exactly true; and that the peculiar certainty ascribed to it, on account of which its propositions are called Necessary Truths, is fictitious and hypothetical, being true in no other sense than that those propositions legitimately follow from the hypothesis of the truth of premises which are avowedly mere approximations to truth.

The inductions of arithmetic are of two sorts: first, those which we have just expounded, such as One and one are two, Two and one are three, etc., which may be called the definitions of the various numbers, in the improper or geometrical sense of the word Definition; and secondly, the two following axioms: The sums of equals are equal, The differences of equals are equal. These two are sufficient; for the corresponding propositions respecting unequals may be proved from these by a *reductio ad absurdum*.

These axioms, and likewise the so-called definitions, are, as has already been said, results of induction; true of all objects whatever, and, as it may seem, exactly true, without the hypothetical assumption of unqualified truth where an approximation to it is all that exists. The conclusions, therefore, it will naturally be inferred, are exactly true, and the science of number is an exception to other demonstrative sciences in this, that the categorical certainty which is predicable of its demonstrations is independent of all hypothesis.

On more accurate investigation, however, it will be found that, even in this case, there is one hypothetical element in the ratiocination. In all propositions concerning numbers, a condition is implied, without which none of them would be true; and that condition is an assumption which may be false. The condition is, that $1 = 1$; that all the numbers are numbers of the same or of equal units. Let this be doubtful, and not one of the propositions of arithmetic will hold true. How can we know that one pound and one pound make two pounds, if one of the pounds may be troy, and the other avoirdupois? They may not make two pounds of either, or of any weight. How can we know that a forty-horse power is always equal to itself, unless we assume that all horses are of equal strength? It is certain that 1 is always equal in *number* to 1; and where the mere number of objects, or of the parts of an object, without supposing them to be equivalent in any other respect, is all that is material, the conclusions of arithmetic, so far as they go to that alone, are true without mixture of hypothesis. There are such cases in statistics; as, for instance, an inquiry into the amount of the population of any country. It is indifferent to that inquiry whether they are grown people or children, strong or weak, tall or short; the only thing we want to ascertain is their number. But whenever, from equality or inequality of number, equality or inequality in any other respect is to be inferred, arithmetic carried into such inquiries becomes as hypothetical a science as geometry. All units must be assumed to be equal in that other respect; and this is never accurately true, for one actual pound weight is not exactly equal to another, nor one measured mile's length to another; a nicer balance, or more accurate measuring instruments, would always detect some difference.

What is commonly called mathematical certainty, therefore, which comprises the twofold conception of unconditional truth and perfect accuracy, is not an attribute of all mathematical truths, but of those only which relate to pure Number, as distinguished from Quantity in the more enlarged sense; and only so long as we abstain from supposing that the numbers are a precise index to actual quantities. The certainty usually ascribed to the conclusions of geometry, and even to those of mechanics, is nothing whatever but certainty of inference. We can have full assurance of particular results under particular suppositions, but we can not have the same assurance that these suppositions are accurately true, nor that they include all the data which may exercise an influence over the result in any given instance.

TWELVE

Are the Laws of Arithmetic Inductive?

GOTTLOB FREGE (1848-1925)

From The Foundations of Arithmetic*

It might well be supposed that numerical formulae would be synthetic or analytic, a posteriori or a priori, according as the general laws on which their proofs depend are so. JOHN STUART MILL, however, is of the opposite opinion. At first, indeed, he seems to mean to base the science, like LEIBNIZ, on definitions,[1] since he defines the individual numbers in the same way as LEIBNIZ; but this spark of sound sense is no sooner lit than extinguished, thanks to his preconception that all knowledge is empirical. He informs us, in fact,[2] that these definitions are not definitions in the logical sense; not only do they fix the meaning of a term, but they also assert along with it an observed matter of fact. But what in the world can be the observed fact, or the physical fact (to use another of MILL's expressions), which is asserted in the definition of the number 777864? Of all the whole wealth of physical facts in his apocalypse, MILL names for us only a solitary one, the one which he holds is asserted in the definition of the number 3. It consists, according to him, in this, that collections of objects exist, which while they impress the senses thus, $\begin{smallmatrix} o & o \\ & o \end{smallmatrix}$ may be separated into two parts, thus, o o o. What a mercy, then, that not everything in the world is nailed down; for if it were, we should not be able to bring off this separation, and 2 + 1 would not be 3! What a pity that MILL did not also illustrate the physical facts underlying the numbers 0 and 1!

"This proposition being granted," MILL goes on, "we term all such parcels Threes." From this we can see that it is really incorrect to speak of three strokes when the clock strikes three, or to call sweet, sour and bitter three sensations of taste; and equally unwarrantable is the expression "three methods of solving an equation." For none of these is a parcel which ever impresses the senses thus,

---

* From The Foundations of Arithmetic, translated by J. L. Austin. Reprinted by kind permission of Basil Blackwell, Oxford.
1 System of Logic, Bk. III, cap. xxiv. § 5.
2 Op. cit., Bk. II, cap. vi, § 2.

If the definition of each individual number did really assert a special physical fact, then we should never be able sufficiently to admire, for his knowledge of nature, a man who calculates with nine-figure numbers. Meantime, perhaps MILL does not mean to go so far as to maintain that all these facts would have to be observed severally, but thinks it would be enough if we had derived through induction a general law in which they were all included together. But try to formulate this law, and it will be found impossible. It is not enough to say: "There exist large collections of things which can be split up." For this does not state that there exist collections of such a size and of such a sort as are required for, say, the number 1,000,000, nor is the manner in which they are to be divided up specified any more precisely. MILL's theory must necessarily lead to the demand that a fact should be observed specially for each number, for in a general law precisely what is peculiar to the number 1,000,000, which necessarily belongs to its definition, would be lost. On MILL's view we could actually not put $1,000,000 = 999,999 + 1$ unless we had observed a collection of things split up in precisely this peculiar way, different from that characteristic of any and every other number whatsoever.

MILL seems to hold that we ought not to form the definitions $2 = 1 + 1, 3 = 2 + 1, 4 = 3 + 1$, and so on, unless and until the facts he refers to have been observed. It is quite true that we ought not to define 3 as $(2 + 1)$, if we attach no sense at all to $(2 + 1)$. But the question is whether, for this, it is necessary to observe his collection and its separation. If it were, the number 0 would be a puzzle; for up to now no one, I take it, has ever seen or touched 0 pebbles. MILL, of course, would explain 0 as something that has no sense, a mere manner of speaking; calculations with 0 would be a mere game, played with empty symbols, and the only wonder would be that anything rational could come of it. If, however, these calculations have a serious meaning, then the symbol 0 cannot be entirely without sense either. And the possibility suggests itself that $2 + 1$, in the same way as 0, might have a sense even without MILL's matter of fact being observed. Who is actually prepared to assert that the fact which, according to MILL, is contained in the definition of an eighteen-figure number has ever been observed, and who is prepared to deny that the symbol for such a number has, none the less, a sense?

Perhaps it is supposed that the physical facts would be used only for the smaller numbers, say up to 10, while the remaining numbers could be constructed out of these. But if we can form 11 from 10 and 1 simply by definition, without having seen the corresponding collection, then there is no reason why we should not also be able in this way to construct 2 out of 1 and 1. If calculations with the number 11 do not follow from any matter of fact uniquely characteristic of that number, how does it happen that calculations with the number 2 must depend on the observation of a particular collection, separated in its own peculiar way?

It may, perhaps, be asked how arithmetic could exist, if we could distinguish nothing whatever by means of our senses, or only three things at most. Now for our knowledge, certainly, of arithmetical propositions and of their applications, such a state of affairs would be somewhat awkward—but would it affect the truth of those propositions? If we call a proposition empirical on the ground that we must have made observations in order to have become conscious of its content, then we are not using the word "empirical" in the sense in which it is opposed to "a priori". We are making a psychological statement, which concerns solely the content of the proposition; the question of its truth is not touched. In this sense, all Münchhausen's tales are empirical too; for certainly all sorts of observations must have been made before they could be invented.

THIRTEEN

The A Priori

A. J. AYER (1910-   )

From *Language, Truth, and Logic**

The view of philosophy which we have adopted may, I think, fairly be described as a form of empiricism. For it is characteristic of an empiricist to eschew metaphysics, on the ground that every factual proposition must refer to sense-experience. And even if the conception of philosophizing as an activity of analysis is not to be discovered in the traditional theories of empiricists, we have seen that it is implicit in their practice. At the same time, it must be made clear that, in calling ourselves empiricists, we are not avowing a belief in any of the psychological doctrines which are commonly associated with empiricism. For, even if these doctrines were valid, their validity would be independent of the validity of any philosophical thesis. It could be established only by observation, and not by the purely logical considerations upon which our empiricism rests.

Having admitted that we are empiricists, we must now deal with the objection that is commonly brought against all forms of empiricism; the objection, namely, that it is impossible on empiricist principles to account for our knowledge of necessary truths. For, as Hume conclusively showed, no general proposition whose validity is subject to the test of actual experience can ever be logically certain. No matter how often it is verified in practice, there still remains the possibility that it will be confuted on some future occasion. The fact that a law has been substantiated in $n - 1$ cases affords no logical guarantee that it will be substantiated in the nth case also, no matter how large we take n to be. And this means that no general proposition referring to a matter of fact can ever be shown to be necessarily and universally true. It can at best be a probable hypothesis. And this, we shall find, applies not only to general propositions, but to all propositions which have a factual content. They can none of them ever become logically certain. This conclusion, which we shall elaborate later on, is one which must be accepted by every consistent empiricist. It is often thought to involve

* From *Language, Truth, and Logic* by A. J. Ayer (London, Victor Gollancz, Ltd., 1936). (New York, Dover Publications, Inc.). Reprinted by permission of Victor Gollancz, Ltd.

him in complete scepticism; but this is not the case. For the fact that the validity of a proposition cannot be logically guaranteed in no way entails that it is irrational for us to believe it. On the contrary, what is irrational is to look for a guarantee where none can be forthcoming; to demand certainty where probability is all that is obtainable. We have already remarked upon this, in referring to the work of Hume. And we shall make the point clearer when we come to treat of probability, in explaining the use which we make of empirical propositions. We shall discover that there is nothing perverse or paradoxical about the view that all the "truths" of science and common sense are hypotheses; and consequently that the fact that it involves this view constitutes no objection to the empiricist thesis.

Where the empiricist does encounter difficulty is in connection with the truths of formal logic and mathematics. For whereas a scientific generalisation is readily admitted to be fallible, the truths of mathematics and logic appear to everyone to be necessary and certain. But if empiricism is correct no proposition which has a factual content can be necessary or certain. Accordingly the empiricist must deal with the truths of logic and mathematics in one of the two following ways; he must say either that they are not necessary truths, in which case he must account for the universal conviction that they are; or he must say that they have no factual content, and then he must explain how a proposition which is empty of all factual content can be true and useful and surprising.

If neither of these courses proves satisfactory, we shall be obliged to give way to rationalism. We shall be obliged to admit that there are some truths about the world which we can know independently of experience; that there are some properties which we can ascribe to all objects, even though we cannot conceivably observe that all objects have them. And we shall have to accept it as a mysterious inexplicable fact that our thought has this power to reveal to us authoritatively the nature of objects which we have never observed. Or else we must accept the Kantian explanation which, apart from the epistemological difficulties which we have already touched on, only pushes the mystery a stage further back.

It is clear that any such concession to rationalism would upset the main argument of this book. For the admission that there were some facts about the world which could be known independently of experience would be incompatible with our fundamental contention that a sentence says nothing unless it is empirically verifiable. And thus the whole force of our attack on metaphysics would be destroyed. It is vital, therefore, for us to be able to show that one or other of the empiricist accounts of the propositions of logic and mathematics is correct. If we are successful in this, we shall have destroyed the foundations of rationalism. For the

is the hope of the author an argumentatively sound book on the truth

fundamental tenet of rationalism is that thought is an independent source of knowledge, and is moreover a more trustworthy source of knowledge than experience; indeed some rationalists have gone so far as to say that thought is the only source of knowledge. And the ground for this view is simply that the only necessary truths about the world which are known to us are known through thought and not through experience. So that if we can show either that the truths in question are not necessary or that they are not "truths about the world," we shall be taking away the support on which rationalism rests. We shall be making good the empiricist contention that there are no "truths of reason" which refer to matters of fact.

[handwritten margin note: the author is taking extreme rationalism as the rule which this extreme form can readily deal with]

The course of maintaining that the truths of logic and mathematics are not necessary or certain was adopted by Mill. He maintained that these propositions were inductive generalizations based on an extremely large number of instances. The fact that the number of supporting instances was so very large accounted, in his view, for our believing these generalizations to be necessarily and universally true. The evidence in their favour was so strong that it seemed incredible to us that a contrary instance should ever arise. Nevertheless it was in principle possible for such generalizations to be confuted. They were highly probable, but, being inductive generalizations, they were not certain. The difference between them and the hypotheses of natural science was a difference in degree and not in kind. Experience gave us very good reason to suppose that a "truth" of mathematics or logic was true universally; but we were not possessed of a guarantee. For these "truths" were only empirical hypotheses which had worked particularly well in the past; and, like all empirical hypotheses, they were theoretically fallible.

I do not think that this solution of the empiricist's difficulty with regard to the propositions of logic and mathematics is acceptable. In discussing it, it is necessary to make a distinction which is perhaps already enshrined in Kant's famous dictum that, although there can be no doubt that all our knowledge begins with experience, it does not follow that it all arises out of experience.[1] When we say that the truths of logic are known independently of experience, we are not of course saying that they are innate, in the sense that we are born knowing them. It is obvious that mathematics and logic have to be learned in the same way as chemistry and history have to be learned. Nor are we denying that the first person to discover a given logical or mathematical truth was led to it by an inductive procedure. It is very probable, for example, that the principle of the syllogism was formulated not before but after the validity of syllogistic reasoning had been observed in a number of particular cases. What we are discussing, however, when we say that logical and mathematical truths are known independently of experience,

[1] *Critique of Pure Reason,* 2nd ed., Introduction, section i.

is not a historical question concerning the way in which these truths were originally discovered, nor a psychological question concerning the way in which each of us comes to learn them, but an epistemological question. The contention of Mill's which we reject is that the propositions of logic and mathematics have the same status as empirical hypotheses; that their validity is determined in the same way. We maintain that they are independent of experience in the sense that they do not owe their validity to empirical verification. We may come to discover them through an inductive process; but once we have apprehended them we see that they are necessarily true, that they hold good for every conceivable instance. And this serves to distinguish them from empirical generalizations. For we know that a proposition whose validity depends upon experience cannot be seen to be necessarily and universally true.

In rejecting Mill's theory, we are obliged to be somewhat dogmatic. We can do no more than state the issue clearly and then trust that his contention will be seen to be discrepant with the relevant logical facts. The following considerations may serve to show that of the two ways of dealing with logic and mathematics which are open to the empiricist, the one which Mill adopted is not the one which is correct.

The best way to substantiate our assertion that the truths of formal logic and pure mathematics are necessarily true is to examine cases in which they might seem to be confuted. It might easily happen, for example, that when I came to count what I had taken to be five pairs of objects, I found that they amounted only to nine. And if I wished to mislead people I might say that on this occasion twice five was not ten. But in that case I should not be using the complex sign "2 × 5 = 10" in the way in which it is ordinarily used. I should be taking it not as the expression of a purely mathematical proposition, but as the expression of an empirical generalization, to the effect that whenever I counted what appeared to me to be five pairs of objects I discovered that they were ten in number. This generalization may very well be false. But if it proved false in a given case, one would not say that the mathematical proposition "2 × 5 = 10" had been confuted. One would say that I was wrong in supposing that there were five pairs of objects to start with, or that one of the objects had been taken away while I was counting, or that two of them had coalesced, or that I had counted wrongly. One would adopt as an explanation whatever empirical hypothesis fitted in best with the accredited facts. The one explanation which would in no circumstances be adopted is that ten is not always the product of two and five.

To take another example: if what appears to be a Euclidean triangle is found by measurement not to have angles totalling 180 degrees, we do not say that we have met with an instance which invalidates the mathematical proposition that the sum of the three angles of a Euclidean triangle is 180 degrees. We say that we have measured wrongly, or, more probably, that the triangle we have been measuring is not Euclidean. And this is our procedure in every case in which a mathematical truth might appear to be confuted. We always preserve its validity by adopting some other explanation of the occurrence.

The same thing applies to the principles of formal logic. We may take an example relating to the so-called law of excluded middle, which states that a proposition must be either true or false, or, in other words, that it is impossible that a proposition and its contradictory should neither of them be true. One might suppose that a proposition of the form "x has stopped doing y" would in certain cases constitute an exception to this law. For instance, if my friend has never yet written to me, it seems fair to say that it is neither true nor false that he has stopped writing to me. But in fact one would refuse to accept such an instance as an invalidation of the law of excluded middle. One would point out that the proposition "My friend has stopped writing to me" is not a simple proposition, but the conjunction of the two propositions "My friend wrote to me in the past" and "My friend does not write to me now": and, furthermore, that the proposition "My friend has not stopped writing to me" is not, as it appears to be, contradictory to "My friend has stopped writing to me," but only contrary to it. For it means "My friend wrote to me in the past, and he still writes to me." When, therefore, we say that such a proposition as "My friend has stopped writing to me" is sometimes neither true nor false, we are speaking inaccurately. For we seem to be saying that neither it nor its contradictory is true. Whereas what we mean, or anyhow should mean, is that neither it nor its apparent contradictory is true. And its apparent contradictory is really only its contrary. Thus we preserve the law of excluded middle by showing that the negating of a sentence does not always yield the contradictory of the proposition originally expressed.

There is no need to give further examples. Whatever instance we care to take, we shall always find that the situations in which a logical or mathematical principle might appear to be confuted are accounted for in such a way as to leave the principle unassailed. And this indicates that Mill was wrong in supposing that a situation could arise which would overthrow a mathematical truth. The principles of logic and mathematics are true universally simply because we never allow them to be anything else. And the reason for this is that we cannot abandon them without contradicting ourselves, without sinning against the rules which govern the use of language, and so making our utterances self-stultifying. In other words, the truths of logic and mathematics are analytic propositions or tautologies. In saying this we are making what will be held to be an extremely controversial statement, and we must now proceed to make its implications clear.

RATIONALISM AND EMPIRICISM

The most familiar definition of an analytic proposition, or judgement, as he called it, is that given by Kant. He said that an analytic judgement was one in which the predicate B belonged to the subject A as something which was covertly contained in the concept of A. He contrasted analytic with synthetic judgements, in which the predicate B lay outside the subject A, although it did stand in connection with it. Analytic judgements, he explains, "add nothing through the predicate to the concept of the subject, but merely break it up into those constituent concepts that have all along been thought in it, although confusedly." Synthetic judgements, on the other hand, "add to the concept of the subject a predicate which has not been in any wise thought in it, and which no analysis could possibly extract from it." Kant gives "all bodies are extended" as an example of an analytic judgement, on the ground that the required predicate can be extracted from the concept of "body," "in accordance with the principle of contradiction"; as an example of a synthetic judgement, he gives "all bodies are heavy." He refers also to "7 + 5 = 12" as a synthetic judgement, on the ground that the concept of twelve is by no means already thought in merely thinking the union of seven and five. And he appears to regard this as tantamount to saying that the judgement does not rest on the principle of contradiction alone. He holds, also, that through analytic judgements our knowledge is not extended as it is through synthetic judgements. For in analytic judgements "the concept which I already have is merely set forth and made intelligible to me."

I think that this is a fair summary of Kant's account of the distinction between analytic and synthetic propositions, but I do not think that it succeeds in making the distinction clear. For even if we pass over the difficulties which arise out of the use of the vague term "concept," and the unwarranted assumption that every judgement, as well as every German or English sentence, can be said to have a subject and a predicate, there remains still this crucial defect. Kant does not give one straightforward criterion for distinguishing between analytic and synthetic propositions; he gives two distinct criteria, which are by no means equivalent. Thus his ground for holding that the proposition "7 + 5 = 12" is synthetic is, as we have seen, that the subjective intension of "7 + 5" does not comprise the subjective intension of "12"; whereas his ground for holding that "all bodies are extended" is an analytic proposition is that it rests on the principle of contradiction alone. That is, he employs a psychological criterion in the first of these examples, and a logical criterion in the second, and takes their equivalence for granted. But, in fact, a proposition which is synthetic according to the former criterion may very well be analytic according to the latter. For, as we have already pointed out, it is possible for symbols to be synonymous without having the same intensional meaning for anyone: and accordingly from the fact that one can think of the sum of seven and five without necessarily thinking of twelve, it by no means follows that the proposition "7 + 5 = 12" can be denied without self-contradiction. From the rest of his argument, it is clear that it is this logical proposition, and not any psychological proposition, that Kant is really anxious to establish. His use of the psychological criterion leads him to think that he has established it, when he has not.

I think that we can preserve the logical import of Kant's distinction between analytic and synthetic propositions, while avoiding the confusions which mar his actual account of it, if we say that a proposition is analytic when its validity depends solely on the definitions of the symbols it contains, and synthetic when its validity is determined by the facts of experience. Thus, the proposition "There are ants which have established a system of slavery" is a synthetic proposition. For we cannot tell whether it is true or false merely by considering the definitions of the symbols which constitute it. We have to resort to actual observation of the behaviour of ants. On the other hand, the proposition "Either some ants are parasitic or none are" is an analytic proposition. For one need not resort to observation to discover that there either are or are not ants which are parasitic. If one knows what is the function of the words "either," "or," and "not," then one can see that any proposition of the form "Either p is true or p is not true" is valid, independently of experience. Accordingly, all such propositions are analytic.

It is to be noticed that the proposition "Either some ants are parasitic or none are" provides no information whatsoever about the behaviour of ants, or, indeed, about any matter of fact. And this applies to all analytic propositions. They none of them provide any information about any matter of fact. In other words, they are entirely devoid of factual content. And it is for this reason that no experience can confute them.

When we say that analytic propositions are devoid of factual content, and consequently that they say nothing, we are not suggesting that they are senseless in the way that metaphysical utterances are senseless. For, although they give us no information about any empirical situation, they do enlighten us by illustrating the way in which we use certain symbols. Thus if I say, "Nothing can be coloured in different ways at the same time with respect to the same part of itself," I am not saying anything about the properties of any actual thing; but I am not talking nonsense. I am expressing an analytic proposition, which records our determination to call a colour expanse which differs in quality from a neighbouring colour expanse a different part of a given thing. In other words, I am simply calling attention to the implications of a certain linguistic usage. Similarly, in saying that if all Bretons are Frenchmen, and all Frenchmen Europeans, then all Bretons are Europeans, I am not

describing any matter of fact. But I am showing that in the statement
that all Bretons are Frenchmen, and all Frenchmen Europeans, the
further statement that all Bretons are Europeans is implicitly contained.
And I am thereby indicating the convention which governs our usage
of the words "if" and "all."

We see, then, that there is a sense in which analytic propositions do
give us new knowledge. They call attention to linguistic usages, of which
we might otherwise not be conscious, and they reveal unsuspected implications in our assertions and beliefs. But we can see also that there
is a sense in which they may be said to add nothing to our knowledge.
For they tell us only what we may be said to know already. Thus, if I
know that the existence of May Queens is a relic of tree-worship, and I
discover that May Queens still exist in England, I can employ the
tautology "If p implies q, and p is true, q is true" to show that there
still exists a relic of tree-worship in England. But in saying that there
are still May Queens in England, and that the existence of May Queens
is a relic of tree-worship, I have already asserted the existence in England
of a relic of tree-worship. The use of the tautology does, indeed, enable
me to make this concealed assertion explicit. But it does not provide
me with any new knowledge, in the sense in which empirical evidence
that the election of May Queens had been forbidden by law would
provide me with new knowledge. If one had to set forth all the information one possessed, with regard to matters of fact, one would not write
down any analytic propositions. But one would make use of analytic
propositions in compiling one's encyclopædia, and would thus come
to include propositions which one would otherwise have overlooked.
And, besides enabling one to make one's list of information complete,
the formulation of analytic propositions would enable one to make
sure that the synthetic propositions of which the list was composed
formed a self-consistent system. By showing which ways of combining
propositions resulted in contradictions, they would prevent one from
including incompatible propositions and so making the list self-stultifying. But in so far as we had actually used such words as "all" and "or"
and "not" without falling into self-contradiction, we might be said
already to know what was revealed in the formulation of analytic
propositions illustrating the rules which govern our usage of these
logical particles. So that here again we are justified in saying that
analytic propositions do not increase our knowledge.

The analytic character of the truths of formal logic was obscured
in the traditional logic through its being insufficiently formalized. For
in speaking always of judgements, instead of propositions, and introducing
irrelevant psychological questions, the traditional logic gave the impression of being concerned in some specially intimate way with the workings of thought. What it was actually concerned with was the formal

relationship of classes, as is shown by the fact that all its principles of inference are subsumed in the Boolean class-calculus, which is subsumed in its turn in the propositional calculus of Russell and Whitehead. Their system, expounded in *Principia Mathematica*, makes it clear that formal logic is not concerned with the properties of men's minds, much less with the properties of material objects, but simply with the possibility of combining propositions by means of logical particles into analytic propositions, and with studying the formal relationship of these analytic propositions, in virtue of which one is deducible from another. Their procedure is to exhibit the propositions of formal logic as a deductive system, based on five primitive propositions, subsequently reduced in number to one. Hereby the distinction between logical truths and principles of inference, which was maintained in the Aristotelian logic, very properly disappears. Every principle of inference is put forward as a logical truth and every logical truth can serve as a principle of inference. The three Aristotelian "laws of thought," the law of identity, the law of excluded middle, and the law of non-contradiction, are incorporated in the system, but they are not considered more important than the other analytic propositions. They are not reckoned among the premises of the system. And the system of Russell and Whitehead itself is probably only one among many possible logics, each of which is composed of tautologies as interesting to the logician as the arbitrarily selected Aristotelian "laws of thought."

A point which is not sufficiently brought out by Russell, if indeed it is recognised by him at all, is that every logical proposition is valid in its own right. Its validity does not depend on its being incorporated in a system, and deduced from certain propositions which are taken as self-evident. The construction of systems of logic is useful as a means of discovering and certifying analytic propositions, but it is not in principle essential even for this purpose. For it is possible to conceive of a symbolism in which every analytic proposition could be seen to be analytic in virtue of its form alone.

The fact that the validity of an analytic proposition in no way depends on its being deducible from other analytic propositions is our justification for disregarding the question whether the propositions of mathematics are reducible to propositions of formal logic, in the way that Russell supposed.[2] For even if it is the case that the definition of a cardinal number as a class of classes similar to a given class is circular, and it is not possible to reduce mathematical notions to purely logical notions, it will still remain true that the propositions of mathematics are analytic propositions. They will form a special class of analytic propositions, containing special terms, but they will be none the less analytic for that. For the criterion of an analytic proposition is that its

2 Vide, *Introduction to Mathematical Philosophy*, Chapter ii.

validity should follow simply from the definition of the terms contained in it, and this condition is fulfilled by the propositions of pure mathematics.

The mathematical propositions which one might most pardonably suppose to be synthetic are the propositions of geometry. For it is natural for us to think, as Kant thought, that geometry is the study of the properties of physical space, and consequently that its propositions have factual content. And if we believe this, and also recognise that the truths of geometry are necessary and certain, then we may be inclined to accept Kant's hypothesis that space is the form of intuition of our outer sense, a form imposed by us on the matter of sensation, as the only possible explanation of our *a priori* knowledge of these synthetic propositions. But while the view that pure geometry is concerned with physical space was plausible enough in Kant's day, when the geometry of Euclid was the only geometry known, the subsequent invention of non-Euclidean geometries has shown it to be mistaken. We see now that the axioms of a geometry are simply definitions, and that the theorems of a geometry are simply the logical consequences of these definitions. A geometry is not in itself about physical space; in itself it cannot be said to be "about" anything. But we can use a geometry to reason about physical space. That is to say, once we have given the axioms a physical interpretation, we can proceed to apply the theorems to the objects which satisfy the axioms. Whether a geometry can be applied to the actual physical world or not, is an empirical question which falls outside the scope of the geometry itself. There is no sense, therefore, in asking which of the various geometries known to us are false and which are true. In so far as they are all free from contradiction, they are all true. What one can ask is which of them is the most useful on any given occasion, which of them can be applied most easily and most fruitfully to an actual empirical situation. But the proposition which states that a certain application of a geometry is possible is not itself a proposition of that geometry. All that the geometry itself tells us is that if anything can be brought under the definitions, it will also satisfy the theorems. It is therefore a purely logical system, and its propositions are purely analytic propositions.

It might be objected that the use made of diagrams in geometrical treatises shows that geometrical reasoning is not purely abstract and logical, but depends on our intuition of the properties of figures. In fact, however, the use of diagrams is not essential to completely rigorous geometry. The diagrams are introduced as an aid to our reason. They provide us with a particular application of the geometry, and so assist us to perceive the more general truth that the axioms of the geometry involve certain consequences. But the fact that most of us need the help of an example to make us aware of those consequences does not show that the relation between them and the axioms is not a purely logical relation. It shows merely that our intellects are unequal to the task of carrying out very abstract processes of reasoning without the assistance of intuition. In other words, it has no bearing on the nature of geometrical propositions, but is simply an empirical fact about ourselves. Moreover, the appeal to intuition, though generally of psychological value, is also a source of danger to the geometer. He is tempted to make assumptions which are accidentally true of the particular figure he is taking as an illustration, but do not follow from his axioms. It has, indeed, been shown that Euclid himself was guilty of this, and consequently that the presence of the figure is essential to some of his proofs. [3] This shows that his system is not, as he presents it, completely rigorous, although of course it can be made so. It does not show that the presence of the figure is essential to a truly rigorous geometrical proof. To suppose that it did would be to take as a necessary feature of all geometries what is really only an incidental defect in one particular geometrical system.

We conclude, then, that the propositions of pure geometry are analytic. And this leads us to reject Kant's hypothesis that geometry deals with the form of intuition of our outer sense. For the ground for this hypothesis was that it alone explained how the propositions of geometry could be both true *a priori* and synthetic: and we have seen that they are not synthetic. Similarly our view that the propositions of arithmetic are not synthetic but analytic leads us to reject the Kantian hypothesis that arithmetic is concerned with our pure intuition of time, the form of our inner sense. And thus we are able to dismiss Kant's transcendental æsthetic without having to bring forward the epistemological difficulties which it is commonly said to involve. For the only argument which can be brought in favour of Kant's theory is that it alone explains certain "facts." And now we have found that the "facts" which it purports to explain are not facts at all. For while it is true that we have *a priori* knowledge of necessary propositions, it is not true, as Kant supposed, that any of these necessary propositions are synthetic. They are without exception analytic propositions, or, in other words, tautologies.

We have already explained how it is that these analytic propositions are necessary and certain. We saw that the reason why they cannot be confuted in experience is that they do not make any assertion about the empirical world. They simply record our determination to use words in a certain fashion. We cannot deny them without infringing the conventions which are presupposed by our very denial, and so falling into self-contradiction. And this is the sole ground of their necessity. As Wittgenstein puts it, our justification for holding that the world could not conceivably disobey the laws of logic is simply that we could not

[3] cf. M. Black, *The Nature of Mathematics*, p. 154.

say of an unlogical world how it would look.[4] And just as the validity of an analytic proposition is independent of the nature of the external world; so is it independent of the nature of our minds. It is perfectly conceivable that we should have employed different linguistic conventions from those which we actually do employ. But whatever these conventions might be, the tautologies in which we recorded them would always be necessary. For any denial of them would be self-stultifying.

We see, then, that there is nothing mysterious about the apodeictic certainty of logic and mathematics. Our knowledge that no observation can ever confute the proposition "7 + 5 = 12" depends simply on the fact that the symbolic expression "7 + 5" is synonymous with "12," just as our knowledge that every oculist is an eye-doctor depends on the fact that the symbol "eye-doctor" is synonymous with "oculist." And the same explanation holds good for every other *a priori* truth.

What is mysterious at first sight is that these tautologies should on occasion be so surprising, that there should be in mathematics and logic the possibility of invention and discovery. As Poincaré says: "If all the assertions which mathematics puts forward can be derived from one another by formal logic, mathematics cannot amount to anything more than an immense tautology. Logical inference can teach us nothing essentially new, and if everything is to proceed from the principle of identity, everything must be reducible to it. But can we really allow that these theorems which fill so many books serve no other purpose than to say in a round-about fashion 'A = A'?"[5] Poincaré finds this incredible. His own theory is that the sense of invention and discovery in mathematics belongs to it in virtue of mathematical induction, the principle that what is true for the number 1, and true for $n + 1$ when it is true for n, is true for all numbers. And he claims that this is a synthetic *a priori* principle. It is, in fact, *a priori,* but it is not synthetic. It is a defining principle of the natural numbers, serving to distinguish them from such numbers as the infinite cardinal numbers, to which it cannot be applied. Moreover, we must remember that discoveries can be made, not only in arithmetic, but also in geometry and formal logic, where no use is made of mathematical induction. So that even if Poincaré were right about mathematical induction, he would not have provided a satisfactory explanation of the paradox that a mere body of tautologies can be so interesting and so surprising.

The true explanation is very simple. The power of logic and mathematics to surprise us depends, like their usefulness, on the limitations of our reason. A being whose intellect was infinitely powerful would take no interest in logic and mathematics. For he would be able to see at a glance everything that his definitions implied, and, accord-

---

[4] *Tractatus Logico-Philosophicus,* 3.031.
[5] *La Science et l'Hypothèse,* Part I, Chapter i.

ingly, could never learn anything from logical inference which he was not fully conscious of already. But our intellects are not of this order. It is only a minute proportion of the consequences of our definitions that we are able to detect at a glance. Even so simple a tautology as "91 × 79 = 7189" is beyond the scope of our immediate apprehension. To assure ourselves that "7189" is synonymous with "91 × 79" we have to resort to calculation, which is simply a process of tautological transformation—that is, a process by which we change the form of expressions without altering their significance. The multiplication tables are rules for carrying out this process in arithmetic, just as the laws of logic are rules for the tautological transformation of sentences expressed in logical symbolism or in ordinary language. As the process of calculation is carried out more or less mechanically, it is easy for us to make a slip and so unwittingly contradict ourselves. And this accounts for the existence of logical and mathematical "falsehoods," which otherwise might appear paradoxical. Clearly the risk of error in logical reasoning is proportionate to the length and the complexity of the process of calculation. And in the same way, the more complex an analytic proposition is, the more chance it has of interesting and surprising us.

It is easy to see that the danger of error in logical reasoning can be minimized by the introduction of symbolic devices, which enable us to express highly complex tautologies in a conveniently simple form. And this gives us an opportunity for the exercise of invention in the pursuit of logical enquiries. For a well-chosen definition will call our attention to analytic truths, which would otherwise have escaped us. And the framing of definitions which are useful and fruitful may well be regarded as a creative act.

Having thus shown that there is no inexplicable paradox involved in the view that the truths of logic and mathematics are all of them analytic, we may safely adopt it as the only satisfactory explanation of their *a priori* necessity. And in adopting it we vindicate the empiricist claim that there can be no *a priori* knowledge of reality. For we show that the truths of pure reason, the propositions which we know to be valid independently of all experience, are so only in virtue of their lack of factual content. To say that a proposition is true *a priori* is to say that it is a tautology. And tautologies, though they may serve to guide us in our empirical search for knowledge, do not in themselves contain any information about any matter of fact.

Further Reading

The following books and papers contain discussions of topics pertinent to this chapter.

BRADLEY, F. H., *Appearance and Reality* (New York, Oxford University Press, 1955).

CARNAP, R., *Meaning and Necessity* (Chicago University Press, 1947).

GRICE, P. and STRAWSON, P. F. "Two Dogmas of Empiricism" *Philosophical Review*, 1956.

GOODMAN, N., *The Structure of Appearance* (Cambridge, Mass., Harvard University Press, 1951).

FEIGL, H. and SELLARS, W. *Readings in Philosophical Analysis* (New York, Appleton-Century-Crofts, 1953).

HUME, D., *Enquiry into Human Understanding* (1748).

———— *Treatise of Human Nature* (1739).

HUSSERL, E., *Logische Untersuchungen* (Halle, Max Neumeyer, 1900).

KANT, I., *Critique of Pure Reason* (1787).

———— *Prolegomena to Any Future Metaphysic* (1783).

KÖRNER, S. *The Philosophy of Mathematics* (New York, Harper & Row, 1960).

LEIBNIZ, G. W., *New Essays Concerning Human Understanding* (New York, The Macmillan Company, 1896).

LOCKE, J., *An Essay Concerning Human Understanding* (1690).

MALCOLM, N., "Are Necessary Propositions Really Verbal?" *Mind*, Vol. 51 (1942).

MILL, J. S., *System of Logic* (1887).

QUINE, W. V., *From a Logical Point of View* (Cambridge, Mass., Harvard University Press, 1953).

Semantics and the Philosophy of Language, L. Linsky, ed. (Urbana, University of Illinois Press, 1952).

SPINOZA, B., *Ethics* (1677).

PART THREE

Truth

Introduction

Aristotle held that to say of what is that it is, or of what is not that it is not, is true. This mirrors a common-sense view that truth consists in a correspondence between our descriptions of what the world is like and the way the world actually is. Since many true statements say not merely that a thing is, or that it is not, but that it has certain characteristics, we may enlarge the definition: truth is a correspondence between propositions and the way the world is, or, in other words, between propositions and facts.

Locke, in the *Essay Concerning Human Understanding*, provides an interesting example of such a correspondence theory of truth. We join words, or "signs", together to form propositions. We have formed a true proposition if the things designated by the words, when joined together, "agree with" the proposition we have formed. Here the relation "agree with" which holds between things and propositions seems to be the same as the relation of correspondence said to hold between propositions and things.

When we begin to examine Locke's definition, however, we get the same feeling Alice must have had when the White Knight told her that "Haddock's Eyes" was not the name of the song he was going to sing for her, but rather the name of the name of the song. For according to Locke, words or signs do not stand for things like tables and chairs, but rather they stand for *ideas*. And only some of these ideas, in turn, designate what we would call real objects. Thus the proposition "Unicorns have horns" would be true even though there are no unicorns, since the proposition agrees with the *ideas* of unicorns and horns which we actually have; our idea of "having horns" is included in our idea of "unicorn." Part of Locke's theory of truth, then, is concerned not with a correspondence between propositions and facts, but between propositions and ideas. Since some ideas stand for material objects, it is possible for a proposition to agree with our ideas, and for our ideas, in turn, to agree with the facts. This possibility leads Locke to make a distinction between "verbal truths," illustrated by the above sentence about unicorns, and "real truths," an example of which would be "Bulls have horns."

The second selection in this chapter, the essay by Franz Brentano (1838–1917), provides a more sophisticated example of a correspondence theory of truth. The selection begins with an examination of some ambiguities in our use of the word "true." Brentano claims, with Aristotle, that although "true" has many meanings, these are all related to one central meaning. The central meaning is the meaning "true" has when applied to judgments. A judgment is true when it corresponds to the facts. Brentano gives a brief summary of the history of this doctrine since Aristotle. In the final part of the essay, Brentano points out some difficulties in the Aristotelian view, and with the aim of avoiding these, he offers a refined formulation.

The selection from Brand Blanshard introduces a second kind of theory of truth, the coherence theory. On this theory, a judgment is true if it coheres with the sum total of our beliefs. All our beliefs, Blanshard supposes, can be arranged in a system; to perfect our knowledge we must strive to make this system as comprehensive and as consistent as possible. If accepting some judgment as true aids us in achieving this goal, then we should provisionally count the judgment as true; if not, not. Our acceptance will be only provisional, since it may happen that later experience will be such that the system's comprehensiveness and consistency would best be achieved by counting the earlier judgment as false, after all. That is, we may be best able to accommodate these later experiences into our system of beliefs by denying the truth of the earlier judgment. It is easily seen that this theory of truth must hold that there are no infallible judgments. If a judgment, for example, the judgment that this paper is white, were infallible—that is, known once and for all to be true—then it would make no sense to submit the judgment to the test of coherence. We would have to say, "It is irrelevant to the question of the truth of this judgment to ask if it coheres with our system of beliefs. If the judgment does not cohere with the system, so much the worse for the system."

The selection from William James represents a third theory of truth, the pragmatic theory. Perhaps the main tenet of pragmatism is its theory of meaning, stated by C. S. Peirce as follows: "Consider what effects, that might conceivably have practical bearings, we conceive the object of our conception to have. Then, our conception of these effects is the whole of our conception of the object." James attempts to outline a theory of truth in keeping with this theory of meaning. He asks us, in validating a judgment, to examine its *consequences,* or its "cash-value in experiential terms."

The final essay in this section is by the contemporary English philosopher P. F. Strawson. Strawson elaborates and defends the view that "to say that an assertion is true is not to make any further assertion at all; it is to make the same assertion." To say, for example, "It is true that the cat is on the mat" is not to say anything in addition to, or anything that has more descriptive content than, "The cat is on the mat." The expresisons "is true," "it is true that," and so on do not have a descriptive use. Rather, they function like performative words. When a person says "I promise" he does not describe anything; rather, he *does* something: he *makes* a promise. "Promise" is a performative. Similarly, when someone says, "It is true that the cat is on the mat," he *gives his assent* to the sentence "The cat is on the mat," or he *concedes* that the cat is on the mat, and so on.

FOURTEEN

On Truth in General

JOHN LOCKE (1632-1704)

From *An Essay Concerning Human Understanding**

1. What is truth? was an inquiry many ages since; and it being that which all mankind either do, or pretend to search after, it cannot but be worth our while carefully to examine wherein it consists; and so acquaint ourselves with the nature of it, as to observe how the mind distinguishes it from falsehood.

2. Truth, then, seems to me, in the proper import of the word, to signify nothing but *the joining or separating of Signs, as the Things signified by them do agree or disagree one with another.* The joining or separating of signs here meant, is what by another name we call *proposition.* So that truth properly belongs only to propositions: whereof there are two sorts, viz. mental and verbal; as there are two sorts of signs commonly made use of, viz. ideas and words.

3. To form a clear notion of truth, it is very necessary to consider truth of thought, and truth of words, distinctly one from another: but yet it is very difficult to treat of them asunder. Because it is unavoidable, in treating of mental propositions, to make use of words: and then the instances given of mental propositions cease immediately to be barely mental, and become verbal. For a *mental proposition* being nothing but a bare consideration of the ideas, as they are in our minds, stripped of names, they lose the nature of purely mental propositions as soon as they are put into words.

4. And that which makes it yet harder to treat of mental and verbal propositions separately is, that most men, if not all, in their thinking and reasonings within themselves, make use of words instead of ideas; at least when the subject of their meditation contains in it complex ideas. Which is a great evidence of the imperfection and uncertainty of our ideas of that kind, and may, if attentively made use of, serve for a mark to show us what are those things we have clear and perfect established ideas of, and what not. For if we will curiously observe the way our mind takes in thinking and reasoning, we shall find, I suppose, that when we make

---

* From *An Essay Concerning Human Understanding* by John Locke (1690).

any propositions within our own thoughts about *white* or *black*, *sweet* or *bitter*, a *triangle* or a *circle*, we can and often do frame in our minds the ideas themselves, without reflecting on the names. But when we would consider, or make propositions about the more complex ideas, as of a *man, vitriol, fortitude, glory*, we usually put the name for the idea: because the ideas these names stand for, being for the most part imperfect, confused, and undetermined, we reflect on the names themselves, because they are more clear, certain, and distinct, and readier occur to our thoughts than the pure ideas: and so we make use of these words instead of the ideas themselves, even when we would meditate and reason within ourselves, and make tacit mental propositions. In substances, as has been already noticed, this is occasioned by the imperfections of our ideas: we making the name stand for the real essence, of which we have no idea at all. In modes, it is occasioned by the great number of simple ideas that go to the making them up. For many of them being compounded, the name occurs much easier than the complex idea itself, which requires time and attention to be recollected, and exactly represented to the mind, even in those men who have formerly been at the pains to do it; and is utterly impossible to be done by those who, though they have ready in their memory the greatest part of the common words of that language, yet perhaps never troubled themselves in all their lives to consider what precise ideas the most of them stood for. Some confused or obscure notions have served their turns; and many who talk very much of *religion* and *conscience*, of *church* and *faith*, of *power* and *right*, of *obstructions* and *humours, melancholy* and *choler*, would perhaps have little left in their thoughts and meditations, if one should desire them to think only of the things themselves, and lay by those words with which they so often confound others, and not seldom themselves also.

5. But to return to the consideration of truth: we must, I say, observe two sorts of propositions that we are capable of making:—

First, *mental*, wherein the ideas in our understandings are without the use of words put together, or separated, by the mind perceiving or judging of their agreement or disagreement.

Secondly, *Verbal* propositions, which are words, the signs of our ideas, put together or separated in affirmative or negative sentences. By which way of affirming or denying, these signs, made by sounds, are, as it were, put together or separated one from another. So that proposition consists in joining or separating signs; and truth consists in the putting together or separating those signs, according as the things which they stand for agree or disagree.

6. Every one's experience will satisfy him, that the mind, either by perceiving, or supposing, the agreement or disagreement of any of its ideas, does tacitly within itself put them into a kind of proposition affirmative or negative; which I have endeavoured to express by the terms putting

together and separating. But this action of the mind, which is so familiar to every thinking and reasoning man, is easier to be conceived by reflecting on what passes in us when we affirm or deny, than to be explained by words. When a man has in his head the idea of two lines, viz. the side and diagonal of a square, whereof the diagonal is an inch long, he may have the idea also of the division of that line into a certain number of equal parts; v.g. into five, ten, a hundred, a thousand, or any other number, and may have the idea of that inch line being divisible, or not divisible, into such equal parts, as a certain number of them will be equal to the sideline. Now, whenever he perceives, believes, or supposes such a kind of divisibility to agree or disagree to his idea of that line, he, as it were, joins or separates those two ideas, viz. the idea of that line, and the idea of that kind of divisibility; and so makes a mental proposition, which is true or false, according as such a kind of divisibility, a divisibility into such *aliquot* parts, does really agree to that line or no. When ideas are so put together, or separated in the mind, as they or the things they stand for do agree or not, that is, as I may call it, *mental truth*. But *truth of words* is something more; and that is the affirming or denying of words one of another, as the ideas they stand for agree or disagree: and this again is two-fold; either purely verbal and trifling, which I shall speak of, (chap. viii.,) or real and instructive; which is the object of that real knowledge which we have spoken of already.

7. But here again will be apt to occur the same doubt about truth, that did about knowledge: and it will be objected, that if truth be nothing but the joining and separating of words in propositions, as the ideas they stand for agree or disagree in men's minds, the knowledge of truth is not so valuable a thing as it is taken to be, nor worth the pains and time men employ in the search of it: since by this account it amounts to no more than the conformity of words to the chimeras of men's brains. Who knows not what odd notions many men's heads are filled with, and what strange ideas all men's brains are capable of? But if we rest here, we know the truth of nothing by this rule, but of the visionary words in our own imaginations; nor have other truth, but what as much concerns harpies and centaurs, as men and horses. For those, and the like, may be ideas in our heads, and have their agreement or disagreement there, as well as the ideas of real beings, and so have as true propositions made about them. And it will be altogether as true a proposition to say *all centaurs are animals,* as that *all men are animals;* and the certainty of one as great as the other. For in both the propositions, the words are put together according to the agreement of the ideas in our minds: and the agreement of the idea of animal with that of centaur is as clear and visible to the mind, as the agreement of the idea of animal with that of man; and so these two propositions are equally true, equally certain. But of what use is all such truth to us?

8. Though what has been said in the foregoing chapter to distinguish real from imaginary knowledge might suffice here, in answer to this doubt, to distinguish real truth from chimerical, or (if you please) barely nominal, they depending both on the same foundation; yet it may not be amiss here again to consider, that though our words signify nothing but our ideas, yet being designed by them to signify things, the truth they contain when put into propositions will be only verbal, when they stand for ideas in the mind that have not an agreement with the reality of things. And therefore truth as well as knowledge may well come under the distinction of verbal and real; that being only verbal truth, wherein terms are joined according to the agreement or disagreement of the ideas they stand for; without regarding whether our ideas are such as really have, or are capable of having, an existence in nature. But then it is they contain *real truth*, when these signs are joined, as our ideas agree; and when our ideas are such as we know are capable of having an existence in nature: which in substances we cannot know, but by knowing that such have existed.

9. Truth is the marking down in words the agreement or disagreement of ideas as it is. Falsehood is the marking down in words the agreement or disagreement of ideas otherwise than it is. And so far as these ideas, thus marked by sounds, agree to their archetypes, so far only is the truth real. The knowledge of this truth consists in knowing what ideas the words stand for, and the perception of the agreement or disagreement of those ideas, according as it is marked by those words.

FIFTEEN

On the Concept of Truth

FRANZ BRENTANO (1838-1917)

From Truth and Evidence*

A lecture delivered to the Vienna Philosophical Society on March 27, 1889

1. When Aristotle laid the foundations of science [*Wissenschaft*], in the broadest sense of this term, he needed a scientific terminology. None existed. He had to invent one himself and his accomplishment showed great perspicacity and a delicate touch.

A whole set of terms was entirely his own invention; other terms he took over from ordinary speech; where these were vague he provided sharp delineation, and where they were ambiguous he distinguished between their various meanings, always attempting to elucidate their content by breaking it up into its conceptual components.

2. Unanticipated equivocations emerged with respect to the term *cause,* with the term *part,* and indeed with the term *Being* itself.

Generally speaking, one would expect to find certain modes of equivocation in any word, or at least in entire classes of words. Consider, for example, the ambiguity which stems from our using one and the same term to designate sometimes an activity, sometimes a power, sometimes a capacity for an activity. We often say of a man that he is seeing [*er ist sehend*] even if his eyes happen to be closed, thus distinguishing him from a blind man; he has the capacity to see. We often say of someone that he doesn't hear [*er höre nicht*], and in saying this we wish to convey that he is deaf. We say that man is a thinking being, and yet without contradiction we count someone a man who has just lost consciousness. We say that knowledge is well-grounded opinion, and yet we attribute knowledge even to the sleeping scholar because of his perduring, acquired dispositions. Again, we may say of a man "I know what he wants" even though he may not be thinking about what it is that he wants. Similarly we say of someone that he plays [*er spielt*] the flute, sometimes when we want to say that he is actually playing, sometimes

* Translated by Kurt R. Fischer and Roderick M. Chisholm. From the forthcoming English edition, edited by Roderick M. Chisholm, of Brentano's *Wahrheit und Evidenz* (Leipzig, 1930), prepared and edited by Oskar Kraus. Reprinted by permission.

when we wish merely to attribute to him the skill of flute-playing, and so on.

3. Aristotle did not eliminate equivocations of this sort; they have a kind of regularity and might be said to belong to the spirit of language. On the contrary, he imitated and multiplied them. No one who properly considers the matter will condemn him for this. The many attacks which have been leveled against Aristotle because of this ambiguity of his terms are therefore without justification. Of course, one can hardly deny that his way of writing often gave rise to misunderstandings; the compression of his style really presupposes another Aristotle as a reader.

4. He was aware of the danger presented to logic by equivocation, and he studied this linguistic phenomenon thoroughly. He distinguished three classes: accidental equivocations, equivocations due to analogy, and equivocations based upon relations of a set of terms to a given term which bears the name in its primary or strict [*eigentlichen*] sense.

5. Accidental equivocations are, for the most part, limited to *one* language. Playing on words is usually lost in translation. Other equivocations, based on a kind of connection among ideas shared by various nations, are likely to be found in the languages of all of them.

6. So it is with the equivocations which Aristotle pointed out in the traditional, important term ἀληθές. What he says about this term would hold equally well had he said it about the Latin *"verum"* or the German *"wahr."* Thus the distinctions between the different senses of "the True", as well as Aristotle's determinations of the concept of truth itself, could, and actually have, become authoritative far beyond the confines of Hellas, holding their sway across millennia in which the torch of philosophy had passed into the hands of foreign nations.

7. Let us then see how the most powerful scientific mind ever to influence the fate of man explained the term "truth".

The expressions "true" and "false", he says, are ambiguous; and their ambiguity is of the type, already mentioned, in which a set of terms stands in diverse relations to a given expression which bears the name in its primary sense.

We call many *presentations* [*Vorstellungen*] true, and we call others false (hallucinations, for example, we call false); we call concepts true and false, we call *judgments* true and false; we call conjectures, hopes, and worries true and false, we call a heart, a mind, true and false (*un esprit faux*); we call outer things true and false; we call sayings true and false, we call conduct true and false; we call expressions, letters of the alphabet, and many other signs, true and false; we call a friend, we call gold, true and false. We speak of true happiness, and of false happiness, and the latter locution, in turn, we may use for very different purposes, sometimes because we only seem to be happy, and sometimes because the happiness we have had has treacherously forsaken us. Similarly, we say on occasion: a false woman, namely when she is a flirtatious girl teasing us; but in another sense a false woman would be a man posing as a woman, as in the case of a thief who was wearing women's clothes when he was arrested; and still in another sense a false woman would be a man who has no thought of pretending to be a woman but nevertheless is taken for one, something that actually happened to me one morning at dawn in the entrance to the Würzburg fortress. At the time I was wearing a cassock, and the horror and bafflement of the man was all the greater, and the more comic.

8. When we thus spell out the various uses of the expression "true" its ambiguity leaps to the eye. But it is equally obvious that these many uses are all related to one use which is standard for the others. A comparable case is provided by the expression "healthy," an expression we sometimes use in connection with a body, at other times in connection with a complexion, and then again in connection with food, medicine, a region, or a walk. It is the healthy body that is healthy in the strict [eigentlichen] sense, and it is everything else that is called healthy by virtue of its relation to the body's health. A complexion is called healthy because it is a sign of health, other things are called healthy because they impart, enhance, or establish health.

What, then, is this one standard use to which all the others are related? Where is truth in the strictest sense to be found? Aristotle says that it is found in judgment.

9. It is with reference to the truth or falsity of judgment that the other things which bear these names may properly be said to be true or false; some things because they express a true or a false judgment, such as a false assertion, or a false utterance; some things because they produce a true or false judgment, as in the case, for instance, of hallucination, a slip in uttering or in writing a word, a metal which because of the resemblance of its color is taken for gold; some things because they intend to produce a true or false judgment, as for instance a true character, a false step (faux pas); some things because one who considers them real judges truly or falsely, for instance a true god, a true, in contrast to a painted, stone; some notions we call true or false with respect to that which coincides, or fails to coincide, with their content, since here a true or erroneous judgment turns upon a discovery about this content; for instance when we speak of rectangular figure as not being the true notion of square, and so forth.

10. Thus truth and falsity in the strict sense apply to judgment. And, moreover, every judgment is either true or false.

11. When, according to Aristotle, is a judgment true, and when false? He answers that a judgment is true if the one who makes the judgment is in a state which corresponds to that of the objects, and that it is false if the one who makes the judgment is in a state contrary to that of

the objects. "He who thinks the separated to be separated and the combined to be combined has the truth, while he whose thought is in a state
contrary to that of the objects is in error." *Metaphysics* IX, 10, 1051, b 3.[a]

12. And thus truth was explained as the correspondence [*Uberein-
stimmung*] of judgment with real objects.

13. A long history had prepared the way for this definition.

a) According to the ancient Ionians we know external stuff and
force by means of the same stuff in us.

> For with earth do we see earth, with water water,
> with air bright air, with fire consuming fire;
> with Love do we see Love, Strife with dread Strife.
>
>   Empedocles [b]

b) And the paradoxical theses of the Sophists also play upon
difficulties bound up with these early opinions. Gorgias comes denying
that anything real can be known, and then adding that if it could be
known the knowledge could not be communicated from one person to
another. There is nothing which corresponds completely to anything other
than itself. What is external to me is not in me, and what is and remains
in me, does not pass over into anyone else. Thus truth, as well as the
communication of truth, is impossible. If any of our thoughts can be said
to be true, then, according to Gorgias, everything else can be said to be
true. For every thought is identical with itself as well as different from all
other thoughts. But that every thought should be called true, even when
I think of a chariot race on the sea, is an absurdity.

c) Nonetheless, another Sophist came forth to present the opposite thesis. Not all of our beliefs are false, said Protagoras; on the contrary,
whatever we happen to believe is true. Whatever one thinks a thing to
be, it is, and whatever one thinks it not to be it is not.

The way Protagoras arrived at this idea, I think, is quite obvious.
If every belief is true by virtue of complete correspondence with something which subsists [*etwas Bestehendem*], then every belief is true since
it is identical with itself. Aristotle, too, in explaining this, points to its
connection with those doctrines of the Ionic school with which Gorgias'
opposite thesis is connected. Protagoras, who was a true Sophist, according to the classical portrait (that is to say, the portrait drawn by Plato
and Aristotle, not the one by Grote,[1] who lived somewhat later), now quite
obviously turns the paradox he had come upon into the starting point
of an ingenious game. The Down-Throwers [c] (καταβάλλοντες) was the
name of the text in which Protagoras defended his thesis. In it, apparently, blows are being dealt out, and threatening objections parried.

---

[a] The translation is by W. D. Ross (Tr.)

[b] Aristotle, *Metaphysics,* B 4, 1000 b 6; W. D. Ross translation.

[c] *die zu Boden streckenden Ringkämpfer,*—translated by R. G. Bury on p. 33 in
Vol. II of the Loeb Classical Library's Sextus Empiricus as "The Down-Throwers" (Tr.)

To the objection that, if his view were right a thing could be said both to be, and not to be, at one and the same time, Protagoras seems to have replied that this was not absurd; the point just is that the thing *is* for one, and *is not* for another.

That Protagoras did not even attempt to justify his position scientifically is suggested by the fact that neither Plato nor Aristotle—to whom the text was surely available—could trace the means by which he arrived at it. Both were guided wholly by conjectures, a procedure in which Aristotle, completely acquainted with the historical antecedents, and certainly more abundantly equipped with an historical sense, was the more successful. I have pointed out the steps on the path towards the Protagorean thesis. Parmenides also says: "What can be thought is only the thought that it is." [d] What could be more obvious than the paradox that every thought is true? Every belief is, obviously, in complete agreement with itself, and thus, under this presupposition, in complete agreement with its object.

14. But let us not remain any longer with the historical antecedents of the Aristotelean definition of truth. Let us rather see the effect it has upon later thinkers. What we find is that, with insignificantly few exceptions, it is standard up to our own time.

15. Medieval thought agrees in saying that true and false in the strict sense is to be found in judgment, and defines truth as *"adaequatio rei et intellectus."*

16. In the Cartesian logic which Arnauld offers us in the *Port Royal Logic* (Part 2, Ch. 3) we read: "Propositions are divided, again, according to their matter, into true and false. And it is clear that there are none which are not either true or false, since every proposition denoting the judgment which we form of things is true when that judgment is conformed to truth, and false when it is not so conformed." [e] Thus the great revolution which Descartes began leaves the Aristotelean definition of truth unshaken.[2]

17. But, if we may believe Windelband, something quite different happened in that other great philosophical revolution which took place in Germany while France was breaking politically with the tradition of her past.

Kant is supposed to have been the one who was then first to reform the Aristotelean, or as Windelband says, the Socratic conception of truth. Kant's great achievement is said to be here—and not elsewhere, as others have thought. "One misunderstands Kant's entire intention," Windelband

[d] Translated by Kirk & Raven, *The Presocratic Philosophers.*

[e] Translated by Thomas Spencer Baynes, 10th edition. The French text reads: "Les propositions se divisent encore selon la matière en vraies et en fausses. Et il est clair, qu'il n'y en peut point avoir, qui ne soient ni vraies ni fausses; puisque toute proposition marquant le jugement que nous faisons de choses est vraie, quand ce jugement est conforme à la verité,[1a] et fausse, lors qu'il n'y est pas conforme."

says in his *Präludien* (p. 140,[1] p. 149 [2]), "and one interprets his doctrine as wrongly as possible if one thinks that he has shown that science can gain a picture of the world of 'appearances', and that, on the other hand, it cannot know anything of things–in–themselves . . . The truth is . . . that, for him, it makes no sense to speak of a picture which copies reality." This concept retains a meaning only for the Socratics who preserved the conception of truth as correspondence of presentation and thing (or, more accurately, judgment and thing). And therefore it retains this meaning for the French philosophers of the eighteenth century who, with a kind of resignation, and a smattering of skepticism, deny man's ability to know things as they are in themselves. Kant does not know of any such barrier to our knowledge. What he did, rather, was to recast the concept of truth. According to him truth is what corresponds with the norm of our mind; not what corresponds with the object (unless one understands by the object nothing but the rule). Moreover, according to Kant, truth is not restricted to judgments or to thought; it may be found equally well in all the other areas of mental activity, in volition and in feeling, provided only that they are normal.

18. Here, then, we at last see accomplished, and in the sublimest fashion, that reformation of the conception of truth which has kept us waiting for so long. What could separate philosophers more than to strive for a quite different sense of truth, one which though nominally the same, in fact serves quite different aims? Accordingly, Windelband classifies all philosophers as either Socratics, who have been left behind, or as Kantians, who are the party of progress. It is to the latter that victory belongs; the others are already non-existent. "All of us who philosophize in the nineteenth century," he says in his Preface, "are pupils of Kant."

19. Now, gentlemen, if you are generous enough to count me a philosopher you may recognize the exaggeration of this pronouncement. I consider Kant's entire philosophy a mistake which gave rise to still greater mistakes, and finally led to complete philosophical chaos. I do believe that I learned a great deal from Kant; I learned, however, not what he wanted to teach me, but, above all, how seductive for the philosophical public, and how deceptive, is the fame which the history of philosophy has tied to names. Every man who has made history must indeed have had a powerful personality; but whether the influence of this personality was beneficial or disastrous, and whether we do well to make him our ideal, and our master, remains much in question.

20. But there are other things which make us suspect Windelband's historical conscience.

How so? Did not Kant teach that there were things in themselves which remain theoretically unknowable for us? Did he not believe that God belonged to these things in themselves—and that this belief was grounded in a practical motive and was indemonstrable only from a theoretical point of view? Did he not believe that he had established a limitation of our knowledge when he said that, since our intuitions are purely sensuous and not intellectual (as they might be for some other being) we could have knowledge of appearances only? Need I say again that the opposite of what Windelband reports has been maintained most emphatically by everyone who knows Kant, as well as by Kant himself?

21. Must we not doubt the views of an author (apparently compelled to make innovations and piquant assertions) who reports Kant's main doctrines in so inventive a manner? And when he comes to Kant's conception of truth, should we not suspect him of entertaining us with a fairy tale? We may ask whether he is not presenting his own brilliant doctrine in the name of Kant. And were we to accept this doctrine, we should not count even Kant among the Kantians, and we would have to classify philosophers, not as Socratics and Kantians, but as Socratics and Windelbandians.

22. The *Critique of Pure Reason* is before us; since Windelband himself says that he has considered this work exclusively, we shall appeal to it for a decision.

And now listen, and be amazed at the way a German historian of philosophy is capable of offering a German philosopher to the public—that philosopher, moreover, whom he declares to be the greatest, and who, in any case, is nowadays most celebrated.

a) Where, according to Kant, is truth in its primary sense to be found? Windelband says: in all regions of mental activity; not only in thinking, but also in volition, and the like.

But what does Kant himself say? In the Second Division of the Transcendental Logic, which he calls "Transcendental Dialectic," we read on the very first page: "Truth or illusion is not in the object, in so far as it is intuited, but in the judgment about it, in so far as it is thought. It is therefore correct to say that the senses do not err—not because they always judge rightly but because they do not judge at all. Truth and error, therefore, and consequently also illusion as leading to error, are only to be found in the judgment, i.e. only in the relation of the object to our understanding. In any knowledge which completely accords with the laws of understanding there is no error." [f]

No further word, I daresay, need be spent on the first question, viz. the question where, according to Kant, truth is to be found.

b) And now, what is this truth which Kant says is to be found solely in judgment?

Does he part from the ancients and no longer understand by it the correspondence of judgment with its object? We heard Windelband's remarks on this topic; let us also hear what Kant has to say.

[f] Immanuel Kant's *Critique of Pure Reason*, translated by Norman Kemp Smith, New York 1933, p. 297.

"What is truth?" he asks in the *Introduction* to the *Transcendental Logic,* Chap. III, p. 97, and he answers: "The nominal definition of truth, that it is the agreement of knowledge with its object, is assumed as granted; the question asked is as to what is the general and sure criterion of the truth of any and every knowledge."

What indeed does Kant teach here? Perhaps that it is false to say, as was said at one time, that truth is the correspondence of a judgment with its object? Quite on the contrary, he presupposes this as generally known, and certainly in the familiar sense. But let us hear what follows immediately (p. 97): "If truth consists in the agreement of knowledge with its object, that object must thereby be distinguished from other objects; for knowledge is false if it does not agree with the object to which it is related, even though it contains something which may be valid of other objects." Windelband says that Kant had altered the traditional definition, at least as far as its meaning is concerned, by understanding something different by object, namely a rule of the mind. But doesn't this passage indicate that Kant is explicitly rejecting Windelband's imputation?

On Windelband's interpretation, what would be the meaning of the expression: "even though it contains something which may be valid of other objects"? Of other *rules?* Of rules perhaps that are valid for another mind? Who is tolerant enough to stand for such tricks of interpretation?—But Kant has not yet finished. He continues by talking just about rules, distinguishing them from objects. (p. 97) "Now a general criterion of truth must be such as would be valid in each and every instance of knowledge, however their objects may vary. It is obvious, however, that such a criterion (being general) cannot take account of the (varying) content of knowledge (relation to its [specific] object). But since truth concerns just this very content, it is quite impossible, and indeed absurd, to ask for a general test of the truth of such content. A sufficient and at the same time general criterion of truth cannot possibly be given. Since we have already entitled the content of knowledge its matter, we must be prepared to recognise that of the truth of knowledge, so far as its matter is concerned, no general criterion can be demanded. Such a criterion would by its very nature be self-contradictory," and he continues in the same vein to the passage containing the words, "however uninstructed we may be with regard to its content" (p. 99).

After this decisive evidence, no one, surely, would require additional confirmation. Nor would we have time to cite it all. Let me therefore simply append one or two passages indicating that Kant does not think of the object as being that which in the manner of a rule, guides and influences the function of thinking.

"All presentations have, as presentations, their object, and can themselves in turn become objects of other presentations. Appearances are the sole objects which can be given to us immediately, and that in them which relates immediately to the object is called intuition. But these appearances are not things in themselves; they are only presentations, which in turn have their object—an object which cannot itself be intuited by us, and which may, therefore, be named the non-empirical, that is transcendental object = x.

"The pure concept of this transcendental object, which in reality throughout all our knowledge is always one and the same, is what can alone confer upon all our empirical concepts in general relation to an object, that is, objective reality." g

"*Understanding* is, to use general terms, *the faculty of knowledge.* This knowledge consists in the determinate relation of given representations to an object; and an *object* is that in the concept of which the manifold of a given intuition is *united.* Now all unification of representations demands unity of consciousness in the synthesis of them. Consequently it is the unity of consciousness that alone constitutes the relation of representations to an object, and therefore their objective validity and the fact that they are modes of knowledge; and upon it therefore rests the very possibility of the understanding." h

23. There is not the slightest doubt! Kant, too, retained the Aristotelean definition of truth as correspondence of judgment with reality. And so, we can assert that all epoch-making thinkers after Aristotle, however revolutionary their procedure when tackling other questions, found no reason to make any change here.

24. But, as Windelband's own case makes clear, attempts to avoid the Aristotelean conception have not been entirely lacking. Others have also tried to find a substitute for the conception of correspondence with an object—if not, with Windelband, in the notion of rule-direction [3] as such, then in that of a rule-directed, normative act of judging. One finds such a view in Sigwart, for example, although he occasionally has recourse to the old conception of truth. The whole of Sigwart's *Logic* is muddy on this point.[4]

25. The alleged attempt at reformation is easily refuted.

If truth were no more than judging according to rule, then all judgments—those which do not have sufficient justification as well as those which are completely blind—must be erroneous. But this is certainly not the case. Insight [*Einsicht*] must always be true; but a frivolously made assumption, a mere prejudice, a view adopted by mere appeal to authority, or because it is fashionable—such judgments as these may turn out either to be true or to be erroneous. Aristotle himself points out that one frequently obtains true conclusions from false premises. If I should happen to reason in this way, my conviction has not been framed according

g This quotation is from page 137 of the Kemp Smith translation.
h This quotation is on page 156 of the Kemp Smith translation.

to rule, and thus, on the view in question, is to be disallowed—and yet the conviction is true.[5]

26. And thus there seems to remain, among traditional definitions, only one which can claim our assent; the ancient one which the founder of logic had already given us.

27. But one cannot deny that this definition is burdened with major difficulties.

28. There is, above all, a consideration which is essentially that of the ancient Gorgias.

Correspondence, where this is meant in the fullest sense, is identity. And this, it would seem, is what must be meant. Some kind of correspondence, a correspondence of certain features, obtains between, say, Peter and Paul. If the judgment asserting Peter's existence corresponded no more closely to Peter than Peter corresponds to Paul, then it would not be true, or at least it would not fully be true of Peter.[i] But if it completely corresponded to Peter, it would be identical with him, it would be Peter himself. Yet Peter is outside my mind, not in it. Thus Professor Dilthey of Berlin uses this position to argue against the possibility of our knowledge of the external world as it really is. In his *Einleitung in die Geisteswissenschaften* [j] he justifies this thesis in the following words. "For a presentation (Dilthey conceives judgment as a connection of presentations) can never be identical with a thing, in as much as the thing is conceived as a reality independent of the presentation. The presentation is not the thing brought inside the mind, and it cannot be made to coincide with an object. If one weakens the concept of sameness to that of similarity, then this concept too, in its precise meaning, cannot be employed: thus the idea of correspondence vanishes into the indefinite."

But, surprisingly enough, Dilthey does not deny the possibility of our knowing the intentions and convictions of others, as these are in themselves. A critic has shrewdly remarked,[6] that Dilthey, in order to remain consistent, would have to maintain the impossibility of the knowledge of someone else's error. "In order to recognize the error of another person, this error would have to be put into my mind. But this is impossible. And even if it were possible, we would still less notice the error, since we would have participated in it." Considering this, it would surely be better to reject the definition of truth as correspondence of thought [*des Denkens*] with its object. As a matter of fact, if Sigwart in his *Logic* seems prepared to reject the definition, he was compelled by a consideration of this sort—one which seems to have influenced Windelband himself.

29. Nonetheless, the argument is completely fallacious. It stems from a failure to recognize the distinction, which Descartes had put as the dis-

i *Wenn mein Urteil das den Peter anerkennt, nicht mehr als der Paul mit ihm übereinstimmte, so wäre es nicht wahr, wenigstens nicht Wahrheit des Peter.*

j On p. 407 of the first volume of Dilthey's *Gesammelte Schriften*, Leipzig, 1922.

tinction between formal and objective reality, but which had been brought fully to light long before by Aristotle, who used it in overcoming the absurdities and sophistries of Parmenides, Gorgias, Protagoras, and others.

If I believe something, then this belief is "formally" in me. When I later recall this belief then it is, according to Descartes' way of speaking, "objectively" in me; the same particular act of belief is in question; but on the one occasion it is my act, and on the other it is only the immanent object of my remembering. Similarly in the case of every other mental function, such as willing, desiring, avoiding, etc. Every mental act, in itself given formally, has its immanent object which, in Descartes' terms, is given objectively. To avoid misunderstandings, we might express this better by saying that the immanent object is given intentionally. It is obvious that no contradiction is involved in saying that something is in me intentionally but not formally, or vice versa, a fact that can be illustrated by the example of remembering, and by thousands of others. A mistake on this point would be a relapse into the crudest stages of the development of the theory of knowledge.

30. But there are other problems which may seem less easy to dispose of. Some of these are due to the particular features of Aristotle's own formulation, stemming from the fact that his conception of judgment is not complete. When the relevant corrections are made, these difficulties disappear. There is another type of case, however, which will not yield to such treatment.

31. First a word about the former. Aristotle states in the *De Interpretatione* that judgment is a combination of thoughts (concepts) (συμπλοκὴ τῶν νοημάτων), that it is a synthesis (σύνθεσις). The synthesis is said to consist in taking one real object to be combined with another, forming a unity, or else in taking one real object to be separated, or different from another. One judges truly when one takes, as combined, objects that really are combined, or, as separate, objects that really are separate. One judges falsely, on the other hand, if one judges in a way that is contrary to the objects.

32. This view is hardly satisfactory. Consider above all the assertion that the separate or distinct existence [*Bestehen*] of the objects, which correspond to the subject and predicate in a judgment, is a condition for the truth of the negative judgment and for the falsity of the affirmative judgment. If I say of a dog that he is a cat then it is indeed the case that the subject (dog) and predicate (cat) have separate existence, and that in taking the dog to be a cat I am judging falsely. But the falsity of my judgment does not lie in the fact that a dog and a cat exist separately; if there were no cat at all—neither combined with nor separated from the dog—my judgment would be still false.

33. We may clarify this point, if it is necessary, by considering other

cases. For example, if I judge that a certain tone "c" is a twentieth octave "a", my judgment is certainly as false as if I had considered it a first octave "a"; the latter tone has a separate existence from the "c"; but the former tone is wholly imaginary. And instead of saying, of a negative judgment, that it is true provided that the predicate exists *separate* from the subject, we ought rather to say that the negative judgment is true provided the predicate does *not* exist *combined* with the subject.

The definition of truth would now become: a judgment is true if it attributes to an object something which, in reality, is combined with it or if it denies of an object something which, in reality, is not combined with it.

34. This change provides us with an essential correction, but the definition is still unsatisfactory. Is it really the case that our affirmative judgments are always concerned with the combination of real determinations? Clearly not: If I believe, of a certain real object, that that object is a dog, or a physical body, or even if I believe that it is round or red, then indeed I do combine real determinations. But consider those cases in which I do not believe, of an object, that it is a dog or that it is a physical body, but believe simply in its existence—those cases in which I judge that a particular object exists. There have been philosophers who really supposed that attributing existence to an object is a case of combining. But when asked what they meant by this existence, they would simply answer that "existent" [*Existierendes*] means no more than "object", taken however in an entirely indeterminate and general sense. From this explanation it would follow that to say "There is a certain object" is to say "A certain object is an object."

Aristotle was quite aware that this strange idea could hardly be correct. Indeed he states in the ninth book of the *Metaphysics* that in such a case there is no belief in anything "being-combined", and certainly no combination of several different thoughts; here the act of thinking is perfectly simple.[7]

35. It is, indeed, just on this account that Aristotle says, of God's apprehension of himself in his own being as a perfectly simple entity, that his act of thought is a simple one which does not combine a subject with a predicate.

36. But let us leave the realm of metaphysics, retaining just the general results it has yielded for the theory of judgment. Evidently we must make a substantial modification. As I think I have shown in my *Psychologie vom empirischen Standpunkt,* the result will be a significant improvement in our theory of judgment.[8]

37. We have noted that what Aristotle said about combining and separating continues to be influential; the result is particularly unhappy in the theory of judgment. While he conceded that affirmative belief is

not always belief in a combination, he felt certain that negation must always involve belief in a separation; hence, according to him, the affirmation of a predicate is opposed to the denial of a predicate, but simple affirmation is not opposed to simple denial. And thus we read in the "Books on the Soul" that while truth is to be found in simple thought, error can be found only in complex thought. And in the *Metaphysics* he states explicitly that what is opposed to a simple, true judgment is not error, but simply ignorance (ἄγνοια).

38. I shall not take the time to show how this mistake is connected with the earlier one. However glaring the present mistake may be, we have ample reason to judge Aristotle more leniently when we consider the obscurity which has surrounded the conception of existential judgments in the views of virtually all philosophers up to the present time.[9]

39. If now we go on to correct the mistake which has just been considered, we arrive at the following modification of the Aristotelian definitions of truth and of error:

The truth of a judgment consists in the fact that: either the judgment attributes to an object some entity with which it is combined, or it denies of the object some entity with which it is *not* combined; or if the judgment is of the simplest sort, then, if it affirms of some entity that it exists, it is true if the thing does exist, and if it affirms of some entity that it does not exist, it is true if the thing does not exist. And this would be the correspondence of true judgment with real objects.

40. But, new difficulties emerge. For there are cases in which even this definition appears inappropriate. I shall restrict myself to the two principal ones.

41. The definition would seem especially inadequate in the case of any negative judgments, including those which wholly deny the object, or deny its existence (as this is usually, but not very happily, expressed). I say "not very happily", because in such cases no one really thinks that perhaps the object subsists [*bestehe*], but without existence [*Existenz*].

42. The difficulty is especially clear in the case of simple denial.

If the truth of "There is no dragon" were to reside in a correspondence between my judgment and an object, what would the object be? Certainly not the dragon, since there isn't any dragon. Nor is there any other concrete thing [*Reale*] which *could* count as the corresponding reality.

43. A similar situation holds when, instead of denying an object simply, the judgment denies it only as being a real determination of another object. Suppose I say, "Some man is not black." What is required for the truth of the statement is, not that there *is* black separated from the man, but rather that there is an absence of black on the man. This absence, this non-black, is clearly not an object; thus again there is no object given in reality which corresponds to my judgment.

It is quite obvious, therefore, that in the case of every true negative judgment—and unmistakably so when the judgment is simple—that that correspondence which is supposed to hold between true judgments and reality is not to be found.

44. The other case, which seems to lead to a similar result, may be seen if we take note of the whole area in which the affirmative function is exercised.

We find, of course, that the affirmative judgment often does apply to things [*Dinge*]; but we also find—I shall make the point clear with examples—that it often applies to objects [*Gegenstände*] which should never be designated as "things." Now whenever a true affirmative judgment *does* apply to a thing—whether the judgment be one which simply accepts or acknowledges [*anerkennt*] the thing or one which attributes to it some further determination—we can indicate a correspondence between the judgment and the thing. But how are we to do this when the judgment does *not* apply to a thing?

45. A true affirmative judgment may apply to a single thing. But it may also apply to a collection of things,[10] or to a part of a thing, or to the limit or boundary of a thing, and such like—all these latter being objects which are not themselves things.[11] Or would one, who ventured to deny all of this, want to say that I could find, as a thing external to me, some entity [*Wesen*] that I know to have perished a long time ago, or to be expected in the distant future.[12]

And still more! What if I recognize the absence of a thing? Will it then be said that this absence, this lack of a thing, is itself a thing? [13] Or again, if I say that there is [*besteht*] a certain impossibility, or that there are certain eternal truths (the laws of mathematics, for example), would it then be supposed that there are eternal entities [*Wesen*], perhaps similar to platonic ideas, which exist in, or outside of, the world? Certainly not! [14] The whole idea of the *adaequatio rei et intellectus* seems to go completely to pieces.[15]

46. And so we realize: the proposition that truth is the correspondence of judgment with fact (or however one may wish to put it) must either be completely false, or else it must be given an interpretation quite different from the one offered by those who think there is a relation of identity, or of sameness, or of similarity, between a true thought and reality.

47. Of these last two possibilities, the second is the one which is correct.[16] And now it should be easy for us to give the proper sense of that formula which has been so long unclear.

To do this we must pay proper attention both to the limits of the area to which judging is applicable, and to the contrast between those judgments which affirm and those which deny.

48. The area to which our judgments may be applied is unlimited, and the content of judgment may be as we like. But it is always "some

thing" [*irgend etwas*] that is judged. And what does "some thing" signify? It is a term that can be applied to God or the world, to any entity
whatever, and to any non-entity.[17]

49. Now this limitless area can be divided into two parts. The opposition between the affirmative and the negative judgment implies, as we
know, that in any given case one, and only one, of the two modes of
judging is appropriate and that the other is inappropriate.[18] This fact
is ordinarily expressed by saying that, of two contradictory judgments,
one and only one is true and the other false.

50. Let us say that the area to which affirmative judgment is appropriate is the area of the existent [*Existierenden*], a concept to be
sharply distinguished from that of the real [*Dinglichen, Wesenhaften,
Realen*]; and that the area to which the negative judgment is appropriate is the area of the non-existent [*Nicht-existierenden*].

51. Following Aristotle's statement that a judgment is true if it takes
as combined what is combined, and so on, we can say: a judgment is true
if it asserts of something that is, that it is, and asserts of something that is
not, that it is not—and a judgment is false if it contradicts that which is,
or that which is not.[19]

52. And this is all there is to the correspondence of true judgment
and object which we have heard so much about. To correspond does not
mean to be the same or to be similar; but it does mean to be adequate,
to fit, to be in agreement with, to be in harmony with, or whatever equivalent expressions one may choose to apply.[20]

53. We may make this concept clearer by drawing another obvious
parallel. In the area of emotion we also find an opposition—that between
loving and hating [*Lieben und Hassen*]. Of everything that may be considered, one of these two attitudes may be said to be appropriate and the
other inappropriate. Accordingly, everything that can be thought about
belongs in either of two classes—the class of things for which love is appropriate, and the class of things for which hate is appropriate. Whatever falls into the first class we call good, and whatever falls into the second we call bad. Thus we can say that love and hate are correct [*richtig*]
if we love what is good and if we hate what is bad, and that love and
hate are *not* correct if we love what is bad and hate what is good. We can
also say that in those cases where our attitude is correct the emotion corresponds with the object, that it is in harmony with the value of the object,
and that in those cases where our attitude is incorrect, the emotion contradicts the object and is not in harmony with its value.[21]

54. We have thus an exact analogue to the correspondence which
holds between a true judgment and its object, or between a true judgment and the existence or non-existence of its object. But the present case
has nothing whatever to do with Being in the sense of that which is a

thing or a substance [*von einem Seienden im Sinne des Realen, Ding-lichen, Wesenhaften*].[22]

55. In the light of all this, if we now ask about the relation between truth and reality, we find a very simple answer.

(1) For one class of true judgments, there is, so to speak, a direct relation between their truth and what is real; these are the judgments which are such that, the idea or thought [*Vorstellung*] which is at their basis has a real content. Clearly the truth of the affirmative judgment—and, in the inverse sense, that of the negative—depends upon the existence, the coming into being, or the passing away, of the respective reality. Without the judgment itself undergoing any change, it may acquire—or lose—its truth if the respective reality should be produced or destroyed.[23]

(2) For the other class of judgments, those whose thoughts or presentations have no real content, there are two possibilities.

(a) It may be that, so far as its truth is concerned, the judgment is not at all dependent upon a reality [*einer Realität*]. This may be said of those judgments whose objects are in themselves necessary or impossible. The law of contradiction, and with it all analytic judgments, belongs to this category.[24]

(b) It may be that the judgment is not directly dependent upon a reality but is *indirectly* dependent upon a reality. The presentation or thought underlying the judgment has no real content, but the object of the judgment belongs to the existent, or to the non-existent, as a result of the fact that a certain real thing, or things, and no other, happens to exist—or did exist, or will exist. Consider an empty space, any kind of lack or deficiency, a capacity, an object of thought, or the like: these exist, and come into being and pass away, as a result of alterations among things that *are* real.[25]

56. Thus I think we have the essential points involved in clarifying the definition of truth as correspondence of judgment with the object—a definition which has been the occasion of so much misunderstanding.

57. I can imagine that many will be disappointed with such a result.

For it may seem that very little is expressed by this definition, no more than would be expressed by saying that a judgment is true if it judges an object suitably or appropriately—if it says, of something that is, that it is, and of something that is not, that it is not.[26]

The expressions "to judge truly" and "to judge appropriately" would seem to be tautologically equivalent [k] and the rest to be only an explication in terms of correlative expressions. If we explicate the conception of the truth of an affirmative judgment by reference to the correlative term "existence of the object," and if we explicate the concept of the truth of

---

k Translators' note: The German reads " '*Wahr beurteilen*' und '*zutreffend beur-teilen*' scheint einfache Tautologie."

a negative judgment by the correlative term, "non-existence of the object," our procedure is like that of one who defines the concept of effect by reference to that of cause, or the concept of the larger by reference to that of the smaller. What does this accomplish? The one expression is just as well known and just as much in use as is the other.

58. Nevertheless there are respects in which our investigation should be instructive.

(1) The fact that we will no longer look for more than is really given in the definition is itself of considerable importance. And the definition is not entirely devoid of value. Tautological expressions, even without conceptual analysis, may be of considerable use in the task of explication, if one of the two synonymous terms is less subject to misunderstanding than the other. But the expression "correspondence with an object" had no such advantage, and we took precautions against going astray by noting the analogue between appropriate affirmation and denial and the kind of appropriateness which applies in the sphere of loving and hating.

And thus we are protected from conceptual confusions and from the blunders to which so many have been led as a result of misunderstanding the definition.

(a) For example, we will not separate formal truth from material truth, as some have done; we see that what is sometimes called formal truth (the lack of inner contradiction) is truth, not in any proper sense, but only in an entirely improper sense—similar to the way in which we sometimes say, of something which is not a judgment at all, that it is true.[27]

(b) Nor are we likely to think, as so many foolishly do, that whenever one is aware of the truth one must *compare* a real thing with a judgment. People who think this way do not realize that our judgments are not always concerned with things that are real. And they don't realize that when our judgments *are* concerned with what is real, we couldn't compare the judgment and the thing unless the thing were already known to us. The theory would thus lead to an infinite regress.[28]

And finally we shall not be tempted, as so many have been, to confuse the concept of the real [des Realen] with the concept of the existent [des Existierenden]. It is a few thousand years since Aristotle investigated the manifold senses of Being; it is regrettable that even today there are many who have not learned from his investigation.[29]

59. (2) Our results are significant in still another respect. We spoke earlier of equivocations, and noticed how, at the outset, Aristotle had recognized the extent to which failure to consider them may impair the success of our intellectual efforts.

Indeed, we gain a clearer picture of the significance of this danger when we see that, because of the equivocal expression "Being," a formula which has been used again and again may yet confuse the most important thinkers and keep them from being clear about something which is, basically, quite simple.

60. (3) Finally, we can derive still another lesson from our investigation, and forever impress it upon our mind. We have been concerned with a definition, i.e., with the elucidation of a concept connected with a name. Many believe such elucidation always requires some general determination, and they forget that the ultimate and most effective means of elucidation must always consist in an appeal to the individual's intuition [*Anschauung*], from which all of our general criteria are derived. What would be the use of trying to elucidate the concepts red or blue if I could not present one with something red or with something blue? All of this has been disregarded by those who were concerned with the nominal definition of truth, whose history we have pursued.

If, as I hope, we have succeeded in clarifying this muddled concept, we have done so only by focussing primarily on examples of true judgments. In so doing we came to see that no such relation as that of sameness or equality could be identified with truth—if only because of the fact that affirmation and negation are frequently without reference to real objects. Even now, after the elimination of confusions and misunderstandings, our definition would convey nothing to one who lacked the necessary intuition.[30] These are our rewards; they are adequate enough if we keep in mind that our modest problem was only that of explicating an expression which, in its ordinary use, is familiar to us all.

NOTES OF THE EDITOR, OSKAR KRAUS

[1] George Grote (1794-1871).

[1a] The Latin text reads: *si iudicium rebus convenit.*

[2] Nevertheless the Cartesian definition "verum est quod clare ac distincte percipio" contained the seed of the right conception, namely, the reference back to evidence and the avoidance of a correspondence theory. This conception is clearly expressed—in spite of some wavering—by Spinoza (*Ethics, II*, prop. 43).

[3] To do complete justice to Windelband one needs to distinguish between two questions: first, whether his exposition and interpretation of Kant's doctrine is historically correct, and, second, whether Windelband did not come close to a correct view in what he said about "the concept of truth." So far as the first question is concerned, Brentano easily succeeds in proving the inaccuracy of Windelband's interpretation of Kant. As for the second question, Windelband had a notion—however vague—which ought not to be rejected out of hand. Brentano himself (§24) calls the proposed interpretation an attempt to shake off the old correspondence theory; opposing this attempt, Brentano puts forward his own interpretation, which is in fact a revision rather than a complete repudiation of the correspondence theory. Windelband, however, faithful to his slogan—

"To understand Kant is to go beyond him" (*Präludien*, p. iv)—goes far beyond the historical Kant by allowing him neither a Ptolemaic nor a Copernican conception of truth; for he would have Kant reject every version of the correspondence theory. With a much finer touch than that of the Marburg Neo-Kantian School, Windelband believes that truth consists in thought which accords with a normative rule (p. 114) and that "the mind brings this norm to its own awareness."

Windelband writes (*Präludien*, p. 47): "The only thing that philosophy can achieve consists in allowing the consciousness which abides by norms to spring from the agitations of the empirical consciousness, and to trust the immediately evident [*unmittelbare Evidenz*] when it presents itself to a clear mind and affects every individual, as it should, with its validity." There is little to quarrel with in this statement, unless one takes too seriously the contention that it is "the *only* thing philosophy can achieve."

All this is certainly fraught with confusion, if "judging" is not distinguished from "thinking about" (*Vorstellen*), and if the logical ought, on the other hand, is identified with the axiological and ethical ought. But this aberration from the intellectual to the emotional, against which Brentano correctly protests in the fourth essay, does show that Windelband looked for the norm—that which is as it ought to be—in consciousness itself. And in doing this he was following the path which indeed Spinoza had taken before him (*Ethics*, II, prop. 43); cf. my detailed review of Cohen's writings on philosophy and the theory of knowledge in *Deutsche Literaturzeitung*, 1929, 30 Heft). To be sure, one still finds in Spinoza traces of the doctrine of correspondence but Freudenthal conceives these traces as merely a gesture towards the venerable principle. Here too Spinoza bases his thought on that of Descartes.

Unfortunately, Windelband and his circle, having set out in the right direction, soon become lost in the chimerical realm of absolute values and validities.

But Brentano, at the time of his lecture on truth, tried merely to modify the correspondence theory. Later he saw that this would not do either. The theory of evidence [*Evidenzlehre*], which Brentano was one of the first to revive, has been developed to the point where it clarifies the concept of truth, and removes the attendant difficulties, without resort to the fiction of ideal objects, "eternal realms of value," and the other non-entities which serve only to restore the correspondence theory in some form or other.

4 Cf. the criticism of Sigwart's doctrine in Essay V [of *Wahrheit und Evidenz*].

5 Cf. Note 3 concerning Windelband's doctrine.

6 Franz Hillebrand in *Grünhut's Zeitschrift für das öffentliche und Privatrecht* (1884, XI, Bd., p. 633).

7 Cf. Franz Brentano, *Von der mannigfachen Bedeutung des Seienden nach Aristoteles* (Freiburg, 1862, p. 22).

8 Compare the new edition of the *Psychologie vom empirischen Standpunkte*, Felix Meiner, *Philosophische Bibliothek*, Vols. I-III, esp. Vol. II.

9 On the so-called "existential judgment" cf. *Psychology*, II (p. 55, 195). Cf. also Hillebrand, *Die neuen Theorien der kategorischen Schlüsse* (Vienna, 1891). Cf. Notes 27 and 42.

10 Brentano later withdrew the assertion that collections of things, and parts

of a thing, are not themselves things. A boundary or limit is indeed not itself a
thing but rather something real which exists only when part of a continuous
thing.

11 Brentano later attacks the doctrine. Everybody calls a house or a chair
a "thing," although it is considered as a joining together of many things (bricks,
pieces of wood, etc.). Certainly the old doctrine is correct in holding that a
collection—a herd or an army, for example—is not something that may be added
to the particular soldiers or sheep as still another entity; it is a real totality in
the sense of a sum whose parts likewise consist of real things.

12 Brentano held at that time that "a past pain," "a former man," "a future man," and the like, are expressions in which the adjective functions as a
modifier converting something real into something non-real. Most of Brentano's
students have remained faithful to this doctrine or have further elaborated upon
it, extending the realm of the non-real into that of the boundless. Husserl's
phenomenology and Meinong's theory of objects both tended to propagate this
realm of non-real entities to an extravagant degree. Marty and Stumpf were
content to defend the traditional stock of non-real entities against Brentano's
elimination of the non-real, whether it be called "non-real essence," "essence,"
"state of affairs," "content," or whatever. So far as "past" and "future" are concerned, Brentano's later doctrine was that differences of praeterital and futural
thinking are differences not in the objects of thought, but in its modality. (He
spoke of *"Vorstellungsmodi"*). The same thing, the same reality, which I think
of in the present mode can be thought of at some other time in the past or in the
future mode. The modes of thinking or presentation also affect the judgments
we make about these things, but in every case what is thought of is something
real [*Reales, Dingliches, Wesenhaftes*]. When we think of a past or a future man,
we are thinking of something real—a man—in the praeterital or in the futural
mode. Cf. Brentano's doctrine of time and temporal modes of presentation
(*Psychologie* II and esp. III). Cf. also Brentano's published letters to Marty [1895]
(*Archiv für Psychologie*, Vol. 75, Heft 1 and 2, 1930). The latter also contains a
discussion of Husserl's later doctrine of modalities.

The question that Brentano raised here—"Does one expect to find, as a real
object [*Ding*] external to oneself, some entity one knows to have perished a long
time ago?"—is a question which, at that time, he answered in the negative; but
he believed then that it was a non-real entity [*irreales Wesen*] that existed and
not a thing.

13 Brentano held at that time that, if I say there is a lack of money, then I
have affirmed something, acknowledged something in judgment; this something
is not a "thing" but is the *lack* of a thing, and the *lack* of a thing is itself something non-real, a non-entity. Things as well as non-things are subsumed under
the concept of "something" [*Etwas*] (cf. § 48 below). But Brentano later realized
that this was a fallacy. The statement "There is a lack of money" is nothing but
the linguistic disguise of a denial—"Money is lacking," "There is no money," or
"No money is there," all of which express my disavowal, or denial, of money.
Such expressions as "lack of money" are not names but pseudo-names. They are
syncategorematic [*mitbedeutende*] expressions; their role in the complete statement is that of expressing a denial and not, as the language might suggest, an
affirmation.

[14] Brentano speaks here of "impossibilities," "eternal truth," which subsist [*bestehen*]; he rejects the idea that one might speak here of "entities" or "things" to which a true judgment corresponds. As may be gathered from the following paragraphs, however, he does allow himself to speak of non-realities [*Irrealitäten*] and he believes that any non-reality may be counted as a "something-or-other" [*Irgendetwas*] which exists and to which our judgment corresponds. At the time Brentano did not consider the "something or other" in such cases to be a real entity; it was a *non-real* entity. Thus he considered mathematical truths as something existent, though he did not consider them to be existing *things*. This is all false; and the fact that it has been exposed as such by Brentano himself has been obstinately ignored. Contemporary theory of knowledge and especially later "phenomenology" (Husserl's *Ideen* and *Transzendentale Logik*) absorbed these thoughts which had long been surmounted by Brentano and developed them into a direction from which Brentano himself had parted.

[15] It seems, says Brentano, that the *adaequatio rei et intellectus* disintegrates because there is no *res*, no "thing," among the "eternal truths," "impossibilities," etc. to which thought would correspond. But then in the following paragraph he holds that entities which are non-real and are yet capable of existing may serve as that to which thought corresponds.

I repeat that this idea is untenable and that Brentano later rejected it categorically. But the theory reigns over the entire epistemological literature without anyone taking note of Brentano's (later) objections.

[16] Brentano believed, then, that the doctrine of the *adaequatio rei et intellectus* is not completely false; it is to be interpreted, however, not as a correspondence of judging with a *res* (fact, reality, real entity, thing), but as a correspondence of the affirming judgment with something existent, and of the denying judgment with something non-existent. Thus not only things, *res*, realities, real entities, but also non-things, *irrealia*, mere objects of thought [*Gedankendinge*] sometimes exist, and sometimes do not exist.

[17] In this context "something" [*Irgendetwas*] is the most fundamental concept for Brentano, under which not only every thing but also every non-thing can be subsumed. Later Brentano rejected this thesis. He attempted to show that "something" must be a unitary concept, since the concept of our consciousness, which always has something as its object, is unitary. But it would be impossible for "something" to be a unitary concept if it were intended to encompass both the real and the non-real, since these would not share a single characteristic. Mental and physical things, indeed *n*-dimensional things, can be subsumed under the concept of 'thing,' or 'real'; but what characteristics could a physical, or mental, thing have in common with the "impossibility of a round square" or a "past pleasure"? These are not to be subsumed under one concept. Otherwise the word "something" would be ambiguous, according to whether something real or something unreal was meant. This question is treated later; cf. Part IV.

[18] The defect in these detailed arguments consists in the following: Brentano proceeds from the concepts of *correct* or *fitting* (as he had done in *Vom Ursprung Sittlicher Erkenntnis*, § 22), instead of proceeding from the concept of the evident or insightful [*einsichtigen*] judgment; but the former concept can be acquired only by an appeal to a judgment which is characterized as correct or is

characterized as evident. He had always held, however, that we can give an account of right and wrong only by reflecting on the evident judgment (or, in the emotive sphere, by reflecting on emotions which are, analogously, correct or right, and incorrect or not-right). In the *Vom Ursprung Sittlicher Erkenntnis,* all reference to "true and false," "right and wrong" is reduced to judging characterized as correct and to loving and hating characterized as correct.

Elements of different theories are lined up here in a somewhat disorderly manner. An older conception which derives from Aristotle connects the correct with the convenient or with the fitting, and a later, more progressive theory reduces the correct to the evident, to that which is insightful.

We must stay with this later doctrine. For it alone sheds light on the question: what is truth?

19 Cf. preceding note. It is clear that Brentano was here trying to improve upon Aristotle's definition of truth—to transform it without completely abandoning it. But this half-way measure is astonishing in view of the fact that, even then, Brentano based the theory of knowledge upon the concept of evident judgment, just as he based the theory of value upon that of correct emotion.

20 We say of a judgment that it fits, corresponds to, or harmonizes with its object provided that the judgment is true; and we say of a judgment that it is true provided that the judgment is evident, or that we believe that it corresponds to an evident judgment with respect to its quality, or that we believe that an evident judgment that is concerned with the same object could not possibly be of a different quality. This is the consequence of Brentano's later doctrine which emerges more and more clearly in the succeeding arguments, and which we must defend against the older doctrine that was advanced in the lecture on truth. Two judgments are said to correspond qualitatively (or formally) if both are affirmative or negative respectively, and have the same temporal mode.

21 What holds of *evident judgment* also holds of correct emotion. Any discussion of *correct* or *right* in the sphere of emotive phenomena derives its meaning from evident judgment. We call an emotion suitable to its object, or fitting to its object, if it is characterized as right, or if we believe that an emotion-characterized-as-right could not possibly have any other quality. In saying of something that it is "good" we mean that no attitude toward the object other than love, or positive evaluation, could possibly be characterized as right. "Good" is a syncategorematic word, like "being" and "non-being." Compare the Introduction and the Notes to our edition of the *Vom Ursprung sittlicher Erkenntnis* and esp. *Psychologie,* Vol. II, as well as the later essays in the present volume.

Hence the complete opposite of what is said in the text is true. It is not that the correctness of loving and hating depends upon whether or not we love the good or hate the bad; the truth of the matter is just the other way around. And to say that our emotion *fits* the object is only to say, again, that the emotion is right or correct. What we recognize primarily is that our emotion-is-characterized-as-right. We say of an object that it is good or bad if it fits an emotion which is right—a correct emotion. One does not first recognize the value and *then* recognize the emotion as right; it is, again, the converse that is true. That which we call a value or a good is that which is an object of a right emotion, and of which any qualitatively differing emotive act could not possibly be correct or right. This was Brentano's later view.

[22] Later Brentano declares this to be false. One can refer only to what is real, thing-like, substantial [*Realem, Dinglichem, Wesenhaftem*]; only these can be the objects of thought [*vorgestellt werden*]. There is a detailed and complete account of this topic in *Psychologie,* Vol. I, Introduction, *Psychologie,* Vol. II, Appendix 9, and in the later essays in the present book.

[23] Truth is not a real property of judgment unless one understands by truth the property of being evident or of being insightful [*einsichtig*]. Since this latter is not the case (and it is not accepted in this lecture), it is clear that in speaking of truth one is concerned with an *apparent* attribute or characteristic. Such apparent attributes are what the scholastics called *denominationes extrinsecae,* extrinsic labels. In speaking of the truth of a judgment that is not evident one has in mind that this blind judgment either corresponds with respect to quality to an evident judgment, or that an evident judgment could not possibly contradict it. All of this is discussed below: compare Note 20 and especially the Introduction.

Brentano says in the text: "Whether the respective external reality is produced or destroyed—without itself changing—, the judgment gains or loses its truth." Suppose, for instance, I judge that it is raining. The rain stops, I do not revise my judgment, and the judgment is thus transformed from one which is true into one which is false. If "true" and "false" were real predicates, or real properties of the judgment, this would constitute a miracle—indeed a contradiction; something would change its real properties without itself undergoing any change other than a temporal one.

Thus "true" and "false" cannot signify real predicates or attributes. Therefore, one might argue, they must signify non-real predicates.

But the great progress of Brentano's thinking consists in showing that there cannot be determinations other than those which are real—indeed that non-real determinations are not even imaginable. What, then, does it mean to say "The judgment is deprived of its truth without its being changed in any way"? I believe the answer is roughly this: "The judgment 'it is raining' ceases to be true." And what this means, when put clearly and explicitly, is: "From now on a judgment which affirms rain cannot possibly be evident." Our sentence is an apodictic rejection of evident judgments affirming rain.

[24] One must object to the view that analytic judgments, and specifically cognitions *a priori,* refer to objects devoid of real content. The principle of contradiction, for instance, no matter how it is formulated, refers to things which are real.

[25] At the time Brentano's view was as follows: The coming into being or passing away of something that has "no real content" [*Gehalt*] and is thus non-real is always tied to the coming into being and passing away of that which *is* real. A deficiency, for instance, comes into being when something real passes away, and a deficiency passes away when the corresponding real thing comes into being. Thus an empty space comes into being when certain bodies pass away or change their location. And an empty space passes away if certain bodies come into being, or change their location. An object of thought comes into existence when one thinks, and it passes away when one stops thinking. It is noteworthy that Brentano had always held that the coming into being and the passing away of the so-called non-real is in fact tied up with what is real. He did believe, at

the time of the lecture on truth, that "An empty space comes into being" conveys something other than "Some physical object passes away," and "My lack of money begins today" conveys something other than "Today I am devoid of all money," or "Today the last of my money is gone." He took the statements to be logically equivalent and yet he considered them to be psychologically and conceptually different. According to the later doctrine, however, the statements express the same thought but in different ways: in each case, there is a relation to something real, in the one example a relation to matter that changes or moves, in the other example a relation to money which changes its owner, and so on. See additional details below and Brentano's *Vom Dasein Gottes*, p. 42.

The seed of Brentano's later view, which rejects the non-real, even as a possible object of thought, is contained in this doctrine of the dependence of non-realities on the real.

26 What Brentano is doing here is essentially this: he replaces the doctrine of correspondence between thought and object (*rei et intellectus*) with that of the adequacy (fittingness, propriety) of thought to the existent *or* non-existent. This is what most of his students designate as adequacy to an "objective" or "state of affairs" (the state of affairs *that* something A is, or that is not). The analogue holds true in the case of the fitting of valuation to value, states-of-value, value-contents, and the like. He had not yet become completely aware of the fictitious character of these modes of speaking.

27 Instead of speaking of a "correct inference" from false premises, one should speak of the correct conception of the so-called "rule of inference." To call the inference itself formally correct or formally true is inadvisable and misleading. Cf. Hillebrand, *Neue Theorien der Kategorischen Schlüsse* (Vienna, 1891; Notes 9 & 42).

28 From this point on the entire theory of adequation [correspondence] may be refuted. Any such theory, including the one presented in the text, is untenable because it is absurd, indeed ridiculous, to hope to compare the thing with the judgment by which the thing is known. For the thing in question would have to be known beforehand. Yet every theory intending to trace back the concept of the "true" to the concepts of "fitting-a-thing," "being in a proper attitude towards a thing," etc., tacitly implies this comparison.

29 The concept of the real [*des Realen*] is not to be confused with that of the existent [*des Existierenden*]. This is to say: we derive the concept of the real from any intuition of outer, or inner, perception. "Real" is synonymous with "thing", "entity" [*Wesen*], "fact" [*Ding, Sachhaltigem*]—the most general concept that there is. But we speak of 'the existent' or of 'that which has being' when we assert of anything that it is; the term is thus related to the judging attitude and especially to affirmation. We will not discuss the ways in which some recent philosophers have played with the words "Being," "Being-there" [*Dasein*], and "Existence," beyond remarking that, if a theory has anything new to offer, then it should not be expressed in words which have traditionally been used in other senses.

30 The principle, according to which any conceptual investigation must ultimately go back to intuition [*Anschauung*], is what finally enabled Brentano to dispose of the doctrine of *irrealia*.

SIXTEEN

The Coherence Theory

BRAND BLANSHARD (1895-   )

From *The Nature of Thought**

. . . 2. The view that truth *is* coherence rests on a theory of the relation of thought to reality, and since this is the central problem of the theory of knowledge, to begin one's discussion by assuming the answer to it or by trying to make one out of whole cloth would be somewhat ridiculous. But as this was our main problem in the long discussions of Book II, we may be pardoned here for brevity. First we shall state in *resume* the relation of thought to reality that we were there driven to accept, and sketch the theory of truth implicit in it. We shall then take up one by one the objections to this theory and ask if they can pass muster.

To think is to seek understanding. And to seek understanding is an activity of mind that is marked off from all other activities by a highly distinctive aim. This aim, as we saw in our chapter on the general nature of understanding, is to achieve systematic vision, so to apprehend what is now unknown to us as to relate it, and relate it necessarily, to what we know already. We think to solve problems; and our method of solving problems is to build a bridge of intelligible relation from the continent of our knowledge to the island we wish to include in it. Sometimes this bridge is causal, as when we try to explain a disease; sometimes teleological, as when we try to fathom the move of an opponent over the chess board; sometimes geometrical, as in Euclid. But it is always systematic; thought in its very nature is the attempt to bring something unknown or imperfectly known into a sub-system of knowledge, and thus also into the larger system that forms the world of accepted beliefs. That is what explanation is. *Why* is it that thought desires this ordered vision? Why should such a vision give satisfaction when it comes? To these questions there is no answer, and if there were, it would be an answer only because it had succeeded in supplying the characteristic satisfaction to this unique desire.

But may it not be that what satisfies thought fails to conform to the real world? Where is the guarantee that when I have brought my

* Reprinted with permission of The Macmillan Company and George Allen & Unwin Ltd from *The Nature of Thought,* Vol. II by Brand Blanshard. First published in 1939.

ideas into the form my ideal requires, they should be *true?* Here we come round again to the tortured problem of Book II. In our long struggle with the relation of thought to reality we saw that if thought and things are conceived as related only externally, then knowledge is luck; there is no necessity whatever that what satisfies intelligence should coincide with what really is. It may do so, or it may not; on the principle that there are many misses to one bull's-eye, it more probably does not. But if we get rid of the misleading analogies through which this relation has been conceived, of copy and original, stimulus and organism, lantern and screen, and go to thought itself with the question what reference to an object means, we get a different and more hopeful answer. To think of a thing is to get that thing itself in some degree within the mind. To think of a colour or an emotion is to have that within us which if it *were developed and completed,* would identify itself with the object. In short, if we accept its own report, thought is related to reality as the partial to the perfect fulfilment of a purpose. The more adequate its grasp the more nearly does it approximate, the more fully does it realize in itself, the nature and relations of its objects.

3. Thought thus appears to have two ends, one immanent, one transcendent. On the one hand it seeks fulfilment in a special kind of satisfaction, the satisfaction of systematic vision. On the other hand it seeks fulfilment in its object. Now it was the chief contention of our second book that these ends are one. Indeed unless they are accepted as one, we could see no alternative to scepticism. If the pursuit of thought's own ideal were merely an elaborate self-indulgence that brought us no nearer to reality, or if the apprehension of reality did not lie in the line of thought's interest, or still more if both of these held at once, the hope of knowledge would be vain. Of course it may really be vain. If anyone cares to doubt whether the framework of human logic has any bearing on the nature of things, he may be silenced perhaps, but he cannot be conclusively answered. One may point out to him that the doubt itself is framed in accordance with that logic, but he can reply that thus we are taking advantage of his logico-centric predicament; further, that any argument we can offer accords equally well with his hypothesis and with ours, with the view that we are merely flies caught in a logical net and the view that knowledge reveals reality. And what accords equally well with both hypotheses does not support either to the exclusion of the other. But while such doubt is beyond reach by argument, neither is there anything in its favour. It is a mere suspicion which is, and by its nature must remain, without any positive ground; and as such it can hardly be discussed. Such suspicions aside, we can throw into the scale for our theory the impressive fact of the advance of knowledge. It has been the steadfast assumption of science whenever it came to an un-solved problem that there was a key to it to be found, that if things

happened thus rather than otherwise they did so for a cause or reason, and that if this were not forthcoming it was never because it was lacking, but always because of a passing blindness in ourselves. Reflection has assumed that pursuit of its own immanent end is not only satisfying but revealing, that so far as the immanent end is achieved we are making progress toward the transcendent end as well. Indeed, that these ends coincide is the assumption of every act of thinking whatever. To think is to raise a question; to raise a question is to seek an explanation; to seek an explanation is to assume that one may be had; so to assume is to take for granted that nature in that region is intelligible. Certainly the story of advancing knowledge unwinds as if self-realization in thought meant also a coming nearer to reality.

4. That these processes are really one is the metaphysical base on which our belief in coherence is founded. If one admits that the pursuit of a coherent system has actually carried us to what everyone would agree to call knowledge, why not take this ideal as a guide that will conduct us farther? What better key can one ask to the structure of the real? Our own conviction is that we should take this immanent end of thought in all seriousness as the clue to the nature of things. We admit that it may prove deceptive, that somewhere thought may end its pilgrimage in frustration and futility before some blank wall of the unintelligible. There are even those who evince their superior insight by taking this as a foregone conclusion and regarding the faith that the real is rational as the wishful thinking of the 'tender-minded'. Their attitude appears to us a compound made up of one part timidity, in the form of a refusal to hope lest they be disillusioned; one part muddled persuasion that to be sceptical is to be sophisticated; one part honest dullness in failing to estimate rightly the weight of the combined postulate and success of knowledge; one part genuine insight into the possibility of surds in nature. But whatever its motives, it is a view that goes less well with the evidence than the opposite and brighter view. That view is that reality is a system, completely ordered and fully intelligible, with which thought in its advance is more and more identifying itself. We may look at the growth of knowledge, individual or social, either as an attempt by our own minds to return to union with things as they are in their ordered wholeness, or the affirmation through our minds of the ordered whole itself. And if we take this view, our notion of truth is marked out for us. Truth is the approximation of thought to reality. It is thought on its way home. Its measure is the distance thought has travelled, under guidance of its inner compass, toward that intelligible system which unites its ultimate object with its ultimate end. Hence at any given time the degree of truth in our experience as a whole is the degree of system it has achieved. The degree of truth of a particular proposition is to be judged in the first instance by its

coherence with experience as a whole, ultimately by its coherence with that further whole, all-comprehensive and fully articulated, in which thought can come to rest.

5. But it is time we defined more explicitly what coherence means. To be sure, no fully satisfactory definition can be given; and as Dr. Ewing says, 'it is wrong to tie down the advocates of the coherence theory to a precise definition. What they are doing is to describe an ideal that has never yet been completely clarified but is none the less immanent in all our thinking.' [1] Certainly this ideal goes far beyond mere consistency. Fully coherent knowledge would be knowledge in which every judgment entailed, and was entailed by, the rest of the system. Probably we never find in fact a system where there is so much of interdependence. What it means may be clearer if we take a number of familiar systems and arrange them in a series tending to such coherence as a limit. At the bottom would be a junk-heap, where we could know every item but one and still be without any clue as to what that remaining item was. Above this would come a stone-pile, for here you could at least infer that what you would find next would be a stone. A machine would be higher again, since from the remaining parts one could deduce not only the general character of a missing part, but also its special form and function. This is a high degree of coherence, but it is very far short of the highest. You could remove the engine from a motor-car while leaving the other parts intact, and replace it with any one of thousands of other engines, but the thought of such an interchange among human heads or hearts shows at once that the interdependence in a machine is far below that of the body. Do we find them in organic bodies the highest conceivable coherence? Clearly not. Though a human hand, as Aristotle said, would hardly be a hand when detached from the body, still it would be something definite enough; and we can conceive systems in which even this something would be gone. Abstract a number from the number series and it would be a mere unrecognizable x; similarly, the very thought of a straight line involves the thought of the Euclidean space in which it falls. It is perhaps in such systems as Euclidean geometry that we get the most perfect examples of coherence that have been constructed. If any proposition were lacking, it could be supplied from the rest; if any were altered, the repercussions would be felt through the length and breadth of the system. Yet even such a system as this falls short of an ideal system. Its postulates are unproved; they are independent of each other, in the sense that none of them could be derived from any other or even from all the others together; its clear necessity is bought by an abstractness so extreme as to have left out nearly everything that belongs to the character of actual things. A completely satisfactory system would have none of these defects. No proposition

[1] *Idealism*, 231.

would be arbitrary, every proposition would be entailed by the others jointly and even singly,[2] no proposition would stand outside the system. The integration would be so complete that no part could be seen for what it was without seeing its relation to the whole, and the whole itself could be understood only through the contribution of every part.

6. It may be granted at once that in common life we are satisfied with far less than this. We accept the demonstrations of the geometer as complete, and do not think of reproaching him because he begins with postulates and leaves us at the end with a system that is a skeleton at the best. In physics, in biology, above all in the social sciences, we are satisfied with less still. We test judgements by the amount of coherence which in that particular subject-matter it seems reasonable to expect. We apply, perhaps unconsciously, the advice of Aristotle, and refrain from asking demonstration in the physical sciences, while in mathematics we refuse to accept less. And such facts may be thought to show that we make no actual use of the ideal standard just described. But however much this standard may be relaxed within the limits of a particular science, its influence is evident in the grading of the sciences generally. It is precisely in those sciences that approach most nearly to system as here defined that we achieve the greatest certainty, and precisely in those that are most remote from such system that our doubt is greatest whether we have achieved scientific truth at all. Our immediate exactions shift with the subject-matter; our ultimate standard is unvarying.

7. Now if we accept coherence as the test of truth, does that commit us to any conclusions about the *nature* of truth or reality? I think it does, though more clearly about reality than about truth. It is past belief that the fidelity of our thought to reality should be rightly measured by coherence if reality itself were not coherent. To say that the nature of things may be *in*coherent, but we shall approach the truth about it precisely so far as our thoughts become coherent, sounds very much like nonsense. And providing we retained coherence as the test, it would still be nonsense even if truth were conceived as correspondence. On this supposition we should have truth when, our thought having achieved coherence, the correspondence was complete between that thought and its object. But complete correspondence between a coherent thought and an incoherent object seems meaningless. It is hard to see, then, how anyone could consistently take coherence as the test of truth unless he took it also as a character of reality.

----

[2] Coherence can be defined without this point, which, as Dr. Ewing remarks (*Idealism*, 231), makes the case harder to establish. In no mathematical system, for example, would anyone dream of trying to deduce all the other propositions from any proposition taken singly. But when we are describing an ideal, such a fact is not decisive, and I follow Joachim in holding that in a perfectly coherent system every proposition would entail all others, if only for the reason that its meaning could never be fully understood without apprehension of the system in its entirety.

8. Does acceptance of coherence as a test commit us not only to a view about the structure of reality but also to a view about the nature of truth? This is a more difficult question. As we saw at the beginning of the chapter, there have been some highly reputable philosophers who have held that the answer to 'What is the test of truth'? is 'Coherence', while the answer to 'What is the nature or meaning of truth'? is 'Correspondence'. These questions are plainly distinct. Nor does there seem to be any direct path from the acceptance of coherence as the test of truth to its acceptance as the nature of truth. Nevertheless there is an indirect path. If we accept coherence as our test, we must use it everywhere. We must therefore use it to test the suggestion that truth *is* other than coherence. But if we do, we shall find that we must reject the suggestion as leading to *in*coherence. Coherence is a pertinacious concept and, like the well-known camel, if one lets it get its nose under the edge of the tent, it will shortly walk off with the whole.

Suppose that, accepting coherence as the test, one rejects it as the nature of truth in favour of some alternative; and let us assume, for example, that this alternative is correspondence. This, we have said, is incoherent; why? Because if one holds that truth is correspondence, one cannot intelligibly hold either that it is tested by coherence or that there is any dependable test at all. Consider the first point. Suppose that we construe experience into the most coherent picture possible, remembering that among the elements included will be such secondary qualities as colours, odours, and sounds. Would the mere fact that such elements as these are coherently arranged prove that anything precisely corresponding to them exists 'out there'? I cannot see that it would, even if we knew that the two arrangements had closely corresponding patterns. If on one side you have a series of elements a, b, c . . . , and on the other a series of elements α, β, γ . . . , arranged in patterns that correspond, you have no proof as yet that the *natures* of these elements correspond. It is therefore impossible to argue from a high degree of coherence within experience to its correspondence in the same degree with anything outside. And this difficulty is typical. If you place the nature of truth in one sort of character and its test in something quite different, you are pretty certain, sooner or later, to find the two falling apart. In the end, the only test of truth that is not misleading is the special nature or character that is itself constitutive of truth.

Feeling that this is so, the adherents of correspondence sometimes insist that correspondence shall be its own test. But then the second difficulty arises. If truth does consist in correspondence, no test can be sufficient. For in order to know that experience corresponds to fact, we must be able to get at that fact, unadulterated with idea, and compare the two sides with each other. And we have seen in the last chapter that such fact is not accessible. When we try to lay hold of it, what we find in our hands is a judgment which is obviously not itself the indubitable fact we are seeking, and which must be checked by some fact beyond it. To this process there is no end. And even if we did get at the fact directly, rather than through the veil of our ideas, that would be no less fatal to correspondence. This direct seizure of fact presumably gives us truth, but since that truth no longer consists in correspondence of idea with fact, the main theory has been abandoned. In short, if we can know fact only through the medium of our own ideas, the original forever eludes us; if we can get at the facts directly, we have knowledge whose truth is not correspondence. The theory is forced to choose between scepticism and self-contradiction.

Thus the attempt to combine coherence as the test of truth with correspondence as the nature of truth will not pass muster by its own test. The result is *in*coherence. We believe that an application of the test to other theories of truth would lead to a like result. The argument is: assume coherence as the test, and you will be driven by the incoherence of your alternatives to the conclusion that it is also the nature of truth.

The theory that truth *consists* in coherence must now be developed more specifically. The theory has been widely attacked, and the average reader will not improbably come to it with numerous and dark suspicions. In presenting the theory we shall therefore follow a somewhat unusual procedure. We shall go down the line of these suspicions and objections, trying to deal with them in roughly the order in which they naturally arise, and seeking in our answers to bring the nature and implications of the theory gradually to light.

9. (1) It is objected, first, that the view entails scepticism. What is it that our judgements must cohere with in order to be true? It is a system of knowledge complete and all-inclusive. But obviously that is beyond us—very probably forever beyond us. If to know anything as true, which means simply to know it, requires that we should see its relation to the total of possible knowledge, then we neither do nor can know anything.

The answer lies partly in an admission, partly in an explanation. The admission is that the theory does involve a degree of scepticism regarding our present knowledge and probably all future knowledge. In all likelihood there will never be a proposition of which we can say, 'This that I am asserting, with precisely the meaning I now attach to it, is absolutely true'. Such a conclusion may bring disappointment, but disappointment is not discredit. And in the light of the history of science, this refusal to claim absoluteness for our knowledge appears even as a merit. For the road of history is so thick with discarded certainties as to suggest that any theory which distributes absolute guarantees is touched with charlatanism. Those who would define truth as

correspondence or self-evidence commonly believe that in certain judgements these characters can be found to the full and hence that the
judgements are true absolutely. But it is easy to point to past judgements
which, in the best opinion of the time, satisfied both definitions at
once—judgements for example about the flatness of the earth or the
rising of the sun—which nevertheless turned out false. In the light of
such facts, theories that give patents of absoluteness to any of our
present truths have antecedent probability against them. It may be
answered that if judgements seeming to be true have turned out
false, this does not show that truth has been wrongly defined but only
that men have made a mistake as to whether its defining character was
present. But the answer is obvious. The objection now before us is that,
in contrast with other theories, coherence leads to scepticism. If it is
now admitted that the other theories themselves are so difficult to apply
that one can have no certainty, even in leading cases, whether the
character they define as truth is present or not, then these theories are
sceptical also.

We may reply, secondly, with an explanation, which comes essentially to this, that the coherence theory, like other theories, needs to be
applied with some common sense. While the truth of a judgement does
consist in the last resort in its relations to a completed system, no
sensible person would claim to know these in detail, or deny the judgement *any* truth till he did know them, any more than he would deny
some beauty to a picture because it failed of beauty absolute. The
system we actually work with is always less than *the* whole; at the best
it is the mass of scientific knowledge bearing on the point in question;
on the average it is a cloudy congeries of memories, suggestions and
inferences, ill-organized in the extreme, and yet capable of subconscious
mobilization and use. And for all of us, except in rare moments, the
interest in truth is satisfied by exercise within these limits. Even the
scientist is commonly satisfied if his theory receives the *imprimatur* of
the organized knowledge of his time, and he would think it fantastic
to attack him on the ground that organized knowledge has been known
to change, that it may do so again, and hence that his theory may have
to change with it. This last he would no doubt admit, adding however
that to allow one's pursuit of science, or one's confidence in it, to be
practically affected by this is merely silly. We agree. For all the ordinary
purposes of life, coherence does not mean coherence with some inaccessible absolute, but with the system of present knowledge; and since
this is by no means beyond determining, to describe the theory as
simply sceptical is misleading. In practice it is not sceptical at all; in
theory it upholds the scepticism that is a mainspring of progress. It
justifies our acceptance of beliefs scientifically tested, while providing
a salutary warning that science itself may become a fetish. While sup-

porting the belief in scientific advance, it refuses to believe that this advance has reached the end of the road. It is absolutistic without dogmatism, and relativistic without countenancing despair.

10. (2) This answers by implication another objection to the theory. It is said that a truth once true must be always true, whereas on the coherence theory what *was* true may now be false, and what is now true may become false with expanding knowledge. That which coheres with the knowledge of an earlier time may conflict with the knowledge of a later time. Thus propositions may put on truth or falsity, and take them off again, with changing scientific fashions; which is absurd.

But the objection is baseless. The measure of truth, which, judged by the ultimate standard, belongs to the proposition 'x is y' is quite unalterable, for the coherence theory as for its critics. But as just admitted, we cannot in practice make use of that ultimate standard, and are compelled to fall back on the second best. What the ultimate standard means *in practice* is the system of present knowledge as apprehended by a particular mind. That system changes; hence what coheres with it at one time may not cohere with it at another; thus in practice we shall be justified in accepting at one time what later we must reject. This is all true, but where is the inconsistency? We have neither said nor implied that truth itself changes. What we have said is that while truth as measured by the ultimate standard is unchanging, our knowledge of that truth does change—which is a very different thing. Our system of knowledge fluctuates; it is not now, for example, what it was in the Dark Ages, or even in the middle of the last century; and if we use as our standard this variable measuring-rod we shall naturally get varying results. But these varying results are in our knowledge, or in truth-as-revealed-in-our-knowledge, not in truth objective and complete. Between a truth that is itself invariant and varying degrees of manifestation of this truth, there is no sort of inconsistency. . . .

13. (5) We come now to an objection more frequently made than any we have been considering. Granting that propositions, to be true, must be coherent with each other, may they not be coherent without being true? Are there not many systems of high unity and inclusiveness, which nevertheless are false? We have seen, for example, that there are various systems of geometry each of which seems to be as coherent internally as the others. Since they are mutually inconsistent, not more than one of them can be true, and there are many mathematicians who would say that *none* of them are true; yet if truth lies merely in coherence, are we not compelled to take all of them as true? Again, a novel, or a succession of novels such as Galsworthy's *Forsyte Saga*, may create a special world of characters and events which is at once extremely complex and internally consistent; does that make it the less fictitious?

To say that it does would imply that if we could only dream constantly enough and consistently enough our dreams would literally come true.

(i) This objection, like so many other annihilating criticisms, would have more point if anyone had ever held the theory it demolishes. But if intended to represent the coherence theory as responsibly advocated, it is a gross misunderstanding. That theory does not hold that any and every system is true, no matter how abstract and limited; it holds that one system only is true, namely the system in which everything real and possible is coherently included. How one can find in this the notion that a system would still give truth if, like some arbitrary geometry, it disregarded experience completely, it is not easy to see.

14. (ii) The objection gains point, however, when it goes on to inquire whether all that is actual might not be embraced in more than one system. When a murder is committed, there may be two theories of the crime which do complete and equal justice to all the known facts and yet are inconsistent with each other. Is it not conceivable similarly that there should be two perfect but conflicting systems in which all known and knowable facts should fall into place? If so, our standard would require us to say that both were true; yet since they conflict, this would be absurd. Now we might reply that such a contingency, though possible, is highly improbable. In the case of the murder, every new bit of evidence narrows the range of available hypotheses, and it does not even occur to us that if we knew *all* the relevant facts we might find ourselves at the end with conflicting theories. If such an issue is improbable where the facts are so few, is it not far more improbable where the facts are infinitely many?

Still, this answer seems inadequate, since a theory that leaves it even possible that in the ultimate nature of truth there should be inconsistency ought to be met, we feel, with some decisive disproof. Can it be shown that such an issue is not only improbable, but impossible? I think it can. There are to be two systems, each including all facts known or knowable, but differing in internal structure. Now if the first system is constructed according to plan A, and the second according to plan B, then the possession by the first of plan A is not a fact that is included in the second, and the possession of plan B by the second is not a fact included in the first. The two systems are thus *not,* as they are supposed to be, each inclusive of all the known facts. To put it otherwise, if the systems differ neither in facts nor in structure, they are not two systems but one. If, with the same facts, they are to differ at all, they must differ in structure, but then there will be at least one fact that each of them must omit, namely, the fact that the other possesses the particular structure it does. Thus that all actual and possible facts should be embraced in conflicting systems is unthinkable.

On the other hand, if the objector lowers his claim and says only that the facts *as so far known* may be ordered in different systems, he is saying nothing against our theory. For this certainly does not show that if all the facts were known these rivals would still stand as rivals; it shows only that with the facts now available we should not on our view be justified in making a choice. And this really confirms our view, through bringing it into line with science. Such suspension of judgement is precisely what is enjoined by scientific practice, which holds that so long as two rival hypotheses equally cover the facts, neither is to be preferred to the other, but that as soon as there appears an *instantia crucis* which one hypothesis can assimilate and the other not, we are justified in adopting the first.[3]

15. (iii) Suppose, however, that no crucial instance ever did arise. Suppose (to put an extreme but conceivable case) that we spent from twelve midnight to twelve noon of every day in dreaming, that our dreams were as vivid and orderly as our waking life, and that when we resumed them every night we did so at exactly the point at which we left off the day before. Would there then be any difference between sleep and waking? Would there be any sense in saying that one world was real and the other unreal, that in the one our perceptions and beliefs were true and in the other delusions merely? I think not. And our inability to make any choice in such a conjuncture confirms our theory. The argument runs: if truth did lie in coherence, then, confronted with two worlds equally coherent, we should be unable to select one as truer than the other; on reflection we can see that such inability is just what we should find; hence the equation of truth with coherence is so far verified.

16. (iv) It is further verified by our way of choosing between systems which in the above sense are *not* equal. There are various cases. Consider *(a)* how we recognize dreams or delusions for what they are. When we are suddenly roused from a vivid dream, we may be momentarily dazed, not knowing the dream from the actuality. How do we establish which is which? Mere vividness does not decide the matter; the dream may be of nightmare intensity while the perception of our familiar surroundings may be comparatively dim. The deciding factor in the battle is what may be called the mass and integration of the household troops. The bureau and windows of our familiar bedroom

---

[3] It may be said that the truth is not established until *all* rivals have been eliminated. But this is not the view on which the natural sciences actually proceed. Of course in formal logic an argument from the affirmation of the consequent is fallacious, and when this is carried over into science it is often said to provide verification without proof; the proof is attained only when it is shown that from no other antecedent could these consequences have sprung. But it will be evident that in the ordinary work of science proof of this kind is seldom if ever practicable; one cannot be sure that *all possible* alternatives have been excluded. 'The character of relativity and non-finality, which attaches to mere verification and causes it to be called the fallacy of the consequent, is really inevitable in the pursuit of truth.'—Bosanquet, *Implication and Lin. Inf.*, 102.

and the sound of a familiar voice throw out innumerable lines of connection that bring our everyday world around us again in irresistible
volume. Against the great bulk of this world, and without any lodgement
in it, the figures of our dream appear unsubstantial and fugitive, quickly
dissolving for want of support; and it is just the recognition that what we
have been experiencing will not fit into our common-sense world that
we mean when we say we wake from dream. The power to measure
such fancies and phantasms against the ordered mass of experience is
the logical meaning of sanity; its disappearance is insanity. There may
be organic differences between the man who thinks himself Napoleon,
the man who is sure he has committed the unpardonable sin, and the
man who is persuaded that there is a universal conspiracy to keep him
down; but intellectually they are alike; there are certain beliefs which
resist appraisal by the mass of their general experience, and stand in
the midst of it like solid capsules impervious to outer influences. In
these cases that is what insanity means. . . .

22. (9) Coherence means more than consistency. It means not only
that the various constituents entering into the system of truth are compatible with each other, but also that they necessitate each other. The
system assumed is a system ideally perfect, for nothing less than this
would satisfy intelligence as stable beyond rectification. In such a
system there would be no loose ends. Difference anywhere would be
reflected in difference everywhere.

Now it has been held that this ideal is merely a cloud-castle, that
it can never be made to embrace the facts of our actual disorderly world.
There are many who would freely admit that nothing exists or occurs
out of relation to *some* other things, but would regard the view that
everything is related by necessity to *everything* else as demonstrably
false. If the fact is that Bishop Stubbs died in his bed, this surely might
be false without everything else being false that is now accepted as true.

23. Now it is obvious that we cannot show *in detail* that a difference
anywhere in the system of truth must be reflected everywhere; we do
not know enough, nor is it likely we ever shall. But we can do something
else that is as near to this as can be reasonably asked. We can show that
in the system of truth, *so far as reflected in our knowledge,* such inter-
connection holds, and that the denial of an apparently isolated judgement
does in fact have implications for every other. The argument is as
follows: When I say that Bishop Stubbs died in his bed, or indeed when
I say anything, I always do so on evidence. This evidence may be hard
or easy to bring to light, but it is there invariably; I never simply
discharge judgements into the air with no ground or warrant at all.
And by the rules of hypothetical argument, to admit the falsity of a
judgement is to throw doubt upon its ground. Indeed it is to do more.

It is to throw doubt, if I am consistent, upon *all* evidence of this kind and degree. Now the evidence on which it is believed that Bishop Stubbs died a natural death is of the kind and degree that would be accepted without hesitation by any historian or scientist. It is the sort of evidence on which science and history generally rest. Hence if I deny this proposition, and thus call in question the value of this sort of evidence, I must in consistency call in question most science and history also. And that would shatter my world of knowledge. Thus the truth about Bishop Stubbs is anything but isolated. However unimportant practically, it is so entangled with my system of beliefs that its denial would send repercussions throughout the whole.[4]

To some this reply may seem an *ignoratio elenchi*. It is one thing, they may say, to show that the abandonment of a *belief* would logically compel the abandonment of other beliefs; it is another thing to show that in the real world about which these beliefs are held, a change in one fact or event would necessitate that all others be different. Suppose I climb the hill behind my farm house in Vermont and look across at Mount Washington. I am wearing a felt hat at the time. Is it sensible or quite sane to argue that if I had worn a straw hat instead, that fact would have made a difference to Mount Washington?

I not only believe it would, but that the argument for this conclusion is strong almost to demonstration. In outline it is as follows: my putting on this particular hat had causes, which lay in part in the workings of my brain; these workings also had causes, which lay in part in the workings of other bodily organs; these in turn depended upon countless physical factors in the way of food, air, light, and temperature, every one of which had its own conditions. It is plain that before we took many steps in this retreat, we should find ourselves involved in millions of conditions, and that if we were able *per impossibile* to traverse all the diverging branches, there would probably be no region of the universe that would remain unpenetrated. Now if we reject, as I suppose we must, the plurality of causes, and hold that the causal relation is reciprocating, then a denial of the causal consequent will require a denial of its antecedent. A different event, then, from that on which these various lines converge would require differences throughout the range of the countless conditions themselves. Very well; let us assume such a different event to have occurred—my wearing a straw hat instead of a felt one—and having ascended the causal lines, let us now descend them. If the antecedents of the present event were scattered throughout the universe, and we suppose them altered throughout, is there any reason whatever to suppose that the present state of the world would be as we find it? The answer is obvious. The world would

4 Contrast Russell, *Philosophical Essays,* on 'The Monistic Theory of Truth' with Bradley, *Essays on Truth,* etc., 212 ff.

not only be different, but so extensively different that we could point neither to Mount Washington nor to anything else and say that it would be exempt from change.

This is the argument in outline. It offers no proof that all events are causally related; still less does it attempt to show that behind such a causal unity there is to be found the unity of logical necessity. Evidence for these points would very much strengthen it. But it is best to leave the statement of such evidence till we consider internal relations, where the present outline will be developed in detail. Meanwhile enough has been said to turn the edge of the objection we have been examining. That objection was that on the coherence theory, a difference anywhere in the system should be reflected everywhere else, whereas a particular fact or event might have been different without entailing any extensive change. We have seen that this contention does not hold.

24. (10) Still the view that everything in the universe is relevant to everything else has been thought by many to be a millstone round the neck of coherence. They say that 'if a judgement cannot be true without reference to all the others, and this is true of all judgements, truth will be a shifting meaningless vortex with no fixed standards anywhere'.[5] The very life of knowledge, they continue, consists in holding to the relevant and excluding the irrelevant; yet we are told that everything is to be relevant and nothing whatever irrelevant. How could thought or discussion go on under such conditions? I can no longer accept what any moralist or economist or literary critic says if I discover that he has omitted from his account 'the sweet influence of the Pleiades'. If a man remarks that it is a fine day, it will be in point to reply, 'Quite so, since umbellifers have imbricated petals', or anything else that may come into my head. What, if possible, is worse is that science will now be indistinguishable from prejudice. Scientific men insist on special connections; they insist, for example, that tuberculosis is caused by a bacillus. But this must now be taken as prejudice, since they have omitted the equally essential fact that Miltiades commanded at Marathon. Now surely all this is nonsense. If everything is to be equally relevant, we shall be asked, how can you argue for your own theory? How can you think at all? Does not thought in its very essence involve the selection of grounds and consequences?

25. One way to meet this onslaught would be to admit that if coherence is true, science and traditional logic are *not* ultimately true, and to ask why they should be taken as arbiters in metaphysical questions. But such a reply would need much explaining, and less provocative replies are at hand. (i) For one thing, the objection contains a bad inference. To say that all things are relevant does not entail that they are all *equally* relevant. When I see an apple fall, I may reflect that if

5 L. A. Reid, *Knowledge and Truth*, 34.

it had been a little larger, a widespread difference would be implied
in the nature of things; but am I therefore committed to saying that no
greater difference would be involved if the law of gravitation itself were
radically different? I do not see that I am. Tuberculosis in a given
patient would not be quite what it is if bacilli and the outer temperature
did not co-operate to the result. Both factors are therefore relevant.
But that does not imply that they contribute equally to causing the
result or explaining it. With the outer temperature replaced by another,
ten degrees lower, we have every reason to think the disease would still
be there, though somewhat different in its complexion; with the bacilli
absent, the disease would not be there at all. Whether our criterion of
relevance is making a difference in the result, or throwing light on it,
the conclusion would appear the same. Admission of relevance is not
the admission of equal relevance.

26. (ii) Nor is there anything here with which scientific theory
need conflict. Probably most scientists would agree with Mill that the
cause of an event is not some single condition, but rather the sum of
the conditions. They would probably also agree with him that to follow
out these conditions would involve, in the long run, the whole state of
the universe. They would therefore admit that in selecting the cause
of an event, they were naming *a* cause rather than *the* cause. Countless
factors are relevant, but this does not prevent their selecting certain
ones, or a certain one, as more relevant than others. It must be admitted
that comparative relevance is often determined for them by considerations other than logical. If *the* cause is identified, as it commonly is,
with the efficient or precipitating cause, it is not seldom because this
is most important in practically controlling the event, or because it is
the most striking of the immediate and constant precursors, or because
it is the only exclusive one. But the selection is not wholly extra-logical,
often as this has been held. If the presence of bacilli is taken as *the* cause
of tuberculosis, it is partly because this is more relevant in the logical as
well as causal sense, because it explains the disease more fully, because
it throws more light on its nature than other concomitant factors.
Reflective science, like coherence, would admit a context of relevance
that is indefinitely extensive. But if coherence does not consider that
this prohibits degrees of relevance, neither does science. There is no
necessary conflict at all. . . .

SEVENTEEN

Pragmatism's Conception of Truth

WILLIAM JAMES (1842-1910)

From *Pragmatism**

Truth, as any dictionary will tell you, is a property of certain of our ideas. It means their 'agreement,' as falsity means their disagreement, with 'reality.' Pragmatists and intellectualists both accept this definition as a matter of course. They begin to quarrel only after the question is raised as to what may precisely be meant by the term 'agreement,' and what by the term 'reality,' when reality is taken as something for our ideas to agree with.

In answering these questions the pragmatists are more analytic and painstaking, the intellectualists more offhand and irreflective. The popular notion is that a true idea must copy its reality. Like other popular views, this one follows the analogy of the most usual experience. Our true ideas of sensible things do indeed copy them. Shut your eyes and think of yonder clock on the wall, and you get just such a true picture or copy of its dial. But your idea of its 'works' (unless you are a clockmaker) is much less of a copy, yet it passes muster, for it in no way clashes with the reality. Even though it should shrink to the mere word 'works,' that word still serves you truly; and when you speak of the 'time-keeping function' of the clock, or of its spring's 'elasticity,' it is hard to see exactly what your ideas can copy.

You perceive that there is a problem here. Where our ideas cannot copy definitely their object, what does agreement with that object mean? Some idealists seem to say that they are true whenever they are what God means that we ought to think about that object. Others hold the copy-view all through, and speak as if our ideas possessed truth just in proportion as they approach to being copies of the Absolute's eternal way of thinking.

These views, you see, invite pragmatistic discussion. But the great assumption of the intellectualists is that truth means essentially an inert static relation. When you've got your true idea of anything, there's an end of the matter. You're in possession; you *know*; you have fulfilled your thinking destiny. You are where you ought to be mentally; you have

* From *Pragmatism* by William James.

obeyed your categorical imperative; and nothing more need follow on that climax of your rational destiny. Epistemologically you are in stable equilibrium.

Pragmatism, on the other hand, asks its usual question. "Grant an idea or belief to be true," it says, "what concrete difference will its being true make in any one's actual life? How will the truth be realized? What experiences will be different from those which would obtain if the belief were false? What, in short, is the truth's cash-value in experiential terms?"

The moment pragmatism asks this question, it sees the answer: *True ideas are those that we can assimilate, validate, corroborate and verify. False ideas are those that we can not.* That is the practical difference it makes to us to have true ideas; that, therefore, is the meaning of truth, for it is all that truth is known-as.

This thesis is what I have to defend. The truth of an idea is not a stagnant property inherent in it. Truth *happens* to an idea. It *becomes* true, is *made* true by events. Its verity *is* in fact an event, a process: the process namely of its verifying itself, its veri-*fication*. Its validity is the process of its valid-*ation*.

But what do the words verification and validation themselves pragmatically mean? They again signify certain practical consequences of the verified and validated idea. It is hard to find any one phrase that characterizes these consequences better than the ordinary agreement-formula—just such consequences being what we have in mind whenever we say that our ideas 'agree' with reality. They lead us, namely, through the acts and other ideas which they instigate, into or up to, or towards, other parts of experience with which we feel all the while—such feeling being among our potentialities—that the original ideas remain in agreement. The connexions and transitions come to us from point to point as being progressive, harmonious, satisfactory. This function of agreeable leading is what we mean by an idea's verification. Such an account is vague and it sounds at first quite trivial, but it has results which it will take the rest of my hour to explain.

Let me begin by reminding you of the fact that the possession of true thoughts means everywhere the possession of invaluable instruments of action; and that our duty to gain truth, so far from being a blank command from out of the blue, or a 'stunt' self-imposed by our intellect, can account for itself by excellent practical reasons.

The importance to human life of having true beliefs about matters of fact is a thing too notorious. We live in a world of realities that can be infinitely useful or infinitely harmful. Ideas that tell us which of them to expect count as the true ideas in all this primary sphere of verification, and the pursuit of such ideas is a primary human duty. The possession of truth, so far from being here an end in itself, is only a preliminary means towards other vital satisfactions. If I am lost in the woods and starved, and find what looks like a cow-path, it is of the utmost importance that I should think of a human habitation at the end of it, for if I do so and follow it, I save myself. The true thought is useful here because the house which is its object is useful. The practical value of true ideas is thus primarily derived from the practical importance of their objects to us. Their objects are, indeed, not important at all times. I may on another occasion have no use for the house; and then my idea of it, however verifiable, will be practically irrelevant, and had better remain latent. Yet since almost any object may some day become temporarily important, the advantage of having a general stock of *extra* truths, of ideas that shall be true of merely possible situations, is obvious. We store such extra truths away in our memories, and with the overflow we fill our books of reference. Whenever such an extra truth becomes practically relevant to one of our emergencies, it passes from cold-storage to do work in the world and our belief in it grows active. You can say of it then either that 'it is useful because it is true' or that 'it is true because it is useful.' Both these phrases mean exactly the same thing, namely that here is an idea that gets fulfilled and can be verified. True is the name for whatever idea starts the verification-process, useful is the name for its completed function in experience. True ideas would never have been singled out as such, would never have acquired a class-name, least of all a name suggesting value, unless they had been useful from the outset in this way.

From this simple cue pragmatism gets her general notion of truth as something essentially bound up with the way in which one moment in our experience may lead us towards other moments which it will be worth while to have been led to. Primarily, and on the common-sense level, the truth of a state of mind means this function of *a leading that is worth while.* When a moment in our experience, of any kind whatever, inspires us with a thought that is true, that means that sooner or later we dip by that thought's guidance into the particulars of experience again and make advantageous connexion with them. This is a vague enough statement, but I beg you to retain it, for it is essential.

Our experience meanwhile is all shot through with regularities. One bit of it can warn us to get ready for another bit, can 'intend' or be 'significant of' that remoter object. The object's advent is the significance's verification. Truth, in these cases, meaning nothing but eventual verification, is manifestly incompatible with waywardness on our part. Woe to him whose beliefs play fast and loose with the order which realities follow in his experience; they will lead him nowhere or else make false connexions.

By 'realities' or 'objects' here, we mean either things of common sense, sensibly present, or else common-sense relations, such as dates, places, distances, kinds, activities. Following our mental image of a house along the cow-path, we actually come to see the house; we get the image's full verification. *Such simply and fully verified leadings are certainly the originals and prototypes of the truth-process.* Experience offers indeed other forms of truth-process, but they are all conceivable as being primary verifications arrested, multiplied or substituted one for another.

Take, for instance, yonder object on the wall. You and I consider it to be a 'clock,' altho no one of us has seen the hidden works that make it one. We let our notion pass for true without attempting to verify. If truths mean verification-process essentially, ought we then to call such unverified truths as this abortive? No, for they form the overwhelmingly large number of the truths we live by. Indirect as well as direct verifications pass muster. Where circumstantial evidence is sufficient, we can go without eye-witnessing. Just as we here assume Japan to exist without ever having been there, because it *works* to do so, everything we know conspiring with the belief, and nothing interfering, so we assume that thing to be a clock. We *use* it as a clock, regulating the length of our lecture by it. The verification of the assumption here means its leading to no frustration or contradiction. Verif*iability* of wheels and weights and pendulum is as good as verification. For one truth-process completed there are a million in our lives that function in this state of nascency. They turn us *towards* direct verification; lead us into the *surroundings* of the objects they envisage; and then, if everything runs on harmoniously, we are so sure that verification is possible that we omit it, and are usually justified by all that happens.

Truth lives, in fact, for the most part on a credit system. Our thoughts and beliefs 'pass,' so long as nothing challenges them, just as bank-notes pass so long as nobody refuses them. But this all points to direct face-to-face verifications somewhere, without which the fabric of truth collapses like a financial system with no cash-basis whatever. You accept my verification of one thing, I yours of another. We trade on each other's truth. But beliefs verified concretely by *somebody* are the posts of the whole superstructure.

Another great reason—beside economy of time—for waiving complete verification in the usual business of life is that all things exist in kinds and not singly. Our world is found once for all to have that peculiarity. So that when we have once directly verified our ideas about one specimen of a kind, we consider ourselves free to apply them to other specimens without verification. A mind that habitually discerns the kind of thing before it, and acts by the law of the kind immediately, without pausing to verify, will be a 'true' mind in ninety-nine out of a hundred emergencies, proved so by its conduct fitting everything it meets, and getting no refutation.

Indirectly or only potentially verifying processes may thus be true as well as full verification-processes. They work as true processes would work, give us the same advantages, and claim our recognition for the same reasons. All this on the common-sense level of matters of fact, which we are alone considering.

But matters of fact are not our only stock in trade. *Relations among purely mental ideas* form another sphere where true and false beliefs obtain, and here the beliefs are absolute, or unconditional. When they are true they bear the name either of definitions or of principles. It is either a principle or a definition that 1 and 1 make 2, that 2 and 1 make 3, and so on; that white differs less from gray than it does from black; that when the cause begins to act the effect also commences. Such propositions hold of all possible 'ones,' of all conceivable 'whites' and 'grays' and 'causes.' The objects here are mental objects. Their relations are perceptually obvious at a glance, and no sense-verification is necessary. Moreover, once true, always true, of those same mental objects. Truth here has an 'eternal' character. If you can find a concrete thing anywhere that is 'one' or 'white' or 'gray' or an 'effect,' then your principles will everlastingly apply to it. It is but a case of ascertaining the kind, and then applying the law of its kind to the particular object. You are sure to get truth if you can but name the kind rightly, for your mental relations hold good of everything of that kind without exception. If you then, nevertheless, failed to get truth concretely, you would say that you had classed your real objects wrongly.

In this realm of mental relations, truth again is an affair of leading. We relate one abstract idea with another, framing in the end great systems of logical and mathematical truth, under the respective terms of which the sensible facts of experience eventually arrange themselves, so that our eternal truths hold good of realities also. This marriage of fact and theory is endlessly fertile. What we say is here already true in advance of special verification, *if we have subsumed our objects rightly.* Our ready-made ideal framework for all sorts of possible objects follows from the very structure of our thinking. We can no more play fast and loose with these abstract relations than we can do so with our sense-experiences. They coerce us; we must treat them consistently, whether or not we like the results. The rules of addition apply to our debts as rigorously as to our assets. The hundredth decimal of π, the ratio of the circumference to its diameter, is predetermined ideally now, tho no one may have computed it. If we should ever need the figure in our dealings with an actual circle we should need to have it given rightly, calculated by the usual rules; for it is the same kind of truth that those rules elsewhere calculate.

Between the coercions of the sensible order and those of the ideal order, our mind is thus wedged tightly. Our ideas must agree with realities, be such realities concrete or abstract, be they facts or be they principles, under penalty of endless inconsistency and frustration.

There is room for metaphysics

So far, intellectualists can raise no protest. They can only say that we have barely touched the skin of the matter.

Realities mean, then, either concrete facts, or abstract kinds of thing and relations perceived intuitively between them. They furthermore and thirdly mean, as things that new ideas of ours must no less take account of, the whole body of other truths already in our possession. But what now does 'agreement' with such threefold realities mean?—to use again the definition that is current.

Here it is that pragmatism and intellectualism begin to part company. Primarily, no doubt, to agree means to copy, but we saw that the mere word 'clock' would do instead of a mental picture of its works, and that of many realities our ideas can only be symbols and not copies. 'Past time,' 'power,' 'spontaneity,'—how can our mind copy such realities?

To 'agree' in the widest sense with a reality *can only mean to be guided either straight up to it or into its surroundings, or to be put into such working touch with it as to handle either it or something connected with it better than if we disagreed.* Better either intellectually or practically! And often agreement will only mean the negative fact that nothing contradictory from the quarter of that reality comes to interfere with the way in which our ideas guide us elsewhere. To copy a reality is, indeed, one very important way of agreeing with it, but it is far from being essential. The essential thing is the process of being guided. Any idea that helps us to *deal, whether* practically or intellectually, with either the reality or its belongings, that doesn't entangle our progress in frustrations, that *fits,* in fact, and adapts our life to the reality's whole setting, will agree sufficiently to meet the requirement. It will hold true of that reality.

Thus, *names* are just as 'true' or 'false' as definite mental pictures are. They set up similar verification-processes, and lead to fully equivalent practical results.

All human thinking gets discursified; we exchange ideas; we lend and borrow verifications, get them from one another by means of social intercourse. All truth thus gets verbally built out, stored up, and made available for every one. Hence, we must *talk* consistently just as we must *think* consistently: for both in talk and thought we deal with kinds. Names are arbitrary, but once understood they must be kept to. We mustn't now call Abel 'Cain' or Cain 'Abel.' If we do, we ungear ourselves from the whole book of Genesis, and from all its connexions with the universe of speech and fact down to the present time. We throw ourselves out of whatever truth that entire system of speech and fact may embody.

The overwhelming majority of our true ideas admit of no direct or face-to-face verification—those of past history, for example, as of Cain and Abel. The stream of time can be remounted only verbally, or verified indirectly by the present prolongations or effects of what the past harbored. Yet if they agree with these verbalities and effects, we can know that our ideas of the past are true. *As true as past time itself was,* so true was Julius Caesar, so true were antediluvian monsters, all in their proper dates and settings. That past time itself was, is guaranteed by its coherence with everything that's present. True as the present *is,* the past *was* also.

Agreement thus turns out to be essentially an affair of leading—leading that is useful because it is into quarters that contain objects that are important. True ideas lead us into useful verbal and conceptual quarters as well as directly up to useful sensible termini. They lead to consistency, stability and flowing human intercourse. They lead away from excentricity and isolation, from foiled and barren thinking. The untrammelled flowing of the leading-process, its general freedom from clash and contradiction, passes for its indirect verification; but all roads lead to Rome, and in the end and eventually, all true processes must lead to the face of directly verifying sensible experiences *somewhere,* which somebody's ideas have copied.

Such is the large loose way in which the pragmatist interprets the word agreement. He treats it altogether practically. He lets it cover any process of conduction from a present idea to a future terminus, provided only it run prosperously. It is only thus that 'scientific' ideas, flying as they do beyond common sense, can be said to agree with their realities. It is, as I have already said, *as if* reality were made of ether, atoms or electrons, but we mustn't think so literally. The term 'energy' doesn't even pretend to stand for anything 'objective.' It is only a way of measuring the surface of phenomena so as to string their changes on a simple formula.

Yet in the choice of these man-made formulas we can not be capricious with impunity any more than we can be capricious on the common-sense practical level. We must find a theory that will *work;* and that means something extremely difficult; for our theory must mediate between all previous truths and certain new experiences. It must derange common sense and previous belief as little as possible, and it must lead to some sensible terminus or other that can be verified exactly. To 'work' means both these things; and the squeeze is so tight that there is little loose play for any hypothesis. Our theories are wedged and controlled as nothing else is. Yet sometimes alternative theoretic formulas are equally compatible with all the truths we know, and then we choose between them for subjective reasons. We choose the kind of theory to which we are already partial; we follow 'elegance' or 'economy.' Clerk-Maxwell somewhere says it would be 'poor scientific taste' to choose the more complicated of two equally well-evidenced conceptions; and you will all agree with him. Truth in science is what gives us the maximum possible sum of satisfactions, taste included, but consistency both with previous truth and with novel fact is always the most imperious claimant.

EIGHTEEN

Truth[1]*

P. F. STRAWSON (1919-   )

In the following discussion, I confine myself to the question of the truth of empirical statements. My positive thesis is an elaboration of what was said, a long time ago, by F. P. Ramsey.[2] My negative purpose is the criticism of a current misconception—the Semantic or Meta-linguistic Theory of Truth—which seems to me to repeat, in a new way, some old mistakes. In so far as this theory is simply a contribution to the construction of artificial languages, and is not intended to be regarded as relevant to the use of actual languages, I am not concerned with it. But I think the theory has been claimed by some, and it has certainly been thought by many, to throw light on the actual use of the word 'true'; or (which I take to be the same claim) on the philosophical problem of truth. I think it *does* throw some light; but I think it is also seriously misleading. Nothing that follows, however, is to be taken as implying that the word 'true' is *never* used in the way described by the semantic theory. It is certainly so used for some technical purposes, and may sometimes be so used for non-technical purposes as well; though I know of no such non-technical purposes.

I

In recent discussions of truth, one or both of two theses are commonly maintained. These are:

First, any sentence beginning 'It is true that . . .' does not change its assertive meaning when the phrase 'It is true that' is omitted. More generally, to say that an assertion is true is not to make any further assertion at all; it is to make the same assertion. This I shall call Thesis 1.

Second, to say that a statement is true is to make a statement about a sentence of a given language, viz., the language in which the first statement was made. It is (in other and more technical terms) to make a statement in a meta-language ascribing the semantic property of truth (or the semantic predicate 'true') to a sentence in an object-language. The object-

---

1 [An extended and in some ways modified version of the views here maintained is to be found in the *Proceedings of the Aristotelian Society,* Supplementary Volume, 1950.]

* From "Truth" by P. F. Strawson, *Analysis,* Vol. 9 (1948-49), pp. 83-97. Reprinted by permission of the author and of the editor and publishers of *Analysis.*

2 Ramsey, *Foundations of Mathematics,* pp. 142-143.

sentence concerned should strictly be written in inverted commas to make it clear that we are talking *about the sentence;* and the phrase 'is true' should strictly be followed by some such phrase as 'in L', where 'L' designates the object-language concerned. This I shall call Thesis 2.

Of these two theses, the first is true, but inadequate; the second is false, but important. The first thesis is right in what it asserts, and wrong in what it suggests. The second thesis is wrong in what it asserts, but right in what it implies. The first thesis is right in asserting that to say that a statement is true is not to make a further statement; but wrong in suggesting that to say that a statement is true is not to do something different from, or additional to, just making the statement. The second thesis is right in implying that to say that a statement is true is to do something different from just making the statement; but wrong in asserting that this 'something different' consists in making a further statement, viz. a statement about a sentence.

Although both theses are sometimes maintained by the same philosopher, it is easy to see that they cannot both be correct. For if it is true that to say (1) "Moths fly by night" is to make the same assertion as to say (2) "It is true that moths fly by night", then it is false that to say (2) is to say anything about the English sentence "Moths fly by night"; i.e. false that (2) ought strictly to be written " 'Moths fly by night' is true in English". If to say (2) is to make the same assertion as to say (1), then to say (2) cannot be to say anything about an English sentence; for to say (1) is not to say anything about an English sentence, but is to say something about moths.

Independently of this, one sees how misleading it is to say that the phrase '. . . is true' is used to talk *about sentences,* by comparing it with other phrases which certainly are used to talk about sentences (or words, or phrases). For example, someone says, in French, "Il pleuve"; and someone else corrects him, saying: " 'Il pleuve' is *incorrect* French. 'Il pleut' is the right way of saying it". Or, criticising the style of a passage, someone says: "The sentence '. . . .' is *badly expressed."* Similarly, one may ask what a sentence *means,* or say that a sentence is *ungrammatical, misspelt, a poor translation.* In all these cases, it is natural to say that one is talking *about a sentence.* If any statement of this kind were correctly translated into any language at all, the sentence which was being discussed would re-appear, quoted and untranslated, in the translation of the statement as a whole. Otherwise the translation would be incorrect. But it is perfectly obvious that a correct translation of any statement containing the phrase 'is true' (used as it is ordinarily used) never contains a quoted and untranslated sentence to which the phrase 'is true' was *applied* in the original sentence. The phrase 'is true' is not *applied* to sentences; for it is not *applied* to anything.

Truth is not a property of symbols; for it is not a property.

II

The habit of calling truth a 'semantic' concept ('true' a 'semantical predicate') does not lessen the confusion involved in saying that 'true' is a predicate of sentences; but it helps to indicate a possible source of the confusion. I shall digress briefly to explore this source. For light on the use of the word 'semantic' I quote the following from Carnap's 'Introduction to Semantics' (p. 22):

> "By a *semantical system* we understand a system of rules, formulated in a meta-language and referring to an object-language, of such a kind that the rules determine a *truth-condition* for every sentence of the object-language. . . . To formulate it in another way: the rules determine the *meaning* or *sense* of the sentences."

It will be noticed that the expressions 'truth-condition' and 'meaning' are used synonymously. And this suggests that even if there is no use of the phrase 'is true' in which that phrase is correctly applied to (used to talk about) sentences, there is, or might be, a use of the phrase 'is true if and only if', in which *this* phrase is correctly applied to (used to talk about) sentences; a use, namely, in which this phrase would be synonymous with the phrase 'means that'; which certainly *is* used to talk about sentences. Suppose, for example, that we wish to give information about the meaning of the sentence "The monarch is deceased". We can do this by making the following meta-statement:

(i) "The monarch is deceased" means that the king is dead. Here we put the sentence "The monarch is deceased" in inverted commas to indicate that we are talking about this sentence. We are making a meta-statement. And the meta-statement is contingent, for it is a contingent matter that the sentence in question has this meaning in English, or, indeed, that it has any meaning at all. To be quite strict, we perhaps ought to write it:

(ia) "The monarch is deceased" in English means that the king is dead.

If we were to translate this meta-statement into another language, none of the expressions occurring in it would remain unchanged except the quoted sentence "The monarch is deceased". That would remain unchanged; otherwise the translation would be incorrect. Now the suggestion is that we might, without unintelligibility, give the same information in exactly the same way, except that we should replace the phrase 'means that' with the phrase 'is true if and only if' obtaining the contingent meta-statement:

(ii) "The monarch is deceased" is true if and only if the king is dead
or, more strictly:

(iia) "The monarch is deceased" is true in English if and only if the king is dead.

This seems to be an intelligible procedure. All that I have said of statements (i) and (ia) will apply to statements (ii) and (iia); we shall be using the phrase 'is true if and only', in a contingent statement, to talk about a sentence. Now consider a degenerate case of such meta-statements: the case exemplified in the sentences:

(iii) "The monarch is deceased" means (in English) that the monarch is deceased.

(iv) "The monarch is deceased" is true (in English) if and only if the monarch is deceased.

It is difficult, and, perhaps, for the present purpose, not very important, to decide what status to assign to such sentences as these. Considerations which might tempt us to describe them firmly as true, contingent meta-statements are the following:

(a) Although they are of no use for telling us what the quoted sentence means, they do give us some information about it. They do at any rate indicate that the quoted sentence has some meaning in English.[3] And this is a contingent matter.

(b) These statements could be obtained from the non-degenerate cases by a quite legitimate process of translation, inference and retranslation. (Or, more simply, their correct translation into, say, French would undoubtedly yield a contingent meta-statement).

(c) It is a contingent matter that any sentence means what it does mean, expresses the proposition it does express.[4]

Although these considerations are decisive against calling (iii) and (iv) 'logically necessary',[5] they are very inadequate grounds for calling them, without qualification, 'true and contingent'. For what contingent matter do they state? If we answer, taking the hint from (a), that they state merely that the quoted sentence has some meaning in English, then their form (the use of the expression 'means that') is utterly misleading. If we demand what contingent matter they state, which falls under the

---

[3] One can imagine another use for statements (iii) and (iv); e.g. if the object-language were written, and the meta-language spoken, English.

[4] Cf. Lewy, "Truth and Significance," *Analysis,* Vol. 9, p. 242.

[5] We might be tempted to call (iii) and (iv) "necessary", because it seems self-contradictory to say:

(iiia) "The monarch is deceased" does not mean in English that the monarch is deceased.

But this would be a mistake. To say that a sentence both has some meaning or other and has no meaning at all would be to say something self-contradictory. To say that a sentence both has and has not some particular, specified meaning would be to say something self-contradictory. But (iiia) does neither of these things. The form of (iii) is appropriate to assigning, and that of (iiia) to withholding, some specific meaning. But since (iii) does not assign, (iiia) does not withhold, any specific meaning. (iiia) is not a self-contradictory, nor a false, contingent, statement; but a pseudo-statement.

head of (c), no answer is possible. One cannot *state* what a sentence means without the help of another sentence.

For these reasons, I propose to continue to refer to statements (or pseudo-statements) like (iii) and (iv) not as necessary, nor as contingent, but simply as 'degenerate cases' of contingent meta-statements of the type of (i) and (ii). The point is not in itself important; though it is important that no confusion should arise from it.

The next step is to notice the deceptive similarity of the use of the phrase 'if and only if' in this type of contingent meta-statement to its use in expressions which are not contingent statements, but necessary or defining formulae. An example of such a formula would be:

The monarch is deceased if and only if the king is dead.

Here the phrase 'is true' does not occur; and no part of this expression is in inverted commas. The formula itself does not give us information about the meaning of the sentence "The monarch is deceased", though the statement that it *was* a necessary formula *would* give us such information. Now the similarity of the use of the phrase 'if and only if' in these necessary formulae to its use as *part* of the phrase 'is true if and only if' in contingent meta-statements, may have constituted a strong temptation to split the degenerate cases of such meta-statements down the middle, and to regard what follows the phrase 'if and only if' as the definiens of what precedes it, i.e. of the phrase "the sentence '. . . .' is true (in L)"; to regard, for example, the whole expression (iii)

"The monarch is deceased" is true if and only if the monarch is deceased

as a specification or consequence or part[6] of a general definition of ". . . . is true" (or of ". . . is true in L"). And this we in fact find; i.e. we find it said that a satisfactory general definition of truth must have as its consequences such expressions as the following:[7]

(v) "To-day is Monday" is true if and only if to-day is Monday.
(vi) "London is a City" is true if and only if London is a City.

Now we have seen that such statements as (v) and (vi) are degenerate cases of those contingent meta-statements of the type of (ii), which make use of the phrase *'is true if and only if'* as a synonym for *'means that'*. It is only *as a part of the former phrase* that the expression *'is true'* is used, in such

[6] E.g. Tarski, in *The Semantic Conception of Truth,* 'Philosophy and Phenomenological Research', Vol. 4, 1943-44, p. 344, says:
"Every equivalence of the form (T) [(T) X is true if and only if p] obtained by replacing 'p' by a particular sentence and 'X' by a name of this sentence, may be considered a partial definition of truth, which explains wherein the truth of this one individual sentence consists. The general definition has to be, in a certain sense, a logical conjunction of all these partial definitions."
[7] Cf. M. Black, expounding and criticising Tarski, *Analysis,* Vol. 9, pp. 245-260.

statements, to talk about sentences. To read the degenerate cases, then, as specification, or parts, of some ideal defining formula for the phrase 'is true' is to separate the phrase from the context which alone confers this meta-linguistic use upon it, and to regard the result as a model for the general use of 'is true'. It is to be committed to the mistake of supposing that the phrase 'is true' is normally (or strictly) used as a meta-linguistic predicate. Thus misinterpreted, as defining formulae, such expressions as (v) are both fascinating and misleading. They mislead because, as we have seen, they crystallise the false Thesis 2. They fascinate because they seem to point to the true Thesis 1; for part of the expression to be defined (namely, the combination of quotation-marks and the phrase 'is true') *disappears* in the definiens without being replaced by anything else. (How odd it is, incidentally, to call this definition-by-disappearance 'definition'!). In this way, the view that 'true' is assertively redundant is represented as somehow combined with, and dependent upon, the view that 'true' is a meta-linguistic predicate of sentences. We may express, then, the main contention of the semantic theory as follows: to say that a statement is true is not to say something further *about the subject-matter* of the statement, but is to say the same thing about the subject-matter of the statement, *by means of a further statement, namely a statement about a sentence.* Now I said that Thesis 1 is true. A fortiori, a modification of Thesis 1 is true, which I shall call Thesis 1A, and which runs as follows:

To say that a statement is true is not to say something further about the subject-matter of the statement, but, in so far as it is to say anything about that subject-matter, is to say the same thing about it.

Now Thesis 1A, but not Thesis 1, is compatible with Thesis 2. The semantic theory consists in the joint assertion of 1A and 2. I suggest that the semantic theory borrows a lot of its plausibility from the truth of 1A. We swallow 2 for the sake of 1A. I now wish to show that the unmodified thesis 1 is true, and that we therefore can and must assert 1A while rejecting 2 and, therefore, rejecting the semantic theory.

As for the muddle I have described above—the muddle of reading a degenerate case of contingent statements meta-linguistically employing the phrase *is true if and only if,* as a pseudo-defining-formula of which the definiendum consists of a quoted sentence followed by the phrase *is true*—I do not claim that this muddle represents the genesis of the semantic theory; but I do think that it, too, may have contributed to the plausibility of the theory.

III

The best way of showing that Thesis 1 is true is to correct its inadequacy. The best way of correcting its inadequacy is to discover the further reasons which have led to Thesis 2. To bring out those features of the situation which lead to the mistake of saying that the word 'true' is used meta-linguistically (to talk about sentences), I want first to compare the use of 'true' with that of 'Yes'. If you and I have been sitting together in silence for some time, and I suddenly say 'Yes', you would, perhaps, look at me with surprise and answer "I didn't say anything". Of course, a man may say 'Yes' to himself; and this will be a sign that he has resolved a doubt in his own mind, or come to a decision. But the normal use of 'Yes' is to answer: and where no question is asked, no answer can be given. Suppose you now ask: "Was Jones there?" and I say 'Yes'; there seems no temptation whatever to say that, in so answering, I am *talking about* the English sentence "Was Jones there?" So, in the case of 'Yes', we have a word of which the normal use requires some linguistic occasion (a question), without there being any temptation at all to say that it is used to *talk about* the sentence of which the utterance is the occasion for its use. There is indeed a temptation to go further in the opposite direction and say that in answering 'Yes' I am not talking *about* anything, not making any assertion, at all; but simply answering. In a way this is correct; but in a way, it's wrong. For it would be perfectly correct for you, reporting our dialogue, to say of me: "He said Jones was there". So of the ordinary use of 'Yes', we may say: first, that it demands a linguistic occasion, namely the asking of a question; second, that it is not used meta-linguistically, to talk about the question, but to answer it; third, that in so far as we are making an assertion at all in using it, the content of the assertion is the same as the content of the question. Now imagine a possible, and perhaps vulgarly current, use of the expression 'Ditto'. You make an assertion, and I say 'Ditto'. In so far as I assert anything, talk about anything, I talk about and assert what you talk about and assert. Of course—and this points to the inadequacy of Thesis 1 and the reason for the meta-linguistic error—to say 'Ditto' is not *the same as* to make the statement in question; for, whereas I might have made the statement before anyone else had spoken, it would be meaningless for me to say 'Ditto' before anyone else had spoken. 'Ditto', like 'Yes', requires a linguistic occasion. But again, and largely, I think, because the expression 'Ditto' does not consist of a grammatical subject and grammatical predicate, there is absolutely no temptation to say that in thus using 'Ditto', I should be talking *about the sentence* you used, and the utterance of which was the linguistic occasion for my use of this expression. I am not talking about what you said (the noise you made, or the sentence you spoke, or the proposition you expressed). I am agreeing with, endorsing, underwriting what you said; and, unless you had said something, I couldn't perform *these* activities, though I could *make the assertion* you made. Now the expression 'That's true' sometimes functions in just the way in which I have suggested the expression 'Ditto' might function. A says "Jones was there" and B says 'That's true'; and C, reporting the conversation, can correctly say: "Both

A and B said that Jones was there". But the point is that B couldn't have said that Jones was there in the way he *did* say it, (i.e. by the use of the expression 'That's true'), unless A had previously uttered the *sentence* "Jones was there", or some equivalent sentence. It is, perhaps, *this* fact about the use *(this* use) of the word 'true', together with the old prejudice that any indicative sentence must describe (be 'about') something, which encourages those who have become chary of saying that truth is a property of propositions to say instead that in using the word 'true', we are talking about sentences. (What I have said about the use of 'That's true' applies, of course, with suitable alterations, to the use of 'That's false').

Now those who assert that 'true' is a predicate of sentences have not, in general, considered these simple cases of the use of 'true' (and 'false'), but the more puzzling cases which lead, or seem to lead, to paradoxes: such as the case where someone uttters the isolated sentence "What I am saying now is false", or writes on an otherwise clean blackboard the sentence "Every statement on this blackboard is false". The solution on meta-linguistic lines is to treat these sentences as making statements of the second order to the effect:

(1) that there is some statement of the first order written on the blackboard (or said by me now);
and (2) that any first-order statement written on the blackboard (or said by me now) is false.

By means of this distinction of orders, the distinction between meta- and object-language, the puzzling sentences are said no longer to engender contradictions: either they are simply false, since the existential part of what they assert is false; or, alternatively, leaving out the existential part of the analysis, and treating them solely as hypotheticals, they are seen to be vacuously true, since no first-order statements occur. This solution is formally successful in avoiding the apparent contradictions. But it seems to me to achieve this success only by repeating the fundamental mistake from which the contradictions themselves arise, and also, and consequently, involving the difficulties mentioned at the beginning of this paper. That is, first, it involves the view that to say that a statement is true (or false) is to make a further, second-order, statement (thus contradicting Thesis 1); and, second, it (usually) involves the unplausibility of saying that this second-order statement is *about* a sentence or sentences. Now the point of the previous discussion of the actual use of 'Yes', the possible use of 'Ditto' and the actual use of 'That's true' is to show that these expedients are unnecessary. When no-one has spoken, and I say 'Ditto', I am not making a false statement to the effect that something true has been said, nor a true statement to the effect that nothing false has been said. I am not making a statement at all; but producing a pointless utterance. When somebody has made an assertion previously, my saying 'Ditto' acquires a point, has an occasion: and, if you like, you may say that I am now making a statement, repeating, in a manner, what the speaker said. But I am not making an additional statement, a meta-statement. It would perhaps be better to say that my utterance is not a statement at all, but a linguistic performance for which in the first case there was not, and in the second case there was, an occasion: so that in the first case it was a spurious, and in the second case a genuine, performance. Similarly, the words 'true' and 'false' normally require, as an occasion for their significant use, that somebody should have made, be making or be about to make (utter or write), some statement. (The making of the statement needs not precede the use of 'true': it may follow it as in the case of the expression "It is true that . . ."—a form of words I shall discuss later). But in all cases the indicative clause of which the grammatical predicate is the phrase 'is true' does not in itself make any kind of statement at all (not even a meta-statement), and a fortiori cannot make the statement, the making of which is required as the occasion for the significant use of the words 'true' or 'false'. This is not, as it stands, quite accurate. For an indicative sentence of which the grammatical predicate is the phrase 'is true' may sometimes, as I shall shortly show, be used to make an implicit meta-statement. But when this is so, the phrase 'is true' plays no part in the making of this meta-statement. The phrase 'is true' *never* has a statement-making role. And when this is seen, the paradoxes vanish without the need for the meta-linguistic machinery; or at least without the need for regarding the words 'true' and 'false' as part of that machinery. The paradoxes arise on the assumption that the words 'true' and 'false' can be used to make first-order assertions. They are formally solved by the declaration that these words can be used only to make second-order assertions. Both paradoxes and solution disappear on the more radical assumption that they are not used to make assertions of any order, are not used to make assertions at all.

I said, however, that indicative sentences of which the grammatical predicate is the phrase 'is true' or the phrase 'is false' may be used to make an implicit meta-statement, in the making of which these phrases themselves play no part. To elucidate this, consider the following sentences:

(1) What I am saying now is false.
(2) All statements made in English are false.
(3) What the policeman said is true.

It is certainly not incorrect to regard each of these sentences as implicitly making an *existential* meta-statement, which does not involve the words 'true' or 'false'. The implicit meta-statements in these cases might be written as follows:

(1a) I have just made (am about to make) a statement.

(2a) Some statements are made in English.
(3a) The policeman made a statement.

These are all second-order assertive sentences to the effect that there are some first-order assertive sentences, uttered (a) by me, (b) in English, (c) by the policeman.

These second-order assertive sentences we can regard as part of the analysis of the sentences (1), (2) and (3).[8] Obviously they are not the whole of their analysis. The sentence "The policeman made a statement" clearly has not the same use as the sentence "What the policeman said is true". To utter the second is to do something more than to assert the first. What is this additional performance? Consider the circumstances in which we might use the expression "What the policeman said is true". Instead of using this expression, I might have *repeated* the policeman's story. In this case, I shall be said to have *confirmed* what the policeman said. I might, however, have made exactly the same set of statements as I made in repeating his story, but have made them *before* the policeman spoke. In this case, though the assertions I have made are no different, I have not done what I did in the other case, namely 'confirmed his story'. So to confirm his story is not to say anything further, *about* his story, or the sentences he used in telling it, though it is to do something that cannot be done unless he has told his story. Now, unlike the confirming narrative which I might have told, the sentence "What the policeman said is true" has no use *except* to confirm the policeman's story [9]; but like the confirming narrative, the sentence does not say anything further *about* the policeman's story or the sentences he used in telling it. It is a device for confirming the story without telling it again. So, in general, in using such expressions, we are confirming, underwriting, admitting, agreeing with, what somebody has said; but (except where we are implicitly making an existential meta-statement, in making which the phrase 'is true' plays no part), we are not making any assertion additional to theirs; and are *never* using 'is true' to talk *about* something which is *what they said,* or the sentences they used in saying it. To complete the analysis, then, of the entire sentence (3) "What the policeman said is true", we have to add, to the existential meta-assertion, a phrase which is not assertive, but (if I may borrow Mr. Austin's word) performatory.[10] We might, e.g., offer, as a complete analysis of one case, the expression: "The policeman made a statement. I confirm it"; where, in uttering the words "I confirm it", I am

[8] [I should now say, not that sentences (1a)—(3a) are parts of the analyses of sentences (1)—(3), but that any statements made by the use of sentences (1)—(3) would presuppose the truth of statements which might be made by the use of sentences (1a)—(3a).]

[9] This needs qualification. Uttered by a witness, the sentence is a *confirmation;* wrung from the culprit, it is an *admission.* No doubt there are other cases.

[10] Cf. J. L. Austin, 'Other Minds', P.S.A. Supp. Vol. XX, pp. 169-175 for an account of some words of this class.

not describing something I do, but *doing* something.[11] There is, then, a difference between the more complicated cases in which the phrase 'is true' is preceded by a descriptive phrase, and the simpler sentences (e.g. 'That's true') in which the phrase 'is true' is preceded by a demonstrative. The former may be regarded as involving an implicit meta-statement, while the latter are purely confirmatory (or purely 'admissive'). But in neither sort of case has the phrase 'is true' any assertive (or meta-assertive) function.

There may still be some uneasiness felt at the denial that the phrase 'is true' has any assertive, or descriptive, function. Partially to allay this uneasiness, I will again say something familiar, that I have said already: that is, that when I say 'That's true' in response to your statement, I am in a manner making an assertion, namely the assertion you made; describing something, namely what you described. But pointing this out is quite consistent with saying that 'That's true' makes no statement in its own right. It makes no meta-statement. If there is any residual uneasiness, it ought not to be allayed. For its source is the ancient prejudice that any indicative sentence is, or makes,[12] a statement. I call it a prejudice: we could, instead, make it a criterion. And there would even be no harm in adopting this criterion for 'statement', if we could simultaneously divorce the word, in this strictly grammatical use, from its logic in other uses: from that logic which leads us, given a 'statement', to enquire: What is it about? What does it describe? What property, or what relation, does it assert to belong to, or hold between, what entity or entities? Asking these questions when confronted with such a sentence as "What Pascal said is true", we are led to look for the entity which is *what Pascal said*; looking with cautious, contemporary eyes, we find only his words; and so are induced to say that, in using this expression, we are talking about the French sentences he wrote or spoke. It is, then, the out-of-date desire that the phrase 'is true' should be some kind of a descriptive phrase, that leads to the up-to-date suggestion that the word 'true' is a second-level predicate of first-level sentences. More important than simply to reject *this* view is to have the right reason for rejecting it: the reason, namely, that the phrase 'is true' is not descriptive at all. If we persist that it describes (is about) something, while denying that it describes (is about) sentences, we shall be left with the old, general questions about the nature of, and tests for, truth, about the nature of the entities related by the truth-relation, and so on. Better than asking "What is the criterion of truth?" is to ask: "What are the grounds for agreement?"—for those we see to be not less various than the subjects on which an agreed opinion

11 Cf. also 'I admit it'. To *say* this *is* to make an admission.
12 Throughout I have used such mild barbarisms as "This sentence makes a statement" as shorthand for such expressions as "Anyone who uttered this sentence would be making a statement".

can be reached. And this will perhaps also discourage us from seeking to mark the difference between one kind of utterance and another by saying, for example, "Ethical utterances are not true or false". It is correct to say that utterances of any kind are true or false, if it is correct usage to signify agreement or disagreement with such utterances by means of the *expressions* 'true' or 'false'.

Of course, the formula that I have adopted in the discussion of one use of 'true' is not immune from another variant of that argument from grammar which leads to treating 'true' as a descriptive word. Someone might say: in order for you to *confirm* anything, there must be some *object* of this activity; a sentence or a proposition: and to perform this activity upon this object is nothing other than to assert that the object has the property, stands in the relation, referred to by the word 'true'. Anyone who says this is misled partly by the fact that the verb 'confirm' takes a grammatical object; and partly by the fact that the linguistic performance (of 'confirming') requires, not an object, but an *occasion*—a fact which I declared to be the misunderstood element of truth in the semantic theory. Even this assertion—that there must be, or be thought to be, some kind of sign-occasion for the significant, or genuine, use of the word 'true' —is not quite correct, if it means that some spoken or written utterance must occur, or be thought to occur. For it would not be incorrect, though it would be unusual, to say: "What you are thinking is true"; when nothing has been said. (But, then, a conversation *can* be carried on by glances and nods).

IV

In philosophical discussion of this whole subject, very little attention has been paid to the actual use of 'true'. And I want to conclude by distinguishing some of its normal uses in a little more detail. The uses mentioned so far I was tempted to call 'performatory'. But this is a misnomer. A performatory word, in Austin's sense, I take to be a verb, the use of which, in the first person present indicative, seems to describe some activity of the speaker, but in fact *is* that activity. Clearly the use of 'is true' does not seem to describe any activity of the speaker; it *has seemed* to describe a sentence, a proposition, or statement. The point of using Austin's word at all is the fact that the phrase 'is true' can sometimes be replaced,[13] without any important change in meaning, by some such phrase as "I confirm it", which is performatory in the strict sense. I shall take the substitute performatory word as a title for each of these cases; and shall speak, e.g., of the 'confirmatory' or 'admissive' use of 'true'. What commends the word as, e.g., a confirmatory device is its economy. By its means we can confirm without repeating.

[13] Of course, not *simply* replaced. Other verbal changes would be necessary.

The word has other, equally non-descriptive, uses. A familiar one is its use in sentences which begin with the phrase "It's true that", followed by a clause, followed by the word 'but', followed by another clause. The words "It's true that . . . but . . ." could, in these sentences, be replaced by the word 'Although'; or, alternatively, by the words "I concede that . . . but . . ." This use of the phrase, then, is concessive. The inappropriateness of the meta-linguistic treatment seems peculiarly apparent here.

The purely confirmatory use is probably no more common than other uses which look much the same, but which are, I think, distinct. A man may make an assertion to you, not wanting you to confirm it, to remove the doubt of others or his own; but wanting to know that you share his belief, or his attitude. If, in this case, you say 'That's true', you are not *saying*, but *indicating*, that you do share his belief. It seems to me natural to describe this simply as 'agreeing'. Again, it seems to me that we very often use the phrase 'That's true' to express, not only agreement with what is said, but also our sense of its novelty and force. We register the impact of what is said, much as we might register it by saying: "I never thought of that". Contrast the ironical 'very true' with which we sometimes rudely greet the obvious. The use of 'true' here is effectively ironical just because we normally use it to express agreement when our agreement is in doubt, or to register a sense of revelation. Sometimes, in sentences beginning "Is it true that . . . ?" or "So it's true that . . .", we could preserve the expressive quality of the utterance by substituting the adverb 'really' for the quoted phrases, at an appropriate point in the sentence; to convey, as they do, incredulity or surprise.

No doubt, the word has other functions; but those I have mentioned are probably as common as any. The important point is that the performance of these functions (and, I suspect, of all other non-technical jobs the word may do) does not involve the use of a meta-linguistic predicate; and that we *could*, with no very great violence to our language, perform them without the need for any expression which *seems* (as 'is true' seems) to make a statement. For instance, the substitution of 'although' for "It's true that . . . but . . ." is an obvious way of dealing with the concessive use; an extension of the practice of the inarticulate election-candidate whose speech consisted of "Ditto to Mr. X" might deal with the confirmatory and, partly, with the expressive uses; and so on. The selection of the substitute-expressions would of course be governed by the propagandist consideration that they should provide the minimum encouragement to anyone anxious to mistake them for statement-making phrases, or descriptive words.

One last point: a suggestion on the reasons why the puzzle about truth has commonly got entangled with the puzzle about certainty. It is above all when a doubt has been raised, when mistakes or deceit seem possible; when the need for confirmation is felt; that we tend to make use of those certifying words of which 'true' is one and of which others are 'certain', 'know', 'prove', 'establish', 'validate', 'confirm', 'evidence' and so on. So that the question "What is the nature of truth?" leads naturally to the question "What are the tests for truth?", and this, in its turn, to the question "What are the conditions of certainty?" The historical or judicial search for truth is the search for the evidence which will set doubt at rest. The philosophical endeavour to characterise truth *in general* has tended to become the endeavour to characterise that which *in general* sets doubt at rest; really and finally at rest. Where you find the indubitable, there you find the true. And this metaphysical road branches into different paths, at the end of one of which you find the Atomic Fact, and, at the end of another, the Absolute.

Finally, I will repeat that in saying that the word 'true' has not in itself any assertive function, I am not of course saying that a sentence like "His statement is true" is incorrect. Of course the word 'statement' may be the grammatical subject of a sentence of which the phrase 'is true' is the grammatical predicate. Nor am I recommending that we drop this usage. But for the usage, there would be no problem.

Further Reading

The following books and papers contain discussions of truth and other topics pertinent to this chapter.

BLACK, M., "The Semantic Definition of Truth." *Analysis,* 8 (1948).

BRADLEY, F. H., *Essays on Truth and Reality* (Oxford, Clarendon Press, 1914).

BRENTANO, F., *Wahrheit und Evidenz,* ed., O. Kraus (Leipzig, Felix Meiner, 1930). (A translation of this book by Roderick M. Chisholm and Kurt Fischer is to be published soon.)

BOSANQUET, B., *Logic* (Oxford, Clarendon Press, 1911).

DEWEY, J., *Reconstruction in Philosophy* (Boston, Beacon Press, 1947).

PITCHER, G. Ed., *Truth* (Englewood Cliffs, Prentice-Hall, 1964).

RUSSELL, B., *Problems of Philosophy* (London, Oxford University Press, 1912).

STRAWSON, P. F., "Truth." *Proceedings of the Aristotelian Society,* Suppl. XXIV, (1950).

TARSKI, A., "The Semantic Conception of Truth." *Philosophy and Phenomenological Research,* 4 (1944).

PART FOUR

The Problem
of Induction

Introduction

If we examine all the members of a class, and if we make an assertion from the results of the examination, our assertion can be said to be based on a "perfect" induction. If, for example, we examine all the parks in the city of Washington, finding that they all contain statues, our assertion "All Washington parks contain statues" rests on a "perfect" induction.

If an assertion about all the members of a class is based on an examination of only *some* of the members of the class, we would ordinarily be said to have made an inductive inference. The problem of induction arises with respect to this type of inference. Suppose, for example, that we examine only thirty Washington parks and find that these thirty all contain statues. Suppose further that, on the basis of this examination, we assert that all Washington parks contain statues. This assertion rests on an inductive inference; that is, an inference from the known properties of some members of a class to a conclusion about the properties of every member of the class. The problem of induction is to justify such inferences.

David Hume is concerned with a particular form of the problem. We see, he says, that like causes are followed by like effects. We then infer that in the future like causes will be followed by like effects. But how can we justify this inference? We cannot *deduce* from our present information that in the future like causes will precede like effects. No entailment relations hold, for example, between the sentences "Today when I tasted a lemon it was sour" and "Tomorrow when I taste a lemon it will be sour." Nor can we inductively infer that because all past instances of like causes were followed by like effects, all future causes will be also. For this inference is itself an inductive inference, and our problem is to justify such inferences. If, then, induction can be justified neither by deductive nor inductive methods, neither *a priori* nor *a posteriori,* how can it be justified?

In the second selection in this chapter, Bertrand Russell applies Hume's points to a wider class of inductive inferences. Like Hume, he also distinguishes between our psychological attitude toward the future—our belief that the future will be like the past—and the question of the *reasonableness* of these attitudes and beliefs.

Hans Reichenbach puts the problem of induction in a new light. Let us call an "inductive rule" any non-deductive rule for drawing conclusions about matters of fact. One such rule might be, "Assume that things will behave in the future the way they did in the past." Another might be, "Assume that things will behave in the future the opposite of the way in which they behaved in the past." For Reichenbach, the problem of induction is to justify the selection of one of the many possible inductive rules over the remaining rules. Reichenbach believes that we can justify on pragmatic grounds the selection of a rule for making inductive inferences.

The article by Paul Edwards, Professor of Philosophy at Columbia University, illustrates a familiar contemporary approach to the problem of induction. He tries to exhibit the meaning that "reason" and "reasonable" have in ordinary language, and argues that when this meaning is grasped, inductive inferences are seen to be reasonable, and hence justified. For a properly made inductive inference is "reasonable" by the very meaning of the word "reasonable"; hence it makes no sense to ask for a proof of the reasonableness of inductive generalizations. If philosophers nevertheless do insist on asking for a demonstration of the reasonableness of inductive inferences, Edwards argues, then they must be using the word "reasonable" in some special, non-ordinary way. Thus their request for such a demonstration means something quite different from what it at first seems to mean, something philosophically much less interesting.

In the last selection in this chapter, Wesley Salmon, of Brown University, argues against the type of approach which Edwards takes to the problem of induction. Salmon bases his argument in part on a distinction between the "validation" as opposed to the "vindication" of such things as principles of conduct and rules of inference.

NINETEEN

There Can Be No Inductive Knowledge

DAVID HUME (1711-1776)

From *An Enquiry Concerning Human Understanding**

PART I

All the objects of human reason or enquiry may naturally be divided into two kinds, to wit, *Relations of Ideas,* and *Matters of Fact.* Of the first kind are the sciences of Geometry, Algebra, and Arithmetic; and in short, every affirmation which is either intuitively or demonstratively certain. *That the square of the hypothenuse is equal to the square of the two sides,* is a proposition which expresses a relation between these figures. *That three times five is equal to half of thirty,* expresses a relation between these numbers. Propositions of this kind are discoverable by the mere operation of thought, without dependence on what is anywhere existent in the universe. Though there never were a circle or triangle in nature, the truths demonstrated by Euclid would for ever retain their certainty and evidence.

Matters of fact, which are the second objects of human reason, are not ascertained in the same manner; nor is our evidence of their truth, however great, of a like nature with the foregoing. The contrary of every matter of fact is still possible; because it can never imply a contradiction, and is conceived by the mind with the same facility and distinctness, as if ever so conformable to reality. *That the sun will not rise to-morrow* is no less intelligible a proposition, and implies no more contradiction than the affirmation, *that it will rise.* We should in vain, therefore, attempt to demonstrate its falsehood. Were it demonstratively false, it would imply a contradiction, and could never be distinctly conceived by the mind.

It may, therefore, be a subject worthy of curiosity, to enquire what is the nature of that evidence which assures us of any real existence and matter of fact, beyond the present testimony of our senses, or the

* From *An Enquiry Concerning Human Understanding* by David Hume (1748).

records of our memory. This part of philosophy, it is observable, has been little cultivated, either by the ancients or moderns; and therefore our doubts and errors, in the prosecution of so important an enquiry, may be the more excusable; while we march through such difficult paths without any guide or direction. They may even prove useful, by exciting curiosity, and destroying that implicit faith and security, which is the bane of all reasoning and free enquiry. The discovery of defects in the common philosophy, if any such there be, will not, I presume, be a discouragement, but rather an incitement, as is usual, to attempt something more full and satisfactory than has yet been proposed to the public.

All reasonings concerning matter of fact seem to be founded on the relation of *Cause and Effect*. By means of that relation alone we can go beyond the evidence of our memory and senses. If you were to ask a man, why he believes any matter of fact, which is absent; for instance, that his friend is in the country, or in France; he would give you a reason; and this reason would be some other fact; as a letter received from him, or the knowledge of his former resolutions and promises. A man finding a watch or any other machine in a desert island, would conclude that there had once been men in that island. All our reasonings concerning fact are of the same nature. And here it is constantly supposed that there is a connexion between the present fact and that which is inferred from it. Were there nothing to bind them together, the inference would be entirely precarious. The hearing of an articulate voice and rational discourse in the dark assures us of the presence of some person: Why? because these are the effects of the human make and fabric, and closely connected with it. If we anatomize all the other reasonings of this nature, we shall find that they are founded on the relation of cause and effect, and that this relation is either near or remote, direct or collateral. Heat and light are collateral effects of fire, and the one effect may justly be inferred from the other.

If we would satisfy ourselves, therefore, concerning the nature of that evidence, which assures us of matters of fact, we must enquire how we arrive at the knowledge of cause and effect.

I shall venture to affirm, as a general proposition, which admits of no exception, that the knowledge of this relation is not, in any instance, attained by reasonings *a priori;* but arises entirely from experience, when we find that any particular objects are constantly conjoined with each other. Let an object be presented to a man of ever so strong natural reason and abilities; if that object be entirely new to him, he will not be able, by the most accurate examination of its sensible qualities, to discover any of its causes or effects. Adam, though his rational faculties be supposed, at the very first, entirely perfect, could not have inferred from the fluidity and transparency of water that it would suffocate him, or from the light and warmth of fire that it would consume him. No object ever discovers, by the qualities which appear to the senses, either the causes which produced it, or the effects which will arise from it; nor can our reason, unassisted by experience, ever draw any inference concerning real existence and matter of fact.

This proposition, *that causes and effects are discoverable, not by reason but by experience,* will readily be admitted with regard to such objects, as we remember to have once been altogether unknown to us; since we must be conscious of the utter inability, which we then lay under, of foretelling what would arise from them. Present two smooth pieces of marble to a man who has no tincture of natural philosophy; he will never discover that they will adhere together in such a manner as to require great force to separate them in a direct line, while they make so small a resistance to a lateral pressure. Such events, as bear little analogy to the common course of nature, are also readily confessed to be known only by experience; nor does any man imagine that the explosion of gunpowder, or the attraction of a load-stone, could ever be discovered by arguments *a priori.* In like manner, when an effect is supposed to depend upon an intricate machinery or secret structure of parts, we make no difficulty in attributing all our knowledge of it to experience. Who will assert that he can give the ultimate reason, why milk or bread is proper nourishment for a man, not for a lion or a tiger?

But the same truth may not appear, at first sight, to have the same evidence with regard to events, which have become familiar to us from our first appearance in the world, which bear a close analogy to the whole course of nature, and which are supposed to depend on the simple qualities of objects, without any secret structure of parts. We are apt to imagine that we could discover these effects by the mere operation of our reason, without experience. We fancy, that were we brought on a sudden into this world, we could at first have inferred that one Billiard-ball would communicate motion to another upon impulse; and that we needed not to have waited for the event, in order to pronounce with certainty concerning it. Such is the influence of custom, that, where it is strongest, it not only covers our natural ignorance, but even conceals itself, and seems not to take place, merely because it is found in the highest degree.

But to convince us that all the laws of nature, and all the operations of bodies without exception, are known only by experience, the following reflections may, perhaps, suffice. Were any object presented to us, and were we required to pronounce concerning the effect, which will result from it, without consulting past observation; after what manner, I beseech you, must the mind proceed in this operation? It must invent or imagine some event, which it ascribes to the object as its effect; and it is plain that this invention must be entirely arbitrary. The mind can never possibly find the effect in the supposed cause, by the most accurate scrutiny and examination. For the effect is totally different from the cause, and consequently can never be discovered in it. Motion in the second Billiard-ball is a quite distinct event from motion in the first; nor is there anything in the one to suggest the smallest hint of the other. A stone or piece of metal raised into the air, and left without any support, immediately falls: but to consider the matter *a priori,* is there anything we discover in this situation which can beget the idea of a downward, rather than an upward, or any other motion, in the stone or metal?

And as the first imagination or invention of a particular effect, in all natural operations, is arbitrary, where we consult not experience; so must we also esteem the supposed tie or connexion between the cause and effect, which binds them together, and renders it impossible that any other effect could result from the operation of that cause. When I see, for instance, a Billiard-ball moving in a straight line towards another; even suppose motion in the second ball should by accident be suggested to me, as the result of their contact or impulse; may I not conceive, that a hundred different events might as well follow from that cause? May not both these balls remain at absolute rest? May not the first ball return in a straight line, or leap off from the second in any line or direction? All these suppositions are consistent and conceivable. Why then should we give the preference to one, which is no more consistent or conceivable than the rest? All our reasonings *a priori* will never be able to show us any foundation for this preference.

In a word, then, every effect is a distinct event from its cause. It could not, therefore, be discovered in the cause, and the first invention or conception of it, *a priori,* must be entirely arbitrary. And even after it is suggested, the conjunction of it with the cause must appear equally arbitrary; since there are always many other effects, which, to reason, must seem fully as consistent and natural. In vain, therefore, should we pretend to determine any single event, or infer any cause or effect, without the assistance of observation and experience.

Hence we may discover the reason why no philosopher, who is rational and modest, has ever pretended to assign the ultimate cause of any natural operation, or to show distinctly the action of that power, which produces any single effect in the universe. It is confessed, that the utmost effort of human reason is to reduce the principles, productive of natural phenomena, to a greater simplicity, and to resolve the many particular effects into a few general causes, by means of reasonings from analogy, experience, and observation. But as to the causes of these general causes, we should in vain attempt their discovery; nor shall we ever be able to satisfy ourselves, by any particular explication of them. These ultimate springs and principles are totally shut up from human curiosity and enquiry. Elasticity, gravity, cohesion of parts, communication of motion by impulse; these are probably the ultimate causes and principles which we shall ever discover in nature; and we may esteem ourselves sufficiently happy, if, by accurate enquiry and reasoning, we can trace up the particular phenomena to, or near to, these general principles. The most perfect philosophy of the natural kind only staves off our ignorance a little longer: as perhaps the most perfect philosophy of the moral or metaphysical kind serves only to discover larger portions of it. Thus the observation of human blindness and weakness is the result of all philosophy, and meets us at every turn, in spite of our endeavours to elude or avoid it.

Nor is geometry, when taken into the assistance of natural philosophy, ever able to remedy this defect, or lead us into the knowledge of ultimate causes, by all that accuracy of reasoning for which it is so justly celebrated. Every part of mixed mathematics proceeds upon the supposition that certain laws are established by nature in her operations; and abstract reasonings are employed, either to assist experience in the discovery of these laws, or to determine their influence in particular instances, where it depends upon any precise degree of distance and quantity. Thus, it is a law of motion, discovered by experience, that the moment or force of any body in motion is in the compound ratio or proportion of its solid contents and its velocity; and consequently, that a small force may remove the greatest obstacle or raise the greatest weight, if, by any contrivance or machinery, we can increase the velocity of that force, so as to make it an overmatch for its antagonist. Geometry assists us in the application of this law, by giving us the just dimensions of all the parts and figures which can enter into any species of machine; but still the discovery of the law itself is owing merely to experience, and all the abstract reasonings in the world could never lead us one step towards the knowledge of it. When we reason *a priori*, and consider merely any object or cause, as it appears to the mind, independent of all observation, it never could suggest to us the notion of any distinct object, such as its effect; much less, show us the inseparable and inviolable connexion between them. A man must be very sagacious who could discover by reasoning that crystal is the effect of heat, and ice of cold, without being previously acquainted with the operation of these qualities.

PART II

But we have not yet attained any tolerable satisfaction with regard to the question first proposed. Each solution still gives rise to a new question as difficult as the foregoing, and leads us on to farther enquiries. When it is asked, *What is the nature of all our reasonings concerning matter of fact?* the proper answer seems to be, that they are founded on the relation of cause and effect. When again it is asked, *What is the foundation of all our reasonings and conclusions concerning that relation?* it may be replied in one word, Experience. But if we still carry on our sifting humour, and ask, *What is the foundation of all conclusions from experience?* this implies a new question, which may be of more difficult solution and explication. Philosophers, that give themselves airs of superior wisdom and sufficiency, have a hard task when they encounter persons of inquisitive dispositions, who push them from every corner to which they retreat, and who are sure at last to bring them to some dangerous dilemma. The best expedient to prevent this confusion, is to be modest in our pretensions; and even to discover the difficulty ourselves before it is objected to us. By this means, we may make a kind of merit of our very ignorance.

I shall content myself, in this section, with an easy task, and shall pretend only to give a negative answer to the question here proposed. I say then, that, even after we have experience of the operations of cause and effect, our conclusions from that experience are *not* founded on reasoning, or any process of the understanding. This answer we must endeavour both to explain and to defend.

It must certainly be allowed, that nature has kept us at a great distance from all her secrets, and has afforded us only the knowledge of a few superficial qualities of objects; while she conceals from us those powers and principles on which the influence of those objects entirely depends. Our senses inform us of the colour, weight, and consistence of bread; but neither sense nor reason can ever inform us of those qualities which fit it for the nourishment and support of a human body. Sight or feeling conveys an idea of the actual motion of bodies; but as to that wonderful force or power, which would carry on a moving body for ever in a continued change of place, and which bodies never lose but by communicating it to others; of this we cannot form the most distant conception. But notwithstanding this ignorance of natural powers [1] and principles, we always presume, when we see like sensible qualities, that they have like secret powers, and expect that effects, similar to those which we have experienced, will follow from them. If a body of like colour and consistence with that bread, which we have formerly eat, be presented to us, we make no scruple of repeating the experiment, and foresee, with certainty, like nourishment and support. Now this is a process of the mind or thought, of which I would willingly know the foundation. It is allowed on all hands that there is no known

---

[1] The word, Power, is here used in a loose and popular sense. The more accurate explication of it would give additional evidence to this argument.

connexion between the sensible qualities and the secret powers; and consequently, that the mind is not led to form such a conclusion concerning their constant and regular conjunction, by anything which it knows of their nature. As to past *Experience,* it can be allowed to give *direct* and *certain* information of those precise objects only, and that precise period of time, which fell under its cognizance: but why this experience should be extended to future times, and to other objects, which for aught we know, may be only in appearance similar; this is the main question on which I would insist. The bread, which I formerly eat, nourished me; that is, a body of such sensible qualities was, at that time, endued with such secret powers: but does it follow, that other bread must also nourish me at another time, and that like sensible qualities must always be attended with like secret powers? The consequence seems nowise necessary. At least, it must be acknowledged that there is here a consequence drawn by the mind; that there is a certain step taken; a process of thought, and an inference, which wants to be explained. These two propositions are far from being the same, *I have found that such an object has always been attended with such an effect,* and *I foresee, that other objects, which are, in appearance, similar, will be attended with similar effects.* I shall allow, if you please, that the one proposition may justly be inferred from the other: I know, in fact, that it always is inferred. But if you insist that the inference is made by a chain of reasoning, I desire you to produce that reasoning. The connexion between these propositions is not intuitive. There is required a medium, which may enable the mind to draw such an inference, if indeed it be drawn by reasoning and argument. What that medium is, I must confess, passes my comprehension; and it is incumbent on those to produce it, who assert that it really exists, and is the origin of all our conclusions concerning matter of fact.

This negative argument must certainly, in process of time, become altogether convincing, if many penetrating and able philosophers shall turn their enquiries this way and no one be ever able to discover any connecting proposition or intermediate step, which supports the understanding in this conclusion. But as the question is yet new, every reader may not trust so far to his own penetration, as to conclude, because an argument escapes his enquiry, that therefore it does not really exist. For this reason it may be requisite to venture upon a more difficult task; and enumerating all the branches of human knowledge, endeavour to show that none of them can afford such an argument.

All reasonings may be divided into two kinds, namely, demonstrative reasoning, or that concerning relations of ideas, and moral reasoning, or that concerning matter of fact and existence. That there are no demonstrative arguments in the case seems evident; since it implies no contradiction that the course of nature may change, and that an object, seemingly like those which we have experienced, may be attended with different or contrary effects. May I not clearly and distinctly conceive that a body, falling from the clouds, and which, in all other respects, resembles snow, has yet the taste of salt or feeling of fire? Is there any more intelligible proposition than to affirm, that all the trees will flourish in December and January, and decay in May and June? Now whatever is intelligible, can be distinctly conceived, implies no contradiction, and can never be proved false by any demonstrative argument or abstract reasoning *à priori.*

If we be, therefore, engaged by arguments to put trust in past experience, and make it the standard of our future judgement, these arguments must be probable only, or such as regard matter of fact and real existence, according to the division above mentioned. But that there is no argument of this kind, must appear, if our explication of that species of reasoning be admitted as solid and satisfactory. We have said that all arguments concerning existence are founded on the relation of cause and effect; that our knowledge of that relation is derived entirely from experience; and that all our experimental conclusions proceed upon the supposition that the future will be conformable to the past. To endeavour, therefore, the proof of this last supposition by probable arguments, or arguments regarding existence, must be evidently going in a circle, and taking that for granted, which is the very point in question.

In reality, all arguments from experience are founded on the similarity which we discover among natural objects, and by which we are induced to expect effects similar to those which we have found to follow from such objects. And though none but a fool or madman will ever pretend to dispute the authority of experience, or to reject that great guide of human life, it may surely be allowed a philosopher to have so much curiosity at least as to examine the principle of human nature, which gives this mighty authority to experience, and makes us draw advantage from that similarity which nature has placed among different objects. From causes which appear *similar* we expect similar effects. This is the sum of all our experimental conclusions. Now it seems evident that, if this conclusion were formed by reason, it would be as perfect at first, and upon one instance, as after ever so long a course of experience. But the case is far otherwise. Nothing so like as eggs; yet no one, on account of this appearing similarity, expects the same taste and relish in all of them. It is only after a long course of uniform experiments in any kind, that we attain a firm reliance and security with regard to a particular event. Now where is that process of reasoning which, from one instance, draws a conclusion, so different from that which it infers from a hundred instances that are nowise different from that single one? This question I propose as much for the sake of information, as with an intention of raising difficulties. I cannot find, I cannot imagine any such reasoning. But I keep my mind still open to instruction, if any one will vouchsafe to bestow it on me.

Should it be said that, from a number of uniform experiments, we *infer* a connexion between the sensible qualities and the secret powers; this, I must confess, seems the same difficulty, couched in different terms. The question still recurs, on what process of argument this *inference* is founded? Where is the medium, the interposing ideas, which join propositions so very wide of each other? It is confessed that the colour, consistence, and other sensible qualities of bread appear not, of themselves, to have any connexion with the secret powers of nourishment and support. For otherwise we could infer these secret powers from the first appearance of these sensible qualities, without the aid of experience; contrary to the sentiment of all philosophers, and contrary to plain matter of fact. Here, then, is our natural state of ignorance with regard to the powers and influence of all objects. How is this remedied by experience? It only shows us a number of uniform effects, resulting from certain objects, and teaches us that those particular objects, at that particular time, were endowed with such powers and forces. When a new object, endowed with similar sensible qualities, is produced, we expect similar powers and forces, and look for a like effect. From a body of like colour and consistence with bread we expect like nourishment and support. But this surely is a step or progress of the mind, which wants to be explained. When a man says, *I have found, in all past instances, such sensible qualities conjoined with such secret powers*: And when he says, *Similar sensible qualities will always be conjoined with similar secret powers,* he is not guilty of a tautology, nor are these propositions in any respect the same. You say that the one proposition is an inference from the other. But you must confess that the inference is not intuitive; neither is it demonstrative: Of what nature is it, then? To say it is experimental, is begging the question. For all inferences from experience suppose, as their foundation, that the future will resemble the past, and that similar powers will be conjoined with similar sensible qualities. If there be any suspicion that the course of nature may change, and that the past may be no rule for the future, all experience becomes useless, and can give rise to no inference or conclusion. It is impossible, therefore, that any arguments from experience can prove this resemblance of the past to the future; since all these arguments are founded on the supposition of that resemblance. Let the course of things be allowed hitherto ever so regular; that alone, without some new argument or inference, proves not that, for the future, it will continue so. In vain do you pretend to have learned the nature of bodies from your past experience. Their secret nature, and consequently all their effects and influence, may change, without any change in their sensible qualities. This happens sometimes, and with regard to some objects: Why may it not happen always, and with regard to all objects? What logic, what process of argument secures you against this supposition? My practice, you say, refutes my doubts. But you mistake the purport of my question. As an agent, I am quite satisfied in the point; but as a philosopher, who has some share of curiosity, I will not say scepticism, I want to learn the foundation of this inference. No reading, no enquiry has yet been able to remove my difficulty, or give me satisfaction in a matter of such importance. Can I do better than propose the difficulty to the public, even though, perhaps, I have small hopes of obtaining a solution? We shall at least, by this means, be sensible of our ignorance, if we do not augment our knowledge.

I must confess that a man is guilty of unpardonable arrogance who concludes, because an argument has escaped his own investigation, that therefore it does not really exist. I must also confess that, though all the learned, for several ages, should have employed themselves in fruitless search upon any subject, it may still, perhaps, be rash to conclude positively that the subject must, therefore, pass all human comprehension. Even though we examine all the sources of our knowledge, and conclude them unfit for such a subject, there may still remain a suspicion, that the enumeration is not complete, or the examination not accurate. But with regard to the present subject, there are some considerations which seem to remove all this accusation of arrogance or suspicion of mistake.

It is certain that the most ignorant and stupid peasants—nay infants, nay even brute beasts—improve by experience, and learn the qualities of natural objects, by observing the effects which result from them. When a child has felt the sensation of pain from touching the flame of a candle, he will be careful not to put his hand near any candle; but will expect a similar effect from a cause which is similar in its sensible qualities and appearance. If you assert, therefore, that the understanding of the child is led into this conclusion by any process of argument or ratiocination, I may justly require you to produce that argument; nor have you any pretence to refuse so equitable a demand. You cannot say that the argument is abstruse, and may possibly escape your enquiry; since you confess that it is obvious to the capacity of a mere infant. If you hesitate, therefore, a moment, or if, after reflection, you produce any intricate or profound argument, you, in a manner, give up the question, and confess that it is not reasoning which engages us to suppose the past resembling the future, and to expect similar effects from causes which are, to appearance, similar. This is the proposition which I intended to enforce in the present section. If I be right, I pretend not to have made any mighty discovery. And if I be wrong, I must acknowledge myself to be indeed a very backward scholar; since I cannot now discover an argument which, it seems, was perfectly familiar to me long before I was out of my cradle.

TWENTY

On Induction*

BERTRAND RUSSELL (1872-   )

From The Problems of Philosophy*

We are all convinced that the sun will rise to-morrow. Why? Is this belief a mere blind outcome of past experience, or can it be justified as a reasonable belief? It is not easy to find a test by which to judge whether a belief of this kind is reasonable or not, but we can at least ascertain what sort of general beliefs would suffice, if true, to justify the judgement that the sun will rise to-morrow, and the many other similar judgements upon which our actions are based.

It is obvious that if we are asked why we believe that the sun will rise to-morrow, we shall naturally answer, 'Because it always has risen every day'. We have a firm belief that it will rise in the future, because it has risen in the past. If we are challenged as to why we believe that it will continue to rise as heretofore, we may appeal to the laws of motion: the earth, we shall say, is a freely rotating body, and such bodies do not cease to rotate unless something interferes from outside, and there is nothing outside to interfere with the earth between now and to-morrow. Of course it might be doubted whether we are quite certain that there is nothing outside to interfere, but this is not the interesting doubt. The interesting doubt is as to whether the laws of motion will remain in operation until to-morrow. If this doubt is raised, we find ourselves in the same position as when the doubt about the sunrise was first raised.

The *only* reason for believing that the laws of motion will remain in operation is that they have operated hitherto, so far as our knowledge of the past enables us to judge. It is true that we have a greater body of evidence from the past in favour of the laws of motion than we have in favour of the sunrise, because the sunrise is merely a particular case of fulfilment of the laws of motion, and there are countless other particular cases. But the real question is: Do *any* number of cases of a law being fulfilled in the past afford evidence that it will be fulfilled in the future? If not, it becomes plain that we have no ground whatever for expecting the sun to rise to-morrow, or for expecting the bread we shall eat at our

* From *The Problems of Philosophy* by Bertrand Russell (Oxford University Press, 1912). Reprinted by permission of the publishers.

next meal not to poison us, or for any of the other scarcely conscious expectations that control our daily lives. It is to be observed that all such expectations are only *probable;* thus we have not to seek for a proof that they *must* be fulfilled, but only for some reason in favour of the view that they are *likely* to be fulfilled.

Now in dealing with this question we must, to begin with, make an important distinction, without which we should soon become involved in hopeless confusions. Experience has shown us that, hitherto, the frequent repetition of some uniform succession or coexistence has been a *cause* of our expecting the same succession or coexistence on the next occasion. Food that has a certain appearance generally has a certain taste, and it is a severe shock to our expectations when the familiar appearance is found to be associated with an unusual taste. Things which we see become associated, by habit, with certain tactile sensations which we expect if we touch them; one of the horrors of a ghost (in many ghost-stories) is that it fails to give us any sensations of touch. Uneducated people who go abroad for the first time are so surprised as to be incredulous when they find their native language not understood.

And this kind of association is not confined to men; in animals also it is very strong. A horse which has been often driven along a certain road resists the attempt to drive him in a different direction. Domestic animals expect food when they see the person who usually feeds them. We know that all these rather crude expectations of uniformity are liable to be misleading. The man who has fed the chicken every day throughout its life at last wrings its neck instead, showing that more refined views as to the uniformity of nature would have been useful to the chicken.

But in spite of the misleadingness of such expectations, they nevertheless exist. The mere fact that something has happened a certain number of times causes animals and men to expect that it will happen again. Thus our instincts certainly cause us to believe that the sun will rise tomorrow, but we may be in no better a position than the chicken which unexpectedly has its neck wrung. We have therefore to distinguish the fact that past uniformities *cause* expectations as to the future, from the question whether there is any reasonable ground for giving weight to such expectations after the question of their validity has been raised.

The problem we have to discuss is whether there is any reason for believing in what is called 'the uniformity of nature'. The belief in the uniformity of nature is the belief that everything that has happened or will happen is an instance of some general law to which there are *no* exceptions. The crude expectations which we have been considering are all subject to exceptions, and therefore liable to disappoint those who entertain them. But science habitually assumes, at least as a working hypothesis, that general rules which have exceptions can be replaced by general rules which have no exceptions. 'Unsupported bodies in air fall' is a general rule to which balloons and aeroplanes are exceptions. But the laws of motion and the law of gravitation, which account for the fact that most bodies fall, also account for the fact that balloons and aeroplanes can rise; thus the laws of motion and the law of gravitation are not subject to these exceptions.

The belief that the sun will rise to-morrow might be falsified if the earth came suddenly into contact with a large body which destroyed its rotation; but the laws of motion and the law of gravitation would not be infringed by such an event. The business of science is to find uniformities, such as the laws of motion and the law of gravitation, to which, so far as our experience extends, there are no exceptions. In this search science has been remarkably successful, and it may be conceded that such uniformities have held hitherto. This brings us back to the question: Have we any reason, assuming that they have always held in the past, to suppose that they will hold in the future?

It has been argued that we have reason to know that the future will resemble the past, because what was the future has constantly become the past, and has always been found to resemble the past, so that we really have experience of the future, namely of times which were formerly future, which we may call past futures. But such an argument really begs the very question at issue. We have experience of past futures, but not of future futures, and the question is: Will future futures resemble past futures? This question is not to be answered by an argument which starts from past futures alone. We have therefore still to seek for some principle which shall enable us to know that the future will follow the same laws as the past.

The reference to the future in this question is not essential. The same question arises when we apply the laws that work in our experience to past things of which we have no experience—as, for example, in geology, or in theories as to the origin of the Solar System. The question we really have to ask is: 'When two things have been found to be often associated, and no instance is known of the one occurring without the other, does the occurrence of one of the two, in a fresh instance, give any good ground for expecting the other?' On our answer to this question must depend the validity of the whole of our expectations as to the future, the whole of the results obtained by induction, and in fact practically all the beliefs upon which our daily life is based.

It must be conceded, to begin with, that the fact that two things have been found often together and never apart does not, by itself, suffice to *prove* demonstratively that they will be found together in the next case we examine. The most we can hope is that the oftener things are found together, the more probable it becomes that they will be found together another time, and that, if they have been found together often enough, the probability will amount *almost* to certainty. It can never quite reach certainty, because we know that in spite of frequent repetitions there sometimes is a failure at the last, as in the case of the chicken whose neck is wrung. Thus probability is all we ought to seek.

It might be urged, as against the view we are advocating, that we know all natural phenomena to be subject to the reign of law, and that sometimes, on the basis of observation, we can see that only one law can possibly fit the facts of the case. Now to this view there are two answers. The first is that, even if *some* law which has no exceptions applies to our case, we can never, in practice, be sure that we have discovered that law and not one to which there are exceptions. The second is that the reign of law would seem to be itself only probable, and that our belief that it will hold in the future, or in unexamined cases in the past, is itself based upon the very principle we are examining.

The principle we are examining may be called the *principle of induction,* and its two parts may be stated as follows:

(a) When a thing of a certain sort A has been found to be associated with a thing of a certain other sort B, and has never been found dissociated from a thing of the sort B, the greater the number of cases in which A and B have been associated, the greater is the probability that they will be associated in a fresh case in which one of them is known to be present;

(b) Under the same circumstances, a sufficient number of cases of association will make the probability of a fresh association nearly a certainty, and will make it approach certainty without limit.

As just stated, the principle applies only to the verification of our expectation in a single fresh instance. But we want also to know that there is a probability in favour of the general law that things of the sort A are *always* associated with things of the sort B, provided a sufficient number of cases of association are known, and no cases of failure of association are known. The probability of the general law is obviously less than the probability of the particular case, since if the general law is true, the particular case must also be true, whereas the particular case may be true without the general law being true. Nevertheless the probability of the general law is increased by repetitions, just as the probability of the particular case is. We may therefore repeat the two parts of our principle as regards the general law, thus:

(a) The greater the number of cases in which a thing of the sort A has been found associated with a thing of the sort B, the more probable it is (if no cases of failure of association are known) that A is always associated with B;

(b) Under the same circumstances, a sufficient number of cases of the association of A with B will make it nearly certain that A is always associated with B, and will make this general law approach certainty without limit.

It should be noted that probability is always relative to certain data.

In our case, the data are merely the known cases of coexistence of A and B. There may be other data, which *might* be taken into account, which would gravely alter the probability. For example, a man who had seen a great many white swans might argue, by our principle, that on the data it was *probable* that all swans were white, and this might be a perfectly sound argument. The argument is not disproved by the fact that some swans are black, because a thing may very well happen in spite of the fact that some data render it improbable. In the case of the swans, a man might know that colour is a very variable characteristic in many species of animals, and that, therefore, an induction as to colour is peculiarly liable to error. But this knowledge would be a fresh datum, by no means proving that the probability relatively to our previous data had been wrongly estimated. The fact, therefore, that things often fail to fulfil our expectations is no evidence that our expectations will not *probably* be fulfilled in a given case or a given class of cases. Thus our inductive principle is at any rate not capable of being *disproved* by an appeal to experience.

The inductive principle, however, is equally incapable of being *proved* by an appeal to experience. Experience might conceivably confirm the inductive principle as regards the cases that have been already examined; but as regards unexamined cases, it is the inductive principle alone that can justify any inference from what has been examined to what has not been examined. All arguments which, on the basis of experience, argue as to the future or the unexperienced parts of the past or present, assume the inductive principle; hence we can never use experience to prove the inductive principle without begging the question. Thus we must either accept the inductive principle on the ground of its intrinsic evidence, or forgo all justification of our expectations about the future. If the principle is unsound, we have no reason to expect the sun to rise to-morrow, to expect bread to be more nourishing than a stone, or to expect that if we throw ourselves off the roof we shall fall. When we see what looks like our best friend approaching us, we shall have no reason to suppose that his body is not inhabited by the mind of our worst enemy or of some total stranger. All our conduct is based upon associations which have worked in the past, and which we therefore regard as likely to work in the future; and this likelihood is dependent for its validity upon the inductive principle.

The general principles of science, such as the belief in the reign of law, and the belief that every event must have a cause, are as completely dependent upon the inductive principle as are the beliefs of daily life. All such general principles are believed because mankind have found innumerable instances of their truth and no instances of their falsehood. But this affords no evidence for their truth in the future, unless the inductive principle is assumed.

Thus all knowledge which, on a basis of experience tells us something about what is not experienced, is based upon a belief which experience can neither confirm nor confute, yet which, at least in its more concrete applications, appears to be as firmly rooted in us as many of the facts of experience. The existence and justification of such beliefs raises some of the most difficult and most debated problems of philosophy.

TWENTY-ONE

The Pragmatic Justification of Induction

HANS REICHENBACH (1891-1953)

From *The Rise of Scientific Philosophy**

Suppose somebody casts a die and you are asked to predict whether or not face "six" will turn up. You will prefer to predict that face "six" will not turn up. Why? You do not know it for certain; but you have a greater probability, namely of $\frac{5}{6}$, for "nonsix" than for "six". You cannot claim that your prediction must come true; but it is advantageous for you to make this prediction rather than the contrary one, because you will be right in the greater number of cases.

A statement of this kind I have called a *posit*. A posit is a statement which we treat as true although we do not know whether it is so. We try to select our posits in such a way that they will be true as often as possible. The degree of probability supplies a *rating* of the posit; it tells us how good the posit is. Such is the only function of a probability. If we have the choice between a posit of the rating $\frac{5}{6}$ and one of the rating $\frac{2}{3}$, we shall prefer the first because this posit will be true more often. We see that the degree of probability has nothing to do with the truth of the individual statement, but that it functions as an advice how to select our posits.

The method of positing is applied to all kinds of probability statements. If we are told that the probability of a rain tomorrow is 80 per cent, we posit that it will rain, and act accordingly; for instance, we tell the gardener that he need not come tomorrow to water our garden. If we have information that the stock market will probably go down, we sell our stock. If the doctor tells us that smoking will probably shorten our lifetime, we stop smoking. If we are told that we shall probably get a job with higher pay by applying for a certain position, we make the application. Although all these statements about what will happen are only maintained as probable, we treat them as true and act accordingly; that is, we employ them in the sense of posits.

* From *The Rise of Scientific Philosophy* by Hans Reichenbach (Berkeley, University of California Press, 1951), pp. 240-248. Reprinted by permission of the publisher.

The concept of posit is the key to the understanding of predictive knowledge. A statement about the future cannot be uttered with the claim that it is true; we can always imagine that the contrary will happen, and we have no guarantee that future experience will not present to us as real what is imagination today. This very fact is the rock on which every rationalist interpretation of knowledge has been wrecked. A prediction of future experiences can be uttered only in the sense of a trial; we take its possible falsehood into account, and if the prediction turns out to be wrong, we are ready for another trial. The method of trial and error is the only existing instrument of prediction. A predictive statement is a posit; instead of knowing its truth we know only its rating, which is measured in terms of its probability.

The interpretation of predictive statements as posits solves the last problem that remains for an empiricist conception of knowledge: the problem of induction. Empiricism broke down under Hume's criticism of induction, because it had not freed itself from a fundamental rationalist postulate, the postulate that all knowledge must be demonstrable as true. For this conception the inductive method is unjustifiable, since there exists no proof that it will lead to true conclusions. It is different when the predictive conclusion is regarded as a posit. In this interpretation it does not require a proof that it is true; all that can be asked for is a proof that it is a good posit, or even the best posit available. Such a proof can be given, and the inductive problem can thus be solved.

The proof requires some further investigation; it cannot be given simply by showing that the inductive conclusion has a high probability. It requires an analysis of the methods of probability and must be based on considerations that are themselves independent of such methods. The justification of induction is to be given outside the theory of probability, because the theory of probability presupposes the use of induction. The meaning of this maxim will be made clear presently.

The proof is preceded by a mathematical investigation. The calculus of probability has been constructed in an axiomatic form, comparable to the geometry of Euclid; this construction shows that all the axioms of probability are purely mathematical theorems and thus analytic statements, if the frequency interpretation of probability is accepted. The only point where a non-analytic principle intervenes is the ascertainment of a degree of probability by means of an inductive inference. We find a certain relative frequency for a series of observed events and assume that the same frequency will hold approximately for further continuation of the series—that is the only synthetic principle on which the application of the calculus of probability is based.

This result is of greatest significance. The manifold forms of induction, including the hypothetico-deductive method, are expressible in terms of deductive methods, with the sole addition of induction by enumeration. The axiomatic method supplies the proof that all forms of induction are reducible to induction by enumeration: the mathematician of our time proves what Hume took for granted.

The result may appear surprising, because the method of constructing explanatory hypotheses, or of indirect evidence, looks so different from a simple induction by enumeration. But since it is possible to construe all forms of indirect evidence as inferences covered by the mathematical calculus of probability, these inferences are included in the result of the axiomatic investigation. By means of the power of deduction, the axiomatic system controls the most remote applications of probability inferences, like the engineer who controls a remote missile by radio waves; even involved inferential structures employed by the detective or by the scientist can be accounted for in terms of the axioms. These structures are superior to a simple induction by enumeration because they contain so much deductive logic—but their inductive content is exhaustively described as a network of inductions of the enumerative type.

I should like to illustrate how enumerative inductions can be combined into a network. For centuries Europeans had known white swans only, and they inferred that all swans in the world were white. One day black swans were discovered in Australia; so the inductive inference was shown to have led to a false conclusion. Would it have been possible to avoid the mistake? It is a matter of fact that other species of birds display a great variety of color among their individuals; so the logician should have objected to the inference by the argument that, if color varies among the individuals of other species, it may also vary among the swans. The example shows that one induction can be corrected by another induction. In fact, practically all inductive inferences are made, not in isolation, but within a network of many inductions.

When I say that all inductive inferences are reducible to induction by enumeration, I mean that they are expressible through a network of such simple inductions. The method by which these elementary inferences are combined can be of a much more complicated structure than the one employed in the preceding example.

Since all inductive inferences are reducible to induction by enumeration, all that is required for making inductive inferences legitimate is a justification of induction by enumeration. Such a justification is possible, when it is realized that inductive conclusions are not claimed to be true statements, but are uttered merely in the sense of posits.

When we count the relative frequency of an event, we find that the percentage found varies with the number of observed cases, but that the variations die down with increasing number. For instance, birth statistics show that of 1,000 births 49 per cent were boys; increasing the number of cases, we find 52 per cent boys among 5,000 births, 51 per cent boys among 10,000 births. Assume for a moment we know that going on we shall finally arrive at a constant percentage—the mathematician speaks of a limit of the frequency—what numerical value should we assume for this final percentage? The best we can do is to consider the last value found as the permanent one and to employ it as our posit. If the posit on further observation turns out to be false, we shall correct it; but if the series converges toward a final percentage, we must eventually arrive at values which are close to the final value. The inductive inference is thus shown to be the best instrument of finding the final percentage, or the probability of an event, if there is such a limiting percentage at all, that is, if the series converges toward a limit.

How do we know that there is a limit of the frequency? Of course, we have no proof for this assumption. But we know: if there is one, we shall find it by the inductive method. So if you want to find a limit of the frequency, use the inductive inference—it is the best instrument you have, because, if your aim can be reached, you will reach it that way. If it cannot be reached, your attempt was in vain; but then any other attempt must also break down.

The man who makes inductive inferences may be compared to a fisherman who casts a net into an unknown part of the ocean—he does not know whether he will catch fish, but he knows that if he wants to catch fish he has to cast his net. Every inductive prediction is like casting a net into the ocean of the happenings of nature; we do not know whether we shall have a good catch, but we try, at least, and try by the help of the best means available.

We try because we want to act—and he who wants to act cannot wait until the future has become observational knowledge. To control the future—to shape future happenings according to a plan—presupposes predictive knowledge of what will happen if certain conditions are realized; and if we do not know the truth about what will happen, we shall employ our best posits in the place of truth. Posits are the instruments of action where truth is not available; the justification of induction is that it is the best instrument of action known to us.

This justification of induction is very simple; it shows that induction is the best means to attain a certain aim. The aim is predicting the future —to formulate it as finding the limit of a frequency is but another version of the same aim. This formulation has the same meaning because predictive knowledge is probable knowledge and probability is the limit of a frequency. The probability theory of knowledge allows us to construct a justification of induction; it supplies a proof that induction is the best way of finding that kind of knowledge which is the only sort attainable. All knowledge is probable knowledge and can be asserted only in the sense of posits; and induction is the instrument of finding the best posits.

This solution of the problem of induction will be clarified if it is confronted with the rationalist theory of probability. The principle of indifference, which occupies a logical position similar to that of the principle of induction because it is used for the ascertainment of a degree of probability, is regarded by the rationalist as a self-evident principle of logic; he thus arrives at a *synthetic self-evidence,* at a synthetic a priori logic. Incidentally, the principle of induction by enumeration is often also regarded as a self-evident principle; this conception represents a second version of a synthetic a priori logic of probability. The empiricist conception of inductive logic is essentially different. The principle of induction by enumeration, which constitutes its only synthetic principle, is not regarded as self-evident, or as a postulate which logic could validate. What logic can prove is that the use of the principle is advisable if a certain aim is envisaged, the aim of predicting the future. This proof, the justification of induction, is constructed in terms of analytic considerations. The empiricist is allowed to use a synthetic principle, because he does not assert that the principle is true or must lead to true conclusions or to correct probabilities or to any kind of success; all he asserts is that employing the principle is the best he can do. This renunciation of any truth claim enables him to incorporate a synthetic principle in an analytic logic and to satisfy the condition that what he *asserts* on the basis of his logic is analytic truth only. He can do so because the conclusion of the inductive inference is not asserted by him, but only posited; what he asserts is that positing the conclusion is a means to his end. The empiricist principle that reason cannot make other than analytic contributions to knowledge, that there is no synthetic self-evidence, is thus fully carried through.

TWENTY-TWO

Bertrand Russell's Doubts About Induction*

PAUL EDWARDS (1925-   )

I

A. In the celebrated chapter on induction in his *Problems of Philosophy*, Bertrand Russell asks the question: "Have we any reason, assuming that they (laws like the law of gravitation) have always held in the past, to suppose that these laws will hold in the future?" [1] Earlier in the same chapter he raises the more specific question: "Do *any* number of cases of a law being fulfilled in the past afford evidence that it will be fulfilled in the future?" [2] We may reformulate these questions in a way which lends itself more easily to critical discussion as follows:

(1) Assuming that we possess n positive instances of a phenomenon, observed in extensively varied circumstances, and that we have not observed a single negative instance (where n is a large number), have we any reason to suppose that the $n + 1$st instance will also be positive?

(2) Is there any number n of observed positive instances of a phenomenon which affords evidence that the $n + 1$st instance will also be positive?

It is clear that Russell uses "reason" synonymously with "good reason" and "evidence" with "sufficient evidence". I shall follow the same procedure throughout this article.

Russell asserts that unless we appeal to a non-empirical principle which he calls the "principle of induction", both of his questions must be answered in the negative. "Those who emphasised the scope of induction", he writes, "wished to maintain that all logic is empirical, and therefore could not be expected to realise that induction itself, their own darling, required a logical principle which obviously could not be proved inductively, and must therefore be *a priori* if it could be known at all". [3] "We must either accept the inductive principle on the ground of its intrinsic evidence or forgo all justification of our expectations about the future". [4]

---

* From "Russell's Doubts about Induction" by Paul Edwards, *Mind*, LVIII (April 1949), pp. 141-163. Reprinted by permission of the editor of *Mind*.

[1] p. 100.
[2] p. 96.
[3] *Our Knowledge of the External World* (2nd edition), p. 226.
[4] *Problems of Philosophy*, p. 106; also *Outline of Philosophy*, p. 286.

In conjunction with the inductive principle, on the other hand, question (1) at least, he contends, can be answered in the affirmative. "Whether inferences from past to future are valid depends wholly, if our discussion has been sound, upon the inductive principle: if it is true, such inferences are valid." [5] Unfortunately Russell does not make it clear whether in his opinion the same is true about question (2).

As against Russell, I shall try to show in this article that question (1) can be answered in the affirmative without in any way appealing to a non-empirical principle. I shall also attempt to show that, without in any way invoking a non-empirical principle, numbers of observed positive instances do frequently afford us evidence that unobserved instances of the same phenomenon are also positive. At the outset, I shall concentrate on question (1) since this is the more general question. Once we have answered question (1) it will require little further effort to answer question (2).

I want to emphasise here that, to keep this paper within manageable bounds, I shall refrain from discussing, at any rate explicitly, the questions "Are any inductive conclusions probable?" and "Are any inductive conclusions certain?" I hope to fill in this gap on another occasion.

It will be well to conduct our discussion in terms of a concrete example. Supposing a man jumps from a window on the fiftieth floor of the Empire State Building. Is there any reason to suppose that his body will move in the direction of the street rather than say in the direction of the sky or in a flat plane? There can be no doubt that any ordinary person and any philosophically unsophisticated scientist, would answer this question in the affirmative without in any way appealing to a non-empirical principle. He would say that there is an excellent reason to suppose that the man's body will move towards the street. This excellent reason, he would say, consists in the fact that whenever in the past a human being jumped out of a window of the Empire State Building his body moved in a downward direction; that whenever any human being anywhere jumped out of a house he moved in the direction of the ground; that, more generally, whenever a human body jumped or was thrown off an elevated locality in the neighbourhood of the earth, it moved downwards and not either upwards or at an angle of 180°; that the only objects which have been observed to be capable of moving upwards by themselves possess certain special characteristics which human beings lack; and finally in all the other observed confirmations of the theory of gravitation.

B. The philosophers who reject commonsense answers like the one just described, have relied mainly on three arguments. Russell himself explicitly employs two of them and some of his remarks make it clear that he also approves of the third. These three arguments are as follows: (a) Defenders of commonsense point to the fact that many inferences to

[5] External World, p. 226.

unobserved events were subsequently, by means of direct observation, found to have resulted in true conclusions. However, any such appeal to observed results of inductive inferences is irrelevant. For the question at stake is: Have we ever a reason, assuming that all the large number of observed instances of a phenomenon are positive, to suppose that an instance which is still unobserved is also positive? The question is not: Have we ever a reason for supposing that instances which have by now been observed but were at one time unobserved are positive? In Russell's own words: "We have experience of past futures, but not of future futures, and the question is: Will future futures resemble past futures? This question is not to be answered by an argument which starts from past futures alone." [6]

(b) Cases are known where at a certain time a large number of positive instances and not a single negative instance had been observed and where the next instance nevertheless turned out to be negative. "We know that in spite of frequent repetitions there sometimes is a failure at the last." [7] The man, for instance, "who has fed the chicken every day throughout its life at last wrings its neck instead." [8] Even in the case of the human being who is jumping out of the Empire State Building, "we may be in no better position than the chicken which unexpectedly has its neck wrung." [9]

(c) The number of positive and negative necessary conditions for the occurrence of any event is infinite or at any rate too large to be directly observed by a human being or indeed by all human beings put together. None of us, for example, has explored every corner of the universe to make sure that there nowhere exists a malicious but powerful individual who controls the movements of the sun by means of wires which are too fine to be detected by any of our microscopes. None of us can be sure that there is no such Controller who, in order to play a joke with the human race, will prevent the sun from rising to-morrow. Equally, none of us can be sure that there is nowhere a powerful individual who can, if he wishes, regulate the movement of human bodies by means of ropes which are too thin to be detected by any of our present instruments. None of us therefore can be sure than when a man jumps out of the Empire State Building he will not be drawn skyward by the Controller of Motion. Hence we have no reason to suppose that the man's body will move in the direction of the street and not in the direction of the sky.

In connexion with the last of these three arguments attention ought to be drawn to a distinction which Russell makes between what he calls the "interesting" and the "uninteresting" doubt about induction.[10] The

6 *Problems of Philosophy*, p. 100.
7 *loc. cit.*, p. 102.
8 *loc. cit.*, p. 98.
9 *Ibid.*
10 *loc. cit.*, p. 95.

uninteresting doubt is doubt about the occurrence of a given event on the
ground that not all the conditions which are known to be necessary are
in fact known to be present. What Russell calls the interesting doubt is
the doubt whether an event will take place although all the conditions
known to be necessary are known to obtain. Russell's "interesting doubt",
if I am not mistaken, is identical with Donald William's "tragic problem
of induction".[11]

II

As I indicated above, it is my object in this article to defend the
commonsense answers to both of Russell's questions. I propose to show,
in other words, that, without in any way calling upon a non-empirical
principle for assistance, we often have a reason for supposing that a generalisation will be confirmed in the future as it has been confirmed in the
past. I also propose to show that numbers "of cases of a law being fulfilled
in the past" do often afford evidence that it will be fulfilled in the future.

However, what I have to say in support of these answers is so exceedingly simple that I am afraid it will not impress the philosophers who
are looking for elaborate and complicated theories to answer these questions. But I think I can make my case appear plausible even in the eyes
of some of these philosophers if I describe at some length the general
method of resolving philosophical puzzles which I shall apply to the problem of induction.

Let us consider a simple statement like "there are several thousand
physicians in New York". We may call this a statement of commonsense,
meaning thereby no more than that anybody above a certain very moderate level of instruction and intelligence would confidently give his assent
to it.

The word "physician", as ordinarily used, is not entirely free from
ambiguity. At times it simply means "person who possesses a medical degree from a recognised academic institution". At other times, though less
often, it means the same as "person who possesses what is by ordinary
standards a considerable skill in curing diseases". On yet other occasions
when people say about somebody that he is a physician they mean both
that he has a medical degree and that he possesses a skill in curing diseases
which considerably exceeds that of the average layman.

Let us suppose that in the commonsense statement "there are several
thousand physicians in New York" the word "physician" is used exclusively in the last-mentioned sense. This assumption will simplify our discussion, but it is not at all essential to any of the points I am about to
make. It is essential, however, to realise that when somebody asserts in
ordinary life that there are several thousand physicians in New York, he

11 "Induction and the Future," *Mind,* 1948, p. 227.

is using the word "physician" in one or other of the ordinary senses just listed. By "physician" he does not mean for example "person who can speedily repair bicycles" or "person who can cure any conceivable illness in less than two minutes".

Now, supposing somebody were to say "Really, there are no physicians at all in New York", in the belief that he was contradicting and refuting commonsense. Supposing that on investigation it turns out that by "physician" he does not mean "person who has a medical degree and who has considerably more skill in curing disease that the average layman". It turns out that by "physician" he means "person who has a medical degree and who can cure any conceivable illness in less than two minutes".

What would be an adequte reply to such an "enemy of commonsense"? Clearly it would be along the following lines: "What you say is true. There are no physicians in New York—in *your* sense of the word. There are no persons in New York who can cure any conceivable disease in less than two minutes. But this in no way contradicts the commonsense view expressed by "there are several thousand physicians in New York". For the latter asserts no more than that there are several thousand people in New York who have a medical degree and who possess a skill in curing disease which considerably exceeds that of the average layman. You are guilty of *ignoratio elenchi* since the proposition you refute is different from the proposition you set out to refute."

Our discussion from here on will be greatly simplified by introducing a few technical terms. Let us, firstly, call *"ignoratio elenchi* by *redefinition"* any instance of *ignoratio elenchi* in which (i) the same sentence expresses both the proposition which ought to be proved and the proposition which is confused with it and where (ii) in the latter employment of the sentence one or more of its parts are used in a sense which is different from their ordinary sense or senses. Secondly, let us refer to any redefinition of a word which includes all that the ordinary definition of the word includes but which includes something else as well as a *"high* redefinition"; and to the sense which is defined by a high redefinition we shall refer as a high sense of the word. Thus "person who has a medical degree and who is capable of curing any conceivable disease in less than two minutes" is a high redefinition of "physician" and anybody using the word in that fashion is using it in a high sense. Thirdly, we shall refer to a redefinition of a word which includes something but not all of what the ordinary definition includes and which includes nothing else as a *"low* redefinition"; and the sense which is defined by a low redefinition we shall call a low sense of the word. "Person capable of giving first aid" or "person who knows means of alleviating pain" would be low redefinitions of "physician". Finally, it will be convenient to call a statement in which a word is used in a high or in a low sense a *redefinitional statement*. If the word is used in a high sense we shall speak of a highdefinitional statement; if it is used in a low sense we shall speak of a lowdefinitional statement.

A short while ago, I pointed out that the man who says "there are no physicians in New York", meaning that there are no people in New York who have a medical degree and who can cure any conceivable illness in less than two minutes, is not really contradicting the commonsense view that there are physicians in New York. I pointed out that he would be guilty of what in our technical language is called an *ignoratio elenchi* by redefinition. Now, it seems to me that the relation between the assertion of various philosophers that past experience never constitutes a reason for prediction or generalisation except perhaps in conjunction with a non-empirical principle and the commonsense view that past experience does often by itself constitute a reason for inferences to unobserved events has some striking resemblances to the relation between the redefinitional statement about physicians in New York and the commonsense view which this redefinitional statement fails to refute. And more generally, it strongly seems to me that almost all the bizarre pronouncements of philosophers—their "paradoxes", their "silly" theories—are in certain respects strikingly like the statement that there are no physicians in New York, made by one who means to assert that there are no people in New York who have medical degrees and who are capable of curing any conceivable disease in less than two minutes.

In making the last statement I do not mean to deny that there are also important differences between philosophical paradoxes and the highdefinitional statement about physicians. There are three differences in particular which have to be mentioned if my subsequent remarks are not to be seriously misleading. Firstly, many of the philosophical paradoxes are not without some point; they do often draw attention to likenesses and differences which ordinary usage obscures. Secondly, the redefinitions which are implicit in philosophical paradoxes do quite often, though by no means always, receive a certain backing from ordinary usage. Frequently, that is to say, there is a secondary sense or trend in ordinary usage which corresponds to the philosophical redefinition, the "real" sense of the word.[12] Thirdly, philosophical paradoxes are invariably ambiguous in a sense in which the highdefinitional statement about the physicians is not ambiguous.[13]

Now, while fully admitting all these (and other) differences, I wish

---

[12] Prominent instances of this phenomenon are "real certainty", "real knowledge", "real sameness", "real freedom", and "really contemporaneous events".

[13] The last of these points seems to me to be of enormous importance for understanding the phenomenon of philosophical paradoxes.

to insist on the great likenesses between philosophical paradoxes and the redefinitional statement about the physicians. And in this article I am mainly concerned with the likenesses, not with the differences. My main object of course is to point out the likenesses between the highdefinitional statement "there are no physicians in New York" and the statement that past experience never by itself affords a reason for making inferences to unobserved events. However, my points there will be clearer if I first make them in connexion with another celebrated paradox.

Following Plato, Berkeley [14] argued in favour of the view that heat and cold are not really "in the object". Ordinary people would unhesitatingly say that water of *e.g.,* 50° Centigrade is hot. Against this, Plato and Berkeley would point out that to a man who a moment before had held his hands in a jug of water with a temperature of 80° C., the water of 50° C. would appear cold. Similarly, to a race of individuals whose body-temperature was say 75° C., water of 50° would regularly appear cold. But the percepts of those to whom the water of 50° appears cold are just as genuine as the percepts of people to whom the water appears hot. Now, since it would be wrong to say that the water of 50° is really cold simply because of these genuine percepts of cold, it cannot any more rationally be said to be hot. The cold has "just as good a right to be considered real" as the hot; and therefore, "to avoid favouritism, we are compelled to deny that in itself" [15] the water is either hot or cold.

It is not difficult to show that this argument is a case of *ignoratio elenchi* by redefinition. When an ordinary person says that water of 50° C. is hot all he means is that human beings, with their body-temperature being what it is, would in *all ordinary circumstances* have sense-impressions of heat on coming into contact with such water. In saying that water of 50° is hot, is *really* hot, an ordinary person in no way denies that under certain *special* conditions a human being would have genuine sense-impressions of cold. He also in no way denies that to a race of individuals whose body-temperature is 75° the water would genuinely appear cold. Pointing to these facts does therefore not refute the ordinary man. Berkeley is clearly guilty of a high redefinition of "hot" or "really hot". To him something is hot only if, in addition to appearing hot to human beings in ordinary circumstances, it also appears hot to them under special circumstances and if it appears hot to beings with a body-temperature which is much greater than the actual body-temperature of human beings.

However, this is not quite accurate since, like most other philosophical paradoxes, the paradox about heat and cold has a double meaning. It would be inaccurate simply to say that Berkeley is guilty of *ignoratio elenchi* by redefinition. On the other hand, without in any

---

14 *Three Dialogues between Hylas and Philonous,* p. 208 (Everyman edit.).
15 The phrases are Russell's, used in a very similar context (*Problems,* p. 14).

way being inaccurate, it can be said that Berkeley and Plato have laid themselves open to the following dilemma: "Either you mean by 'hot' what is ordinarily meant by it—if you do, then what you say is plainly false; or else you are using 'hot' in a high sense—if so what you say is true, but in that case you are guilty of *ignoratio elenchi* by redefinition. In either event you have failed to refute commonsense." Very similar answers can also be made to Berkeley's and Russell's arguments concerning colours, shapes, and the other qualities which commonsense believes to exist independently of being perceived.

At the same time it must be admitted that Berkeley's arguments have a certain value. In ordinary speech we make a fairly rigid distinction between "real" and "unreal" data. Among the unreal data we lump together both the percepts which we have under special conditions (and percepts which do and would appear to beings differently constituted from ourselves) and what we experience *e.g.,* in dreams and hallucinations. "Real" we call only those percepts which a normal observer has under certain standard conditions.

A classification of this sort obscures the many likenesses between the "real" percepts and percepts appearing under special conditions, while also hiding the many differences between the latter and data which are experienced in dreams and hallucinations.

The situation becomes quite clear if we divide data into three and not merely into two groups, as follows:

the R-data: percepts appearing to a normal observer under standard conditions,

the A-data: percepts appearing to a normal observer under special conditions or to an abnormal observer in certain normal or special circumstances, and

the D-data: data appearing in dreams, hallucinations, etc.

It is unnecessary for our purposes to discuss exactly what are the likenesses between the R-data and the A-data. It is unnecessary, too, to discuss what exactly are the differences between the A-data and the D-data. It is sufficient to point out that while Berkeley is wrong in believing or suggesting that there are no differences between the R-data and the A-data, he is right in insisting that the differences between the R-data and the A-data are not nearly as great as ordinary speech suggests. In the case of colours, Berkeley's argument has the further merit of bringing out the fact that the expression "X's real colour" has *two* perfectly proper senses. His argument helps one to realise that "X's real colours" may mean "the colour which X exhibits to a normal observer under certain standard conditions" *as well as* "the colour which X exhibits to a normal observer under a finer instrument than the human eye, *e.g.,* a microscope".

III

A. Supposing a man, let us call him M, said to us "I have not yet found any physicians in New York". Suppose we take him to Park Avenue and introduce him to Brown, a man who has a medical degree and who has cured many people suffering from diseases of the ear. Brown admits, however, that he has not been able to cure *all* the patients who ever consulted him. He also admits that many of his cures took a long time, some as long as eight years. On hearing this, M says "Brown certainly isn't a physician".

Supposing we next take M to meet Black who has a medical degree and who can prove to M's and to our satisfaction that he has cured every patient who ever consulted him. Moreover, none of Black's cures took more than three years. However, on hearing that some of Black's cures took as long as two years and ten months, M says "Black certainly isn't a physician either".

Finally we introduce M to White who has a medical degree and who has cured every one of his patients in less than six months. When M hears that some of White's cures took as long as five and a half months, he is adamant and exclaims "White—what a ridiculous error to call him a physician!"

At this stage, if not much sooner, all of us would impatiently ask M: What on earth do you mean by "physician"? And we would plainly be justified in adding: Whatever you may mean by "physician", in any sense in which we ever use the word, Black and Brown and White are physicians and very excellent ones at that.

Let us return now to Russell's doubt about the sun's rising to-morrow or about what would happen to a man who jumps out of the Empire State Building. Let us consider what Russell would say in reply to the following question: Supposing that the observed confirmatory instances for the theory of gravitation were a million or ten million times as extensive as they now are and that they were drawn from a very much wider field; would we then have a reason to suppose that the man will fall into the street and not move up into the sky? It is obvious that Russell and anybody taking his view would say "No". He would reply that though our *expectation* that the man's body will move in the direction of the street would be even stronger then than it is at present, we would still be without a *reason*.

Next, let us imagine ouselves to be putting the following question to Russell: Supposing the world were such that no accumulation of more than five hundred observed positive instances of a phenomenon has ever been found to be followed by a negative instance; supposing, for instance, that all the chickens who have ever been fed by the same man for 501 days in succession or more are still alive and that all the men too are still alive feeding the chickens every day—would the observed confirmations of the law of gravity in that case be a reason to suppose that the man jumping out of the Empire State Building will move in the direction of the street and not in the direction of the sky? I am not quite sure what Russell would say in reply to this question. Let us assume he would once again answer "No—past experience would not even then ever be a *reason*".

Thirdly and finally, we have to consider what Russell would say to the following question: Supposing we had explored every corner of the universe with instruments millions of times as fine and accurate as any we now possess and that we had yet failed to discover any Controller of the movements of human bodies—would we then in our predictions about the man jumping out of the Empire State Building be in a better position than the chicken is in predicting its meals? Would our past observations then be a reason for our prediction? Whatever Russell would in fact say to this, it is clear that his remarks concerning the "interesting" doubt about induction require him to answer our question in the negative. He would have to say something like this: "Our *expectation* that the man's body will move in a downward direction will be even stronger than it is now. However, without invoking a non-empirical principle, we shall not *really* be in a better position than the chicken. We should still fail to possess a *reason*."

As in the case of the man who refused to say that Brown, Black, and White were doctors, our natural response to all this will be to turn to Russell and say: What do you mean by "being in a better position"? What on earth do you mean by "a reason"? And, furthermore, why should anybody be interested in a reason in your sense of the word?

Russell's remarks about the need for a general principle like his principle of induction to serve as major premiss in every inductive argument make it clear what he means by a reason: like the Rationalists and Hume (in most places), he means by "reason" a *logically conclusive* reason and by "evidence" *deductively conclusive* evidence. When "reason" is used in this sense, it must be admitted that past observations can never by themselves be a reason for any prediction whatsoever. But "reason" is not used in this sense when, in science or in ordinary life, people claim to have a reason for a prediction.

So far as I can see, there are three different trends in the ordinary usage of "reason for an inductive conclusion" and according to none of them does the word mean "logically conclusive reason". Among the three trends one is much more prominent than the others. It may fitly be called the main sense of the word. According to this main sense, what we mean when we claim that we have a reason for a prediction is that the past observations of this phenomenon or of analogical phenomena are of a certain kind: they are exclusively or predominantly positive, the number of the positive observations is at least fairly large, and they come from extensively varied sets of circumstances. This is of course a very crude formulation. But for the purposes of this article it is, I think, sufficient.[16]

Next, there is a number of trends according to which we mean very much less than this. Occasionally, for instance, we simply mean that it is *reasonable* to infer the inductive conclusion. And clearly it may be reasonable to infer an inductive conclusion for which we have no reason in the main sense. Thus let us suppose I know that Parker will meet Schroeder in a game in the near future and that it is imperative for me not to suspend my judgment but to come to a conclusion as to who will win. Supposing I know nothing about their present form and nothing also about the type of court on which the match is to be played. All I know is that Parker and Schroeder have in the previous two seasons met six times, Parker scoring four victories to Schroeder's two. In these circumstances it would be reasonable for me to predict that Parker will win and unreasonable to predict that Schroeder will win. Clearly however, in the main sense of the word I have no reason for either prediction.

Again there is a trend according to which any positive instance of a phenomenon is *a* reason for concluding that the next instance of the phenomenon will be positive. Thus in the circumstances described in the preceding paragraph, it would be quite proper to say we have *more reason* for supposing that Parker will win than for predicting Schroeder's victory. It would be quite proper also to say that we have *some reason* for supposing that Schroeder will win. It would be proper to say this even if Schroeder had won only one of the six matches. To all these and similar trends in the ordinary usage of "reason for an inductive conclusion" I shall from now on refer as the second ordinary sense of the word.

There can be no doubt that in both these ordinary senses of the word, we frequently have a reason for an inductive conclusion. In these senses we have an excellent reason for supposing that the man jumping out of the Empire State Building will move in the direction of the street, that the sun will rise to-morrow and that Stalin will die before the year 2000. The answer to question (1) is therefore a firm and clear "Yes": in many domains we have a multitude of exclusively positive instances coming from extensively different circumstances.

The same is true if "reason" is used in the third ordinary sense. However, I propose to reserve our discussion of that sense for Section V below. For the time being it will be convenient and, I think, not at all

---

[16] I have so far left out one important element in the main sense of "reason for an inductive conclusion". I shall come to that in Section IV. In the meantime this omission will not affect any of my points.

misleading to speak as if what I have called the main sense is the *only* ordinary sense of "reason for an inductive conclusion".

It should now be clear that, when Russell says that observed instances are never by themselves a reason for an inductive conclusion, he is guilty of an *ignoratio elenchi* by redefinition. His assertion that the premises of an inductive argument never by themselves constitute a *logically conclusive* reason for an inductive conclusion in no way contradicts the commonsense assertion that they frequently constitute a reason *in the ordinary sense of the word*. Russell's definition of "reason" is indeed in one respect not a redefinition since in certain contexts we do use "reason" to mean "deductively conclusive reason". However, it is a redefinition in that we never in ordinary life use "reason" in Russell's sense when we are talking about inductive arguments.

Moreover, if "reason" means "deductively conclusive reason", Russell's questions are no more genuinely questions than *e.g.,* the sentence "Is a father a female parent?" For, since part of the definition of "inductive inference" is inference from something observed to something unobserved, it is a *contradiction* to say that an inference is both inductive and at the same time in the same respect deductively conclusive. Russell's "interesting" doubt, then, is no more sensible or interesting than the "doubt" whether we shall ever see something invisible or find an object which is a father and also female or an object which is a man but not a human being.

In a similar fashion, Russell's remarks about the future future which we quoted in Section 1B constitute an *ignoratio elenchi* by redefinition.[17] If the word "future" is used in its ordinary sense in the statement "the future will resemble the past and the present in certain respects" then we have plenty of evidence to support it. For in the ordinary sense of the word, "future" simply means "period which has to the past and the present the relation of happening after it". In its ordinary sense, "future" does *not* mean "period which has to the past and the present the relation of happening after it *and* which can never itself be experienced *as a present*". The period which is referred to by "future" in its ordinary sense may very well one day be experienced as a present.

In the ordinary sense of the word "future" therefore, what Russell calls past futures *are* futures. They are futures in relation to certain other periods which preceded them. Now, the appeal to the fact that past futures resembled past pasts and past presents constitutes excellent inductive evidence for the conclusion that the future will resemble the past and the present. Stated fully, the argument is as follows: a period which has to the past and present the relation of happening after it

---

[17] The paragraphs which follow are a summary in my own words of the main point of F. L. Will's delightful article "Will the Future be like the Past?" (*Mind*, 1947).

will resemble the past and the present in certain respects because in the past periods which stood in the same temporal relation to other periods were found to resemble those periods in these respects.

It should be emphasised that in the conclusion of this argument "future" means "future future", as that phrase would normally be understood. It refers to a period which by the time at which the statement is made has not yet been experienced, *i.e.*, has not yet become a present or a past.

The appeal to the resemblance between past futures and past pasts and presents is not to the point only if in the sentence "the future will resemble the past and the present" the word "future" means "period which has to the present the relation of occurring after it *and* which can never be experienced as a present". In that case, of course past futures are not really futures. For, when they were experienced they were experienced as presents. However, anybody who in ordinary life or in science says or implies that the future will resemble the past and the present does not use "future" in this sense. He means to assert something about a future which may one day be experienced as a present.

B. If Russell had answered in the affirmative any of the three questions which we imagined ourselves to be addressing to him, his question (1) would be a genuine question in the sense that it could then not be disposed of by an examination of definitions alone. But even then Russell would have been guilty of *ignoratio elenchi* by high redefinition. For in order to have a reason, in the ordinary sense of the word, for inferring that the next instance of a certain phenomenon is positive it is not necessary to observe all the positive and negative necessary conditions for the occurrence of this instance. Nor is it necessary that the collection of positive observed instances should be larger or taken from more extensively different circumstances than many we actually have. Nor, finally, is it necessary that breakdowns should never have occurred in *any* domain. All that is necssary in this connexion is that there should have been no breakdowns in the same domain. Or if any did occur in the same domain they must have proved capable of correlation with certain special features which are known not to be present in the subject of the prediction.

Anybody who takes the trouble to observe the ordinary usage of the word "reason" in connexion with inductive arguments can easily check up on these claims.

It may be interesting to return for a moment to the case of the chicken which finally had its neck wrung. If we had explored every corner of the universe with wonderfully fine instruments and failed to discover a Controller of human movements, then in any ordinary sense of "being in a better position" we should undoubtedly, be in a better position in the case of the man jumping out of the Empire State Building than the chicken in regard to its meals. If Russell even then denied that we are in a better position he is surely using the phrase "being in a better position" in a strange sense. Or else he is asserting a very plain falsehood. For to say that possession of one set of observed facts, say P, puts one in a better position with regard to a certain inductive conclusion, say c, than possession of another set of observed facts, say Q, simply means that P is a reason for c while Q is not, or that P is a better reason than Q.

Moreover, even without having explored every corner of the universe, we *are* in a very much better position in the case of predicting the sun's rising or the movement of a man jumping from the Empire State Building than the chicken is regarding its meals. The truth is that Russell's analogy, although it is not wholly pointless, is very weak indeed. Its only merit consists in bringing out the fact that neither we nor the chicken have explored every corner of the universe. On the other hand, there are two important differences which Russell obscures when he says that even in the case of our most trusted scientific theories we may be in no better a position than the chicken. Firstly, the number of observed instances supporting our prediction in a case like the man's jumping from the Empire State Building is obviously much greater than the number of positive instances observed by the chicken. And secondly, although we cannot definitely say that there is nowhere a Controller of human motions, we certainly have no reason whatsoever to suppose that one exists. We have no reason whatsoever to suppose that a living individual, in any ordinary sense of "control", controls the movements of human beings who jump out of a house. The chicken, on the other hand, if it knows anything, knows that it depends for its meals on another living object.

C. Let us now turn to question (2): Is there any number, n, of observed positive instances of a phenomenon which affords evidence that the $n + 1$st instance will also be positive? I have already mentioned the familiar fact that scientists as well as ordinary people of a certain level of intelligence do not rely for their inductive conclusions on the number of observed positive instances exclusively. However, it will be easier to discuss the question before us if we proceed on the assumption that according to commonsense the strength of the past experience as evidence depends on the number of observed positive instances and on nothing else. All important points can be made more easily if we proceed on this assumption.

Now, in two senses the answer to question (2) must be admitted to be a clear "No". Firstly, even if there were in every domain or in some domains a number of observed positive instances which constitutes the dividing line between evidence and non-evidence or, as it is more commonly expressed, between sufficient and insufficient evidence, there is no reason whatsoever to suppose that the number would be the same for different domains. There is no reason to suppose that in the domain of animal learning, for example, the number is the same as in the domain of the movements of the heavenly bodies. But, secondly, there is no such number in *any* domain. For we are here clearly faced with a case of what is sometimes called "continuous variation". There is no more *a* number dividing sufficient from insufficient evidence than there is a number dividing bald people from those who are not bald or poor people from people who are not poor.

These facts, however, imply nothing against commonsense. For, from the fact that there is no rigid division between sufficient and insufficient evidence it does not follow that there are no cases of sufficient evidence. From the fact that there is no number which constitutes the borderline between adequate collections of positive instances and those which are not adequate it does not follow that no number of positive instances is adequate. Although we cannot point to a number which divides bald people from people who are not bald, we can without any hesitation say that a man without a single hair on his head is bald while one with a million hairs on his head is not bald.

Furthermore, just as we can say about many people that they are bald and about many others that they are not bald although we have not counted the number of hairs on their heads and just as we can say that Rockefeller is rich although we cannot even approximately say what is the dollar-equivalent of his total possessions, so we can very often say *that* a number of observed instances constitutes sufficient evidence although we cannot say *what* this number is. The number of instances supporting the theory of gravitation which human beings have observed is for example more than sufficient evidence—in any ordinary sense of the word—for supposing that the man jumping out of the Empire State Building will move in a downward direction. But nobody knows what this number is. Human beings simply do not bother to keep records of all instances which confirm the law of gravity.

*   *   *   *   *

TWENTY-THREE

Should We Attempt To Justify Induction?*

WESLEY C. SALMON (1925-   )

According to [a common argument for the impossibility of justifying induction], justification consists in showing that whatever is to be justified conforms to certain already accepted principles or rules. In particular, an inference is justified if it can be shown to conform to the relevant rules of inference. Sometimes these rules can, in turn, be justified by reference to other rules or principles. But to ask for a justification of all rules of inference is without sense, for no rules or principles are available in terms of which a justification could possibly be given. When we have called into question so much that there no longer remain any rules or principles to which a justification could be referred, then we have reached the limits of justifiability. Thus, to question any particular inductive inference is legitimate, for it can be justified or refuted in terms of the general canons of induction, whereas, to question induction in general leaves no canons in terms of which the justification can occur. This view is held by Strawson.[1]

If the foregoing theory is correct, empirical knowledge is, at bottom, a matter of convention. We choose, quite arbitrarily it would seem, some basic canons of induction; there is no possibility of justifying the choice. They are arbitrary in the sense that cognitive considerations do not force their acceptance. It is perfectly conceivable that someone else might select a different set of inductive canons, and if so, there would be no way of showing that one set was better than another for purposes of gaining factual knowledge. Yet, such a person would regard certain inferences as justified which we would regard as unjustified. He would hold certain conclusions to be well established while we would hold the same conclusions to be disconfirmed. This is the sense in which conventionalism follows from the Strawson theory.

Herbert Feigl has given an answer to this contention of Strawson, and it consists in providing a clear sense for the question of the justification of induction in general. Feigl distinguishes two kinds of justifi-

---

* From "Should We Attempt to Justify Induction?" by Wesley C. Salmon, *Philosophical Studies*, Vol. VIII, No. 3 (April 1957), pp. 38-42. Reprinted by permission of the editors and the publisher.

[1] P. F. Strawson, *Introduction to Logical Theory*, New York, 1952.

cation. He calls the first of these "validation"; it is the kind of justification Strawson describes. An inference is validated by showing that it is governed by an accepted rule. A rule of inference is validated by showing that it can be derived from other accepted rules or principles. There is, however, a second form of justification called "vindication." This kind of justification consists in showing that a given decision, policy, or act is well adapted to achieving a certain end. Translated into Feigl's terminology, Strawson's thesis becomes the innocuous claim that it is impossible to validate induction in general; only particular inductive rules and inferences can be validated. However, the warrantist is not attempting to validate the basic inductive canons; he seeks to vindicate them. The warrantist intentionally goes beyond the limits of validation, but he does not go beyond the limits of justification. To maintain that he transgresses the limits of justification would be tantamount to a denial that vindication is a kind of justification. It is difficult to imagine any argument that could possibly support such a denial.

The appeal to vindication requires, obviously, some aims or goals in terms of which a vindication can be given. It is at this point that one of the main controversies in the whole philosophy of induction occurs. The practicalist wants to vindicate induction by reference to the aim of attaining correct predictions and true conclusions. The critic will immediately point out that it is impossible to prove that induction will ever achieve this goal. It might therefore be concluded that there is no possibility of ever vindicating induction.

There are two major alternatives at this point. On the one hand, we may revise our conception of the aim of induction in an attempt to escape the necessity of proving that induction is well suited to the aforementioned purpose of arriving at true conclusions. On the other hand, we may hold, as the practicalist does, that it is possible to show that some inductive rules are better suited than others to the purpose of arriving at true results, even though it is impossible to prove that one will be successful while another will not. Let us consider the first of these alternatives. A large number of authors have suggested that we might justify induction as a tool for establishing *reasonable* beliefs, since it is impossible to show that induction will lead to *true* beliefs. According to this view, induction could be vindicated as leading, not necessarily to true conclusions, but rather to reasonable ones. Strawson, not really content with a view which implies sheer conventionalism, argues for this kind of justification when he is not busy arguing that no justification is needed. The argument is based chiefly upon an analysis of the meaning of "reasonable" which purports to establish that reasonable beliefs, by definition, are beliefs which have good inductive support. Strawson says (1, p. 249), "to call a particular belief reasonable or unreasonable is to apply inductive standards . . ." A little later, he further comments (1, p. 257): "to ask whether it is reasonable to place reliance on inductive procedures is like asking whether it is reasonable to proportion the degree of one's convictions to the strength of the evidence. Doing this is what 'being reasonable' *means* in such a context."

It seems to me that there are fatal objections to this approach. The term "reasonable" is, after all, virtually a synonym of "justifiable." To have reasonable beliefs is to have beliefs that are well grounded by justifiable methods. "Reasonable," then, partakes of the same ambiguity as "justifiable"—one sense referring to validation, the other to vindication. Thus, believing reasonably in one sense means holding beliefs which are sanctioned by inductive and deductive canons. In this sense, reasonable beliefs are beliefs which have been arrived at by methods which can be *validated* by reference to the accepted principles of inductive and deductive inference. In the second sense, "reasonable" means the adoption of methods and techniques which will most efficiently bring about one's ends and goals. This sense of "reasonable" corresponds to *vindication*. It is clear that using inductive methods is reasonable in the sense of "reasonable" which corresponds to *validation*. Now the problem of the justification of induction assumes the form "Is there any justification for being reasonable?" It will not do to reply that this question has the obvious tautological answer "It is reasonable to be reasonable." In view of the two distinct meanings of "reasonable" this answer may be no tautology at all, for it may contain an equivocation on the term "reasonable." Therefore, we must not lightly dismiss the question about a justification for being reasonable.

If we ask, "Why be reasonable?" construing "reasonable" in the sense related to vindication, the answer is easy to find. Being reasonable, in this sense, means adopting methods which are best suited to the attainment of our ends. Since we are motivated to achieve our ends, the realization that a method is reasonable constitutes a sufficient reason for adopting that method. To be unreasonable, in this sense, is to invite frustration. If, however, we shift to the sense of "reasonable" which is associated with validation, the answer to the question "Why be reasonable?" is much less clear. Presumably, the answer would be that to be reasonable is to be scientific and to use methods which have worked well for us. To be unreasonable would be to hold beliefs which are ill grounded and which run great danger of being false. But in so saying, have we not begged the very question which is at issue in the problem of induction? Surely there is no particular intrinsic value in being scientific or proceeding in accord with the standard inductive methods. We adopt these methods because we regard them as the best methods for establishing matter of fact conclusions. But when the problem of induction is raised, the question at issue is whether the standard inductive methods are, in fact, well suited to the purpose of establishing these factual conclusions.

It may be that the two senses of "reasonable" which we have distinguished are extensionally equivalent—that procedures are reasonable in the one sense if and only if they are reasonable in the other. But it would be a mistake merely to assume that this is the case. When a term has two distinct definitions it is not permissible to assume that the two definitions are equivalent; if there is such equivalence it must be shown. This is especially true when there are arguments which indicate that the supposed equivalence may not hold. Hume's arguments are just such arguments. If we try to show that such equivalence does hold—if we try to show that the standard inductive methods are those best suited to the purpose of arriving at correct beliefs—we are undertaking the task of the warrantist.

In accord with the philosophic fashion of the times one may be tempted to ask what is the ordinary meaning of "reasonable." Perhaps the ordinary sense of "reasonable" ensures that proceeding according to the standard inductive rules is reasonable. This is probably true of the ordinary sense. But this only shows that ordinary usage is established by people who are unaware of Hume's arguments. To say that ordinary people are untroubled by Humean doubts about induction may simply mean that ordinary people are philosophically ignorant. They assume that the two senses of reasonable distinguished above are equivalent partly because they have never thought of the distinction and partly because, had they thought of the distinction, they would have been unaware of any considerations which would lead to the conclusion that possibly the two senses are not equivalent. To cite ordinary use in this context, then, does not solve the philosophic question. It sanctions neglect of the philosophic question by virtue of an equivocation.

The attempt to vindicate inductive methods by showing that they lead to reasonable belief is a failure. If we assume that inductive beliefs are reasonable in the sense of being based on justifiable methods of inference, we are begging the question. If we regard beliefs as reasonable simply because they are arrived at inductively, we still have the problem of showing that reasonable beliefs are valuable. This is the problem of induction stated in new words. If we regard beliefs as reasonable simply because they are arrived at inductively and we hold that reasonable beliefs are valuable for their own sake, it appears that we have elevated inductive method to the place of an intrinsic good. On this latter alternative it would seem that we use inductive methods, not because they enable us to make correct predictions or arrive at true explanations, but simply because we like to use them. It sounds very much as if the whole argument (that reasonable beliefs are, by definition, beliefs which are inductively supported) has the function of transferring to the word "inductive" all of the honorific connotations of the word "reasonable," quite apart from whether induction is good for anything. The resulting justification of induction amounts to this: If you use inductive procedures you can call yourself "reasonable"—*and isn't that nice!*

Further Reading

BLACK, M., *Problems of Analysis* (Ithaca, Cornell University Press, 1954).

CARNAP, R., *Logical Foundations of Probability* (Chicago, University of Chicago Press, 1950).

GOODMAN, N., *Fact, Fiction and Forecast* (Cambridge, Mass., Harvard University Press, 1955).

HUME, D., *Enquiry Concerning Human Understanding* (1748).

————, *Treatise on Human Nature* (1739).

KNEALE, W., *Probability and Induction* (Oxford, Clarendon Press, 1949).

REICHENBACH, H., *Theory of Probability* (Berkeley, Calif., University of California Press, 1954).

STRAWSON, P. F., *Introduction to Logical Theory* (New York, John Wiley and Sons, Inc., 1952).

VON WRIGHT, G. H., *Logical Problem of Induction* (Oxford, Basil Blackwell, 1957).

PART FIVE

Perception

Introduction

Philosophers have often said that our knowledge must be limited because seeing, hearing, and the other forms of sensory perception are systematically defective, or at least are by nature incapable of disclosing to us anything with the characteristics we ordinarily suppose physical objects have. Justification for these claims is offered in a number of different arguments, examples of which are presented in the initial section of this chapter, "Arguments for the Introduction of Sense Data." All these arguments lend support to the views just mentioned by directly supporting still others: that there is only one kind of thing we can ever really or strictly perceive—sensory qualities—and that sensory qualities are entities entirely different in character from physical objects. Such true or proper objects of perception have been variously called "ideas" (Locke and Berkeley), "impressions," "sensibilia," and "sense data." Though different philosophers have given different descriptions of these special entities (which will here be called simply sense data), one thing generally said of them is that their existence is dependent upon the specific perceptual situation. Obviously any such dependence is foreign to our notion of a physical object; we do not suppose that the existence of trees and chairs depends upon their being perceived. If it is true that perception really discloses to us only such special entities, then our assumption that sensory perception can give information about the world is rendered problematic; for what we constantly take ourselves to be seeing—things independent of experience—cannot be what we actually do see.

In contrast to the direct, or "naive," realist (a philosopher who contends that what we really perceive are physical objects), the defender of sense data, will have to say how these entities are related to the trees, buildings, people, and other objects that we ordinarily suppose to be what we see. One account of the matter is that of representational (indirect) realism. According to this view seeing an object like a tree involves apprehending or sensing a datum that represents a certain kind of physical object or configuration of matter. The representative character of the datum, which stems from the fact that it has some traits in common with what it represents, explains how we can find out about the physical world by having sense experience. It is often said that the datum has the further characteristic of being caused by the physical object (depending upon a certain state of the eyes, nervous system, and so forth; see Locke). Berkeley, however, shows difficulties in this account of perception. Chief among them, perhaps, is the problem of how the existence of any such independent objects could ever be verified, if in perception we are confined to sense data. One way of handling this difficulty might be to show that the existence of such independent entities is a supposition we must make in order to have any knowledge at all (see Whitely, pp. 440-447). Another course is to reject realism and adopt phenomenalism.

In view of this problem of how, screened in by sense data, we can know of an external world, phenomenalism is an obvious successor to realism. For the phenomenalist maintains that our ordinary beliefs about trees and buildings are nothing but beliefs about sense data and their relations. The seeing of a tree, on this view, is not to be thought of as a relation between person, sense datum, and material object; it is a relation between person, sense datum, and still other data of suitable kinds. In the text various forms of phenomenalism are presented, as well as some of its difficulties. As an answer to scepticism, phenomenalism may have much to recommend it. Yet efforts to analyze trees and buildings (or statements about them) in terms of sense data have results that seem inescapably queer; and provocative reasons have been given for questioning the possibility of such analyses on technical grounds, however willing we might be to set aside queerness as an objection.

The final section of this chapter contains criticisms of the arguments originally given for the introduction of sense data. The first paper attacks the supposition that seeing can involve entities whose character is independent of belief or judgment about them, and presents a point of view often found in idealist epistemology (for certain companion doctrines see Bosanquet, pp. 95-111, and Blanshard, pp. 285-299). If the original arguments for sense data could be effectively countered, then some of the most important grounds for maintaining that we cannot strictly perceive physical objects would be disestablished. Of course this view could still be true, even though these arguments for it were to be found inadequate. The burden of proof must rest on its defender, however, for it is incompatible with some of our most fundamental assumptions about experience.

SECTION ONE

Arguments for Introducing Sense Data in Analyzing Perception

TWENTY-FOUR

Arguments from Relativity of Perception

GEORGE BERKELEY (1685-1753)

From *Three Dialogues Between Hylas and Philonous**

PHILONOUS. What mean you by Sensible Things?

HYLAS. Those things which are perceived by the senses. Can you imagine that I mean anything else?

PHIL. Pardon me, Hylas, if I am desirous clearly to apprehend your notions, since this may much shorten our inquiry. Suffer me then to ask you this farther question. Are those things only perceived by the senses which are perceived immediately? Or, may those things properly be said to be *sensible* which are perceived mediately, or not without the intervention of others?

HYL. I do not sufficiently understand you.

PHIL. In reading a book, what I immediately perceive are the letters; but mediately, or by means of these, are suggested to my mind the notions of God, virtue, truth, &c. Now, that the letters are truly sensible things, or perceived by sense, there is no doubt: but I would know whether you take the things suggested by them to be so too.

HYL. No, certainly: it were absurd to think *God* or *virtue* sensible things; though they may be signified and suggested to the mind by sensible marks, with which they have an arbitrary connexion.

* From *Three Dialogues Between Hylas and Philonous* by George Berkeley.

PHIL. It seems then, that by *sensible things* you mean those only which can be perceived *immediately* by sense?

HYL. Right.

PHIL. Doth it not follow from this, that although I see one part of the sky red, and another blue, and that my reason doth thence evidently conclude there must be some cause of that diversity of colours, yet that cause cannot be said to be a sensible thing, or perceived by the sense of seeing?

HYL. It doth.

PHIL. In like manner, though I hear variety of sounds, yet I cannot be said to hear the causes of those sounds?

HYL. You cannot.

PHIL. And when by my touch I perceive a thing to be hot and heavy, I cannot say, with any truth or propriety, that I feel the cause of its heat or weight?

HYL. To prevent any more questions of this kind, I tell you once for all, that by *sensible things* I mean those only which are perceived by sense; and that in truth the senses perceive nothing which they do not perceive *immediately*: for they make no inferences. The deducting therefore of causes or occasions from effects and appearances, which alone are perceived by sense, entirely relates to reason.

PHIL. This point then is agreed between us—That *sensible things are those only which are immediately perceived by sense.* You will farther inform me, whether we immediately perceive by sight anything beside light, and colours, and figures; or by hearing, anything but sounds; by the palate, anything beside taste; by the smell, beside odours; or by the touch, more than tangible qualities.

HYL. We do not.

PHIL. It seems, therefore, that if you take away all sensible qualities, there remains nothing sensible?

HYL. I grant it.

PHIL. Sensible things therefore are nothing else but so many sensible qualities, or combinations of sensible qualities?

HYL. Nothing else.

PHIL. *Heat* then is a sensible thing?

HYL. Certainly.

PHIL. Doth the *reality* of sensible things consist in being perceived? or, is it something distinct from their being perceived, and that bears no relation to the mind?

HYL. To *exist* is one thing, and to be *perceived* is another.

PHIL. I speak with regard to sensible things only. And of these I ask, whether by their real existence you mean a subsistence exterior to the mind, and distinct from their being perceived?

HYL. I mean a real absolute being, distinct from, and without any relation to, their being perceived.

PHIL. Heat therefore, if it be allowed a real being, must exist without the mind?

HYL. It must.

PHIL. Tell me, Hylas, is this real existence equally compatible to all degrees of heat, which we perceive; or is there any reason why we should attribute it to some, and deny it to others? And if there be, pray let me know that reason.

HYL. Whatever degree of heat we perceive by sense, we may be sure the same exists in the object that occasions it.

PHIL. What! the greatest as well as the least?

HYL. I tell you, the reason is plainly the same in respect of both. They are both perceived by sense; nay, the greater degree of heat is more sensibly perceived; and consequently, if there is any difference, we are more certain of its real existence than we can be of the reality of a lesser degree.

PHIL. But is not the most vehement and intense degree of heat a very great pain?

HYL. No one can deny it.

PHIL. And is any unperceiving thing capable of pain or pleasure?

HYL. No, certainly.

PHIL. Is your material substance a senseless being, or a being endowed with sense and perception?

HYL. It is senseless without doubt.

PHIL. It cannot therefore be the subject of pain?

HYL. By no means.

PHIL. Nor consequently of the greatest heat perceived by sense, since you acknowledge this to be no small pain?

HYL. I grant it.

PHIL. What shall we say then of your external object; is it a material substance, or no?

HYL. It is a material substance with the sensible qualities inhering in it.

PHIL. How then can a great heat exist in it, since you own it cannot in a material substance? I desire you would clear this point.

HYL. Hold, Philonous, I fear I was out in yielding intense heat to be a pain. It should seem rather, that pain is something distinct from heat, and the consequence or effect of it.

PHIL. Upon putting your hand near the fire, do you perceive one simple uniform sensation, or two distinct sensations?

HYL. But one simple sensation.

PHIL. Is not the heat immediately perceived?

HYL. It is.

PHIL. And the pain?

HYL. True.

PHIL. Seeing therefore they are both immediately perceived at the same time, and the fire affects you only with one simple or uncompounded idea, it follows that this same simple idea is both the intense heat immediately perceived, and the pain; and, consequently, that the intense heat immediately perceived is nothing distinct from a particular sort of pain.

HYL. It seems so.

PHIL. Again, try in your thoughts, Hylas, if you can conceive a vehement sensation to be without pain or pleasure.

HYL. I cannot.

PHIL. Or can you frame to yourself an idea of sensible pain or pleasure in general, abstracted from every particular idea of heat, cold, tastes, smells, &c.?

HYL. I do not find that I can.

PHIL. Doth it not therefore follow, that sensible pain is nothing distinct from those sensations or ideas, in an intense degree?

HYL. It is undeniable; and, to speak the truth, I begin to suspect a very great heat cannot exist but in a mind perceiving it.

PHIL. What! are you then in that sceptical state of suspense, between affirming and denying?

HYL. I think I may be positive in the point. A very violent and painful heat cannot exist without the mind.

PHIL. It hath not, therefore, according to you, any *real* being?

HYL. I own it.

PHIL. Is it therefore certain, that there is no body in nature really hot?

HYL. I have not denied there is any real heat in bodies. I only say, there is no such thing as an intense real heat.

PHIL. But, did you not say before that all degrees of heat were equally real; or, if there was any difference, that the greater were more undoubtedly real than the lesser?

HYL. True: but it was because I did not then consider the ground there is for distinguishing between them, which I now plainly see. And it is this: because intense heat is nothing else but a particular kind of painful sensation; and pain cannot exist but in a perceiving being; it follows that no intense heat can really exist in an unperceiving corporeal substance. But this is no reason why we should deny heat in an inferior degree to exist in such a substance.

PHIL. But how shall we be able to discern those degrees of heat which exist only in the mind from those which exist without it?

HYL. That is no difficult matter. You know the least pain cannot exist unperceived; whatever, therefore, degree of heat is a pain exists only in the mind. But, as for all other degrees of heat, nothing obliges us to think the same of them.

PHIL. I think you granted before that no unperceiving being was capable of pleasure, any more than of pain.

HYL. I did.

PHIL. And is not warmth, or a more gentle degree of heat than what causes uneasiness, a pleasure?

HYL. What then?

PHIL. Consequently, it cannot exist without the mind in an unperceiving substance, or body.

HYL. So it seems.

PHIL. Since, therefore, as well those degrees of heat that are not painful, as those that are, can exist only in a thinking substance; may we not conclude that external bodies are absolutely incapable of any degree of heat whatsoever?

HYL. On second thoughts, I do not think it so evident that warmth is a pleasure as that a great degree of heat is a pain.

PHIL. I do not pretend that warmth is as great a pleasure as heat is a pain. But, if you grant it to be even a small pleasure, it serves to make good my conclusion.

HYL. I could rather call it an *indolence*. It seems to be nothing more than a privation of both pain and pleasure. And that such a quality or state as this may agree to an unthinking substance, I hope you will not deny.

PHIL. If you are resolved to maintain that warmth, or a gentle degree of heat, is no pleasure, I know not how to convince you otherwise than by appealing to your own sense. But what think you of cold?

HYL. The same that I do of heat. An intense degree of cold is a pain; for to feel a very great cold, is to perceive a great uneasiness: it cannot therefore exist without the mind; but a lesser degree of cold may, as well as a lesser degree of heat.

PHIL. Those bodies, therefore, upon whose application to our own, we perceive a moderate degree of heat, must be concluded to have a moderate degree of heat or warmth in them; and those, upon whose application we feel a like degree of cold, must be thought to have cold in them.

HYL. They must.

PHIL. Can any doctrine be true that necessarily leads a man into an absurdity?

HYL. Without doubt it cannot.

PHIL. Is it not an absurdity to think that the same thing should be at the same time both cold and warm?

HYL. It is.

PHIL. Suppose now one of your hands hot, and the other cold, and that they are both at once put into the same vessel of water, in an intermediate state; will not the water seem cold to one hand, and warm to the other?

HYL. It will.

PHIL. Ought we not therefore, by your principles, to conclude it is really both cold and warm at the same time, that is, according to your own concession, to believe an absurdity?

HYL. I confess it seems so.

PHIL. Consequently, the principles themselves are false, since you have granted that no true principle leads to an absurdity.

HYL. But, after all, can anything be more absurd than to say, *there is no heat in the fire?*

PHIL. To make the point still clearer; tell me whether in two cases exactly alike, we ought not to make the same judgment?

HYL. We ought.

PHIL. When a pin pricks your finger, doth it not rend and divide the fibres of your flesh?

HYL. It doth.

PHIL. And when a coal burns your finger, doth it any more?

HYL. It doth not.

PHIL. Since, therefore, you neither judge the sensation itself occasioned by the pin, nor anything like it to be in the pin; you should not, conformably to what you have now granted, judge the sensation occasioned by the fire, or anything like it, to be in the fire.

HYL. Well, since it must be so, I am content to yield this point, and acknowledge that heat and cold are only sensations existing in our minds. But there still remain qualities enough to secure the reality of external things.

PHIL. But what will you say, Hylas, if it shall appear that the case is the same with regard to all other sensible qualities, and that they can no more be supposed to exist without the mind, than heat and cold?

HYL. Then indeed you will have done something to the purpose; but that is what I despair of seeing proved.

PHIL. Let us examine them in order. What think you of *tastes*—do they exist without the mind, or no?

HYL. Can any man in his senses doubt whether sugar is sweet, or wormwood bitter?

PHIL. Inform me, Hylas. Is a sweet taste a particular kind of pleasure or pleasant sensation, or is it not?

HYL. It is.

PHIL. And is not bitterness some kind of uneasiness or pain?

HYL. I grant it.

PHIL. If therefore sugar and wormwood are unthinking corporeal substances existing without the mind, how can sweetness and bitterness, that is, pleasure and pain, agree to them?

HYL. Hold, Philonous, I now see what it is deluded me all this time. You asked whether heat and cold, sweetness and bitterness, were not particular sorts of pleasure and pain; to which I answered simply, that they were. Whereas I should have thus distinguished:—those qualities, as perceived by us, are pleasures or pains; but not as existing in the external objects. We must not therefore conclude absolutely, that there is no heat in the fire, or sweetness in the sugar, but only that heat or sweetness, as perceived by us, are not in the fire or sugar. What say you to this?

PHIL. I say it is nothing to the purpose. Our discourse proceeded altogether concerning sensible things, which you defined to be, *the things we immediately perceive by our senses.* Whatever other qualities, therefore, you speak of, as distinct from these, I know nothing of them, neither do they at all belong to the point in dispute. You may, indeed, pretend to have discovered certain qualities which you do not perceive, and assert those insensible qualities exist in fire and sugar. But what use can be made of this to your present purpose, I am at a loss to conceive. Tell me then once more, do you acknowledge that heat and cold, sweetness and bitterness (meaning those qualities which are perceived by the senses), do not exist without the mind?

HYL. I see it is to no purpose to hold out, so I give up the cause as to those mentioned qualities. Though I profess it sounds oddly, to say that sugar is not sweet.

PHIL. But, for your farther satisfaction, take this along with you: that which at other times seems sweet, shall, to a distempered palate, appear bitter. And, nothing can be plainer than that divers persons perceive different tastes in the same food; since that which one man delights in, another abhors. And how could this be, if the taste was something really inherent in the food?

HYL. I acknowledge I know not how.

PHIL. In the next place, *odours* are to be considered. And, with regard to these, I would fain know whether what hath been said of tastes doth not exactly agree to them? Are they not so many pleasing or displeasing sensations?

HYL. They are.

PHIL. Can you then conceive it possible that they should exist in an unperceiving thing?

HYL. I cannot.

PHIL. Or, can you imagine that filth and ordure affect those brute animals that feed on them out of choice, with the same smells which we perceive in them?

HYL. By no means.

PHIL. May we not therefore conclude of smells, as of the other fore-mentioned qualities, that they cannot exist in any but a perceiving substance or mind?

HYL. I think so.

PHIL. Then as to *sounds,* what must we think of them: are they accidents really inherent in external bodies, or not?

HYL. That they inhere not in the sonorous bodies is plain from hence: because a bell struck in the exhausted receiver of an air-pump sends forth no sound. The air, therefore, must be thought the subject of sound.

PHIL. What reason is there for that, Hylas?

HYL. Because, when any motion is raised in the air, we perceive a sound greater or lesser, according to the air's motion; but without some motion in the air, we never hear any sound at all.

PHIL. And granting that we never hear a sound but when some motion is produced in the air, yet I do not see how you can infer from thence, that the sound itself is in the air.

HYL. It is this very motion in the external air that produces in the mind the sensation of *sound.* For, striking on the drum of the ear, it causeth a vibration, which by the auditory nerves being communicated to the brain, the soul is thereupon affected with the sensation called *sound.*

PHIL. What! is sound then a sensation?

HYL. I tell you, as perceived by us, it is a particular sensation in the mind.

PHIL. And can any sensation exist without the mind?

HYL. No, certainly.

PHIL. How then can sound, being a sensation, exist in the air, if by the *air* you mean a senseless substance existing without the mind?

HYL. You must distinguish, Philonous, between sound as it is perceived by us, and as it is in itself; or (which is the same thing) between the sound we immediately perceive, and that which exists without us. The former, indeed, is a particular kind of sensation, but the latter is merely a vibrative or undulatory motion in the air.

PHIL. I thought I had already obviated that distinction, by the answer I gave when you were applying it in a like case before. But, to say no more of that, are you sure then that sound is really nothing but motion?

HYL. I am.

PHIL. Whatever therefore agrees to real sound, may with truth be attributed to motion?

HYL. It may.

PHIL. It is then good sense to speak of *motion* as of a thing that is *loud, sweet, acute,* or *grave.*

HYL. I see you are resolved not to understand me. Is it not evident those accidents or modes belong only to sensible sound, or *sound* in the common acceptation of the word, but not to *sound* in the real and philosophic sense; which, as I just now told you, is nothing but a certain motion of the air?

PHIL. It seems then there are two sorts of sound—the one vulgar, or that which is heard, the other philosophical and real?

HYL. Even so.

PHIL. And the latter consists in motion?

HYL. I told you so before.

PHIL. Tell me, Hylas, to which of the senses, think you, the idea of motion belongs? to the hearing?

HYL. No, certainly; but to the sight and touch.

PHIL. It should follow then, that, according to you, real sounds may possibly be *seen* or *felt,* but never *heard.*

HYL. Look you, Philonous, you may, if you please, make a jest of my opinion, but that will not alter the truth of things. I own, indeed, the inferences you draw me into sound something oddly; but common language, you know, is framed by, and for the use of the vulgar: we must not therefore wonder if expressions adapted to exact philosophic notions seem uncouth and out of the way.

PHIL. Is it come to that? I assure you, I imagine myself to have gained no small point, since you make so light of departing from common phrases and opinions; it being a main part of our inquiry, to examine whose notions are widest of the common road, and most repugnant to the general sense of the world. But, can you think it no more than a philosophical paradox, to say that *real sounds are never heard,* and that the idea of them is obtained by some other sense? And is there nothing in this contrary to nature and the truth of things?

HYL. To deal ingenuously, I do not like it. And, after the concessions already made, I had as well grant that sounds too have no real being without the mind.

PHIL. And I hope you will make no difficulty to acknowledge the same of *colours.*

HYL. Pardon me: the case of colours is very different. Can anything be plainer than that we see them on the objects?

PHIL. The objects you speak of are, I suppose, corporeal Substances existing without the mind?

HYL. They are.

PHIL. And have true and real colours inhering in them?

HYL. Each visible object hath that colour which we see in it.

PHIL. How! is there anything visible but what we perceive by sight?

HYL. There is not.

PHIL. And, do we perceive anything by sense which we do not perceive immediately?

HYL. How often must I be obliged to repeat the same thing? I tell you, we do not.

PHIL. Have patience, good Hylas; and tell me once more, whether there is anything immediately perceived by the senses, except sensible qualities. I know you asserted there was not; but I would now be informed, whether you still persist in the same opinion.

HYL. I do.

PHIL. Pray, is your corporeal substance either a sensible quality, or made up of sensible qualities?

HYL. What a question that is! who ever thought it was?

PHIL. My reason for asking was, because in saying, *each visible object hath that colour which we see in it* you make visible objects to be corporeal substances; which implies either that corporeal substances are sensible qualities, or else that there is something beside sensible qualities perceived by sight: but, as this point was formerly agreed between us, and is still maintained by you, it is a clear consequence, that your *corporeal substance* is nothing distinct from *sensible qualities.*

HYL. You may draw as many absurd consequences as you please, and endeavour to perplex the plainest things; but you shall never persuade me out of my senses. I clearly understand my own meaning.

PHIL. I wish you would make me understand it too. But, since you are unwilling to have your notion of corporeal substance examined, I shall urge that point no farther. Only be pleased to let me know, whether the same colours which we see exist in external bodies, or some other.

HYL. The very same.

PHIL. What! are then the beautiful red and purple we see on yonder clouds really in them? Or do you imagine they have in themselves any other form than that of a dark mist or vapour?

HYL. I must own, Philonous, those colours are not really in the clouds as they seem to be at this distance. They are only apparent colours.

PHIL. *Apparent* call you them? How shall we distinguish these apparent colours from real?

HYL. Very easily. Those are to be thought apparent which, appearing only at a distance, vanish upon a nearer approach.

PHIL. And those, I suppose, are to be thought real which are discovered by the most near and exact survey.

HYL. Right.

PHIL. Is the nearest and exactest survey made by the help of a microscope, or by the naked eye?

HYL. By a microscope, doubtless.

PHIL. But a microscope often discovers colours in an object different from those perceived by the unassisted sight. And, in case we had microscopes magnifying to any assigned degree, it is certain that no object whatsoever, viewed through them, would appear in the same colour which it exhibits to the naked eye.

Hyl. And what will you conclude from all this? You cannot argue that there are really and naturally no colours on objects: because by artificial managements they may be altered, or made to vanish.

Phil. I think it may evidently be concluded from your own concessions, that all of the colours we see with our naked eyes are only apparent as those on the clouds, since they vanish upon a more close and accurate inspection which is afforded us by a microscope. Then, as to what you say by way of prevention: I ask you whether the real and natural state of an object is better discovered by a very sharp and piercing sight, or by one which is less sharp?

Hyl. By the former without doubt.

Phil. Is it not plain from *Dioptrics* that microscopes make the sight more penetrating, and represent objects as they would appear to the eye in case it were naturally endowed with a most exquisite sharpness.

Hyl. It is.

Phil. Consequently the microscopical representation is to be thought that which best sets forth the real nature of the thing, or what it is in itself. The colours, therefore, by it perceived are more genuine and real than those perceived otherwise.

Hyl. I confess there is something in what you say.

Phil. Besides, it is not only possible but manifest, that there actually are animals whose eyes are by nature framed to perceive those things which by reason of their minuteness escape our sight. What think you of those inconceivably small animals perceived by glasses? must we suppose they are all stark blind? Or, in case they see, can it be imagined their sight hath not the same use in preserving their bodies from injuries, which appears in that of all other animals? And if it hath, is it not evident they must see particles less than their own bodies; which will present them with a far different view in each object from that which strikes our senses? Even our own eyes do not always represent objects to us after the same manner. In the jaundice every one knows that all things seem yellow. Is it not therefore highly probable those animals in whose eyes we discern a very different texture from that of ours, and whose bodies abound with different humours, do not see the same colours in every object that we do? From all which, should it not seem to follow that all colours are equally apparent, and that none of those which we perceive are really inherent in any outward object?

Hyl. It should.

Phil. The point will be past all doubt, if you consider that, in case colours were real properties or affections inherent in external bodies, they could admit of no alteration without some change wrought in the very bodies themselves: but, is it not evident from what hath been said that, upon the use of microscopes, upon a change happening in the humours of the eye, or a variation of distance, without any manner of real alteration in the thing itself, the colours of any object are either changed, or totally disappear? Nay, all other circumstances remaining the same, change but the situation of some objects, and they shall present different colours to the eye. The same thing happens upon viewing an object in various degrees of light. And what is more known than that the same bodies appear differently coloured by candlelight from what they do in the open day? Add to these the experiment of a prism which, separating the heterogeneous rays of light, alters the colour of any object, and will cause the whitest to appear of a deep blue or red to the naked eye. And now tell me whether you are still of opinion that every body hath its true real colour inhering in it; and, if you think it hath, I would fain know farther from you, what certain distance and position of the object, what peculiar texture and formation of the eye, what degree or kind of light is necessary for ascertaining that true colour, and distinguishing it from apparent ones.

HYL. I own myself entirely satisfied, that they are all equally apparent, and that there is no such thing as colour really inhering in external bodies, but that it is altogether in the light. And what confirms me in this opinion is, that in proportion to the light colours are still more or less vivid; and if there be no light, then are there no colours perceived. Besides, allowing there are colours on external objects, yet, how is it possible for us to perceive them? For no external body affects the mind, unless it acts first on our organs of sense. But the only action of bodies is motion; and motion cannot be communicated otherwise than by impulse. A distant object therefore cannot act on the eye; nor consequently make itself or its properties perceivable to the soul. Whence it plainly follows that it is immediately some contiguous substance, which, operating on the eye, occasions a perception of colours: and such is light.

PHIL. How! is light then a substance?

HYL. I tell you, Philonous, external light is nothing but a thin fluid substance, whose minute particles being agitated with a brisk motion, and in various manners reflected from the different surfaces of outward objects to the eyes, communicate different motions to the optic nerves; which, being propagated to the brain, cause therein various impressions; and these are attended with the sensations of red, blue, yellow, &c.

PHIL. It seems then the light doth no more than shake the optic nerves.

HYL. Nothing else.

PHIL. And consequent to each particular motion of the nerves, the mind is affected with a sensation, which is some particular colour.

HYL. Right.

PHIL. And these sensations have no existence without the mind.

HYL. They have not.

PHIL. How then do you affirm that colours are in the light; since by *light* you understand a corporeal substance external to the mind?

HYL. Light and colours, as immediately perceived by us, I grant cannot exist without the mind. But in themselves they are only the motions and configurations of certain insensible particles of matter.

PHIL. Colours then, in the vulgar sense, or taken for the immediate objects of sight, cannot agree to any but a perceiving substance.

HYL. That is what I say.

PHIL. Well then, since you give up the point as to those sensible qualities which are alone thought colours by all mankind beside, you may hold what you please with regard to those invisible ones of the philosophers. It is not my business to dispute about *them;* only I would advise you to bethink yourself, whether, considering the inquiry we are upon, it be prudent for you to affirm—*the red and blue which we see are not real colours, but certain unknown motions and figures which no man ever did or can see are truly so.* Are not these shocking notions, and are not they subject to as many ridiculous inferences, as those you were obliged to renounce before in the case of sounds?

TWENTY-FIVE

Sense Data

GEORGE EDWARD MOORE (1873-1958)

From *Some Main Problems of Philosophy**

My first question is, then: What exactly is it that happens, when (as we should say) we *see* a material object? And I should explain, perhaps, to avoid misunderstanding, that the occurrence which I mean here to analyse is merely the *mental* occurrence—the act of consciousness—which we call *seeing*. I do not mean to say anything at all about the bodily processes which occur in the eye and the optic nerves and the brain. I have no doubt, myself, that these bodily processes *do* occur, when we see; and that physiologists really do *know* a great deal about them. But all that I shall mean by *"seeing,"* and all that I wish to talk about, is the mental occurrence—the act of consciousness—which occurs (as is supposed) as a consequence of or accompaniment of these bodily processes. This mental occurrence, which I call "seeing," is known to us in a much more simple and direct way, than are the complicated physiological processes which go on in our eyes and nerves and brains. A man cannot directly observe the minute processes which go on in his own eyes and nerves and brain when he sees; but all of us who are not blind can directly observe this mental occurrence, which we mean by seeing. And it is solely with *seeing,* in this sense—seeing, as an act of consciousness which we can all of us directly observe as happening in our own minds—that I am now concerned.

And I wish to illustrate what I have to say about seeing by a direct practical example; because, though I dare say many of you are perfectly familiar with the sort of points I wish to raise, it is, I think, very important for every one, in these subjects, to consider carefully single concrete instances, so that there may be no mistake as to exactly what it is that is being talked about. Such mistakes are, I think, very apt to happen, if one talks merely in generalities; and moreover one is apt to overlook important points. I propose, therefore, to hold up an envelope in my hand, and to ask you all to look at it for a moment; and then to consider with me exactly what it is that happens, when you

* Reprinted with permission of George Allen & Unwin Ltd and The Macmillan Company from *Some Main Problems of Philosophy* by George Edward Moore. First published in 1953.

see it: *what* this occurrence, which we call the *seeing* of it, *is*.

I hold up this envelope, then: I look at it, and I hope you all will look at it. And now I put it down again. Now what has happened? We should certainly say (if you have looked at it) that we all *saw* that envelope, that we all saw it, *the same* envelope: I saw it, and you all saw it. We all saw *the same* object. And by the *it*, which we all saw, we mean an object, which, at any one of the moments when we were looking at it, occupied just *one* of the many places that constitute the whole of space. Even during the short time in which we were looking at it, it may have moved—occupied successively several different places; for the earth, we believe, is constantly going round on its axis, and carrying with it all the objects on its surface, so that, even while we looked at the envelope, it probably moved and changed its position in space, though we did not see it move. But at any *one* moment, we should say, this *it*, the envelope, which we say we all saw, was at some *one* definite place in space.

But now, what happened to each of us, when we saw that envelope? I will begin by describing *part* of what happened to me. I saw a patch [1] of a particular whitish colour, having a certain size, and a certain shape, a shape with rather sharp angles or corners and bounded by fairly straight lines. These things: this patch of a whitish colour, and its size and shape I did actually see. And I propose to call these things, the colour and size and shape, *sense-data*,[2] things *given* or presented by the senses—given, in this case, by my sense of sight. Many philosophers have called these things which I call sense-data, *sensations*. They would say, for instance, that that particular patch of colour was a sensation. But it seems to me that this term "sensation" is liable to be misleading. We should certainly say that I *had* a sensation, when I saw that colour. But when we say that I *had* a sensation, what we mean is, I think, that I had the experience which consisted in my *seeing* the colour. That is to say, what we mean by a "sensation" in this phrase, is my *seeing* of the colour, not the colour which I saw: this colour does not seem to be what I mean to say that I *had*, when I say I *had* a sensation of colour. It is very unnatural to say that I *had* the colour, that I *had* that particular whitish grey or that I *had* the patch which was of that colour. What I certainly did *have* is the experience which consisted in my seeing the colour and the patch. And when, therefore, we talk of *having* sensations,

---

[1] I am so extending the use of the word "patch" that, *e.g.*, the very small black dot which I directly apprehend when I see a full-stop, or the small black line which I directly apprehend when I see a hyphen, are, each of them, in the sense in which I am using the word, a "patch of colour." (1952).

[2] I should now make, and have for many years made, a sharp distinction between what I have called the "patch," on the one hand, and the colour, size and shape, *of* which it is, on the other; and should call, and have called, *only* the patch, *not* its colour, size or shape, a "sense-datum." (1952).

I think what we mean by "sensations" is the experiences which consist
in apprehending certain sense-data, *not* these sense-data themselves.
I think, then, that the term "sensation" is liable to be misleading,
because it may be used in two different senses, which it is very important
to distinguish from one another. It may be used *either* for the colour
which I saw or for the experience which consisted in my seeing it. And
it is, I think, very important, for several reasons, to distinguish these
two things. I will mention only two of these reasons. In the first place,
it is, I think, quite conceivable (I do not say it is actually true) but
conceivable that the patch of colour which I saw may have continued
to exist after I saw it: whereas, of course, when I ceased to see it, *my
seeing* of it ceased to exist. I will illustrate what I mean, by holding up
the envelope again, and looking at it. I look at it, and I again see a
sense-datum, a patch of a whitish colour. But now I immediately turn
away my eyes, and I no longer see that sense-datum: my seeing of it
has ceased to exist. But I am by no means sure that the sense-datum—that
very same patch of whitish colour which I saw—is not still *existing* and
still there. I do not say, for certain, that it is: I think very likely it is
not. But I have a strong inclination to believe that it is. And it seems
to me at least *conceivable* that it should be still existing, whereas my
seeing of it certainly has ceased to exist. This is one reason for distinguishing between the sense-data which I see, and my seeing of them.
And here is another. It seems to me *conceivable*—here again I do not
say it is true but *conceivable*—that some sense-data—this whitish colour
for instance—are in the place in which the material object—the envelope, is. It seems to me *conceivable* that this whitish colour is really
on the surface of the material envelope. Whereas it does not seem to
me that my *seeing* of it is in that place. My seeing of it is in another
place—somewhere within my body. Here, then, are two reasons for
distinguishing between the *sense-data* which I see, and my *seeing* of
them. And it seems to me that both of these two very different things
are often meant when people talk about "sensations." In fact, when you
are reading any philosopher who is talking about sensations (or about
sense-*impressions* or *ideas* either), you need to look very carefully to
see which of the two he is talking about in any particular passage—
whether of the sense-data themselves or of our apprehension of them:
you will, I think, almost invariably find that he is talking now of the
one and now of the other, and very often that he is assuming that what
is true of the one must also be true of the other—an assumption which
does not seem to be at all justified. I think, therefore, that the term
"sensation" is liable to be very misleading. And I shall, therefore, never
use it. I shall always talk of *sense-data,* when what I mean is such things
as this colour and size and shape or the patch which is *of* this colour
and size and shape, which I actually see. And when I want to talk of

my seeing of them, I shall expressly call this the seeing of sense-data; or, if I want a term which will apply equally to all the senses, I shall speak of the *direct apprehension* of sense-data. Thus when I see this whitish colour, I am *directly apprehending* this whitish colour; my seeing of it, as a mental act, an act of consciousness, just consists in my direct apprehension of it;—so too when I hear a sound, I directly apprehend the sound; when I feel a toothache I directly apprehend the ache: and all these things—the whitish colour, the sound and the ache are *sense-data*.

To return, then, to what happened to us, when we all saw the same envelope. Part, at least, of what happened to me, I can now express by saying that I saw certain sense-data: I saw a whitish patch of colour, of a particular size and shape. And I have no doubt whatever that this is part, at least, of what happened to all of you. You also saw certain sense-data; and I expect also that the sense-data which you saw were more or less similar to those which I saw. You also saw a patch of colour which might be described as whitish, of a size not very different from the size of the patch which I saw, and of a shape similar at least in this that it had rather sharp corners and was bounded by fairly straight lines. But now, what I want to emphasize is this. Though we all did (as we should say) see *the same* envelope, no two of us, in all probability, saw exactly the *same sense-data*. Each of us, in all probability, saw, to begin with, a slightly different shade of colour. All these colours may have been whitish; but each was probably at least slightly different from all the rest, according to the way in which the light fell upon the paper, relatively to the different positions you are sitting in; and again according to differences in the strength of your eye-sight, or your distance from the paper. And so too, with regard to the size of the patch of colour which you saw: differences in the strength of your eyes and in your distance from the envelope probably made slight differences in the size of the patch of colour, which you saw. And so again with regard to the shape. Those of you on that side of the room will have seen a rhomboidal figure, while those in front of me will have seen a figure more nearly rectangular. Those on my left will have seen a figure more like this which you in front now see, and which you see is different from *this* which you then saw. And those in front of me will have seen a figure like that which you on the left now see, and which, you see, is different from *this*, which you saw before. Those directly in front of me, may, indeed, have all seen very nearly the same figure—perhaps, even, exactly the same. But we should not say we *knew* that any two did; whereas we should say we did *know* that we all saw the *same* envelope. That you did all see the same envelope, would, indeed, be accepted in ordinary life as a certainty of the strongest kind. Had you all seen me commit a murder, as clearly as you all saw this envelope, your evidence would be accepted by any jury as sufficient to hang me. Such evidence would be accepted in any court of law as quite conclusive; we should take such a responsibility as that of hanging a man, upon it. It would be accepted, that is, that you had all seen me, *the same man,* commit a murder; and not merely that you had all seen some man or other, possibly each of you a different man in each case, commit one. And yet, in this case, as in the case of the envelope, the sense-data which you had all seen, would have been different sense-data: you could not swear in a court of law that you had all seen exactly the *same sense-data.*

Now all this seems to me to show very clearly, that, *if* we *did* all see the same envelope, the envelope which we saw was not *identical with* the sense-data which we saw: the envelope cannot be exactly the same thing as each of the sets of sense-data, which we each of us saw; for these were in all probability each of them slightly different from all the rest, and they cannot, therefore, *all* be exactly the same thing as the envelope.

But it might be said: Of course, when we say that we all saw the envelope, we do not mean that we all saw the *whole* of it. I, for instance, only saw *this* side of it, whereas all of you only saw *that* side. And generally, when we talk of seeing an object we only mean seeing some *part* of it. There is always more in any object which we see, than the *part* of it which we see.

And this, I think, is quite true. Whenever we talk roughly of seeing any object, it is true that, in another and stricter sense of the word *see,* we only see *a part of* it. And it might, therefore, be suggested that why we say we all saw this envelope, when we each, in fact, saw a different set of sense-data, is because each of these *sets of sense-data* is, in fact, a *part* of the envelope.

But it seems to me there is a great difficulty even in maintaining that the different sense-data we all saw are parts of the envelope. What do we mean by a *part* of a material object? We mean, I think, at least this. What we call a part of a material object must be something which occupies a part of the volume in space occupied by the whole object. For instance, this envelope occupies a certain volume in space: that is to say, it occupies a space which has breadth and thickness as well as length. And anything which is a *part* of the envelope at any moment, must be *in* some part of the volume of space occupied by the whole envelope at that moment: it must be somewhere within that volume, or at some point in the surfaces bounding that volume.

Are, then, any of the sense-data we saw *parts* of the envelope in this sense?

The sense-data I mentioned were these three—the colour— the whitish colour: the *size* of this colour; its *shape.*[3] And of these three it is only the

---

[3] I had here forgotten that one of the sense-data mentioned was the *patch* which *has* that colour and shape and size—the *patch* which, I should now say, is the *only* "sense-datum," having to do with the envelope, which I then saw. (1952).

colour, which could, in the sense defined, possibly be supposed to be a *part* of the envelope. The colour might be supposed to occupy a *part* of the volume occupied by the envelope—one of its bounding surfaces,[4] for instance. But the size and shape could hardly be said to *occupy* any part of this volume. What might be true of them is that the size I saw *is* the size of one surface of the envelope; and that the shape *is* the shape of this surface of the envelope. The side of the envelope which I say I saw certainly *has* some size and some shape; and the sense-data—the size and shape, which I saw as the size and shape of a patch of colour—might possibly *be* the size and shape of this side of the envelope.

Let us consider whether these things are so.

And, first, as to the colours. Can these possibly be parts of the envelope? What we supposed is that each of you probably saw a slightly different colour. And if we are to suppose that *all* those colours are parts of the envelope, then we must suppose that *all* of them are in the same place. We must suppose that ever so many different colours all of them occupy the same surface—this surface of the envelope which you now see. And I think it is certainly difficult to suppose this, though not absolutely impossible. It is not absolutely impossible, I think, that all the different colours which you see are really all of them in the same place. But I myself find it difficult to believe that this is so; and you can understand, I think, why most philosophers should have declared it to be impossible. They have declared, chiefly, I think, on grounds like this, that none of the colours which any of us ever see are ever parts of material objects: they have declared that none of them are ever in any part of the places where material objects (if there are any material objects) are. This conclusion does, indeed, go beyond what the premisses justify, even if we accept the premiss that several different colours cannot all be in exactly the same place. For it remains possible that the colour, which some *one* of you sees, is really on the surface of the envelope; whereas the colours which all the rest of you see are *not* there. But if so, then we must say that though all of you are seeing the same side of the envelope, yet only one of you is seeing a sense-datum which is a part of that side: the sense-data seen by all the rest are *not* parts of the envelope. And this also, I think, is difficult to believe. It might be, indeed, that those of you who are seeing a colour, which is *not* a part of the envelope, might yet be seeing a size and a shape which really *is* the size and shape of one side of the envelope; and we will go on to consider whether *this* is so.

And, first, as to the size. I assumed that the sense-given sizes, which you see, are all of them probably slightly different from one another. And, if this be so, then certainly it seems to be absolutely impossible that they should *all* of them be the size of this side of the envelope. This side of the

---

[4] I should now say that any part of the *surface* of a volume is *not* a part of the volume, because it is not itself a volume. (1952).

envelope can only really have *one* size; it cannot have several different sizes. But it may not seem quite clear, that you all do see different sizes; the differences between the different distances at which you are from the envelope are not so great, but what the patches of colour you all see might be, at least, of *much the same* size. So I will give a hypothetical instance to make my point clearer. Suppose this room were so large that I could carry the envelope two or three hundred yards away from you. The sense-given size which you would then see, when I was three hundred yards off, would certainly be appreciably smaller than what you see now. And yet you would still be seeing this same envelope. It seems quite impossible that these two very different sizes should both of them be *the* size of the envelope. So that here the *only* possibility is that the size which you see at some *one* definite distance or set of distances, should be the envelope's real size, *if* you ever see its real size at all. This may be so: it may be that some one of the sense-given sizes which we see is the envelope's real size. But it seems also possible that none of them are; and in any case we all see the envelope, just the same, *whether* we see its real size or not.

And now for the shape. Here again it seems quite impossible that *all* the shapes we see can be the envelope's real shape. This side of the envelope can have but *one* shape: it cannot be both rhomboidal, as is the shape which you on the left see, and also rectangular, as is the shape seen by those in front; the angles at its corners cannot be both right angles and also very far from right angles. Certainly, therefore, the sense-given shape which some of you see is *not* the shape of this side of the envelope. But here it may be said, it is plain enough that one of the sense-given shapes seen *is* its real shape. You may say: The shape seen by those in front *is* its real shape; the envelope *is* rectangular. And I quite admit that this is so: I think we do know, in fact, that the envelope really is *roughly* rectangular. But here I want to introduce a distinction. There are two different senses in which we may talk of *the* shape of anything. A rectangle of the size of this envelope, and a rectangle of the size of this blackboard, may both, in a sense, have exactly *the same* shape. They may have the same shape in the sense, that all the angles of both are right angles, and that the proportions between the sides of the one, and those between the sides of the other, are the same. They may, in fact, have the same shape, in the sense in which a big square always has the same shape as a small square, however big the one may be and however small the other. But there is another sense in which *the* shape of a big square is obviously not *the same* as that of a small square. We may mean by *the* shape of a big square the actual lines bounding it; and if we mean this, *the* shape of a big square cannot possibly be the *same* as *the* shape of a smaller one. The lines bounding the two cannot possibly be the *same* lines. And the same thing may be true, even when there is no difference in size between two shapes. Imagine *two* squares, of the same size, side by side. The lines bounding the one are *not* the same lines as those bounding the other: though each is both *of* the same shape and *of* the same size as the other. The difference between these two senses in which we may talk of *the* shape of anything, may be expressed by saying that the shape of the big square is the same *in quality*—qualitatively identical—with that of the small square, but is not *numerically* the same—not numerically identical: the shape of the big square is *numerically* different from that of the small, in the sense that they are *two* shapes, and not one only, of which we are talking, though both are the same in quality: both are *squares,* but the one is *one* square and the other is *another* square. There is, then, a difference between two different kinds of identity: qualitative identity and numerical identity; and we are all perfectly familiar with the difference between the two, though the names may sound strange. I shall in future use these names: qualitative identity and numerical identity. And now to return to the case of the envelope. Even supposing that the sense-given shape which you in front see is rectangular, and that the real shape of the envelope is also rectangular, and that both are rectangles of exactly the same shape; it still does not follow that the sense-given shape which you see is *the* shape of the envelope. The sense-given shape and the shape of the envelope, even if they are qualitatively the same, *must* still be *two* different shapes, *numerically* different, unless they are *of the same size;* just as *the* shape of a large square must be numerically different from *the* shape of a smaller one. And we saw before how difficult it was to be sure that any of the sizes which you saw were the *real* size of the envelope. And even if the sense-given size which some one of you sees *is* the real size of the envelope, it still does not follow that the sense-given *shape* which you see is numerically the same as the shape of the envelope. The two may be numerically different, just as in the case of two different squares, side by side, of the same shape and size, *the* shape of the one *is* not *the* shape of the other; they are two numerically different shapes. We may say, then, that if those of you who see rectangular shapes, do see rectangular shapes of different sizes, only one of these can possibly be *the* shape of the envelope: all the others may be *of* the same shape—the same in quality—but they cannot be *the* shape of the envelope. And even if some *one* of you does see a shape, which is of the same size as *the* shape of the envelope, as well as being of the same shape (and it is very doubtful whether any of you does) it would yet be by no means certain that this sense-given shape which you saw was *the* shape of the envelope. It might be a shape *numerically* different from *the* shape of the envelope, although exactly similar both in shape and size. And finally there is some reason to suppose that none of the sense-given shapes which any of you see are *exactly* the same, even in quality, as *the* shape of the envelope. The envelope itself probably has a more or less irregular edge; there are probably ups and downs in the line bounding its side, which you at that distance cannot see.

Of the three kinds of sense-data,[5] then, which you all of you saw, when I held up the envelope, namely, the whitish colour, its size, and its shape, the following things seem to be true. First, as regards the colour, no one of you can be sure that the exact colour which you saw was really a part of the envelope—was really in any part of the space, which the real envelope (if there was a real envelope) occupied. Then as regards the size, no one of you can be sure that the size which you saw was the real size of the envelope. And finally as regards the shape, no one of you can be sure that the shape which you saw was really of exactly the same shape as that of the envelope; still less can you be sure that it *was the* shape of the envelope, that the bounding lines which composed it were numerically the same bounding lines as those which enclosed the envelope. And not only can none of you be sure of these things. As regards the sizes and shapes which you saw, it seems quite certain that some of you saw sizes and shapes which were *not* the real size and shape of the envelope; because it seems quite certain that some of you saw sizes and shapes different from those seen by others, and that these different sizes and shapes cannot possibly *all* be *the* size and shape of the envelope. And as regards the colours it seems fairly certain, that the colours which you saw cannot all have been *in* the envelope; since it seems fairly certain that you all saw slightly different colours, and it is difficult to believe, though not absolutely impossible, that all these different colours were really in the same place at the same time.

This seems to be the state of things with regard to these sense-data— the colour, the size and the shape. They seem, in a sense, to have had very little to do with the real envelope, if there *was* a real envelope. It seems very probable that *none* of the colours seen was really a part of the envelope; and that *none* of the sizes and shapes seen were the size or the shape of the real envelope.

But now I wish to mention one other sense-datum, of a kind that we all saw, which might be thought to have more to do with the real envelope. Besides the patch of colour and its shape and size, we did, in a sense, all see the *space* which this patch of colour occupied. The patch of colour seemed to occupy a certain area; and we can by abstraction distinguish this area from the patch of colour occupying it. This area was also a sense-datum. And in this area we can distinguish parts—this part, and this part, and this. And it might be thought with regard to parts, at least, of this area, that two things are true. Firstly, that part at least of the sense-given area which each of you saw, is really numerically identical with some part of that seen by all the rest. And secondly, that *this* part, which you all saw, is also a part of the area occupied by the real envelope. In other words, you might comfort yourselves by supposing, that even if the colour presented by your senses is *not* a part of the real envelope, and even if the shape and size presented by your senses are not

5 The *patch* itself, which *has* that colour and shape and size, again forgotten! (1952).

the shape and size of the real envelope, yet at least there is presented by your senses a *part* of the *space occupied by* the real envelope. And against this supposition I confess I cannot find any argument, which seems to me very strong. We are all, I think, very strongly tempted to suppose that this is so. That, for instance, this space which I touch is really seen by all of you—this very same place—and that it also is part of the space which the real envelope occupies. The best argument I can think of against this supposition is the following; and I think it is enough to render the supposition doubtful. If we are to say that part of this sense-given area which I see is really numerically the same with part of those which you see, and that it is also numerically the same as part of the area occupied by the real envelope, then we must either again accept the hypothesis that all the different colours which we see as occupying the area are really in the same place and in the same place as the real envelope, or else we must say that the colours only *seem* to be in this sense-given area and are not really there. But there is the former objection to supposing that several different colours are all really in the same place. And as to the only remaining possibility, namely, that they only *seem* to be in this sense-given area; it may be objected that so far as the sense-given area is concerned, the colours we see *really do* occupy it—that they not only seem to be but *really are* there—that there can be no doubt about this. If we are talking of the area really presented by the senses as occupied by the colours, *this* area, it may be said, undoubtedly *is* occupied by the colours: it *is* nothing but the space over which the colour is spread. So that, if the area, which I see, really is numerically the same as those which you see, then it will follow that all the different colours we see really are in the same place. This argument, I say, does not seem to me to be absolutely conclusive. It does seem to me possible that the colour I see only *seems* to be in the sense-given area, which I see. But it is, I think, sufficient to suggest a doubt whether any part of this sense-given area seen by me really is numerically the same as any part of any of those seen by you.

Well now: Chiefly, I think, for reasons of the sort which I have given you, an overwhelming majority of philosophers have adopted the following views. Reasons of the sort which I have given are not the only ones which have been alleged as reasons for holding these views, but they are, I think, the ones which really had most influence in getting them adopted, and they are, it seems to me, by far the strongest reasons for adopting them. However that may be, whatever the reasons, an overwhelming majority of philosophers have, I think, adopted the following views; and I wish you to realise these views as clearly as possible.

They have held with regard to absolutely *all* the sense-data [6] and

---

[6] These three propositions about what philosophers have held are only true if the word "sense-datum" be understood in the sense explained in footnote 2 on p. 44, *i.e.* in such a sense that "patches" are sense-data, but their colour, size and shape, are not. (1952).

every part of any sense-datum, which we ever apprehend by any of our senses, the following things.

They have held (1) that absolutely no part of the sense-data, which I ever apprehend, exists at all except at the moment when I am apprehending it. They have held, that is to say, that except at the moment when I am apprehending it, there simply *is not* in the Universe any particular sense-datum which I ever apprehend. If, for instance, I look at this envelope again and now turn away my eyes for a moment, then while I saw that particular patch of whitish colour, there *was* that particular patch of colour in the Universe: there certainly *was,* for I saw it. But now that I no longer see it, that particular patch of colour has ceased to exist. It no longer *is* in the Universe, any more than my seeing of it is. They are both of them, both the colour and my seeing of it, things which *were,* but which are no longer: both of them equally and in the same sense have completely ceased to be. These philosophers would not deny, indeed, that there *may* still be in the Universe a patch of colour *exactly like* that which I saw. For instance, some one else might at this moment be seeing a patch of colour exactly like it. But this other patch of colour, though exactly like, they would say, is certainly not the same: they may be exactly the same in quality, but they are *not* numerically the same. *The* patch of colour which I saw cannot be now existing even though another exactly like it may be. And they would say this with regard to absolutely all the sense-data, which any of us ever apprehends. Each of them only *is,* so long as the person apprehending it *is* apprehending it. And they would say this not only with regard to sense-data like colours, sounds, hardness, smoothness, heat, cold, aches, which seem to us to occupy space—to be localised. They would say it also with regard to the sense-given spaces which these things seem to occupy. For instance, the sense-given area, occupied by this patch of colour: I see it now, and while I see it, it *is:* that particular area is one among the contents of the Universe. But now that I turn my head away, *it,* that particular area I saw, has entirely ceased to exist. With my seeing of it, *it* also has ceased to be. I may indeed be still seeing an area exactly like it: this area for instance, which I now see, seems to be exactly like, and only distinguishable by the fact that it is occupied by a different colour. But these two areas, they would say, though perhaps exactly like, are not the *same.* They are no more the *same* than is this part of the total area which I now see the same as *that* part. *The* particular sense-given area which I just now saw has entirely ceased to be.

This, then, is one view, which an overwhelming majority of philosophers have held with regard to sense-data. They have held that every sense-datum, of *every* kind, and every part of every sense-datum, is something which only *is* or *exists,* so long as the person apprehending it is apprehending it.

(2) And they have held too this second view. Namely, that no two of us ever apprehend exactly the same sense-datum. They would allow that we might, perhaps, apprehend sense-data exactly *alike;* but they would say that even though exactly alike—the same in quality—they cannot ever be *numerically* the same. That this is so with regard to sense-data which exist at different times, would, indeed, follow from the first view. If this particular patch of colour which I see now, has *now,* when I turn away my head, entirely ceased to be, it follows that nobody can be seeing it now. But it is worth while to emphasize that this is the view actually held by most philosophers. It is held, for instance, that if somebody were to come and look at this envelope, immediately after I had looked at it, standing at exactly the same distance from it and in the same direction, having exactly the same power of eyesight, and the light also not having changed at all, so that he saw a patch of colour exactly similar to that which I had just seen; nevertheless the patch of colour which he saw would not be *the same* as that which I had just seen. It would be numerically different from it, in the same sense, in which, supposing you see two spots of colour, of exactly the same size and shape side by side, the one spot, though exactly like the other, is yet *not* the same, is numerically different from it. And it is held too, that no two persons can see the same sense-datum, or any part of the same sense-datum, even *at the same time:* a point which does not follow from the last view. For though it might be true that all the sense-data, which any of you now sees in looking at this envelope ceased to exist the moment you ceased to see it; yet it might be true that, *while* you were seeing and while, therefore, it exists, some other of you might be seeing at least a part of one of them too. But this is what is denied by this second view. It is denied that any two of you are at this moment seeing, even in part, the same sense-data. It is asserted that every part of every sense-datum which any one of you sees now, is numerically different from any part of any sense-datum seen by any other of you.

And the third view, which is held by an overwhelming majority of philosophers about sense-data is this.

They hold, namely (3) that none of the sense-data apprehended by any one person can ever be situated either in the same place with, or at any distance in any direction from, those apprehended by any other person. In other words, they hold that any sense-datum apprehended by me cannot possibly be in the *same place* as any sense-datum apprehended by any one of you: and that this is true of any pair of persons you like to take. That is to say, this patch of colour seen by me is neither in the same place with, nor at any distance in any direction from, any that is seen by any of you: the two simply have no spatial relations of any kind to one another. With regard to the different sense-data seen by me at any one moment, they would indeed admit that these have, in a sense, spatial relations *to one another.* This corner of the patch of colour which I see really is at a certain distance, in a certain direction, from this corner; and at another distance in another direction from this other corner. But they would say that all the different sense-data within my field of vision at any one time have distance and direction from one another only within a *private space of my own.* That is to say, no point in this private space of mine is either identical with, nor at any distance from, any point within the field of vision of any other person. The sense-given field of vision of each of us, at any moment, constitutes a private space of that person's own;—no two points in any two of these spaces, can be related to one another in any of the ways in which two points in any *one* of them are related.

These three views have, I think, been held by an overwhelming majority of philosophers. They have held, that is (1) that absolutely every sense-datum that any person ever directly apprehends exists only so long as he apprehends it, (2) that no sense-datum which any one person directly apprehends ever is directly apprehended by any other person, and (3) that no sense-datum that is directly apprehended by one person can be in *the same space with* any sense-datum apprehended by any other person —that no sense-datum that is seen or heard or felt by me can possibly be either in the same place with or at any distance from any that is seen or heard or felt by any one else. These three things are, I think, the chief things that are meant, when it is said that all sense-data exist only *in the mind of* the person who apprehends them; and it is certainly the common view in philosophy that all sense-data do only exist *in our minds.* I do not think myself that this is a good way of expressing what is meant. Even if all these three things are true of all the sense-data which I ever directly apprehend; it does not seem to me to follow that they exist only in my mind, or indeed are *in* my mind in any sense at all except that they are apprehended by me. They are, so far as I can see, not in my mind in the sense in which my apprehension of them is in my mind: for instance, this whitish colour, even if it does only exist while I see it, and cannot be seen by any one else, does not seem to me to be *in* my mind in the sense in which my seeing of it is *in my mind.* My seeing of it is, it seems to me, related to my mind in a way in which this which I see is not related to it: and I should prefer to confine the phrase *"in* the mind" to those things which are related to my mind, in the way in which my seeing of this colour, and my other acts of consciousness are related to it. But whether they could be properly said to be in my mind or not, certainly all the sense-data, which I ever directly apprehend, are, if these three things are true of them, *dependent* upon my mind in a most intimate sense. If it is really true of all of them that they exist only while I am conscious of them, that nobody else ever is directly conscious of them, and that they are situated only in a private space of my own, which also exists only while I am conscious of it, and of which no one else is ever directly conscious—then certainly nothing could well be more thoroughly dependent on my mind than they are. Most philosophers have, I think, certainly held that all sense-data are dependent on our minds in this sense. This has been held both by philosophers who believe that there are material objects and that we know of their existence, and by those who believe that there are no such things as material objects, or, that, if there are, we do not know it. It has, in fact, an overwhelming weight of authority in its favour. And I am going to call it for the moment *the accepted view*.

And as regards the question whether this accepted view is true or not, I confess I cannot make up my mind. I think it may very likely be true. But I have never seen any arguments in its favour which seem to me to be absolutely conclusive. The strongest arguments in its favour, as I said, seem to me to be arguments of the sort which I have given you. This one, for instance: That if we are to say that any portion of the sense-given spaces apprehended by each of us at the same time, really is numerically the same portion of space, then we must hold *either* that the very same portion of space may be occupied at the same time by several different colours *or* that it only really is occupied by the colour which *one* of us sees and only *seems* to be so by those which the rest of us see *or* that it only *seems* to be and is not really occupied by any of the colours which any of us see. There do seem to me objections to saying any of these three things but, on the other hand, the objection to none of them seems to me perfectly conclusive: it seems to me *possible* that any one of them *might* be the truth. One argument which has been urged by some philosophers as being conclusive seems to me to have absolutely no weight at all. It has been urged, namely, that we can see directly, without the need of any argument, if we will but think of it, that all sense-data are a sort of thing which can only exist while the person perceiving them is perceiving them; it is urged that this is a self-evident truth like the truth that $2 + 2 = 4$. This argument seems to me to have no weight at all. It seems to me that it is simply false that what it says is self-evident. I can perfectly well conceive that the very same sense-data, which I see at one time, should exist even when I am not seeing them: and I cannot, by merely considering the possibility, determine whether it is true or not. And moreover, I think, that the apparent strength of this argument has been largely due to the confusion I spoke of above—the confusion between the sense-data which I see and my seeing of them. Many philosophers have, as I said, not only called both of these two very different things "sensations," but have treated them as if they were the same thing. And, of course, when I cease to see a given sense-datum, I do cease to see it: my seeing of it certainly does cease to exist. They have, then, argued, treating the sense-datum as if it were the same thing as my seeing of it, that the sense-datum ceases to exist too. But this is surely mere confusion. We are, then, I think, if we are to find conclusive arguments in favour of this accepted view, thrown back upon such questions as whether many different colours can all occupy the same space; and whether, when the space we are talking of is the sense-given space presented with the colours, it can be true that these colours only *seem* to occupy this sense-given space, and do not *really* occupy it. And no arguments of this kind seem to me to be perfectly conclusive, though they do seem to me to have weight. And on the other side, in favour of the contrary view, there seems to me the fact that we all have a very strong tendency to believe it. I find it very difficult not to believe that when I look at this, and turn away my head, the colour which I just saw is not still existing; that the space in which I saw it is not still existing too; and that the colour is not still *in* that space. And so too, I find it very difficult to believe that this space, which I see—this very same portion of space—is not also seen by all of you. I point at it; and what I point at seems to be a part of the sense-given space which I see; and I cannot believe that by pointing at it I do not make plain to you also, which portion of space I am pointing at. We all constantly assume that pointing at a thing is of some use; that if I point at a thing, that serves to show you *which* thing I am talking about; that you will see the same thing, which I see, and will thus know what it is that I see. And it certainly seems as if *the* thing at which I am pointing now is part of the sense-given space which I see; and that, therefore, if you see *what* I am pointing at, some portion of the sense-given space which each of us sees *must* be the same. But on the other hand, I can imagine that I am mistaken about this. I can imagine that what I am sure that you see is *not* a part of my *sense-given* space; and that what you see, when you see the place I am pointing at, is *not* a part of your sense-given space either: and that the supposition that some portion of our sense-given spaces must be identical, arises from our confusion of sense-given space with the real space, which we do really all of us see—but see in another sense. I can, therefore, not find any arguments, either, which seem to me conclusive *against* the accepted view: the view that all the sense-data I see, including every portion of my sense-given space, are private sense-data of my own, which exist only while I directly apprehend them, and no part of which can be directly apprehended by any one of you. And what I wish to do in the rest of this lecture is this. I wish for the moment to *suppose* that this accepted view is true; to *suppose* that absolutely all the sense-data of each of us are private to that person, in the sense I have explained; and then to consider what, supposing this view is true, can be the nature of our knowledge of material objects by means of the senses, if we have such knowledge at all.

TWENTY-SIX

Argument from Hallucination

SIR RUSSELL BRAIN (1895-   )

From *The Nature of Experience**

Now let us turn to such abnormal experiences as illusions and hallucinations. These phenomena are relevant to the sense-datum theory of perception, because if having an hallucination to which no object corresponds is a sensory experience in itself indistinguishable from seeing a real object, this is a strong argument for the view that seeing a real object also involves experiencing a sense-datum which is generated by the brain and is therefore independent of the object. Some philosophers, as we shall see, have devoted much ingenuity to providing different descriptions of these two experiences, but the problem is not primarily a semantic but an empirical one. We must therefore begin by finding out what these experiences are and how those who experience them describe and regard them.

I shall begin by giving a fairly detailed description of the phenomena which both parties to the philosophical dispute are seeking to interpret. This is all the more important because it is evident that most philosophers who discuss the nature of hallucinations have had no personal experience of them. I do not mean by that merely that they themselves have never been hallucinated, but that they seem not to have had the opportunity of discussing hallucinations with those who have experienced them, nor even, to judge from their writings, to have read the accounts given by the subjects of hallucinations.

I shall leave on one side for the present what may be termed everyday illusions, for example, the oval appearance of a penny seen from an angle and the colour of distant hills, which are much discussed in philosophical arguments about perception. These are experiences which no doubt must find an interpretation in any theory of perception, but they are common to all of us, and if a philosopher gives a wrong account of them this can easily be detected. That, however, is not the case with all other types of perceptual experience, some normal and others abnormal. Some such experiences cannot be fully described, or properly interpreted, without training of a special kind which most philosophers lack.

* Sir Russell Brain: *The Nature of Experience,* pp. 10-22. Published in 1959 for the University of Durham by the Oxford University Press, London.

I shall begin by describing some common visual experiences, and then turn to the illusions and hallucinations produced by drugs and disease of the nervous system. In doing so I shall use the word 'see' as it is actually used by those who describe these experiences. I shall leave for subsequent discussion whether in such circumstances the word 'see' is rightly used.

There are different kinds of visual after-image, but one will be sufficient for our present purpose. Hanging on the wall opposite me is a picture with a black frame. I look at it steadily for a few seconds, and then without closing my eyes look to one side. I now see against the wall a white rectangle, which is the same shape and size as the picture frame, but is white instead of black. This white rectangle lasts for a few seconds before fading away. While it lasts, if I either turn my eyes without turning my head, or turn my head and my eyes at the same time, I see the white rectangle in a different position in relation to the opposite wall, namely, in the direction in which I am at the time looking. Furthermore, if I tilt my head, the white rectangle also becomes tilted and is now seen at an angle to the black picture frame. Finally, if during the experience of the white rectangle I close my eyes I continue to see it, and if I then move my head, the white rectangle is again seen in a different position in relation to the position of my body, but no longer in relation to my visual experience of the wall opposite, since, my eyes being closed, I have none.

Now let us turn to some accounts of visual hallucinations. The following quotations are taken from the account of his experiences given by a man who had taken lysergic acid.

Then my attention became preoccupied with the dull, gold stars on the lamp shade. These stars began to be filled with colour; they *lived* with colour. One star, I now saw, was a very small (and wholly attractive) *turtle* on its back, its body a maze of distinct colours—the colours which must actually be involved in the gold paint itself. These little turtles—stars—or highwaymen with two huge pistols!—lived and moved in their firmament of illumined paper. . . . Then my eyes went to the whitish-gold distempered wall above, where the lamp-light fell. The wall began to be covered with an incredibly beautiful series of patterns—embossed, drawn, painted, but *continuously changing*. More colour. Indescribable colour. And all the colours, all the patterns, *were in the wall* in any case —only we don't usually see them, for we haven't eyes to. . . . Looking at my bright blue pyjamas on the bed eight feet away, I saw that the blue was *edged with flame:* a narrow flickering, shifting nimbus, incredibly beautiful, which it filled me with delight to watch. Clear flame; golden-scarlet. Then I understood that this flame *was music,* that I was *seeing sound.*

Here is the account given by another observer of his experience under the influence of mescaline.

I received two subcutaneous injections between nine and ten in the morning. . . . At about 11 a.m. changes in the *colour* of objects were noted and the increased intensity of after-images became disturbing. With closed eyes visions of moving constantly changing patterns appeared and attracted the whole attention. Oriental tapestry, mosaic-like wallpapers, kaleidoscopic-coloured geometric patterns, lines in brilliant luminescent colours or in black and white, etc. . . . The colours of real objects appeared more pure, more clean, untarnished by dirt . . . There were also visual hallucinations unconnected with my conscious thinking, especially friendly animals, little demons and dwarfs, fairytale ornaments and mythology from the aquarium such as one sees sometimes on the walls of inns. The faces of people around me were slightly distorted as if drawn by a cartoonist, often with the emphasis on some small, humorous, but, nevertheless, rather characteristic feature.

Writers on the philosophical aspects of perception rarely concern themselves with illusions or hallucinations involving any other sense than vision, but if we are to learn about the status of hallucinations in general this is unduly restricting, and may be actually misleading, if there turn out to be certain features peculiar to hallucinations in the sphere of vision which, in the absence of information about other forms of hallucinations, might be taken to be characteristic of hallucinations in general. Let me, therefore, now describe the experiences of two patients who suffered from hallucinations of smell. One experienced what he described as 'a smell of rubber burning' which would last for hours at a time. He said: 'I would wake up at night and smell burning, and I woke my wife and said there is something on fire—and I'd heard of a beam in those old farmhouses smouldering for days. And then,' he went on, 'I realized it wasn't the house that was on fire—it was me!' I asked him how he discovered this, and he replied: 'Well, when I went somewhere else and found I could still smell it.' Another patient had her first attack of hallucination of smell while driving her car. Thinking the car battery was leaking she stopped the car to look at it. And here is the account which another patient gave me of her experience of a buzzing in the ears. 'It sounded like the bombers coming over during the war. It was a long time before I found out it was me.'

Disease of the brain may produce illusions and hallucinations over the whole range of sensory experience which do not differ in character from those which can be produced by the administration of drugs. Let me now quote a few examples of illusions and hallucinations occurring as part of the manifestations of an epileptic attack or elicited by electrical stimulation of the brain in the fully conscious patient. First, here is an account of a visual illusion as part of an epileptic attack recorded by his doctor. 'While I was visiting him this evening the patient said: "Wait a minute! You are getting bigger. The nurse is standing beside you. She is getting

bigger. Watch me!" I asked, "Are you having an attack now?" No reply.'
Then follows a description of the attack. And here is an account of an
hallucination of hearing.

In these later attacks, she heard voices which seemed to be coming
from her right. They were not the voices of her children. Indeed she said
she could not hear her children speak to her during an attack. Once, on
getting up at night to go to the bathroom, she heard music. She thought
it came from the radio in the living room. It was a song she had frequently
heard on the radio. She could not hear the words.

Another patient said that she would hear music at the beginning of
her seizure 'and the music was always the same, a lullaby her mother had
sung, "Hushabye my baby." ' When this patient's brain was stimulated
she said 'I hear people coming in, I hear music now, a funny little piece.'
Stimulation was continued. She became more talkative than usual, explaining that the music was something she had heard on the radio, that
it was the theme song of a children's programme.

Now consider some illusions and hallucinations arising in connexion
with awareness of the body. The simplest and commonest of these is the
'phantom limb,' which is the name for the persistent feeling of the presence of a limb which has been amputated. Phantom limbs must have been
known to humanity ever since injury or warfare led to the loss of a part
of the body. This strange experience is not limited to limbs, but can
apply to many parts, including the nose or tooth. The phenomenon interested Descartes, and Nelson, after losing his arm, had a phantom one,
which for some reason he regarded as a proof of the existence of the soul.
Of course a phantom limb can only be felt and not seen, but the feeling
may be so convincing that a man who has a phantom leg may fall down
because he attempts to stand on it. The subject may feel that he is able
to move his phantom limb, and it may be the site of severe and persistent
pain. In most cases a painless phantom limb gradually shortens and after
a time disappears into the amputation stump.

But amputation is not the only cause of phantom limbs. If certain
sensory nerve-paths between a normal limb and the brain are interrupted
the patient may feel that he has a second limb in a different place from
the real one. Suppose this happens in the case of an arm. Since the inter-
ruption of the nerve-paths takes away the feeling from his arm, he now
says that he has one arm which he can see, but not feel, and another arm
which he can feel, but not see.

Drugs which cause hallucinations may produce the most bizarre
effects upon the subject's awareness of his body. One who had taken mescaline said: 'I felt my body particularly plastic and minutely carved. At
once I had a sensation as if my foot was being taken off. Then I felt as
if my head had been turned by 180 degrees. . . . My feet turned spirals
and scrolls, my jaw was like a hook and my chest seemed to melt away.'

Not only may the body feel enlarged; it may enter into a complicated scene. One subject, also under mescaline and lying with his arms crossed, said: 'My right arm is a street with a group of toy soldiers. My left arm goes across the street like a bridge and carries a railway.'

To complete this account of the perceptual changes produced by mescaline intoxication I must mention the occurrence of synaesthesiae, that is the irradiation of sensation from one sense to another. For example, one subject found that the colours of his visual hallucinations were altered by changes in the rhythm of the music being played on the radio. Mayer-Gross quotes an experience of a subject under mescaline which illustrates what he calls not only 'the peculiar result of the synaesthetic perception, but also the inadequacy of ordinary language for such experiences'. 'What I see, I hear; what I smell, I think. I am music, I am the lattice-work. I see an idea of mine going out of me into the lattice-work. . . . I felt, saw, tasted and smelled the noise of the trumpet, was myself the noise. . . . Everything was clear and absolutely certain. All criticism is nonsense in the face of experience.'

But lest it be thought that these results of the administration of drugs are quite remote from the experiences of normal people, let me quote Grey Walter's observations on the effect of exposing normal individuals to a flickering light. At certain frequencies around ten per second some subjects see whirling spirals, whirlpools, explosions, Catherine wheels which do not correspond to any causal physical event. There may be organized hallucinations, and all sorts of emotions are experienced. Sometimes the sense of time is lost or disturbed. One subject said that he had been 'pushed sideways in time'—yesterday was at one side, instead of behind, and tomorrow was off the port bow.

If I am to give a comprehensive account of hallucinations, that is to provide all the data which a philosophical explanation of them needs to take into account, there are some further points which I must add. An hallucination may be present to one sense, but not to another, as in the case of a phantom limb. Perhaps the best-known example of this is Macbeth's dagger.

> Is this a dagger which I see before me
> The handle toward my hand? Come, let me clutch thee.
> I have thee not, and yet I see thee still.
> Art thou not, fatal vision, sensible
> To feeling as to sight? or art thou but
> A dagger of the mind, a false creation,
> Proceeding from the heat-oppressed brain?

Similar experiences are common in psychiatry. On the other hand an hallucination may be present to more than one sense. For example, a person may think that he sees a coin on the floor. He may then stoop and pick up the hallucinatory coin and say that he can feel its milled edge with his finger. Or he may say that he sees a human figure and that the figure speaks to him, and he can hear its words. Probably the most elaborate hallucinatory experiences are those of so-called apparitions. Smythies gives an excellent summary of the characteristics of these hallucinations. He says:

The hallucinated object or person purports to be a physical object—i.e. it looks and behaves very like a physical object or person. And 'an apparition' usually looks solid, throws a proper shadow, gets smaller as it moves away from the observer, moves around the room with respect of the furniture, gets dimmer as it moves into the more dimly lit parts of the room, may speak to the observer or even touch him. In nearly one half of the reported cases the 'apparition' has been seen by more than one observer at the same time—i.e. there are collective hallucinations. These features of this class of hallucinations may be summarized by stating that the internal and external organization of the hallucination *approaches* that of veridical perception. An 'apparition' may be so 'life-like' as to be frequently confused with the biological person it purports to be. They frequently satisfy the criteria by which we judge what is and what is not a veridical perception and are accepted as members of the class of veridical perceptions—at any rate for a time—although this membership is usually cancelled by subsequent experience, as when the apparition suddenly disappears or information is later obtained that the person hallucinated was actually at that time in a distant part of the country.

I have given a by no means exhaustive account of the rich variety of hallucinatory experiences, but I have described enough to be able to draw attention to certain points. First, no hard-and-fast line can be drawn introspectively between normal perception, illusions, and hallucinations. The subject under the influence of mescaline or lysergic acid describes modifications in the appearance of the objects around him. 'The wall began to be covered with an incredibly beautiful series of patterns.' 'Looking at my bright blue pyjamas . . . I saw that the blue was edged with flame.' 'The colours of real objects appeared more fine.' 'The faces of people around me were slightly distorted.' These experiences merge into others in which the change involves the nature of the object itself. 'These stars on the lampshade began to be filled with colour . . . the star, I now saw, was a very small (and wholly attractive) turtle . . . These little turtles—stars—or highway-men with two huge pistols!—lived and moved in their firmament of illumined paper.' From this a step takes us to visual hallucinations which seem independent of any object in the environment —animals, demons, and dwarfs, for example—and finally to 'visions' of coloured patterns seen with closed eyes.

Secondly, in describing illusions and hallucinations the subjects, whether normal or abnormal, frequently use the words 'see,' 'hear,' and 'smell,' and not the phrases 'seem to see,' 'seem to hear,' and 'seem to smell.' When I am describing my own experience of visual after-images it seems natural to say that I see them. I do not mean by that that I believe that I am seeing any physical object, but that the after-images have sensory quality in common with the seeing of the object which has immediately preceded them, that they are describable in similar terms in respect of colour and spatial extension, and moreover they have some relationship to my eyes since they move when I move my eyes. Similarly the patient who had a visual illusion in an epileptic attack did not say: 'You seem to be growing bigger,' but 'You are growing bigger.' Thus the patient describing an illusion often uses the same terms with which he describes the reality. He does not discriminate the illusion as a sensory experience from the reality as a sensory experience, and he describes both in the same way. How, then, does he distinguish between them when he does so? By reasoning. He compares the appearance or behaviour of the illusory object with what he knows is its normal appearance or behaviour, and concludes that he is experiencing an illusion.

Thirdly, both the drug-induced illusions and the hallucinatory 'apparitions' show that these abnormal experiences are often associated with a modification of normal perception such that the abnormal appearance is integrated into the subject's perception of his environment. When an apparition hides from view an object in front of which it is standing, or opens and passes through a door known to be locked, it provides the strongest evidence that the sense-data comprising the apparition and those comprising the environment possess the same perceptual status, and that those events, whatever they may be, which are causing the subject to see the apparition are at the same time appropriately modifying his perception of the rest of his environment. Perhaps I should add at this point that I am concerned with these phenomena purely as hallucinations and express no views as to the epistemological status of apparitions.

Now although there are many hallucinatory states which present themselves with the same sensory vividness as veridical perceptions, and of which the subject naturally, and in my view appropriately, says 'I see,' 'I hear,' or 'I smell' so-and-so, there are other experiences which are usually and appropriately described by the subject with the words 'I seemed to see,' 'I seemed to hear,' or 'I seemed to smell.' The commonest example of this is a dream. If we relate our dreams, we commonly do so in some such words as Bottom's: 'Methought I was,—and methought I had,—.' Our account of our dreams is usually retrospective, though I do not know whether philosophers in their dreams give themselves an account of their experiences. But although in our dreams most of us have experiences which we describe in visual terms—and in what other terms could we discuss, for example, whether an object seen in a dream is coloured or not?—we do, looking back on a dream in memory, regard it as having a sensory quality which distinguishes it from a waking experience. And the same applies to visual imagery and visual memory in a subject who has these faculties strongly developed. However vividly he may see an object in his memory or in his imagination he is never likely to make the mistake of thinking he is seeing it in reality: he will recognize that he is seeing it in his 'mind's eye.' No doubt the perceptual character of the experience is only one reason for this: the subject knows that he is himself responsible for remembering, or for imagining, in a way in which he is not responsible for the appearance of things he perceives or his hallucinations. However, there are disorders of sleep in which the subject, who may be described as half-awake, fails to distinguish between the events of his dream and the reality of his environment which he also perceives. He may then, as it were, act out his dream in his ordinary surroundings. This, though rare in adults, is by no means uncommon in a child awakening from a nightmare. In some mental disorders, too, the patient's phantasies may not have the vivid perceptual external location of hallucinations, but rather the quality of dreams or imagination mingling with the everyday environment. Thus, while there are many perceptual experiences in which a hallucination has sensory qualities indistinguishable to the subject from veridical perceptual experiences and which are naturally, and appropriately, described in the same terms, there are also both normal and abnormal mental states in which images may play a part which are not naturally or appropriately so described.

TWENTY-SEVEN

Argument from Physiology

J. C. ECCLES (1903-   )

From *The Neurophysiological Basis of Mind**

E. NEUROPHYSIOLOGICAL PROBLEMS IN PERCEPTION

The usual sequence of events is that some stimulus to a receptor organ causes the discharge of impulses along afferent nerve-fibres, which, after various synaptic relays, eventually evoke specific spatio-temporal patterns of impulses in the neuronal network of the cerebral cortex. The transmission from receptor organ to cerebral cortex is by a coded pattern that is quite unlike the original stimulus and the spatio-temporal pattern evoked in the cerebral cortex would be again different. Yet, as a consequence of this cerebral pattern of activity, we experience a sensation (more properly the complex constructs called percepts) which are 'projected' to somewhere outside the cortex; it may be to the surface of the body or even within it, or, as with visual, acoustic, and olfactory receptors, to the outside world. However, the only necessary condition for an observer to see colours, hear sounds, or experience the existence of his own body is that appropriate patterns of neuronal activity shall occur in appropriate regions of his brain, as was first clearly seen by Descartes. It is immaterial whether these events are caused by local stimulation of the cerebral cortex or some part of the afferent nervous pathway, or whether they are, as is usual, generated by afferent impulses discharged by receptor organs.

In the first instance, therefore, the observer will experience a private perceptual world which is an interpretation of specific events in his brain. This interpretation occurs according to conventions both inherited and acquired, that, as it were, are built into the micro-structure of the cerebral cortex, so that all kinds of diverse patterned sensory inputs are co-ordinated and linked together to give some coherent synthesis. We can regard the perceptual world of each observer as a kind of map built upon

---

* From J. C. Eccles, *The Neurophysiological Basis of Mind,* by permission of the Clarendon Press, Oxford.

the spatial relations between objects of the external world, but also giving us symbolic information in terms of the secondary qualities, as is customary in ordinary maps with their conventions for rivers, towns, railways, &c. For example, colours, sounds, smells, heat, and cold as such belong only to the perceptual world of an observer and are merely symbolic of events in the physical world which they are quite unlike.

However, in various ways all the observers each with his private and unique perceptual world come to agree on the existence of a single physical world, which provides an explanation more or less complete and satisfactory of these manifold perceptual worlds. Personal experiment from earliest childhood onwards, and communication with other observers, are the standard procedures by which we learn to interpret a part of our private perceptual experience as events in a single physical world common to other observers. Furthermore, the task of scientists has been to attempt to build up a progressively more valid or real physical world, i.e. a world more and more purified from the symbolic bias that is necessarily introduced into the perceptual world by the manner in which it is derived from the physical world. This is done by the discovery of rules by which the real physical world may be inferred from the symbolic data of the perceptual world, as for example the correlation of wave frequency in the physical world with colour of light in the perceptual world.

But the key problem in perception has remained so far beyond this discussion. We may ask: how can some specific spatio-temporal pattern of neuronal activity in the cerebral cortex evoke a percept in the mind?

In brain-mind liaison the traffic is both ways, from brain to mind in perception no less than from mind to brain in willed action. Existing knowledge of the brain provides the basis for the hypothesis relating to the operation of the mind on the brain. The reverse traffic—specific patterns of activity in the brain to percepts in the mind—is still more perplexing; but, presumably, if the mind can operate on dynamic spatio-temporal patterns of activity in the cortex, and itself have some spatio-temporal patterning, it would be expected to be susceptible to operation in the reverse sense. That would be the operational path in all perception and in the memory of events. Perhaps electromagnetic interaction may provide a model that is valuable in this respect. For the interaction is symmetrical, from electrical to magnetic phenomena and vice versa, and yet each has a certain autonomy, just as is assumed for mind and brain. Yet this analogy can be helpful merely in giving a general picture of a reciprocal interaction. It throws no light on the 'how' of the interaction of brain and mind, for it would be gratuitous to assume any similarity in this respect.

TWENTY-EIGHT

An Argument from the Nature
of Empirical Knowledge

C. I. LEWIS (1883-   )

From *An Analysis of Knowledge and Valuation**

. . . Empirical truth cannot be known except, finally, through presentations of sense. Most affirmations of empirical knowledge are to be justified, proximately, by others already accepted or believed: such justification involves a step or steps depending on logical truth. The classification as empirical will still be correct, however, if amongst such statements required to support the one in question, either deductively or inductively, there are some which cannot be assured by logic or analysis of meaning but only by reference to the content of given experience. Our empirical knowledge rises as a structure of enormous complexity, most parts of which are stabilized in measure by their mutual support, but all of which rest, at bottom, on direct findings of sense. Unless there should be some statements, or rather something apprehensible and stable, whose truth is determined by given experience and is not determinable in any other way, there would be no non-analytic affirmation whose truth could be determined at all, and no such thing as empirical knowledge. But also there could be no empirical knowledge if there were not meanings capable of being entertained without dependence on particular occasions. No experience or set of experiences will determine truth of a statement or a belief unless, prior to such experience, we know what we mean; know what experiences will corroborate our affirmation or supposition and what experiences will discredit it. Apprehension of the criteria by which what we intend may be recognized, must be antecedent to any verification or disproof.

We shall find, however, that most empirical statements—all those ordinarily made, in fact—are such that no single experience could decisively prove them true; and it can be doubted that any experience would conclusively prove them false. We *do* entertain assertable meanings of a sort

* From *An Analysis of Knowledge and Valuation* by Clarence Irving Lewis (LaSalle, Illinois, The Open Court Publishing Co., 1946), pp. 171-190. Reprinted by permission of the publisher.

which *can* be decisively determined to hold or not to hold; but statements having that kind of significance are not usually expressed, both because there is seldom occasion to express them and because there is no language in which they can be easily expressed without ambiguity. It is items which belong somewhere in the upper stories of our structure of empirical beliefs which can be clearly put: it is those which are at or near the bottom, required to support the whole edifice, which there is difficulty to state without implying what does not genuinely belong to the import of them. Thus the analysis of an ordinary empirical judgment such as might indicate the foundations of it in given experience, encounters a difficulty which is primarily one of formulation. The reason for this is something which must be understood and appreciated at the start, if we are not to fall into some kind of misconception which would be fatal for the understanding of empirical knowledge in general.

2. Let us turn to the simplest kind of empirical cognition; knowledge by direct perception. And let us take two examples.

I am descending the steps of Emerson Hall, and using my eyes to guide my feet. This is a habitual and ordinarily automatic action. But for this occasion, and in order that it may clearly constitute an instance of perceptual cognition instead of unconsidered behavior, I put enough attention on the process to bring the major features of it to clear consciousness. There is a certain visual pattern presented to me, a feeling of pressure on the soles of my feet, and certain muscle-sensations and feelings of balance and motion. And these items mentioned are fused together with others in one moving whole of presentation, within which they can be genuinely elicited but in which they do not exist as separate. Much of this presented content, I should find it difficult to put in words. I should find it difficult because, for one reason, if I tried to express it precisely in objectively intelligible fashion, I should have to specify such items as particular muscles which are involved and the behavior of them, and other things of this kind; and I do not in fact know which muscles I am using and just how. But one does not have to study physiology in order to walk down stairs. I know by my feelings when I am walking erect—or I think I do. And you, by putting yourself in my place, know how I feel—or think you do. That is all that is necessary, because we are here speaking of direct experience. You will follow me through the example by using your imagination, and understand what I mean—or what *you* would mean by the same language—in terms of your own experience.

The experience I have as I approach the steps and look down is familiar: it is qualitatively specific, and undoubtedly supplies the clues on which I act. For example, if I had approached the steps with eyes shut, I should have been obliged to behave quite differently in order to avoid falling. Let us single out the visual part of the presentation for particular consideration. Ordinarily I have no occasion to express empirical content of this sort: it performs its office of guiding my behavior and thereupon lapses from consciousness. But if I attempt to express it, I might say: "I see what looks like a flight of granite steps, fifteen inches wide and seven inches deep, in front of me." The locution 'looks like' represents my attempt to signalize the fact that I do not mean to assert that the steps *are* granite, or have the dimensions mentioned, or even that in point of absolutely certain fact there are any steps at all. Language is largely preempted to do the assertion of objective realities and events. If I wish, as I now do, to confine it to expression of a presented content, my best recourse is, very likely, to express what I take to be the objective facts this presentation signalizes and use locutions such as 'looks like,' tastes like,' 'feels like,' or some other contextual cue, to mark the intention on this occasion to restrict what I say to the fact of presentation itself as contrasted with the objective state of affairs more usually signified by the rest of my statement.

This given presentation—what looks like a flight of granite steps before me—leads to a prediction: "If I step forward and down, I shall come safely to rest on the step below." Ordinarily this prediction is unexpressed and would not even be explicitly thought. When so formulated, it is altogether too pedantic and portentous to fit the simple forward-looking quality of my conscious attitude. But unless I were prepared to assent to it, in case my attention were drawn to the matter, I should not now proceed as I do. Here again, the language I use would ordinarily be meant to express an objective process involving my body and a physical environment. But for the present occasion, I am trying to express the direct and indubitable content of my experience only, and, particularly, to elicit exemplary items which mark this conscious procedure as cognitive. As I stand momentarily poised and looking before me, the presented visual pattern leads me to predict that acting in a certain manner—stepping forward and down—will be followed by a further empirical content, equally specific and recognizable but equally difficult to express without suggesting more than I now mean—the felt experience of coming to balance on the step below.

I adopt the mode of action envisaged; and the expected empirical sequent actually follows. My prediction is verified. The cognitive significance of the visual presentation which operated as cue, is found valid. This functioning of it was a genuine case of perceptual knowledge.

Let us take another and different example; different not in any important character of the situation involved, but different in the manner in which we shall consider it.

I believe there is a piece of white paper now before me. The reason that I believe this is that I see it: a certain visual presentation is given. But my belief includes the expectation that so long as I continue to look in the same direction, this presentation, with its qualitative character essentially unchanged, will persist; that if I move my eyes right, it will be displaced to the left in the visual field; that if I close them, it will disappear; and so on. If any of these predictions should, upon trial, be disproved, I should abandon my present belief in a real piece of paper before me, in favor of belief in some extraordinary after-image or some puzzling reflection or some disconcerting hallucination.

I do look in the same direction for a time; then turn my eyes; and after that try closing them: all with the expected results. My belief is so far corroborated. And these corroborations give me even greater assurance in any further predictions based upon it. But theoretically and ideally it is not completely verified, because the belief in a real piece of white paper now before me has further implications not yet tested: that what I see could be folded without cracking, as a piece of celluloid could not; that it would tear easily, as architect's drawing-cloth would not; that this experience will not be followed by waking in quite different surroundings; and others too numerous to mention. If it is a real piece of paper before me now, then I shall expect to find it here tomorrow with the number I just put on the corner: its reality and the real character I attribute in my belief imply innumerable possible verifications, or partial verifications, tomorrow and later on.

But looking back over what I have just written, I observe that I have succumbed to precisely those difficulties of formulation which have been mentioned. I have here spoken of predictable results of further tests I am not now making; of folding the paper and trying to tear it, and so on. Finding these predictions borne out would, in each case, be only a partial test, theoretically, of my belief in a real piece of paper. But it was my intention to mention predictions which, though only partial verification of the objective fact I believe in, could themselves be decisively tested. And there I have failed. That the paper, upon trial, would really be torn, will no more be evidenced with perfect certainty than is the presence of real paper before me now. It—provided it take place—will be a real objective event about which, theoretically, my momentary experience could deceive me. What I meant to speak of was certain expected experiences—of the *appearance and feeling* of paper being folded; of its *seeming* to be torn. These predictions of *experience,* would be decisively and indubitably borne out or disproved if I make trial of them. But on this point, the reader will most likely have caught my intent and improved upon my statement as made.

3. Let us return to the point we were discussing. We had just noted that even if the mentioned tests of the empirical belief about the paper should have been made, the result would not be a theoretically complete verification of it because there would be further and similar implications of the belief which would still not have been tested. In the case of an

important piece of paper like a deed or a will, or an important issue like the question whether "Midsummer Night's Dream" was written by Shakspere or by Bacon, such implications might be subject to test years or even centuries afterward. And a negative result might then rationally lead to doubt that a particular piece of paper lay on a certain desk at a certain time. My present example is no different except in importance: what I now believe has consequences which will be determinable indefinitely in the future.

Further, my belief must extend to any predictions such that I should accept the failure of them as disproof of the belief, however far in the future the time may be which they concern. And my belief must imply as probable, anything the failure of which I should accept as tending to discredit this belief.

Also it is the case that such future contingencies, implied by the belief, are not such that failure of them can be absolutely precluded in the light of prior empirical corroborations of what is believed. However improbable, it remains thinkable that such later tests could have a negative result. Though truth of the belief itself implies a positive result of such later tests, the evidence to date does not imply this as more than probable, even though the difference of this probability from theoretical certainty should be so slight that practically it would be foolish to hesitate over it. Indeed we could be too deprecatory about this difference: if we interrogate experience we shall find plenty of occasions when we have felt quite sure of an objective fact perceived but later circumstance has shocked us out of our assurance and obliged us to retract or modify our belief.

If now we ask ourselves how extensive such implied consequences of the belief are, it seems clear that in so simple a case as the white paper supposedly now before me, the number of them is inexhaustible. For one thing, they presumably will never come to an end in point of time: there will never be a time when the fact—or non-fact—of this piece of paper now lying on my desk will not make some trivial difference. If that were not the case, then it must be that at some future date it will become not only practically but theoretically impossible that there should be a scintilla of evidence either for or against this supposed present fact. It would not be possible for anyone even to think of something which, if it should then occur, would be such evidence. That even the least important of real events will thus make no conceivable difference after a certain time, is not plausible. If that should be so, then what belongs to the past, beyond a certain stretch, could be something worse than an unknowable thing in itself; it could be such that the very supposition of it could make no conceivable difference to anyone's rational behavior; and any alleged interest in its truth or falsity could be shown to be fictitious or pointless, or to be confined to having others assert or assent to a certain form of words. In that sense, this belief would then become meaningless, having no con-

ceivable consequence of its truth or falsity which would be testable or
bear upon any rational interest.

It will be well for the reader to come to his own clear decision on
this question; whether it is or is not the case that the truth of an objective
empirical belief has consequences which are inexhaustible and are such
that there is no limited number of them whose determination theoretically and absolutely precludes a negative result of further tests and hence
deductively implies all further and as yet untested consequences. It will
be well to become thus clear because this point has decisive consequences
for the nature of empirical knowledge. Also these consequences are disconcerting: those who are more interested in pretty theories than in facts
will be sure to repudiate this conception, whether they acknowledge such
repudiation or merely pass this point without making any uncomfortable
admissions.

In fact, one objection to this conception is likely to occur to us
promptly. It will strike us as dubious that we can believe, all in a minute,
something whose consequences—which by implication we must also be
believing—are not finitely enumerable. But that objection is not one
which offers serious difficulty: what it reflects is principally a necessary
comment on 'believing' and 'knowing'; and it cannot be more implausible
than that we can know anything at all. This difficulty concerns the sense
in which the 'consequences' of a belief—those statements whose proven
falsity would discredit it—are 'included in' the belief. A little reflection
will remind us that *every* proposition has innumerable consequences, deducible from it by laws of logic: or if that fact has escaped us, the logicians
can easily make it clear, by providing us with formulas by which we can,
from any given premise you please, deduce different conclusions without
limit, so long as we can think of new terms to write in certain places in
these formulas. The kind of deducible consequences of a proposition
which such formulas would give are not entirely comparable to the kind
we are here thinking of: the nature of the kind of consequences here in
question will call for further examination; and other important questions
are suggested, though we would best not pause upon them here. But on
the point at issue, the comparison holds: it cannot be doubted that belief
in *any* proposition commits us to innumerable consequences, disproof of
any one of which would require rationally that the belief be retracted,
whether we explicitly think of these consequences in believing what implies them or not. And surely, what is supposed to be or asserted to be
empirical fact, cannot be supposed or asserted irrespective of what would,
at some future time, be evidence concerning it, and irrespective of further
possible tests the failure of which would discredit our supposition or
assertion. The fact that such consequences of what we affirm are inex-
haustibly numerous, cannot stand as a valid objection to this conception.

4. Let us now give attention to our two examples, and especially to

the different manner in which the two have been considered. Both represent cases of knowledge by perception. And in both, while the sensory cues to this knowledge are provided by the given presentation, the cognitive significance is seen to lie not in the mere givenness of these sensory cues but in prediction based upon them. In both cases, it is such prediction the verification of which would mark the judgment made as true or as false.

In the first case, of using my eyes to guide me down the steps, the prediction made was a single one. Or if more than one was made, the others would presumably be like the one considered and this was taken as exemplary. This judgment is of the form, "If I act in manner A, the empirical eventuation will include E." We found difficulty in expressing, in language which would not say more than was intended, the content of the presentation which functioned as sensory cue. We encountered the same difficulty in expressing the mode of action, A, as we envisaged it in terms of our own felt experience and as we should recognize it, when performed, as the act we intended. And again this difficulty attended our attempt to express that expected presentational eventuality, E, the accrual of which was anticipated in our prediction.

As we considered this first example, the attempt was to portray it as a case in which a directly apprehensible presentation of a recognizable sort functioned as cue to a single prediction; the prediction that a certain directly recognizable act would lead to a particular and directly recognizable result. If we are to describe this cognitive situation truly, all three of these elements—the presentation, the envisaged action, and the expected consequence—must be described in language which will denote immediately presented or directly presentable contents of experience. We attempted to make clear this intent of the language used by locutions such as 'looks like,' 'feels like'; thus restricting it to what would fall completely within the passage of experience in question and what this passage of experience could completely and directly determine as true. For example, if I should say, "There is a flight of granite steps before me," I should not merely report my experience but assert what it would require a great deal of further experience to corroborate fully. Indeed, it is questionable whether any amount of further experience could put this assertion theoretically beyond all possibility of a rational doubt. But when I say, "I see what *looks like* granite steps before me," I restrict myself to what is given; and what I intend by this language is something of which I can have no possible doubt. And the only possible doubt *you* could have of it—since it concerns a present experience of mine—is a doubt whether you grasp correctly what I intend to report, or a doubt whether I am telling the truth or a lie.

This use of language to formulate a directly presented or presentable content of experience, may be called its *expressive* use. This is in contrast to that more common intent of language, exemplified by, "I see (what in fact *is*) a flight of granite steps before me," which may be called its *objective use*. The distinctive character of expressive language, or the expressive use of language, is that such language signifies *appearances*. And in thus referring to appearances, or affirming what appears, such expressive language *neither asserts any objective reality of what appears nor denies any*. It is confined to description of the content of presentation itself.

In such expressive language, the cognitive judgment, "If I act in manner *A*, the empirical eventuality will include *E*," is one which can be verified by putting it to the test—supposing I can in fact put it to the test; can act in manner *A*. When the hypothesis of this hypothetical judgment is made true by my volition, the consequent is found true or found false by what follows; and this verification is decisive and complete, because nothing beyond the content of this passage of experience was implied in the judgment.

In the second example, as we considered it, what was judged was an *objective fact:* "A piece of white paper is now before me." This judgment will be false if the presentation is illusory; it will be false if what I see is not really paper; false if it is not really white but only looks white. This objective judgment also is one capable of corroboration. As in the other example, so here too, any test of the judgment would pretty surely involve some way of acting—*making* the test, as by continuing to look, or turning my eyes, or grasping to tear, etc.—and would be determined by finding or failing to find some expected result in experience. But in this example, if the result of any single test is as expected, it constitutes a partial verification of the judgment only; never one which is absolutely decisive and theoretically complete. This is so because, while the judgment, so far as it is significant, contains nothing which could not be tested, still it has a significance which outruns what any single test, or any limited set of tests, could exhaust. No matter how fully I may have investigated this objective fact, there will remain some theoretical possibility of mistake; there will be further consequences which must be thus and so if the judgment is true, and not all of these will have been determined. The possibility that such further tests, if made, might have a negative result, cannot be altogether precluded; and this possibility marks the judgment as, at the time in question, not fully verified and less than absolutely certain. To quibble about such possible doubts will not, in most cases, be common sense. But we are not trying to weigh the degree of theoretical dubiety which common-sense practicality should take account of, but to arrive at an accurate analysis of knowledge. This character of being further testable and less than theoretically certain characterizes every judgment of objective fact at all times; every judgment that such and such a real thing exists or has a certain objectively factual property, or that a certain objective event actually occurs, or that any objective state of affairs actually is the case.

A judgment of the type of the first example—prediction of a particular passage of experience, describable in expressive language—may be called *terminating*. It admits of decisive and complete verification or falsification. One of the type of the second example—judgment of objective fact which is always further verifiable and never completely verified—may be called *non-terminating*.

However, if the suggested account should be correct, then the judgment of objective fact implies nothing which is not theoretically verifiable. And since any, even partial, verification could be made only by something disclosed in *some* passage of experience, such an objective and non-terminating judgment must be translatable into judgments of the terminating kind. Only so could confirmation of it in experience come about. If particular experiences should not serve as its corroborations, then it cannot be confirmed at all; experience in general would be irrelevant to its truth or falsity; and it must be either analytic or meaningless. Its non-terminating character reflects the fact, not that the statement implies anything which is not expressible in some terminating judgment or other, but that no limited set of such terminating judgments could be sufficient to exhaust its empirical significance.

To be sure, the sense of 'verifiable' which is appropriate to the principle that a statement of supposed objective fact which should not be verifiable would be meaningless, is one which will call for further consideration. 'Verifiable', like most 'able' words, is a highly ambiguous term, connoting conditions which are implied but unexpressed. For example, the sense in which it is verifiable that there are lines on the other side of this paper, is somewhat different from the sense in which it is verifiable that there are mountains on the other side of the moon. But such various senses in which 'verifiable' may be taken, concern the sense in which the verifying experience is 'possible'; not the character of the experience which would constitute verification. And in general we may safely say that for *any* sense in which statement of objective fact is 'meaningful', there is a coordinate and indicated sense in which it is 'verifiable'.

It may also be the case that, for some judgments at least—those called 'practically certain'—a degree of verification may be attained such that no later confirmation can render what is presently judged more certain than it is at the moment. That turns on considerations which we are not yet ready to examine. But as will appear, these postponed considerations further corroborate, instead of casting doubt upon, the conclusion that no objective statement is theoretically and completely certain. For that conclusion—which is the present point—the grounds mentioned would seem to be sufficient.

5. The conception is, thus, that there are three classes of empirical statements. First, there are formulations of what is presently given in experience. Only infrequently are such statements of the given actually made: there is seldom need to formulate what is directly and indubitably presented. They are also difficult or—it might plausibly be said—impossible to state in ordinary language, which, as usually understood, carries implications of something more and further verifiable which *ipso facto* is not given. But this difficulty of formulating precisely and only a given content of experience, is a relatively inessential consideration for the analysis of knowledge. That which we should thus attempt to formulate plays the same role whether it is expressed, or could be precisely expressed, or not. Without such apprehensions of direct and indubitable content of experience, there could be no basis for any empirical judgment, and no verification of one.

To this there is no alternative. Even if one should wish to suppose that *all* empirical statements are affected by uncertainty; one could not—short of an absurd kind of skepticism—suppose them all to be doubtful in the same degree that they would be if there were no experience. And if there are some empirical statements not thus utterly doubtful, then there must be something which imparts to them this status of better-than-utterly-doubtful. And that something must be an apprehended fact, or facts, of experience. If facts of this order should not be clearly expressible in language, they would still be the absolutely essential bases of all empirical knowledge.

Those thinkers who approach all problems of analysis from the point of view of language, have raised numerous difficulties over this conception of the empirically given. We shall not pause to clear away all the irrelevant issues with which the point has thus been surrounded. That point is simply that there is such a thing as experience, the content of which we do not invent and cannot have as we will but merely find. And that this given is an element in perception but not the whole of perceptual cognition. Subtract, in what we say that we see, or hear, or otherwise learn from direct experience, *all that conceivably could be mistaken;* the remainder is the given content of the experience inducing this belief. If there were no such hard kernel in experience—e.g., what we *see* when we think we see a deer but there is no deer—then the word 'experience' would have nothing to refer to.

It is essential to remember that in the statement or formulation of what is given (if such formulation be attempted), one uses language to *convey* this content, but what is *asserted* is what the language is intended to convey, not the correctness of the language used. If, for example, one says, "I see a red round something," one assumes but does *not* assert, "The words 'red' and 'round' correctly apply to something now given." This last is not a given fact of present experience but a generalization from past experience indicating the customary use of English words. But one does not have to know English in order to see red; and that the word 'red' applies to this presently given appearance, is not a fact given in that experience.

Knowledge itself might well get on without the formulation of the immediately given: what is thus directly presented does not require verbalization. But the *discussion* of knowledge hardly can, since it must be able somehow to refer to such basic factualities of experience. If there should be no understood linguistic mode of telling what is given, the analysis of knowledge would have to invent one, if only by arbitrary figure of speech. But our situation is hardly so bad as that: such formulations can be made, in a manner the intent of which, at least, is recognizable by what we have called the expressive use of language, in which its reference is restricted to appearances—to what is given, as such.

Apprehensions of the given which such expressive statements formulate, are not judgments; and they are not here classed as knowledge, because they are not subject to any possible error. Statement of such apprehension is, however, true or false: there could be no doubt about the presented content of experience as such at the time when it is given, but it would be possible to tell lies about it.[1]

Second, there are terminating judgments, and statements of them. These represent some prediction of further possible experience. They find their cue in what is given: but what they state is something taken to be verifiable by some test which involves a way of acting. Thus terminating judgments are, in general, of the form, "If A then E," or "S being given, if A then E," where 'A' represents some mode of action taken to be possible, 'E' some expected consequent in experience, and 'S' the sensory cue. The hypothesis 'A' must here express something which, if made true by adopted action, will be *indubitably* true, and not, like a condition of my musculature in relation to the environment, an objective state of affairs only partially verified and not completely certain at the time. And the consequent 'E' represents an eventuality of *experience,* directly and certainly recognizable in case it accrues; not a resultant objective event, whose factuality could have, and would call for, further verification. Thus both antecedent and consequent of this judgment, "If A then E," require to be formulated in expressive language; though we shall not call it an expressive statement, reserving that phrase for formulations of the given.

[1] It would be possible to take statements of the given as involving judgment of correspondence between the character of the given itself and a fixed (expressive) meaning of words. But a judgment, "What is given is what '———' expresses," is not expression of the given but of a relation between it and a certain form of words. There is such a 'judgment of formulation' in the case of *any* statable fact. Let 'P' be an empirical statement which says nothing about language. "This fact is correctly stated by 'P'" is then a different statement, stating a relation between the fact which 'P' asserts and the verbal formulation 'P.' Correlatively, it is always possible to make a mistake of formulation, even where there could be no possible error concerning what is formulated.

Also, unlike statements of the given, what such terminating judgments express is to be classed as knowledge: the prediction in question calls for verification, and is subject to possible error.

Third, there are non-terminating judgments which assert objective reality; some state of affairs as actual. These are so named because, while there is nothing in the import of such objective statements which is intrinsically unverifiable, and hence nothing included in them which is not expressible by some terminating judgment, nevertheless no limited set of particular predictions of empirical eventualities can completely exhaust the significance of such an objective statement. This is true of the simplest and most trivial, as much as of the most important. The statement that something is blue, for example, or is square—as contrasted with merely looking blue or appearing to be square—has, always, implications of further possible experience, beyond what should, at any particular time, have been found true. Theoretically complete and absolute verification of any objective judgment would be a never-ending task: any actual verification of them is no more than partial; and our assurance of them is always, theoretically, less than certain.

Non-terminating judgments represent an enormous class; they include, in fact, pretty much all the empirical statements we habitually make. They range in type from the simplest assertion of perceived fact— "There is a piece of white paper now before me"—to the most impressive of scientific generalizations—"The universe is expanding." In general, the more important an assertion of empirical objective fact, the more remote it is from its eventual grounds. The laws of science, for example, are arrived at by induction from inductions from inductions - - -. But objective judgments are all alike in being non-terminating, and in having no other eventual foundation than data of given experience.

6. The point of distinguishing expressive statements of given data of experience from predictive and verifiable statements of terminating judgments, and both of them from statements of objective fact, representing non-terminating judgments, is that without such distinctions it is almost impossible so to analyze empirical knowledge as to discover the grounds of it in experience, and the manner of its derivation from such grounds.

All empirical knowledge rests ultimately upon this kind of evidence and calls for the corroboration constituted by the facts of presentation. The cue to any statement of perceived actuality is in such presentation; and if there is to be any further confirmation of such statement, that can come about only through some further presentation. But unless the fact of presentation itself be distinguished from the objective fact it is cue to or corroborates, we shall never be able to understand or formulate the manner in which objective belief receives its warrant, or to explain how a belief which has some justification may nevertheless prove later to have been mistaken.

One says, for example, "I see a sheet of white paper," "I hear a bell," "I smell honeysuckle." Some datum of sense gives rise to the belief expressed. But what is believed does not coincide with the fact of sense: the belief expressed may be mistaken and the experience, as we say, 'illusory'; whereas the actual character of the given datum as such, is indubitable. If the belief expressed is corroborated by further investigation, there will be, again, data of sense. But these additional and corroborating data will not be the totality of the objective fact believed in and corroborated; and expression of the verifying event of experience will not coincide with expression of this objective fact.

Again; if the statement of objective fact, in whatever degree it may have become already assured, is further significant—if it implies what could be further and empirically determined but is not strictly deducible from past and present findings—then always it signifies something verifiable but as yet unverified, and is, in corresponding measure, itself subject to some theoretical uncertainty. We have concluded that all statements of objective fact do have this character. That conclusion being premised, it becomes essential to distinguish statements of the given and presently certain, as well as statements of terminating judgments which later experience may render certain, from such statements of objective fact. Otherwise it becomes impossible to assure objective truth as even probable. If what is to confirm the objective belief and thus show it probable, were itself an objective belief and hence no more than probable, then the objective belief to be confirmed would only probably be rendered probable. Thus unless we distinguish the objective truths belief in which experience may render probable, from those presentations and passages of experience which provide this warrant, any citation of evidence for a statement about objective reality, and any mentionable corroboration of it, will become involved in an indefinite regress of the merely probable—or else it will go round in a circle—and the probability will fail to be genuine. If anything is to be probable, then something must be certain. The data which eventually support a genuine probability, must themselves be certainties. We do have such absolute certainties, in the sense data initiating belief and in those passages of experience which later may confirm it. But neither such initial data nor such later verifying passages of experience can be phrased in the language of objective statement—because what can be so phrased is never more than probable. Our sense certainties can only be formulated by the expressive use of language, in which what is signified is a content of experience and what is asserted is the givenness of this content. . . .

SECTION TWO

Representative Realism and Its Problems

TWENTY-NINE

The Independent Existence of Body

JOHN LOCKE (1632-1704)

From *An Essay Concerning Human Understanding**

II, viii, 7. To discover the nature of our *ideas* the better, and to discourse of them intelligibly, it will be convenient to distinguish them *as they are ideas or perceptions in our minds;* and *as they are modifications of matter in the bodies that cause such perceptions in us:* that so we may not think (as perhaps usually is done) that they are exactly the images and resemblances of something inherent in the subject; most of those of sensation being in the mind no more the likeness of something existing without us, than the names that stand for them are the likeness of our ideas, which yet upon hearing they are apt to excite in us.

8. Whatsoever the mind perceives *in itself,* or is the immediate object of perception, thought, or understanding, that I call *idea;* and the power to produce any idea in our mind, I call *quality* of the subject wherein that power is. Thus a snowball having the power to produce in us the ideas of white, cold, and round,—the power to produce those ideas in us, as they are in the snowball, I call qualities; and as they are sensations or perceptions in our understandings, I call them ideas; which *ideas,* if I speak of sometimes as in the things themselves, I would be understood to mean those qualities in the objects which produce them in us.

* From *An Essay Concerning Human Understanding* by John Locke (1690).

9. [Qualities thus considered in bodies are,

First, such as are utterly inseparable from the body, in what state soever it be]: and such as in all the alterations and changes it suffers, all the force can be used upon it, it constantly keeps; and such as sense constantly finds in every particle of matter which has bulk enough to be perceived; and the mind finds inseparable from every particle of matter, though less than to make itself singly be perceived by our senses: v.g. Take a grain of wheat, divide it into two parts; each part has still solidity, extension, figure, and mobility: divide it again, and it retains still the same qualities; and so divide it on, till the parts become insensible; they must retain still each of them all those qualities. For division (which is all that a mill, or pestle, or any other body, does upon another, in reducing it to insensible parts) can never take away either solidity, extension, figure, or mobility from any body, but only makes two or more distinct separate masses of matter, of that which was but one before; all which distinct masses, reckoned as so many distinct bodies, after division, make a certain number. [These I call *original* or *primary* *qualities* of body, which I think we may observe to produce simple ideas in us, viz. solidity, extension, figure, motion or rest, and number.

10. *Secondly,* such qualities which in truth are nothing in the objects themselves but powers to produce various sensations in us by their primary qualities, i.e. by the bulk, figure, texture, and motion of their insensible parts, as colours, sounds, tastes, &c. These I call *secondary* *qualities.* To these might be added a *third* sort, which are allowed to be barely powers; though they are as much real qualities in the subject as those which I, to comply with the common way of speaking, call qualities, but for distinction, secondary qualities. For the power in fire to produce a new colour, or consistency, in *wax* or *clay,*—by its primary qualities, is as much a quality in fire, as the power it has to produce in *me* a new idea or sensation of warmth or burning, which I felt not before,—by the same primary qualities, viz. the bulk, texture, and motion of its insensible parts].

11. [The next thing to be considered is, how bodies produce ideas in us; and that is manifestly by impulse, the only way which we can conceive bodies to operate in].

12. If then external objects be not united to our minds when they produce ideas therein; and yet we perceive these *original* qualities in such of them as singly fall under our senses, it is evident that some motion must be thence continued by our nerves, or animal spirits, by some parts of our bodies, to the brains or the seat of sensation, there to produce in our minds the particular ideas we have of them. And since the extension, figure, number, and motion of bodies of an observable bigness, may be perceived at a distance by the sight, it is evident some singly imperceptible bodies must come from them to the eyes, and thereby convey to the brain

some motion; which produces these ideas which we have of them in us.

13. After the same manner that the ideas of these original qualities are produced in us, we may conceive that the ideas of *secondary* qualities are also produced, viz. by the operation of insensible particles on our senses. For, it being manifest that there are bodies and good store of bodies, each whereof are so small, that we cannot by any of our senses discover either their bulk, figure, or motion,—as is evident in the particles of the air and water, and others extremely smaller than those: perhaps as much smaller than the particles of air and water, as the particles of air and water are smaller than peas or hail-stones;—let us suppose at present that the different motions and figures, bulk and number, of such particles, affecting the several organs of our senses, produce in us those different sensations which we have from the colours and smells of bodies; v.g. that a violet, by the impulse of such insensible particles of matter, of peculiar figures and bulks, and in different degrees and modifications of their motions, causes the ideas of the blue colour, and sweet scent of that flower to be produced in our minds. It being no more impossible to conceive that God should annex such ideas to such motions, with which they have no similitude, than that he should annex the idea of pain to the motion of a piece of steel dividing our flesh, with which that idea hath no resemblance.

14. What I have said concerning colours and smells may be understood also of tastes and sounds, and other the like sensible qualities; which, whatever reality we by mistake attribute to them, are in truth nothing in the objects themselves, but powers to produce various sensations in us; and depend on those primary qualities, viz. bulk, figure, texture, and motion of parts [as I have said].

15. From whence I think it easy to draw this observation,—that the ideas of primary qualities of bodies are resemblances of them, and their patterns do really exist in the bodies themselves, but the ideas produced in us by these secondary qualities have no resemblance of them at all. There is nothing like our ideas, existing in the bodies themselves. They are, in the bodies we denominate from them, only a power to produce those sensations in us: and what is sweet, blue, or warm in idea, is but the certain bulk, figure, and motion of the insensible parts, in the bodies themselves, which we call so.

16. Flame is denominated hot and light; snow, white and cold; and manna, white and sweet, from the ideas they produce in us. Which qualities are commonly thought to be the same in those bodies that those ideas are in us, the one the perfect resemblance of the other, as they are in a mirror, and it would by most men be judged very extravagant if one should say otherwise. And yet he that will consider that the same fire that, at one distance produces in us the sensation of warmth, does, at a nearer

approach, produce in us the far different sensation of pain, ought to be-think himself what reason he has to say—that this idea of warmth, which was produced in him by the fire, is *actually in the fire;* and his idea of pain, which the same fire produced in him the same way, is *not* in the fire. Why are whiteness and coldness in snow, and pain not, when it produces the one and the other idea in us; and can do neither, but by the bulk, figure, number, and motion of its solid parts?

17. The particular bulk, number, figure, and motion of the parts of fire or snow are really in them,—whether any one's senses perceive them or no: and therefore they may be called *real* qualities, because they really exist in those bodies. But light, heat, whiteness, or coldness, are no more really in them than sickness or pain is in manna. Take away the sensation of them; let not the eyes see light or colours, nor the ears hear sounds; let the palate not taste, nor the nose smell, and all colours, tastes, odours, and sounds, *as they are such particular ideas,* vanish and cease, and are reduced to their causes, i.e. bulk, figure, and motion of parts.

18. A piece of manna of a sensible bulk is able to produce in us the idea of a round or square figure; and by being removed from one place to another, the idea of motion. This idea of motion represents it as it really is in manna moving: a circle or square are the same, whether in idea or existence, in the mind or in the manna. And this, both motion and figure, are really in the manna, whether we take notice of them or no: this everybody is ready to agree to. Besides, manna, by the bulk, fig-ure, texture, and motion of its parts, has a power to produce the sensa-tions of sickness, and sometimes of acute pains or gripings in us. That these ideas of sickness and pain are *not* in the manna, but effects of its operations on us, and are nowhere when we feel them not; this also every one readily agrees to. And yet men are hardly to be brought to think that sweetness and whiteness are not really in manna; which are but the effects of the operations of manna, by the motion, size, and figure of its particles, on the eyes and palate: as the pain and sickness caused by manna are confessedly nothing but the effects of its operations on the stomach and guts, by the size, motion, and figure of its insensible parts, (for by nothing else can a body operate, as has been proved): as if it could not operate on the eyes and palate, and thereby produce in the mind particular distinct ideas, which in itself it has not, as well as we allow it can operate on the guts and stomach, and thereby produce distinct ideas, which in itself it has not. These ideas, being all effects of the operations of manna on several parts of our bodies, by the size, figure, number, and motion of its parts;— why those produced by the eyes and palate should rather be thought to be really in the manna, than those produced by the stomach and guts; or why the pain and sickness, ideas that are the effect of manna, should be thought to be nowhere when they are not felt; and yet the sweetness and

whiteness, effects of the same manna on other parts of the body, by ways equally as unknown, should be thought to exist in the manna, when they are not seen or tasted, would need some reason to explain.

19. Let us consider the red and white colours in porphyry. Hinder light from striking on it, and its colours vanish; it no longer produces any such ideas in us: upon the return of light it produces these appearances on us again. Can any one think any real alterations are made in the porphyry by the presence or absence of light; and that those ideas of whiteness and redness are really in porphyry in the light, when it is plain *it has no colour in the dark?* It has, indeed, such a configuration of particles, both night and day, as are apt, by the rays of light rebounding from some parts of that hard stone, to produce in us the idea of redness, and from others the idea of whiteness; but whiteness or redness are not in it at any time, but such a texture that hath the power to produce such a sensation in us.

20. Pound an almond, and the clear white colour will be altered into a dirty one, and the sweet taste into an oily one. What real alteration can the beating of the pestle make in any body, but an alteration of the texture of it?

21. Ideas being thus distinguished and understood, we may be able to give an account how the same water, at the same time, may produce the idea of cold by one hand and of heat by the other: whereas it is impossible that the same water, if those ideas were really in it, should at the same time be both hot and cold. For, if we imagine *warmth,* as it is in our hands, to be nothing but a certain sort and degree of motion in the minute particles of our nerves or animal spirits, we may understand how it is possible that the same water may, at the same time, produce the sensations of heat in one hand and cold in the other; which yet *figure* never does, that never producing the idea of a square by one hand which has produced the idea of a globe by another. But if the sensation of heat and cold be nothing but the increase or diminution of the motion of the minute parts of our bodies, caused by the corpuscles of any other body, it is easy to be understood, that if that motion be greater in one hand than in the other; if a body be applied to the two hands, which has in its minute particles a greater motion than in those of one of the hands, and a less than in those of the other, it will increase the motion of the one hand and lessen it in the other; and so cause the different sensations of heat and cold that depend thereon.

22. I have in what just goes before been engaged in physical inquiries a little further than perhaps I intended. But, it being necessary to make the nature of sensation a little understood; and to make the difference between the *qualities* in bodies, and the *ideas* produced by them in the mind, to be distinctly conceived, without which it were impossible to discourse intelligibly of them;—I hope I shall be pardoned

this little excursion into natural philosophy; it being necessary in our present inquiry to distinguish the *primary* and *real* qualities of bodies, which are always in them (viz. solidity, extension, figure, number, and motion, or rest, and are sometimes perceived by us, viz. when the bodies they are in are big enough singly to be discerned), from those *secondary* and *imputed* qualities, which are but the powers of several combinations of those primary ones, when they operate without being distinctly discerned;—whereby we may also come to know what ideas are, and what are not, resemblances of something really existing in the bodies we denominate from them.

23. The qualities, then, that are in bodies, rightly considered, are of three sorts:—

First, The bulk, figure, number, situation, and motion or rest of their solid parts. Those are in them, whether we perceive them or not; and when they are of that size that we can discover them, we have by these an idea of the thing as it is in itself; as is plain in artificial things. These I call *primary qualities.*

Secondly, The power that is in any body, by reason of its insensible primary qualities, to operate after a peculiar manner on any of our senses, and thereby produce in *us* the different ideas of several colours, sounds, smells, tastes, &c. These are usually called *sensible qualities.*

Thirdly, The power that is in any body, by reason of the particular constitution of its primary qualities, to make such a change in the bulk, figure, texture, and motion of *another body,* as to make it operate on our senses differently from what it did before. Thus the sun has a power to make wax white, and fire to make lead fluid. [These are usually called *powers*].

The first of these, as has been said, I think may be properly called real, original, or primary qualities; because they are in the things themselves, whether they are perceived or not: and upon their different modifications it is that the secondary qualities depend.

The other two are only powers to act differently upon other things: which powers result from the different modifications of those primary qualities.

24. But, though the two latter sorts of qualities are powers barely, and nothing but powers, relating to several other bodies, and resulting from the different modifications of the original qualities, yet they are generally otherwise thought of. For the *second* sort, viz. the powers to produce several ideas in us, by our senses, are looked upon as real qualities in the things thus affecting us: but the *third* sort are called and esteemed barely powers. v.g. The idea of heat or light, which we receive by our eyes, or touch, from the sun, are commonly thought real qualities existing in the sun, and something more than mere powers in it. But when we consider the sun in reference to wax, which it melts or blanches,

we look on the whiteness and softness produced in the wax, not as qualities in the sun, but effects produced by powers in it. Whereas, if rightly considered, these qualities of light and warmth, which are perceptions in me when I am warmed or enlightened by the sun, are no otherwise in the sun, than the changes made in the wax, when it is blanched or melted, are in the sun. They are all of them equally *powers in the sun, depending on its primary qualities;* whereby it is able, in the one case, so to alter the bulk, figure, texture, or motion of some of the insensible parts of my eyes or hands, as thereby to produce in me the idea of light or heat; and in the other, it is able so to alter the bulk, figure, texture, or motion of the insensible parts of the wax, as to make them fit to produce in me the distinct ideas of white and fluid.

25. The reason why the one are ordinarily taken for real qualities, and the other only for bare powers, seems to be, because the ideas we have of distinct colours, sounds, &c., containing nothing at all in them of bulk, figure, or motion, we are not apt to think them the effects of these primary qualities; which appear not, to our senses, to operate in their production, and with which they have not any apparent congruity or conceivable connexion. Hence it is that we are so forward to imagine, that those ideas are the resemblances of something really existing in the objects themselves: since sensation discovers nothing of bulk, figure, or motion of parts in their production; nor can reason show how bodies, *by their bulk, figure, and motion,* should produce in the mind the ideas of blue or yellow, &c. But, in the other case, in the operations of bodies changing the qualities one of another, we plainly discover that the quality produced hath commonly no resemblance with anything in the thing producing it; wherefore we look on it as a bare effect of power. For, through receiving the idea of heat or light from the sun, we are apt to think *it* is a perception and resemblance of such a quality in the sun; yet when we see wax, or a fair face, receive change of colour from the sun, we cannot imagine *that* to be the reception or resemblance of anything in the sun, because we find not those different colours in the sun itself. For, our senses being able to observe a likeness or unlikeness of sensible qualities in two different external objects, we forwardly enough conclude the production of any sensible quality in any subject to be an effect of bare power, and not the communication of any quality which was really in the efficient, when we find no such sensible quality in the thing that produced it. But our senses, not being able to discover any unlikeness between the idea produced in us, and the quality of the object producing it, we are apt to imagine that our ideas are resemblances of something in the objects, and not the effects of certain powers placed in the modification of their primary qualities, with which primary qualities the ideas produced in us have no resemblance.

26. To conclude. Beside those before-mentioned primary qualities in bodies, viz. bulk, figure, extension, number, and motion of their solid

parts; all the rest, whereby we take notice of bodies, and distinguish them one from another, are nothing else but several powers in them, depending on those primary qualities; whereby they are fitted, either by immediately operating on our bodies to produce several different ideas in us; or else, by operating on other bodies, so to change their primary qualities as to render them capable of producing ideas in us different from what before they did. The former of these, I think, may be called secondary qualities *immediately perceivable:* the latter, secondary qualities, *mediately perceivable.*

THIRTY

Criticisms of Representative Realism

GEORGE BERKELEY (1685-1753)

From *Three Dialogues Between Hylas and Philonous**

HYLAS. I frankly own, Philonous, that it is in vain to stand out any longer. Colours, sounds, tastes, in a word all those termed *secondary qualities,* have certainly no existence without the mind. But by this acknowledgment I must not be supposed to derogate anything from the reality of Matter, or external objects; seeing it is no more than several philosophers maintain, who nevertheless are the farthest imaginable from denying Matter. For the clearer understanding of this, you must know sensible qualities are by philosophers divided into *Primary* and *Secondary.* The former are Extension, Figure, Solidity, Gravity, Motion, and Rest; and these they hold exist really in bodies. The latter are those above enumerated; or, briefly, *all sensible qualities beside the Primary;* which they assert are only so many sensations or ideas existing nowhere but in the mind. But all this, I doubt not, you are apprised of. For my part, I have been a long time sensible there was such an opinion current among philosophers, but was never thoroughly convinced of its truth until now.

PHILONOUS. You are still then of opinion that *extension* and *figures* are inherent in external unthinking substances?

HYL. I am.

PHIL. But what if the same arguments which are brought against Secondary Qualities will hold good against these also?

HYL. Why then I shall be obliged to think, they too exist only in the mind.

PHIL. Is it your opinion the very figure and extension which you perceive by sense exist in the outward object or material substance?

HYL. It is.

PHIL. Have all other animals as good grounds to think the same of the figure and extension which they see and feel?

HYL. Without doubt, if they have any thought at all.

* From *Three Dialogues Between Hylas and Philonous* by George Berkeley.

PHIL. Answer me, Hylas. Think you the senses were bestowed upon all animals for their preservation and well-being in life? or were they given to men alone for this end?

HYL. I make no question but they have the same use in all other animals.

PHIL. If so, is it not necessary they should be enabled by them to perceive their own limbs, and those bodies which are capable of harming them?

HYL. Certainly.

PHIL. A mite therefore must be supposed to see his own foot, and things equal or even less than it, as bodies of some considerable dimension; though at the same time they appear to you scarce discernible, or at best as so many visible points?

HYL. I cannot deny it.

PHIL. And to creatures less than the mite they will seem yet larger?

HYL. They will.

PHIL. Insomuch that what you can hardly discern will to another extremely minute animal appear as some huge mountain?

HYL. All this I grant.

PHIL. Can one and the same thing be at the same time in itself of different dimensions?

HYL. That were absurd to imagine.

PHIL. But, from what you have laid down it follows that both the extension by you perceived, and that perceived by the mite itself, as likewise all those perceived by lesser animals, are each of them the true extension of the mite's foot; that is to say, by your own principles you are led into an absurdity.

HYL. There seems to be some difficulty in the point.

PHIL. Again, have you not acknowledged that no real inherent property of any object can be changed without some change in the thing itself?

HYL. I have.

PHIL. But, as we approach to or recede from an object, the visible extension varies, being at one distance ten or a hundred times greater than at another. Doth it not therefore follow from hence likewise that it is not really inherent in the object?

HYL. I own I am at a loss what to think.

PHIL. Your judgment will soon be determined, if you will venture to think as freely concerning this quality as you have done concerning the rest. Was it not admitted as a good argument, that neither heat nor cold was in the water, because it seemed warm to one hand and cold to the other?

HYL. It was.

PHIL. Is it not the very same reasoning to conclude, there is no extension or figure in an object, because to one eye it shall seem little, smooth, and round, when at the same time it appears to the other, great, uneven, and angular?

HYL. The very same. But does this latter fact ever happen?

PHIL. You may at any time make the experiment, by looking with one eye bare, and with the other through a microscope.

HYL. I know not how to maintain it; and yet I am loath to give up *extension,* I see so many odd consequences following upon such a concession.

PHIL. Odd, say you? After the concessions already made, I hope you will stick at nothing for its oddness. [But, on the other hand, should it not seem very odd, if the general reasoning which includes all other sensible qualities did not also include extension? If it be allowed that no idea, nor anything like an idea, can exist in an unperceiving substance, then surely it follows that no figure, or mode of extension, which we can either perceive, or imagine, or have any idea of, can be really inherent in Matter; not to mention the peculiar difficulty there must be in conceiving a material substance, prior to and distinct from extension, to be the *substratum* of extension. Be the sensible quality what it will—figure, or sound, or colour, it seems alike impossible it should subsist in that which doth not perceive it.]

HYL. I give up the point for the present, reserving still a right to retract my opinion, in case I shall hereafter discover any false step in my progress to it.

PHIL. That is a right you cannot be denied. Figures and extension being despatched, we proceed next to *motion.* Can a real motion in any external body be at the same time both very swift and very slow?

HYL. It cannot.

PHIL. Is not the motion of a body swift in a reciprocal proportion to the time it takes up in describing any given space? Thus a body that describes a mile in an hour moves three times faster than it would in case it described only a mile in three hours.

HYL. I agree with you.

PHIL. And is not time measured by the succession of ideas in our minds?

HYL. It is.

PHIL. And is it not possible ideas should succeed one another twice as fast in your mind as they do in mine, or in that of some spirit of another kind?

HYL. I own it.

PHIL. Consequently the same body may to another seem to perform its motion over any space in half the time that it doth to you. And the same reasoning will hold as to any other proportion: that is to say, according to your principles (since the motions perceived are both really in the object) it is possible one and the same body shall be really moved the same way at once, both very swift and very slow. How is this consistent either with common sense, or with what you just now granted?

HYL. I have nothing to say to it.

PHIL. Then as for *solidity;* either you do not mean any sensible quality by that word, and so it is beside our inquiry: or if you do, it must be either hardness or resistance. But both the one and the other are plainly relative to our senses: it being evident that what seems hard to one animal may appear soft to another, who hath greater force and firmness of limbs. Nor is it less plain that the resistance I feel is not in the body.

HYL. I own the very *sensation* of resistance, which is all you immediately perceive, is not in the body; but the *cause* of that sensation is.

PHIL. But the causes of our sensations are not things immediately perceived, and therefore are not sensible. This point I thought had been already determined.

HYL. I own it was; but you will pardon me if I seem a little embarrassed: I know not how to quit my old notions.

PHIL. To help you out, do but consider that if *extension* be once acknowledged to have no existence without the mind, the same must necessarily be granted of motion, solidity, and gravity; since they all evidently suppose extension. It is therefore superfluous to inquire particularly concerning each of them. In denying extension, you have denied them all to have any real existence.

HYL. I wonder, Philonous, if what you say be true, why those philosophers who deny the Secondary Qualities any real existence should yet attribute it to the Primary. If there is no difference between them, how can this be accounted for?

PHIL. It is not my business to account for every opinion of the philosophers. But, among other reasons which may be assigned for this, it seems probable that pleasure and pain being rather annexed to the former than the latter may be one. Heat and cold, tastes and smells, have something more vividly pleasing or disagreeable than the ideas of extension, figure, and motion affect us with. And, it being too visibly absurd to hold that pain or pleasure can be in an unperceiving Substance, men are more easily weaned from believing the external existence of the Secondary than the Primary Qualities. You will be satisfied there is something in this, if you recollect the difference you made between an intense and more moderate degree of heat; allowing the one a real existence, while you denied it to the other. But, after all, there is no rational ground for that distinction; for, surely an indifferent sensation is as truly *a sensation* as one more pleasing or painful; and consequently should not any more than they be supposed to exist in an unthinking subject.

HYL. It is just come into my head, Philonous, that I have somewhere heard of a distinction between absolute and sensible extension. Now, though it be acknowledged that *great* and *small,* consisting merely in the relation which other extended beings have to the parts of our own bodies, do not really inhere in the substances themselves: yet nothing obliges us to hold the same with regard to *absolute extension,* which is something abstracted from *great* and *small,* from this or that particular magnitude or figure. So likewise as to motion; *swift* and *slow* are altogether relative to the succession of ideas in our own minds. But, it doth not follow, because those modifications of motion exist not without the mind, that therefore absolute motion abstracted from them doth not.

PHIL. Pray what is it that distinguishes one motion, or one part of extension, from another? Is it not something sensible, as some degree of swiftness or slowness, some certain magnitude or figure peculiar to each?

HYL. I think so.

PHIL. These qualities, therefore, stripped of all sensible properties, are without all specific and numerical differences, as the schools call them.

HYL. They are.

PHIL. That is to say, they are extension in general, and motion in general.

HYL. Let it be so.

PHIL. But it is a universally received maxim that *Everything which exists is particular.* How then can motion in general, or extension in general, exist in any corporeal substance?

HYL. I will take time to solve your difficulty.

PHIL. But I think the point may be speedily decided. Without doubt you can tell whether you are able to frame this or that idea. Now I am content to put our dispute on this issue. If you can frame in your thoughts a distinct *abstract idea* of motion or extension, divested of all those sensible modes, as swift and slow, great and small, round and square, and the like, which are acknowledged to exist only in the mind, I will then yield the point you contend for. But if you cannot, it will be unreasonable on your side to insist any longer upon what you have no notion of.

HYL. To confess ingenuously, I cannot.

PHIL. Can you even separate the ideas of extension and motion from the ideas of all those qualities which they who make the distinction term *secondary?*

HYL. What! is it not an easy matter to consider extension and motion by themselves, abstracted from all other sensible qualities? Pray how do the mathematicians treat of them?

PHIL. I acknowledge, Hylas, it is not difficult to form general propositions and reasonings about those qualities, without mentioning any other; and, in this sense, to consider or treat of them abstractedly. But, how doth it follow that, because I can pronounce the word *motion* by itself, I can form the idea of it in my mind exclusive of body? or, because theorems may be great of extension and figures, without any mention of *great* or *small,* or any other sensible mode or quality, that therefore it is possible such an abstract idea of extension, without any particular size or figure, or sensible quality, should be distinctly formed, and apprehended by the mind? Mathematicians treat of quantity, without regarding what other sensible qualities it is attended with, as being altogether indifferent to their demonstrations. But, when laying aside the words, they contemplate the bare ideas, I believe you will find, they are not the pure abstracted ideas of extension.

HYL. But what say you to *pure intellect?* May not abstracted ideas be framed by that faculty?

PHIL. Since I cannot frame abstract ideas at all, it is plain I cannot frame them by the help of *pure intellect,* whatsoever faculty you understand by those words. Besides, not to inquire into the nature of pure intellect and its spiritual objects, as *virtue, reason, God,* or the like, thus much seems manifest—that sensible things are only to be perceived by sense, or represented by the imagination. Figures, therefore, and extension, being originally perceived by sense, do not belong to pure intellect: but, for your farther satisfaction, try if you can frame the idea of any figure, abstracted from all particularities of size, or even from other sensible qualities.

HYL. Let me think a little—I do not find that I can.

PHIL. And can you think it possible that should really exist in nature which implies a repugnancy in its conception?

HYL. By no means.

PHIL. Since therefore it is impossible even for the mind to disunite the ideas of extension and motion from all other sensible qualities, doth it not follow, that where the one exist there necessarily the other exist likewise?

HYL. It should seem so.

PHIL. Consequently, the very same arguments which you admitted as conclusive against the Secondary Qualities are, without any farther application of force, against the Primary too. Besides, if you will trust your senses, is it not plain all sensible qualities coexist, or to them appear as being in the same place? Do they ever represent a motion, or figure, as being divested of all other visible and tangible qualities?

HYL. You need say no more on this head. I am free to own, if there be no secret error or oversight in our proceedings hitherto, that *all* sensible qualities are alike to be denied existence without the mind. . . .

PHIL. *Material substratum* call you it? Pray, by which of your senses came you acquainted with that being?

HYL. It is not itself sensible; its modes and qualities only being perceived by the senses.

PHIL. I presume then it was by reflexion and reason you obtained the idea of it?

Hyl. I do not pretend to any proper positive *idea* of it. However, I conclude it exists, because qualities cannot be conceived to exist without a support.

Phil. It seems then you have only a relative *notion* of it, or that you conceive it not otherwise than by conceiving the relation it bears to sensible qualities?

Hyl. Right.

Phil. Be pleased therefore to let me know wherein that relation consists.

Hyl. Is it not sufficiently expressed in the term *substratum,* or *substance?*

Phil. If so, the word *substratum* should import that it is spread under the sensible qualities or accidents?

Hyl. True.

Phil. And consequently under extension?

Hyl. I own it.

Phil. It is therefore somewhat in its own nature entirely distinct from extension?

Hyl. I tell you, extension is only a mode, and Matter is something that supports modes. And is it not evident the thing supported is different from the thing supporting?

Phil. So that something distinct from, and exclusive of, extension is supposed to be the *substratum* of extension?

Hyl. Just so.

Phil. Answer me, Hylas. Can a thing be spread without extension? or is not the idea of extension necessarily included in *spreading?*

Hyl. It is.

Phil. Whatsoever therefore you suppose spread under anything must have in itself an extension distinct from the extension of that thing under which it is spread?

Hyl. It must.

Phil. Consequently, every corporeal substance, being the *substratum* of extension, must have in itself another extension, by which it is qualified to be a *substratum:* and so on to infinity? And I ask whether this be not absurd in itself, and repugnant to what you granted just now, to wit, that the *substratum* was something distinct from and exclusive of extension?

Hyl. Aye but, Philonous, you take me wrong. I do not mean that Matter is *spread* in a gross literal sense under extension. The word *substratum* is used only to express in general the same thing with *substance.*

Phil. Well then, let us examine the relation implied in the term *substance.* Is it not that it stands under accidents?

Hyl. The very same.

PHIL. But, that one thing may stand under or support another, must it not be extended?

HYL. It must.

PHIL. Is not therefore this supposition liable to the same absurdity with the former?

HYL. You still take things in a strict literal sense. That is not fair, Philonous.

PHIL. I am not for imposing any sense on your words: you are at liberty to explain them as you please. Only, I beseech you, make me understand something by them. You tell me Matter supports or stands under accidents. How! is it as your legs support your body?

HYL. No; that is the literal sense.

PHIL. Pray let me know any sense, literal or not literal, that you understand it in.—How long must I wait for an answer, Hylas?

HYL. I declare I know not what to say. I once thought I understood well enough what was meant by Matter's supporting accidents. But now, the more I think on it the less can I comprehend it: in short I find that I know nothing of it.

PHIL. It seems then you have no idea at all, neither relative nor positive, of Matter; you know neither what it is in itself, nor what relation it bears to accidents?

HYL. I acknowledge it.

PHIL. And yet you asserted that you could not conceive how qualities or accidents should really exist, without conceiving at the same time a material support of them?

HYL. I did.

PHIL. That is to say, when you conceive the *real* existence of qualities, you do withal conceive Something which you cannot conceive?

HYL. It was wrong, I own.

THIRTY-ONE

Physical Objects*

C. H. WHITELY (1911-   )

The problem I shall discuss is What reason have we for believing that there are physical objects? My purpose is not either to raise or to dispel doubts as to the existence of physical objects; this doubt constitutes a medical rather than a philosophical problem. The point of asking the question is that, while there can be no reasonable difference of opinion as to whether there are physical objects, there can be and is reasonable difference of opinion as to how the notion of a physical object is to be analysed; and if we are clear as to what grounds there are for believing in physical objects, we shall also be clearer as to what sort of physical objects we have grounds for believing in. Also, it is worth while to inquire which other beliefs are logically connected with, and which are logically independent of, the belief in physical objects.

I make one important assumption at the outset: namely, that by a physical object or process we mean something that exists or occurs apart from and independently of our perceptions, and of our experiences of other kinds. The distinction between the physical or "real" world and the "subjective" or "imaginary"—illusions, hallucinations, after-images, shadows, rainbows, mental pictures, what we merely suppose, imagine or expect—is a distinction between things and events which exist or occur whether anybody is aware of them or not, and things and events which have their being only as and when somebody is aware of them. A belief in physical objects is a belief in things which are sometimes at least unobserved by the believer.

It is obvious that the existence of such things is not a question to be settled by sense-perception alone. That there is a material world cannot be established or even made plausible merely by looking, listening, touching; it is not *given* in the way in which the existence of something red and something round, of sounds, smells, aches, feelings of sadness, can be given. I do not mean that the something red or round cannot be a physical object; I mean that it cannot be known to be a physical object just by looking at it or otherwise perceiving it. For I cannot, simply by perceiving something, tell whether that something continues to exist when I cease to perceive it. This logical necessity is not evaded by naive

* Reproduced, by permission of C. H. Whitely and the editor of *Philosophy*, from *Philosophy*, Vol. XXXIV, April 1959.

realism, which holds that the something red or round which appears to sight is (usually at least) identical with a physical object; for though this may be so, we cannot know it just by looking. Nor is it evaded by phenomenalism; for no phenomenalist does or plausibly could analyse statements about physical objects into statements asserting the *actual* occurrence of sense-data; he must add statements about what sense-data *would* be sensed if certain conditions were fulfilled; and this fact is not given by sense-perception, but reasons for it are required. That there are physical objects is not something we observe or perceive, but something we suppose or assume (to call it a "hypothesis" or "postulate" is to suggest something rather too deliberate and self-conscious). In old-fashioned language, it is a transcendent belief; it goes beyond the evidence.

Thus there is no logical absurdity in denying or refusing to admit the existence of a material world. To say that there are no physical objects, while doubtless very foolish, does not involve a man in any logical contradiction, nor does it force him to shut his eyes to any patent and indisputable facts. An intellectually indolent percipient, whose few wants were supplied independently of his own efforts, might well abstain from supposing that there was a physical world. There is some evidence that young babies, who are more or less in this situation, do not believe that there are any material things—do not believe, for instance, that the rattle just dropped from the hand and the visitor just departed from the room are now anywhere at all.

If somebody did behave like this, in what way would he be worse off, and what other beliefs would he be debarred from entertaining? I answer —and this is my principal point—that he would be unable to make valid generalizations, or reliable forecasts of his future experience. He would have to do without the belief in an order in nature, in regular sequences of events, in casual laws. For if I confine myself to what I myself observe or am aware of, I can make no valid generalizations concerning the concomitance or sequence of types of phenomena. I find only that phenomena of one type are quite often accompanied or followed by phenomena of another type, but sometimes not. There is no type of sense-datum A of which it is true that whenever it occurs another type of sense-datum B accompanies or follows or precedes it. And this is the case however complex you make your A and your B. This point has often been overlooked. People know quite well that lightning is always accompanied by thunder, barking by the presence of dogs, that green apples are always sour, and the ground always gets dark and sticky after a heavy fall of rain; and they talk about these as though they were *phenomenal* regularities—as though the seeing of lightning always went along with the hearing of thunder, and so forth. But this is of course not the case. If, as some people have said, it was the business of science to disclose the order or regularity in phenomena, meaning by phenomena what we see and hear and feel, science would be a very unrewarding pursuit. For phenomena are disorderly and irregular, and scientists cannot make them out any different.

Many philosophers have indeed thought that natural regularities could be conceived without the postulation of actual unobserved things and events, if instead we postulate that certain phenomena would occur or would have occurred, given certain unfulfilled conditions. Instead of saying that whenever I hear barking there exists an actual dog, perceived or unperceived, I am to say that whenever I hear barking, I should perceive a dog if certain conditions were fulfilled—if my eyes were open and my sight normal, if there was an adequate amount of light, if I looked in the right direction and there was no opaque obstacle in my line of vision, etc. Such an interpretation in terms of possible phenomena would relieve us of any need to postulate another order of physical events over and above perceptual events, and would in this way be more economical. There are, however, three ways in which phenomenal generalizations of this kind cannot take the place of physical generalizations.

(1) A physical generalization associates one uniform property with another uniform property: I mean that when something is asserted to be universally true of dogs, or pieces of iron, or cases of pneumonia, or falling bodies of a weight of ten pounds, it is assumed that there is some physical property or group of properties which is common to all dogs, pieces of iron, etc. Phenomenal generalizations, however, concern associations between sets of diverse phenomena. If we wish to correlate the auditory phenomenon of barking with visual phenomena we must specify a set of canine sense-data, or views of dogs, which are not all alike in any sensory property, but form one class only in virtue of a very complex set of relations.

(2) A physical generalization applies to *all* cases of a given type, and the study of nature aims at reducing to laws all events and all features of events. But phenomenal generalizations can never apply to all cases of a given type, but only to some of them, namely to those cases in which the supplementary conditions for observation are fulfilled. The physical generalization "There's no smoke without fire" applies to all instances of smoke, whether or not either the smoke or the fire is observed. But the corresponding phenomenal generalization brings under a uniformity-rule only those cases in which both the smoke and the fire are observed. Observed smoke can be correlated with observed fire; but when I observe the smoke but not the fire, the observed smoke is correlated with nothing, and is an instance of no natural law (except in the forced and trivial sense in which a white cat with brown eyes and quick hearing is an instance of the law that all white cats with blue eyes are deaf); it forms no part of the order of nature.

(3) A phenomenal generalization must always include a reference to

conditions of observation, whereas physical generalizations are independent of these. We can say without qualification "Whenever it thunders, it lightens". But we can say "Whenever thunder is heard, lightning is seen" only if we add "provided that there is an observer with adequate eyesight, facing in the appropriate direction, having his eyes open and his view not obscured by any opaque object, etc." This difference does not merely prevent the phenomenal generalization from adequately replacing the physical one. It also means that there can be no generalizations on the phenomenal level which are universally valid. For it is impossible to give in purely phenomenal terms an adequate statement of all the conditions required for perceiving lightning besides the occurrence of lightning. It is curious that the analysis of physical-object statements in terms of sense-data and the analysis of causation in terms of regular sequence should have been so often advocated by the same philosophers. For if we restrict our attention to phenomena, we can find no instances for the regular-sequence concept of cause to apply to.

If, therefore, I am to make reliable generalizations about the course of events, and reliable forecasts about my future experiences, I must suppose that there are unperceived as well as perceived events. Thus the connection between the category of substance and that of cause is, as Kant suggested, not fortuitous but necessary. We do not discover that there are (perfect) regularities in nature, that is, in the physical world, as we discover that there are (imperfect) regularities amongst phenomena. On the contrary, the regularity is essential to the concept of nature; the assumption that the physical world is orderly is inseparable from the assumption that the physical world exists. It is only to the extent that I assume it to be orderly that I have any grounds for believing that there is a physical world at all. This may help to account for our strong inclination to regard physical determinism as a necessary *a priori* truth.

What, then, is the sort of supposition which will make it possible to believe in regular sequences and concomitances in the world, and to regulate our expectations accordingly? A simple and comprehensive answer cannot be given to this question. The precise character of the suppositions we make about physical objects and processes is subject to variation for different kinds of cases, and to modification with the improvement of our knowledge. One can, however, indicate the general line which must be followed.

There are, amongst the events which we are aware of, certain associations of characteristics which, while not invariable, are very common: for example, the association between the sound of barking and the sight of dogs, between the visual appearance of oranges and their characteristic flavour, between the brightness of sunshine and felt warmth, between the kinaesthetic sensations of speech and the sound of my own voice, between the visible immersion of a lump of sugar in a cup of tea and its gradual disappearance, between the various members of the visible sequence black-coal . . . flame . . . red-coal . . . ashes, between the patter of raindrops, the sight of rain falling, the feeling of dampness on exposed parts of the body, and the darkening of the soil or pavement. (These are, of course, examples of several different kinds of association.)

The supposition required has two parts: (1) That to these imperfect phenomenal regularities there corresponds in each case a perfect physical regularity, that is, in each case in which there is a frequent association between phenomenal characteristics there are some corresponding physical characteristics which are invariably associated. Whereas the sound of barking is often but not always accompanied by the sight of a dog, there is some type of event, physical barking, which is always accompanied by the presence of some one type of physical object, a dog. Whereas the visual brightness of sunshine is only sometimes accompanied by a feeling of warmth, there is a physical entity, sunlight, and a physical entity, heat, which always goes with it. Whereas a person may be seen setting off from A and arriving at B without being seen at intermediate places at intermediate times, physical passage from A to B involves the temporally continuous traversing of a spatially continuous path. In general, whenever there is an imperfect but frequent association between a phenomenal characteristic A and a phenomenal characteristic B, there is a thing or process having a characteristic corresponding to A which is invariably associated with a thing or process having a characteristic corresponding to B. Thus whenever I hear barking, there exists a physical dog, whether or not there also occurs the experience of my seeing him.

(2) The existence of the corresponding physical thing, or the occurrence of the corresponding physical process, is a necessary but not a sufficient condition for the awareness of the phenomenal characteristic. There can be no hearing of barks without there being (physical) barks; but there can be barks without the hearing of barks. The further conditions, other than the existence of the dog or the occurrence of the bark, which are required if I am to have the corresponding perception of the dog or the bark, may be called the observation-conditions. Some of these conditions are pretty easy to discover. For instance, if I am to see anything at all, there must be a certain amount of light (but not enough to dazzle), and my vision must not be blocked by any obstacle. Other observation-conditions can only be discovered by much experimental research: for instance, the need for air or some other transmitting medium in the case of hearing, the need for integrity of the optic nerves in the case of sight. The occurrence of the appropriate sense experience is determined jointly by the corresponding physical process and the relevant observation-conditions. (These conditions, of course, concern the properties of other physical things and processes, so that we cannot say just what they are without knowing something about physical things other than the one to be per-

ceived. Learning about the properties of dogs, and learning about the properties of light and the human sense-organs, go hand in hand.) Thus the assumption of a physical world involves two supposed sets of regularities: an association between one physical characteristic and another, and an association between physical processes together with observation-conditions on the one hand and sense-experiences on the other.

So far, the physical world has been presented as a set of processes which occur independently of perceptions, which are related by laws of sequence and concomitance to other processes, and which together with the relevant observation-conditions determine specific sense-experiences of ours. These are purely relational properties; and nothing has been said so far about any other properties that physical objects may possess. On the view here advocated, namely that the justification of a belief in a physical world is that it makes possible the formulation of laws of nature, the only positive reason for attributing a property to physical objects would be that by assuming physical objects to possess this property we can account for the character of our perceptions, and explain how we come to perceive this rather than that, now rather than then. One way of accounting for the character of our perceptions would be to suppose that the sensory qualities which are present in them (the particular colours, sounds, tastes, etc.) are properties of physical objects, and persist unperceived just as they appear when perceived. This is naive realism. A completely naive-realist theory would hold that all sensory qualities are properties of physical objects, and exist independently of perception; other theories are naively realistic to the extent that they identify the properties of physical things with those properties which are present in sense-experience.

Now the investigation of the properties of physical things is the business of the science of physics. And contemporary physics is not naively realistic in any degree. The properties which it attributes to physical objects are not sensory properties, but hypothetical properties defined by their relations to one another and to certain kinds of perceptions. The reason for this is often misunderstood. Philosophical criticism of naive realism is apt to concentrate on the "argument from illusion", that is, on the *deceptiveness* of sense-perception. This is the wrong sort of criticism. Our perceptions can sometimes mislead us (that is, lead us to form false expectations about other perceptions to come) only because they also, and more often, lead us to form true expectations; perception could not be systematically misleading. But the question whether our perceptions induce in us true or false expectations is quite independent of the question whether they show us the permanent characteristics of material things. The damaging criticisms of naive realism rest on this principle: given that the physical object corresponding to a given sense-datum is something which, in conjunction with the relevant observation-conditions, determines the characteristics of that sense-datum, then if a given characteristic can be shown to be determined by the observation-conditions, there can be no reason for attributing it to the corresponding physical object. The successive modifications in our concept of the physical world arise from our increasing knowledge of the dependence of sensory properties upon observation-conditions. The challenge to naive realism with respect to colours comes from optics. The challenge to naive realism with respect to space and time comes from relativity-theory. The challenge to naive realism with respect to beauty and ugliness comes from our understanding of the dependence of aesthetic delight and disgust upon the dispositions and past experiences of the subject.

In abandoning naive realism, scientific theory only carries further a process which pre-scientific common sense has already begun. The common-sense view of the physical world is by no means a purely naive-realist view. When I look at an object from different angles and in different lights successively, the sensory properties which appear to me are many and various. Common sense does not hold that all these various sensory properties belong to the physical object and exist apart from my perception. Were that so, there would have to be either a multitude of physical objects or a constantly changing object to possess all these different properties. Common sense holds, on the contrary, that there is but one object with one shape, size, colour etc., which are unchanging throughout my changing perceptions. This postulation of a single set of physical properties corresponding to a multiplicity of sensory properties is the first and fundamental step away from naive realism. A Berkeleian analysis, which reverses this step, is a greater affront to common sense and provokes more resistance from it than a Lockean analysis which takes a step or two further in the same direction.

It is a belief of common sense that at least some sensory properties are *not* properties of physical objects, but are due to conditions of observation (quantity and quality of light, distance, defects of vision, etc.). As to whether *any* sensory properties are also physical properties, I am not convinced that common sense has any clear and consistent view. Of course we say that grass is green and roses are red. But does this mean more than that if we look at them under suitable conditions green and red are the colours we shall see? It is not clear to me that common sense is committed to the belief that objects have any colours when unperceived. (Examining the way we talk about the matter is of no help. Given that a certain piece of cloth looks bluish in artificial light and greyish in daylight, are we to presume that its colour changes with changes in the light, and say "It *is* blue in artificial light and grey in daylight", or are we to presume that it has a colour independently of the light, and say "It is really grey, but it looks blue in artificial light"? Ordinary idiom allows us to say either of these things indifferently.) By contrast, there are some properties which common sense does attribute to physical objects apart from perception—size and weight, for instance. When I conclude that this brick must have made that hole in the window, though nobody saw it do so, I credit the brick with having a size and weight at a time when it was not being perceived. But size and weight are not sensory properties. Blueness is a way things look; but heaviness is not a way things look or feel. A thing can, of course, look or feel heavy; but its *being* heavy is something different—it is heavy if it will hold down or make dents in other objects, if you can't lift it with one hand, and so on; and these casual characteristics are not ways of looking or feeling. Properties like size and weight, which common sense does attribute to unperceived objects, bear the same sort of relation to sense-experience as the concepts of modern physics. Thus it seems to me that one can abandon naive realism in all its forms without abandoning any belief to which common sense is committed.

To sum up. That there are physical objects is a supposition, not a datum. The use of the supposition is to account for the regularities in sensory phenomena, to enable the course of events to be set in a framework of regular sequences and concomitances. It is confirmed by the success we achieve in ordering our experiences by its aid, in making our generalizations continually more extensive and more exact. Being a supposition, and not an inevitable and invariable category of thought, it is subject to modification as we learn more about the conditions under which perception takes place. Scientific concepts are related to sense-experience in a remoter and more complex fashion than common-sense concepts of physical objects. But they are not of an entirely different order. The common-sense concept of "table" is not, like "blue" or "bang" or "stench", a merely phenomenal concept; it is explanatory and theoretical.

Phenomenalism and Its Problems

THIRTY-TWO

Physical Objects As Congeries of Ideas

GEORGE BERKELEY (1685-1753)

From *A Treatise Concerning
the Principles of Human Knowledge**

22. I am afraid I have given cause to think I am needlessly prolix in handling this subject. For, to what purpose is it to dilate on that which may be demonstrated with the utmost evidence in a line or two, to any one that is capable of the least reflexion? It is but looking into your own thoughts, and so trying whether you can conceive it possible for a sound, or figure, or motion, or colour to exist without the mind or unperceived. This easy trial may perhaps make you see that what you contend for is a downright contradiction. Insomuch that I am content to put the whole upon this issue:—If you can but conceive it possible for one extended moveable substance, or in general for any one idea, or anything like an idea, to exist otherwise than in a mind perceiving it, I shall readily give up the cause. And, as for all that compages of external bodies you contend for, I shall grant you its existence, though you cannot either give me any reason why you believe it exists, or assign any use to it when it is supposed to exist. I say, the bare possibility of your opinions being true shall pass for an argument that it is so.

23. But, say you, surely there is nothing easier than for me to

---

* From *A Treatise Concerning the Principles of Human Knowledge* by George Berkeley.

imagine trees, for instance, in a park, or books existing in a closet, and nobody by to perceive them. I answer, you may so, there is no difficulty in it. But what is all this, I beseech you, more than framing in your mind certain ideas which you call *books* and *trees,* and at the same time omitting to frame the idea of any one that may perceive them? But do not you yourself perceive or think of them all the while? This therefore is nothing to the purpose: it only shews you have the power of imagining, or forming ideas in your mind; but it does not shew that you can conceive it possible the objects of your thought may exist without the mind. To make out this, it is necessary that you conceive them existing unconceived or unthought of; which is a manifest repugnancy. When we do our utmost to conceive the existence of external bodies, we are all the while only contemplating our own ideas. But the mind, taking no notice of itself, is deluded to think it can and does conceive bodies existing unthought of, or without the mind, though at the same time they are apprehended by, or exist in, itself. A little attention will discover to any one the truth and evidence of what is here said, and make it unnecessary to insist on any other proofs against the existence of *material substance.*

24. [Could men but forbear to amuse themselves with words, we should, I believe, soon come to an agreement in this point.] It is very obvious, upon the least inquiry into our own thoughts, to know whether it be possible for us to understand what is meant by the *absolute existence of sensible objects in themselves,* or *without the mind.* To me it is evident those words mark out either a direct contradiction, or else nothing at all. And to convince others of this, I know no readier or fairer way than to entreat they would calmly attend to their own thoughts; and if by this attention the emptiness or repugnancy of those expressions does appear, surely nothing more is requisite for their conviction. It is on this therefore that I insist, to wit, that the *absolute existence of unthinking things* are words without a meaning, or which include a contradiction. This is what I repeat and inculcate, and earnestly recommend to the attentive thoughts of the reader.

29. But, whatever power I may have over my own thoughts, I find the ideas actually perceived by Sense have not a like dependence of *my* will. When in broad daylight I open my eyes, it is not in my power to choose whether I shall see or no, or to determine what particular objects shall present themselves to my view: and so likewise as to the hearing and other senses; the ideas imprinted on them are not creatures of *my* will. There is therefore some other Will or Spirit that produces them.

30. The ideas of Sense are more strong, lively, and distinct than those of the Imagination; they have likewise a steadiness, order, and coherence, and are not excited at random, as those which are the effects of human wills often are, but in a regular train or series—the admirable connexion

whereof sufficiently testifies the wisdom and benevolence of its Author. Now the set rules, or established methods, wherein the Mind we depend on excites in us the ideas of Sense, are called *the laws of nature;* and these we learn by experience, which teaches us that such and such ideas are attended with such and such other ideas, in the ordinary course of things.

31. This gives us a sort of foresight, which enables us to regulate our actions for the benefit of life. And without this we should be externally at a loss: we could not know how to act anything that might procure us the least pleasure, or remove the least pain of sense. That food nourishes, sleep refreshes, and fire warms us; that to sow in the seed-time is the way to reap in the harvest; and in general that to obtain such or such ends, such or such means are conducive—all this we know, not by discovering any *necessary connexion* between our ideas, but only by the observation of the *settled laws* of nature; without which we should be all in uncertainty and confusion, and a grown man no more know how to manage himself in the affairs of life than an infant just born.

32. And yet this consistent uniform working, which so evidently displays the Goodness and Wisdom of that Governing Spirit whose Will constitutes the laws of nature, is so far from leading our thoughts to Him, that it rather sends them wandering after second causes. For, when we perceive certain ideas of Sense constantly followed by other ideas, and we know this is not of our own doing, we forthwith attribute power and agency to the ideas themselves, and make one the cause of another, than which nothing can be more absurd and unintelligible. Thus, for example, having observed that when we perceive by sight a certain round luminous figure, we at the same time perceive by touch the idea or sensation called heat, we do from thence conclude the sun to be the *cause* of heat. And in like manner perceiving the motion and collision of bodies to be attended with sound, we are inclined to think the latter the *effect* of the former.

33. The ideas imprinted on the Senses by the Author of nature are called *real things:* and those excited in the imagination, being less regular, vivid, and constant, are more properly termed *ideas* or *images of* things, which they copy and represent. But then our *sensations,* be they never so vivid and distinct, are nevertheless ideas: that is, they exist in the mind, or are perceived by it, as truly as the ideas of its own framing. The ideas of Sense are allowed to have more reality in them, that is, to be more strong, orderly, and coherent than the creatures of the mind; but this is no argument that they exist without the mind. They are also less dependent on the spirit or thinking substance which perceives them, in that they are excited by the will of another and more powerful Spirit: yet still they are *ideas:* and certainly no idea, whether faint or strong, can exist otherwise than in a mind perceiving it.

34. Before we proceed any farther it is necessary we spend some time

in answering Objections which may probably be made against the Principles we have hitherto laid down. In doing of which, if I seem too prolix to those of quick apprehensions, I desire I may be excused, since all men do not equally apprehend things of this nature; and I am willing to be understood by every one.

First, then, it will be objected that by the foregoing principles all that is real and substantial in nature is banished out of the world, and instead thereof a chimerical scheme of *ideas* takes place. All things that exist exist only in the mind; that is, they are purely notional. What therefore becomes of the sun, moon, and stars? What must we think of houses, rivers, mountains, trees, stones; nay, even of our own bodies? Are all these but so many chimeras and illusions of the fancy?—To all which, and whatever else of the same sort may be objected, I answer, that by the Principles premised we are not deprived of any one thing in nature. Whatever we see, feel, hear, or any wise conceive or understand, remains as secure as ever, and is as real as ever. There is a *rerum natura,* and the distinction between realities and chimeras retains its full force. This is evident from sect. 29, 30, and 33, where we have shewn what is meant by *real things,* in opposition to *chimeras* or *ideas of our own framing;* but then they both equally exist in the mind, and in that sense are alike *ideas.*

35. I do not argue against the existence of any one thing that we can apprehend, either by sense or reflection. That the things I see with my eyes and touch with my hands do exist, really exist, I make not the least question. The only thing whose existence we deny is that which *philosophers* call Matter or corporeal substance. And in doing of this there is no damage done to the rest of mankind, who, I dare say, will never miss it. The Atheist indeed will want the colour of an empty name to support his impiety; and the Philosophers may possibly find they have lost a great handle for trifling and disputation. [But that is all the harm that I can see done.]

36. If any man thinks this detracts from the existence or reality of things, he is very far from understanding what hath been premised in the plainest terms I could think of. Take here an abstract of what has been said:—There are spiritual substances, minds, or human souls, which will or excite ideas in themselves at pleasure; but these are faint, weak, and unsteady in respect of others they perceive by sense; which, being impressed upon them according to certain rules or laws of nature, speak themselves the effects of a Mind more powerful and wise than human spirits. These latter are said to have *more reality* in them than the former; —by which is meant that they are more affecting, orderly, and distinct, and that they are not fictions of the mind perceiving them. And in this sense the sun that I see by day is the real sun, and that which I imagine by night is the idea of the former. In the sense here given of *reality,* it is evident that every vegetable, star, mineral, and in general each part of

the mundane system, is as much a *real being* by our principles as by any other. Whether others mean anything by the term *reality* different from what I do, I entreat them to look into their own thoughts and see.

37. It will be urged that thus much at least is true, to wit, that we take away all *corporeal substances.* To this my answer is, that if the word *substance* be taken in the vulgar sense, for a *combination* of sensible qualities, such as extension, solidity, weight, and the like—this we cannot be accused of taking away: but if it be taken in a philosophic sense, for the support of accidents or qualities without the mind—then indeed I acknowledge that we take it away, if one may be said to take away that which never had any existence, not even in the imagination.

38. But after all, say you, it sounds very harsh to say we eat and drink ideas, and are clothed with ideas. I acknowledge it does so—the word *idea* not being used in common discourse to signify the several combinations of sensible qualities which are called *things;* and it is certain that any expression which varies from the familiar use of language will seem harsh and ridiculous. But this doth not concern the truth of the proposition, which in other words is no more than to say, we are fed and clothed with those things which we perceive immediately by our senses. The hardness or softness, the colour, taste, warmth, figure, and suchlike qualities, which combined together constitute the several sorts of victuals and apparel, have been shewn to exist only in the mind that perceives them: and this is all that is meant by calling them *ideas;* which word, if it was as ordinarily used as *thing,* would sound no harsher nor more ridiculous than it. I am not for disputing about the propriety, but the truth of the expression. If therefore you agree with me that we eat and drink and are clad with the immediate objects of sense, which cannot exist unperceived or without the mind, I shall readily grant it is more proper or conformable to custom that they should be called *things* rather than *ideas.*

39. If it be demanded why I make use of the word *idea,* and do not rather in compliance with custom call them *things;* I answer, I do it for two reasons:—First, because the term *thing,* in contradistinction to *idea,* is generally supposed to denote somewhat existing without the mind: Secondly, because *thing* hath a more comprehensive signification than *idea,* including spirits, or thinking things, as well as ideas. Since therefore the objects of sense exist only in the mind, and are withal thoughtless and inactive, I chose to mark them by the word *idea;* which implies those properties.

40. But, say what we can, some one perhaps may be apt to reply, he will still believe his senses, and never suffer any arguments, how plausible soever, to prevail over the certainty of them. Be it so; assert the evidence of sense as high as you please, we are willing to do the same. That what I see, hear, and feel doth exist, that is to say, is perceived by me, I no more doubt than I do of my own being. But I do not see how the testimony of

sense can be alleged as a proof for the existence of anything which is *not* perceived by sense. We are not for having any man turn sceptic and disbelieve his senses; on the contrary, we give them all the stress and assurance imaginable; nor are there any principles more opposite to Scepticism than those we have laid down, as shall be hereafter clearly shewn.

41. *Secondly,* it will be objected that there is a great difference betwixt real fire for instance, and the idea of fire, betwixt dreaming or imagining oneself burnt, and actually being so. [ᵢ⁻ᶠ you suspect it to be only the idea of fire which you see, do but put your hand into it and you will be convinced with a witness.] This and the like may be urged in opposition to our tenets.—To all which the answer is evident from what hath been already said; and I shall only add in this place, that if real fire be very different from the idea of fire, so also is the real pain that it occasions very different from the idea of the same pain, and yet nobody will pretend that real pain either is, or can possibly be, in an unperceiving thing, or without the mind, any more than its idea.

42. *Thirdly,* it will be objected that we see things actually without or at a distance from us, and which consequently do not exist in the mind; it being absurd that those things which are seen at the distance of several miles should be as near to us as our own thoughts.—In answer to this, I desire it may be considered that in a dream we do oft perceive things as existing at a great distance off, and yet for all that, those things are acknowledged to have their existence only in the mind.

43. But, for the fuller clearing of this point, it may be worth while to consider how it is that we perceive distance, and things placed at a distance, by sight. For, that we should in truth *see* external space, and bodies actually existing in it, some nearer, others farther off, seems to carry with it some opposition to what hath been said of their existing nowhere without the mind. The consideration of this difficulty it was that gave birth to my *Essay towards a New Theory of Vision,* which was published not long since. Wherein it is shewn that distance or outness is neither immediately of itself perceived by sight, nor yet apprehended or judged of by lines and angles, or anything that hath a necessary connexion with it; but that it is only suggested to our thoughts by certain visible ideas, and sensations attending vision, which in their own nature have no manner of similitude or relation either with distance or things placed at a distance; but, by a connexion taught us by experience, they come to signify and suggest them to us, after the same manner that words of any language suggest the ideas they are made to stand for. Insomuch that a man born blind, and afterwards made to see, would not, at first sight, think the things he saw to be without his mind, or at any distance from him. See sect. 41 of the forementioned treatise.

44. The ideas of sight and touch make two species entirely distinct and heterogeneous. The former are marks and prognostics of the latter.

That the proper objects of sight neither exist without the mind, nor are the images of external things, was shewn even in that treatise. Though throughout the same the contrary be supposed true of *tangible objects;*— not that to suppose that vulgar error was necessary for establishing the notion therein laid down, but because it was beside my purpose to examine and refute it, in a discourse concerning *Vision.* So that in strict truth the ideas of sight, when we apprehend by them distance, and things placed at a distance, do not suggest or mark out to us things actually existing at a distance, but only admonish us what ideas of touch will be imprinted in our minds at such and such distances of time, and in consequence of such or such actions. It is, I say, evident, from what has been said in the foregoing parts of this Treatise, and in sect. 147 and elsewhere of the Essay concerning Vision, that visible ideas are the Language whereby the Governing Spirit on whom we depend informs us what tangible ideas he is about to imprint upon us, in case we excite this or that motion in our own bodies. But for a fuller information in this point I refer to the Essay itself.

45. *Fourthly,* it will be objected that from the foregoing principles it follows things are every moment annihilated and created anew. The objects of sense exist only when they are perceived: the trees therefore are in the garden, or the chairs in the parlour, no longer than while there is somebody by to perceive them. Upon shutting my eyes all the furniture in the room is reduced to nothing, and barely upon opening them it is again created.—In answer to all which, I refer the reader to what has been said in sect. 3, 4, &c.; and desire he will consider whether he means anything by the actual existence of an idea distinct from its being perceived. For my part, after the nicest inquiry I could make, I am not able to discover that anything else is meant by those words; and I once more entreat the reader to sound his own thoughts, and not suffer himself to be imposed on by words. If he can conceive it possible either for his ideas or their archetypes to exist without being perceived, then I give up the cause. But if he cannot, he will acknowledge it is unreasonable for him to stand up in defence of he knows not what, and pretend to charge on me as an absurdity, the not assenting to those propositions which at bottom have no meaning in them.

THIRTY-THREE

Physical Objects As Permanent Possibilities of Sensation

JOHN STUART MILL (1803-1873)

From An Examination of Sir William Hamilton's Philosophy*

We have seen Sir W. Hamilton [1] at work on the question of the reality of Matter, by the introspective method, and, as it seems, with little result. Let us now approach the same subject by the psychological. I proceed, therefore, to state the case of those who hold that the belief in an external world is not intuitive, but an acquired product.

This theory postulates the following psychological truths, all of which are proved by experience, and are not contested, though their force is seldom adequately felt, by Sir W. Hamilton and the other thinkers of the introspective school.

It postulates, first, that the human mind is capable of Expectation. In other words, that after having had actual sensations, we are capable of forming the conception of Possible sensations; sensations which we are not feeling at the present moment, but which we might feel, and should feel if certain conditions were present, the nature of which conditions we have, in many cases, learned by experience.

It postulates, secondly, the laws of the Association of Ideas. So far as we are here concerned, these laws are the following: 1st. Similar phenomena tend to be thought of together. 2d. Phenomena which have either been experienced or conceived in close contiguity to one another, tend to be thought of together. The contiguity is of two kinds; simultaneity, and immediate succession. Facts which have been experienced or thought of simultaneously, recall the thought of one another. Of facts which have been experienced or thought of in immediate succession, the antecedent, or the thought of it, recalls the thought of the consequent, but not conversely. 3d. Associations produced by contiguity become more

* From *An Examination of Sir William Hamilton's Philosophy* by John Stuart Mill (1865).

[1] An important Scottish philosopher (1788-1856) who maintained that the belief that independent objects are present to us in perception rests on intuition and is a 'direct deliverance of consciousness'. (ed.)

certain and rapid by repetition. When two phenomena have been very often experienced in conjunction, and have not, in any single instance, occurred separately either in experience or in thought, there is produced between them what has been called Inseparable, or less correctly, Indissoluble Association: by which is not meant that the association must inevitably last to the end of life—that no subsequent experience or process of thought can possibly avail to dissolve it; but only that as long as no such experience or process of thought has taken place, the association is irresistible; it is impossible for us to think the one thing disjoined from the other. 4th. When an association has acquired this character of inseparability—when the bond between the two ideas has been thus firmly riveted, not only does the idea called up by association become, in our consciousness, inseparable from the idea which suggested it, but the facts or phenomena answering to those ideas, come at last to seem inseparable in existence: things which we are unable to conceive apart, appear incapable of existing apart; and the belief we have in their co-existence, though really a product of experience, seems intuitive. Innumerable examples might be given of this law. One of the most familiar, as well as the most striking, is that of our acquired perceptions of sight. Even those who . . . consider the perception of distance by the eye as not acquired, but intuitive, admit that there are many perceptions of sight which, though instantaneous and unhesitating, are not intuitive. What we see is a very minute fragment of what we think we see. We see artificially that one thing is hard, another soft. We see artificially that one thing is hot, another cold. We see artificially that what we see is a book, or a stone, each of these being not merely an inference, but a heap of inferences, from the signs which we see, to things not visible.

Setting out from these premises, the Psychological Theory maintains, that there are associations naturally and even necessarily generated by the order of our sensations and of our reminiscences of sensation, which, supposing no intuition of an external world to have existed in consciousness, would inevitably generate the belief, and would cause it to be regarded as an intuition.

What is it we mean when we say that the object we perceive is external to us, and not a part of our own thoughts? We mean, that there is in our perceptions something which exists when we are not thinking of it; which existed before we had ever thought of it, and would exist if we were annihilated; and further, that there exist things which we never saw, touched, or otherwise perceived, and things which never have been perceived by man. This idea of something which is distinguished from our fleeting impressions by what, in Kantian language, is called Perdurability; something which is fixed and the same, while our impressions vary; something which exists whether we are aware of it or not, and which is always square (or of some other given figure) whether it appears to us square or round, constitutes altogether our idea of external substance. Whoever can assign an origin to this complex conception, has accounted for what we mean by the belief in matter. Now, all this, according to the Psychological Theory, is but the form impressed by the known laws of association, upon the conception or notion, obtained by experience, of Contingent Sensations; by which are meant, sensations that are not in our present consciousness, and perhaps never were in our consciousness at all, but which, in virtue of the laws to which we have learned by experience that our sensations are subject, we know that we should have felt under given supposable circumstances, and under these same circumstances, might still feel.

I see a piece of white paper on a table. I go into another room, and though I have ceased to see it, I am persuaded that the paper is still there. I no longer have the sensations which it gave me; but I believe that when I again place myself in the circumstances in which I had those sensations, that is, when I go again into the room, I shall again have them; and further, that there has been no intervening moment at which this would not have been the case. Owing to this law of my mind, my conception of the world at any given instant consists, in only a small proportion, of present sensations. Of these I may at the time have none at all, and they are in any case a most insignificant portion of the whole which I apprehend. The conception I form of the world existing at any moment, comprises, along with the sensations I am feeling, a countless variety of possibilities of sensation; namely, the whole of those which past observation tells me that I could, under any supposable circumstances, experience at this moment, together with an indefinite and illimitable multitude of others which though I do not know that I could, yet it is possible that I might, experience in circumstances not known to me. These various possibilities are the important thing to me in the world. My present sensations are generally of little importance, and are moreover fugitive: the possibilities, on the contrary, are permanent, which is the character that mainly distinguishes our idea of Substance or Matter from our notion of sensation. These possibilities, which are conditional certainties, need a special name to distinguish them from mere vague possibilities, which experience gives no warrant for reckoning upon. Now, as soon as a distinguishing name is given, though it be only to the same thing regarded in a different aspect, one of the most familiar experiences of our mental nature teaches us, that the different name comes to be considered as the name of a different thing.

There is another important peculiarity of these certified or guaranteed possibilities of sensation; namely, that they have reference, not to single sensations, but to sensations joined together in groups. When we think of anything as a material substance, or body, we either have had, or we think that on some given supposition we should have, not some *one* sensation, but a great and even an indefinite number and variety of sensations, generally belonging to different senses, but so linked together, that the presence of one announces the possible presence at the very same instant of any or all of the rest. In our mind, therefore, not only is this particular possibility of sensation invested with the quality of permanence when we are not actually feeling any of the sensations at all; but when we are feeling some of them, the remaining sensations of the group are conceived by us in the form of Present Possibilities, which might be realized at the very moment. And as this happens in turn to all of them, the group as a whole presents itself to the mind as permanent, in contrast not solely with the temporariness of my bodily presence, but also with the temporary character of each of the sensations composing the group; in other words, as a kind of permanent substratum, under a set of passing experiences or manifestations: which is another leading character of our idea of substance or matter, as distinguished from sensation.

Let us now take into consideration another of the general characters of our experience, namely, that in addition to fixed groups, we also recognize a fixed Order in our sensations; an Order of succession, which, when ascertained by observation, gives rise to the ideas of Cause and Effect, according to what I hold to be the true theory of that relation, and is in any case the source of all our knowledge *what* causes produce what effects. Now, of what nature is this fixed order among our sensations? It is a constancy of antecedence and sequence. But the constant antecedence and sequence do not generally exist between one actual sensation and another. Very few such sequences are presented to us by experience. In almost all the constant sequences which occur in Nature, the antecedence and consequence do not obtain between sensations, but between the groups we have been speaking about, of which a very small portion is actual sensation, the greater part being permanent possibilities of sensation, evidenced to us by a small and variable number of sensations actually present. Hence, our ideas of causation, power, activity, do not become connected in thought with our sensations as *actual* at all, save in the few physiological cases where these figure by themselves as the antecedents in some uniform sequence. Those ideas become connected, not with sensations, but with groups of possibilities of sensation. The sensations conceived do not, to our habitual thoughts, present themselves as sensations actually experienced, inasmuch as not only any one or any number of them may be supposed absent, but none of them need be present. We find that the modifications which are taking place more or less regularly in our possibilities of sensation, are mostly quite independent of our consciousness, and of our presence or absence. Whether we are asleep or awake, the fire goes out, and puts an end to one particular possibility of warmth and light. Whether we are present or absent, the corn ripens, and brings a new possibility of food. Hence we speedily think to learn of Nature as made up solely of these groups of possibilities, and the active force in Nature as manifested in the modification of some of these by others. The sensations, though the original foundation of the whole, come to be looked upon as a sort of accident depending on us, and the possibilities as much more real than the actual sensations, nay, as the very realities of which these are only the representations, appearances, or effects. When this state of mind has been arrived at, then, and from that time forward, we are never conscious of a present sensation without instantaneously referring it to some one of the groups of possibilities into which a sensation of that particular description enters; and if we do not yet know to what group to refer it, we at least feel an irresistible conviction that it must belong to some group or other; i.e., that its presence proves the existence, here and now, of a great number and variety of possibilities of sensation, without which it would not have been. The whole set of sensations as possible, form a permanent background to any one or more of them that are, at a given moment, actual; and the possibilities are conceived as standing to the actual sensations in the relation of a cause to its effects, or of canvas to the figures painted on it, or of a root to the trunk, leaves, and flowers, or of a substratum to that which is spread over it, or, in transcendental language, of Matter to Form.

When this point has been reached, the permanent Possibilities in question have assumed such unlikeness of aspect, and such difference of position relatively to us, from any sensations, that it would be contrary to all we know of the constitution of human nature that they should not be conceived as, and believed to be, at least as different from sensations as sensations are from one another. Their groundwork in sensation is forgotten, and they are supposed to be something intrinsically distinct from it. We can withdraw ourselves from any of our (external) sensations, or we can be withdrawn from them by some other agency. But though the sensations cease, the possibilities remain in existence; they are independent of our will, our presence, and everything which belongs to us. We find, too, that they belong as much to other human or sentient beings as to ourselves. We find other people grounding their expectations and conduct upon the same permanent possibilities on which we ground ours. But we do not find them experiencing the same actual sensations. Other people do not have our sensations exactly when and as we have them: but they have our possibilities of sensation; whatever indicates a present possibility of sensations to ourselves, indicates a present possibility of similar sensations to them, except so far as their organs of sensation may vary from the type of ours. This puts the final seal to our conception of the groups of possibilities as the fundamental reality in Nature. The permanent possibilities are common to us and to our fellow-creatures; the actual sensations are not. That which other people become aware of when, and on the same grounds as I do, seems more real to me than that which they do not know of unless I tell them. The world of Possible Sensations succeeding one another according to laws, is as much in other beings as it is in me; it has therefore an existence outside me; it is an External World. . . .

Matter, then, may be defined, a Permanent Possibility of Sensation. If I am asked whether I believe in matter, I ask whether the questioner accepts this definition of it. If he does, I believe in matter: and so do all Berkeleians. In any other sense than this, I do not. But I affirm with confidence, that this conception of Matter includes the whole meaning attached to it by the common world, apart from philosophical, and sometimes from theological, theories. The reliance of mankind on the real existence of visible and tangible objects, means reliance on the reality and permanence of Possibilities of visual and tactual sensations, when no such sensations are actually experienced. We are warranted in believing that this is the meaning of Matter in the minds of many of its most esteemed metaphysical champions, though they themselves would not admit as much: for example, of Reid, Stewart, and Brown. For these three philosophers alleged that all mankind, including Berkeley and Hume, really believed in Matter, inasmuch as unless they did, they would not have turned aside to save themselves from running against a post. Now, all which this manœuver really proved is, that they believed in Permanent Possibilities of Sensation. We have therefore the sanction of these three eminent defenders of the existence of matter, for affirming, that to believe in Permanent Possibilities of Sensation *is* believing in Matter. It is hardly necessary, after such authorities, to mention Dr. Johnson, or any one else who resorts to the *argumentum baculinum* of knocking a stick against the ground. Sir W. Hamilton, a far subtler thinker than any of these, never reasons in this manner. He never supposes that a disbeliever in what he means by Matter, ought in consistency to act in any different mode from those who believe in it. He knew that the belief on which all the practical consequences depend, is the belief in Permanent Possibilities of Sensation, and that if nobody believed in a material universe in any other sense, life would go on exactly as it now does. He, however, did believe in more than this, but, I think, only because it had never occurred to him that mere Possibilities of Sensation could, to our artificialized consciousness, present the character of objectivity which, as we have now shown, they not only can, but unless the known laws of the human mind were suspended, must necessarily, present.

THIRTY-FOUR

Linguistic Phenomenalism

A. J. AYER (1910-   )

From *The Foundations of Empirical Knowledge*[*]

CONCERNING PHENOMENALISM

The problem of specifying the relationship of material things to sense-data, to which the causal theory of perception has been shown to provide so unsatisfactory an answer, is apt to be obscured by being represented as a problem about the inter-relationship of two different classes of objects. There is, indeed, a sense in which it is correct to say that both sense-data and material things exist, inasmuch as sentences that are used to describe sense-data and sentences that are used to describe material things both very frequently express true propositions. But it would not be correct to infer from this that there really were both material things and sense-data, in the sense in which it can truly be said that there really are chairs as well as tables, or that there are tastes as well as sounds. For whereas, in these cases, the existential propositions refer to different empirical "facts", this does not hold good in the case of sense-data and material things. All the same, the term "material thing" is not synonymous with any term or set of terms that stand for species of sense-data. It is indeed logically necessary that any situation that in any degree establishes the existence of a material thing should also establish the existence of a sense-datum; for we have constructed the sense-datum language in such a way that whenever it is true that a material thing is perceived, it must also be true that a sense-datum is sensed; and this applies also to the cases where the existence of the material thing is inferred from observations of its "physical effects". But it is not wholly a matter of convention that a situation which establishes the existence of a sense-datum should also be evidence in some degree for the existence of a material thing. For this depends, as I shall show, upon certain special features of our sensory experience, which it might conceivably not have possessed. Moreover, while a situation which directly establishes the existence of a sense-datum does so conclusively,

[*] From *The Foundations of Empirical Knowledge* by A. J. Ayer (London, Macmillan & Co. Ltd., 1940). Reprinted by permission of the author, St. Martin's Press, Inc., New York, The Macmillan Company of Canada Ltd, and Macmillan & Co. Ltd, London.

461

no such situations can conclusively establish the existence of a material thing. The degree to which the existence of the material thing is established will depend upon the character of the sense-data in question, and especially upon the nature of the contexts in which they occur; but whatever the strength of this evidence may be, it will always be logically compatible with the hypothesis that this material thing is not in all respects what it appears to be, or even that it does not exist at all. Additional evidence may weaken this hypothesis to an extent that makes it very foolish still to entertain it; but it may also substantiate it, as the fact that there are illusions shows. At the same time, it is to be remarked that this additional evidence, whether favourable or not, will always consist in the occurrence of further sense-data. Indeed there is nothing else in which one can legitimately suppose it to consist, once one has accepted the rule that the word "sense-datum" is to be used to stand for whatever is, in fact, observed. And since it is impossible, by any valid process of inference, to make a transition from what is observed to anything that is conceived as being, in principle, unobservable, all that the evidence in question will be evidence for or against is the possible occurrence of further sense-data still. And from this it seems to follow that, even though the term "material thing" is not synonymous with any set of terms that stand for species of sense-data, any proposition that refers to a material thing must somehow be expressible in terms of sense-data, if it is to be empirically significant.

A common way of expressing this conclusion is to say that the material things are nothing but collections of actual and possible sense-data. But this is a misleading formula and one that provokes objections which a more accurate way of speaking might avoid. Thus, it is sometimes argued, by those who reject this "phenomenalistic" analysis of the nature of material things, that to conceive of such things as houses or trees or stones as mere collections of actual and possible sense-data is to ignore their "unity" and "substantiality", and that, in any case, it is hard to see how anything can be composed of so shadowy a being as a possible sense-datum. But these objections are founded upon the mistaken assumption that a material thing is supposed to consist of sense-data, as a patchwork quilt consists of different coloured pieces of silk. To remove this misconception, it must be made clear that what the statement that material things consist of sense-data must be understood to designate is not a factual but a linguistic relationship. What is being claimed is simply that the propositions which are ordinarily expressed by sentences which refer to material things could also be expressed by sentences which referred exclusively to sense-data; and the inclusion of possible as well as actual sense-data among the elements of the material things must be taken only to imply a recognition that some of these statements about sense-data will have to be hypothetical. As for the belief in the "unity" and "substantiality" of material things, I shall show that it may be correctly represented as involving no more than the attribution to visual and tactual sense-data of certain relations which do, in fact, obtain in our experience. And I shall show that it is only the contingent fact that there are these relations between sense-data that makes it profitable to describe the course of our experience in terms of the existence and behaviour of material things.

It may seem that an attempt to carry out this plan of "reducing" material things to sense-data would be at variance with my previous attempt to draw a sharp distinction between them. But the purpose of making this distinction was simply to increase the utility and clarity of the sense-datum language by ensuring that its sentences should not be of the same logical form as those that refer to material things. And here it may be explained that two sentences may be said to have the same logical form if they can be correlated in such a way that to each expression that occurs in either one of them there corresponds in the other an expression of the same logical type; and that two expressions may be said to be of the same logical type if any sentence that significantly contains either one of them remains significant when the other is put in its place. It follows that if sentences referring to sense-data are of a different logical form from sentences referring to material things, it must not be assumed that precisely the same things can be said about them. To say, for example, that this was being written with a "pennish" group of sense-data, instead of saying that it was being written with a pen, would be neither true nor false but nonsensical. But this does not rule out the possibility that a proposition which is expressed by a sentence referring to a material thing can equally well be expressed by an entirely different set of sentences, which refer to sense-data; and this is what those who assert that material things are "logical constructions" out of sense-data must be understood to claim. Their view is sometimes put in the form of an assertion that "to say anything about a material thing is to say something, but not the same thing about classes of sense-data";[1] but if this is taken to imply that any significant statement about a material thing can actually be translated, without alteration of meaning, into a definite set of statements about sense-data, it is not strictly accurate, for a reason I shall presently give.

An objection which is often brought against phenomenalists is that they begin with a false conception of the nature of "perceptual situations". Thus, it is held by some philosophers that what is directly observed is usually not a sense-datum at all, but a material thing; so that the view that material things must be reducible to sense-data, on the ground that these alone are observable, is fundamentally erroneous. But this, as I have shown,[2] is not the expression of a disagreement about any

[1] Vide A. E. Duncan-Jones, "Does Philosophy Analyse Common Sense?" Aristotelian Society Supplementary Proceedings, 1937, pp. 140-41.
[2] In Part I.

matter of fact, but only of a preference for a different form of language. It is indeed legitimate to use the phrase "direct observation" in such a way that things like houses and trees and stones can properly be said to be directly observable; and this usage can perfectly well be made to cover the case of delusive as well as veridical perceptions, provided that it is allowed that what is "directly observed" may not in fact exist, and that it may not really have the properties that it appears to have. But I have shown that it is also legitimate to use the phrase "direct observation" in such a way that it is only what is designated by the term "sense-datum", or some equivalent term, that can be said to be directly observable; and that it is this usage that, for my present purpose, is to be preferred. And one reason why it is to be preferred is to be found in the fact, which I have already mentioned, that whereas the proposition that a sense-datum is veridically sensed does not entail that any material thing is veridically perceived, the proposition that a material thing is veridically perceived can always be represented as entailing that some sense-datum or other is veridically sensed. Indeed, it is inconceivable that any sense-datum should not be sensed veridically, since it has been made self-contradictory to say of an experienced sense-datum that it does not exist or that it does not really have the properties that it appears to have. And because there is this logical relationship between "perceiving a material thing" and "sensing a sense-datum", it follows that, while a reference to a material thing will not elucidate the meaning of a sentence which is used to describe a sense-datum, except in so far as the poverty of our language may make it convenient to identify this sense-datum as one of a type that is ordinarily associated with a special sort of material thing, a reference to sense-data will provide a general elucidation of the meaning of statements about material things by showing what is the kind of evidence by which they may be verified. And this may be regarded as the purpose of the phenomenalist analysis.

Besides the philosophers who maintain that material things are themselves "directly observed", there are others who object to phenomenalism on the ground that even if the occurrence of illusions shows that what is directly observed is not a material thing, it is still not just a sense-datum. Thus Professor Stout, for one, has argued that "the evidence of sense-perception flatly contradicts phenomenalism", on the ground that to regard what is immediately experienced as being just a sensible appearance is to ignore an essential factor which he calls "perceptual seeming".[3] According to him, it is because of "perceptual seeming" that one is able to "perceive one thing as behind another, although it is so hidden that there is no sensible appearance of it", or that one can "perceive things as having insides, when they are not transparent".[4] But while this line of

---

[3] "Phenomenalism", *Proceedings of the Aristotelian Society,* 1938-9, pp. 1-18.
[4] *Loc. cit.* pp. 10-11.

argument may have some force against those who employ a physiological criterion for determining the character of sense-data, it does not affect us at all, inasmuch as our use of the word sense-datum is not bound up with any special empirical theory about the nature of what is given. If one accepts the view of certain psychologists that there are experiences that may properly be described as experiences of "seeing the inside of a solid object" or "seeing an object when it is screened by another", then the inference one must draw is not that what is observed on such occasions is "more than a mere sense-datum", but that the character of people's visual sense-fields is empirically different from what a misplaced attention to the laws of physiology might lead one to suppose. It is true that the terms in which the psychologists describe such experiences are not purely sensory; but the reason for this is that it is only by referring to material things that they can actually expect to make their meaning understood. We must not, therefore, be misled into supposing that what they are intending to describe is anything more than a sensory phenomenon. The statement that someone is having the experience of "seeing the inside of a solid object" must not, in this context, be taken to exclude the possibility that no such physical object is actually there.

It may, however, be admitted that not only in cases of this sort, but in the vast majority of cases in which one senses a visual or tactual sense-datum, one tends to take it for granted that there is a physical object "there"; and it may be that this is what Professor Stout is referring to when he talks of "perceptual seeming". But this is a fact that I do not think any phenomenalist would wish to deny. The view that material things are, in the sense I have just explained, logical constructions out of sense-data does not imply that "perceiving a material thing" need involve any conscious process of inference from the occurrence of one sense-datum to the possible occurrence of another. The phenomenalist is perfectly free to admit that the sensing of a visual or tactual sense-datum is, in most cases, accompanied by an unreflecting assumption of the existence of some material thing. But the question in which he is interested is, What exactly is it that is here unreflectingly assumed? And his answer, which certainly cannot be refuted by any such appeal to psychology as Professor Stout relies on, is that it is the possibility of obtaining further sense-data.

It would seem that the best way to justify the claim that "to say anything about a material thing is always to say something, though not the same thing, about certain sense-data", would be to provide a number of specimen translations. But this is what no one has ever yet been able to do. It may be suggested that the reason why it has never been done is that no one has yet devised a sufficiently elaborate vocabulary. With our current resources of language we are able to classify visual sense-data only in a very general way, tactual data even less specifically, and kinaesthetic data hardly at all: and the result is that when we wish to distinguish the sense-data that belong to one sort of material thing from those that belong to another we are unable to achieve it except by referring to the material things in question. But suppose that someone took the trouble to name all the different varieties of sensible characteristics with which he was acquainted. Even so, he would still not be able to translate any statement about a material thing into a finite set of statements about sense-data. It is not inconceivable that someone should construct and make use of such a sensory language, though in practice he would find it very difficult to make himself understood; but what he succeeded in expressing by these means would never be precisely equivalent even to the singular statements that we make about material things. For when statements are equivalent to one another, they can always be represented as standing in a relationship of mutual entailment. And, in the case I am now considering, this condition cannot be fulfilled.

I have indeed already submitted that no finite set of singular statements about sense-data can ever formally entail a statement about a material thing, inasmuch as I have recognized that statements about material things are not conclusively verifiable. For when we try to reproduce the content of a statement about a material thing by specifying the empirical situations that would furnish us with direct tests of its validity, we find that the number of these possible tests is infinite. Admittedly, when someone makes a statement of this kind he does not actually envisage an infinite series of possible verifications. He may very well be satisfied, in familiar circumstances, with the single sense-experience on which his statement is based; and if he does think it necessary to test it further, the subsequent occurrence, in the appropriate conditions, of only a limited number of "favourable" sense-data will be sufficient, in the absence of contrary evidence, to convince him that it is true. And this is an entirely reasonable procedure, as I have shown.[5] But the fact remains that however many favourable tests he may make he can never reach a stage at which it ceases to be conceivable that further sense-experience will reverse the verdict of the previous evidence. He will never be in a position to demonstrate that he will not subsequently have experiences that will entitle him to conclude that his original statement was false after all. And this implies that the content of a statement about a material thing cannot be exhaustively specified by any finite number of references to sense-data. This difficulty could indeed be met by introducing into the sense-datum language a suitable set of expressions which would be understood to refer to infinite series of sense-data. But I am afraid that most philosophers would not admit that this gave them the sort of translation that they wanted. For all that would seem to be achieved by the introduction of these new expressions would be a mere renaming of material things.

[5] Part I, section 4.

But not only is the occurrence of any one particular, finite series of sense-data never formally sufficient to establish the truth of a statement about a material thing; it is never even necessary. There is, indeed, a sense in which it can be said that every statement about a material thing entails some set of statements or other about sense-data, inasmuch as it is only by the occurrence of some sense-datum that any statement about a material thing is ever in any degree verified. But there is no set of statements about the occurrence of particular sense-data of which it can truly be said that precisely this is entailed by a given statement about a material thing. And the reason for this is that what is required to verify a statement about a material thing is never just the occurrence of a sense-datum of an absolutely specific kind, but only the occurrence of one or other of the sense-data that fall within a fairly indefinite range. In other words, not only can we go on testing a statement about a material thing as long as we like without being able to arrive at a formal demonstration of its truth; but for any test that we actually do carry out there are always an indefinite number of other tests, differing to some extent either in respect of their conditions or their results, which would have done just as well. And this means that if we try to describe what at any given moment would afford us direct evidence for the truth of a statement about a material thing by putting forward a disjunction of statements about sense-data, we shall find once again that this disjunction will have to be infinite.[6]

But if one infers from this that sentences referring to material things cannot be translated, without alteration of meaning, into sentences referring to sense-data, one must not then conclude that to speak about a material thing is to speak about something altogether different from sense-data, or that it is to speak about sense-data but about something else besides. For that would be a mistake analogous to that of supposing that because sentences referring indefinitely to what is red cannot be translated into a finite number of sentences referring to particular red things, therefore "redness" is the name of an object with a distinct existence of its own, or that because sentences referring to "someone" cannot be translated into a finite disjunction of sentences referring to particular persons, therefore "someone" is the name of a peculiar being, a "subsistent entity" perhaps, who is distinct from any person that one can actually meet. If we cannot produce the required translations of sentences referring to material things into sentences referring to sense-data, the reason is not that it is untrue that "to say anything about a material thing is always to say something about sense-data", but only that one's references to material things are vague in their application to phenomena and that the series of sense-data that they may be understood to specify are composed of infinite sets of terms.

This does not mean, however, that nothing can be done in the way

6 Cf. John Wisdom, "Metaphysics and Verification", *Mind*, October 1938, pp. 478-81.

of "analysing material things in terms of sense-data". It would not, indeed, be profitable to seek in any such analysis a means of distinguishing one material thing from another. It is not by a verbal analysis in terms of sense-data that one can hope to make clear what is meant, for example, by "a pen" as opposed to "a pencil", or by "a steamship" as opposed to "a canoe". One can give a verbal, as well as an ostensive, indication of the meaning of such words; but it will not exclude the use of other expressions that belong to a physical rather than to a purely sensory terminology. At the same time, there are certain general features about the way in which any expression referring to a material thing applies to phenomena that one can profitably undertake to analyse. That is to say, one may be able to explain what are the relations between sense-data that make it possible for us successfully to employ the physical terminology that we do. If I may now use the metaphor of construction without being misunderstood, I can describe the task I am about to undertake as that of showing what are the general principles on which, from our resources of sense-data, we "construct" the world of material things.

THIRTY-FIVE

Problems of Phenomenalism

R. M. CHISHOLM (1906-   )

From *Perceiving**

1. Ernst Mach expressed *phenomenalism* by saying that "all bodies are but thought-symbols for complexes of sensations." [1] Where Mach uses "sensations" other phenomenalists may use "appearances" or "sense-data." And where Mach uses "thought-symbols," others may talk about language and "rules of translation." [2] But every form of phenomenalism involves the thesis that anything we know about material things may be expressed in statements referring solely to appearances. Since many of the problems I have discussed in this book would require a very different treatment if this thesis were true, I shall now state my reasons for believing it to be false.

2. I have said that whenever we perceive anything *x* to have some property *f* we have certain beliefs about the ways in which *x* appears. If a man now takes something to be a tree, he believes that, under the conditions now obtaining, he would *not* be appeared to in just the way he is appeared to unless the thing were a tree. And he believes that if he were now to act in certain ways—if he were to approach the thing he takes to be a tree, or if he were to reach out and touch it—he would be appeared to in still other ways characteristic of a tree. It is accurate to say, I think, that phenomenalism is based upon an interpretation of such facts as these.

The phenomenalist contends that, if we ask ourselves just what it is we are believing when we think we perceive something to have a certain characteristic, we will find that our beliefs really pertain only to the *appearances* of the thing we think we are perceiving. He then infers that our ordinary statements about physical things—such statements as "That is a tree" and "This thing is red"—logically *entail* many statements referring solely to appearances. And he concludes that, if only we were to list the

* From *Perceiving* by Roderick M. Chisholm (Ithaca, New York, Cornell University Press, 1957), pp. 189-197. Reprinted by permission of the publisher.

[1] Ernst Mach, *The Analysis of Sensations* (Chicago, 1897), p. 22.

[2] Compare A. J. Ayer, *The Foundations of Empirical Knowledge*: "What is being claimed is simply that the propositions which are ordinarily expressed by sentences which refer to material things could also be expressed by sentences which referred exclusively to sense-data" (p. 232).

appearance statements entailed by any thing statement, we would have
for that thing statement the type of translation the phenomenalistic thesis
requires: we would have a set of appearance statements expressing everything that the thing statement is ordinarily used to express.

But is it true that such statements as "That is a tree" and "This thing
is red" *entail* any statements referring solely to appearances—to ways of
sensing? The familiar facts of "perceptual relativity" suggest that our
ordinary thing statements do *not* entail any statements referring solely to
appearances.[3]

Whether a material thing will ever present, say, a red appearance
depends partly upon the nature of the thing and partly upon the conditions under which the thing is perceived. If one knew that the thing was
red and that the lighting conditions were normal, one could predict that,
to a normal observer, the thing would present a red appearance; if one
knew that the lights were out, or that the perceiver had a certain kind of
color blindness, one could predict that the thing would present some other
appearance; and so on, for any other thing and its possible appearances.
To calculate the appearances, it is necessary to know both the thing perceived and the observation conditions, for it is the thing perceived and
the observation conditions working jointly which determine the way the
thing is to appear.

The facts of perceptual relativity thus suggest that even the simple
thing statement, "This thing is red," doesn't entail *any* statement about
appearances; an appearance statement is entailed only when "This thing
is red" is taken in conjunction with *another* thing statement referring to
observation conditions. This may be seen further if we compare first the
thing statement

This is red *(P)*

and a categorical appearance statement

Redness will be sensed *(R)*

(In his use of such words as "appearance" and "sense," the phenomenalist
may allow himself more freedom than would be condoned by the view
about appearing advocated in Chapter Eight. But I shall not presuppose
this view in what follows.)

May we say, then, that the statement *P* above entails *R*, as these statements would ordinarily be interpreted? Possibly it is obvious that no contradiction is involved in affirming *P* and denying *R*. The following considerations, however, may make the matter clearer.

Taken in conjunction with certain *other* thing statements *Q*, referring to observation conditions, *P* does entail *R*. The following is such a
statement *Q:*

---

[3] We should say, more exactly, that such thing statements entail no *synthetic*, or
nonlogical, statements referring solely to appearances.

This is perceived under normal conditions; and if this is red and is perceived under normal conditions, redness will be sensed. *(Q)*

(So far as our present point is concerned, it does not particularly matter how the expression "normal conditions" is defined.)

Taken in conjunction, not with *Q*, but with still *other* thing statements *S*, also referring to observation conditions, *P* entails not-*R*. An example of *S* would be:

This is perceived under conditions which are normal except for the presence of blue lights; and if this is red and is perceived under conditions which are normal except for the presence of blue lights, redness will not be sensed. *(S)*

As these statements would ordinarily be interpreted, *S* is logically consistent with *P*; there is no contradiction involved in affirming one and denying the other. But the conjunction of *P* and *S*, if it is logically consistent, must entail everything that *P* entails and cannot entail anything logically incompatible with what *P* entails. If *P* and *S* entail not-*R*, it is impossible that *P* entail *R*. Hence "This is red" *(P)* does not entail "Redness will be sensed" *(R)*. Similarly, "Redness will not be sensed" is not sufficient to *falsify* "This is red." We may draw a similar conclusion with respect to any other categorical appearance statement *R'*. Although there may be a statement about observation conditions, *Q'*, such that "This is red" *(P)* and *Q'* entail *R'*, there is also a statement about observation conditions, *S'*, such that *P* and *S'* entail not-*R'*; hence *P* does not entail *R'*.

According to some phenomenalists, the appearance statements entailed by statements describing a physical thing would be considerably more complicated than "Redness will be sensed"; they would be conjunctions of conditionals of the form "If such and such should be sensed, then such and such would be sensed." The phenomenalist might hold, for example, that the thing statement

There is really a door in front of me *(P)*

entails a conditional appearance statement of this sort:

If such-and-such visual appearances should be sensed (namely, those associated with reaching), then such-and-such tactual appearances would be sensed. *(R)*

Again, if *P* entails *R*, then it is logically impossible that there be a statement S, consistent with *P* and such that *P* and *S* entail not-*R*. Clearly there are many such statements *S*. One might be:

I am subject to delusions such that, whenever a door is in front of me, then such-and-such visual appearances are sensed and such-and-such tactual appearances are not sensed. *(S)*

This statement, in conjunction with P, entails not-R. Since S is consistent with P, it is false that P entails R.

By similar reasoning it would seem possible to formulate, for any complex appearance statement R' that might be thought to be an analytic consequence of P, some statement S' consistent with P and such that P and S' entail not-R'.

I believe we may say, therefore, that no synthetic thing statement P entails any appearance statement unless P is taken in conjunction with some *other* thing statement referring to observation conditions. In our earlier example, "This is red" *(P)* does entail an appearance statement when P is conjoined with Q: "This is perceived under normal conditions; and if this is red and is perceived under normal conditions redness will be sensed." And we have seen that, when conjoined with statements about different observation conditions, "This is red" may entail a different statement about appearances. Thus when John Stuart Mill tried to show, with respect to his belief that Calcutta exists, that it can be expressed phenomenalistically, in terms of "permanent possibilities of sensations," he specified these possibilities by reference to himself and to the banks of the Hooghly:

I believe that Calcutta exists, though I do not perceive it, and that it would still exist if every percipient inhabitant were suddenly to leave the place, or be struck dead. But when I analyze the belief, all I find in it is, that were these events to take place, the Permanent Possibility of Sensation which I call Calcutta would still remain; that if I were suddenly transported to the banks of the Hooghly, I should still have the sensations which, if now present, would lead me to affirm that Calcutta exists here and now.[4]

But this method of deriving appearance statements from thing statements does not suggest any way of expressing "Calcutta exists" or "This thing is red" in terms referring solely to permanent possibilities of sensation, or to appearances. For we obtain our appearance statements only by referring to still other physical things.[5]

[4] John Stuart Mill, *An Examination of Sir William Hamilton's Philosophy* (New York, 1884), p. 246. Compare H. H. Price's criticism of such theories in *Hume's Theory of the External World* (Oxford, 1940), pp. 183-188. Roderick Firth has proposed a rather complex theory about the meaning of ordinary thing statements in order to deal with such problems (*op. cit.,* especially pp. 319-323). I cannot here do justice to his theory, but I believe it is fair to say: (i) the theory has some implausible consequences; (ii) it was designed with the purpose of adapting phenomenalism to considerations such as the above; and (iii) if the criticism of the ostensible *grounds* of phenomenalism, in Section 3 below, is accurate, then there is no positive reason for accepting Firth's theory.

[5] In *Berkeley* (pp. 183-189), G. J .Warnock compares the relation between thing statements and appearance statements to that between the *verdict* a jury makes and the *evidence* to which the jury appeals. But any verdict that is just and reasonable is probable—more probable than not—in relation to its evidence. And I have suggested in Chapter Six that there is no statement about a material thing which is more probable than not in relation to any set of statements referring merely to appearances.

3. Why should one think that phenomenalism is true? If we look to the reasons phenomenalists have proposed, we will find, I think, that each is inconsistent with at least one of the conclusions of the present book. The most important of these reasons are the following three.[6]

(i) Professor Lewis has said that, if phenomenalism cannot be successfully defended, "then there will be nothing left for us but skepticism." [7] In saying this, he assumed, I think, that some form of *empiricism* (as defined in Chapter Six) is true. He assumed, first, with respect to those statements we would ordinarily justify by reference to perceiving, that no such statement is evident unless it is more probable than not in relation to statements about appearing. He assumed, secondly, that if we are thus confined to appearances and if phenomenalism is false then skepticism is true. And he assumed, thirdly, that if phenomenalism is true then, even though we may be so confined, skepticism is false. But according to the theory of evidence I attempted to defend in Chapter Six, there is no reason to accept the first of these assumptions. The statements we would ordinarily defend by reference to perceiving may be evident even though they are not probable in relation to statements about appearing. And therefore we need not accept the thesis that if phenomenalism cannot be successfully defended "there is nothing left for us but skepticism."

(ii) I think that many philosophers have been led to accept phenomenalism because of what they believe about the genesis of our knowledge. They have assumed: first, that "before we can learn about the things that appear to us, we must learn about their appearances"; secondly, that the psychological process of perceiving developed from the more simple process of sensing appearances; and, thirdly, that this process could not have taken place unless phenomenalism is true. In Chapter Nine, Section 4, I discussed the first of these assumptions and suggested an alternative. If the suggested alternative is true, then, I think, there is no reason for supposing that the *second* of these assumptions is true. Moreover, the second assumption does not seem to me to be plausible. It would be difficult to show *how* the process of perceiving might have developed from that of sensing. The difficulty would be very much like that of showing how the process of remembering might have developed from perceiving, or from sensing.

---

[6] Phenomenalism has been defended by saying that, if statements about physical things have any *meaning* at all, they are translatable into statements about appearances. Little is gained by introducing the concept of *meaning* into the discussion, however, inasmuch as the positive grounds for this view of meaning are presumably the same as those for phenomenalism. And when phenomenalism is expressed this way, the phenomenalist's problem becomes that of showing that thing statements *do* have meaning, in this sense of "meaning"; for it would be misleading to use the word "meaning" in such a way that the statement "This thing is red" could *not* be said to mean anything.

[7] C. I. Lewis, "Professor Chisholm and Empiricism," *Journal of Philosophy*, XLV (1948), 519.

(iii) At one time Professor Ayer defended phenomenalism on the ground that "the only alternative to it, once we have agreed to the use of the sense-datum terminology is the iron-curtain theory of perception: that physical objects are there sure enough but we can never get at them, because all we can observe is sense-data: and surely this theory at least can be shown to be untenable." [8] The doubtful step in this argument, I think, is the premise that, once we have adopted the sense-datum terminology, we must say that "all we can observe is sense-data." If Ayer took "observe" to be synonymous with "perceive," then his argument was an instance of what, in Chapter Ten, we called the sense-datum fallacy. And in this case, the statement "All we can observe is sense-data" is false. But if he took "observe" to be synonymous with "sense" (as we have been using "sense" and as he used it in *The Foundations of Empirical Knowledge*), then, although it is now true to say that all one can observe—all one can *sense*— is sense-data, this statement no longer implies that, if phenomenalism is false, one "can never get at" physical objects. For we may now say, what might have been less appropriate at the beginning of this book, that one *can* get at them—in the only relevant sense of this expression—by *perceiving* them.

[8] A. J. Ayer, *Philosophical Essays* (London, 1954), p. 143.

Criticisms of the Introduction of Sense Data

THIRTY-SIX

Sense Data and Judgment in Sensory Cognition*

C. A. CAMPBELL (1897-   )

COGNITION AS JUDGMENT

'All cognition is judgment.' That is the thesis we have to try to recommend. And it may be as well first of all to make it clear that 'cognition' in this statement is not a synonym for that strict 'knowing' which excludes the possibility of error. It is being used rather in the sense in which it has been customary in Psychology to distinguish cognition from conation and feeling as basic modes of experience. In this use of the term it is no more necessary that a cognition be true than that a conation be good. Those who advocate our doctrine have given expression to this aspect of it by equating cognition with *any* 'awareness of meaning', *any* 'significant apprehension'.

These latter expressions, 'awareness of meaning' and 'significant apprehension', throw some light, I think, on the nature of cognition. But they are not all self-explanatory expressions, and we shall not at this stage avail ourselves of them. Their identity with cognition will emerge in the course of the argument for the identity of cognition with judgment.

As to this central argument, there is, I think, only one really sound course to follow—an 'empirical' course. If we are to understand what cognition essentially is and entails, we must start from an actual instance in regard to which we should all be agreed that our minds pass from a non-

---

* From "Sense Data and Judgment in Sensory Cognition" by C. A. Campbell, *Mind,* Volume LVI (1947), pp. 292-311. Reprinted by permission of the author and the editor of *Mind.*

cognitive state to a state of cognition; and we must endeavour to observe the characteristic marks of that transition.

Let the reader, then, suppose himself to be lying out on the open hill-side on a fine summer day, completely absorbed in his own thoughts. All sorts of sights and sounds and smells assail his senses, but they 'mean nothing' to him. So far as awareness of his physical surroundings is concerned, he might equally well be sitting in his easy-chair before his study fire. Suddenly, something occurs to awaken him abruptly from his reverie —perhaps the whirr of an approaching aeroplane. He 'comes back to life' (as the saying is) and begins to 'notice' what is before him and about him. What he was previously 'looking at', but without awareness, is registered now in his conscious mind, and now, in sharp contrast with a moment ago, it has what would ordinarily be called a *meaning* for him.

Everyone will doubtless concede that we have here a case in which the mind passes from a non-cognitive to a cognitive state with respect to its owner's physical environment. Now let us select some particular item in the cognised field, for preference some very simple item like a patch of green, and let us consider what is involved in its thus becoming 'cognised' or (for I think we may already accept the identity) 'meaningful'.

I suggest that it is not really so very difficult, if we conduct our 'ideal experiment' with care, to detect the most important thing that happens when the 'green', which previously 'meant nothing' to us, suddenly acquires meaning or is cognised. It acquires meaning, or is cognised, *when and only when it is apprehended* [1] *as characterising the objective world,* and as related, accordingly, to other constituents of that world.

The key term in this statement is pretty clearly 'objective world', and we must leave no doubt about what it means for us. By 'objective world' I mean that independent reality which is the postulate of all knowing and all attempts to know. All knowing and all attempts to know presuppose a reality to be known whose existence and nature are independent of the knowing mind. The cognitive life in general may be said to consist in the progressive articulation of that independent objective reality. To be 'cognised' is, I am suggesting, to be apprehended as characterising this independent objective reality.

This view of the matter is strongly confirmed, I think, when we consider the cognitive development of our rudimentary 'objects'. Our coming to think of them as having complex relational meanings seems to depend absolutely upon their first satisfying this minimal condition, that they be apprehended as characterising the objective reality. Only thus could the 'cognised green' play the role that it actually does play in the later life of cognition. For only thus could we link it up or relate it to other items in our characterised objective reality, and eventually arrive at the devel-

[1] It should perhaps be made clear that the term 'apprehend' is used throughout this paper in a sense which does not exclude the possibility of erroneous apprehension.

oped cognition of it as, perhaps, 'a green shrub in the middle of a stretch of moor-land half a mile to the northwest of us'. And this is the sort of thing we do in fact do with whatever comes within the orbit of genuine 'cognition'.

It may be allowed, indeed, that it is possible for an entity to be in *some* sense 'present' to the mind and yet not apprehended as characterising the objective world: as, *e.g.,* in certain kinds of subconscious mental process. But it seems perfectly evident that in such cases we should not, on reflection, be prepared to speak of the object as being 'cognised'. So far as cognition is concerned, the entity is just nothing at all, conveys no kind of meaning. It has precisely the same status, in this respect, as the unnoticed, uncognised 'green' which becomes cognised only when, emerging from our 'day-dream', we are aware of it as characterising the objective world.

It is also possible, of course, for an entity to be quite genuinely 'cognised', and yet, even if a 'sensible' entity, not to be apprehended as characterising the *physical* world. At a certain level of philosophical sophistication we are plainly able to regard the cognised 'green' as characterising the *mental* world, or perhaps a *neutral* world sacred to sense-data. But the 'mental' and 'neutral' worlds fall within the sphere of 'objective reality' just as much as the 'physical' world does. We are still, in cognising the 'green', characterising the objective reality, whether we assign it to the physical, the mental, or the neutral realm of that reality (or, in a state of 'philosophic doubt', disjunctively to the physical-or-mental-or-neutral realm). The one thing we *cannot* do is to cognise the green and ascribe it to *no* realm of objective reality. To be 'just green' is to be, for our minds, just nothing.

The view for which I have been arguing is, or at least is like, the view that 'all cognition is judgment'. I am of opinion that it is not merely like, but the same. Where we have a character ('green' in our illustration) affirmed (or accepted—it makes not the least difference, as I shall argue below) as predicate of the independent reality as subject, there it seems natural and proper to speak of a 'judgment'. The name, of course, is a matter of indifference. So long as we are agreed about what is involved in cognition, the terms we use are a mere question of convenience. But there really seems to be no good reason for departing from the traditional nomenclature. The term 'belief', which has found a certain amount of favour as an alternative, seems to me to have serious disadvantages. Among these is the fact that belief, as we ordinarily use the term, admits of degrees of intensity. We speak of having strong, and not so strong, beliefs. But that which we are preferring here to designate by the term 'judgment' does *not* thus admit of degrees. So far as the strictly mental assertion that A is B is concerned (assertion by word of mouth or other physical medium is of course another matter, but is not to the point), the distinction between strong and weak has no application. Without doubt our degree of confidence about the B-ness of A can be very different at different times. But this difference in our state of mind does not manifest itself in a difference in the degree of assertiveness in the corresponding judgments: it manifests itself in a difference in the contents of the judgments. If we are in no doubt as to the B-ness of A, our mental assertion or judgment is that A *is* B; if we are doubtful, but only slightly doubtful, it is that there is a high probability that A is B; and so on.

But is it always the case in cognition that we *assert* characters of reality? It might be urged against our identification of cognition with judgment (as was hinted a moment ago) that there are many cognitions in everyday life in which nothing that can properly be called 'asserting' occurs: cognitions in which we merely 'accept', and do not 'assert', the B-ness of A.

One might answer the objection by pointing out that even cognitions which merely 'accept' are capable of being true or false, and that the possession of this mark places them at once in the class of 'judgments'. But, apart from that, it seems to me that to 'accept' the B-ness of A *is* to 'assert' the B-ness of A, but to assert it in a relatively inexplicit fashion. For though we cannot assert 'more or less', we can assuredly be 'more or less' clearly conscious of asserting. We are, as a rule, *most* clearly conscious of asserting when the B-ness is a feature of A that is unfamiliar to us, or when there has been a prior period of doubt as to whether A is B. We are, as a rule, *least* clearly conscious of asserting, when the B-ness of A is a feature to which we have long been accustomed. We may say, if we please, that cognitions at the lower end of the scale 'accept', and that those at the higher end 'assert': but there is no clean line of demarcation, rather a shading of the one into the other at certain intermediate stages at which we should be hard put to it to know whether it is more proper to speak of 'asserting' or 'accepting'. In short, the distinction is wholly a matter of degree.

The application which we are proposing to make of our doctrine in the sequel is solely to the field of *sensory* cognition, and we may—indeed must—limit our exposition accordingly, ignoring objections which might possibly be raised (and also, I believe, met) in respect of other spheres of cognition. It is now time that we turned to look more closely at the judgment-form in which (we are contending) all cognition is cast. We shall follow the same economical procedure as before, considering only those general characteristics of judgment which will have to be borne in mind as a background in order to appreciate the full implications of the doctrine for sensory cognition.

First, then, as to the *subject* of judgment. An answer to this has already been given by implication. It is always the *objective reality* which cognition seeks to characterise. All knowing and all attempts to know

are a knowing of or attempts to know *reality*. A simple way of bringing
out this point in relation to judgment is by consideration of the fact that
the judgment by its very form claims to be *true*. (Otherwise the claim of
a judgment would not be felt to be denied by the rejoinder that what
was asserted was false: it would be open to the person who made the
judgment to retort that he never thought it wasn't.) But to be 'true' is to
be true of *reality*. There is nothing else of which anything *can* be true.
Hence the judgment must be held to claim that what it asserts—its 'ideal
content', in the terminology of the tradition we are following—is true of
or correctly characterises reality. Another way of establishing the same
conclusion is by pointing out that any judgment 'S is P' whatsoever can
be cast, without change of meaning, into the form 'Reality is such that
S is P'. This formulation has the incidental value of bringing out an
important truth, *viz.*, that the whole ideal content of the judgment can
legitimately be regarded as a *single* complex idea—the P-ness of S—which
is predicated of reality.

To this aspect of judgment we shall be returning presently. But we
may just note in passing how it affords an easy, yet for our purposes
sufficient, way of dealing with a type of judgment which is, at the first
look, more than any other type incompatible with the doctrine that
reality is the subject of all judgments. I mean those judgments which
are 'about' purely fanciful beings, products of the creative imagination.
Take, *e.g.*, the judgment 'The Lilliputians were about the size of a man's
finger'. On the surface it seems mere paradox to claim that the subject of
this judgment is 'reality'. But if we re-state the judgment according to
the formula given above, at the same time expanding the verbal expression sufficiently to bring out clearly the real meaning of what is being
asserted, we get some such judgment as 'Reality is such that, in the world
of things and people projected by the imagination of Swift and depicted
in the pages of Gulliver's Travels, the Lilliputians were about the size
of a man's finger'. *This* judgment is certainly about 'reality' as subject.
Yet it differs only verbally, and not in meaning, from the earlier judgment,
which seemed to be about *un*realities.

Reality, then, is the ultimate subject of all judgment. But although
this is the case, it is possible, and convenient, to distinguish also a
proximate subject of judgment. If I assert that Scotland is mountainous,
it is true that I am ascribing the mountainousness of Scotland, as predicate,
to reality as subject. But there is also obvious truth in the ordinary notion
that what I am doing is to ascribe mountainousness as predicate to
Scotland as subject. But how can both be true? How can 'Scotland' in the
judgment belong with truth both to the subject and to the predicate?
Let us consider this question.

The convenience of distinguishing a proximate from an ultimate
subject in judgment arises from the fact that while we are always, in

judgment, seeking to characterise reality, it is normally upon reality already characterised in some particular phase or aspect of it that our cognitive attention is focussed. Not indeed *always*. Exceptions exist both at the lowest and at the highest reaches of cognition (and perhaps elsewhere): in the most rudimentary cognitions, before discrimination within the real takes effect, and, at the other extreme, in those flights of philosophical or religious speculation in which we expressly seek to know the *general* character of reality. But the existence of exceptions does not affect our present point. Normally in judgment it is reality already characterised in some particular phase or aspect that we seek to characterise *further*. It is this particular phase or aspect that constitutes the *proximate* as distinct from the *ultimate* subject of judgment.

Now the proximate subject, thus understood, can be readily seen to be, in an important sense, both 'ideal' and 'real'. 'Scotland', the proximate subject in the judgment 'Scotland is mountainous', is 'ideal' in so far as it consists of a more or less definitive complex of significant terms-in-relation; but it is 'real' as well, in that this ideal complex is accepted by the judging mind, on the basis of past experience, as already accurately characterising reality so far, and as thus 'one with' the real. In the proximate subject, we may say, the opposition between ideal and real is for the judging mind partially reconciled.

Thus the judgment 'Scotland is mountainous', more fully articulated, becomes "Reality, already so far correctly characterised by what we mean by 'Scotland', is further characterised by what we mean by 'mountainous' ". And we can now see, I think, how it is that 'Scotland' can be said with equal truth to belong to the side of the subject and to belong to the side of the predicate. It falls on the side of the predicate because it is ideal content affirmed of reality. But it falls on the side of the subject also, because its 'affirmation' is the affirmation involved in *acceptance*, and as an 'accepted' character of reality it serves in the judgment as the basis for further characterisation; *i.e.*, as 'proximate' subject.

With these perhaps too brief observations upon the judgment-form in which all cognition is cast, we must pass on to the special problem of the paper, the application of our general theory of cognition to the field of sensory experience. Let us begin by trying to get clear ideas about the conception of 'sense-data', in terms of which the problems of sensory cognition are now almost universally discussed.

THE NOTION OF 'SENSE-DATA'

The difficulty of giving a short account of the judgment-doctrine was much lessened by the fact that its advocates are practically unanimous as to what it means. Unfortunately this advantage is lacking in the case of the conception of 'sense-data' or 'sensa'. (I shall use these terms as synonyms. The distinction which philosophers have sometimes drawn between them does not, I think, affect anything I have to say.) There is no agreed definition of the term 'sense-datum', and there is very marked variety in the properties and relationships which different philosophers have thought fit to ascribe to the entity. As might be expected, however, there is a fair measure of agreement—by no means total agreement—as to the *denotation* of the term. As is also to be expected, there is what may fairly be described as a 'common doctrine' which, so far as it goes, all or almost all the votaries of sense-data would accept. In the present Section I shall state what I take to be the chief items in that common doctrine.

(a) I think that all sense-data philosophers would agree that the sensing by which sense-data are apprehended is a separate cognitive function, quite distinct from, though no doubt closely related to, intellection. Some of these philosophers are prepared to concede that sensing is always in fact, and perhaps even of necessity, accompanied by intellection: that, *e.g.*, the sensum is always judged about as well as sensed. But they would still insist that within this 'total' act of cognition it is always possible in principle to distinguish the sensing with its sensum on the one hand from the judging with what is judged on the other hand. And indeed it is not easy to see how on any view which denied this autonomy to sensing the use of the terms 'sensa' and 'sense-data' could be felt to be appropriate.

This view represents, of course, the most radical possible departure from the epistemological tradition of the previous half-century, and the return to a doctrine which was subjected in the late nineteenth century to about as fierce a bombardment of heavy artillery as any philosophical doctrine has ever had to face. Many, probably most, of the philosophers of a generation ago firmly believed that the refutation of the claim of sensing to yield *per se* any kind of cognition constituted one of the few really permanent advances which the history of philosophy was able to show. The contemporary advocate of sensing, however, seldom allows himself to be disturbed by the criticisms of philosophers who lived before the great twentieth century *Aufklärung*.[2]

(b) There is almost universal agreement, I think, that the sensing of sensa is not merely a distinct mode of *cognition*, but a distinct mode of *knowing*. The sensing of sensa is, so far as it goes, *infallible*. This is

[2] Nor, perhaps, by the criticisms of later philosophers either, if these happen to have drawn their inspiration from the Idealist tradition. A significant case is the article called 'Sensation and Thought' which the late Professor R. G. Collingwood contributed to the *Aristotelian Proceedings* of 1923-1924. In that article all the traditional arguments against 'pure sense' are marshalled with the author's well-known skill and vigour, and the conclusion is roundly stated that 'sense-data' are sheer mythology. I have not seen a reference to, much less a reply to, this attack by any of the sense-data philosophers in the twenty-odd years that have since elapsed.

equally the case whether the sensum is the constituent in a veridical or in an illusory perception. If under certain conditions I see a pink cloud, and under certain other conditions a pink elephant, the existence of the object of my sensing—the pink shape which is my sensum—is as indubitable in the one case as in the other.

On the other hand, although there is almost no support for the view that sensing can be fallible in the sense that the sensum can appear to be something which it is not, there is some influential support for the view that it can be fallible in the sense that the sensum can fail to appear to be something that it is. Some philosophers have held that there may well be more properties in a sensum than are actually noticed in a particular sensing of it. But this cannot be said to be, as yet at any rate, part of 'the common doctrine'. We must be content here merely to record a domestic difference which seems to us to have rather far-reaching consequences for the way in which the term 'sensum' is to be defined.

(c) The third item in what I have called the common doctrine is that sensa are *actual existents*. On this there is, I believe, absolute unanimity—whatever differences of opinion there may be as to the *mode* of existence which these entities enjoy. Nor is this unanimity at all surprising. If sense-data do not have actual existence, they cannot meet the theoretical need out of which they primarily arose. A chief begetter of the sense-datum theory was the problem set by illusory sense-appearances: *e.g.,* the elliptical appearance (from certain angles) of the 'round' penny. We know that the elliptical shape does not belong to the penny. Yet even while we are knowing this, we still continue to 'see' *some*thing as elliptical. How could this be so (it is asked), if there were not something elliptical 'there' to be seen? The conclusion is drawn that there does exist an elliptical something which, though evidently in very intimate relationship with, cannot be identified with, the penny. As an immediate object of sensing it may be named (with all else of its kind) a *sensum*. Whether this sensum be mental in character, or physical, or neither mental nor physical, are questions open to debate. But that it has existence in *some* mode is of the essence of its being a sensum at all.

From this central characteristic of sensa—actual existence—arise almost all the familiar and desperately intractable problems about sense-perception that have been agitating the philosophical world for the last quarter of a century. If sense-data are existents, how are they related to certain other ostensible existents in our universe? How in particular are they related to 'physical objects', which we know, apparently, only through their instrumentality? At least *some* sensa, we seem bound to agree, cannot be, or be constituents of, physical objects. And if *some* are not, does not the strong 'family resemblance' among sensa, and the identity in the conditions of their production, rather strongly suggest that *none* of them are? But if so, how by their means (or *without* their means) do we 'know' physical objects? Or have we perhaps been going too fast in supposing that we *do* know physical objects, in any sense of that term at any rate which is not reducible to a set of statements about sense-data? After all, once we grant the conception of sensa, the *prima facie* strength of the case for Phenomenalism cannot be gainsaid. For the evidence which is taken to support the existence of sensa—direct acquaintance—seems a good deal stronger than the evidence for the existence of 'physical objects', and perhaps stronger than the evidence for the existence of any other entity whatsoever. Quite naturally, therefore, sense-data tend to acquire a privileged position as the ultimate bases of metaphysical construction, and legitimate enquiries (wholly legitimate once the notion of sense-data is accepted) are set on foot as to whether all other ostensible realities are not in the last resort explainable in terms of the one indubitable reality—the 'sense-datum'. And so the debate goes on—no nearer an agreed solution on any major point after twenty-five years, so far as the present writer can see, than it was at the beginning: which is only what one should expect if sense-data are not actual existences at all but just the fictitious products of a faulty epistemological analysis.

ON THE NATURE OF SENSORY COGNITION

By those who followed, even though they may not have agreed with our development of the thesis that all cognition is judgment, our main reason for contending that sense-data just do not exist will have been already anticipated. For if the argument for this thesis was sound, sensing is not a mode of cognition at all, much less a mode of knowing. The so-called 'sensum' can have being only as an element within the unity of the judgment, an element logically distinguishable but not otherwise separable. The question of its 'real existence' (and *a fortiori* of its relation as a real existent to other real existents) just does not arise.

Such was the implication of our analysis of the mind's passage from the unnoticed, uncognised 'green' to the noticed, cognised 'green'. The 'green' acquires a meaning for our minds, is something for cognition, when and only when it is apprehended as a colour characterising some part (possibly in certain rare cases the whole) of what we take to be the objective reality. That is, it functions as a predicate in a judgment. A 'green' *not* thus apprehended as characterising the objective reality, a 'green' with *no* apprehended relationship to the world we partially know and seek to know more fully, can play no conceivable part in the life of cognition. It is, so far as cognitive experience is concerned, sheer nonentity.

But obviously this view stands in need of much elaboration and defence if it is to appear at all plausible to those who remain sceptical (to say the least of it) about the soundness of its premises. I shall deal

with the difficulties which seem to me the most formidable as faithfully as I can. I propose to begin by answering a question which may very
reasonably be in the minds of many readers; and I am hopeful that, in the
course of its discussion, the nature and implications of the view that is
being defended will be appreciably clarified.

The question is this. "Are you" ,it may be asked, "denying that in
what is commonly called 'sensory' cognition there is any such thing as
'sensing' at all? Are you really hoping to persuade us that there is nothing
involved save an intellectual act of judgment?"

The answer is emphatically in the negative. I have denied 'sensing'
only as a *mode of cognition:* I do not believe that there is a sensing
whereby we apprehend a significant sensum. But I do not for a moment
dispute that there is in the experience of sensory cognition something
besides sheer intellection, something for which the title 'sensing' is appropriate. On the contrary, I believe this sensing to be highly important
—not as a *mode* of cognition, but as a *basis* of cognition. Let me now try
to explain what I understand by this 'sensory basis' of cognition.

The way can best be prepared, I think, by considering why it is
that, even if one has ceased to believe in 'sensa', one still has no real
doubt that there is more in sensory cognition than mere judgment. The
paramount reason appears to me to lie in what one may perhaps call the
'extra-logical compulsoriness' of the judgment in sensory cognition. I look
at the tree and feel 'obliged' to affirm its greenness. But the obligation is
not felt as a 'logical' obligation. The connexion of greenness with the
tree is, intellectually, neither self-evident nor the implication of anything that is self-evident. And yet I do feel 'compelled' so to judge. Now
if the source of this compulsion is taken to fall outside the field of the
intellect, and yet to fall (as presumably it must) within the field of experience, we are clearly driven to recognise in sensory cognition the
operation of some kind of non-intellectual mode of experience. And there
is, so far as I can see, little against, and sound traditional reasons for,
calling this non-intellectual mode of experience by the name of 'sensation'.

But what positive meaning are we to give to 'sensation' in this
context? Obviously not a physical meaning, such as the reaction of sense-
organs to material stimuli: for our 'sensation' is a mode of 'experience'.
We are likewise forbidden by our own doctrine to regard it as a mode of
cognition—the sensing of a significant sensum. From the point of view
we have reached there is, I think, only one proper way of understanding
'sensation', *viz.,* as an *immediate experience,* in which sensing and what
is sensed are indissolubly one.

This seems to me to be in principle the solution. In all sensory
cognition there is a *basis* of immediate experience—'sensation'—which
evokes in us, by extra-logical compulsion, the appropriate judgment:

which *obliges* us to ascribe greenness to the tree, smoothness to the billiard ball, and so on. This is what must be opposed to the doctrine that we are moved to affirm greenness of the tree because we 'sense a green sensum'. One may, if one cares, retain the term 'sensing' for the immediate experience looked at from the side of the experiencing subject; though it would be wise, if one wishes to give a name to its objective correlate, to speak of that as the 'sensed', or even the 'given', and not as a 'sensum'. But the vital thing to recognise is that this immediate sensory experience is in itself indivisible, sensing and sensed in one without distinction.

What has been said applies to sensing in general (in so far as sensing is a factor in sensory cognition). At a certain stage in the development of our cognitive life, of course, we come to discriminate, within sensing, different sensory capacities connected with different classes of cognised characters—seeing with colours, hearing with sounds, and so on—and we come to correlate these different sensory capacities with processes in different parts of our bodies ('sense organs') which condition their exercise. At a later stage, psycho-physical analysis may reveal more detailed correlations, of determinate species within a class of cognised character (*e.g.,* a particular shade of colour) with a determinate species of physical reaction in the organ of sense. Such empirically discovered psycho-physical relations in the region of sensory cognition are not, I think, incompatible with anything in the general view of sensory cognition I have been putting forward. It can be accepted as simple matter of fact that sensory cognition is conditioned by bodily processes, and (as an implication of this) that the underlying 'sensing' is likewise so conditioned. Adoption of the thesis that all cognition is judgment has not, despite the circumstance that those who have been foremost in advocating the thesis happen to have been idealist in their metaphysic, any intrinsic connexion with denial of the existence of physical bodies. Indeed, a case could be made for the direct contrary. At least *one* serious barrier to belief in the existence of physical bodies is removed if we can accept the view that our primary sensory cognition is not of 'sensa', but of sensible qualities (including those that define 'the physical') as characterising subjects in reality. But we have enough on our hands without raising issues of this sort. What we are immediately concerned to do is to give an account of sensory cognition which, while true to our doctrine that all cognition is judgment, gives due recognition to that aspect of passivity, compulsiveness, or giveness which is rightly regarded as ineluctable in sensory cognition.

Our acceptance of a definite role for 'sensing' in sensory cognition will, we trust, have persuaded the reader that our theory is not so excessively 'intellectualist' as may have at first appeared. But the main burden of the reader's discontent, I am aware, may still remain. It is not difficult to imagine objections couched in some such form as this. "You are still, despite your lip-service to sensing, failing disastrously to do justice to the difference, manifest to everyone, between contents of sense and contents of thought. On your view, *all* content at the cognitive level, even what is universally called 'sensible' content, falls within the field of judgment, and is thus a content of thought. But surely direct reference to actual experience discloses characteristics in 'sensible content' which mark it off in kind, and not merely in degree, from anything that can properly be called a 'content of thought'. Suppose, for example, we attend to the red colour of a 'seen' tomato, perhaps with a view to comparing this shade of red with other shades of red. Must it not be admitted (*a*) that there is an unique sensible 'quality', a vividness or tang, about the 'seen red' which is altogether lacking in any content of thought—in 'justice', 'triangularity' and the like. And must it not also be admitted (and this would seem to be a decisive objection to your view), (*b*) that this red which we see has that definite location in space and time which is universally accepted as the mark of a particular existent? If it has—and *that* it has seems obvious—the 'seen red' cannot possibly discharge the function which you would accord to it of a character ascribed in judgment to a subject in reality—a 'character' which is necessarily a *universal*."

Let us look at each of these points in turn.

(*a*) First, as to this 'sensible vividness' which is alleged to mark off contents of sense from contents of thought.

I do not at all deny that there is something fairly enough described as sensible vividness which is discoverable in some cognised contents and not in others. What I do deny is that the possession of this feature disqualifies a content from being a content of *thought*. The proper interpretation of sensible vividness I believe to be this. It does *not* serve to mark off 'contents of sense' from 'contents of thought'. It *does* serve to mark off a specific *kind* of thought-content, *viz.*, that specific kind which is thought under the direct impulsion of immediate sensory experience. Let me explain by way of an illustration.

Suppose that, instead of attending to the 'seen red' with a view to comparing it with other reds, I am looking at the tomato and making the straightforward judgment 'this tomato is red'. Presumably the 'redness' I ascribe to the tomato is a universal. And presumably also, as a universal, it is a content of thought. Now can it really be maintained that the thought-content here, the 'universal' redness, as it functions in my mind, lacks the 'sensible vividness' supposed to be the exclusive property of contents of sense? Has it not, on the contrary, precisely the *same* sensible vividness as the red that we say we 'see'? It seems to me that the test of inspection, the appeal to direct experience, reveals very plainly that the sensible vividness is present identically in the two cases.

Nor of course is there, for us, anything in the least surprising in this identity between the universal 'redness' in the judgment 'this tomato is red' and the 'seen red' upon which one may focus one's attention as a prospective subject of a comparative judgment. For in our view the latter content, despite first appearances, is every bit as much a universal as the "redness" in the judgment cited. Indeed it is the same universal. The difference is merely that whereas in the one case (in the judgment 'this tomato is red') it is a character *affirmed* as qualifying a subject in reality, in the other case it is a character *accepted* as qualifying a subject in reality. Its alleged status as a 'particular existent' is, in our view, a delusion. But with this we come to topics better dealt with under (*b*) below.

(*b*) The second objection we were to deal with is, we believe, much less formidable than it looks. It looks formidable because, by dint of constant repetition, it has come to be regarded as just plain matter of fact, beyond dispute, that a sensible *quale* like the 'red' we see has position in space and time. It is, indeed, obvious that *something* in the 'objective field' of such cognitions has position in space and time. But need that 'something' be the sensible *quale?* Holding as we do that the sensible *quale* is in *truth* a universal affirmed as characterising a subject in reality, it is obviously incumbent upon us to suggest a tenable alternative to the common view. The alternative we suggest is that it is the '*subject in reality*', not the sensible *quale,* that possesses these spatio-temporal relations. In other words, it is not the red of the tomato that stands to the right of the sprig of lettuce in the salad bowl. It is the tomato which so stands—the tomato, to which both this shade of redness and a particular position in space (and time) are ascribed.

The example just used, however, must not be taken as committing us to the view that the entity which is characterised by the sensible *quale,* and which (we hold) alone has spatio-temporal position, is necessarily a *material* entity like the tomato. Such a view is untenable: for it is certain that one can cognise a 'red' while firmly convinced, on one or other of a number of possible grounds, that there is no material entity there to be characterised. If, then, we admit (as we do) that in such cases *something* is taken to have position in space and time, what can that 'something' be save the sensible *quale* itself? If not the 'red', what is it?

The answer is, I suggest, that it is a *specific spatial expanse.* For whatever the sentient subject may believe about the status of the red he cognises, however esoteric or bizarre the epistemological or ontological theory that he favours, it can be affirmed with confidence that he just is not capable of cognising a red without cognising it as characterising *at least* a specific spatial expanse. And a specific spatial expanse is, of course, a 'particular existent', with spatio-temporal position, just as much as a material entity is. . . .

To sum up this part of our discussion. Our claim is that the seeing of a red patch is still, even where there is disbelief in the existence of a material object that is red, a judgment in which the universal redness (or some shade of redness) is ascribed to a subject in reality. The 'subject in reality' is a specific spatial expanse which is an object neither of thought, nor of sense, but of intuition. It is the spatio-temporal position of the specific spatial expanse characterised by redness which tends to be misattributed to the 'seen red' itself, with the natural consequence of engendering, or reinforcing, the false belief that the seen red is a 'particular'.

THIRTY-SEVEN

Argument from Physiology

GILBERT RYLE (1900-   )

From *Dilemmas**

. . . It is now time to turn to a much more difficult and important source of theoretical lawsuits.

As anatomy, physiology and, later, psychology have developed into more or less well-organized sciences, they have necessarily and rightly come to incorporate the study of, among other things, the structures, mechanisms, and functionings of animal and human bodies *qua* percipient. Answers are looked for and found to questions of the general pattern With what organs in our bodies do we see, hear, taste and feel things? and What lesions, diseases and fatigues in these organs diminish or destroy our capacity to see, hear, smell, taste and feel things? Harm need not result, though it can result from formulating the general programme of these inquiries in the question-patterns 'How do we perceive?' and 'Of what is seeing the effect?'

I say that harm can result from so formulating the programme of these inquiries. For these questions, so formulated, easily lend themselves to being construed after the pattern of other familiar and well-behaved questions; and when so construed they worry us by behaving extremely badly. I mean this. The questions 'How do we digest our food?' and 'What happens in us when we drink milk or alcohol?' have discoverable and largely discovered answers. The experts know well enough what happens to the milk or alcohol after we have consumed it and what differences the absorption of them make to our blood-streams, our reaction-times and so on. Doubtless there is more to be found out, but we can think what it will be like to have this extra knowledge. We know where it will fit in.

So when we ask 'How do we see trees?' or 'What happens in us when we see trees?' we are predisposed to expect the same sorts of answers, namely reports of modifications in some of our internal states and processes. Further than that, we are predisposed to think that these reports will tell us not only what happens in us when we perceive but what perceiving is, in the way in which the answer to the question 'What

* From *Dilemmas* by Gilbert Ryle (Cambridge University Press, 1954). Reprinted by permission of the publisher.

happens in us when we eat poison?' does tell us what being poisoned is. As eating results in nourishment and as haemorrhage results, sometimes, in fainting or in death, so, we fancy, some other external happenings result *via* some other complex internal happenings in the special internal happening of seeing a tree.

Yet, however its details may be filled in, this sort of story leaves us uneasy. When asked whether I do or do not see a tree, I do not dream of postponing my reply until an anatomist or physiologist has probed my insides, any more than he, when asked whether he has seen the zigzag lines on his encephalogram, postpones replying until some other anatomist or physiologist has tested him by a second encephalogram. The question whether I have or have not seen a tree is not itself a question about the occurrence or non-occurrence of experimentally discoverable processes or states some way behind my eyelids, else no one could even make sense of the question whether he had seen a tree until he had been taught complicated lessons about what exists and occurs behind the eyelids.

'No', it might be said 'of course seeing a tree is not just a physiological state or a physiological process. Such states and processes can indeed occur without their owner knowing anything at all about them, where seeing, hearing and smelling belong where remembering, yearning and wondering belong, namely to the field or stream of consciousness. A person can suffer from a vitamin-deficiency without knowing what vitamins are, much less that he is short of them. But he cannot see or remember or wonder without knowing both that he is doing so and what it is that he is doing. These are not bodily states or processes but mental states or processes, and the questions "How do we see trees?" and "What takes place in us when we see trees?" need not anatomical or physiological answers but psychological answers or, perhaps, a conjunction of psychological with physiological answers.'

It is the regular lament of physiologists from Sydenham to Sherrington, not merely that they cannot trace but, worse, that they cannot think how they even might trace the whole chain of processes from the arrival of the initial external physical impulse at the ear-drum, say, the whole way through to the subject detecting the note of a flute. But, the suggestion is, the lament is gratuitous, for somehow, we do not yet know how, the chain of processes at a certain point changes over from having its links in the body to having its latest link or links in the mind. That is where the terminal process has its seat.

There are, I think, a number of objections to this way of retaining our seeings and hearings as the concluding stages of chain-processes while rendering them inaccessible to observation and experimentation in laboratories. But I do not want to go into them here. What I do hope to do is to show that there is something which is drastically wrong with the whole programme of trying to schedule my seeing a tree either as a physiological or as a psychological end-stage of processes. It is not a question of my seeing the tree evading observation and experiment, but of its not being the sort of thing that can be found *or* missed in either the one place or the other. It is not an intractably shy phenomenon, even an introspective phenomenon, because it is not a phenomenon at all. Neither the physiologist nor the psychologist nor I myself can catch me in the act of seeing a tree—for seeing a tree is not the sort of thing in which I can be caught. When I report, perhaps to an oculist, that at a certain moment I saw something, what I report does not qualify to be the filling of any statement of the pattern 'The needle gave me a twinge of pain' or 'His haemorrhage caused him to faint'. To put the point much too crudely, seeing a tree is not an effect—but this is not because it is an eccentric sort of state or process which happens to be exempt from causal explanations but because it is not a state or process at all.

In this one negative respect seeing and hearing are like enjoying. It was partly for this reason that on a former occasion I discussed the notion of enjoyment at such length, namely to familiarize you with the idea that well understood autobiographical verbs can still be grossly misclassified. I argued that some theorists had tried to fit the notions of liking and disliking into the conceptual harness which suits such terms as 'pain' and 'tickle'. They had misclassified *liking* and *disliking* with sensations or feelings. In somewhat the same way, many theorists have tried to subjugate the notions of seeing, hearing and the rest to marching in step either with such notions as *pain* and *tickle,* or else with such notions as *inflammation* or *knee-jerk*. It is tacitly assumed that seeing and hearing must be what stimuli stimulate, only, unfortunately, we have not yet found the way to correlate with these stimuli the perceptions which they stimulate.

I want to satisfy you that verbs like 'see' and 'hear' are not verbs of those sorts. Their functions are quite unlike the functions of verbs like 'tingle', 'wince', 'turn pale' or 'faint'; and answerable questions like 'What made him faint or flinch?' become unaskable questions when 'see' or 'taste' replace 'faint' and 'flinch'.

To begin with, seeing and hearing are not processes. Aristotle points out, quite correctly (*Met.* ix, vi. 7-10) that I can say 'I have seen it' as soon as I can say 'I see it'. To generalize the point that I think he is making, there are many verbs part of the business of which is to declare a terminus. To find something puts 'Finis' to searching for it; to win a race brings the race to an end. Other verbs are verbs of starting. To launch a boat is to inaugurate its career on the water; to found a college is to get it to exist from then on. Now starting and stopping cannot themselves have starts or stops, or, *a fortiori,* middles either. Noon does not begin, go on and finish. It is itself the end of the morning, the beginning of the afternoon and the half-way point of the day. It cannot itself go on for a time, however short. It is not a process or a state. Similarly though we can ask how long a poem is, we cannot ask how long its beginning and end are. They are not sub-stretches of the poem.

We can ask how long it was before the team scored its first goal; or how long the centre-forward spent in manœuvring the ball towards the goal; and even how long the ball was in flight between his kicking it and its going between the goal-posts. But we cannot ask how many seconds were occupied in the scoring of the goal. Up to a certain moment the team was goal-less; from that moment it had scored a goal. But there was no interim moment at which it had half-scored, or scored half of its first goal. Scoring a goal is not a process, but the termination of one and the beginning of another condition of the game. The beginning of a process, such as the start of the motion of an avalanche, is not the cause of that motion; the end of a process, such as the going out of a fire, is the termination but not an effect of the combustion.

It will, I think, be apparent why, with certain reservations, verbs which in this way declare termini cannot be used and are in fact not used in the continuous present or past tenses. The judge may say that he has been trying a man all the morning but not that he has spent the morning or any stretch of the morning in convicting him. I can say that I am occupied in searching for a pencil or trying to solve an anagram, but not that I am occupied in finding the pencil or getting the solution of the anagram. In the same way I can be looking for or looking at something, but I cannot be seeing it. At any given moment either I have not yet seen it or I have now seen it. The verb 'to see' does not signify an experience, i.e. something that I go through, am engaged in. It does not signify a sub-stretch of my life-story.

For safety, let me just mention the reservations. I could certainly say that I was finding misprints all the morning, though not that I was finding some one misprint for any part of that morning. If I found one misprint after another, and the sequence of discoveries went on from breakfast to lunch, then I was finding misprints all the morning. Or, when asked what I am busy about, I could reply that I am occupied in solving anagrams. I have solved some and I have some more which I hope to solve. But I could not say 'I am at present solving this anagram'. Either I have now got the solution or I have not yet got it. In short, a lot of biographical verbs like 'find', 'see', 'detect', and 'solve' share with a lot of other verbs of starting and stopping, which have no special biographical connotations, the negative property of not standing for processes taking place in or to things, or for states in which things remain. The programme, therefore, of locating, inspecting and measuring the process or state of seeing, and of correlating it with other states and processes, is a hopeless programme—hopeless not because the quarry wears seven-leagued boots or a cloak of invisibility, but because the idea that there was such a quarry was the product, almost, of inattention to grammar.

To say that verbs of perceptual detection, unlike those of perceptual exploration, have this resemblance to verbs of stopping and starting is, of course, not to say very much about their business. Checkmating also resembles midnight in this one respect, but a person who knew only this would not know much about checkmating. Let us consider a half-way-house pair of cases. Reaching the end of the measured mile of a race-track takes no time. The runner was running for some five minutes before he reached this point, but his reaching this point did not prolong his running-time. His reaching it is not something with its own beginning, middle and termination. The same is true of winning a mile race. Yet winning involves much more than reaching the end of the measured mile. To win a mile-race, the winner must have been running in competition with at least one other runner; he must not have started before the gun or taken a short-cut or used a bicycle or tripped up his opponent; and he must have reached the end of the measured mile ahead of any op-ponent. His winning the race comes with his reaching the end of the mile, but to be a victory it has to satisfy quite a lot of additional requirements. Both are attainings, but they are not homogeneous with one another.

Suppose a man, flying in terror from a bull, crossed the start-line of a race-track as the gun was fired, and in his terror reached the tape ahead of the racers. Should we say that he had won the race? or that as he did not know that there was a race on, or anyhow had no intention of match-ing his speed against anybody save the bull, therefore he was not in the race and so did not win it? Has the careless chess-player whose cuff ac-cidentally pushes his Queen into a square which puts his opponent's King in checkmate, defeated his opponent? We are inclined to require some intention or purpose of a runner or player before we will use the heavily loaded terminus-verbs 'win' and 'checkmate'.

We may imagine an athletics coach with a scientific training research-ing into the physiology and the psychology of runners. He finds out how men of different bodily builds and different temperaments race over different distances. He finds out the effects of fatigue, of alcohol, of tobacco, of lumbago and of depression upon their performances. He finds out about muscular co-ordination, rhythm, length of stride, and rates of breathing. He finds out about adrenalin, reaction-times and elec-trical impulses in nerve-fibres. But then he laments that he can find no physiological phenomenon answering to his subject's winning a race, or losing it. Between his terminal output of energy and his victory or defeat there is a mysterious crevasse. Physiology is baffled. Then for a moment our experimentally minded coach cheers up. Perhaps winning and losing are not physiological states or processes having their being under the athlete's skin; perhaps they are mental states or processes, experiences which the athlete himself can unearth by careful introspection. Indeed this looks very plausible, since runners, who know nothing of what goes on under their own skins, seem often to have no difficulty in discovering that they have won or lost a race. So presumably they discover these facts by introspection upon their mental states and processes. But then, alas, it turns out that this hypothesis will not do either. A runner's victory, though it is tied up, in lots of important ways, with his muscles, nerves and frame of mind, with his early training and the briefing received just before the race, still refuses to be listed among these or kindred phases of his private career. However fast, resolutely and cleverly he has run, he has not won the race unless he had at least one rival, did not cheat and got to the tape first. That these conditions were satisfied cannot be ascertained by probing still further into him. Winning is not a physiological phenomenon, like perspiring or panting, nor yet is it a psychological phenomenon, e.g. an experience like a surge of confidence or a spasm of annoyance. It happens, but, to put it in a way which is not my way, it does not happen in either of those two places, for all that its happening has a great deal to do with what happened in those two places.

In some respects, though certainly not in very many, the verbs 'see' and 'hear' function like the verb 'win'. They do not stand for bodily or psychological states, processes or conditions. They do not stand for anything that goes on, i.e. has a beginning, a middle and an end. The assertion that a subject has seen a misprint carries with it the assertion that there was a misprint for him to see, somewhat as the assertion that a runner has been victorious or defeated carries with it the assertion that there was at least one other runner. The fact that he has seen a misprint has a great deal to do with facts about the light, the condition and position of his eyes and their distance from the page and the absence of screens, the condition of his retina, nerves, etc., the nature of his early education and his present interests, mood and so on. But his seeing or missing the misprint is not itself among the facts about him which can be established in the ways in which these physiological and psychological facts are established. It is not a fact of any of those sorts. None the less, it is not a mysterious fact, any more than winning or losing a race is rendered a mysterious fact by the failure of experiments upon the runner to establish it.

This partial analogy between the business of the verb 'win' and the business of verbs like 'see' and 'hear' of course breaks down quickly and in a number of places. I want to draw attention to two of these collapses, which are, I think, especially illuminating. First, no one would in fact ever suppose that 'winning' stood for a physiological or psychological condition or process, whereas all of us are under strong pressure to assimilate seeing and hearing to having pangs and twinges. Our immunity from the ludicrous blunder which I have invented is partly due to the fact that we know not merely implicitly and in practice, but explicitly and in theory what are the connotations of the verb 'to win'. We were taught the rules of racing when we were taught to race. We not only knew but could say what constituted cheating and not cheating, what constituted competing and what constituted the finish of a race. Even more conspicuously, we had been explicitly taught the rules of chess before we began to use the word 'checkmate'. But verbs of perceiving, though they also carry complex connotations, partly similar to those of 'win' and 'checkmate', were not and could not have been taught to us in this way. We picked up the ways of handling them without being told what these ways were, much as we picked up the pronunciation of the words of our native tongue without any lessons in phonetic theory.

Secondly, whereas the question whether I have won the race, check-mated my opponent or scored a bull's-eye can be decided at least not worse and often better by someone else than by myself, the question whether I have seen or heard something does not ordinarily get or need an umpire. In the vast majority of everyday situations, the person who claims to have found or detected something is excellently placed for upholding that claim. He is as expert an umpire and as favourably situated an umpire as anyone could be. But, and it is an important 'but', not always. The reader who claims to have found a misprint or alternatively to have found a passage correctly printed is not to be trusted if he is a bad speller or not well versed in the language of the passage; the child who claims to see the railway lines meeting just beyond the signal-box is not the person to adjudicate on his claim; and the question whether or not the spectators saw the doves emerging from the conjuror's pocket is for him, not them, to decide. Notice that the conjuror is in a position to reject the claim of the spectators that they saw something happen, if he knows that it did not happen. But if they claim to have seen something happen which did happen, then he cannot, on this score alone, concede their claim. If the thing happened, but happened behind a screen, then their claim to have seen it must be rejected. They could not have seen it unless it happened, and unless it happened in such a place, and at such a distance and in such a light that it was visible to them and unless their eyes were open, properly directed and focused and so on. But when he has conceded that they could have seen it happen, the question whether they did see it happen is not one which he can decide without interrogating them.

What sorts of questions will be put to them? He will not ask them to describe, in retrospect, what experiences they had had, for example what feelings they had felt, what ideas had crossed their minds or what after-images, if any, interfered with their subsequent vision; and of course he will not ask them intricate questions of physiological or psychological sorts, to which they are in no position to give any answers. No answers to such questions would go any way towards deciding whether they had seen what they claimed to have seen. No, he will ask them questions about what they claim to have witnessed happening. If they can tell him facts about the happening which they could not have found out without seeing it happen, their possession of this knowledge is what will satisfy him that they did see it. But sometimes they will not be able to satisfy him in this way, and the question whether they did see what they claimed to see remains undecidable for him. It may also remain undecidable for them too. The anxious mother, listening for the doctor's car, is not sure whether or not she faintly hears the noise of the car a few moments before it does in fact arrive. Perhaps it is imagination—it often is. Perhaps she does just hear it—we often do. But there need be no way of deciding the question after the event.

But in general it is true—we could even say that *of course* in general it is true—that an observer has seen or heard what he says that he has seen or heard. Sometimes he is deceived, for example, by the quickness of the conjuror's hand; but he can be deceived in this abnormal situation only because he is not deceived when witnessing the relatively slow motions of the hands of the people with whom he has ordinarily to do. The child, on his first visit to a skyscraper, may mistakenly judge the vehicles in the street below to be the size of beetles—but for this misestimate to be possible he must have learned to get right, in ordinary situations, the sizes of cars and beetles. The point is that where winning is the scoring of an athletic success, perceiving is the scoring of an investigational success. We find things out or come to know them by seeing and hearing. Of course we know what we have discovered, since to discover that something is the case is to come to know that it is the case. Normally, too, though not necessarily, we know how we discovered it, e.g. by sight and not by smell, or by touch and not by ear; though there are fringe-cases in which we are in doubt whether we found out that she was angry from the look on her face or from the tone of her voice; or whether we detected the proximity of the tree-trunk in the dark from a sort of sudden thickening in the sounds of things or from a sort of nameless hint given by the skin of our faces.

In this chapter I have tried to show at least part of the way out of a certain kind of dilemma about perception. From some well-known facts of optics, acoustics and physiology it seemed to follow that what we see, hear or smell cannot be, as we ordinarily suppose, things and happenings outside us, but are on the contrary, things or happenings inside us. Where we ordinarily speak confidently of seeing other people's faces, we ought, apparently, to speak instead of seeing some things going on behind our own faces, or else, more guardedly, inside our own minds. Where we ordinarily suppose that we cannot see inside our own heads, and that only unusually situated surgeons could possibly get a look at what exists and happens there, we ought instead to allow that all the sights, sounds, and smells available to us are literally or else metaphorically internal to us; and that what the surgeon sees, when peering inside our skulls is, in its turn, nothing that exists or happens in our skulls but something existing or happening inside his own skull, or else inside some other more ethereal chamber, totally private to him.

One source of this dilemma is, I have tried to show, the natural but mistaken assumption that perceiving is a bodily process or state, as perspiring is; or that it is a non-bodily, or psychological process or state; or, perhaps, that it is somehow jointly a bodily and non-bodily process or state. That is, we have yielded to the temptation to push the concepts of seeing, hearing and the rest through the sorts of hoops that are the proper ones for the concepts which belong to the sciences of optics, acoustics, physiology and psychology. The unscheduled but well-disciplined conduct in ratiocination of the notions of seeing, hearing and the rest diverges sharply from the conduct that we have been induced to schedule for them.

To say this is not to disparage the admirable conduct of the concepts of optics, acoustics or physiology. It is no slur on the harness that fits the team-horse to perfection to say that it is an impediment when borrowed for the sleigh-dog. But more than this. There are all sorts of important connexions between the things that we all know, and have to know, about seeing and hearing and the things which have been and will be discovered in the sciences of optics, acoustics, neurophysiology and the rest.

To say that a person's seeing a tree is in principle the same sort of affair as a negative in a camera being exposed, or a gramophone-disc being indented certainly will not do at all. But a great deal has been found out about seeing by working on analogies like this. It is, indeed, the good repute of these discoveries which bribes us to try to subjugate our untechnical generalities about seeing and hearing to the codes that govern so well our technical generalities about cameras, gramophones and galvanometers. Nor is there anything to warn us beforehand whether or where the attempted subjugation will fail.

THIRTY-EIGHT

The Problem of Perception*

A. M. QUINTON (1926-   )

I

The problem of perception is to give an account of the relationship of sense-experience to material objects. This relationship has traditionally been seen as logical, a matter of showing how beliefs about objects can be established or supported by what we know in immediate experience. For, it is held, only our knowledge of experience is direct, immediate, by acquaintance; what we know or claim to know about objects is indirect, derivative, by inference from what we know directly. Consequently if our beliefs about objects are to have any secure foundation, it must consist in what we know directly, by acquaintance, about sense-data. From this starting-point philosophers have gone on to present varying accounts of the type of inference involved. An extreme view is Hume's, that the passage from experiences to objects rests on 'a kind of fallacy or illusion'. Lockean causal theories assert that the connexion between experiences and objects is contingent and that knowledge of experience is good inductive evidence for beliefs, logically distinct from it about objects. The species of inference involved is transcendental hypothesis of the type to be found in scientific arguments for the existence of such unobservables as electrons or chromosomes. For phenomenalism the connexion between experiences and objects is necessary, to speak of objects is to speak in an abbreviated way about certain pervasive kinds of regularity in experience. The species of inference involved is simple inductive extrapolation. There are not two worlds, an inner and an outer, but two terminologies. The terminology of objects is used to refer to what is invariant as between the private worlds of experience.

Each view derives strength from the weaknesses of its opponent. The most emphasised weakness of phenomenalism is that, if it were true, un-observed objects would be mere possibilities and actual effects would have to arise from merely potential causes. Mill's view that objects are permanent possibilities of sensation is confronted by a fundamental and unargued incredulity. A more serious difficulty arises about the antecedents of the hypothetical statements which describe the permanent possibilities

* From "The Problem of Perception" by A. M. Quinton, *Mind*, LXIV (1955), pp. 28-51. Reprinted by permission of the author and the editor of *Mind*.

in question. For these antecedents mention objects. To assume, as phenomenalists often cheerfully do, that these references can be replaced by references to 'orienting experiences' is to beg the very question at issue. One cannot *assume* that statements about experiences are equivalent in meaning to statements about objects in order to *show* that they are. Against the causal theory it is argued that, given the sense-datum theory, it would be impossible ever to know that the logically distinct, unobservable, transcendental causes existed. For a causal inference is only legitimate if it is at least possible to obtain evidence for the existence of the cause which is independent of the events it is held to explain.

In the face of this impasse sense-datum theorists have tended to adopt a middle position of compromise. Causal theorists liken their procedure to the 'model-building' of natural scientists. The external world is a theoretical construction, fruitful and various in its predictive and explanatory consequences. Phenomenalists modify their thesis of the strict logical equivalence of statements about experiences and about objects, in view of the difficulties, in principle and practice, of translating one into the other. Both extremes are abandoned in favour of the view that it is a simple, convenient and fruitful theoretical construction. But this is rather a method of refusing to face the difficulties than of overcoming them. For what sort of theoretical construction is involved, a substantial model of the not-yet-observed like a theory of atomic structure or a mere *façon de parler* like theories of magnetic and gravitational fields?

My purpose in this paper is to overcome these difficulties by a more radical procedure, that of refuting the premise from which both problematic doctrines derive, that we are never directly aware of or acquainted with objects.

My principal target will be the conception of direct awareness or acquaintance itself. The sense-datum theory holds that corresponding to the two kinds of objects of knowledge are two kinds of knowledge—direct and indirect. Thus while no knowledge of material objects is direct, all or only knowledge of experience is direct. In more linguistic terms, while no statements about objects are basic, all or only statements about experience are basic. A piece of knowledge, then, is direct if, and only if, it can be expressed by a basic statement. But this translation is of little help since neither of the crucial terms, 'direct' and 'basic', is clearly intelligible, let alone more intelligible than the other.

Two main kinds of definition are commonly offered of these expressions, one in terms of certainty, the other in terms of inference. By the former I directly know that p (or 'p' is a basic statement) if I know for certain that p. It is held that beliefs about objects are never certain, beliefs about experience are always certain and that for any uncertain belief to be even probable something else must be certain. Consequently all beliefs about objects that are to any extent probable must be logically derived

from beliefs about experience. I shall hold that all three of the premises
for this conclusion are false. The incorrigibility of statements about experience has been defended, notably by Ayer, on the ground that the only
mistakes to which we are liable in making such statements are 'verbal'. I
shall attempt to show that this too is false. Sometimes a definition in terms
of inference is preferred. I directly know that p (or 'p' is a basic statement)
if I know that p without inference. It is not, of course, maintained that
in coming to form a belief about an object I undertake any conscious
process of reasoning. What is involved is 'implicit' inference. Nevertheless,
it is held, reasons exist for beliefs about objects which it is the philosopher's business to render explicit and without reference to which no
justification of these beliefs can be provided. I shall argue that there is no
relevant sense of 'reason' in which a reason for them always exists.

Why should this have been thought to be so? The sense-datum theory,
seemingly a variant of the empiricist principle that all our knowledge of
matters of fact is based on sense-experience, tends to assume that principle's authority. But this, like other oracles, owes much of its reputation
to ambiguity. It can be taken to assert three different things, two of which
are uncontentious while the third deserves close inspection. First, it is
an unexciting truth of physiology that sensations, physical stimulations
of the sense-organs, are causally necessary conditions of our knowledge of
matters of fact. Second, the establishment of any truth about objects logically requires that someone shall have seen, touched or otherwise perceived
something. The chains of inference and testimony cannot hang unsupported but must terminate in observation. In this use 'sense-experience'
does not mean anything so definite as 'sense-datum', it has no phenomenological flavour. Seeing a tomato is just as much an observation as seeing
a round, red, shiny patch. Finally, 'based on sense-experience' can be
taken to mean 'logically derived from sense-experience'. The logical derivation in question here is of statements about objects from statements
about experiences. It is this third interpretation of the principle that
constitutes the sense-datum theory and which I shall attempt to refute.

These definitions of 'direct' and 'basic' in terms of certainty and
inference are not, however, the starting-points of sense-datum theories of
perception. They are rather conclusions to the argument from illusion
in terms of which the expressions 'direct' and 'basic' are normally introduced. This argument holds that objects are not always what they appear
to be and that there need be no discoverable difference between two situations in one of which an object is and in the other is not what it appears to be. In consequence, all that we really know is what appears to
be the case, since, even when what appears to be the case *is* the case, we
cannot there and then tell whether it is or not. Since we know only what
appears to be the case, the only things we really perceive are appear-

ances. Some philosophers have protested weakly against the later stages of this argument. I hope to substantiate and fortify their protest.

The mistake lies in the identification of what appears to be the case with our sense-experience. We always know what appears to be the case. So it is appearances, not objects, that we really perceive. But what else are these appearances but our current sense-fields, our sense-experience? The three forms of words; 'this appears to be ϕ', 'there is a ϕ appearance', 'there is a ϕ sense-datum', are held to be equivalent in meaning. I shall argue that a statement of what appears to be the case is rarely a description of our sense-experience and is normally a modified, guarded claim about what *is* the case, expressing an inclination to believe something about objects. The ostensible firmness and incorrigibility of these assertions is a consequence, not of their referring to a class of private, given entities, but rather of the modesty of the claim they make. So what the argument from illusion establishes is not that we always infallibly know what our sense-experience is like, but only that, whether or not we *know* what is the case, we can always say, without much fear of contradiction, what we are inclined to *believe* is the case. These statements do not, then, express a special kind of direct knowledge by acquaintance nor are they premises from which statements about objects could be inferred. For they are not claims to knowledge at all, but more or less tentative expressions of belief, and what is tentatively affirmed is precisely the same as, and thus cannot be a premise for, what, in the conclusion of the supposed inference, we claim to know without hesitation. I shall argue, however, that we can, and rather infrequently do, describe our experience and that we can do this in statements containing such expressions as 'look', 'appear' and 'seem'.

The consequences of this distinction of 'appearances' from sense-data are that knowledge about experience is much less common than is widely supposed and that the greater part of our 'knowledge of appearances' is not capable of figuring as premises in inferences to beliefs about objects.

Before embarking on this another familiar argument for the sense-datum theory must be considered: what may be called the argument from scientific knowledge. There is conclusive evidence for the fact that many of our sense-experiences occur appreciably later than the events of which they give us knowledge, in particular the experiences caused by what is astronomically visible or less remotely audible. More generally, every sense-experience is at the end of a temporally extended causal chain whose first member is the supposedly perceived occurrence. Consequently, what we directly perceive, the object of acquaintance, cannot be the same as that about which we claim knowledge. But this involves no new issue of principle. It shows objects and experiences to be temporally distinct where the argument from illusion shows them to be much more generally different in character. It only shows that we do not directly perceive objects if the supposed consequence of the argument from illusion—that we perceive only our sense-experience directly—is already accepted.

The view common to all versions of the sense-datum theory that the perception of objects is really a kind of inference seems to arise from a belief that, while perception proper must be infallible, inference need not be, and thus that all mistakes are fallacies. But both perception and inference are learnt, intelligent activities which we can presumably perform with varying degrees of efficiency and success. That perception is an acquired skill has perhaps been an inducement to regard it as inference to those who suppose all intelligent activities to be species of reasoning.

Ultimately the problem of perception is that of the relation of thought or language to the world. There is a distressing correspondence with primitive cosmology. Some statements are supported by others, but what supports these others, what is tortoise to their elephant? For the whole system of knowledge cannot support itself in mid-air; it is not self-contained. There is a dilemma here. Either the ultimate support is logically related to the body of knowledge and is thus automatically brought inside the body of knowledge, since only statements can stand in logical relations, and, if so, the question of dependence on the extra-linguistic world breaks out again. Or it is not and there is no answer in terms of correct inference to the request for a justification of reliance on this ultimate support.

Philosophers have sought to evade this dilemma by recourse to the Janus-faced notion of experience. The fact that we cannot, it seems, have an experience without somehow being conscious or aware of it has seemed to provide foundation-stones for the edifice of knowledge which are at once statements, capable of standing in logical relations to the rest of the structure, and parts, perhaps the sole constituents, of the extralinguistic world, self-describing entities. I shall contend that there are no such things and opt for the second horn of the dilemma which, as I hope to show, is a less painful resting-place than it might seem.

II

Our first problem is to evaluate the argument from illusion. From the unexceptionable premises that things are not always what they appear to be and that we cannot always tell, there and then, whether they are or not, it is concluded that we have direct knowledge only of appearances, never of objects. For there need be no immediately discoverable difference between two appearances of which one is in fact 'veridical' and the other 'delusive'. So what we really perceive are appearances, whether they are veridical or not depends on something that lies outside the perceptual situation. But what are these appearances that we perceive? They are, it is said, sense-data, the given, immediate experience, they are the current states of our sense-fields.

Of some uses of 'appear', 'seem', etc. it is clearly untrue to say that they figure in descriptions of experience. 'They appear to be away', said when the twice-rung doorbell of a house with drawn curtains remains unanswered, means much the same as 'they must be away' or 'they are probably away'. We are not here describing, but drawing conclusions from, what we observe. The word 'appear' serves to indicate that these conclusions are drawn with less than full confidence. There is nothing 'basic' about them.

But there is another use of 'appear' in which no reason can be given for statements containing it and which do report observations. 'It appears to be green' we might say of a distant house. If challenged we can only repeat, or perhaps correct, ourselves or protest, 'well, that is how it appears to me'. But such a statement would normally be made in answer to such questions as 'what colour is that house' and could be replaced by 'it's green, I think' or 'it's green, isn't it?' They report observations in a tentative way where we know, believe or suspect that the circumstances are unfavourable to an accurate report, that there is something wrong with or abnormal about the conditions of observation. They resemble ordinary categorical descriptions, 'that house is green', in subject-matter, but differ from them in expressing inclinations to believe rather than full beliefs.

There is a third use of 'appear', which resembles the one last mentioned, in that no reasons or evidence can be given for statements containing it, but differs from it in that certain conventional conditions of observation are supposed to obtain, whether they do or not. 'It looks to me (here, now) elliptical' we say of a plate we know to be tilted and round, supposing it to be at right angles to our line of vision. This statement answers the question 'how does it strike you, look to you, what exactly do you see?' It is replaceable by 'there is an elliptical patch in the centre of my visual field'. It is in this type of case only that the description of appearances and experience coincide.

Consider that old friend the stick half in, half out, of water. One might say of it (a) 'it is straight', (b) 'it looks bent but is really straight', (c) 'it looks bent', (d) 'it is bent'. Statement (a) is true, (b) describes the stick correctly and points out how one might be led to make a mistake about it if unaware of an abnormality (a refracting medium) in the conditions of observation, (c) gives tentative expression to the inclination mistakenly to believe (d) which is straightforwardly false. 'It looks bent' is the puzzling case. For it may be a guarded way of saying 'it is bent' (denied by 'it isn't bent') or a way of saying 'most people would be inclined to say it was bent' (denied by 'it doesn't') or a way of saying 'it looks bent to me, here now' (which can only be denied by 'oh surely not').

So, even when not used to give tentative conclusions from evidence, the verb 'appear' and its cognates are seldom used to describe experience, but primarily to give tentative descriptions of objects. In other words, the 'appearances' that survive the argument from illusion as the proper objects of acquaintance are not ordinarily sense-experiences. These seemingly rock-bottom matters of fact are, in a way, incorrigible and, *ex hypothesi*, uninferred. But their incorrigibility is imperfect and spurious. Imperfect because both 'this is ϕ, I think' and 'this is ϕ, most people would say' can be contradicted (by 'it isn't' and 'they wouldn't') and revised accordingly. Spurious because it arises, not from their making a definite claim about something private, but from their making a weak, indefinite claim about something public. And, though uninferred, they cannot play the part of premises in inferences to categorical descriptions of objects. 'This appears to be ϕ' is no more evidence or a reason for 'this is ϕ' than are 'this may be ϕ' or 'this is probably ϕ'. All three are simply modified ways of saying 'this is ϕ', appropriate for one who is inclined, but not inclined quite confidently enough, to make the categorical statement itself.

This is not to deny that we can and do describe our experience. All I have tried to show is that we describe it very much less often than is usually supposed. Being unsure about the circumstances is a common enough occurrence. But the description of experience proper is a sophisticated procedure and one seldom called for. It is an essential accomplishment for painters, broadcasting engineers, doctors of the eye and ear, cooks and experimental psychologists. But unless we fall into their hands there is little need for us to become proficient in it. The sophistication arises with the deliberate supposition that conditions obtain which we have no reason to suppose do so in fact and perhaps every reason to suppose do not. The fact that we have laboriously to learn perspective drawing is an indication of this, as is the notorious unreliability of eye-witnesses.

That we seldom do describe our experience and then usually with difficulty does not entail that we could not set up and become proficient in the use of a private language. But it would involve a remarkable change in our attitude to the world. Normally we observe in a context of beliefs about where we are and what we are doing that the sophisticated naivete of phenomenology would exclude. To attend to one's experience involves a radical shift in attitude, a determined effort to resist the solicitations of that submerged constellation of beliefs within which our perceptual discoveries are made.

To this extent, then, I am in sympathy with those who have argued that if the stick half in water looks bent then something really *is* bent. When I say the stick looks bent, I should discover, if I were to direct my attention to it, that my visual field contained a bent brown line. Whether it follows from this that I am in some way aware of this feature of my visual field is a question that will be answered later. But there is something to be said against this line of argument which is commonly ignored. No doubt when the stick looks bent, something else is bent. But consider these cases. I see a small glassy object in a radio shop and say 'that looks like a valve'. But in fact it is a wineglass. For this error there is no sensory cue; it is the outcome of my general beliefs about the contents of radio shops. Again, I see what is in fact half a pair of spectacles beside a box which I mistakenly suppose to be obscuring the rest. Even when I know better, it still looks just like a pair to me but it is unlikely that my visual field contains anything corresponding to the second lens.

I have been at pains to emphasise the uncommon and sophisticated nature of the description of experience because of the supposed consequence of the argument from illusion, that in every perceptual situation, even if no object is in fact perceived or if objects are misperceived, still something is perceived, our sense-experience. It would seem *prima facie* that one cannot be said to perceive something unless one is in a position to describe it. But I am not in a position to describe my experience unless I am in the appropriate, sophisticated, phenomenological frame of mind.

Normally if someone says mistakenly that he sees something we are not inclined to say that he really saw something else. We should say of Macbeth that he thought he saw the dagger, imagined he could see it, was under the impression he could see it, but that he did not actually see it at all. In cases of illusion, as against hallucination, there will be something that really is perceived, but it will be a perfectly ordinary public object, not a private experience. If I take a piece of mud on the doormat to be a letter, it will be said that what I actually saw was a piece of mud.

In general, it is not the case, when I am mistaken about what I claim to perceive, either that I am in a position to describe my experience or that I would be said really to have perceived my experience. There are reasons, nevertheless, which have led philosophers to believe that I am aware of my experience, acquainted with it, in such circumstances.

It is not only when in the hands of those professionally concerned with it that we attend to and describe our experience. We are sometimes forced to do so by total ignorance of the conditions of observation. Waking up in unfamiliar circumstances we may, if no other assumption seems inviting, suppose that the conventional phenomenological conditions obtain. In exceptional circumstances of this kind, as we come round from an anaesthetic for example, a description of our visual experience is a possible answer to the question 'can you see anything?' But it is worth noticing that in such cases we can also say, with even better warrant perhaps, 'no, just a lot of yellow streaks' instead of 'yes, a lot of yellow streaks'. Only in a very marginal sense is a description of one's visual experience to be called 'seeing' at all.

In a way, then, we can be said sometimes to 'see' our visual experience: when we are trying to describe it or when we are not in a position to describe anything else. But what of the case of a man lying in the sun on his back with his eyes open and his mind far away? Does he see the blue expanse with shifting white patches on it that he could describe if he were to turn his attention to his visual field? And what of the man who is carefully watching a hen to discover where the gap in the hen-run is? Does he see the green expanse of the downs beyond, that he would in fact find occupying the greater part of his visual field if he were to attend to it? Compare these cases with a less problematic kind of seeing. Suppose you show me round your garden and afterwards ask me 'did you see the tulip tree?' If I say 'no', you may say 'you must have done, it's right beside the summer-house I showed you'. If I still deny seeing it, even after another look to refresh my memory, then I cannot have seen it. Yet one might be inclined here to think that I must have seen it all the same. There it was, ten yards away, in broad daylight, right in the middle of my field of vision. But perhaps I was concentrating on the summer-house or thinking of something else altogether. One's visual field is in much the same case as the tulip tree in this example. However far one's attention may have strayed, it seems, nevertheless, that one is inescapably *confronted* by it. So philosophers have said that whenever we think we see anything we really do see the contents of our visual fields. But this is an extremely hypothetical kind of seeing. All we can say is that if I had been in a different frame of mind I should have noticed the tree; I should have been able to describe the contents of my visual field.

In every perceptual situation, then, we know what appears to be the case, but this is not usually to be in a position to describe our experience. It may be true that we can be said to have sense-experiences in every perceptual situation (they are, no doubt, the *causes* of our inclinations to believe) but this is quite another matter from being aware of them, noticing them, being in a position to describe them, and nothing less than this can be involved in the claim of the sense-datum theory that it is our experience which we really perceive.

But can having experiences and being aware of them be clearly distinguished in this way? For having an experience is a mental event of the kind, it would be argued, the only direct evidence for whose existence is its presence in consciousness. One might distinguish two senses of 'awareness'. In the wider sense I am aware of any mental event that I am in any way conscious of. In the narrower sense I am only aware of what I notice or attend to, of what I am in a position to describe, of what, in fact, I have some statable knowledge of. Now it might be argued that one was aware of all experience in the wider sense and that this was sufficient reason for saying that all experience was really perceived. I do not think that this distinction can be maintained. It is not that we are really aware of a great many things which we do not notice or attend to but rather that we suppose ourselves to have a great deal of experience for whose existence we have little or no direct evidence. For ordinarily 'be aware of' and 'notice' are largely interchangeable. Both imply claims to knowledge. There are differences of nuance: to become aware of a smell of decay is to have it borne in upon one, to notice a smell of decay is to have discovered it. In implying claims to knowledge both words resemble the perceptual verbs 'see', 'hear', etc. One cannot be aware *of* something without knowing something about it, being aware *that* something is the case.

Now we are, perhaps, usually vaguely aware of the character of our experience, but far too indefinitely for the knowledge involved to support the complicated structure of beliefs that the sense-datum theory would erect on it. The faint and undetailed nature of this underlying awareness of experience is attested to by the fact that when asked to recall our experience we have more or less to reconstruct it from the objects perceived. We attend to experience often enough to know the sort of experiences normally associated with various kinds of objects in various conditions. When we transfer our attention from objects to experience an enormously richer awareness of the latter is obtained. We then suppose that we were in fact having experiences of as complex and detailed a kind while attending to the objects, although we were unaware of the complexity and detail. This move is not inference supported by recollection, but a convention. It is assumed that, given unchanged objects, medium, and sense-organs, a change of attention brings about no change in the associated experiences. The idealist's problem 'does attention alter its object'? is thus a matter of convention not of fact. The convention described here lays down that it does not. By this a distinction is introduced between experiences which we have and which we are aware of. It gives a sense to the expression 'unnoticed experience'. One could equally well, if not better, opt for the other alternative and speak, not of 'unnoticed', but of 'possible' experiences, that is the experiences one would be aware of were one to adopt the phenomenological frame of mind. There is a close analogy with the problem of unsensed sense-data. Should we speak with Russell of 'sensibilia' or with Ayer of 'possible sense-data'? In each case considerations of continuity urge one convention, conceptual economy and epistemological rigour the other. In our problem continuity makes a stronger claim. For while there is a clear distinction between sensed and unsensed sense-data, there would seem to be an unbroken continuum of grades of awareness. At any rate to have an experience of which one is not aware is not so much an event as the possibility of an event, it is to be able, by appropriately directing one's attention, to become aware of an experience. The nature of these possibilities is discovered inductively. I conclude that, whether we decide to say we have experiences of which we are not aware or merely that we could have them, anything we can say about them or their possibility depends on the limited number we are aware of. It is only these, meagre or absent in most perceptual situations, which we can be said to perceive.

III

I have argued that experience cannot be the sole object of acquaintance since it is not the case that in every perceptual situation we are aware of it. If this argument is accepted it can be reinforced—if not replaced—by considering what is *meant* by saying that experience alone is the object of acquaintance. I shall first consider the view that this is so because only of experience can we have certain knowledge.

That statements about objects can never be certain (an elliptical way of saying that we can never know for certain that they are true) is sometimes affirmed on the ground that they are empirical. For it is an essential feature of empirical statements that they can be shown to be false and, it is argued, if a statement can be false there can be reasonable doubt of its truth. But if there can be reasonable doubt of its truth it cannot be certain. This argument has the notorious consequence that only necessary truths can be certain. This is not, as some have argued, merely inconvenient in assimilating one useful distinction to another, it is the outcome of a definite mistake. For it is not correct to say that a statement is certain only if there *can* be no reasonable doubt of its truth; a statement is certain, rather, if there *is* no reasonable doubt of its truth.

This familiar argument, in trying to prove that no empirical statement is certain, tries to prove too much. For, if it were correct, the supposed differences in epistemological status between objects and experiences could not consist in a difference in respect of certainty between the statements describing them. I shall consider two arguments designed to show that, in fact, there is always reasonable doubt about descriptions of objects. Both assert that descriptions of objects have implications which inevitably 'go beyond' or 'lie outside' the current observation.

The first holds that there is no limit to the set of other statements which follow from a given statement about objects. For at any time, however remote from the time to which the original statement refers, evidence will exist and could be obtained for or against it. If at any time there is no evidence, however tenuous, for or against it, it is then untestable and, therefore, without meaning. At any rate the possibility of evidence arising for any statement, however remote its reference, cannot be ruled out. So, it is argued, however much favourable evidence for the truth of a statement may have accumulated, it is always possible that all the evidence to come may point to and, in the end, enforce the opposite conclusion.

If, as I shall argue later, it is also the case that descriptions of experience can be revised, that there can be evidence for and against them distinct from the occurrence of the experience itself, then precisely the same argument can be applied to them and so no difference in epistemological status is established. In effect this argument comes to the same as the previous one; revision in the face of unfavourable evidence is as much a universal feature of empirical statements as falsifiability.

But, waiving this point for the moment, the argument is fallacious in concluding that statements with 'open consequences' are never certain. For if the statement of unfavourable evidence q is remote, in the way described, from the original statement p, then q alone will not entail the falsity of p but only in conjunction with some generalization or law of nature r. So q will only falsify or disconfirm p to the extent that r is accepted as true and applicable. It is not p and q simply that are incompatible but p, q and r. If q turns out to be true we are not therefore compelled to abandon p. The more remote q is from p, the more tenuous the connexion, the more we shall be inclined to abandon r. This critical point between abandoning p and abandoning r in face of q may be hard to locate, but for every statement it will exist and for every statement circumstances can be indicated in which its 'logical neighbourhood' is so densely populated with favourable evidence that no remote unfavourable evidence whatever would be taken as refuting it. So it does not follow from the fact that the set of a statement's consequences is open that there is always reasonable doubt of its truth.

The second argument about implications asserts that statements about objects are always and necessarily predictive, that they always logically imply something which the current observation is not sufficient to establish. A statement about objects always forms part of a system of beliefs of varying size, at least including assumptions about the normality —or controllable abnormality—of the conditions of observation. But this has no disastrous consequences. In the first place, no infinite regress is generated. The entailed consequences (or assumptions about the conditions of observation) are themselves statements about objects, but *their* entailed consequences (or conditions) will not all be distinct from the original statement. The implications do not fray off endlessly into the unknown, they are, rather, elements in finite, and indeed decently small, systems of mutual support. And in the second place, arising out of this, it is wrong to regard statements about objects as necessarily predictive under all circumstances. For it is perfectly possible to establish all the members of such a set of mutually supporting statements. Knowledge of the conditions of observation constitutes just such a framework which a statement about objects completes, supports and is supported by. I am not here going back on my earlier criticism of the coherence theory. These coherent sets of statements are not self-sufficient. For their members are conventionally correlated with observed situations. Loose talk about semantic or ostensive rules has ignored the indeterminacy of this correlation, the existence of slack in the application of statements about objects which the systems in which they figure take up.

In the normal course of events it is not that the entailed consequences or conditions are yet to be discovered but that they are known already. This 'systematic' character of our knowledge of objects does indeed distinguish it from our knowledge of experience, consistently with what has gone before since it is the logical correlate of the perceptual as against the phenomenological frame of mind. In the extreme, limiting case (waking up, etc.), where we have no knowledge of the conditions, all descriptions of objects are likely to be less than certain. But we are not usually in this unfortunate position and single observations can give us certain knowledge about objects.

Even if statements about objects were never certain this would not prove them to be derived from statements about experience, if being less than certain were not identified with being probable and if it were not held that nothing can be probable unless something else is certain.

The crucial error in these interconnected doctrines is the supposition that certainty and probability are exhaustive as well as mutually exclusive. Any assertion made with full confidence may be called certain but only one kind of assertion made with less than full confidence is called probable. 'It appears to be cloudy over there' is perfectly good, if weak, evidence for 'it will probably rain'. Yet the whole point of saying that it appears to be, rather than that it is, cloudy over there is to indicate lack of confidence, uncertainty. That is, a less than certain conclusion can be based on less than certain premises which are not themselves the result of inference. The word 'probably' qualifies assertions which are both tentatively advanced, held to be less than certain, and are the conclusions of inferences. This latter characteristic allows us always to challenge, to ask for the reasons for, a statement that something is probably the case and warrants the view that probability is always relative to evidence. But this evidence may itself be tentative and less than certain. To express just this 'uninferred' hesitancy is, as was shown earlier, the principal office of the words 'look', 'appear' and 'seem'. But can we describe experience in this way? The sole use we have for forms of words where these verbs are re-iterated (it seems to look ϕ) is where neither verb is used to describe experience (I am inclined to think that most people would say it was ϕ). But this does not entail that phenomenological uses of these verbs cannot be tentative, that 'this looks to me, here, now, ϕ' must be certain. To modify these we use adverbial devices like 'roughly', 'more or less', 'sort of' or add the rider 'I think'. We avoid 'appear' and its kin because they suggest assignable reservations, that we realise or suspect something to be amiss with the conditions of observation or, in non-perceptual uses ('he appears to have died about 300 B.C.'), that we realise that better evidence could, in principle, be obtained. But there are no **better** conditions in

which to describe our experiences than those in which they occur, no better evidence than that they occur. The corrigibility of a statement, in
other words, does not entail that 'appear' and the rest apply to it; they
apply only where assignable reservations are indicated.

Less than certain statements are not all probable; they are so only
if they are the conclusions of inferences, and the premises of these inferences may be less than certain without themselves being inferred. They
will be what appears to be the case if I can assign the reservations from
which my tentativeness arises or what is, I think, roughly the case, if I
cannot.

Finally we must consider a familiar argument against the view that
all descriptions of experience are certain. A statement of fact must be
expressed by a sentence containing a predicate, a general or descriptive
word, and must, therefore, involve the classification of what it refers to,
the discrimination of this from other things to which the predicate does
not apply. Things, including experiences, do not confront us already
sorted out, classified, discriminated. And like any other learnt, regular
procedure classification can be carried out wrongly. The use of predicates
in classifying and discriminating is essentially a matter of relating what
we are describing to the things which are the standard for the application
of the predicate, with which it is conventionally correlated, by which it
is 'ostensively defined'.

For we can and do revise our descriptions of experience, however
convinced we were of their correctness at the time we made them. Such
revision could only be excluded by the presumption that recollected experiences, formerly described as ϕ, and now recalled as noticeably different
from something else we want to call ϕ, must always be misrecollected. But
our recollections have a credibility of their own which does not depend
on what is recollected matching something which we now describe with
the same predicate we applied to it. Not only can we revise past descriptions of experience, we can also be hesitant about present descriptions.
Sometimes we can find no precedent for a perfectly distinct and definite
but unique impression; sometimes, while inclined to give a certain description, there is some peculiarity in the situation which we cannot precisely identify and which makes us hesitate. There is a range of cases between these extremes of inadequate vocabulary and indistinct experience.

Against this view it is argued that the errors corrected by such a
revision are merely *verbal*. 'All that one can properly mean . . . by saying that one doubts whether this (sense-datum) is green is that one is
doubting whether "green" is the correct word to use.' (Ayer). But what
else is one doubting when one doubts whether this *object* is green? There
is a difference, of course, in that one can have another, better, look at the
object but not at the sense-datum. But it does not follow from this that all
mistakes that do not depend on unfavourable conditions of observation

are not really mistakes at all. What, after all, is a 'merely verbal' error? Properly speaking, only mistaken expressions of belief due to slips of the tongue or pen or laziness and inattention. Linguistic incapacity, the source of mistaken descriptions of experience, is quite another matter. Professor Ayer has recently argued that experience is described 'not by relating it to anything else but by indicating that a certain word applies to it in virtue of a meaning-rule of the language'. The suggestion is that the application of meaning-rules is such a simple matter that it is impossible to perform it wrongly except by a slip. But meaning-rules do not have the bemusing simplicity of their 'semantic' formulation (the word 'red' applies to red things). The class of things to which a predicate applies is indeterminately bounded. Some blue things are more obviously blue than others. Again we are not equally and perfectly accomplished in the application of all predicates. We can manage 'red' and 'round' fairly well, but are less efficient with 'mauve' and 'rhomboidal'. Even if we were trained up to the highest pitch of descriptive efficiency with the predicates we do understand, it is wrong to imagine that that notoriously blunt instrument, our descriptive vocabulary, would provide a precisely appropriate caption for every situation, that it could deal exhaustively with the fecundity of experience. Behind this theory of semantic rules lurks a pair of metaphysical assumptions: that universals, in one-one correlation wtih predicates, are wide open to some kind of direct apprehension and that there is a decent limit to their variety. The implied analogy with the rules by means of which the truths of mathematics and logic are established is misleading. These rules are precise, definite and can be clearly stated and communicated; careful tests can be made of whether they have been employed correctly. No such laborious check of the correct employment of 'meaning-rules' is possible with the private, fluid and unstable constituents of our sense-experience.

Lack of clarity about the relation between the mere occurrence of an experience and its description has contributed to the view that we cannot, without lying or slips, misdescribe experience. Experience just happens. But being what it is we cannot help being aware of it. Yet it occurs in every perceptual situation. This confusion of the phenomenologically scrutinised with the more or less hypothetical unnoticed experience is responsible for the view that simply to have an experience is to know it for what it is. Those who have, consistently enough, denied that experience as such is properly speaking either a kind of knowledge or true or false at all, have avoided the confusion at the cost of abolishing their problem. For from mere events nothing can be logically derived; only from statements, from what can be known to be true, can other statements be inferred.

I conclude that statements about objects and about experience are sometimes certain, sometimes not. In this respect there is no sharp distinction between the two. Whether a description of objects is certain will depend largely on the circumstances in which it is given and what is known about them. Its familiarity and stability will no doubt determine whether a description of experience is certain. We can err about both from linguistic incapacity and the loose correlation of language and the world, about objects on account of unfavourable conditions of observation and about experiences (and occasionally objects) on account of their evanescence. Such difference as there is between the respective sources of error is not sufficient to substantiate a theory of acquaintance or to show one category to be logically prior to the other.

IV

Some philosophers, realising that certainty as a criterion of acquaintance or basic statements is not sufficient to distinguish objects and experience in the way the sense-datum theory requires, have proposed a different definition in terms of inference. On this view we know directly, by acquaintance, what we know without inference; basic statements are primitive, uninferred; and, while no descriptions of experience are inferred, all descriptions of objects are. The task of theory of knowledge, it is held, is to make a rational reconstruction of our knowledge of matters of fact in which the uninferred premises from which alone this knowledge can be validly derived are explicitly set out. It is agreed that we are rarely, if ever, conscious of carrying out these inferences. It is thought, nevertheless, that experiential premises must somehow 'underlie' what we believe about objects.

If this account is correct two conditions must be satisfied. Statements about experience must count as reasons or evidence for statements about objects and they must in some, no doubt rather obscure, sense be accepted by those who make statements about objects. This second, seemingly platitudinous, requirement deserves emphasis. A fact cannot be a man's reason or evidence for an assertion unless, however implicitly, he is aware of it. Someone's implicit or unconscious awareness of facts about objects can be established by observation of his behaviour. But there is no such criterion available for detecting his awareness of his experience. The view, mistaken as I have argued, that we cannot help being aware of our experience no doubt explains why it has not been thought necessary to provide any criterion for the occurrence of this supposed awareness. If my argument against the view that in every perceptual situation we are aware of our own experience is accepted, it follows that the second condition of the inference theory is unsatisfied and that the theory is mistaken. For our experiences could only be our reasons or evidence for our beliefs about objects if we were to become aware of them through adopting a completely different, phenomenological, frame of mind in our traffic with the external world. Like any other facts, facts about experience must be discovered before they can be appealed to. But even if my argument on this is not accepted, the inference theory is mistaken since the first condition mentioned is not satisfied either.

The best proof that statements about experience were reasons or evidence for statements about objects would be that we did in fact commonly infer from the one to the other. This, however, is admittedly not the case. But, as it stands, this is of little importance. In the first place, the psychological criterion involved is exceedingly vague, seeming to do no more than mark off as cases of inference those in which a thoughtful pause supervenes between observation and announcement. Furthermore, there are many cases, unquestionably of knowledge by inference, where it is not in the least likely that any conscious process of reasoning has taken place. A girl, sitting in the drawing-room, hears the front door slam and says 'Father's home'. I hear a pattering on the roof and say 'it's raining'. I see a small pool on the kitchen floor and say 'the dog has misbehaved'. We only infer consciously in situations that are unfamiliar or complex, in the predicament of the weekend guest or the new boy on the first day of term. The detective, the busybody, the scientist are more or less professionally concerned to make the most of a small stock of data. Conscious, deliberate thinking is both exhausting and infrequent, a last resort to be appealed to only when all habitual capacities have failed. But most of our perceptual knowledge is of familiar states of affairs and acquired in familiar conditions.

That a statement is employed as a premise in a conscious process of reasoning is not the only feature of our use of that statement which shows it to count as a reason or evidence for the conclusion. More fundamental surely, is that we *give* it as our reason when challenged on the other.

Consider these five cases. I can at once reproduce the course of reasoning that led me to say that it is Mother's hat on top of the garage. This is conscious inference, where the reason given is a premise already consciously affirmed. Secondly, I can, without hesitation, answer 'by the way he sways about' when asked how I can tell someone is drunk, although I recollect no process of inferring. Thirdly, I may take some time over or require assistance in accounting for my claim that Towzer is ill by the glazed look in his eye. Fourthly, I may be unable to give any reason of my own and unwilling to accept any reason offered by another for my assertion that X dislikes Y. Yet commonly in this type of case I may be sure a reason does exist for my belief, may be extremely confident of the truth of my belief and turn out, in the end, to be quite right. Finally, consider standing in broad daylight three feet away from a large and perfectly normal chestnut cart-horse and saying 'that is a horse' or, more adventurously, 'that horse is brown'. This resembles the previous case in that one would be quite unable to give or accept any reason whatever for one's assertion. It differs from it in that one would not be in the very least abashed or apologetic about this. For, in these conditions, the challenge 'how can you tell?' is simply devoid of sense.

Still, if it were made, one might perhaps answer 'well, because it looks like a horse'. If this were intended as a description of one's experience, as interchangeable with 'there is now a shiny brown patch of a characteristic shape in the centre of my visual field', it would not be to answer the question but rather to change the subject, perhaps to offer a causal explanation of one's belief. But this interpretation proposed by the sense-datum theory, a wildly unnatural interpretation of what is, in the circumstances, a wildly unnatural remark, is surely mistaken. The statement would more naturally be intended and understood as a modification of, an infusion of tentativeness into, the original claim, expressing a lack of confidence inspired by the nagging question. As such it is not a reason. To repeat oneself in a more cautious way is not to substantiate but merely to attenuate one's original assertion. 'It looks like a horse' resembles 'it is probably a horse' or 'I think it's a horse' and not 'it has thick legs and no horns' which might be advanced to support the claim that some comparatively distant animal was a horse. For there are, of course, plenty of situations in which reasons do exist for statements about objects.

A statement cannot be inferred, then, if no reason or evidence for it exists, or, more exactly, if it does not make sense to ask for or give a reason for it. Whether or not it does make sense to ask for a reason depends on the circumstances in which the statement is made. The sentence, the form of words, 'that is a horse', may be used in an enormous variety of circumstances. In some of these it will make sense to ask 'how can you tell', in others not. The latter may be called the standard conditions of its use. It will be in such circumstances that the use of the sentence will normally be learnt. This accomplished, it will be possible to use it in an increasingly adventurous way in increasingly non-standard conditions. Connexions are established between assertions and their reasons through the discovery of a vast array of factual concomitances. That standard conditions are those in which we learn how to use a sentence helps to explain why the statements they are used to make are basic and uninferred. For in these conditions they are directly correlated with an observable situation, they are not introduced by means of other statements. (This explains 'implicit inference'. I implicitly infer, acknowledge a reason for, a statement if I was introduced to it by means of other statements but can now make it without conscious consideration of them.) For some sentences there are no standard conditions (generalizations or such implicitly general sentences as 'she is naturally shy'). With others the nature of their standard conditions may vary from person to person. A wife will be able to tell at once that her husband is depressed where others have no inkling of the fact. (A difference in capacity that leads us to speak of intuition.) Again prolonged success in a certain nonstandard use of a sentence may lead us to incorporate the conditions of this use into the standard. I say 'it is raining' when I cannot actually see the rain falling but only drops of water bouncing off the wet street. The addition of unwillingness to inability to answer the question 'how can you tell?' shows that these conditions have become standard. Standard conditions are those in which we have a right to feel certain of the truth of an assertion. The suggestion of uncertainty conveyed by the protest 'that's only an inference' would be made more obviously by the equivalent protest 'you are in no position to be sure' (*i.e.* 'these are not standard conditions'.) The lawyer, who asks for a description of what one *actually* saw, devoid of inference and conjecture, is asking for a standard description, that is, a description for which the conditions one was then in were standard.

The notions of acquaintance and of the basic statements which it warrants have, therefore, a foundation in our ordinary way of thinking and speaking. The failure to locate them in their right place is due in part to the failure to distinguish between sentences and statements. For because of multiplicity of uses there are no 'basic sentences'. What we know for certain and without inference in any situation is what the circumstances we are in are the standard conditions for. This will normally be a statement about objects. But there are circumstances in which, knowing nothing about the conditions or that they are highly abnormal, we can take no description of objects as standard. In such a situation we can do no more than tentatively say what appears to be the case. If we are not prepared to do this we can, by an appropriate shift of attention, describe our experience. This last-ditch feature of statements about experience is another encouragement to the sense-datum theorist.

More important is the fact that standard conditions are not a perfect guarantee of the truth of a statement made in them. For standard conditions do not involve that all of a statement's entailed consequences have been established. The horse in the example may just possibly be a brilliantly contrived deception, a flat painted board. We could make our standard stringent enough to cater for this, by insisting on the establishment of entailed consequences, without abandoning statements about objects as basic. But it would be laborious and inconvenient to do so. The programme of convenience embodied in our actual standards is abetted by the order of nature which is uniform enough to make the risks of standard description negligible. Our standards depend on contingencies but some contingencies are highly reliable and regular. Error, as Descartes pointed out, is a product of the will rather than the understanding and arises almost entirely with nonstandard descriptions.

This minute residual imperfection is the ulimate source of the sense-datum theory. The metaphysical demand behind the theory is for an infallible basis for knowledge. So a new standard is proposed which is thought to be perfect. The justification of the new standard is that the knowledge of conditions required is always available, conditions are always standard for the description of experience. I have argued that we are not, in fact, always in standard conditions for the description of experience but rather that it is always in our power, by an appropriate shift of attention, to produce such conditions. If this is so, the sense-datum theory can be no more than the proposal of a new and exceedingly cumbrous way of thinking and speaking to be adopted from fear of a very minor risk. But whether it is true or not, whether the sense-datum theory is a proposal or, what it claims to be, an account of what actually occurs, the supposed improvement is illusory. For, in taking steps to set one exaggerated doubt at rest, it provides the opportunity for another to arise. Admittedly descriptions of experience, for which conditions are always standard, do not depend on a knowledge of conditions which may not be forthcoming. But they have weaknesses of their own. The objects we describe are largely stable and persistent; if we are unsure about them we can always look again. But experience is fleeting and momentary; to attend to it again is to make the insecure hypothesis that it has not changed. The systematic, mutually corroborative character of our beliefs about objects is not a weakness but a strength. Similarly the atomic, disconnected character of experiences, which has encouraged the view that they are self-describing entities, is a weakness. I conclude, then, that experiences are not only not in fact the basis of our empirical knowledge but that they would be inferior to the basis we have, since we are just as much open to error about them, though not entirely the same way; and we should have to revise our way of thinking and speaking completely to use them as a basis.

The relation between experiences and objects, then, neither is nor should be logical. On the contrary it is causal, a matter of psychological fact. Our beliefs about objects are based on experience in a way that requires not justification but explanation. Experiences are not *my* reasons for my beliefs about objects—to have an experience is not to know or believe anything which could be a reason in this sense—though they may be *the* reasons for my believing what I do from the point of view of the psychologist. They may, that is, be the causes of my beliefs and explain them. But they could only be my reasons for my beliefs about objects if I already knew something independently about the relations between experiences and objects.

We learn, it is said, to interpret our experiences, to give rein to Hume's principle of the imagination, to apply Kant's schematized category of substance. These forms of words at least point out that perception is an intelligent activity (not an infallible reflex), but they point it out so uncompromisingly that it is over-intellectualized. Interpreting experi-

ences suggests literary scholarship or detective work. But not all intellectual processes are types of reasoning. These phrases refer to the psychological preconditions of recognizing objects for what they are. They point
out that we must learn to use the language we do use, that this is an
exercise of skill not an automatism and, further, that the situations in
which any one sentence may be correctly uttered are extremely various.
But they do not demand and could not evoke any logical justification of
our practice of thinking and speaking of a common world of objects. We
cannot set out the logical relation of an assertion about objects with the
experiences that occasion it, because there is no such relation. This is not
to sever language from the world altogether, the sin of the coherence
theory. It is simply to say that the relations that obtain within the body
of our knowledge do not also connect it with what is outside.

I have considered the three principal methods of establishing the
sense-datum theory: the arguments from illusion, certainty and inference.
Those who hold statements about experience to be basic have miscon-
strued all three. Statements about experience are not known in every perceptual situation, for we cannot know what we are not aware of, they are
no more certain than statements about objects and they do not differ from
all statements about objects in being uninferred. Doctrines about acquaintance and basic statements are the outcome of a search for perfect
standard conditions. But no standard conditions are perfect and there is
no reason to say that descriptions of experience are or ought to be our
standard. Our empirical knowledge already has a basis and as good a
one as we can obtain. It is to be found, as we should expect, in those situations in which the use of our language is taught and learnt.

Further Reading

The following books and papers contain discussions of perception. Books marked with an asterisk are primarily concerned with the psychology or physiology of perception.

ADRIAN, E. D., *The Physical Background of Perception* * (Oxford, Clarendon Press, 1947).

ARMSTRONG, D. M., *Perception of the Physical World* (London, Routledge & Kegan Paul Ltd., 1961).

AUSTIN, J. L., *Sense and Sensibilia* (Oxford, Clarendon Press, 1962).

AYER, A. J., *The Foundations of Empirical Knowledge* (New York, The Macmillan Company, 1940).

————, *Philosophical Essays* (London, Macmillan & Co., 1954).

————, *The Problem of Knowledge* (London, Macmillan & Co., 1956).

BROAD, C. D., *Perception, Physics and Reality* (Cambridge University Press, 1914).

————, *Scientific Thought* (London, Routledge & Kegan Paul Ltd., 1923). (Paterson, N.J., Littlefield, Adams & Company).

CHISHOLM, R., *Perceiving* (Ithaca, New York, Cornell University Press, 1957).

GIBSON, J. J., *The Perception of the Physical World* * (Boston, Houghton Mifflin Company, 1950).

HAMLYN, D. W., *The Psychology of Perception: A Philosophical Examination of Gestalt Theory and Derivative Theories of Perception* (London, Routledge & Kegan Paul Ltd., 1957).

HAYEK, F. A., *The Sensory Order* (London, Routledge & Kegan Paul Ltd.; Chicago, University of Chicago Press, 1952).

HICKS, G. D., *Critical Realism* (London, Macmillan & Co., 1938).

HIRST, R. J., *The Problems of Perception* (New York, The Macmillan Company, 1959).

LEWIS, C. I., *An Analysis of Knowledge and Valuation* (LaSalle, Ill., Open Court Publishing Co., 1946).

MACH, E., *The Analysis of Sensations* (New York, Dover Publications, Inc.).

MARC-WOGAU, K., *Die Theorie der Sinnesdaten* (Upsala, Sweden, 1945).

MERLEAU-PONTY, M., *Phénoménologie de la perception* (Callimard, Paris, 1945).

MOORE, G. E., *Philosophical Studies* (London, Routledge & Kegan Paul Ltd., 1922). (New York, Littlefield, Adams & Company, 1959).

————, *Proof of an External World,* proceedings of the British Academy (1939).

PRICE, H. H., *Perception* (London, Methuen, 1932).

REID, T., *Essay on the Intellectual Powers of Man.* A. D. Woozley ed. (London, Macmillan & Co., 1941).

RUSSELL, B., *Our Knowledge of the External World* (New York, W. W. Norton, & Company, 1929).

SMITH, N. K., *Prolegomena to an Idealist Theory of Knowledge* (London, Macmillan & Co., 1924).

STACE, W. T., *The Theory of Knowledge and Existence* (Oxford University Press, 1932).

VERNON, M. D., *A Further Study of Visual Perception* * (Cambridge University Press, 1952).